The Women's Movement Today

The Women's Movement Today

An Encyclopedia of Third-Wave Feminism

Volume 1, A–Z

Edited by
Leslie L. Heywood

GREENWOOD PRESS
Westport, Connecticut • London

Library of Congress Cataloging-in-Publication Data

The women's movement today : an encyclopedia of third-wave feminism / edited by Leslie
L. Heywood.

    p. cm.

  Includes bibliographical references and index.

  ISBN 0–313–33133–2 (set: alk. paper)—ISBN 0–313–33134–0 (v. 1: alk. paper)—ISBN
0–313–33135–9 (v. 2: alk. paper)

  1. Feminism—Encyclopedias. 2. Women—Social conditions—21st century—Encyclopedias.
I. Heywood, Leslie.
HQ1115.W644   2006
305.42'03—dc22   2005019217

British Library Cataloguing in Publication Data is available.

Library of Congress Catalog Card Number: 2005019217
ISBN: 0–313–33133–2 (Set)
      0–313–33134–0 (Vol. 1)
      0–313–33135–9 (Vol. 2)

First published in 2006

Greenwood Press, 88 Post Road West, Westport, CT 06881
An imprint of Greenwood Publishing Group, Inc.
www.greenwood.com

Printed in the United States of America

The paper used in this book complies with the
Permanent Paper Standard issued by the National
Information Standards Organization (Z39.48–1984).

10 9 8 7 6 5 4 3 2 1

Contents

Part II   Consumerism, Globalization, and Third-Wave Lives

Part III   Resisting Culture

Preface

The Women's Movement Today: An Encyclopedia of Third-Wave Feminism introduces the third wave's key issues, members, visions, writings, and more. A major collective effort has been made by more than seventy contributors to present as much information about third-wave feminism as possible, and they have conveyed the dynamism and excitement that often characterize work in the third wave. Some contributors, such as Amy Richards, Jennifer Baumgardner, and Lisa Jervis, are leading activist voices in the movement. Others, such as Rebecca Hurdis, Sarah Gamble, Rebecca Munford, Stacy Gillis, Gillian Howie, Alison Piepmeier, Rory Dicker, Deborah Siegel, Leslie Heywood, and Jennifer Drake, have been influential in academia. This is meant to be the essential reference work on the current movement as it charts, describes, and clarifies what has been a much debated and misunderstood phenomenon. The scope of the more than 200 entries is multidisciplinary and multicultural, inclusive of diverse gender orientations and sexualities, with a focus primarily on the movement in the United States.

A chronology and historical introduction put the movement and the encyclopedia and primary documents into perspective. The encyclopedia entries are presented alphabetically. To help readers find entries of interest, the front matter contains an Alphabetical List of Entries and a Topical List of Entries. Many entries have **boldfaced** cross-references to other entries and list other related entries as well. The comprehensive subject and person index also provides more options to access the information quickly. Most entries have a Further Reading section with print and/or Web sources. A Selected Bibliography lists classic third-wave books, Web sites, and films.

The Primary Documents volume showcases a wide variety of writings from some of the leading third-wavers. The selection criteria involved multiple considerations. On a pragmatic level, the documents had to be available for reproduction, the authors locatable, and the permissions attainable. For this reason, I focused on nonfiction pieces from crucial books and magazines rather than on fiction, poetry, or zine contributions. On a conceptual level, I chose to include pieces that were definitional in some way, that represented fundamental aspects of third-wave feminist thinking, and that articulated the broad parameters of the many ideas that contribute to what has come to be termed "third wave." Because of availability, the pieces are limited to those from the United States, Canada, the United Kingdom, and Australia. In the end, I have made every effort to be inclusive and representative of the rich and wide range of voices that have contributed to what, fifteen years later, is now a significant body of third-wave feminist work.

LESLIE HEYWOOD

Acknowledgments

I would like to thank Darlene Gold and Denise Parillo for their editorial assistance, and Gwendolyn Beetham for the third-wave chronology. Deborah Siegel provided much needed consultation at various stages in the project, and many referrals for contributors, which was much appreciated. Thanks as well to all the contributors, who made this such a great project, and to Wendi Schnaufer, Senior Acquisitions Editor, who recognized the need for this work and asked me to edit it, and for her patience and assistance throughout its development.

Introduction: A Fifteen-Year History of Third-Wave Feminism

Like any term that carries cultural and emotional weight and touches on people's lives and beliefs, the term "third-wave feminism" has had a dynamic, controversial history that now spans fifteen years. Popularized by author and activist Rebecca Walker in 1992 in an article for Ms. magazine called "Becoming the Third Wave," which was a critical response to the Anita Hill–Clarence Thomas hearings and the widely circulated media claim that America had now entered an era of postfeminism, the term "third wave" has been a part of conversations around feminism and women's issues in the United States ever since. Like other social movements, third-wave feminism has developed and changed in response to world events and to debates within the movement itself, and can now be described roughly in terms of three stages.

EARLY THIRD WAVE

Third-wave feminism, both the definition and the term itself, was controversial from the beginning. In the United States, what might be termed its early, formational period (roughly 1991–1995) was marked by a debate about whether or not "third wave" and "postfeminist" were synonymous, and which term applied to authors such as Naomi Wolf, Katie Roiphe, and Rene Denfeld, who were overtly critical of second-wave feminism. "Postfeminist," in this sense, meant literally "after feminism," whereas "third wave" implied a continuation of feminism with a difference. The two terms were often conflated both in the media and academia. The popular, media-friendly work of Naomi Wolf is particularly instructive in understanding how "third wave" was initially defined, and why it was so often conflated with postfeminism.

Wolf first came to prominence with 1991's *The Beauty Myth*, a critical look at the beauty industry which stated that "after the success of the women's movement's second wave, the beauty myth was perfected to checkmate power at every level in individual women's lives." This argument struck a nerve and received massive media coverage and positive reviews. Published in the same year as Susan Faludi's *Backlash*, which got even more attention (and which argued that American women's status is deteriorating because the media worked steadily through the 1980s to convince women that their feelings of dissatisfaction and overwork were the result of too much feminism and independence while simultaneously undermining what progress women had made), Wolf's book made a similar case but focused more on beauty standards as a form of social control. Both Faludi and Wolf described American civic life and culture in the 1980s, which resonated with third-wave feminists who had come of age in those years. Wolf became a household name, and it was in *The Beauty Myth* that she used the term "feminist third wave" to refer to women who were in her own age group (their twenties). But contradictory conditions, such as the new hope for change inspired by the Clinton presidency beginning in 1992, the progress that had been made in some institutions for some women, and a growing backlash against those changes, all affected how third-wave feminism developed in those years.

Wolf's 1993 follow-up to *The Beauty Myth* was *Fire with Fire: The New Female Power and How It Will Change the 21st Century*. In it she coined the terms "victim feminism" and "power feminism." "Victim feminism" referred largely to academic feminism and what she saw as its formulations of women as victims of patriarchy and patriarchal institutions. Wolf claimed this version of feminism alienated young women, and she proposed what she saw as a more positively oriented alternative, "power feminism." Power feminism was similar to classic liberal feminism in that it argued for a feminism that would motivate women to claim their individual power and achieve as much as men within the current social structure. Since Wolf had become identified in the media as the most visible representative of third-wave feminism, the term "third wave" became synonymous with a new version of liberal feminism and was roundly criticized for being apolitical, individualistic, self-promotional, and applicable only to white, middle-class women who have more economic opportunities, not to women as a whole. It was also sometimes seen as "postfeminist" because of its overt criticisms of second-wave feminism.

The attention given to Wolf as the representative, third-wave feminist obscured other versions of third wave that were very much in development during that time. Rebecca Walker, whose essay "Becoming the Third Wave" articulated a very different version of third-wave feminism than Wolf's, cofounded Third Wave Direct Action Corporation with Shannon Liss in 1992. This national, nonprofit organization was devoted to cultivating young women's leadership and activism. In 1998, this organization became the Third Wave Foundation and is still active and influential today. In her essay, Walker described pushing herself "to figure out what it means to be part of the Third Wave of feminism .... My involvement must reach beyond my own voice in discussion, beyond voting, beyond reading feminist theory ... I am not a post feminism feminist. I am the Third Wave."[1] Walker's declaration of a difference between postfeminism and third wave was seminal, as was the work of The Third Wave Direct Action Corporation, which was designed to "support the leadership of young women 15 to 30 by providing resources, public education, and relationship building opportunities." Because "each year less than 7% of all philanthropic dollars are directed to programs for women and girls," Third Wave addressed this need. Third Wave's grants and scholarships give "direct financial support to young women activists and the organizations they lead, helping ensure that their cutting edge strategies get the resources needed to help change our communities." Third Wave also has an educational mission, which "highlights issues that concern young women and their allies," and "amplify[ies] the voices and concerns of young women to decision makers, the media, and other institutions."[2] Self-described as multiracial, multicultural, multiethnic, multisexual, and containing members with various religious orientations, the Third Wave was the first organization to articulate the views and concerns of a new demographic with identities that could not easily be broken down into opposing categories such as black/white, gay/straight, female/male. The ideas they forwarded addressed these complexities and the need for new forms of social justice activism that could address this kind of hybridity within individual identity.

The early to mid-1990s was a time of heightened interest in feminism, both within the United States and worldwide. New organizations and forums developed, including EMILY's list, a national network of political donors devoted to helping pro-choice, democratic women, which began to effect election outcomes. An international movement centered around nongovernmental organizations gained membership all over the world, defining women's rights as human rights and gaining headlines in the Fourth World Conference on Women in Beijing in 1995. And the early 1990s saw the development of many feminist-oriented listservs and spaces for cultural production organized around the Internet.

The ideas and concerns of the third wave were also expressed through another form of activism that called itself third wave: Riot Grrrl. Beginning in Olympia, Washington, and Washington, D.C., in the early 1990s, the punk-grunge DIY (do it yourself) musicians known as Riot Grrrl became visible as the cultural expression of third-wave ideals. Musicians who also produced what became influential zines such as *Girl Germs, Satan Wears a Bra,* and *Quit Whining,* Riot Grrrl started as a way to encourage women to become a more powerful presence in music—to break through the stereotype of women singer-songwriters who did not play instruments and to replace it with loud electric guitar and bass and with uninhibited lyrics unafraid to express anger or discontent. The musical dimension of Riot Grrrl encouraged female self-expression and creativity and demanded that women be taken more seriously as artists, while the cultural dimension engaged with third-wave feminism and its ideals of using mass culture as a venue for activism to bring about social change. It was one of the most visible forms of third-wave feminism during this time but was limited in its scope (largely white, middle-class girls participated) and did little to affect civic institutions or legislation.

Another important development for third-wave feminism at the time was the race and gender activism of hip-hop, rap, and R&B artists such as Roxanne Shante, Salt-n-Pepa, Queen Latifah, MC Lyte, and Me'shell Ndegéocello. The artists themselves, however, would not necessarily claim that label. In her book *Black Noise: Rap Music and Black Culture in Contemporary America* (1994), Tricia Rose wrote that "during my conversations with Salt, MC Lyte, and Queen Latifah, it became clear that these women were uncomfortable with being labeled feminist and perceived feminism as a signifier for a movement that related specifically to white women."[3] This has often been a criticism of second-wave feminism and, in some cases, of the third. Many third-wave writers would argue that black women's presence in hip-hop was an influential form of expression that many young girls relate to, and that a major part of third-wave identity involves not just the inclusion of multiple racial and ethnic perspectives but a concern with multi- and bi-raciality and all of its complications, making hip-hop a central expression of and concern to the third wave.

THIRD WAVE IN THE DOT COM ERA (1995–2000)

Beginning in the mid-1990s, the countercultural energy of Riot Grrrl and the progressive hip-hop of artists such as Salt-n-Pepa and Me'shell Ndegéocello was replaced by more gender-conventional musicians such as Sarah McLachlan and the traditional singer-songwriters who performed as part of her woman-only Lilith Fair, and artists such as Mariah Carey and the more controversial raps of Lil' Kim and Foxy Brown. At the same time, the Spice Girls popularized the phrase "girl power," and, though debatably very different from it, "girl power" also became conflated with third wave. These developments in popular culture were directly related to economic developments such as the so-called new economy, the optimism attached to the dot com bubble and the Wall Street surge, and the marketing of "girl power" as a commercial slogan—that is, corporate multinational's attempts to court girls as consumer audiences. Research on girls, such as the American Association of University Women's study *Short-changing Girls, Shortchanging America* (1994), Mary Pipher's *Reviving Ophelia* (1994), Carol Gilligan's earlier edited work, *Making Connections* (1990), and Peggy Orenstein's *Schoolgirls* (1995), all called attention to the negative impact of traditional feminine socialization for girls and to the fact that they were not treated with as much seriousness as boys in educational settings. The results of the research also led to the development of many girl-centered programs that used the language of girl power, but were, initially at least, distinct from its consumer orientation. For most third-wavers, girl power and feminism were different, and feminism was more than a lifestyle choice circulating around the consumption of products. But in the mass media and the academy, the third wave was often represented as "lipstick feminism," "consumer feminism," or "feminism lite."

It was in this period, however, that third-wave feminism began to have a more public presence in terms of its writings and to develop a recognizable identity and set of goals and ideals. Although the term "third wave" was still confused with postfeminism in some circles, and although it was often dismissed by writers such as Anna Quindlen as "babe feminism" because of its emphasis on using popular culture as a tool rather than trying to remain outside it, foundational popular anthologies such as Rebecca Walker's *To Be Real: Telling the Truth and Changing the Face of Feminism* (1995) and Barbara Findlen's *Listen Up: Voices From the Next Feminist Generation* (1995) began to appear and to distinguish the third wave from the more controversial and possibly postfeminist work of writers like Naomi Wolf and Katie Roiphe. *To Be Real* explored how younger feminists defined themselves against both traditional stereotypes of race, gender, sexuality, religion, and class, and the ideas and ideals of second-wave feminism. *Listen Up* discussed issues such as blending careers and family with feminist politics, the inability of a single feminism to speak for all women, the ways traditional culture and third-wave sensibilities can intersect, and the connections between sexuality, identity, and ideas about gender. Heywood and Drake's *Third Wave Agenda: Being Feminist, Doing Feminism* (1997) was the first academic collection to fully present an account of the third wave and to attempt to chart both its debts to and differences from the second, as well as to attempt to bridge academic and popular feminisms. *Hypatia*, the journal of feminist philosophy, devoted a special issue to the third wave in 1997, and Devoney Looser and E. Ann Kaplan's *Generations: Academic Feminists in Dialogue* (1997) explored the question of whether second and third waves were based on a generational divide.

Highly successful third-wave magazines also gained a large audience in this period and included *Bust: For Women with Something to Get Off Their Chests* and *Bitch: Feminist Response to Pop Culture*. *Bust* describes itself as having "an attitude that is fierce, funny, and proud to be female, providing an uncensored view on the female experience." *Bitch* describes itself as "a print magazine devoted to incisive commentary on our media-driven world. We feature critiques of TV, movies, magazines, advertising, and more—plus interviews with and profiles of cool, smart women in all areas of pop culture."[4] Both *Bust* and *Bitch* began as zines, giving strength to the DIY (do it yourself) philosophy and still have strong followings today, and the names of both are a good example of the way third wave interacts with popular culture: taking old stereotypes about women and redefining them in a positive way, as well as admitting complicity with and a place inside popular culture that is simultaneously critical, and that sees the third-wave mission as making use of popular culture to effect social change.

THE THIRD WAVE TODAY

Perhaps one of the reasons that the term "third wave" has been so easy to conflate with other, very different terms such as "postfeminism" and "girl power" is because third-wave feminism has never had a monolithically identifiable, single-issue agenda that distinguishes it from other movements for social justice. One of its main emphases, in fact, has been on feminism and gender activism as only one part of a much larger agenda for environmental, economic, and social justice, and one of its main arguments is that it is counterproductive to isolate gender as a single variable. Furthermore, for the third wave, feminism is a form of inclusiveness; a feminism that allows for identities that previously may have been seen to clash with feminism. For example, one can be a devout Christian or a Muslim and also be feminist, one can identify with "male" cultures like sport and also be feminist, or one can participate in as well as critique beauty culture and also be feminist. A third-wave feminist often occupies "the rock-and-hard place of wanting-to-get-those-good-ass-jeans-without-giving-[your]-money-to-the-Gap."[5] Since race, gender, class, religion, and social location are all seen to intersect in third-wave feminism, different identities and different issues emerge as being important at different times. Furthermore, since the third wave came of age and is increasingly aware of its place in a globalized world, whose ideas of "development" and modes of production often promote overt discrimination against and exploitation of women in the non-Western world, most recently third wave has seen the importance of turning to, in third-wave feminist Winifred Woodhull's words, "an engagement with women's movements the world over."[6] The early third-wave feminist adoption of the idea that a single person occupies multiple social locations and identities simultaneously, and that, especially in the Western world, this means that one can be exploitative in one context while being exploited in another, makes it impossible to ever see oneself in a position of an absolute moral high ground.

Therefore, third-wave goals continue to center around the creation of an inclusive feminism that respects not only differences between women based on race, ethnicity, religion, and economic standing but also makes allowance for different identities within a single person. Third wave seeks to create a feminism that is not only critical of media and its representations of women but also produces media itself and makes use of that media and its representations to bring about social change. Online women's studies journals such as Krista Jacob's *Sexing the Political*, Barnard College's *Scholar and Feminist Online*, and the Canadian journal *Third Space* are all devoted to developing third-wave perspectives. Third wave also seeks to create a feminism that includes men and looks at gender as something that men have as well as women, and it seeks to address inequalities in multiple forums such as the growing gap between the rich and poor within this country, and between the "First World" and "Third World" globally.

Beyond these goals and others, most recently there has been significant agreement among practitioners of third wave that the term "third wave" itself has become a problem. In the Winter 2004 issue of *Ms.* magazine, Lisa Jervis, one of the founders of *Bitch*, wrote that "we've reached the end of the wave terminology's usefulness … Here's what we all need to recognize so that we can move on: Those in their twenties and thirties who don't see their concerns reflected in the feminism of their elders are ignorant of history; those in their fifties and beyond who think that young women aren't politically active—or active enough, or active around the right issues—don't know where to look. We all want the same thing: To borrow bell hooks' phrase, we want gender justice."[7] The third wave is concerned with gender justice and other, interrelated forms of justice such as environmental justice, economic justice, racial justice, and justice around sexuality, religion, and physical ability. Hannah Miyamoto, co-chair of the National Women's Studies Association (NWSA) Third Wave Feminisms group, echoed Jervis when she wrote that "at the 2004 meeting … many members felt that the time for manifestoes on behalf of the generation had passed, and the time has come to emphasize dialogue with Second Wave women." Parallel to the sense that distinguishing third wave from second wave is counterproductive in the current political climate is the sense that the focus of third-wave activism itself needs to change. According to Miyamoto, in the NWSA third-wave feminisms group, there was "a feeling that North American feminism focuses so much on issues like sex, beauty standards, and career that the movement has become excessively de-politicized…. At least as I see it, this project must focus on action by American feminists as U.S. citizens and scholars, and avoid directly interfering in less-developed states. Furthermore, critically examining laissez-faire global capitalism or perhaps, neo-fascist corporatism, unmistakably differentiates this approach to generational identity in U.S. feminism with that of Katie Roiphe and perhaps Naomi Wolf."[8] Miyamoto's comments echo the ideas about bridging generations and problems with the wave metaphor, as well as on the need for a transnational activist focus, expressed by many recent third-wave thinkers such as Jennifer Baumgardner and Amy Richards in *Grassroots* (2005); Stacy Gillis, Rebecca Munford, and Gillian Howie in the edited collection called *Third Wave Feminism: A Critical Exploration* (2004); and Rory Dicker and Alison Piepmeier in *Catching a Wave: Reclaiming Feminism for the 21st Century* (2003). Today more than ever, third-wave activists link gender concerns with concerns related to the environment, economic and social justice, and women's movements worldwide—linking third wave all the more fully with activists in the second wave. Directly aligned with activism in the second wave, third-wave feminism contributes to a wide range of social justice struggles today that include gender as one important variable of identity among others.

NOTES

1. Rebecca Walker, "Becoming Third Wave," *Ms.*, January/February 1992, p. 41.

2. All quotations are from the Third Wave Foundation Web site, "What We Do," http://www.thirdwavefoundation.org/programs/default.htm.

3. Tricia Rose, "Bad Sistas: Black Women Rappers and Sexual Politics in Black Music," *Black Noise: Rap Music and Black Culture in Contemporary America* (Hanover, NH: Wesleyan University Press, 1994), p. 176.

4. From "About *Bitch*" on the *Bitch* Web site, http://bitchmagazine.com.

5. From a post by Sarah Rasmusson sent January 21, 2005, to wmst-l@listserv.umd.edu.

6. Winifred Woodhull, "Global Feminisms, Transnational Political Economies, Third World Cultural Production," *Third Wave Feminism: A Critical Exploration* (London: Palgrave, 2004), p. 252.

7. Lisa Jervis, "The End of Feminism's Third Wave," *Ms.*, Winter 2004, http://www.msmagazine.com.

8. Post from Hannah Miyamoto sent January 21, 2005, to wmst-l@listserv.umd.edu.

Chronology

1991   Anita Hill charges Clarence Thomas with sexual harassment at his Senate Confirmation hearings for his appointment as Supreme Court Justice.

Naomi Wolf publishes *The Beauty Myth*.

Generation X: Tales for an Accelerated Culture is published by Douglas Coupland, and "Gen X" hits the public lexicon.

Susan Faludi publishes *Backlash*.

700 young women converge in Akron, Ohio, for the National Organization of Women's Young Feminist Conference.

Thelma and Louise, starring Geena Davis and Susan Sarandon, hits theaters.

The National Council for Research on Women and the Ms. Foundation publish the report, "Risk, Resiliency, and Resistance: Current Research on Adolescent Girls."

1992   Rebecca Walker writes in Ms. magazine (in response to both Clarence Thomas hearings and *New York Times* article proclaiming, "feminism is dead"), "I am not a post-feminist feminist. I am the Third Wave."

750,000 march on Washington for reproductive rights.

Third Wave Foundation founding project "Freedom Summer '92" takes place. The voter registration drive registers over 20,000 people.

A record 2,370 Democrat and Republican women run for state legislative office and the "Year of the Woman" is declared.

Four white cops are acquitted of assaulting black motorist Rodney King, whose beating was caught on videotape by a passer-by. Violent riots in Los Angeles follow the verdict.

"Riot Grrrls" break onto the mainstream media scene, catapulting bands like Bikini Kill and Bratmobile into the spotlight and calling for "Revolution Girl Style Now!" Riot Grrrl bands, zines, groups, and clubs are founded all across the country and a Riot Grrrl Convention takes place in Washington, D.C.

Women win all five of the U.S. gold medals at the Winter Olympics.

The American Association of University Women (AAUW) publishes the report "How Schools Shortchange Girls."

1993   Debbie Stoller and Marcella Karp start *Bust* magazine. Then a Xeroxed and stapled "zine," *Bust* had a circulation of 50,000 by 1999.

The Ms. Foundation introduces Take Our Daughters to Work Day.

Naomi Wolf coins the terms "victim feminism" and "power feminism" in her book *Fire with Fire: The New Female Power and How It Changed the 21st Century.*

David Gunn, a physician, is shot outside his clinic in Pensacola, Florida, marking the first in several serious violence acts aimed at women's health clinics and doctors who provide abortions that would escalate through the late 1990s.

"Army of God" manual describing sixty-five ways to destroy abortion clinics is found in the backyard of an anti-choice extremist indicted on nine clinic attacks.

Katie Roiphe publishes *The Morning After: Sex, Fear and Feminism* and sparks controversy with her indictment of the feminist movement.

1994   Violence Against Women Act is passed in Congress.

Lisa Jones publishes *Bulletproof Divas: Tales of Race, Sex, and Hair.*

Ani DiFranco's Righteous Records label, created in 1990, becomes Righteous Babe Records.

Tricia Rose publishes *Black Noise: Rap Music and Black Culture in Contemporary America.*

Congress passes the Freedom of Access to Clinic Entrances (FACE) Act, establishing federal criminal and financial penalties for those who use violence and intimidation to prevent persons from obtaining or providing reproductive health services.

1995   Barbara Findlen publishes the anthology *Listen Up: Voices from the Next Feminist Generation.*

Rebecca Walker publishes the anthology *To Be Real: Telling the Truth and Changing the Face of Feminism.*

The United Nations holds its Fourth World Conference in Beijing. There is a strong young feminist presence among the 50,000 attendees. The conference resulted in both a Beijing Declaration and a Platform for Action, which highlighted twelve key areas of concern for women around the world, and called upon the 189 governments who unanimously adopted the Beijing Declaration and Platform for Action to take strategic action in those areas.

Lisa Miya-Jervis and Andi Zeisler found *Bitch* magazine.

First all-female rap group, Salt-n-Pepa, wins a Grammy for Best Rap Performance for their single, "None of Your Business," from the 1993 album *Very Necessary.*

Anti-choice extremist kills two and injures five when he opens fire at two Brookline, Massachusetts, women's health clinics.

Former football star O.J. Simpson goes to trial for the murder of his former wife, Nicole Brown Simpson, and her friend, Ron Goldman. The trial, which was televised for its full 133 days, captivated the country and brought the issue of domestic violence into the public. Simpson was acquitted.

1996 U.S. women win nineteen gold, ten silver, and nine bronze medals at the Summer Olympics. The success is largely attributed to huge increase of girls and women participating in sports since the passage of Title IX (1972).

Laurel Gilbert and Crystal Kile publish *Surfergrrrls: Look, Ethel! An Internet Guide for Us!*

"Wannabe," the first single from the Spice Girls' debut album *Spice,* hits airwaves in the United States.

Female rapper Lil' Kim releases her first album, *Hard Core.*

1997 Leslie Heywood and Jennifer Drake publish the anthology *Third Wave Agenda: Being Feminist, Doing Feminism.*

The feminist journal *Hypatia* publishes "Special Edition: Third Wave Feminism."

Karen Green and Tristan Taormino edit *A Girl's Guide to Taking Over the World: Writings from the Girl Zine Revolution.*

Missy "Misdemeanor" Elliott releases *Supa Dupa Fly,* her first album.

The televisions series *Buffy the Vampire Slayer* begins its first season.

1998 White House intern Monica Lewinsky reveals that she has had an affair with President Bill Clinton.

Elizabeth Wurtzel publishes *Bitch: In Praise of Difficult Women*.

Anti-choice fanatic kills Barnett Slepian, a physician who performed abortions, in his home.

Bridget Jones's Diary by Helen Fielding is published in the United States.

Building on the success of *The Vagina Monologues*, playwright Eve Ensler starts "V-Day." The global campaign names Valentine's Day V-Day until violence against women and girls stops.

1999   *The Bust Guide to the New Girl Order* is published.

Activists from around the world converge in Seattle, Washington, to protest against the World Trade Organization, expressing discontent with global economic inequity.

The Independent Media Center is born when hundreds of people join together to cover the Seattle Protests via the World Wide Web. By 2002 there are more than 200 Independent Media (Indymedia) Centers all over the world.

Joan Morgan publishes *When Chickenheads Come Home to Roost: My Life as a Hip-Hop Feminist*.

Eric Robert Rudolph is charged with the January 1998 bombing of a women's health clinic in Birmingham, Alabama, that killed one security guard and seriously injured a nurse, as well as the 1996 bombing of a lesbian bar during the 1996 Olympic games in Atlanta, Georgia, and the bombing of another clinic in Georgia.

The world is introduced to Mia Hamm and the U.S. Women's Soccer Team when they win the Women's World Cup. Tearing off her shirt after scoring the winning goal for the team, Brandi Chastain stirs up debate about Title IX, women's involvement in sports, and the combination of feminine power and beauty.

2000   Jennifer Baumgardner and Amy Richards publish *Manifesta: Young Women, Feminism, and the Future*.

Beijing +5 Review takes place at the United Nations Headquarters in New York to review the progress made and to assess the work needed to be done since the 1995 Conference.

The Presidential election of 2000 between George W. Bush and Al Gore results in a highly contested recount in Florida and charges of voting fraud in that state. The U.S. Supreme Court decides nearly a month after the November elections that the recount of votes in Florida should not continue, and that Bush be declared president.

Bust magazine publishes "The F-Word: Feminist Issue" featuring an interview between second-wave feminist Gloria Steinem and third-wave feminist Kathleen Hanna (of Riot Grrrl band Bikini Kill).

No Logo: No Space No Choice No Jobs is published by Naomi Klein, making clear the impact of globalization on the lives of young people and the importance of youth in the "new global" movement.

2001 New York and Washington, D.C., are the targets of a terrorist attack on September 11. Nearly three thousand people are killed.

The United States declares war on Afghanistan and the American public learns of the plight of Afghan women under the Islamic fundamentalist Taliban regime, which feminists in the United States (and Europe) had been advocating about for quite some time.

Ariel Gore and Bee Lavendar edit *Breeder: Real-Life Stories from the New Generation of Mothers*, a book culminating from the work of their magazine, *Hip Mama*, which had been in print since 1993.

YELL-Oh Girls!: Emerging Voices Explore Culture, Identity, and Growing Up Asian American edited by Vickie Nam is published.

Medea Benjamin and others found CODEPINK Alert, a women's grassroots peace and social justice activists group, named in response to the Bush Administration's color-coded "terror alert" system.

2002 Lisa Merri Johnson edits *Jane Sexes It Up: True Confessions of Feminist Desire*.

The anthology *Colonize This! Young Women of Color on Today's Feminism* is edited by Daisy Hernández and Bushra Rehman.

Conference held at Barnard College results in what Women's Enews calls a "clash over the future" between second- and third-wave feminists.

Purdue University hosts a Third Wave Feminism conference.

The University of Exeter (UK) hosts a Third Wave Feminism International Conference.

Kimberly Springer questions the relevance of the concept "third wave" for young black women in her article "Third Wave Black Feminism?" in the Summer 2002 edition of *Signs*.

2003 Rory Dicker and Alison Piepmeier edit *Catching a Wave: Reclaiming Feminism for the 21st Century*.

The United States declares war on Iraq. Millions of people worldwide march against the war.

The Barnard Center for Research on Women launches *The Scholar & Feminist Online*, the first online-only, refereed women's studies journal in the United States. It is designed and managed by third-wave feminists.

2004 Lisa Jervis' article "The End of Feminism's Third Wave" appears in *Ms.* magazine's Winter 2004 edition.

Astrid Henry publishes *Not My Mother's Sister: Generational Conflict and Third-Wave Feminism.*

Beloit College holds a Third Wave Feminist Conference.

More than 1 million women and men take part in the March for Women's Lives in Washington, D.C.

Vivien Labaton and Dawn Lundy Martin edit *The Fire This Time: Young Activists and the New Feminism.*

Single young women are courted in the 2004 Presidential election by George W. Bush and John Kerry, after much is made over the fact that 22 million single women did not vote in the 2000 election. More than 7 million more single women vote in 2004 than in 2000. Sixty-two percent of single women voted for John Kerry.

Eleven states vote to pass amendments banning same-sex marriage in the 2004 election

Mattel introduces "Barbie for President" after Marie Wilson, President of The White House Project, asked Mattel to complement The White House Project's efforts to get more girls to aspire to be president. Mattel agrees but refuses to remove the doll's high heels or the wording on the box that reads, "Doll cannot stand alone."

Third Wave Feminism: A Critical Exploration, edited by Stacy Gillis, Gillian Howie, and Rebecca Munford, is published.

The Feminist Press publishes *The W Effect: Bush's War on Women*, edited by Laura Flanders.

2005   Jennifer Baumgardner and Amy Richards publish *Grassroots: A Field Guide to Feminist Activism.*

Younger Women's Task Force of the National Council of Women's Organizations holds its founding "Meet-up" in Washington, D.C., drawing 100 women ages nineteen to thirty-nine from around the country.

The Beijing +10 Review takes place during the annual Commission on the Status of Women meeting at UN Headquarters in New York. The two-week meetings are stalled for the first week when the U.S. delegation tries to include an amendment specifying that the Beijing Platform for Action does not include the right to abortion.

College-going feminists from around the country attend The Feminist Majority Foundation's National Collegiate Global Women's and Human Rights Conference in Washington, D.C.

Alphabetical List of Entries

Topical List of Entries

Academia

Academic Activism
Academic Feminism
Butler, Judith
Cultural Studies
Deconstruction
Education
Feminist Theory
Gilligan, Carol
Haraway, Donna
History, Postmodern
hooks, bell
McRobbie, Angela
Postmodern Theory
Queer Theory
Rose, Tricia
Women's Colleges
Women's Studies versus Gender Studies

Activism/Political Participation

Academic Activism
Baumgardner, Jennifer, and Richards, Amy

Clinton, Hillary
CODEPINK
Consciousness Raising
Cultural Activism
Environmentalism
Political Participation
Seattle Protests
Third Wave Foundation
Walker, Rebecca

Athletics

Hamm, Mia
National Girls and Women in Sports Day
Nike
Sports
Williams, Venus, and Williams, Serena
Women's Professional Sports Organizations

Body

Advertising
Beauty Ideals

McLachlan, Sarah
McRobbie, Angela
Morgan, Joan
Moss, Kate
Oprah
Phair, Liz
Roberts, Tara
Rose, Tricia
RuPaul
Tea, Michelle
Walker, Rebecca
Wallace, Michele
Whedon, Joss
Williams, Venus, and Williams,
    Serena
Wolf, Naomi

Religion

Islamic Feminism
Manji, Irshad
Religion and Spirituality
Religious Fundamentalism
Virginity Movement
Wicca

Sexuality and Gender

Bright, Susie
Butch/Femme
Butler, Judith
Compulsory Heterosexuality
Desire, Feminist
Drag Kings

Femininity/Masculinity
Halberstam, Judith
Haraway, Donna
Lipstick Lesbian
Multisexuality
Pornography, Feminism and
Pornography, Feminist
Queer
Queer Theory
Sex Shops, Feminist
Sexuality
Transgender

Terminology

Backlash
Bitch
Chick
DIY
Feminazi
Girl/Girlies
Girl Power
Hip-Hop Terms for Women
Queer
Third-Wave Catch Phrases
Womanism/Womanist

Violence

Domestic Abuse
Military, Women in the
Rape
Sexual Harassment
War

A

ABORTION. Abortion is a controversial surgical procedure that ends an unwanted pregnancy. For feminists of all "waves," it is seen as a cornerstone to women's rights. Around the world, 46 million women undergo abortion each year, with 26 million women doing so in countries where abortion is legal. Despite legality, 85 percent of countries do not have abortion providers. The CDC reports that in the United States in 2000, there were 246 legal abortions per 1,000 live births. Most women in the United States who have an abortion are twenty-five or younger, are white, and unmarried. Historically, abortion has at times been forced on minority, low-income, and physically and mentally challenged women. The right to abortion—secured by the Supreme Court decision in *Roe v. Wade* in 1973 but continually being challenged—is only one aspect to the issue of reproductive rights. Third-wave **feminism** has also focused on increasing the safety of legal abortion, access issues, free choice for all women, availability of over-the-counter emergency contraception, increasing the number of providers by including midwives, remembering abortion issues globally, and the importance of preserving the right while acknowledging the real world experiences of women and abortion.

Technologies. Numerous medical technologies exist for performing abortion. The morning-after pill and emergency contraceptive drugs are taken shortly after sex to prevent the ovary from releasing an egg or from the egg being fertilized and, although some anti-choice groups disagree, their use is generally not seen as abortion. Pregnancy in medical terms means a fertilized egg has implanted in the uterus, so emergency contraceptives do not end but rather prevent pregnancy.

Chemical Abortion. Depending on the stage of pregnancy, an abortion can be performed via numerous methods. Chemical abortion with the "abortion pill"—the drug Mifepristone (RU-486)—was approved after a long battle by the U.S. Food and Drug Administration in 2000 for use within the first seven weeks of pregnancy. Mifepristone works successfully by blocking the hormone progesterone, which a fertilized egg needs to develop. Ingested early on, Mifepristone begins the menstrual cycle, and the fertilized egg is shed from the uterus. Subsequently, misoprostol is taken to start uterine contractions and complete the abortion. Advocates of chemical abortion explain that it is safe and that many women prefer it to surgical abortion when it is available. Access to chemical abortion remains key to third-wave feminists because it is not widely available.

Surgical Abortion. In the first fifteen weeks, vacuum abortion is one of the most common methods and is extremely safe. This method consists of emptying the uterus by suction. From the fifteenth week until about week eighteen, a surgical dilation and extraction (D&E) is used.

As the fetus size increases, other techniques must be used to secure abortion. The drug prostaglandin in combination with injecting the amniotic fluid with saline may be used as an abortion method. Later-term abortions can be brought about by the controversial intact dilation and extraction (D&X) technique, named by physicians Martin Haskell, who developed the procedure as an alternative to D&E, and James McMahon. This procedure is controversially termed "partial-birth abortion" by anti-choice activists but is more appropriately called late-term abortion. President George W. Bush signed the Partial-Birth Abortion Ban Act into law on November 5, 2003, and many women's groups see this as a significant step toward reversing *Roe v. Wade* and eliminating a woman's right to choose.

Access to Abortion. Abortion can be elective or medically necessary, but regardless of the reason, abortion has been a controversial subject throughout history. Abortion has been regularly banned and otherwise limited, yet women have continued to have abortions. Abortion laws in the United States can vary widely by state, but thanks to *Roe v. Wade*, abortions are legal in the first trimester in all states and with certain restrictions in the second trimester. Before *Roe v. Wade*, unsafe abortions were the only option for most women. Estimates of illegal abortions in the 1950s and 1960s ranged from 200,000 to 1.2 million, with many women dying. Poor women and their families were disproportionately impacted by not having a choice about pregnancy and not being able to afford an illegal abortion. The long-distance travel required for some women made obtaining an abortion impossible. Racial disparity was also clear, with the rate of death during abortion being higher for women of color than for white women. Even now, with abortion safe and legal, many populations do not have the means or information to attain a safe abortion.

Roe v. Wade. The reproductive rights movement, in combination with the U.S. Supreme Court's ruling in *Roe v. Wade* (1973), relaxed or eliminated restrictions on abortion. The *Roe v. Wade* decision ruled that the restrictive regulation of abortion was unconstitutional. Abortion was safe, so it should be legal. A countermovement called for strict control over abortions, and social and political conflict ensued. Opponents of abortion argue that there is no rational basis for distinguishing the fetus from a newborn infant, believing that each has rights. For second- and third-wave feminists alike, reproductive rights involve a woman's right, not the state's right, to manage her pregnancy. Women's lives are at risk without access to legal, medically supervised abortion.

The public reacted to the landmark *Roe v. Wade* decision, with reproductive rights advocates applauding and anti-choice advocates campaigning to restore abortion restrictions. The *Roe v. Wade* decision is arguably the most controversial one in the Court's history. Views on abortion influence elections. Most Republicans remain anti-choice, whereas Democrats generally support a woman's right to choose, although many remain unclear where they stand. Republican administrations use an anti-*Roe* litmus test for judicial appointments.

Anti-choice activists broadly attack reproductive rights by working to enact state restrictions that include waiting periods, informed consent laws, restricting minors' access to reproductive services, biased counseling, measures giving legal status to fetuses or embryos, bans on public funding, insurance prohibitions, refusal clauses, laws imposing Targeted Regulation of Abortion Providers (TRAP laws), and unnecessary clinic regulations, in addition to staging clinic protests.

Importance of Abortion. The right to a safe and legal abortion was a major gain for American women and is key to saving women's lives. It is an issue of personal freedom for women to have a right to bear or not bear children and to have a right to accessible and affordable services. The right to abortion ensures that women, not the government or particular religious groups, have control of their bodies.

Abortion is typically framed by second-wave feminists as an issue of choice, but many third-wave feminists note that it is not a simple choice and that there may be financial, geographical, cultural, and/or familial hindrances on that choice. Third-wavers want to maintain the right for a safe legal abortion—and acknowledge the second wave's success in this—while simultaneously discussing what choice means. The third wave insists on listening to more women's voices and notes that there are contradictions surrounding "free" and "choice."

Since abortion is safe, increased access and availability of abortion are key issues. Where and how to have an abortion and the availability of this information, while simultaneously preventing women from being forced into abortion and respecting that choice, encompass important reproductive rights concerns. Be it financial coercion or otherwise, abortion is not always a free choice. It is also seen to be important to include women's personal history and experience in defining the issue of abortion and on how to be active on this issue. Women's emotional and physical experiences should be acknowledged in discussions of abortion.

Third-wave feminists demand that midwives be allowed to perform abortions, which would give women more options when it came to choosing a provider.

Fewer health care professionals are being trained in abortion techniques and increasing restrictions in states limit who can provide abortion services and with what funds. Younger women face increased difficulty in receiving proper care if there are waiting periods and parental notification requirements, which may lead to desperate solutions or problematic time delays. Continuing to re-solve these issues is important to third-wave feminists.

In April 2004, more than a million people participated in the "**March for Women's Lives**" in Washington, D.C., fighting for the many issues surround-ing abortion and reproductive rights. The name of the march was initially going to be March for Choice, but the diversity of groups in the coalition of the march organizers and the complexity of the choice issue led to the realiza-tion that the new title was more encompassing and focusing on the national and global issues involved in reproductive rights.

See also Women's Health; Volume 2, Primary Document 56

Further Reading: Feldt, Gloria, *The War on Choice: The Right-Wing Attack on Women's Rights and How to Fight Back*, New York: Bantam Books, 2004; National Abortion Federation, http://www.prochoice.org; National Abortion Rights Action League, Pro-Choice America, NARAL, http://www.naral.org; Planned Parenthood Federation of America, http://www.plannedparenthood.org; Solinger, Rickie, *Abortion Wars: A Half Century of Struggle 1950–2000*, Berkeley: University of California Press, 1998.

AMI LYNCH

ACADEMIC ACTIVISM. Academic activism can be defined as activities un-dertaken in and around educational institutions with the intent to advance one or more social justice agendas. Academic activism has been around almost as long as academic institutions have, and its recent history in the United States includes the student-labor coalitions in the 1930s, anti-nuclear prolif-eration organizing of the 1950s, civil rights campaigns and anti-war protests of the 1960s, women's movement activities of the 1970s, anti-apartheid rallies of the 1980s, and anti-sweatshop campaigns of the 1990s. Students, their teachers, and others who work in educational institutions are often at the heart of social change endeavors that call for transformations both in the larger culture and their own campuses.

Even a cursory look at the production and consumption of third-wave doc-uments (anthologies, Web sites, **zines**) reveals that academic institutions are primary locations where third-wavers cultivate both their feminist and activist identities. It makes sense, then, that academic activism—its functions, its meth-ods, its effects—should be central to understanding third-wave feminists as social change agents. Yet, as with so many ideas and practices that are part of the third wave, contradictions, tensions, and paradoxes surround academic ac-tivism.

College and university campuses, especially, have been the site of recent academic activism that includes visibility campaigns, efforts to expand and deepen student political involvement, and coalition work with larger social movements. In visibility campaigns, students and teachers explore, expose, and educate themselves and others about populations or concepts that are often invisible, taboo, or unpopular in dominant culture. Raising awareness about **queer** identities, naming and working against racial discrimination, and combating sexual coercion and violence are common examples. Other academics organize around issues that demand increased political involvement, focusing their efforts on voter registration drives, electoral campaigns, and proposed legislation. Finally, students are among the most dedicated participants in loosely organized coalitions that form national or international social movements against corporate **globalization**. Their efforts include anti-sweatshop campaigns that demand their schools use only clothing manufactured where workers are paid fair wages and allowed to organize unions, fair trade campaigns that demand their schools only buy and consume fair trade products such as coffee, tea, and chocolate, and anti-war campaigns that call for changes in U.S. foreign policy toward countries such as Afghanistan and Iraq.

The prevalence of activism on campuses derives from the unique mission of higher **education**. Colleges and universities, most of which are based to some extent in the Western tradition of the liberal arts, provide one of the few spaces in society where the independent pursuit of knowledge and critical thinking is valued *in and of itself*. In other words, the central purpose of the academy is the production and dissemination of knowledge; it does not have to produce a concrete "product" per se or, for that matter, turn a profit. Its often state-subsidized rationale is to encourage its members, more or less, to be critical of ideas, practices, other institutions (**media**, religion, **family**, the state, health care, etc.), and even itself while generating knowledge that will benefit society. The ideal of higher learning is to foster a civic society.

This heady mandate means that those who inhabit the academy have some cultural authority to raise concerns or advance ideas that are antithetical to the interests of other powerful constituencies, like business or government, in the larger culture. So, one can find, for example, serious considerations of Marxist (anti-capitalist) ideas, extensive critiques about the excesses of military culture, and historical treatments of society's failure to address racial discrimination and violence. Given this mandate to raise questions about the world, it seems almost inevitable that the people who move through these institutions would be inspired to act on behalf of a more just society. In addition, given that college students are often at a developmental stage in which they are questioning others' expectations of them and forming their own identities, the academy often becomes a place of simultaneous self-discovery and vigorous engagement with the issues of the day. This confluence of individuals and institutions produces students who are, in every sense, activists for social justice.

At the same time, academic institutions can limit the scope and effectiveness of social justice work in a number of ways. For example, the academy is a primary site for the (re)production of the middle class and, thus, implicated in sustaining particular class-based power relations. No matter what one's class background, a university education is a prerequisite for acceptance into the middle-class ranks of managerial and professional positions that hold legitimized forms of power in our society: law, business, science, teaching, etc. These positions come with all sorts of privileges that too frequently exclude others based on their income, race, lack of personal or professional connections, gender expression, cultural habits, immigrant status, physical characteristics, criminal record, etc. Therefore, the students learning about how society perpetuates inequities to protect middle-class access to privileges are often the same people who stand to benefit most from this protection. With an awareness of injustice frequently comes an awareness of one's own culpability in perpetuating it. Thus, the motivation to *avoid* questions about equity and justice can be equally compelling. And social class is just one example of the privileges that are both interrogated by and yet embedded within academic institutions.

The manifestation and negotiation of these sorts of paradoxes of position are principal objects of study for newer, **identity**-based academic disciplines such as **women's studies**, ethnic studies (African American studies, Chicano studies, American Indian studies, etc.), lesbian/gay/bi/**transgender**/queer studies, postcolonial studies, and working-class studies. These disciplines are the concrete results of academic activism and seek to focus attention on the powerful connections between identities, social justice, and knowledge production. Typically, students and faculty who are members of or in solidarity with these demographic groups argue that lacking visibility, suffering injustices, and enduring violence in the dominant culture not only warrant academic attention but also lead to new understandings of cultures, institutions, and theories based on the perspectives gleaned from these marginalized locations. This new knowledge, in turn, can then inform activist struggles for justice out of which the disciplines initially emerged.

For these same disciplines, however, a tension exists between their activist origins and their need to be seen as academically legitimate. Without demonstrating its legitimacy—through defining and policing the boundaries around a unique object of analysis, promoting standardized methodologies, constructing a canon of primary texts, and organizing disciplinary-specific outlets for publication—a discipline cannot make demands on institutions for its inclusion. Yet, this quest for academic legitimacy, by definition, must disavow or at least sideline social justice as the discipline's foundational objective. The question that confronts scholars, then, is about the relevant values between theorizing social change and practicing it. No matter what the discipline, students are more likely to be asked by their professors to study a social movement, not join one. And it is the skills of a theoretician and researcher—one who transforms something in the outside world into an *object* of study—that tend to be rewarded in the academy. So often, then, students who study and are therefore inspired by activists and activism in the "real world" simultaneously feel alienated from that world through the very act of studying it.

For example, students who identify as third-wave feminists might take a **feminist theory** class and get frustrated with the level of abstraction that theorizing requires. "How is this stuff going to have an effect on 'real women'?" or "Instead of studying this stuff, we should be doing something about it!" Anxieties about moving farther and farther away from practicing meaningful social change exist alongside of a kind of *idealization of activism* as that which is more "real" than what goes on in any classroom. In a way, by studying activism, and therefore turning it into an object of study, academic feminist practices transform feminist activism into something outside of themselves. It can become a kind of unattainable state of being or idealized identity rather than a set of practices that change in both meaning and effect as the contexts in which they are contained shift and change.

At the same time, a contradictory yet equally debilitating process occurs when one's own gendered, raced, sexualized, nationalized identity is the focus of intellectual interrogation. Frequently in this process, the preoccupation with the self becomes paramount. This is the case in many feminist classrooms where students may fret over their own identities as activists or feminists or anti-racists or anti-capitalists, etc. A comfortable boundary between students and their object of study is dissolved as the feminist classroom collapses the difference between learning about the world "out there" and thinking about the ways they themselves are implicated in that world. Therefore, social activism is transformed into a sort of cultural politics of the self, where self-**empowerment** and self-transformation become the primary mode of activist activity. This politics of the self can include alternative forms of personal adornment, sexual practices, and lifestyle choices that attempt to rework cultural ideals of, say, femininity or whiteness or consumption. The tension here is between the assumption that social change is about engaging in the world beyond the self and the assumption that transformation of the self inevitably leads to transformation of society.

Academic activism has also taken on new forms of legitimacy through the recent popularity of service learning, community-based learning, and internship programs promoted by increasing numbers of institutions. These programs can be administered either through disciplinary departments or through campus-wide initiatives supported by the school's administration, alumni organizations, community leaders, and even corporations. Students combine course work with work in the community beyond the campus to bridge the gaps between academic knowledge and its potential applications. Although these programs can enrich students' academic experiences immensely and offer much needed assistance to under-resourced social programs, they can also be exploitative of the very communities they are intended to help. This is especially true when students enter communities with little or no understanding of the people in that community, their histories of struggle, or the long-term commitment that is so often required to both work through differences of race, class, and culture and facilitate positive social change.

Academic activism is shot through with contradictions, tensions, and paradoxes. Although institutions of higher learning offer third-wave feminists opportunities for social justice work and to forge their identities as activists, they also can present limitations that are murky, difficult to negotiate, and propose no simple solutions. By their nature, then, academic institutions are both uniquely positioned to foster activism and problematic as agencies of genuine social change.

Further Reading: "Academy/Community Connections," *Feminist Collections: A Quarterly of Women's Studies Resources* (Special Issue) 20(3) (1999); Ayers, William, Jean Ann Hunt, and Therese Quinn, eds., *Teaching for Social Justice: A Democracy and Education Reader*, New York: New Press, 1998; Boren, Mark Edelman, *Student Resistance: A History of the Unruly Subject*, New York: Routledge, 2001; Campus Compact, http://www.compact.org; "Expanding the Classroom: Fostering Active Learning and Activism," *Women's Studies Quarterly* (Special Issue) 27(3/4) (1999); Kaufman, Cynthia, *Ideas for Action: Relevant Theory for Radical Change*, Boston: South End Press, 2003; MacDonald, Amie A., and Susan Sanchez-Casal, eds., *Twenty-First-Century Classrooms: Pedagogies of Identity and Difference*, New York: Palgrave Macmillan, 2002; Orr, Catherine M., "Challenging the 'Academic/Real World' Divide," in *Teaching Feminist Activism: Strategies from the Field*, Nancy Naples and Karen Bojar, eds. New York: Routledge, 2002; Readings, Bill, *The University in Ruins*, Cambridge, MA: Harvard University Press, 1996.

CATHERINE M. ORR

ACADEMIC FEMINISM. Academic **feminism** is an institutionalization of feminism in academia (universities and other educational arenas). It is an intellectual movement engaged with academic and political issues, perspectives, and approaches. Academic feminism began with women who created feminist scholarship in their disciplines and, more broadly, in the academy. Often in the form of **women's studies** programs and departments in universities, academic feminism articulates and houses **feminist theory**, gender theory, and **queer theory** and more explicitly brings feminist politics into the academy as an integral part of university departments, systems, and culture. Academic feminism combines the academic and the political, encouraging feminist and women-centered scholarship. As third-wave feminists build on the academic and political work of previous feminist movements, they emphasize the connection between academics and feminist practice, more overtly integrating community and social activism into the classroom and scholarship.

Feminism's presence in academia was (and still is) heavily influenced by women's liberation movements of the sixties and seventies, which provided a catalyst for women to pursue feminist issues in academic settings and to analyze and critique their broader contexts. Although those within the academy did not always believe that feminism was "academic" or rigorous enough, the more explicitly political, "real" world thought academic feminism was over-intellectualized; more theory than practice. Academic feminism and women's studies programs developed concurrently, as both insisted on making women the center of academic inquiry at a time when they were virtually invisible, particularly in university settings. As women's studies programs became more prominent in academia, feminism and interdisciplinary programs (encompassing multiple disciplines) existed on the margins of most college curriculums. In part because of their interdisciplinarity, women's studies programs were not always valued as legitimate parts of universities, and while academic feminism is a vital component of individual disciplines such as English, philosophy, psychology, and sociology (among others), it is not usually recognized as a discipline itself. Many feminists in academia believe that interdisciplinary programs thrive because they are not limited to one academic field or method of inquiry, providing limitless perspectives and possibilities. Others wanted to establish legitimacy for feminist work within the boundaries of disciplinary significance, trying to reconcile the tension between their feminist interests and the scholarship in their disciplines, while many third-wave feminists and academics argue that feminism can be academic without being institutionalized—disseminating meaning through intellectual and political frameworks and thinking critically about issues through feminist lenses and analysis, without relying on formally structured systems.

Third-wave academic feminism draws from prior movements but further blurs the lines between the academy and the real world, transgressing the borders of both by intertwining theory with practice, scholarship with activism, and intellect with politic. Third-wave feminists in academia insist on blending theoretical analysis and social movement and encouraging academics to write comprehensible theory (intellectual philosophies and ideas articulated in a way that students, and perhaps the general public, can understand), making it more useful and meaningful to women outside of academia. Third-wave feminists do this in much of their writing, particularly by framing the personal in political contexts in collections such as *Listen Up: Voices from the Next Feminist Generation* (Findlen, 1995) and *To Be Real: Telling the Truth and Changing the Face of Feminism* (Walker, 1995), and while some academic and second-wave feminists argue that these narratives are not "academic" or "theoretical" enough or are solely grounded in the personal, the tension between third-wave feminists and other feminists is clear: many second-wave and contemporary academic feminists do not view the personal as academic enough, despite the feminist mantra, "the personal is political."

Academic feminism speaks with multiple voices, simultaneously critiquing and enmeshed in institution(s) and forced to confront the institutional realities of feminism in academia. While feminism challenges traditional notions of power and hierarchy (as well as tradition itself), academic feminism is a part of a greater system rooted in those very elements, and challenging such systems from within those very systems inevitably creates tension. Ideally, systems change, but in many cases feminist politics become institutionalized, compromising their very foundation and threatening the most potentially revolutionary aspects of feminist theory and practice.

Critics of academic feminism (some of whom are feminists themselves) cite the institutionalization inherent in educational systems, arguing that feminist politics are relegated to administrative duties and responsibilities, negotiating their radical potential. Women's studies and academic feminism, critics claim, are more elitist and bureaucratic than feminist. Charges also include that academic feminists theorize about issues they should be working to change, depleting energy from movements addressing broader areas of social concern. Academic feminists, however, contend that **education** does address such concerns, whether through direct action or **consciousness raising,** increasing awareness about women's issues through course curriculums and educational programs.

As feminist thought has developed in academia, criticism has come from individuals who strongly oppose academic feminism beyond its institutional structures, in its social and political role(s) and position(s).

Critics such as Camille Paglia and Katie Roiphe (who most would consider anti-feminist) harshly criticize academic feminism, charging that such feminism relies on representing women as helpless victims (referring to academic feminism as "**victim feminism**") and therefore propagates falsehoods about women's condition in American culture. Such criticism is generally a response to academic feminist discussion and activism surrounding sexual violence and **rape** (specifically on college campuses), and Paglia and Roiphe both challenge the prevalence and seriousness of rape, claiming that feminism has blown such crimes out of proportion by encouraging women to call any sexual act rape and going so far as to deem such crimes the fault of the women themselves. The popularity of such critics has been part of feminist **backlash,** as these critics reinforce popular notions and stereotypes of feminism and elicit a strong response from both academic and not-so-academic feminists, who claim that such critics uphold oppressive and sexist conservative ideologies.

The third-wave movement in academia is crucial to maintain the feminist progress of second-wave academic feminists, as third-wave feminism asks scholars to re-imagine, revisit, and revise what counts as "inside" or "outside" the academy, illuminate the more common overlaps between the two, and encourage academic feminists to rethink the relationship between feminist scholarship and the public and that between activism and academic theory. Third-wave activity links feminism, the academy, and grassroots activism, thereby sustaining feminist struggle within and without institutionalized educational systems. As third-wave feminism continues to evolve, so does academic feminism, infusing education and academia with a new set of considerations, keeping feminism central—and anything but dead.

Further Reading: Findlen, Barbara, ed., *Listen Up: Voices of the Next Feminist Generation*, Seattle: Seal Press, 1995; Gupport, Patricia J., *Academic Pathfinders: Knowledge Creation and Feminist Scholarship*, Westport, CT: Greenwood Press, 2002; *Is Academic Feminism Dead?: Theory in Practice*, New York: New York University Press, 2000; Messer-Davidow, Ellen, *Disciplining Feminism: From Social Activism to Academic Discourse*, Durham, NC: Duke University Press, 2002; Walker, Rebecca, ed., *To Be Real: Telling the Truth and Changing the Face of Feminism*, New York: Doubleday, 1995.

Leandra Preston

ACTIVISM. *See* Academic Activism; CODEPINK; Cultural Activism; DiFranco, Ani; Globalization; Guerrilla Girls; Seattle Protests; *The Vagina Monologues; Volume 2, Primary Document 13*.

ADVERTISING. Today, advertising permeates virtually all aspects of our lives. Advertising is a third-wave feminist concern because through this marketing technique, negative and stereotypical messages about race, class, and gender are conveyed. Feminists argue that these components of advertising contribute to an ideologically oppressive culture by re-enforcing and recreating sexism, racism, classism, ageism, heterosexism, and ableism. Because women make 83 percent of all consumer purchases, advertising agencies accordingly gear their ads to appeal to female consumers. Corporate advertising does more than simply sell a product. Corporations advertise a way of life and teach consumers to think in certain ways. We are constantly bombarded by advertisements through radio and television commercials, logos on T-shirts, billboards, and computer pop-up ads. We are exposed to advertising when we use our ATM machines, see a bus drive by, go to the movies, or read a magazine. Advertising includes ads, product placement, undercover marketing, and entertainment that is heavily tied to products (e.g., the **Powerpuff Girls**, a cartoon television series). Advertisers increasingly blur the line between marketing and entertainment. The term "advertainment" has been created to describe this phenomenon. For example, MTV was originated as an entertaining format for recording labels to display their artists and entice consumers to buy their records. In this market-driven culture, no aspect of daily living is immune from advertising.

The relation between advertising and mass **media** has a long history. The advertising industry uses techniques similar to the tools of propaganda that were developed after World War I, such as the use of spokespeople, euphemism, glittering generalities, fear inducements, and testimonials from "just plain folks." Early soap operas first appeared as radio shows that were designed to appeal to women who were presumed to be homemakers. These serial shows were sponsored by soap companies that placed their ads throughout the shows. In fact, soap operas were designed for the purpose of selling soap. Today this practice of advertising through corporate sponsorship of entertainment continues, with the advertising industry spending more than $200 billion a year to promote consumer products. Twelve billion dollars is spent each year on ads targeting kids. Cosmetics and beauty aid manufacturers, which primarily market to women, spend more than $600 million yearly on magazine and newspaper advertising. Concert tours and sporting events are commonly sponsored by advertisers. This advertising practice teaches the public to equate an image or **desire** with various consumer products themselves. For example, Vans shoes sponsors the Warped Tour, thus sending the message to young consumers that certain shoe brands are hip and alternative.

A contrary view of advertising and corporate sponsorship of events such as extreme **sports** or **music** festivals is that such financial support allows artists to gain exposure and allows fans to gain access to entertainment. Because the effects of advertising are so powerful, critics of the third wave are concerned with how ideas about women, people of color, **sexuality**, and **identity** are conveyed through ads. One primary concern is the objectification of women (i.e., how advertising portrays women as objects or as sexual objects, and how it often portrays women of color as animal-like objects). Writer Alice Walker points out that in a society that considers nonhuman animals a lesser species, women of color are often animalized in modern advertising. **Fashion** advertisers have done this by using makeup to transform a woman into a tiger or zebra or by posing women in jungle scenes or in "untamed" land. The message here is that women of color, too, are "untamed" or "primitive" in their sexual appetites. This message ties in with pre-existing stereotypes about the sexuality of black and Latina women and other women of color.

Objectification occurs when women's bodies are used to sell products on the market, even when a product has no relation to the human form. Billboards display bikini-clad women selling cell phones, cars, or alcohol. Magazines and television ads use women's bodies to sell everything from new kitchen interiors to a band's latest CD. Often, **body** parts are used instead of the entire body. Objectification is particularly damaging because it takes place within a culture that devalues women's abilities and in which women, people of color, gays, lesbians, and **transgenders** often face hostility or outright violence. For example, one ad for Bitch Skateboards portrayed cartoon figures of a man and a woman, and the man was holding a gun to the woman's head and the word **"bitch"** was written above. One of the powerful and simultaneously dangerous aspects of advertising images is the way in which they are everywhere, and yet are consciously unnoticed. Current feminist efforts involve a focus on learning to view media and advertising in a conscious and politically informed manner. An important component of this project is learning to understand that mass media makes its money by selling audiences to advertisers who pay billions of dollars to run their ads so they can sell their products. Third-wave **feminism** understands the importance of learning how to "read" advertising and how to be active participants in the process of consuming all forms of mass media.

Advertising and Body Image. Jean Kilbourne writes that advertising promotes an unrealistic standard of beauty and an unhealthy preoccupation with body image. Advertising bombards us with images of impossibly rail-thin models. These models are often pre-pubescent and the visual images are digitally altered to create, quite literally, an image that is unattainable for women who have breasts and hips. Today, nearly 5 percent of young women in America are affected by **eating disorders**. Research indicates that approximately 15 percent of young women have unhealthy behaviors regarding food, ranging from starvation to compulsive overeating. One recent study (http://www.girlpower.gov/girlarea/bodywise/eatingdisorders/statistics.htm) found that 30–55 percent of girls started dieting between the ages of twelve and fifteen; 70 percent of sixth-grade girls surveyed said that they first became concerned about their weight between the ages of nine and eleven.

Although advertising does not directly cause eating disorders, there is an unmistakable link between the two, and advertising certainly contributes to the body hatred that many young women experience. As Kilbourne points out, when television was introduced to the Pacific island of Fiji, a significant increase in eating disorders among young women soon followed. The problem of weight and body image is exacerbated in women's or girls' magazines by the fact that images of extremely skinny models are often interspersed with ads for calorie-laden desserts and articles on weight loss. These mixed messages simultaneously entice and chastise women by telling women both to eat and be thin. Studies suggest that about 60 percent of all adult Americans are overweight. According to the Archives of Pediatrics and Adolescent Medicine, about 31 percent of American teenage girls and 28 percent of American boys are somewhat overweight. (Fifteen percent of American teen girls and nearly 14 percent of American teen boys are obese.) Many of these people have binge eating disorders that parallel the "binge-purge" patterns found in media advertising.

Young men are increasingly objectified in advertisements through the display of men's naked or partially nude bodies. Although cases of anorexia and bulimia occur disproportionately among women and girls, the increased objectification of men in ads corresponds to recent increases of eating disorders among men, as well. Currently, an estimated 10–15 percent of anorexics and bulimics are male. As men are more frequently objectified in advertisements, this becomes a feminist concern because the objectification of anyone diminishes humanity and puts people at risk for stereotyping and even physical danger. However, few white, heterosexual men are in danger of violence at the hands of women, while women remain at risk of attack by men through **rape**, battery, assault, or sexual harassment. Consequently, a core concern regarding the objectification of women in advertising is that this takes place within a cultural context that discriminates against women, and often this culture is not a safe place for women and girls. Some feminist arguments point out that ads for implants and **cosmetic surgery** send messages that women's bodies are inadequate and that they, quite literally, must be sliced and diced to conform to a socially constructed image of acceptability. On the other hand, there are also feminist arguments taking the position that an individual who chooses cosmetic surgery is exercising free will. Sometimes, explicit and ideological components of advertising coexist. An ad for an herbal weight-loss product may read, "I am half the woman I used to be and I love it." This ad is clearly addressing women's body size, but it can also be looked at in terms of power. Less than 10 percent of Congress is female and the top leadership of Fortune 1,000 companies is 98 percent male. Therefore, a feminist critique of an ad like this would look at women's unequal access to power and the fact that women do not want to be half their size or half their power; women must be full size—literally and figuratively—with full power and full voice.

Cultural studies and semiotics are two approaches to understanding how advertising contains symbolic and ideological messages that have political components or effects. These ideological messages include **compulsory hetero-sexuality**, monoamory, racism, ableism, and sexism and the idea that having more things makes people better. Each of these ideological messages is conveyed and re-enforced in advertising images. In contemporary society, for example, the concept that menstruating women are unclean is repeatedly broadcast through advertisements for feminine hygiene products. Ad copy for these products uses words such as "fresh" or "discreet," the implication being that without these products, menstruating women are dirty or vulgar in regard to bodily functions. The idea that a diamond engagement ring signifies true love was an invention of the De Beers diamond company and is another example of how ideological messages are created and conveyed through advertising. Today, the diamond industry is targeting women with its "right-hand ring" campaign. It tells consumers that the left-hand ring signifies love or **marriage**, but a woman who buys herself a ring to wear on the right hand signifies her independence through her ability to purchase consumer goods.

Many times men in ads are active. Men or boys are jumping, skateboarding, running, etc., while women and girls are portrayed more passively (sitting, smiling, laughing, or talking). Often ads show women with their mouths covered by their hands, clothing, or other objects. This recreates regressive **ideology** regarding women's roles and behavior in society. Feminism is linked directly to this issue because feminism is concerned with women finding the **empowerment** to speak out about what they think and believe in. Yet repeatedly in advertisements women's voices are symbolically muffled.

Everyday Pornography. Advertising frequently eroticizes dominance and submission, violence, and the objectification women and people of color. Feminist writer Jane Caputi calls this advertising phenomenon "everyday pornography." From a feminist perspective, ads are developed around the exploitation, objectification, and denigration of women and the female body. This reinforces fundamental precepts of mainstream morality, which is not only sexist and oftentimes racist but also heterosexist. This form of advertising conveys political messages about domination and imbalanced power dynamics that currently exist throughout society and are reflected and perpetuated through advertising (among other avenues). Advertising images that sexualize children or infantilize adults are examples of everyday child pornography. Feminists point out that these depictions portray women as being without power (as children in our society rarely get to make decisions for themselves), and furthermore they normalize the serious problem of sexual child abuse in our culture and then use this imagery to sell a product such as perfume or shoes.

Another feminist perspective argues that sexuality and pornography are liberating and sex-positive. However, many third-wave feminists who are working to increase media and advertising literacy argue that it is challenging to recognize manifestations of **misogyny** in advertising and pop culture because these images are naturalized in society; that is, they are so prevalent that it seems natural and we no longer notice or question the ideological messages.

This latter view is often misunderstood and contributes to the mistaken idea that feminism is anti-sex. Caputi and others argue this is not the case and distinguish between sex and pornography, where sex is something that takes place between mutually agreeing partners and pornography involves force or coercion. Feminists argue that pornography itself is sex-negative and misogynist because it sexualizes brutalities such as the humiliation, capture, and possession of women. Arising from the complicated, intersecting issues of feminism and sexuality are **pro-sex** feminists who claim that the consequences of censorship would be worse than objectionably sexualized imagery in advertising.

Further Arguments within Feminism. In addition to feminist critiques of mainstream media's relation to advertising, the issue is a serious one within feminism itself. For years the magazine Ms. alternated between selling ad space in its pages and remaining ad free. The conflict over advertising is encapsulated by a controversy at *Bust* magazine in the late 1990s over accepting money for cigarette ads. Many readers were angry about the magazine's decision because it was an independent magazine taking money from a profit-seeking corporation that was hawking a harmful and addictive product. The magazine's editors argued that feminism includes the freedom to make all choices as women see fit, including the choice to smoke or to accept tobacco advertising money.

The conflict at *Bust* exemplifies core concerns of contemporary feminism. On the one hand, people argue that if progressive ventures accept advertising money from large corporations, then it means feminism has lost to the status quo. On the other hand, perhaps the existing power structure can be transformed by using advertising dollars for progressive causes. Oftentimes, major companies that run ads in magazines have certain stipulations regarding placement of their ads near editorial content. For example, it is unlikely that a shoe company would accept having its ad near an article on sweatshop labor because of the implications that may be drawn regarding that company's labor practices. Magazines and other media rely on advertising dollars to exist or earn profits. Because the relationship between magazines' editorial content and advertising dollars is political, third-wave feminists pay attention to this issue.

See also Beauty Ideals; Consumerism; Discrimination against Women; Heterosexism; Magazines, Women's; Male Body; Pro-Sex Feminism

Further Reading: *Bitch* magazine, http://www.bitchmagazine.com; *Bust* magazine, http://www.bust.com; Kilbourne, Jean, *Can't Buy My Love*, New York: Touchstone, 1999; Klein, Naomi, *No Logo*, New York: Picador, 1999.

SHIRA TARRANT

AGING. "Aging" is a demographic term defined as the organic or biological process of growing older and showing the effects of increasing age. The aging process starts from the moment of birth and continues throughout the life span. In contemporary North American popular culture, the word "age" often means the categorization of particular groups, born at particular times, into cohorts (e.g., "Generation Y," "**Generation X**," and the "Baby Boomers") with particular wants, needs, interests, and norms. Similarly, "aging" generally translates into the marketing of products—usually targeting women but increasingly pursuing men—to counteract the physical signs of getting older.

"Population aging" (also known as demographic aging) occurs when the age distribution of older people relative to younger people in a society increases or when the overall average age of a particular group rises. This can mean that for a period of time, the ratio of "old" to "young" becomes higher than average. Expected to be one of the more prominent demographic trends across the globe in the next century, population aging presents challenges for Western health care, **education**, and social security programs, as the number of people using such systems will shift.

From a feminist perspective, the term is much more complex and its importance has become even more marked in recent years. Although third-wave feminists and **feminism** are not necessarily defined by demographics (as the authors of the classic third-wave text *Manifesta* [2000] write, it is "more an attitude than a rigid age"), age and the process of aging have played a significant role in their historical emergence. Leslie Heywood and Jennifer Drake's *Third Wave Agenda* (1997), for instance, characterizes those feminists born between the years 1964 and 1973 as third wave. *Manifesta* defines them as those born with feminism as their birthright: "therefore anyone born after 1965." Their coming-of-age (in essence, their *aging*) fostered a reconceptualization of what feminism could mean, and their foci—as diverse as the women who constitute the cohort—reflect their particular stage in life. Generational and intergenerational discourse has also emerged from the aging of the women's movement and the aging of its constituency, and it has received widespread **media** attention in recent years. The relationship between the second wave (the older generation, usually associated with the Baby Boomers) and the younger, third wave (often conflated with "Generation X") has revealed conflict—including anxieties and hostilities—within the women's movement.

However, intergenerational attachments between and among women have also become significant, as many women try to use the "generation gap" to their advantage. In 1993, the discipline of "age studies" was born from the increased popular and academic attention focused on age in the previous decade. Although it is a burgeoning field, it has attempted to resituate "age" and "aging" (as well as the social, cultural, and economic implications of those terms) not only within feminism as a whole, but with existing power structures in the movement and beyond. The goal has been to integrate age and aging into the common feminist lexicon of theory-building as a useful and timely analytical tool. The stress then would not only be on the biological processes associated with aging but also on the cultural, social, and economic factors involved.

Further Reading: Baumgardner, Jennifer, and Amy Richards, *Manifesta: Young Women, Feminism, and the Future*, New York: Farrar, Straus and Giroux, 2000; Gullette, Margaret Morganroth, *Aged by Culture*, Chicago: University of Chicago Press, 2004; Heywood, Leslie, and Jennifer Drake, eds., *Third Wave Agenda: Being Feminist, Doing Feminism*,

Minneapolis: University of Minnesota Press, 1997; Søland, Birgitte, ed., "Ages of Women: Age as a Category of Analysis in Women's History," *Journal of Women's History* (special issue) 12(3) (2001); Woodward, Kathleen, *Aging and Its Discontents: Freud and Other Fictions*, Bloomington: Indiana University Press, 1991; Woodward, Kathleen, *Figuring Age: Women, Bodies, Generations*, Bloomington: Indiana University Press, 1999.

CANDIS STEENBERGEN

AIDS. On June 5, 1981, the Centers for Disease Control (CDC) announced a new disease, Acquired Immune Deficiency Syndrome (AIDS), which is transmitted through sexual intercourse, blood, and infected needles. The third-wavers were the first generation to grow up during the discovery and epidemic of human immunodeficiency virus (HIV), which leads to the development of AIDS. Twenty years into the epidemic, women, especially young women, make up nearly half the population infected with HIV/AIDS. According to the CDC, infection rates among women tripled between 1985 and 1999, from 7 percent to 25 percent. Black and Hispanic women have been hit the hardest by the epidemic, making up three-fourths of new cases among women between the ages 13 and 24, and AIDS is the leading cause of death for black women between the ages of 25 and 44. Today despite **media** attention, publicity campaigns, and community services providing **education** and prevention advice, young women still do not get the information they need to protect themselves from HIV/AIDS. Stigmas about young women's sexual lives continue to persist, leaving young women at risk—especially as young women's sexual behavior evolves. In 2000, the CDC finally published information about lesbian and bisexual women's possible risks for transmitting HIV/AIDS, and **transgender** young women still receive little to no information about their risks and sexual health needs.

Because of women's invisibility in the AIDS epidemic, women quickly became active and vocal about the lack of proper medical diagnosis, care, and prevention education during the late 1980s and early 1990s. Women's activism began to pay off during the 1990s as the U.S. government, medical researchers, and organizations began to recognize the growing numbers of women and minorities being infected with HIV/AIDS. In 1990, the first National Conference on Women and AIDS was held in Boston, and in 1991 ACT UP's Women's Caucus, an early AIDS activist organization, published *Women, AIDS, and Activism* (1991), the first book about women and AIDS. By 1993, women and minorities were integrated into medical research through the National Institute of Health's (NIH) Revitalization Act, which broadened researchers to include women and minorities in federally funded studies. Recognition of the spread of AIDS among young women led to the research and the avail of more forms of women-controlled contraceptives and preventative methods, such as the female condom in 1993 and the development of microbicides (a new gel, **film**, or foam that women insert into their vaginas that attacks or blocks the HIV virus and/or other sexually transmitted diseases and infections).

Further Reading: The ACT UP/NY Women and AIDS Book Group, *Women, AIDS, and Activism*, New York: Between the Lines, 1991; Bockting, Walter, and Sheila Kirk, eds., *Transgender and HIV: Risks, Prevention, and Care*, New York: Haworth Press, 2001; Roth, Nancy L., *Gendered Epidemic: Representations of Women in the Age of AIDS*, New York: Routledge 1998.

HEATHER CASSELL

ALT CULTURE. From Riot Grrrls to Suicide Girls, debates about what is and is not "alternative culture" have become commonplace in third-wave feminist forums. Often underlying these debates is the question, "Alternative to what?" As many feminists point out, the answer to this question is not so simple. Often what is considered to be alternative to some people (and in certain ways) may not be seen as alternative to everyone (in the same ways). Taking into account such differences, what feminist alternative cultures and their critics share is a commitment to producing culture that does not simply rely on conventional images and ideas about how *all* women should think, look, and act.

For example, the Riot Grrrls' 1990s feminist movement offered an exciting alternative to punk rock's **misogyny** and made **feminism** accessible to many young people. At the same time it was criticized for failing to include the voices and perspectives of nonwhite, non–middle-class women. Likewise, the subculture Web site Suicide Girls, which displays its models' punky pinups alongside daily dairy entries, is frequently hailed as the apex of "alternative porn." Yet some feminists argue that most of the girls look more like Britney Spears with a "bod-mod" makeover than a revolutionary revision of beauty and **body** ideals.

Tensions like these are not new to the third wave. Rather, current debates are informed, directly and indirectly, by earlier generations of feminists. One example is the magazine *Off Our Backs*. Founded in 1970, it provided a space for women's voices and issues outside of the mainstream press. However, in 1984 an alternative to this "alternative" was created. Objecting to the anti-pornography position dominant in feminism at the time, Debi Sundahl and Nan Kinney founded *On Our Backs*, a sex-positive magazine written for and by lesbian feminists.

One of *On Our Backs*' controversial columnists, **Susie "Sexpert" Bright**, later began writing for *Bust* magazine. Created by Debbie Stoller and Marcelle Karp in 1993, *Bust* offers readers an alternative to glossies like *Cosmopolitan* and *Jane*. Once again, questions were raised about how "alternative" this cultural production is. Embraced for its savvy attitude, the magazine also faces criticism for giving more coverage to **DIY** (do it yourself) purses than DIY politics. In all of these cases, the question of commodification—or how feminist politics can turn into consumer products—prompts criticism. The Riot Grrrls' **"girl power"** became a mantra of the Spice Girls, while the Suicide Girls now boast an "army" that does their **advertising** in exchange for autographs and hooded sweatshirts.

However, as young feminists continue to resist racist, classist, and sexist practices, the importance of the term "alternative culture" prevails. Often it is the shortcomings of existing cultures that drive people to create new movements. Thus, the legacies of feminist alternative culture carry on in offshoots and counter-productions: women organize Riot Grrrl–inspired Ladyfest concerts across the globe, transpositive porn site www.nofauxxx.com explodes the boundaries of conventional beauty, and racially diverse *Fierce* magazine gives voice to women who are often marginalized in other feminist forums. These are just some recent examples of how feminists continue to create alternatives to the alternatives, helping strengthen and broaden the third wave's offerings of alternative culture.

Further Reading: *Bust* magazine, http://www.bust.com; *Fierce* magazine, http://www.fiercemag.com; http://www.girlzinenetwork.com; http://www.ladyfest.org; Nguyen, Mimi, "Riot Grrrl Worse than Queer Web site," http://www.worsethanqueer.com/slander/pp40.html; Tomlin, Annie, "Sex, Dreads, and Rock 'n' Roll," July 2004, *Bitch* magazine, http://www.bitchmagazine.com/archives/12_02sg/sg.shtml.

ANNA FEIGENBAUM

ANIMAL RIGHTS. Animal rights has become a concern for a number of feminists who have linked human's violence against animals with sexist manifestations of violence against women, claiming that both stem from a mentality that makes animals and women the "other." Although third-wave **feminism** has no unified stance on the issue, a number of feminists who identify as third wave also identify as ecofeminists and animal rights activists. The process of making women and animals into the "other" is seen in language and behavior. Household companions such as dogs and cats are seen as possessions and are often referred to as "it" instead of him or her. At the same time, conversations that center on **rape** or sexism often mention that women are "treated like meat," as well as objectified like animals in situations where spouses treat them as property and tell them to "shut up," often using physical violence. This is much like the abused dog who learns to stop barking to avoid getting hit or, thanks to newer technology, is cowed into submission by a shock collar. Indeed, everything from whips to collars to chains has been used to restrain and abuse not just animals, but humans as well, in times of slavery and in current sexual abuse and **"sex tourism."** In the dairy industry, cows are held in what the industry refers to as "rape racks" to be artificially inseminated, only to have their male offspring ripped away to become veal. The cows are then milked three times a day for several months, and the process is repeated again in an unending cycle for about a third of their natural life span, until finally the now "spent" cows are sent to slaughter. These individuals are reduced to something less than human, where human could be understood as including only the select few who demonize all others deviating from the white (male) norm. Ecofeminists argue that because discussions of oppression have repeatedly used the simile of humans being "treated like animals," without ever addressing the

implicit message that it is okay to treat animals as such, oppression will continue for both humans and animals. As a consequence, even when progressive struggles have made strides against oppression, these advancements must be measured against continuing violence against animals, as violence against animals is often the first step toward the use of violence against people. Instead, animal rights feminists argue that questioning a system of thought and a practice that makes living beings into property, and recognizing the intrinsic worth of living beings in general, would immediately improve the conditions of oppressed humans. Once one recognizes the need to treat a cow as a feeling, self-directing being, it becomes that much harder to discriminate or mistreat other humans simply because they differ in race, gender, nationality, and so on.
See also Environmentalism

Further Reading: Adams, Carol, *The Sexual Politics of Meat: A Feminist-Vegetarian Critical Theory*, New York: Continuum, 1990; Singer, Peter, *Animal Liberation*, New York: Avon Books, 1990; Spiegel, Marjorie, *The Dreaded Comparison: Human and Animal Slavery*, New York: Mirror Books, 1996.

JOSEPH SCHATZ

ART, THIRD-WAVE FEMINIST. A third-wave feminist approach to art can be distinguished from second-wave feminist ideas in its effort to transform "essentialist" ways of creating and consuming art and cultural productions. **Essentialism** is any perspective that claims that all women, regardless of their cultural differences, have certain fundamental, innate characteristics that can be attributed to their biology (e.g., the idea that women are "naturally" more nurturing than men). In a third-wave framework, the category of "women" cannot be reduced to assumptions that make all women the same. The third wave demands a perspective that takes account of issues of race, class, **sexuality**, nation, age, and ability, among other factors of social **identity** in relationship to gender. Third-wave feminist approaches to art also attend to what can be called "postmodern" cultural ideas and understandings of identity and culture. In this view, everyone has many aspects of identity, and those aspects can also sometimes appear to be at odds with each other. For instance, one person may have aspects of her identity that are privileged and aspects that are marginalized at the same time. For women who are identified as belonging to a "racialized" category of "nonwhite," the notion that she may be discriminated against on the basis of her gender might not seem as pressing as her experience of racial discrimination. The notion of "woman" as a universal category is challenged by third-wave ideas of speaking across differences and taking these differences into account when discussing social inequality and diversity. Third-wave feminist ideas about art, like other aspects of third-wave **feminism**, strive to translate, interpret, and adapt earlier and second-wave feminist politics and then practice to transform art and a range of cultural practices and identity productions. Third-wave feminist ideas about art can encompass a range of scholarly, artistic, and activist cultural productions and activities. They can include plays such as Eve Ensler's *The Vagina Monologues* and productions that center around feminist ideas, questions, and expressive cultures, and they may also include distinctive and diverse feminist cultures that are also defined by a liberal, conservative, or radical approach. Third-wave feminist art and cultural productions may also reflect distinctive cultural groups defined by ethnicity, sexuality, grassroots activism, and more. A third-wave approach to art acknowledges that "feminist art" might include a wide range of mainstream art (**visual art**, **music**, dance, **theater**, **film**) but would also recognize grassroots and regional and urban feminist subculture arts that can be found in Web sites, **zines**, comics, and performances.

Third-wave feminist approaches can also be seen in the cultural criticism of the arts that speaks back to mass-marketed cultural commodities such as Andy Warhol's ironic image of Marilyn Monroe. Third-wave feminist ideas may also attempt to subvert or question the meanings of gendered cultural objects, images, and performances that are typically connected to mainstream and mass popular culture. Feminist dance and performance art troupes such as Urban Bushwomen in the 1990s and the **Guerrilla Girls** in the 2000s are examples of black **womanist** and politicized cultural productions that "talk back" to mainstream cultural perceptions of women from a third-wave feminist point of view.

Although the term "art" does not always denote visual forms of artistry, it most commonly refers to cultural output that can be seen. An interdisciplinary arts perspective is valuable when considering third-wave feminism because third-wave feminist ideas may also be found in nonvisual and nonmaterial arts productions such as music and dance. In the academy, third-wave feminist approaches to art have emerged alongside the development of feminist film theory, **cultural studies**, and now feminist visual culture studies. The entire domain of art and art history has been challenged by questions of who is look-ing, who has produced the art, the global economy of visual images sold as products, and the politics of the ways different groups are represented. Feminist film theory has played a key role in developing important questions about who is looking at who in mass-marketed popular culture and about how women tend to be represented in visual cultures as "hot babes" or the objects of a male heterosexual gaze. Although there have been changes in traditions of representation since it was published in 1975, Laura Mulvey's widely reprinted essay, "Visual Pleasure and Narrative Cinema," is widely considered to be a ground-breaking article for feminist film criticism. Using **feminist theory** and psychoanalysis, Mulvey argued that the women's image in film as a "not-male" defined women as a passive "other," who only exists in relation to men (the main actors). The film's audience (including women) identify with this male gaze, so they are positioned to look at the women on the screen with pleasure and **desire**, and if they are women they will see also see themselves as objects of desire. According to Mulvey, the view of the camera and the audience's viewpoint are from the perspective of the film's male hero. The audience is meant to view women as he does. Therefore, the audience's gaze is always identified with the male ego. To disrupt this oppressive representation, Mulvey suggested that feminist views must detach from this tradition of desire and pleasure and make present women who are more active in terms of having desires of their own that are independent of the male heroes. Mulvey's essay remains a key text for studies of feminism and art and has been incorporated into cultural studies and film studies. It is also a useful essay for separating second- and third-wave approaches to art and the idea of seeing through a feminist lens. The black feminist writer **bell hooks** reread Mulvey's thesis almost two decades later. In hooks' 1992 essay, "The Oppositional Gaze: Black Female Spectators," she argued that Mulvey erred in the assumption that "women" identify with the desire and pleasure of looking through the patriarchal gaze. Hooks asserted that black women spectators had a history of resisting identification with an oppressive and also racist, white patriarchal gaze. She suggested that mainstream feminist film criticism had overlooked black female spectatorship. Black women looked at cultural productions differently, therefore resisting both the sexism and **racism** embedded in Hollywood films. This attention to difference and racialized aspects of women's experiences and identities illustrates how third-wave feminist approaches to art involve an ongoing discussion of how women have multiple forms of social identity, which can also involve race, class, sexuality, ability, age, etc. Discussions of identity and subjectivity have informed and characterized third-wave sensibilities about making, seeing, and reading visual art forms. However, the discussion of fluidity and multiplicity in terms of identity are also an important part of the postmodern revision that has become widespread in the Western academy since the 1970s.

The emergence of visual culture as a field of study follows the postmodern influence on art studies in universities. The concept of postmodern arts usually involves a sense that there has been a blurring of boundaries between "high" and "low" art forms and the divisions between disciplines and formal genres such as art, theater, art history, photography, film and **television** studies, communications, semiotics, aesthetics, and cultural studies. The notion of visuality has emerged as a critical location from which to question how vision itself—the way we see things—is a cultural construction. The act of perception is now understood as a process that involves history, culture, and memory as much as it involves human biology. Visuality broadly recognizes that the act of seeing and understanding what we see must involve all of the other senses that mediate acts of seeing and vision. The third-wave approach to visual arts is inherently postmodern in the way it blurs simple ideas about "good" or "bad" approaches to reading and understanding artistic and cultural productions in relationship to feminist goals and social identities. In other words, what seems "sexist" to one feminist may not seem so to another. The notion of a singular feminist critical reading of a "pro-" or "anti-" feminist art has been replaced by a more complex understanding of identity, arts, and cultural representations that can include multilayered ways of seeing and reading.

The idea of reading against the grain and the possibility that different audiences read a single work of art or cultural text differently suggest a greater emphasis on identity and culture in the act of reading and interpreting artistic productions. Such an idea represents a marked difference from second-wave mainstream perspectives, which suggested that a work of art or film bore an essential meaning, derived from the authority of the artist and patriarchal culture. An example of how different feminists interpret works of art as "pro-" or "anti-" women may be seen in the controversy over the art of Kara Walker (specifically whether stereotypes of African American women are affirmed or disrupted). The third-wave approach to art accepts that there is no one essential meaning to be found in a work of art and that there is no "essential" identity of the female spectator. If vision is a socially constructed idea of perception, then it is never fixed but rather always connected to a particular cultural context. This means that there are no "right" or "wrong" ways of seeing through a feminist lens and that vision itself is a part of a larger cultural experience that is fluid, multiple, and may reveal how different social identities may produce many different ways of seeing art.

See also Binary Oppositions; Deconstruction; Postmodern Theory; *Volume 2, Primary Documents 48 and 49*

Further Reading: Bloom, Lisa, ed., *With Other Eyes: Looking at Race and Gender in Visual Culture*, Minneapolis: University of Minneapolis, 1999; hooks, bell, "The Oppositional Gaze: Black Female Spectators," *Black Looks: Race and Representation*, Boston: South End Press, 1992; Jones, Amelia, ed., *The Feminism and Visual Culture Reader*, New York: Routledge, 2003; Mulvey, Laura, "Narrative Cinema and Visual Pleasure," *Screen* 16(3) (Autumn 1975): 6–18.

STEFANIE SAMUELS

ASIAN AMERICAN FEMINISM. The third wave of Asian American **feminism** encompasses more than a single movement or idea. Asian Americans are in a perpetual and constant state of "becoming," as well. This idea of "becoming" means that there is not one fixed or universal **identity** for Asian Americans. Becoming then represents the way in which their identities are constantly changing. Additionally, in the tradition of women of color feminism, Asian American feminism also uses the lens of "intersectionality" to examine social factors such as race, class, gender, and **sexuality**. (That is, instead of seeing these as individual factors, they are seen to be intersecting and simultaneous.) It also uses the lens of "**hybridity**," which is the multiple and often dichotomous (either/or) ways in which people exist in the world to examine the issues of Asian American women. (Many individuals such as transracial adoptees and those of mixed race speak of a "hybrid" existence.) This helps to account for the diversity of Asian Americans by including those from East Asia, Southeast Asia, and South Asia. It includes women who are born in the United States, refugees, and still others who have immigrated. It ranges from the working class to the highly privileged, from the noneducated to those with professional degrees.

The unifying issue of Asian American feminism is representation. Representation and the issues of objectification and invisibility have propelled third-wave Asian American feminism. The third-wave Asian American feminists have learned from second-wave mothers the importance of breaking silences and speaking truths. Maxine Hong Kingston's pivotal novel, *The Woman Warrior* (1976), helped to empower not only Chinese American women but also many other Asian American women. This fictional memoir acknowledges how Asian American women are often mistaken for passive, but in actuality they come from a long line of women who have transgressed social and familial restrictions.

The third-wave Asian American feminists have been extremely active in continuing to talk about things that are typically viewed as taboo. Issues of gender inequality, sexuality, invisibility, exotification (looking at Asian American women in a sexually stereotypical way that turns them into objects), and **racism** are being confronted by these feminists. Many Asian American feminists have found a creative medium to express these realities. The comedienne Margaret Cho has been extremely successful in finding a way to talk about serious issues such as **body** image, **eating disorders**, sexual exploration, and self-hatred through her comedy routines. She speaks from her own experiences, yet her audience is still able to identify with her. She has become a source of great pride for Asian American women, as she continues to push the envelope of what defines an Asian American woman, as well as her limitless possibilities. The cartoonist/actress Lela Lee has also found an effective way to convey her frustrations with society through her comic strip, *Angry Asian Girl*. This comic strip subverts the stereotype of the unconditionally accepting Asian girl to show her anger at being mistreated. **Zines** (underground and self-published mini-**magazines** either in paper or online) have also been a popular forum for Asian American women to express themselves without censor. Sabrina Sandata is a mixed-race Filipino writer who publishes the zine *Bamboo Girl*. *Bamboo Girl* confronts sexism, racism, and homophobia with a voice that differs from and combats white **patriarchy**.

Asian American feminists have also been extremely politically active in their communities. With organizations such as the San Francisco Bay area's Asian Immigrant Women's Advocates (AIWA) and Los Angeles' Korean Immigrant Women's Advocacy (KIWA), ties between Asian American and Asian immigrant women have been cultivated to fight against the exploitation of women workers, specifically in the garment industry, the hotel housekeeping business, and the production of computer chips. AIWA had an extremely successful campaign in the mid-1990s against several large clothing manufactures such as Esprit Corporation and Jessica McClintock. AIWA also founded the Youth Build Immigrant Power (YBIP) organization, which addresses the issues of the children of immigrant women workers. This project aims to build leadership qualities for immigrant youth and develop connections and understanding between mothers and their children.

Overall, the third wave of Asian American feminists is extremely diverse in population as well as in their interests. Asian American feminists continue to work at the local community level as well as at the transnational and global levels.

See also Volume 2, Primary Documents 8, 10, 27, and 58–60

Further Reading: Cho, Margaret, *I Am the One That I Want*, New York: Ballantine Books, 2002; Kim, Elaine H., ed., *Making More Waves: New Writings by Asian American Women*, Boston: Beacon Press, 1997; Nam, Vickie, ed., *YELL-Oh Girls!: Emerging Voices Explore Culture, Identity, and Growing up Asian American*, New York: Quill, 2001; Shah, Sonia, ed., *Dragon Ladies: Asian American Feminists Breathe Fire*, Boston: South End Press, 1997.

REBECCA HURDIS

B

BABE FEMINISM. First coined by journalist Anna Quindlen in her 1994 *New York Times* article entitled, "And Now, Babe Feminism," the term "babe feminism" refers to the heavily **pro-sex** agenda articulated by a politically diverse group of American feminists in the 1990s. "Babe feminism" has often been confused or conflated with third-wave **feminism**, but it is more accurately described as "post-feminist." Quindlen was responding to an *Esquire* **magazine** cover story on the new face of feminism, as represented by predominantly young, heterosexual, middle-class women who champion a feminist rhetoric of sexy and fun **empowerment**. Citing Camille Paglia (1992), **Naomi Wolf** (1994), and Katie Roiphe (1993) among others, *Esquire* proclaimed the arrival of a new feminist zeitgeist, wherein babe (or "do-me") feminists reclaim women's right to celebrate their sexual agency.

In her book *Prime Time Feminism* (1996), Bonnie Dow notes that these feminists, in their rejection of difference feminism, argue that women be as "sexually aggressive and power seeking as men are presumed to be." Babe feminists advocate an autonomous, empowered femininity that both welcomes and confronts contradictions stemming from the differences between what is perceived as the prescribed politics of an appropriately feminist **sexuality** and women's experiences. These authors argue against the "victim feminism" promulgated by the so-called feminist establishment. Strongly critical of the perceived dogmatism of academic feminism, babe feminists contend that their feminist foremothers espouse an **ideology** of sexual Puritanism that arises from the inaccurate and all too frequent portrayal of women as helpless victims of sexual violence, **beauty ideals**, and economic inequality.

These feminists claim to speak on behalf of the current generation of twenty- and thirty-something women who refuse the feminist label because they believe that "traditional feminism" has lost its relevance to their lives. For instance, Rene Denfeld, in her 1995 book, *The New Victorians*, posits that feminism has become so convoluted and complicated in its challenge to oppressive social institutions that formerly feminist agendas are actually patriarchal traps. Traditional feminism, she concludes, is discriminatory, right wing, anti-male, and anti-(hetero)sexual and advocates gender separatism and compulsory lesbianism. In the **media** and the academy, these ideological differences between feminisms has been constructed as a generation gap, in which the older generation of feminists is characterized as overly serious and prescriptive. Babe feminists purport to offer a realistic alternative for young women seeking livable feminist politics, but this form of feminism should be distinguished from third-wave feminism.

Babe feminists' successful engagement with the media also sets them apart from their predecessors. However, given that they tend to situate women's empowerment at the nexus of (hetero)sexuality, "Girlie" culture, and anti-feminist establishment rhetoric, critics question the mainstream media's complicity in promoting a **backlash** agenda via this sexy, readily commodifiable "feminism lite."

Critics argue that by locating the means to women's empowerment in the bedroom, babe feminism reduces the basis of feminist praxis from collective political questions to individual sexual lifestyle choices. Detractors also challenge that babe feminists ignore issues of difference by failing to address race, class, nationality, and sexual orientation in their texts, speaking to a homogenous demographic of white, middle-/upper-class, well-educated, American, and heterosexual women. Babe feminists are faulted for mounting their strongest attacks on the monolithic "feminist establishment"—a move that overlooks the diversity, plurality, and dissent present within contemporary feminisms. Largely associated with early 1990s writers such as Wolf, Denfeld, and Roiphe, the term "babe feminism" has fallen out of popular usage, and though it debatably may have represented one small part of the third wave, it was not representative of third-wave feminism in general.

See also Empowerment; Girl/Girlies; Patriarchy; *Volume 2, Primary Documents 4 and 52*

Further Reading: Denfeld, Rene, *The New Victorians*, New York: Warner Books, 1995; Johnson, Lisa, ed., *Jane Sexes It Up: True Confessions of Feminist Desire*, New York: Four Walls, Eight Windows, 2002; Siegel, Deborah L., "Reading Between the Waves: Feminist Historiography in a 'Postfeminist' Moment," in *Third Wave Agenda: Being Feminist, Doing Feminism*, eds. Leslie Heywood and Jennifer Drake, Minneapolis: University of Minnesota Press, 1997; Wolf, Naomi, *Fire with Fire: The New Female Power and How It Will Change the 21st Century*, New York: Random House, 1994.

SAMANTHA C. THRIFT

BACKLASH. Sir Isaac Newton's famous Third Law of Motion states that "for every action there is an equal and opposite reaction." This is precisely the process described by the term "backlash," which denotes a counteraction not against physical forces but against social or political events. The word took on a specifically feminist slant with the publication of **Susan Faludi**'s book, *Backlash*, in 1992. The main thrust of her argument is that **feminism** has become the victim of its own success, since the immense social changes it has instigated are being attacked by a reactionary, or conservative, counter-ideology. According to "backlash" thinking, women may now have greater social freedom and responsibility, but this has forced them to contend with a whole new set of potentially destructive problems. What precisely these dilemmas are, however, depends on the origin of the critique, which Faludi sees issuing from a wide variety of sources within the **media** and academia. Her debate is therefore impressively wide-ranging, encompassing a whole range of references—such as the **fashion** and beauty industry, **film**s and novels, medical journals, and employment legislation—and she makes the point that women are being inhibited by "scare" stories and seduced back into retrogressive models of feminine appearance and behavior.

According to Faludi, one of the most insidious aspects of the backlash is the notion of **postfeminism**, which she regards as merely a way of repackaging backlash **ideology** in such a way that makes it more attractive to women, and it encourages them to dismiss the concept of feminist activism that was so central to the second wave as unnecessary and outdated. In this way, women are repositioned as consumers rather than activists—their attention is turned to issues of **body** image and **sexuality** rather than political or social change.

The concept of "postfeminism" has increased in popularity since the publication of Faludi's book, and it has gained a number of prominent and contentious spokeswomen such as **Naomi Wolf**, Rene Denfeld, and Christina Hoff Somers. Although not functioning as a unified group with a centralized agenda, all these women have published works that, in their critiques of the second-wave feminist movement, might seem to exemplify the problematic politics of the backlash. In *Who Stole Feminism?: How Women Have Betrayed Women* (1994), Hoff Sommers writes admiringly of first-wave feminism, which she portrays as a liberal movement with the specific aim of achieving social equality for women, but she attacks the second wave for its self-righteous, radical, and socially disruptive politics. Sommers' argument is echoed by Denfeld in *The New Victorians: A Young Woman's Challenge to the Old Feminist Order* (1995), in which she asserts that feminism has lost touch with the very women the movement was meant to liberate, retreating into loony extremism on the one hand and academic obscurity on the other. Tellingly, both Sommers and Denfeld explicitly target Faludi's concept of the backlash, dismissing it as an example of modern feminism's dangerously misguided tactic of making women identify themselves as victims of a hostile patriarchal system bent on maintaining their subjugation at all costs. Opponents of such an idea would, of course, argue that in their refusal to admit that the backlash exists, Sommers and Denfeld are attempting to deny the very grounds on which their work could be most forcefully critiqued.

The backlash concept has thus become a fault line running through the center of contemporary feminism. Whereas conservative postfeminism attacks or ignores the backlash, second-wavers continue to publicize and resist the social and political practices they identify as oppressive to women. Feminists of the third wave follow their second-wave predecessors in taking the existence of the backlash for granted. However, they adopt a characteristically ironic and multifaceted approach to the issue, blurring the boundaries that divide "pro-" and "anti-" feminist positions. For example, the fashion industry is unequivocally condemned in *Backlash* for luring women back into a restrictive beauty culture, whereas a typical third-wave argument would be that women can enjoy control over the production of self-image by playing with different costumes and roles in a way that is personally empowering. From a third-wave point of view, the adoption of such a tactic would not mean to deny that the backlash does exist and that there are real forces in society that operate to keep women in a subordinate position. However, some third-wave feminists' apparent willingness to negotiate and appropriate in this way has led more conservative feminists to identify them as merely another aspect of the backlash.

See also Victim/Power Feminism

Further Reading: Baumgardner, Jennifer, and Richards, Amy, *Manifesta: Young Women, Feminism, and the Future*, New York: Farrar, Straus and Giroux, 2000; Denfeld, Rene, *The New Victorians*, New York: Warner Books, 1995; Faludi, Susan, *Backlash*, New York: Anchor Books, 1992.

SARAH GAMBLE

BARBIE. Barbie is a plastic doll originally created in 1959 by Mattel cofounder Ruth Handler after she discovered and then bought the rights to a cartoon prostitute character named Lillie, who was beloved by German men. Barbie was named after Handler's daughter, Barbara. Other dolls were added later, such as Barbie's boyfriend, Ken, who was named after Handler's son. To create the ideal life for Barbie, as well as the ideal marketing scheme for Mattel, set pieces and accessories (clothes, cars, the "Dream House," etc.) were developed.

Barbie is an American icon. She has been a topic of interest since the late 1960s among feminists who want to better understand the role children's toys play in the construction of gender **identity**. Barbie's effect on society is presumably even greater because in recent decades she has become popular among adult women.

Third-wave feminists have a love/hate relationship with this doll. To understand Barbie and third-wave **feminism** is to understand Barbie in a postmodern sense in which there is no negative or positive value placed upon her. The historical feminist critique typically lambastes the Barbie doll because she represents an unrealistic **body** ideal for women. If applied to a human body, Barbie's measurements would translate to a 39-inch bust, an 18-inch waist, and

33-inch hips. It has been argued that in real life, a woman with Barbie's proportions would not have the strength to stand upright. Second-wave feminism has critiqued Barbie for imposing unrealistic expectations of physical beauty and limited professional aspirations.

Third-wave feminist discussion about Barbie recognizes these concerns but also accepts that some people may find pleasure in Barbie and her aesthetic. Some third-wave feminists embrace Barbie for the camp value derived from her hyperfemininity. However, third-wave feminism also critiques Barbie for being an Anglocentric proponent of binary gender, **racism**, and **heterosexism**. The Barbie Liberation Front (BLF) is a group of culture jammers who oppose the oppressive gender messages conveyed by Barbie. BLF takes public action to convey their argument. For example, they have switched the voice boxes of talking GI Joes with those of talking Barbies on store shelves so that GI Joe asks, "Coming to my party Saturday?" while Barbie says, "Dead men tell no lies." This act exposes the dolls' perpetration of gender stereotypes. **Ophira Edut**'s 2002 edited collection of essays on body image and women (now known as *Body Outlaws: Young Women Write about Body Image and Identity Because Mattel Sued*) was originally titled *Adios, Barbie* to reflect the powerful impact the doll has on society's expectations of women's bodies and standards of beauty. Some third-wave feminists experiment with the concept of Barbie as an over-the-top example of gender as a social construction and gender as performance. Los Angeles–based artist Kari French has created entire exhibits around Barbie, with pieces in which the doll is used to create objects such as bowling pins and hanging mobiles. The intersection of the love/hate relationship with Barbie seems to have been a point of unification among zinesters and Riot Grrrls. Much zine writing and Internet chatter has been dedicated to sharing childhood stories of detaching Barbie's head and other nonconformist versions of Barbie play. Third-wave feminism generally believes that individuals are capable of making their own decisions and that only by understanding the political implications of how Barbie conveys ideas about race, gender, beauty, ability, class, and **sexuality** can they make an informed choice about whether to participate in "Barbie play."

Flava Dolls and Bratz have recently achieved enormous popularity among young girls. These ethnically diverse dolls reflect current youth trends (particularly **hip-hop** culture). These dolls especially appeal to those who are critical of the fact that Barbie and her friends are white or are dolls of color with white features, thereby contributing to hegemonic ideals about race and beauty. The popularity of Bratz and Flava Dolls both reflects the demand for broader ideas about what "pretty" looks like and at the same time contributes to the liberation of beauty from imitating Barbie's blonde hair and white skin. However, like Barbie, Flava Dolls and Bratz can be very expensive. Even though third-wave feminists tend to embrace the free expression of sexuality, many are concerned that Flava Dolls and Bratz encourage young girls to express an age-inappropriate sexuality and, like Barbie, perpetrate the objectification of female sexuality. Concerns regarding consumerism, identity, and hegemonic expectations of gender remain even, while Flava Dolls and Bratz have perhaps improved on Barbie's race and gender issues.

See also Binary Oppositions; Body; *Volume 2, Primary Documents 36 and 37*

Further Reading: Edut, Ophira, ed., *Body Outlaws: Young Women Write About Body Image and Identity*, Seattle: Seal Press, 2000; Lord, M.G., *Forever Barbie: The Unauthorized Biography of a Real Doll*, New York: William Morrow, 1994.

EMILIE TARRANT

BAUMGARDNER, JENNIFER, AND RICHARDS, AMY. Amy Richards (1970–) and Jennifer Baumgardner (1970–) are leading voices in the third-wave movement and have worked together since they met when they were twenty-two years old at *Ms.* **magazine**, where Baumgardner was an editor and Richards was a contributing editor and Gloria Steinem's personal assistant. They cowrote *Manifesta: Young Women, Feminism, and the Future* (2000) and founded **Soapbox, Inc.**, a national progressive speakers' bureau representing current events and cultural experts, after completing their national book tour for *Manifesta*. Richards and Baumgardner have spoken together at conferences, universities, and lecture halls about issues such as abortion, **media**, and other political topics that affect young women, as well as at events bringing together second- and third-wave feminists.

Richards is now a writer, activist, researcher, and organizational consultant. She cofounded the **Third Wave Foundation** with **Rebecca Walker** in 1993, and she is a political consultant to Gloria Steinem, the Ms. Foundation for Women, First Peoples Worldwide, Voters for Choice, and Scenarios USA. Her work has been published in *Bitch, Bust, The Nation, Ms.*, and other magazines and in numerous anthologies addressing third-wave feminist issues. Richards is also the columnist for "Ask Amy," an online activist advice column on http://www.feminist.com and a columnist for *Work for Change*, Working Assets' progressive e-magazine. In 1997, Richards was named by *Ms.* magazine as "21 for the 21st: Leaders for the Next Century," and in 1995, *Who Cares* magazine named her as one of twenty-five Young Visionaries.

Baumgardner is a writer, editor, fundraiser, and feminist and political public speaker. She is a political contributor for "She Span," a political discussion and debate program on the Oxygen Network. Baumgardner works actively with publisher Farrar, Straus and Giroux, reprinting feminist classics that have long been out of print (such as Germaine Greer's *The Female Eunuch*, 1971), and she is the author of *Look Both Ways: Girls and Sex* (2004), which explores bisexuality among young women. Baumgardner writes for *Bust, Bitch, Rockrgrl, Elle, Jane, The Nation*, and other magazines.

Baumgardner organizes, sometimes with Richards, intergenerational speaking events to bridge the generation gap between second- and third-wave feminists. Baumgardner actively raises money and awareness for the New York Abortion Access Fund and works with Haven, a small organization that, by raising money

and awareness, serves as a network for women seeking abortions and provides a safe place for many women. She is an active member of the Third Wave Foundation and works with the Ms. Foundation and Planned Parenthood.
See also Writing, Third-Wave Feminist; *Volume 2, Primary Document 41*

Further Reading: Baumgardner, Jennifer, and Amy Richards, *Manifesta: Young Women, Feminism and the Future*, New York: Farrar, Straus and Giroux, 2000; Dicker, Rory, and Alison Piepmeier, *Catching a Wave: Reclaiming Feminism for the 21st Century*, Boston: Northeastern University Press, 2003; Edut, Ophira, *Body Outlaws: Young Women Write About Body Image and Identity*, Seattle: Seal Press, 1998; Findlen, Barbara, *Listen Up: Voices from the Next Feminist Generation*, Seattle: Seal Press, 1994; Karp, Marcelle, and Debbie Stoller, *The Bust Guide to the New Girl Order*, New York: Penguin Books, 1999.

HEATHER CASSELL

BEAUTY IDEALS. Beauty ideals are a standardized set of physical characteristics used to judge whether a person is beautiful or attractive. These standards vary over time and across cultures according to societal values, but they are viewed as natural and unchanging. Female **body** types that have gone in and out of **fashion** in the last century include the thin, flat-chested frame of the flapper; the "classic hourglass" with full hips, small waist, and full bust of the 1940s and 1950s; and the current ideal, which is a thin body with large breasts. Historically, American beauty standards have been strongly linked to race and class, with preferred features being strongly associated with European whiteness: blonde and/or flowing hair, big blue eyes, and a small nose. Pale skin was an ideal when it signified upper-class status (i.e., not working outside in the sun), but with the rise of factory work, having a tan indicated not outdoor manual labor but leisure time and the resources to vacation in sunny climates, and thus came to be seen as an attractive physical trait. Standards for both women and men tend to shore up traditional ideas about proper femininity and masculinity as well: for example, "pretty" includes having delicate features and long hair on one's head but very little hair on one's body; "handsome" includes being tall and having a strong jaw line.

These ideals are reproduced and perpetuated in all sorts of complicated chicken-or-egg-type ways through individuals, families and communities, and institutions. Pop culture and the entertainment industry are seen as primary agents in the manufacture and promotion of beauty standards. The glorification of models and actresses, plus **magazine** cover lines touting "Seductress Hair: Tips for Lush, Tousled Waves" and "40 Hot Beauty Tips" are obvious examples of the ways in which ideas about attractiveness are purposefully disseminated. To place too much blame for such on the **media**, however, is to greatly oversimplify ways in which beauty standards are woven into our lives. Media messages surely exert a strong influence, but pop culture is as much a reflection of the world as a determinant of it. Furthermore, there are many other businesses and industries that, although they are connected to the media (particularly fashion and beauty magazines aimed at women) are separate from it and are heavily invested in beauty standards (e.g., makeup companies, plastic surgeons, and pharmaceutical companies that make weight-loss drugs). On an individual and **family** level, a friend might tell another how lucky she is to have "good hair" (a phrase used to describe straight, nonkinky hair in African American communities); or a mother might tell her daughter that she would be pretty if she would only lose that "extra" twenty pounds.

Feminists have always been critical of the concept of beauty ideals. One of the actions widely seen as having kicked off the second wave of **feminism** was the protest at the 1968 Miss America Pageant, which took issue not only with judging women based on appearance and the specific criteria used to do so but also with the rigidity inherent in having beauty standards in the first place. Protesters filled a "freedom trash can" with girdles, bras, makeup, and high heels in a symbolic casting off of societal expectations for feminine beauty. The Black Power movement also recognized the political value of challenging beauty ideals, with the slogan "Black is beautiful" designed to counteract racist messages of the culture at large and instill pride. More recently, the fat-acceptance movement has emerged specifically around issues of body size, **queer** movements have sought to make room for alternative expressions of gender, and Riot Grrrls have self-consciously challenged traditional notions of prettiness by combining elements of typically girlish appearance with decidedly unladylike items (e.g., baby-doll dresses and combat boots).

Current mainstream standards of beauty have, to some degree, been broadened through these and other efforts. There is much more racial diversity and a variety of features among those considered beautiful today than, say, fifty years ago: for example, actress/singer Jennifer Lopez, actress Julia Roberts, and model Tyra Banks are all emblematic of today's beauty standards, and all deviate from the traditional white, blonde, blue-eyed beauty "norm." Furthermore, some famous women's nonstereotypical attributes are often exaggerated: for example, Jennifer Lopez's butt is famously large, and singer Beyoncé Knowles is touted as "voluptuous."

Though there may be an increased spectrum of beauty ideals to choose from, pressure to maintain one's own looks has only intensified in recent years. Reasons for this increased pressure include a growing saturation of public space with **advertising** messages; an increasing number of available publications both in print and on the Internet (which also leads to more advertising messages); and "advances" in medical technology, particularly in the realm of plastic surgery, which have made cosmetic procedures more common and more affordable.

The issue of how much to partake in beauty culture is a difficult and complicated one for feminists. One extreme—the view that all participation in living up to any standard of beauty shores up sexist expectations and thus perpetuates sexism—overlooks the very real pleasure that many women take in grooming, fashion, and a style that sometimes overlaps with traditional femininity. The other extreme—the view that any choice that is pleasurable or fun for the chooser is automatically free from sexist cultural influence—ignores the way that gendered and commercial forces act to form the ways we make choices.

For these reasons and the attendant complexities, third-wave feminism takes beauty ideals as a central issue more often than did earlier social movements. Tactics for tackling it vary widely. Some reject the trappings of beauty ideals altogether by eschewing makeup, dieting, and the like. Others reclaim some of the elements of the beauty ideal, picking and choosing from those trappings while self-consciously refusing the entire package of traditional femininity. Many younger women, in reaction to a perceived anti-beauty bent among older feminists, argue that because beauty ideals are less restrictive nowadays, lipstick and other items often described as "girlie" can be actively feminist. They assert that making an informed choice, not the content of the choice itself, is what constitutes the politics of one's actions.

The tactic of reclaiming elements of traditionally feminine beauty culture has created a fair amount of controversy among feminists on a number of levels. Most straightforwardly, this conflict is seen as a generational one: second-wavers demonized (for example) lipstick, third-wavers have reclaimed lipstick for its pleasure and cast the doing so as a feminist act, and second-wavers do not take it seriously. However, the reality is, as always, much more complicated. First, this is not an entirely accurate view on either side. Second-wavers did not reject all things beauty related as completely as many younger women think they did, and third-wavers are more critical, or less embracing of beauty culture in its entirety, than their critics seem to think they are. Second, attitudes about beauty do not break down neatly along generational or second-/third-wave lines. Nonetheless, inaccurate perceptions can be stubborn, and feminist discourse about beauty culture tends to be set up oppositionally, with false consciousness and a killjoy nature flying.

Interestingly, many of these arguments echo those within feminist communities about topics such as pornography and sexual expression, bringing up the same issues of pleasure, choice, and sexist cultural influence and fueled by generational myths and misperceptions on both sides. Also, many feminists of all ages do not choose to politicize the choices they make regarding their appearance; perhaps the most common attitude is a recognition of both the flaws and the pleasures of partaking in beauty culture and a view that allows for participation that is cast as neither feminist nor anti-feminist.

Complicating matters even further is one measure of feminism's success. Feminist rhetoric, most notably the notion of making choices about one's body as a primary value, has made it into mainstream culture in many ways. Though originally used in the realm of reproductive rights, to support the idea that women should be able to choose if and when to become mothers, "choice" has come to be a buzzword that lends a feminist tinge to any decision. A statement that breast implants or facelifts, for instance, are perhaps capitulations to unrealistic cultural expectations for women's bodies and/of the **aging** process is often met with a counter-argument that women should be able to make their own choices about what to do with their bodies. Women who make these choices are doing it for their own reasons and should not be criticized. Another feminist ideal is that women should not judge each other's choices, which makes it difficult to talk deeply and honestly about the effects beauty ideals have on their decisions.

Some third-wave feminists make more of an economic argument, pointing out that beauty ideals are no longer as much about upholding a specific standard for women as they are about driving the consumerist economy. This makes the argument less personal but no less complicated.

Furthermore, some observers and critics see too much of a focus on beauty standards and pop culture within third-wave feminism and believe it is a detriment to other longtime areas of feminist activism that still demand attention. However, others note that attention to these issues is not given at the expense of others and that the intense mediation of our world and the sheer volume of advertising and marketing messages we are deluged with every day create conditions that demand such a response.

See also Girl/Girlies; Magazines, Women's; Male Body; *Volume 2, Primary Documents 19 and 38*

Further Reading: *Bitch* magazine, http://www.bitchmagazine.com; Bordo, Susan, *Unbearable Weight: Feminism, Western Culture, and the Body*, Berkeley: University of California Press, 1993; Edut, Ophira, ed., *Body Outlaws: Young Women Write about Body Image and Identity*, Seattle: Seal Press, 2000.

LISA MIYA-JERVIS

BEIJING FOURTH WORLD CONFERENCE ON WOMEN AND BEIJING +10.

The Fourth World Conference on Women (FWCW), attended by more than 30,000 participants, was held in Beijing, China, from September 4 to 15, 1995, and developed two important documents: the "Platform for Action" and the "Beijing Declaration," which stated that women's rights are human rights and simultaneously created a plan to advance goals of equality, development, and peace for women transnationally. After this conference, all countries in the United Nations joined the consensus to adopt and implement most of these documents. The "Beijing Declaration" acknowledges women and their achievements and looks toward the future to further empower and advance women so they can reach their full potential in society and their lives. It also ensures that human rights are inalienable, integral, and indivisible for women and girls. The "Platform for Action" established a set of actions for institutions to cease inequalities in various arenas. These actions also sought to address other issues related to women and girls including poverty, violence, rights violations, stereotyping, and the lack of respect for, promotion of, and protection of the human rights of women.

The 49th session of the UN Commission on the Status of Women (UNCSW) convened from February 28 to March 11, 2005, in New York to conduct a ten-year review (Beijing +10) of earlier gender equality commitments and to talk about remaining challenges and forward-looking strategies for the advancement and empowerment of women and girls. A declaration reaffirming the commitments made ten years ago in Beijing and calling for further action from governments was adopted at the end of the first week. This was the most significant outcome of the meeting.

See also Volume 2, Primary Document 47

Further Reading: Auth, Janice, *To Beijing and Beyond: Pittsburgh and the United Nations Fourth World Conference on Women*, Pittsburgh: University of Pittsburgh Press, 1998; Blea, Irene I., *U.S. Chicanas and Latinas within a Global Context: Women of Color at the Fourth World Women's Conference*, Westport, CT: Praeger, 1997; United Nations Division for the Advancement of Women (DAW), The United Nations Forth World Conference on Women, http://www.un.org/womenwatch/daw/beijing/index.html.

LAURA MADELINE WISEMAN

BIKINI KILL. Bikini Kill (1991–1998) was a Washington, D.C.–based Riot Grrrl band. Members included Tobi Vail (drummer), Billy "Boredom" Karren (guitar), Kathi Wilcox (bass), and Kathleen Hanna (vocals). In response to a male-dominated punk rock **music** scene, Bikini Kill helped to create the Riot Grrrl movement that formed to empower women through music, support groups, **zines**, and guerrilla art. Their basic, aggressive, punk-styled songs spread ideas about what they named "revolution girl style"; a call for women to speak out about violence, **domestic violence**, **rape**, **feminism**, and the importance of female friendships. Incorrectly dubbed the leaders of the movement, Bikini Kill dismissed the idea by insisting that Riot Grrrl was nonhierarchical. After the press portrayed the movement as a cute girl fad, Bikini Kill and the rest of the Riot Grrrl movement ceased giving interviews to corporate **media** sources. When playing live, Bikini Kill set up women-only areas at the front, passed out lyric sheets, and confronted violent male audience members. In the spirit of the movement, they maintained a nonhierarchical band structure by switching instruments and band responsibilities (such as booking tours or creating band-related graphics).

Further Listening: Bikini Kill, *The Anti-Pleasure Dissertation*, CD, 1995, Kill Rock Stars; Bikini Kill, *Bikini Kill*, 1991, EP, Kill Rock Stars; Bikini Kill, *Boy/Girl*, split 7" with Slim Moon, 1991; Bikini Kill, *Give Me Back*, compilation, 1991, Ebullition Records; *I Like Fucking/I Hate Danger*, 1995, 7", Kill Rock Stars; Bikini Kill, *Pussy Whipped*, CD/LP, 1993, Kill Rock Stars; Bikini Kill, *Rebel Girl*, 7", 1994, Kill Rock Stars; Bikini Kill, *Reject All American*, CD/LP, 1996, Kill Rock Stars; Bikini Kill, *Revolution Girl Style Now*, 1991, demo tape; Bikini Kill, *There's a Dyke in the Pit*, 1991, Outpunk Records; Bikini Kill, *Yeah Yeah, Yeah, Yeah, Yeah*, split album with Huggy Bear, LP, 1992, Kill Rock Stars.

Further Reading: Bikini Kill Factsheet, Kill Rock Stars, http://www.killrockstars.com/bands/factsheets/bikinikill; Juno, Andrea, *Angry Women in Rock*, New York: Juno Books, 1996; O'Dair, Barbara, ed., *Trouble Girls: The Rolling Stone Book of Women in Rock*, New York: Random House, 1997.

BREA GRANT

BINARY OPPOSITIONS. A key concept for third-wave feminists, "binary opposition" refers to any pair of terms defined by opposites, such as male/female, masculine/feminine, white/black, rich/poor, mind/**body**, reason/emotion, good/evil, active/passive, and subject/object. The late French theorist Jacques Derrida became known for his work of "deconstructing" (or taking apart) binary oppositions, particularly what he saw as their innately hierarchical nature. Derrida argued that both language and culture have been organized by entire systems of binary opposites and that the paired terms are never of equal worth: one side is usually considered to be more valuable than the other. For example, one side of the binary (white/rich/reason) is generally invested with greater value than its opposite (black/poor/emotion), one (masculine/male) is more privileged than the other (feminine/female). Interestingly, even though dualisms are in a constant state of conflicting value, they rely upon each other for their continued existence. In other words, there could be no hierarchy without their opposition: the linguistically and culturally dominant side of the binary (active) needs the other side of the binary (passive) to give it meaning. For instance, "light" is meaningless without "dark." To Derrida, the work of **deconstruction** was to move beyond the limitations of binaries. His work has been significant for feminist theorists in that it provided a way in which power relations (and their social, cultural, and political meanings) such as **patriarchy, racism,** and/or class could be analyzed and complicated. The work of French philosopher and writer Hélène Cixous also tackles binary oppositions, arguing more specifically that a patriarchal hierarchy organizes language and sex into positively and negatively charged binary terms (woman/man, passive/active), always favoring the masculine side. Going further, Cixous notes that these definitions are socially constructed and that the negative associations could be changed by actively writing against them to create new identities for women first, and then for social institutions and systems. She seeks a disruption of the structures that have established rigid sexual differences.

Since the early 1990s, however, there has been a wave of retrospection and rethinking of binary oppositions in these terms. Following the work of **Judith Butler,** a postmodern theorist best known for her work on gender as a performance, third-wave feminists have begun critiquing both deconstruction and French **feminism:** the former because it tends to impose its own limiting terms (i.e., "the Other") and often simplifies rather than complexifies, and the latter because it seems to rely on a return to a form of **essentialism** that remains deeply problematic. Some third-wave feminists, such as Jeannine De Lombard, have sought to challenge binary oppositions by challenging the terms themselves instead (her "femmenism" includes self-identifying as a "girly-girl" while insisting that others call her a "woman"). By evoking multiplicity, both contradictions and falsities emerge, which could shift **feminist theory** and practice into a more self-conscious, self-reflexive, and "provisional" place than before.

Further Reading: Butler, Judith, *Gender Trouble: Feminism and the Subversion of Identity*, New York: Routledge, 1990; Cixous, Hélène, and Catherine Clemént, *The Newly Born Woman*, trans. Betsy Wing, Manchester, UK: Manchester University Press, 1986; De Lombard, Jeannine, "femmenism," in *To Be Real: Telling the Truth and Changing the Face of Feminism*, ed. Rebecca Walker, New York: Bantam, 1995, 21–34; Derrida, Jacques, *Of Grammatology*, trans. Gayatri Chakravorty Spivak, Baltimore: Johns Hopkins University Press, 1976; Derrida, Jacques, *Writing and Difference*, trans. Alan Bass, Chicago: University of Chicago Press, 1978; McDonald, Kristie, "New Choreographies of Gender," an interview with Jacques Derrida, *Diacritics* 12 (1982): 66–76.

CANDIS STEENBERGEN

BIOLOGICAL DETERMINISM. Biological determinism is the belief that one's biological traits necessarily inform one's performance so that, for example, women are better suited to raise children because of their biology. This view is rejected by all forms of third-wave **feminism**, as well as by some feminists in other waves, who, while recognizing biological differences, argue that surrounding social structures and norms have more to do with one's performance than with biology alone. Hence, some feminists would revise the previous stereotype to say that women have become better suited to raise children because that was how they themselves were raised and that, if given different conditions, men can become just as good or better at raising children. Not only have biologically deterministic viewpoints been central to sexist beliefs and practices, but they have also taken a central role in **racism** by creating stereotypes of certain races as innately less intelligent, less hard working, or less "civilized." In short, biological determinism finds its home squarely on the nature side of the age-old nature versus nurture debate, claiming to stand for what is "natural." In regard to women's rights, fighting a biologically deterministic viewpoint has become an essential strategy, because in the past it has been used to deny women the right to work in certain professions because they supposedly require "the strength or business skills only a man can have." Biological determinism has also created boundaries that attempt to prevent women and girls from playing certain **sports** or competing on an even playing field. Such beliefs create assumptions that *no* females can fairly compete for certain jobs or in sports against males simply because *some* cannot, entirely ignoring the fact some females can indeed outperform numerous males in those same instances. Hence, while the average NBA player might compete at a higher level than the average WNBA player in basketball, the average WNBA player can still outperform the majority of men despite the biologically deterministic view that men are intrinsically better suited to play sports than women are. Interestingly enough, recently a number of evolutionary scientists have come out to discredit biological determinism by pointing out that, although biological characteristics do have an effect on an organism's behavior, the surrounding environment, both social and otherwise, also has an enormous impact on how an organism responds. Indeed, many scientists have concluded that the interaction between genetic characteristics and the environment is so strong that one cannot have a complete understanding by focusing on only one side, because certain environmental characteristics will cause certain biological functions to act differently depending on the given conditions. Therefore, biological determinism is a point of view discredited by all third-wave feminists and most contemporary scientists.

Further Reading: Burstyn, Varda, *The Rites of Men: Manhood, Politics, and the Culture of Sport*, Toronto: University of Toronto Press, 1999; Ridley, Matt, *Nature Via Nurture: Genes, Experience, and What Makes Us Human*, New York: HarperCollins, 2003.

JOSEPH SCHATZ

BITCH. A woman who is a "bitch" contradicts the submissive nature of female socialization. Third-wave feminists run the risk of being called a "bitch" for resisting cultural norms, but they actively work to redefine the term in a positive way so that a "bitch" is seen as any woman who stands up for herself. *Bitch* magazine is a good example of this redefinition. The magazine is part of the third-wave feminist movement adoption of the term, and it serves as another example of third-wave feminists co-opting the language of sexism and transforming its meaning into something empowering. What is of importance is not the word itself, but who wields its usage and how they define it. Founded in 1996, *Bitch* magazine is a contemporary feminist critique of pop culture and uses many of the techniques of alternative analysis and challenging accepted ideas about women.

Before the third-wave redefinition of the term, however, the word primarily functioned as an expletive used for women and was (and still is) often aimed at girls in adolescent attacks. The context of its usage can be varied. In popular rap **music**, "bitch" has become known as a synonym for a sexually available female. The outward expression of anger or **desire** is seen as violating the old female code of conduct. By the stereotypical definition, a "bitch" is a selfish woman who has learned to please herself instead of accommodating others. She has an appetite, which may be an appetite for food, sex, or power. Or that appetite may be for self-expression, in the case of a woman who refuses to be silent about her position and the position of other women. Former First Lady and now New York Senator **Hillary Clinton** has been repeatedly referred to as a "bitch" by **media** pundits for simply being a competent, outspoken, and self-determined adult. The word, in both its stereotypical uses and its redefinition by third-wave feminists, points to the ways in which language can be used to both control and empower.

See also Volume 2, Primary Documents 25 and 41

Further Reading: Baumgardner, Jennifer, and Amy Richards, *Manifesta: Young Women, Feminism, and the Future*, New York: Farrar, Straus, and Giroux, 2000; Wurtzel, Elizabeth, *Bitch: In Praise of Difficult Women*, New York: Anchor Books, 1998.

LEIGH PHILLIPS

BLACK FEMINISM. Because of the historical **racism** and classism of the women's movement, it is often debated whether or how black **feminism** is a part of third-wave feminism. Women of African descent, since the time of their original enslavement in the United States, have resisted as individuals and in organized groups. What they resist is an intersection of inequality that is represented by the multiple injustices of sexism, racism, and classism—all of which, in many cases, they suffer. After emancipation, when this intersection of inequality manifested itself into institutionalized, "Jim Crow" racism, black women began building a tradition of courage and resilience for themselves, not only on their own behalf but also on the behalf of the men and children of their community. This tradition is in stark contrast to Eurocentric or white feminism, which historically excluded men.

The term "black feminism" can be traced back to the 1970s and the crescendo of the women's movement, or the second-wave feminist movement. At the time, black women often accused white feminists of focusing on gender issues and ignoring those issues of race and class. They disagreed with white feminists' insular approach and their tendency to speak universally about sexist issues affecting "all" women, while ignoring the triple threat to black women formed along axes of sexism, racism, *and* class oppression. As a result, black women often thought their concerns were marginalized—even outright ignored—by the women's movement.

The concept of black feminism has a longer history than the term and can be traced to the nineteenth century, when as early the 1800s free black women such as Maria Stewart, Frances E.W. Harper, and Sojourner Truth worked on behalf of both the abolitionist movement and the women's movement, or the (first-wave) feminist movement. It was in 1851 that Truth made her often-quoted, if not misquoted, "Ain't I a Woman?" speech. Given that the rhetoric dominating the abolitionist movement often emphasized the right of enslaved "men" to be free, and because white women of the women's movement appealed to white men's greed for power by pointing out that their vote would fortify white political dominance, black women were marginalized by both movements and excluded from circles of political power. In her 1981 book, *Ain't I a Woman*, black feminist scholar **bell hooks** wrote that "the women's movement had not drawn black and white women close together; instead it exposed the fact that white women were not willing to relinquish their support of white supremacy to support the issues of all women."

By the close of the nineteenth century, black women, led by brave stalwarts such as Josephine St. Pierre Ruffin, Mary Church Terrell, and Anna Julia Cooper, began to organize what would become known as the Black Women's Club movement. In 1896 these women were instrumental in the formation of The National Association of Colored Women (NACW). The forerunner of today's National Council of Negro Women, NACW consisted of more than 100 black women's clubs from across the country with an outspoken mission to advocate on behalf of women, children, and the elderly, many of whom were former slaves still laboring under Jim Crow racism.

As the civil rights movement picked up steam in the 1950s and 1960s, black women continued to publicly advocate on behalf of their community in lieu of joining, en masse, white women who were simultaneously arguing for the increased rights of middle-class white women. The choice was made by many black women active in the civil rights movement to subvert their own needs in favor of the greater good of the entire community.

However, despite this willingness to sacrifice their own interests, black women's leaderships skills, efforts, and aspirations often went unrecognized and unappreciated by the black men dominating the Black Panthers, the Student Nonviolent Coordinating Committee, the National Association for the Advancement of Colored People (NAACP), and the movement's other various factions. Black women did not begin to publicly champion their own unique needs until after the turbulent 1960s, and in 1973 black feminists in New York City formed the National Black Feminist Organization (NBFO). Later they would hold a national conference, drawing for the first time hundreds of black feminists from across the country to one place for the stated purpose of addressing their own issues.

If the 1960s witnessed significant civil rights progress for the black community as a whole, then the 1970s belonged to black women as they began to focus on the specific issues that affect and shape the lives of women of color. It was during the 1970s that increasing numbers of black women began to publicly and privately question sexual oppression as manifested within the black community and the wider society. It was during this decade that black feminist writers, scholars, and theorists such as Alice Walker, Ntozake Shange, Toni Cade Bambara, Angela Davis, Toni Morrison, June Jordan, Michele Wallace, and other black women stepped forward to start the national debate about sexual politics in the black community. Census bureau population statistics from the 1970s reveal a significant increase in black single mother households, for instance, as black women privately began to assert their independence in the home.

In 1977, a grassroots black feminist organization, the Combahee River Collective, which began as a chapter of NBFO, issued a position paper on behalf of black women. By this time black lesbians led by Audre Lorde, Pat Parker, Margaret Sloan, and Barbara Smith were also publicly addressing the issue of homophobia in the black community. According to its black feminist statement, the Combahee River Collective stated its politics to be an active commitment to struggling against racial, sexual, heterosexual, and class oppression, all as interlocking and interrelated forms of oppression.

Lorde wrote in her 1984 book, *Sister Outsider*, that "black feminism is not white feminism in black face," and in 1983 Alice Walker went a step further by coining the term "**womanist**" to describe a black or of color feminist. Black women would continue to name themselves throughout the 1980s and into the 1990s and more vocally advocate on their own behalf in **theater**, in **fiction**, and in political and social arenas. They struggled against entrenched racism among white colleagues, argued for the expansion of a U.S. feminist agenda that included issues important to poor women and Third World women, and appealed for broader opportunities for black feminist academics. In 1991, black feminists organized nationally in defense of Anita Hill during the Clarence Thomas Supreme Court confirmation hearings, and in 1995 they organized to protest the exclusion of black women from the Million Man March. Although the struggle to be heard has historically been difficult and into the twenty-first century remains so, black feminists continue to defend the rights of black women and uphold as worthy of respect their valuable and unique citizenship in the United States. Although third-wave feminism claims that it has a vision of feminism that is by definition multiracial, and that it looks at the intersections of race, class, gender, economics, and religion, sometimes feminists most identified as third wave by the **media** still seem to put forward a white, middle-class agenda.

See also Womanism/Womanist; *Volume 2, Primary Documents 3, 7, 9, 20, 23, 26, 27, and 30*

Further Reading: Collins, Patricia Hill, *Black Feminist Thought: Knowledge, Consciousness and the Politics of Empowerment*, New York: Routledge, 1990; Guy-Sheftall, Beverly, ed., *Words of Fire: An Anthology of African-American Feminist Thought*, New York: New Press, 1995; hooks, bell, *Ain't I A Woman: Black Women and Feminism*, Boston: South End Press, 1981; Hull, Gloria T., and Patricia Bell Scott, eds., *All the Women Are White, All the Blacks Are Men, But Some of Use Are Brave: Black Women's Studies*, New York: Feminist Press, 1982; Lorde, Audre, *Sister Outsider: Essays and Speeches*, Berkeley: The Crossing Press, 1984; Smith, Barbara, ed., *Home Girls: A Black Feminist Anthology*, New Brunswick, NJ: Rutgers University Press, 2000.

MURIEL L. WHETSTONE-SIMS

BODY. In third-wave **feminism**, the female body continues to be a subject of great interest because it carries the burden of current cultural, social, political, and economic values. In fact, third-waver **Amy Richards** once called it "third-wave feminism's issue" for the variety of contexts in which it is of importance.

The third-wave movement openly rejects long-standing historical constructs, such as the idea that women are closer to nature and more controlled by their bodies than are men, and instead it focuses on the power relationships that stigmatize and devalue the female body. Drawing on the concept that the personal is political, and adding that nothing is more personal than the body, third-wave feminists confront the notion of "the perfect body" and celebrate the body in its diverse abilities, shapes, sizes, races, ethnicities, sexualities, genders, and classes. There is an expansion of ways to discuss the body. Third-wave feminism focuses on what the body can do and mean in the context of women's daily lives.

Body Image and Objectification. Although body image has long been a concern of feminism, third-wave feminism questions the role of dominant culture in the production and consumption of the "ideal" or "perfect" body. This body image that is produced and reproduced in U.S. **media** is male-supremacist, racist, ageist, heterosexist, anti-Semitic, ableist, and class biased in that the image is produced for the typically white male viewer (e.g., beer advertisements) who judges the body of the woman (for instance, when a woman is said to be a "5" or a "10"). Violence is unnecessary to subjugate women; just an appraising look will do it because it positions women as objects of male consumption. The only thing that is important is what women look like and that men think they are "hot."

Women can be negatively affected by the portrayal of the "ideal" body that is everywhere in **advertising**, the media, and private conversations. The "ideal" female body is fashioned by dominant cultural ideals about beauty that are supposedly superior to the reality of "flawed" bodies of real women. This idea of the "ideal body" versus "flawed body" makes people examine themselves and those around them for how closely they approximate the ideal, with the highest value attributed to those who come close to the idea. This kind of self-policing perpetuates the myth of what a "woman" is, the construction of what it means to be "feminine," and it makes women and men unconsciously accept dominant cultural ideals. As women compare their body and others with media representations of the "perfect" body, they participate in their own objectification as well as in the objectification of others. They see themselves and others as objects with the potential to become "better" or "more desirable" objects. In this way, body image is complicated as women come to be seen by themselves, other women, and men as malleable objects that must be cleaned up, stylized, shaped, colored, cut, groomed, tailored, and fit into the current "ideal" body image. Since the early 1990s, with the advent of male beauty culture and the proliferation of beauty products for men, this problem has become widespread in men as well, though not to the same degree as in women.

However, this feminist analysis of body image has done little to alter the ongoing struggle that women have with their bodies. A clear example of objectification can be seen in the fair-skinned, straight-haired, light-eyed images of African American, Asian, and Latina models in advertising, which only serve to reinforce the privileging of Eurocentric and Caucasian characteristics. The altering of racial features through plastic surgery, such as double-eyelid surgeries and nose bridges, also exemplifies the extent to which racial ideologies influence women to have unnecessary surgery via the Western medical system.

In fact, when women seek to achieve the "ideal" or "perfect" body image, they are at a greater risk for **eating disorders**; complications of extreme and unnecessary cosmetic surgeries; over exercising; exposure to drugs, which can permanently damage their hearts, lungs, livers, and other organs; and social anxiety and low self-esteem, which can be an effect of continuously falling short of achieving the "ideal" body image.

Resistance. The third wave critiques but also plays with body image. In fact, the third wave, perhaps more than any other wave, has opened up the space for women to play with their own images and step outside of rigid categories of appearance. Third-wave feminism calls for empowering subversive images of women so as to change the vision of our culture. Women need alternative body images to stop measuring their own bodies against idealized body images.

The political implications of a dominant, normative femininity and its body image—white, heterosexual, wealthy, and thin—operates in developed countries in a way that limits the potential for resistant and subversive modes of femininity, or anything that is different from the ideal. Still, many women struggle every day to resist **racism, heterosexism**, and classism in their workplaces, communities, families, and relationships.

Third-wave feminists maintain that resistance and the potential for subversive actions rest within the feminist movement as women recognize and celebrate the power of their bodies; however, subversion of traditional or even contemporary "ideal" body images has not yet freed all women from the bonds of objectification.

Body Politics. The politics of women's bodies continues to be a central feminist concern in the third wave. As noted, women are frequently measured according to their appearance, but women's bodies are also subject to social control. Disciplining women's bodies to conform to social norms and standards is one of the greatest issues facing third-wave feminism. Controlling women's bodies is a way of controlling women. Battles over reproductive rights are perhaps the most obvious example of the social control of women's bodies. Women of all races and classes face daily the specter of governmental control and interference in their health care, including access to a range of birth-control methods, abortion, fertility treatments, hysterectomies, and more.

American women also confront sexual harassment, objectification, and sexual, racial, and ableist discrimination both at home and in the workplace. Such discrimination actually prevents women from fully experiencing the capacities of their bodies.

Sporting Bodies. With regard to this issue of social control of women's bodies, historically female athletes have been subjected to the so-called female apologetic that mandates they perform like men and thus exercise a kind of masculinity while competing. Outside of **sports**, however, they are pressured to demonstrate a normalized and ideal femininity. The female apologetic is a term used for athletes who in their self-presentation conform to these norms. As such, it functions as an "apology" for aggressiveness, muscularity, and competitiveness and helps deflect negative criticism that female athlete comes dangerously close to crossing the boundaries between masculine and feminine. Women athletes have been subjected to two primary criticisms: that their physical differences make them incapable of performing sports competently, and that sports masculinize females and make them abnormal/lesbian women. Bodies of female athletes are subjected to close scrutiny because they "should," according to old stereotypes, avoid being too masculine looking. The emphasis on a slight feminine appearance in many women's sports (gymnastics, synchronized swimming, figure skating, and diving) has brought about significant health risks for female athletes who are encouraged to maintain dangerously low proportions of fat, even if this means training while anorexic or bulimic.

This female apologetic is used to restrict female athletes to the frames of normalized femininity and heterosexuality. Feminine appearance is emphasized everywhere in women's sports, and the negative stigmas of "mannishness," "muscle moll," and "lesbian" continue to plague female athletes. To this end, heterosexual women may actually be afraid to participate in sports because of the lesbian label. Although the "butch" body and "muscle moll" have traditionally been cast in opposition to the hyperfeminized body, the current trend in conjunction with the female apologetic suggests that muscles are acceptable, so long as female athletes publicly advertise their heterosexuality.

Since the advent of Title IX in 1972 in the United States, which banned sex discrimination in schools, female athletic participation has increased 800 percent. Since the early 1990s, two positive changes have occurred: gays and lesbians have enjoyed increased visibility and wider cultural acceptance, even as there is a virulent **backlash** against this visibility and acceptance; and female athletes have become more the norm than an exception. As a result, old stereotypes about female athletes have started to break down even as they continue to haunt the way female athletes are represented in newspapers, **magazines**, and **television**.

See also Beauty Ideals; Male Body; *Volume 2, Primary Documents 19, 26, 37–39, and 57*

Further Reading: Bordo, Susan, *Unbearable Weight: Feminism, Western Culture and the Body*, Berkeley: University of California Press, 1993; Edut, Ophira, ed., *Body Outlaws: Young Women Write about Body Image and Identity*, Seattle: Seal Press, 2000; Heywood, Leslie, and Shari Dworkin, *Built to Win: The Female Athlete as Cultural Icon*, Minneapolis: University of Minnesota Press, 2003; Kuo, Lenore, "SWIP Suggested Readings on Feminism and Body Image," The Society for Women in Philosophy, http://www. uh.edu/~cfreelan/SWIP/bodyimage.html; Switala, Kristin, "Body Studies in Feminist Theory," Center for Digital Discourse and Culture, http://www.cddc.vt.edu/feminism/bod. html; Weitz, Rose, ed., *The Politics of Women's Bodies: Sexuality, Appearance and Behavior*, New York: Oxford University Press, 1998.

WENDY A. BURNS-ARDOLINO

BORDO, SUSAN. Susan Bordo is a theorist embraced by many third-wave feminists for her analysis of the **body** and beauty norms. For women especially, Bordo describes the body as a battleground, caught in a **war** between cultural forces and the self. Bordo warns her readers that beauty culture has created culture of self-discipline, where women must constantly "police" their bodies in an effort to meet ideals of whiteness, wealth, and sexual propriety. Advertisements that depict waifish models not only idealize slenderness and promote a culture of anorexia, but they also idealize vulnerability, teaching women that they have to suppress their physical and emotional appetites. These ads warn women against being or wanting "too much." Bordo does not see women as

helpless victims of their culture; however, she acknowledges that, on a daily basis, women are faced with rigid beauty expectations. Therefore, although she is critical of the inflexible culture, she is sympathetic to women's compromises as they work within their culture. Like many third-wave feminists, Bordo would argue that women could actively participate in beauty culture without compromising their **feminism**: although it is admirable to protest culture by refusing to operate by its rules (not wearing makeup, gaining weight, and rejecting **fashion**), ultimately, women are always limited by the culture. Bordo suggests that a more useful means of protest is one in which feminists must constantly evaluate the implications of both cultural and personal **beauty ideals**.
See also Volume 2, Primary Document 19

Further Reading: Bordo, Susan, *Twilight Zones: The Hidden Life of Cultural Images from Plato to O.J.*, Berkeley: University of California Press, 1997; Bordo, Susan, *Unbearable Weight: Feminism, Western Culture, and the Body*, Berkeley: University of California Press, 1993; Bordo, Susan, and Alison Jaggar, eds., *Gender-Body Knowledge: Feminist Reconstruction of Being and Knowing*, New Brunswick, NJ: Rutgers University Press, 1989.

BETH KREYDATUS

BRIDGET JONES'S DIARY. The 1996 novel *Bridget Jones's Diary* originated from a newspaper column written for the *Independent* newspaper by the British author Helen Fielding. A *Pride and Prejudice* (first published in 1813) for the postfeminist generation, it tells the story of the misadventures of a thirty-something single woman in search of her Mr. Darcy. Although it is a comic and entertaining piece of light, romantic **fiction**, the novel polarized its readers from the start. Many readers found Bridget a heroine with whom they could identify, arguing that her anxieties concerning her **body** image and her problems in finding a boyfriend were an accurate reflection of their own experiences. For them, she was a realistic depiction of a generation striving to balance personal aspirations with a career. Others, however, were appalled, regarding the novel as nothing less than an example of the **backlash** in action. Viewed from this perspective, Bridget is a retrogressive heroine who possesses, but does not appreciate, the social and financial independence for which the activists of the second wave fought. Instead, her ambitions stretch no further than finding the perfect mate. Nevertheless, the novel instigated a whole new subgenre of romantic fiction—the so-called chick-lit novel—and terms in Bridget's vocabulary such as "singleton" (an unmarried woman over thirty) and "fuckwittage" (men's emotional manipulation of women) are now in widespread use. In 1999, Fielding published a sequel, *Bridget Jones: The Edge of Reason*, and the novel's popularity has further been maintained by the appearance of a **film** adaptation in 2001 starring Renée Zellwegger.

Further Reading: Fielding, Helen, *Bridget Jones's Diary*, New York: Penguin, 1999; Fielding, Helen, *Bridget Jones: The Edge of Reason*, New York: Penguin, 2001; Gamble, Sarah, "Growing up Single: The Postfeminist Novel," *Studies in the Literary Imagination* 38(1) (2005).

SARAH GAMBLE

BRIGHT, SUSIE. Susie Bright (1958–) is an American sex educator, author, editor, and performer. Nicknamed "Susie Sexpert," Bright is one of the most prominent sex-positive feminist figures and has played an integral role in promoting **pro-sex** ideas within the third wave. Bright cofounded and edited *On Our Backs*, the first **magazine** about sex for lesbians by lesbians, she has written columns for *Playboy*, *Salon*, and *Libida*, and reviewed pornography for *Penthouse*. Additionally, she was a contributing editor and advice columnist for *Bust*, a premier third-wave feminist magazine. Bright currently edits *The Best American Erotica* series, writes books, and gives speeches across the country. Her work explores all aspects of **sexuality** and the erotic through analyses of politics, culture, literature, and her own experiences. Committed to "erotic truth-telling," Bright works in opposition to American sexual Puritanism and repression because she "know[s] that sexual repression in our lives is a powerful weapon that is as antidemocratic and anti-egalitarian as any bayonet, and its vulgar origins are bigotry, opportunism, and superstition at its worse" (http://www.susiebright. com/why.html). The advocacy of individual sexual **empowerment**, a trademark of Bright's work, is very much a defining part of third-wave culture. Her critics claim that she is too simple in her analyses, investing heavily in individual pleasurable for social change and too readily offering sexual **consumerism** as an answer for complex sexual and cultural problems. However, the many fans of Bright's work, particularly women, laud her for empowering them through knowledge and helping them accept their own sexualities.

Further Reading: Bright, Susie, *The Sexual State of the Union*, New York: Simon & Schuster, 1997; Bright, Susie, "Why Susie," Susie Bright's Web site, http://www. susiebright.com/why.html.

HELENA KVARNSTROM

BUTCH/FEMME. Butch and femme are terms used to refer to sexual **identity** and gender presentation. A "butch" embodies masculinity in her/his style of dress, demeanor, and sexual practice; and a "femme" dresses and acts in ways traditionally associated with femininity. The terms "butch" and "femme" most often refer to lesbian norms and contexts. The practices and politics of butch/ femme can be traced back to the lesbian and bisexual communities in the Harlem Renaissance of the 1920s. Masculine black lesbians often referred to each other as "bulldaggers" or "studs." The later terminology used more by whites was "butch."

In the 1950s, working-class lesbian subcultures popularized a polarized political aesthetics that celebrated the intimate pairing of masculine women with feminine partners. The working-class butch was esteemed for her gender nonconformity in lesbian communities, and femmes, too, found invitation and acceptance for loving butch women. During the rise of lesbian and gay liberation politics, groups such as the Daughters of Bilitis argued that butch/femme appearances gave lesbians a bad name, casting them out of society. The Daughters of Bilitis pleaded for lesbian and gay assimilation into mainstream heterosexual culture. As the gay liberation movement gained momentum in the late 1960s and early 1970s, lesbian feminists argued that butch/femme lesbians were the antithesis to lesbian liberation. Many second-wave lesbian feminists claimed that butch/femme representations perpetuated lesbian oppression by imitating heterosexual gender roles. Likewise, in the 1980s, anti-pornography feminists contended that butch/femme lesbians were enacting patriarchal sexual practices oppressive to women. But, the 1980s also fostered a sex-positive movement that affirmed the erotic elements of butch/femme relationships and broke away from limiting orthodoxies of lesbian-feminists and middle-class lesbians who suggested that sex acts, such as vaginal penetration and sexual role-playing, served to reinforce patriarchal oppression of women. In *Odd Girls and Twilight Lovers: A History of Lesbian Life in Twentieth-Century America* (1991), Lillian Faderman noted that lesbian historians, such as Joan Nestle and Judy Grahn, recognized that butch and femme roles and relationships were not imitations of hetero-sexuality but were unique in themselves. She stated that Grahn has argued that butches were not copying males but rather they were saying, "Here is another way of being a woman," and that what they learned in the lesbian subculture was to "imitate dykes, not men" (169).

In the 1990s, in context of **queer** theorist **Judith Butler**'s groundbreaking argument highlighting the performative nature of gender, butch/femme was considered a form of play that disrupts socially prescribed notions of gender. And in the twenty-first century, third-wave feminists and queer scholars and activists continue to recognize butch/femme as subversion—a performative counter to the heterosexist **gender binary** that perpetuates oppressive and limiting roles. Many third-wavers connect butch lesbian expression with **transgender** identities and affirm that variation in gender is sometimes tied to **sexuality** but that gender and sexuality do not depend on each other.
See also Lipstick Lesbian; Queer Theory

Further Reading: Davis, Madeline, and Elizabeth Kennedy, "Oral History and the Study of Sexuality in the Lesbian Community: Buffalo, NY, 1940–1960" in *Hidden from History: Reclaiming the Gay and Lesbian Past*, eds. Martin Duberman, Martha Vicinus, George Chauncey, New York: New American Library, 1989; Faderman, Lilian, *Odd Girls and Twilight Lovers: A History of Lesbian Life in Twentieth-Century America*, New York: Penguin, 1991; Grahn, Judy, *Another Mother Tongue: Gay Words, Gay Worlds*, Boston: Beacon Press, 1984; Munt, Sally, *Butch/Femme: Inside Lesbian Gender*, London: Cassell, 1998; Nestle, Joan, "Butch/Fem Relationships: Sexual Courage in the 1950s," *Heresies: Sex Issue* 12(3) (1981): 21–24.

KRIS GANDARA

BUTLER, JUDITH. Judith Butler (1956–) is well known as a theorist of power, gender, **sexuality**, and **identity**. In her most influential book, *Gender Trouble: Feminism and the Subversion of Identity* (1990), Butler introduced the notion of "gender **performativity**." She wrote, "There is no gender identity behind the expressions of gender; [that] identity is performatively constituted by the very 'expressions' that are said to be its results" (25). Butler argues that gender is not a fixed or stable identity, but that it is a fluid and provisional performance dependent on time, place, and audience; that gender is created through the repetition of ideas about what men and women "are" that presume heterosexuality and a set of stereotypical characteristics. Butler's critique of the identity-based politics sometimes associated with **feminism** that insists on women's "essential" natures is one of the key ideas distinguishing **queer theory** from **feminist theory**. She (along with Gayle Rubin and Eve Kosofsky Sedgwick) is considered a founder of queer theory, which looks at how gender and sexuality are constructions rather than given natures.

Butler received her PhD in Philosophy from Yale University in 1984 and is a professor in the Department of Comparative Literature and Rhetoric at the University of California, Berkeley. She has received numerous awards and fellowships, including the Guggenheim Fellowship (1999) and the Rockefeller Fellowship (2001–2002). She is the author of several books including: *Antigone's Claim: Kinship between Life and Death* (2000); *Bodies That Matter: On the Discursive Limits of "Sex"* (1993); *The Psychic Life of Power: Theories of Subjection* (1997); and *Excitable Speech* (1997). She has also written numerous other books and articles on feminist and queer theory.

See also Essentialism

Further Reading: Butler, Judith, *Bodies That Matter: On the Discursive Limits of "Sex,"* New York: Routledge, 1993; Butler, Judith, *Excitable Speech: A Politics of the Performative*, New York: Routledge, 1997; Butler, Judith, *Gender Trouble: Feminism and the Subversion of Identity*, New York: Routledge, 1990; Butler, Judith, and Joan W. Scott, *Feminists Theorize the Political*, New York: Routledge, 1992.

KRIS GANDARA

C

CAPITALIST PATRIARCHY. Third-wave **feminism** has a divided position on issues of what has been called capitalist **patriarchy**. Patriarchy can be defined as the systematic subordination of one class (women), to another class (men), where men control women's (re)productive power, extracting and exploiting women's **sexuality**. Capitalism is defined by Marxists as the organization of social production for profit where one class (the bourgeoisie) owns and controls the means of production and extracts surplus labor from another class (the proletariat). The term "capitalist patriarchy," a synthesis of Marxist class analysis and feminist patriarchal analysis, indicates a historically specific form of patriarchy, functioning through class and productive relations. Some theorists argue that patriarchy and capitalism are two historically distinct systems that may be in conflict but today intersect, and others argue that theories of capitalism and patriarchy describe aspects of a single social system: gendered capitalism. The problem was how to explain the relation of production to reproduction: is male dominance the creation of capitalism, or is capitalism one expression of male domination?

Marxism and feminism are both theories of power and its distribution, and for feminist legal scholar Catharine MacKinnon, sexuality is to feminism what work is to Marxism: that which is most one's own, most taken away, and most alienated. Seizures of state and productive power may overturn work relations but would not overturn sex relations: a class analysis of sex would revolutionize Marxism. Heidi Hartmann argued that if all relations of oppression were reduced to relations of production, then the point that all women are and have been oppressed by men (and that this control assumes differing historical forms but is distinct from a woman's relation to production) would be missed. Juliet

Mitchell contended that women's relation to production—low pay, part-time work, and economic dependency—is one cause of oppression, but that biological and social factors and society's ideas concerning masculinity and femininity are also causes, which are often unconscious. By implication, an economic revolution would do nothing to alter these psychological facts.

Theorist Iris Young argued that women do not constitute a class and are not oppressed as women within the **family** and as workers within the economy but rather as women workers—capitalism is at its core gender biased. By replacing the Marxist category "class" with "division of labor," she found that the secondary role women play in production is an essential and fundamental characteristic of capitalism. Selma James and Dalla Costa suggested that, because domestic labor is necessary to the reproduction of capitalism, housewives ought to receive a wage, thereby making transparent the "socially" productive nature of "private" domestic labor and freeing women from economic dependency on men. Lise Vogel argued that for capitalism to reproduce itself, the conditions for production must themselves be reproduced: sexual reproduction is an essential component of social reproduction. Women fulfill a dual role because they are economically productive and sexually generative. This role is a source of contradiction, because when a woman is reproductively active, her economic productivity is reduced. This contradiction is resolved in three ways: (1) women's form of labor allows for greater flexibility; (2) by paying women paid two-thirds of a male wage for the same work, their economic dependency is reinforced; and (3) the ruling class enlists the support of working-class men to ensure that when a woman is economically less active, she "freely'" performs the necessary domestic labor required to guarantee the maximum economic labor from men. Men consent to the general system, which also exploits them, because they reap sex-based rewards: sanctioned advantage (economic privilege) and sanctioned domination (patriarchal authority). Vogel's account allows the fact of sex-specific oppression within a general framework of economic exploitation.

Finding Marxism and feminism increasingly incompatible, and Marxism itself a redundant modernist theory, a new wave of historical materialist feminism emerged, which was grounded upon women's bodies and concerned with differences—especially race and ethnicity. Some third-wavers believe that technoculture and **globalization** mark the end of patriarchy, and others believe that the harsh economic truths of global processes have meant that anti-capitalist activism must become part of a reinvigorated feminism. Third-wave feminists interested in the shifting economic relations of global capitalist production and the specific roles women occupy will find the disputes between these theorists still relevant.

See also Wage Gap

Further Reading: Einstein, Zillah, ed., *Capitalist Patriarchy and the Case for Socialist Feminism*, New York: Monthly Review Press, 1979; MacKinnon, Catharine, "Feminism, Marxism, Method: An Agenda for Theory," in *Feminist Theory: A Critique of Ideology*, eds. Barbara C. Gelpi, Nannerl Keohane, and Michelle Z. Rosaldo, Sussex,

UK: Harvester, 1982; Tong, Rosemary, *Feminist Thought: A Comprehensive Introduction*, London: Unwin Hyman, 1989.

GILLIAN HOWIE

CEDAW. During the second-wave era, Third World women initiated efforts to gain international acknowledgment of basic human rights to food, health services, and subsistence wages. In 1967, the United Nations Commission on the Status of Women began work on CEDAW (Convention on the Elimination of All Forms of Discrimination Against Women), the world's first comprehensive treaty on women's rights, and endorsed it in June 1975. Since then, a multicultural network of grassroots activists, including third-wave feminists, has supported CEDAW. CEDAW's goal is a more just world via the transformation of cultural infrastructures that shape the quality of women's lives and opportunities.

CEDAW catalogs specific forms of **discrimination against women**, including **domestic violence**, female infanticide, genital mutilation, slavery, and systematic **rape** as a military strategy. The U.N. General Assembly adopted CEDAW on December 18, 1979. In signing the treaty on July 17, 1980, Jimmy Carter became the first U.S. president to advocate human rights as a primary factor in setting foreign policy. Women whose lives were blighted by state-condoned discrimination testified in international hearings from 1982 to 1987. By May 2004, 177 U.N. member nations had ratified CEDAW, but 8 percent (including the United States) had not. This stance continues to reflect poorly on the United States in the international human rights arena.

Further Reading: Bunch, Charlotte, and Niamh Reilly, *Demanding Accountability: The Global Campaign and Vienna Tribunal for Women's Human Rights*, New Jersey: Center for Women's Global Leadership, Rutgers University Press, 1994; CEDAW: Treaty for the Rights of Women, http://www.womenstreaty.org; U.N. Centre for Social Development and Humanitarian Affairs, *The Work of CEDAW*, (ST/CSDHA/5), Vienna, 1990; Zoelle, Diana G., *Globalizing Concern for Women's Human Rights: The Failure of the American Model*, New York: St. Martin's Press, 2000.

BETTY J. GLASS

CHICK. Many women of the third-wave feminist movement have grown up in a cartoon-land "Beavis and Butthead" culture where women are often referred to as "chicks." The original usage labeled the female a commodity or item to appraise and reinforced gender inferiority. The term has been traditionally used to imply a woman's availability as a vulnerable, sexually charged object. Reappropriation has resulted in the term having a certain level of self-contained irony. Calling oneself a "chick" signals power and cancels out the term's function as an insult. As noted in the introduction of the 1995 book *Girlpower*, "Part of claiming and reclaiming our power as girls and women is taking back those words that once were ours and have been abused and misused, and giving them a new and different connotation: girl, chick, broad—even words that aren't necessarily female oriented, but used as labels to alienate or ridicule such as outcast, jock, **queer**, and others."

Though its common usage is still a subject of debate, "chicks" is an example of how language can change and eventually come to communicate something very different from what was originally meant. Change in this recent usage of "chick" shows how meaning depends on the context and that power and gender are always in the process of being questioned.

Further Reading: Carlip, Hillary, *Girlpower: Young Women Speak Out*, New York: Warner Books, 1995; Karaian, Lara, ed., *Turbo Chicks: Talking Young Feminisms*, Toronto: Sumarch Press, 2001.

LEIGH PHILLIPS

CLINTON, HILLARY. Hillary Diane Rodham Clinton (1948–), New York state senator, is a former First Lady of the United States and the State of Arkansas, attorney, activist, author, mother of Chelsea Clinton, wife to former President Bill Clinton, and role model for third-wave feminists. Born in Chicago, Illinois, on October 26, Clinton was the first of three children and the only daughter of Dorothy and Hugh Rodham. After a public school **education** where she excelled academically and as a student leader, she attended Wellesley College and then Yale Law School, where she met Bill Clinton.

When Clinton "followed her heart" to Arkansas to marry Bill Clinton in 1975, she chose to maintain a professional career as a law professor at the University of Arkansas and a practitioner at the Rose Law Firm. She also was a political wife and activist and mother. Her only child, Chelsea, was born in 1980.

Clinton used her First Lady status of Arkansas and the United States to tirelessly advocate on behalf of women and children, both domestically and internationally, and continues to do so as New York state senator. Clinton's form of **feminism** has stressed **empowerment** by way of economic and educational advances for women.

Clinton has been a role model for many women who watched her balance her career, **family**, and public service. Beyond that, Clinton has brought the issue of women's rights to the table in arenas where policy is made. She is particularly important to third-wave feminists because she supports the third-wave contention that the public sphere has substantively changed. Clinton is one of the few First Ladies who had more than a decorative, supportive function in the White House, and she is the first to have gone on to have her own political career.

See also Political Participation

Further Reading: Clinton, Hillary Rodham, *Living History*, New York: Simon & Schuster, 2003; Hillary Clinton Web site, http://clinton.senate.gov.

LAURA GLADNEY-LEMON

CODEPINK. CODEPINK is a grassroots peace group that organized in November 2002 as a reaction to the **war** on Iraq. The group's name is an ironic comment on the president's color-coded system to relay the level of terrorist threat in the United States. The Bush Administration's militaristic actions, for the group, "signifies extreme danger to all the values of nurturing, caring, and compassion that women and loving men have held." Like the third-wave appropriation of the terms "**bitch**" or "**chick**," here the color pink is the third-wave **feminism**'s reclamation of things that have been labeled "feminine" (such as peace). Approximately 100 women helped form the group. It began with a march through the streets of Washington, D.C., and then culminated in a four-month vigil in front of the White House. Today, there are more than eighty CODEPINK groups throughout the United States, and each group acts independently of CODEPINK-Central. CODEPINK-Central seeks to connect the groups via e-mail alerts and keeps them supplied with pink scarves, buttons, bumper stickers, and T-shirts to maintain their visibility.

Rather than focus on reacting violently to the war and the government, CODEPINK addresses global peace in a pacifistic way. They have used classic demonstration techniques such as marches and sit-ins but have also cleverly devised ways to address their dissatisfaction of some political representatives. They deliver pink slips (women's lingerie), "firing" political representatives for not doing their job of representing the people. The war on Iraq is only one focus. They have several priority areas: peacemaking and militarism, life-affirming economic priorities, civil liberties, environmental sustainability, responsible **media** and reporting, and elections and voter registration. According to their Web site, "Women have been the guardians of life—not because we are better or purer or more innately nurturing than men, but because the men have busied themselves making war. Because of our responsibility to the next generation, because of our own love for our families and communities and this country that we are a part of, we understand the love of a mother in Iraq for her children, and the driving **desire** of that child for life." CODEPINK is representative of third-wave feminist thinking because they claim that women are not innately more peaceful than men and that peace should be a goal for every human, regardless of gender.
See also Military, Women in the

Further Reading: Boylan, Anne M., *The Origins of Women's Activism: New York and Boston, 1797–1840*, Chapel Hill, NC: University of North Carolina Press, 2003; CODEPINK, http://www.codepink.org; Hamill, Sam, *Poets against the War*, New York: Nation Books, 2003; Sen, Rinku, and Kim Klein, *Stir It Up: Lessons in Community Organizing and Advocacy*, San Francisco: Jossey Bass, 2003.

KRISTINE SISBARRO

COMEDY, FEMINIST. Feminist comedy takes shape in a variety of mediums and is as individual as the novelist, playwright, troupe, or comedian who writes or performs it. It is personal and political. Some have argued that **feminism**

dates back to the humanitarian movements of the eighteenth century; thus, the idea that feminist comedy has its roots in the early nineteenth-century writings of authors such as Jane Austen is plausible. Her use of satire and parody and the creation of independent female characters allowed for a new kind of subversive comedy to form. This comedy interjected feminist **ideology** or ideas at a time when making obvious statements of such were not accepted. Not only did her writings seek to question and critique patriarchal practices, they also attempted to draw a clear line between myth and reality.

Feminism and comedy seem like unlikely allies. However, the use of humor as a subversive tool to expose the difficult subjects of **patriarchy**, sexism, **sexuality, rape**, etc., implies the possibility that new and different audiences can be reached through this medium. Since then, novelists, playwrights, artists, comedy troupes, and comedians have, like Austen, found a way to combine humor with feminism. The novelist Charlotte Perkins Gilman (1860–1935), author of the classic story *The Yellow Wallpaper*, also penned a feminist utopian comedy entitled *Herland*. Gilman, classified as both a feminist and a socialist, used satire in *Herland* to question masculine and feminine assumptions. In the story, the seeming matriarchal world created by Gilman is penetrated by three men who land in an all-female utopia where procreation is thwarted for virgin birth by vegetarian mothers. Gilman uses the medium of feminist satiric comedy to critique American society.

Contemporary feminist comedians and comedic troupes include Kathy Najimy, Kate Clinton, Margaret Cho, and the **Guerrilla Girls**. What is interesting about feminist comedians or comedic troupes is that each is vastly different. Feminist comedy ties these individuals and groups together through a commitment to activism, inclusion, and accessibility. Contemporary feminist comedy addresses issues relevant to feminism, or more specifically the second and now third waves of the feminist movement: women and the workplace, sexuality, politics, law, **family**, representations of women in the **media**, and **education**.

Kathy Najimy is a feminist, activist, writer, and comic. She was a member of the feminist comedy troupe *Sisters on Stage* for five years and is most known for her role in the 1992 **film** *Sister Act*. She has gained notoriety for her feminist approach to comedy over recent years. Najimy seeks to use feminist comedy as a medium to diffuse the stigma associated with feminism.

Kate Clinton is a lesbian comic. She describes herself as a "fumerist"; more accurately, a feminist humorist, or a humorist who fumes. Clinton is also writer, columnist, and actress. She has appeared in numerous **television** spots, documentaries, and movie roles. Clinton's feminist humor focuses on both political and women's comedy. In addition to a book and essays, she has six comedy albums out. Clinton seeks to divorce the idea of feminism as being exclusive but rather as something that is inclusive and open to all.

The modern feminist comedy troupe *The Guerrilla Girls*, an anonymous group of women whose identities are concealed by gorilla masks, use humor and improvisational comedy to enlighten audiences about contemporary issues, critique culture, and expose sexism. Each guerrilla girl adopts the name of a dead female artist as a pseudonym in her performances.

Feminist humor has also been more silent but not less comical. The combination of humor, artistic talent, and feminism has come together to create feminist comedy in the form of comic strips. Pulitzer Prize (for an editorial cartoon) winner Ann Telnaes' political cartoons, namely *Six Chix*, satirize politics, women's issues, reproductive rights, church and state issues, feminism, terrorism, and the environment, to name a few.

Feminist comedy is a growing and evolving medium in which personal and political material introduces feminism to an audience. It is sometimes subtle and subversive, and other times out loud and in your face. For feminist comedy, the former f-word was "feminism": now it is "funny."

Further Reading: Bilger, Audrey, *Laughing Feminism: Subversive Comedy in Frances Burney, Maria Edgeworth, and Jane Austen*, Detroit: Wayne State University Press, 1998; Clinton, Kate, *Don't Get Me Started*, New York: Ballantine Books, 2000; Gilman, Charlotte Perkins, *Herland*, New York: Penguin Books, 1999; Robins, Tina, *From Girls to Grrrlz: A History of Woman Comics From Teens to Zines*, San Francisco: Chronicle Books, 1999.

JESSICA A. YORK

COMMUNICATIONS TECHNOLOGY. It is hard to imagine how third-wave **feminism** would have occurred without the incredible developments in electronic technology at the end of the twentieth century. These advances are mostly Internet-related and include the World Wide Web, e-mail, blogs, chat rooms, and discussion lists, but they also include the expansion of cell phone use, including text messaging. Together, the Internet and cell phones have enabled communication that is fast, can potentially reach a vast audience, and facilitates new forms of art as well as encourages ordinary people to present their ideas to others in creative ways. Where the Internet was once hailed as an "information superhighway," for third-wave feminists the focus is on its role as a communication network, enabling interactivity and an exchange of ideas rather than a one-way flow of information. Key ideas of third-wave feminism—**media** representation, active and innovative politics, the involvement of "any woman," gender playfulness—are emphasized and shaped by contemporary communications technology.

Communications technologies were developing and expanding in the Westernized world in the late 1980s, 1990s, and into the twenty-first century, at the same time that younger generations of women were assessing second-wave feminism of the 1960s and 1970s. It was a coincidence, but these two huge cultural shifts—in gender relations and in communication—happened to occur at the same time in the same cultures. Women can circulate ideas by Internet or phone and not only share but also get, speedy responses. Communities are increasingly formed not by geographical location but by ideas transmitted electronically. These "digital neighborhoods" are becoming an integral part of people's lives, and women who previously felt isolated in their locality can find kindred spirits to talk to and be challenged by. Some of these communities center around everyday issues (e.g., **television** programs and shopping), while others have more obvious political agendas and allow the details of feminist activism to spread quickly.

While the cost of hardware such as computers and telephones means that only some people have access to these new technologies, the distribution of electronic communication is not explained by a simple linkage to issues of poverty or gender, as might be expected. For instance, working-class communities have traditionally spent a large proportion of their income on consumer goods such as televisions and computers. And although many more people have Internet access in North America, Oceania, and Europe than in Africa and most of Asia and South America (Japan and Brazil being exceptions here, with high usage), these statistics change rapidly and also present different sorts of gendered patterns. In addition, once hardware is acquired at home, in schools, or in local community centers, the cost of communicating is relatively cheap, and in poor communities, one networked computer can give hundreds of people access to the Internet.

Communications Technology and Culture. Many see that it is necessary to always consider who uses particular technologies and for what purposes and to recognize the social influences on the deployment of technology. This is one reason why third-wave feminists want to be "in there," affecting the practices of communications technologies. Yet third-wave feminism is not one movement; it has many manifestations that have differing relations to mainstream thinking and culture. For instance, all feminists seek to change existing ideas and practices: some third-wavers attempt to "open up" more areas of life to women, and others work toward a more radical transformation of society. These kinds of variations are reflected in feminist engagements with communications technologies, which could be divided into three areas: "women and technology," "**cyberfeminism**," and "cyborg feminism."

The women and technology strand seeks more equal gender access to technology, both at home and within the job market. Girls and women are encouraged to play with computers; girl-centered games are devised, such as those from the company Purple Moon; extensive online resources are developed, such as those provided by the Center for Women and Information Technology (CWIT) at the University of Maryland, in Baltimore; and feminist debate is encouraged (e.g., in journals such as the UK-based "*The F Word*"). This kind of "equal opportunities" third-wave feminism has advocates in all countries. Although some women may wish for more radical interventions, many women have benefited from this form of advocacy.

Cyberfeminism emerged from the Australian group VNS Matrix in 1991 via their graphic "Cyberfeminist Manifesto for the 21st Century" and continued to actively develop throughout the 1990s, particularly in Oceania, the United States, Western Europe, and Japan. Cyberfeminists assert that the Internet, with its multiple nodes and webbed hyperlinks, is capable of disrupting masculine, linear thinking and practices and thus enables women to communicate in multiple, playful ways. For cyberfeminists, the Internet liberates women, and they applaud the Web's imaginative potential as a space for creative communication. Unlike the "women and technology" school of thought, this form of third-wave feminism does not see women as lacking the skills for working with communications technology but as already having these abilities. Interestingly, cyberfeminism is not just for girls and women but also for boys and men who can "behave" in a nonpatriarchal way and enter into this radical interpretation of communications technology.

Cyborg feminism stems from **Donna Haraway**'s mid-1980s "Cyborg Manifesto," and this version of third-wave feminism understands communications technology as an inseparable part of contemporary everyday life. It is argued that feminists cannot ignore the spread of new technologies, so they must participate and make sure that technologies work for women and not against them. Cyborg feminism focuses on three main aspects of communications technologies: **identity** (how women label themselves, or are labeled by others); bodies (how technology affects what counts as a **body**); and epistemology (how we come to know things). The cyborg identity is post-gender in that the old traditions of masculine and feminine behavior are broken down, and cyborg almost becomes a gender in itself.

Forms of Communications Technology. Third-wave feminism relates to communications technology in practical ways (encouraging women to grab the tools of new media and computing) and theoretical ways (seeking to understand how communications technologies make us different sorts of human beings). However, it is also true to say that different types of technology enable and relate to different sorts of third-wave practices.

The Internet is a good example of how third-wave feminists take something that could be seen as oppressive to women and, rather than ignore it or fight against it, use it to their advantage, finding pleasure and fun in the process. The origin of the Internet (U.S. military work in the 1960s) does not seem as though it would be promising for feminists. Yet the intrinsic decentralization of the Internet, which was developed as a defense against a "one-strike" attack by a foreign power, gave rise to a system that relates well to third-wave practices of networking. Alongside military interest, other institutions such as universities were also working on aspects of the Internet, and by the mid-1980s and into the 1990s the system was rapidly spreading to companies as well as individuals through the development of cheap computers. The Internet is basically a network of networks that has become a worldwide communication tool: an ideal method for third-wave feminist interaction. It offers a number of communication methods, the most common of which are the World Wide Web (WWW), chat rooms, e-mail, and discussion lists.

The WWW is often seen as the Internet, but it is actually only one part. Third-wave feminists have been quick to exploit the wealth of information and provocative ideas available on the Web. Although some might say there is a surfeit of data, making it difficult to decide what to believe, the counter-argument is that at least it is the individual, in consultation with others, who gets to decide what is true or useful, and her source material is less likely to be filtered by an authority who may have a different political agenda from her own. Today, with access to a networked computer, it is relatively easy to find out about anything (e.g., **sexuality**, careers, radical thinking, and ethical **fashion**). While all governments censor the Web to some extent, the decentralized and global nature of this technology makes total censorship difficult, and ideas continue to proliferate. Yet, interestingly, the WWW, with its multiple Web sites (connected via clickable links called hyperlinks), is actually one of the most passive features of the Internet. Despite hyperlinks, most Web sites involve reading information without actually being able to respond to the data. Where intervention is possible, this is usually via buying goods or by filling in forms attached to the Web site. Thus, Web sites are largely a one-way communication technology, offering goods or information for the buyer or reader to access and use. This is a far cry from the type of interactivity planned by Tim Berners-Lee, who invented hyperlinks and therefore the WWW. He envisaged Web pages that anyone could not only access but also edit—a vision that has been taken up in a limited way by http://openwiki.com Web sites. Nevertheless, the feeling of freedom that occurs when browsing the Web is an important aspect of third-wave feminism, and learning not only how to travel in **cyberspace** but also how and when to linger are key feminist skills of the twenty-first century. Interaction is also developed by combining Web sites with other media, as produced in China on the Web site http://www.stopdv.org.cn, an anti-**domestic violence** site that recognized that access to the Internet for Chinese women was limited and successfully used the site to instigate a relevant and powerful television soap opera storyline.

And of course, third-wave feminists do not just browse the Web; they also publish their own sites. Most Web pages are created using hypertext markup language (HTML), which in its basic form is fairly simple to learn. Moreover, corporate Web companies such as Yahoo offer easy-to-use templates and free Web space, making Web site production a cheap and effective means of communicating ideas. These "home pages" were popular in the 1990s, with girls and young women offering details of their lives, hopes, and dreams, and they also served as resources for different sorts of political activism and for **family**, friends, and beyond. Since the late 1990s, key functions of home pages have been taken over by the use of Web logs, or blogs. These began as sites that offered links, commentary, and personal thoughts, usually with dated entries. They were a form of active and activist participation in the media, presenting links to sites evaluated by the writer, or blogger. At first these were HTML-coded sites, similar to home pages, but in 1999 companies such as Pittas and Blogger launched their free-to-use blog templates, and now there are thousands of blogs on the Web. Their original function has shifted from media filtering sites offering thoughtful links alongside commentary to something more akin to an online personal journal with links. However, the key factor for the interactivity so important to third-wavers is that blogs solicit responses from their readers. Just by pressing a "comment" link, any reader can contribute to the blog. It is also possible to produce collective blogs that are written by a group of people. Although these seem like ideal feminist tools, this method is much less popular than individual blogging.

One of the clichés about the Internet is that people can be anyone they want when online, an attribute that seems to offer great potential for third-wave feminists to pretend to be different sorts of people, to cross gender, and to meet with a variety of people in a way not feasible in local communities. It is in the interactive forums of chat rooms and particularly MOOs that such serious playfulness becomes possible. Chat rooms are virtual rooms in cyberspace where at least two people and usually more meet to talk in real time: it is a little like a phone conversation where people can respond immediately to the words of another, but text is used rather than voice. There are thousands of chat rooms. They often focus on specific topics, both serious and frivolous, just as in real-life chat. There are chat rooms that center around anorexia, or Britney Spears, or coming out as a lesbian. Here, the third-wave belief that the power of communication between ordinary women can affect change can be realized, as ideas, facts, (mis)information, and "chat" are exchanged between people who may never meet in real life.

MOOs offer an even more complex experience. They are telnet-based applications, and one of the most famous MOOs is LambdaMOO (on telnet:// lambda.moo.mud.org:8888/). Lambda is a virtual city where users, or "citizens," create their own characters and homes that remain at all times, even when the user is logged off. Although there are some image-based MOOs, most, like Lambda, use words. LambdaMOO offers a choice of ten genders—female, male, spivak (ambiguous), neuter, splat (a kind of "thing"), plural, 2nd, royal ("we"), egotistical, either—and each has its own associated pronouns. A MOO allows for a kind of performance of gender that can help to challenge traditional ideas and that offers an environment where imagination becomes a tool for change. Rather than read a story about different ways of living, a MOO allows users to create their own collective fantasy using words, and to live, in some small way, the experience of those dreams. For many women, this participatory **fiction** has been as life changing as reading a novel.

But while chat rooms and MOOs are exciting, two other more straightforward forms of the Internet are important feminist tools: e-mail and discussion lists. Both offer the potential for communicating with many people but, unlike chat rooms, they do not support instantaneous messaging. This can lead to more reflexive debate, especially on discussion lists, which, like chatting rooms, focus on specific topics. E-mails are rather like electronic postcards: short messages sent between friends and colleagues, with the facility to send one message to an individual or to thousands.

Cell Phones. Although computers are becoming more portable, even more so with the increase in wireless technology, laptops are far from being small enough to fit into an average-sized purse. Use is therefore largely restricted to home, workplace, or schools and community establishments, and this is partly why cell phones have become such an important communications technology for feminists wishing to have a more convenient way of keeping in touch with friends and colleagues. Based on a combination of radio and telephone technology and offering both voice and text messaging, they are widespread in Europe and Asia, where an estimated 90 percent of people own a cell phone, as opposed to approximately 50 percent in the United States. Although they started as business devices, they are now almost essential tools for everyday life, and there is evidence that women are possibly more likely than men to carry and use one. As long as there is a suitable transmitter, cell phones offer availability all of the time. They give feminists flexibility in leisure and political activities, as plans can be made at the last minute and changed easily. Such portability is, however, double-edged. As cell phones are carried "all the time" they provide a degree of personal safety, but they can also act as a kind of personal monitoring system—an aspect of cell phone technology that is a serious and as yet unresolved issue for civil liberties.

Further Reading: Center for Women and Information Technology University of Maryland, Baltimore, http://www.umbc.edu/cwit; Cherney, Lynn, and Elizabeth Reba Wise, *Wired Women: Gender and New Realities in Cyberspace*, Seattle, WA: Seal Press, 1996; "The F Word: Contemporary UK Feminism," http://www.thefword.org.uk; Haraway, Donna, "A Cyborg Manifesto: Science, Technology and Socialist-Feminism in the Late Twentieth Century," in *Simians, Cyborgs, and Women: The Reinvention of Nature*, New York: Routledge, 1991, 149–181; Hawthorne, Susan, and Renate Klein, eds., *Cyberfeminism: Connectivity, Critique and Creativity*, North Melbourne, AUS: Spinifex Press, 1999; Turkle, Sherry, *Life on the Screen: Identity in the Age of the Internet*, New York: Simon and Schuster, 1995; VNS Matrix, http://lx.sysx.org/vnsmatrix.html; Wajcman, Judy, *TechnoFeminism*, Williston, VT: Blackwell Publishing, 2004;

ANN KALOSKI-NAYLOR

COMPETITION, WOMEN AND. It is commonly believed that boys and men are more competitive and aggressive than girls and women. This belief is inaccurate. Males and females both feel the need to compete and be aggressive in various contexts in their lives, yet males in our culture are socially encouraged to compete and be aggressive, while females in our culture are discouraged from doing the same. As a result, females have a complex relationship with competition and aggression and tend to either deny their competitive/aggressive impulses or express them in unhealthy ways. Moreover, competition and aggression in women are particularly complicated for many feminists because these motivations violate the feminist belief, popularized during the second wave, that competing is in and of itself a destructive activity that promotes ego and hierarchy (which have been associated with sexism). Third-wave feminists, on the other hand, have discussed the destructive consequences that can occur when competitive and aggressive **desires** are stymied.

Some feminists of the first wave believed that competition is inherently a destructive force. In her utopian novel, *Herland* (1915), Charlotte Perkins Gilman (1860–1935) imagined a country with only girls and women and no boys and men. In this country, the perfect civilization, there was no competition at all. Gilman expressed her belief that societal evils, including competition, are caused by men and that if women ruled the world it would consist of one great sisterhood. Activists in the early days of the second wave of **feminism** likewise consciously tried to avoid a hierarchical leadership model that was prevalent at the time in the male-dominated New Left. Feminism, as they saw it, would be a nonhierarchical movement of equals without any leaders. However, this optimistic vision was impossible to put into practice. Eventually, many second-wave feminists realized that no matter how successful feminism is, women would always have differences in income, **education**, ability to conceive, physical attractiveness, and health. Therefore, there will always be a hierarchy of status along with a desire to achieve and obtain more through competitive behavior.

However, one strand of second-wave feminism continued to explore the idea that women are more sensitive and gentle and more empathetic and interconnected than men. Often referred to as "essentialists" because they posit that there exists an essential feminine and an essential masculine nature, these feminists have maintained that women are more sharing and caring than men, that they operate on a higher moral plane, and that they are more attuned to others' feelings than men are. In her influential feminist treatise, *Maternal Thinking* (1989), author Sara Ruddick (1935–) wrote that only women can become mothers, mothers are more nurturing than fathers, and mothers are necessarily pacifist. Psychoanalyst Nancy Chodorow (1944–) has theorized that females have a stronger sense of connectedness to others, which results from being cared for as young children by their mothers rather than by their fathers. Psychologist **Carol Gilligan** (1936–) has built on Chodorow's theory and advanced the idea that females' relational character makes them feel a stronger sense of justice and responsibility to the world than men do. The ideas of Chodorow and Gilligan have been enormously popular among feminists, especially those who identify with the second wave.

Third-wave feminists have attempted to initiate dialog about competition and aggression, particularly competition and aggression among women, and dispel the myth that women are less competitive and aggressive than men. Phyllis Chesler (1940–), a second-wave thinker and author who has continued to advance her ideas during the period of the third wave, has argued that women's relations with one another are often contentious because they reflect the mother–daughter relationship. In her book, *Woman's Inhumanity to Woman* (2002), she claimed that most women expect other women to mother them and hold them to the ideal standards for motherhood. Chesler also pointed out that, contrary to the ideas of Ruddick et al., women can be very aggressive and violent toward women and children, as well as toward men. She described instances of violence and manipulation by women in every culture worldwide every day.

Several third-wave authors have further explored the ways in which females are competitive and aggressive with one another. In her book about girls who are labeled "sluts," *Slut!: Growing Up Female with a Bad Reputation* (1999), Leora Tanenbaum (1969–) advanced the idea that girls, not boys, are the primary bullies who ostracize, ridicule, and harass so-called sluts. A few years later, this idea that girls can be "mean" toward one another became the subject of several books that also focused on the pre-adolescent and adolescent years. Rosalind Wiseman, in her book *Queen Bees and Wannabes* (2002), and Rachel Simmons, in her book *Odd Girl Out* (2002), acknowledged the long-taboo truth that, far from being "made of sugar and spice and everything nice," girls in fact can be extremely aggressive, especially toward one another.

In a follow-up to *Slut!*, Tanenbaum wrote about adult women's rivalries with one another and the ways in which they tend to compete in destructive ways. In her book *Catfight: Rivalries Among Women—From Diets to Dating, from the Boardroom to the Delivery Room* (2002), Tanenbaum argued that there is a **double standard** in competition. Girls and women internalize the idea that being aggressive is acceptable only for men, so they direct their aggression underground. Rather than confront others openly, girls and women tend to express their aggression indirectly, through social sabotage, gossip, vague double entendres, and other underhanded forms of manipulation. Tanenbaum focused on four areas in a woman's life in which she may be involved in this behavior, either as a target or as an actor. The first is beauty, in which women feel pressured to look prettier, thinner, or more fashionable than other females. The second is dating, in which heterosexual women are set up as rivals competing over a man. The third is the workplace, in which women may be particularly aggressive toward one another because they must struggle for recognition in a discriminatory environment. Finally, Tanenbaum analyzed the arena of motherhood, in which mothers feel judged and pressured to compete over who is the "better" mother.

Third-wave feminists have struck an optimistic tone, advancing the idea that competition and aggression are not inherently bad; only their primary expression is destructive. Wiseman and Simmons have educated girls on healthy ways to interact, while Tanenbaum has encouraged adult women to get in touch with and become unashamed of their competitive and aggressive motivations, so that they can avoid resorting to underhanded manipulations. She has also urged women to learn from the example of first-wave feminists, who unified to fight for their rights as citizens even though they experienced internal disagreements and divisions. These leaders knew that the only way their agenda would be realized was if they cooperated with rather than competed against one another. As a result of their ability to transcend destructive competition with one another, the right to vote was signed into law in 1920.

See also Volume 2, Primary Documents 42 and 43

Further Reading: Chesler, Phyllis, *Woman's Inhumanity to Woman*, New York: Thunder's Mouth/Nation Books, 2002; Chodorow, Nancy, *Feminism and Psychoanalytic Theory*, New Haven, CT: Yale University Press, 1989; Gilligan, Carol, *In a Different Voice: Psychological Theory and Women's Development*, Cambridge, MA: Harvard University Press, 1993 (originally published in 1982); Gilman, Charlotte Perkins, *Herland: A Lost Feminist Utopian Novel*, New York: Pantheon, 1979 (originally published in 1915); Ruddick, Sara, *Maternal Thinking: Toward a Politics of Peace*, Boston: Beacon, 1989; Simmons, Rachel, *Odd Girl Out: The Hidden Culture of Aggression in Girls*, New York: Harcourt, 2002; Tanenbaum, Leora, *Catfight: Rivalries Among Women— From Diets to Dating, from the Boardroom to the Delivery Room*, New York: Harper-Perennial, 2003 (originally published in 2002 as *Catfight: Competition among Women*); Tanenbaum, Leora, *Slut! Growing Up Female with a Bad Reputation*, New York: Seven Stories, 1999; Wiseman, Rosalind, *Queen Bees and Wannabes: Helping Your Daughter Survive Cliques, Gossip, Boyfriends, and Other Realities of Adolescence*, New York: Crown, 2002.

LEORA TANENBAUM

COMPULSORY HETEROSEXUALITY. The term "compulsory heterosexuality"— meaning that heterosexuality is the only "normal" or acceptable form of sexual expression—is targeted by **queer** and feminist activists for its role in granting straight men more power and privilege than women and sexual minorities. It is one of the ideas third-wave **feminism** questions. The term refers to the ways in which heterosexuality is made out to be the only option one has to express his or her **sexuality**. According to this concept, attraction to the "opposite" sex is the one true, natural, and universal mode of sexuality that has ever existed. Same-sex **desire** is seen as unnatural, unhealthy, and immoral and, in many cases, made illegal. The powers that keep this view firmly entrenched include institutions such as schools, churches, governments, businesses, the **media**, and the health profession and can operate subtly or openly. The most apparent example is the push at both the federal and state levels in the United States to define **marriage** exclusively as the bond between a man and a woman, thus curtailing many civil rights for same-sex couples. Employers who extend benefits only to heterosexual couples, faiths that denounce homosexuality as an abomination, and schools that refuse to address homosexuality are also complicit in bolstering compulsory heterosexuality. Perhaps less obvious is the impact of **film**, **television**, and popular **music**, all of which rarely touch on homosexual themes, or if they dare to do so, it is done only in a derogatory manner. Instead, such media regularly bombard audiences with images of boyfriends and girlfriends, husbands and wives, and straight wedding ceremonies and anniversaries, therefore creating the illusion of heterosexuality as the inevitable, fated path of all "normal," healthy individuals.

Ironically, the very fact that heterosexuality requires institutional and media power to enforce its exclusive acceptance and practice reveals how it is far from the natural, universal mode of sexual expression. The consequences of this artificial imposition are far-reaching, impacting both sexual minorities and people who claim heterosexual identities. Lesbians, gays, bisexuals, and **transgender** individuals arguably suffer the most from society's compulsive heterosexuality, as their sexual attractions and desires are ignored, silenced, mocked, prohibited, and violently opposed by others. **Depression**, internalized shame, denial, repression, and suicidal thoughts and actions are among the many painful emotional responses triggered by societal demands to be straight. Guarded public behavior and extreme reluctance to reveal one's sexual **identity** to **family**, friends, and coworkers demonstrate how the "closet" can affect society as a whole. However, if it is accepted that sexuality does not exist simply as a pair of polar opposites (i.e., gay versus straight) but rather as a continuum ranging through a variety of degrees from same-sex to "opposite-sex" attraction, then it follows that a large percentage of the entire population is made to monitor their thoughts, feelings, speech, and behavior for fear of experiencing and/or revealing homosexual interest. This self-surveillance ultimately reinforces stereotypical gender roles, requiring women to accept traditionally feminine traits such as passivity and men to take on conventional masculine characteristics including aggressiveness and emotional coolness.

Consequently, feminists, including those belonging to the third wave, have aligned themselves with queer activists who are striving to expose the suffering wrought by compulsory heterosexuality and thereby bring it to an end. In addition to sexual repression and bolstering gender roles, the enforcement of heterosexuality is believed to be a major factor in maintaining an imbalance of power between men and women. According to this feminist critique, compulsory heterosexuality closes off many possibilities for women, effectively forcing them to opt for the traditional family life, which has been long seen as an institution that inherently oppresses women with its emphasis on childbearing, child-rearing, economic dependence, and subservience to men.

In fact, it was the feminist poet Adrienne Rich who coined the term "compulsory heterosexuality" in the early 1980s. She reasoned that because an individual's first intimate bonding experience is with the mother, women possess a fundamental attraction to other women, thus creating an argument that weakens the notion of heterosexuality as *the* natural sexual orientation. However, for several reasons, Rich's case has been opposed, even by those holding strong feminist views. First, the argument that lesbianism has a natural basis is problematic for the same reason that assuming heterosexuality's natural status is faulty. Claiming a natural cause for a variety of identity issues, whether they are race, gender, or sexuality, always opens the door to elevating certain groups to a privileged position while labeling others as deviant. Second, Rich's position depicts sexuality as a masculine trait as compared with lesbianism, which has more to do with the woman-identification process initiated during early childhood. This stance ultimately casts sexuality in negative terms, rather than exploring the ways in which sexual expression can grant pleasure and fulfillment to those wishing to escape the confines of compulsory heterosexuality. Finally, Rich's argument ironically creates a notion of normalcy (i.e., a certain kind of lesbian identification) that constrains feminists, rather than encouraging a spectrum of sexual options from which to choose.

See also Heterosexism

Further Reading: Gay, Lesbian, Bisexual, Transgender, and Queer Encyclopedia, http://www.glbtq.com; Rich, Adrienne, "Compulsory Heterosexuality and Lesbian Existence," http://www.terry.uga.edu/~dawndba/4500compulsoryhet.htm.

SEAN MURRAY

CONSCIOUSNESS RAISING. Once seen as a characteristic second-wave feminist strategy, consciousness raising (CR) has recently become important to the third wave. The recent third-wave feminist anthology, *Catching a Wave* (2003), organizes itself around that strategy. CR is a practice used by feminists to uncover truths about the oppressions experienced by women as a result of sexism and **patriarchy**. Although CR grew more mainstream in 1972 after *Ms.* magazine published a guide to CR in its first issue, initially CR was a tool used by radical women's liberation groups. Starting in the mid- to late 1960s, women met in CR groups of between ten and fifteen members to talk about their feelings and experiences. Typically sitting in a circle to emphasize CR's rejection of hierarchy, women discussed topics ranging from love, **marriage**, sex, femininity, and motherhood to work, female **competition**, and **aging**.

As it was originally understood, CR was neither merely rap session nor therapy; women joined CR groups not to learn about themselves but to gain new insights about the causes of women's oppression. By pooling information about their personal experiences, women came to see that many of the things they considered to be private problems actually had public or political causes and consequences. In other words, they discovered that the "personal is political." For instance, as group members discovered how angry they all were both about the unequal distribution of housework in their families and about sex lives that privileged men's pleasure over women's, they gained insight into inequalities that were socially and culturally created and perpetuated. In the process, their consciousnesses were raised.

The goals of CR were analysis and action. Interpreting the causes and effects of women's oppression was the first goal. After listening to all participants' ideas and feelings, women analyzed the connections they saw among all of their experiences. The analyses they performed yielded some of the first **feminist theory** produced during the second wave. Authors such as Shulamith Firestone (*The Dialectic of Sex* [1970]), Anne Koedt ("The Myth of the Vaginal Orgasm" [1970]), and Pat Mainardi ("The Politics of Housework" [1970]) arrived at their insights as a result of CR. Although this writing crystallized new ideas, radical feminists saw activism and organizing as the most crucial goals of CR. The publication of *Our Bodies, Ourselves* in 1973 by the Boston Women's Health Book Collective is an example of CR-inspired activism. However,

CR often did not lead to public projects, mainly because the nonhierarchical organization of CR groups typically inhibited the formation of structures that would promote activism. In addition, as CR grew in popularity, its focus shifted toward "softer" goals of therapy and self-examination instead of the "harder" goals of theory development and organizing.

As feminist consciousness and literacy began to be achieved by more women in the late 1970s and early 1980s, CR declined in prominence. Although CR is not often seen in its "hard" form very often anymore, the technique has been implemented in a variety of mainstream arenas, including **television** talk shows, Web sites and chat rooms, alternative **music**, and **zines**. It is also the cornerstone of the **women's studies** classroom: as college students are introduced to women's studies and discover the sources of the inequalities they see around them, they are participating, even unknowingly, in a kind of CR.

Further Reading: Dicker, Rory, and Alison Piepmeier, eds., *Catching a Wave: Reclaiming Feminism for the 21st Century*, Boston: Northeastern University Press, 2003; Gornick, Vivian, "Consciousness," in *Radical Feminism: A Documentary Reader*, ed. Barbara A. Crow, New York: New York University Press, 2000, 287–300; Hogeland, Lisa Maria, *Feminism and Its Fictions: The Consciousness-Raising Novel and the Women's Liberation Movement*, Philadelphia: University of Pennsylvania Press, 1998; Sarachild, Kathie, "Consciousness-Raising: A Radical Weapon," in *Feminist Revolution*, New York: Random House, 1978, 144–150, http://scriptorium.lib.duke.edu/wlm/fem/sarachild.html.

RORY DICKER

CONSUMERISM. Broadly stated, consumerism refers to the shopping, **advertising**, and production practices that exist within economic systems based on global capitalism. Consumerism describes what people buy, how advertisers convince consumers to buy their goods and services, and the practices of major corporations worldwide that produce these consumer goods. Consumerism is also part of the ways people form identities through the things they buy, such as clothes or **music**. Increasingly, the major corporations producing consumer goods are multinational. As labor is exported from the United States to developing countries, these companies may take advantage of comparatively lenient labor and environmental laws and thus may exploit indigenous peoples by paying less than a living wage or providing unsafe work environments.

Third-wave **feminism** is concerned with consumerism because of its links to issues of **identity**, exploitation, imperialism, **racism**, and gender. Third-wave feminism has opposed the practices of companies such as Levi's and **Nike** for their sweatshop labor practices. One issue that feminists raise focuses on consumerism as a display of false consciousness versus a form of pleasure. In other words, shopping and buying recreates the sexism, classism, **heterosexism**, racism, and imperialism that third-wave feminism struggles against, yet it can also be the source of fun and may even help form individual and group identities and help to tell the world who we are, what we think, and what we believe in. Within third-wave feminism there is no unified response to these issues. For example, buying panties with "pussy power" printed on the front can be seen as literally buying into sexist ideas about womanhood. On the other hand, third-wave feminists can take this same product and argue that the phrase "pussy power" reclaims and redefines the concept of **girl power** and femininity through the use of irony. Still others argue that feminism has no right to criticize the popular activities that so many women enjoy, whether this means reading chick-lit romances or wearing trendy clothes.

While many might think that shopping for jeans is fun, important questions remain: Where did those jeans come from? Who made them? Under what sorts of conditions were they made? Do we really want to buy a certain pair of jeans because we genuinely like them, or have we been convinced by the tools of multinational corporations and the practices of global branding that we "need" this particular brand or style of jeans? According to current feminist arguments, what we buy is part of a larger political struggle. One solution that third-wavers have adopted to help battle the problems of consumerism is to "reduce, reuse, recycle." Instead of buying new things at large corporate chains (Wal-Mart or Old Navy, for example), third-wavers might buy from independently owned and operated stores, from second-hand thrift stores, or from other resale shops. They might also reuse what they have by mending and repairing broken items, or they might simply buy less in the first place. Third-wave feminism is interested in reconstructing or changing the consumer market. A predominant third-wave approach to addressing the problems of consumerism is not rejecting shopping or consumption entirely, but conducting a *different kind* of shopping, such as buying green, earth-friendly products: nontoxic menstrual products; non-leather, cruelty-free shoes; non-sweatshop labor clothing; fair trade coffee; or retro **DIY** (do it yourself) products and supplies (for knitting, sewing, cooking, building, etc.).

Many third-wave feminists embrace consumer culture by arguing that liberation includes the freedom to buy what they want. Since advertisers create false wants and needs amongst consumers, third-wavers construct alternative patterns of consumption. This might include buying Hello Kitty paraphernalia and glitter makeup or getting tattoos or **body** piercings. These are each a statement of personal identity and individuality in a culture largely defined by advertisers asking consumers to buy the same products and take on similar **fashion** trends. However, even if today's feminists oppose consumerism through alternative shopping, third-wavers recognize that any feminist perspective on consumerism must involve a critique of the status quo in regard to employment practices, sexualized violence, health, **sexuality**, and the law, as well as the interrelationships between capitalism, **patriarchy**, imperialism, racism, and how they shop and spend. According to this perspective, any critical sociopolitical analysis must go beyond the viewpoint that women have finally achieved liberation or equality because they can choose to wear makeup or current fashions.

A final aspect of third-wave focus on consumerism concerns how street culture, "alternative," or independent trends are co-opted by corporate interests,

packaged, and then sold back to the youth market. This would include celebrities such as Madonna and **Missy Elliott** wearing street gear and singing in a **television** ad for the Gap, or skate- and snowboarders who seem to be independent but who actually have corporate sponsorship from companies such as Vans, which sells shoes. This image of independence then becomes closely controlled and in some sense contrived and works in the interest of capitalist consumption and profit. The Urban Outfitters clothing store chain makes billions of dollars from pretending it has street cred by taking street fashion, repackaging it, and selling it back to the youth market it came from.
See also Capitalist Patriarchy

Further Reading: *Adbusters* magazine, Vancouver, BC: Media Foundation; Klein, Naomi, *No Logo*, New York: Picador, 1999; Schor, Juliet B., and Douglas B. Holt, eds., *The Consumer Society Reader*, New York: The New Press, 2000.

SHIRA TARRANT

COOPERATIVE ECONOMICS. Cooperative economics stresses community cooperation in economic situations usually dominated by the "winner-take-all" mantra of economic **globalization**. Michelle Sidler voices the concerns of many third-wave feminists in her essay, "Living in McJobdom: Third Wave Feminism and Class Inequality," when she argues that processes associated with globalization have overtaken the social structures that second-wave feminists struggled against, and that this means, "third wave feminism needs a new economy" (1997, 38). For many young women and men, cooperative economics has provided just such an alternative. Instead of competing against each other for the biggest piece of the pie, those who participate in cooperative economics join together in co-ownership of a grocery store, an apartment building, or even a strip club, which is a process that benefits all individuals involved as well as contributes to the local economy.

Historically, women have much to gain from cooperative economics. It was not until 1974, through the Equal Credit Opportunity Act, that it became illegal to discriminate against women who applied for loans and other forms of credit. Before this time, women were often denied loans, credit, and the like without a male cosigner. Unmarried women, young people, and people of color are still often discriminated against. The negative effects of globalization on both young women and men have made cooperative economics even more appealing. Today, many cooperative organizations give small business loans and credit to women and others who are otherwise left out of the global economy or negatively affected by it.

Cooperatives also deal with much more than credit. WAGES (Women's Action to Gain Economic Security), based in California, helps low-income Latinas gain economic and social **empowerment** through cooperative ownership of eco-friendly cleaning businesses. Influenced by the indigenous cooperative movement of the Zapatistas in Chiapas, Mexico, the volunteer-run Indymedia allows *all* socially conscious people to become reporters who speak truth to the power of mainstream media. In 2003, the Lusty Lady Theater in San Francisco became the first cooperatively run strip club, owned by club workers themselves. The Self Employed Women's Association in India combines labor, cooperative, and women's movements to organize for women workers.

See also Downsizing; McJob; Outsourcing

Further Reading: Breitbart, Joshua, and Ana Nogueira, "An Independent Media Center of One's Own: A Feminist Alternative to Corporate Media," in *The Fire This Time: Young Activists and the New Feminism*, eds. Vivien Labaton and Dawn Lundy Martin, New York: Anchor Books, 2004, 19–41; Folbre, Nancy, *Who Pays for the Kids?: Gender and the Structures of Constraint*, New York: Routledge, 1994; Godfred, Joline, *No More Frogs to Kiss: 99 Ways to Give Economic Power to Girls*, New York: HarpersBusiness, 1995; Hayden, Tom, *The Zapatista Reader*, New York: Nation Books, 2001; Indymedia, http://www.indymedia.org; International Co-operative Alliance (ICA), http://www.ica.coop; Kabeer, Naila, *Reversed Realities: Gender Hierarchies in Development Thought*, London: Verso, 1994; Self Employed Women's Association (SEWA), http://www.sewa.org; Sidler, Michelle, "Living in McJobdom: Third Wave Feminism and Class Inequality," in *Third Wave Agenda: Being Feminist, Doing Feminism*, eds. Leslie Heywood and Jennifer Drake, Minneapolis: University of Minnesota Press, 1997, 25–39; Women's Action to Gain Economic Security (WAGES), http://www.wagescooperatives.org; Women and the Economy, U.N. Platform for Action Committee, http://www.unpac.ca.

GWENDOLYN BEETHAM

COSMETIC SURGERY. Cosmetic surgery is a type of plastic surgery performed for aesthetic reasons. According to research conducted by the American Society for Aesthetic Plastic Surgery (ASAPS), there were nearly 8.3 million cosmetic procedures performed in 2003, which cost Americans just under $9.4 billion (not including the fees for surgical facilities, anesthesia, medical tests, prescriptions, surgical garments, or other related miscellaneous expenses). These procedures included surgery, such as liposuction and breast implants, and nonsurgical procedures such as Botox injection, peels, and other injections. Women represented 87 percent of cosmetic surgery patients. Third-wave feminists grapple with the ethics of cosmetic surgery. Although most feminists might suggest that society's emphasis on female appearance drives women to endure expensive and oftentimes risky procedures, some third-wave feminists suggest that choosing cosmetic surgery can be a "liberating" personal decision for individual women.

Because cosmetic surgery is performed for aesthetic purposes only, physicians have justified these procedures by arguing the patient has a psychological need for the surgery. Cosmetic surgeons and their patients would argue that the psychological discomfort of living with a "deformity" such as sagging flesh, a large nose, or small breasts can create an inferiority complex and limit a person's potential. Practitioners distinguish between "cosmetic" surgery and "reconstructive" surgery, which usually refers to operations performed to hide the effects of disease (including reconstruction of a breast after a mastectomy) or a trauma. By distinguishing between aesthetically motivated surgeries and reconstructive surgery, physicians and the public at large imply that cosmetic surgery is frivolous (explaining why most insurance companies will pay for reconstructive surgery but not cosmetic surgery). In the United States, any physician (regardless of specialty) can perform cosmetic surgery, a policy that critics suggest results in inferior treatment.

Among feminists, much of the controversy over cosmetic surgery has centered on the practice of breast augmentation. During the early 1990s, breast augmentation came under increasing scrutiny and federal regulation as critics drew attention to the dangers of silicon implants. Silicon has been used as a breast implant device since the early 1960s; however, the procedure still involves numerous risks. Surgeons acknowledge that women with implants frequently experience a painful condition known as capsular contracture, where scar tissue around the implant hardens, requiring the physician to either remove the implant or put pressure on the woman's implanted breast until the mass of hardened tissue essentially tears apart. Sensation in the breast and nipple is regularly lost in women with implants. Research has proven that implants interfere with diagnosing (and therefore delay the treatment of) breast cancer. Also, as with any surgery, the patient is at risk of reacting badly to the anesthesia. Most ominously, studies have linked silicone implants to autoimmune diseases. Physicians, researchers, and patients still hotly debate the link between implants and autoimmune disease, but by 1971, the FDA reported that at least four women had died from silicone embolisms. While Ms. magazine wrote an exposé about silicone in 1978, most **media** downplayed risks of silicone implants until the early 1990s. In 1991, Dow Corning, a silicon-implant manufacturer, lost a multimillion-dollar lawsuit that linked the implants to autoimmune disorders. Public outcry led the FDA to restrict the use of silicon gel implants to reconstructive surgery in 1992. This decision implies that only the "moral" imperative of reconstructing a breast after a mastectomy necessitates using a silicone as an implant. Women seeking aesthetic breast augmentations have since been limited to saline-filled implants. Nevertheless, the saline is often enclosed in a silicone pouch.

Third-wave feminists have not come to a consensus on the issue of breast augmentation. Most would agree that implants do involve significant risk. They would also agree that unfair gender norms that equate femininity with large, youthful-looking breasts provide the cultural context for this decision. While masculinity is evaluated based on what men *do*, femininity is evaluated based on how women *look*, leaving women to struggle with genetics and the process of **aging** as best they can.

However, feminists dispute the best course of action for women within these cultural inequalities.

Kathy Davis, author of *Reshaping the Female Body: The Dilemma of Cosmetic Surgery* (1995), found that women with breast implants chose to undergo surgery fully aware they were pursuing unrealistic norms of beauty with a risky procedure. According to Davis, these women had implants to feel like complete, worthwhile, and beautiful human beings. Davis explained that her feminist background initially led her to assess this decision as evidence of a "false consciousness." In other words, women would "choose" breast surgery because they were tricked into compliance with Western beauty norms. However, many feminists have accused Davis of misinterpreting the nature of feminist criticism. Theorist **Susan Bordo** has argued that **feminism** protests a *cultural norm*—the combination of rigid beauty standards and simplistic surgical "solutions"—not the individual women who operate within those norms. Should a woman decide to have breast augmentation, feminists would respect her choice to negotiate a place within a repressive cultural climate. Nevertheless, Bordo would argue that this respect for individual choice does not require a sanctioning of what is, essentially, a risky and painful surgical procedure that perpetuates unrealistic beauty standards.

The controversy over cosmetic surgery is not limited to breast augmentation. Feminists point to the use of surgery to obliterate racial and ethnic characteristics that deviate from the white Anglo-Saxon "norm." Significant numbers of Jewish and African American women undergo rhinoplasty ("nose jobs"), and some Asian Americans undergo eye blepharoplasty (having a fold added to the upper eyelid in imitation of the "Western eye") to try to achieve a beauty standard that idealizes white Anglo-Saxon features. However, just as with breast augmentation, feminists disagree as to whether conformity to these ideals is an act of individual **empowerment** on the part of the patient or a capitulation to oppressive beauty standards dictated by a racist, sexist society.

See also Beauty Ideals; Body; Racism; Women's Health

Further Reading: American Society for Aesthetic Plastic Surgery "Press Center," http://www.surgery.org/press/statistics-2003.php; Bordo, Susan, *Unbearable Weight: Feminism, Western Culture, and the Body*, Berkeley: University of California Press, 1993; Davis, Kathy, *Reshaping the Female Body: The Dilemma of Cosmetic Surgery*, New York: Routledge, 1995; Karp, Marcelle, and Debbie Stoller, *The Bust Guide to the New Girl Order*, New York: Penguin Books, 1999; Wolf, Naomi, *The Beauty Myth: How Images of Beauty Are Used against Women*, New York: W. Morrow, 1991.

BETH KREYDATUS

CULTURAL ACTIVISM. Cultural activism encompasses a range of activist strategies that may be carried out by individuals or groups. A significant difference between political and cultural activism is in their intended scopes and methods. The aim of cultural activism typically addresses culture-producing arenas and elements of popular culture, such as large **media** corporations that have a stronghold on information and entertainment venues. Cultural activist actions are distinct from traditional sorts of political activism, which commonly include protest rallies, information gathering and distribution, and other actions that are primarily guaranteed by democratic social practice in basic rights to assembly and free speech. Instead, cultural activism may go beyond legally sanctioned activities and expands on these basic approaches.

Cultural activism works to resist and counteract oppressive social conditions that are held to be basic consequences of cultural habits and assumptions, such as U.S. **consumerism**, rather than the kinds of policies and procedures targeted by traditional political activism. The trends toward commercialism and consumerism are identified by cultural activists as basic cultural problems that attempt to substitute active participation and citizenship with material goods. In efforts to call attention to the invalidity and moral problems of the pro-corporate mindset, cultural activists often create "alternative" advertisements as visual images that work on a different level from argumentation and debate. These alternate ads function to disrupt the continuity of marketing messages and question the companies, products, and purposes of mainstream commercials.

Third-wave feminist research and practice often shares a perspective of cultural criticism that is held by cultural activists. Third-wave feminist work draws on multiple connections between individuals and social groups and also stresses actions and practices that counter oppressive ideologies rooted in cultural assumptions, especially those dealing with media-driven portrayals and characterizations that rely on and perpetuate sexist and racist ideas. The critical stance toward cultural habits widens the perspectives of third-wave analysis of systemic oppression to include cultural attitudes and standards and behaviors, such as images and ideas in mainstream media sources. Cultural activism is used by many third-wave feminists who engage directly in the criticism and interruption of dominant cultural productions by creating alternatives to culture-producing sources such as the media networks, radio stations, and publishing companies.

Cultural activism includes attention to the major methods of cultural production as a means to expose, criticize, and resist the promotion of unjust and repressive practices such as marketing, **advertising**, and other profit-driven practices of the multinational corporations that dominate the marketplace. For third-wave feminists, the critiques of cultural attitudes frequently rely on connections that include critical perspectives on **racism**, classism, homophobia, xenophobia, and other forms of oppression that are experienced and supported by systems of power. Frequently, third-wave efforts involve coalition strategies and close attention to multiple categories of oppression. Also, third-wave work often rejects single-focus efforts that suppose sexism is a primary or fundamental form of oppression. Rejecting a "single axis" approach to oppression creates a space for a multifaceted reading of popular culture and resistant activism for third-wave feminists.

Cultural activism aims to create space for resisting the constant barrage of corporate marketing that has become a part of daily life in the United States. By embarking in ongoing cultural critiques, cultural activists move beyond single issues and single policy approaches to activism. Often cultural activism involves a connect-the-dots approach to examining contemporary issues that includes attention to individual- and social-level concerns. For instance, consumerism, a frequent target of cultural activism, calls attention to the co-option of ideals like individuality, authenticity, and other values. Activists may point out the falsity of products that are marketed as one of a kind or unique, when in fact they are mass marketed and sold by the millions.

The hypocrisy of trying to market values in advertising is coupled with serious concentration on the detailed facts about the businesses producing the advertisements, slogans, and perpetual images that inundate cultural life. By examining the effects of **globalization** and consumerism, cultural activists are able to link issues that bring into focus the myriad forms of oppression perpetuated by cultural habits. For instance, the exploitation of labor and the environment, racism, and colonization can be identified as direct side effects of so-called first world capitalist consumerism.

The critique of culture includes an examination of all aspects of culture production, including advertising. Advertisers try to sell more than the product, often promoting images, states of mind, and ways of life that advertisers associate with the material goods described. While promoting "the good life" for instance, companies may be spending a fraction of their budget on fair compensation and even less on the safe disposal of waste, thus contributing to pollution and exploitation while serving their primary interest of making high profits. When the work of cultural activists takes on these (and other) hypocrisies, attention is called to the basic inequities promoted and sustained by the very practices (like shopping) that are associated with the "way of life." In taking companies and consumers to task regarding the culture of innocence promoted by "free market **individualism**," cultural activists spell out the direct role consumers have in creating fair market choices and a healthier environment, thus promoting concerns that evoke a sense of responsible choice.

In drawing out the potential for coalitions between these specific areas, the insights and efforts of activists in various movements can be aligned. The effect for third-wave feminists, in particular, provides an array of opportunities to engage in forward-looking activism that aims to create ongoing social movements centered on goals of ending multiple forms of oppression and exploitation. The methods of cultural activists, while varied, frequently involve visual elements such as those found in anti-corporate advertising. Such efforts work toward exposing hypocrisy, but they also work in providing viewers with an alternative understanding of advertising that functions differently from rational arguments or factual discussions of corporate wrongdoings. Whether working on isolated projects, in community events, or online, cultural activists work toward developing a consistent and keen focus on debunking the mental colonization associated with large companies that dominate popular realms of culture.

As noted, the methods of cultural activism include diverse techniques and strategies. For instance, "culture jamming" is a technique designed to interrupt the flow of corporate-controlled media and marketing. Culture jamming may involve producing **zines** as alternatives to mainstream publishers' **magazines** that may be reluctant to print articles that are critical of mainstream culture; producing billboards or alternative advertisements that criticize the ideological grip of marketing strategies; producing online sites devoted to undermining the credibility of corporations, which thrive on image-production; or producing forms of "hacktivism," which are designed to interrupt the dependency of humans on computers. Cultural activism may also include activities that are not legally sanctioned—such as forms of political graffiti that deface corporate billboards—with the intent to make viewers recognize an inconsistency or falsity promoted by the company (e.g., spray painting the word "sweatshop" on the billboard of a company known to exploit its workers).

See also Capitalist Patriarchy

Further Reading: *Adbusters* magazine, www.adbusters.org; Ehrenreich, Barbara, and Arlie Russell Hochschild, eds., *Global Woman: Nannies, Maids, and Sex Workers in the New Economy*, New York: Henry Holt, 2004; hooks, bell, *Outlaw Culture*, New York: Routledge, 1994; James, Joy, *Resisting State Violence in the U.S.*, Minneapolis: University of Minnesota Press, 1996; Klein, Naomi, *No Logo*, New York: Picador USA, 2000; Lipsitz, George, *The Possessive Investment in Whiteness: How White People Profit from Identity Politics*, Philadelphia: Temple University Press, 1998.

ERIKA FEIGENBAUM

CULTURAL CAPITAL/CELEBRITY. For third-wave feminists who came of age in a media-saturated culture, the idea of cultural capital or celebrity has been as central to their lives as their cell phones. Celebrity status is not determined by the quality of a person's cultural contributions as much as it is by the quantity. Aesthetics are not as important as saturation. In other words, it does not matter if one is a good actor or a bad one or a good writer or a bad one. What matters is the degree to which one is recognized and cited in what is loosely called mass **media** (newspapers, **magazines**, **television**, radio, etc.), and the greater the number of citations, the greater the status.

The concept of a "celebrity" really came to fruition during the twentieth century, particularly when television and radio enabled information to be more quickly relayed to larger numbers of people simultaneously. And now with cyberculture as dominant as it is, the rate at which celebrities are created has increased even more. In theoretical terms, its identification can be traced to Guy DeBord's influential *Society of the Spectacle* (1967), which identified the "accumulation of representations" as the primary way in which status was determined in capitalist society. According to DeBord, representation rather than some essentialist notion of subjectivity is what matters in post-capitalist society.

For third-wave feminists, this means that whatever status one attains is often double-edged. On the one hand, it can break down gender-based power dynamics. On the other, it can work to reinforce stereotypes. When one considers that celebrities now include activists, politicians, movie stars, musicians, athletes, and critics, as well as porn stars and even **rape** victims, it means there is a wide range of possibilities open to various interpretations. It is not easy to say one's status as a celebrity is progressive or regressive based on definition alone. While pornographic **films** are generally considered sexist, there is an entire segment of the porn industry that identifies itself as feminist.

Although DeBord was concerned with resisting spectacle, and someone like **Susan Faludi** has critiqued "consumer feminists" for being too concerned with celebrity status, it is hard to see a way in which one could stand outside the world of cultural capital. Faludi herself is a celebrity who has appeared on talk shows and written for *Ms.* magazine. And even an activist such as Michael Moore (director of leftist documentaries, such as *Bowling for Columbine* [2002] and *Fahrenheit 9/11* [2004], and author of *Stupid White Men . . . And Other Sorry Excuses for the State of the Nation* [2002]) has embraced the mass media machine, employing every possible outlet in the attempt to get the most possible exposure. They have used their status in different ways—Faludi to promote her brand of **feminism** and Moore to launch an assault against the conservative politics of the Republican Party—but both have the kind of celebrity status that is essential to maintaining any sort of sociopolitical power, whether it be third wave or otherwise.

Further Reading: DeBord, Guy, *Society of the Spectacle*, New York: Zone Books, 1995; Faludi, Susan, *Stiffed: The Betrayal of the American Man*, New York: W. Morrow, 1999.

JEFF NIESEL

CULTURAL STUDIES. One of the primary sites of struggle for third-wave **feminism** is "culture" in the cultural studies sense of the term. Cultural studies is the study of the meanings people attach to a wide range of objects and activities—teen **magazines**, novels, pop **music**, soap operas, snapshots, Internet blogging, holiday celebrations, graffiti, and so on—in their everyday lives. With the emergence of cultural studies as an academic field (in the 1970s at the Birmingham Centre for Cultural Studies and in the late 1980s and early 1990s in the United States), the meaning of long-held distinctions between high and low culture in academic study was seriously challenged. For cultural studies, "culture" refers to culture as it is *lived* and *used* (or *cultural practices*), which always includes the very important role that popular culture plays in everyday life. Cultural studies, in other words, insists that such topics as shopping or the teen **television** favorite *Buffy the Vampire Slayer* are worthy of academic study. It shows that popular culture is a very complicated place where gender norms, for example, can be strengthened by dominant groups, but also where they might be questioned and even undermined. To study how people use a wide range of cultural forms, cultural studies often combines different approaches from sociology, literary studies, **film** studies, and cultural anthropology, to name just a few.

Although it is impossible to make strict generalizations about cultural studies' theories and methods because they vary widely, it is safe to say that cultural studies (and the third wave) share the following basic beliefs about culture: (1) all cultural forms carry messages about the world. They are vehicles of meaning, and these meanings actively shape perceptions of our surroundings and ourselves. This is an inevitable fact of life; (2) when studying the meanings of any particular cultural form, such as **Barbie** or a women's magazine, how people *use* that cultural form in their daily lives is important; (3) it should not be assumed that people passively consume the messages that are handed to them in the news, in movies, or in music. For example, people interact with culture all the time as *active consumers*. Third-wave feminists launch harsh critiques of narrow ideals of beauty and femininity in contemporary culture. An example is when they view girls and women as smart and creative users of popular culture, rather than as powerless victims of it. Furthermore, the third wave does not consider the stuff of popular culture to be all bad, and many young feminists have reclaimed the most girly elements of pop culture as part of their politics; (4) users of culture can also be producers of culture. This is especially true for the third wave, where cultural production—the making of **zines**, music, books, films, and more—is considered a powerful feminist tool. For the Riot Grrrls of the early 1990s and others that have followed in their footsteps, such cultural forms not only provide alternative places to the main-stream where girls can express themselves, but they are also valuable devices for collectivizing and networking (here the Internet has become especially sig-nificant) and are important instruments in feminists' political fight for gender equality. Along these lines, the third wave sees equal access to the institutions and means of cultural production as an extremely important goal for feminism; and (5) the meanings people attach to any kind of everyday object or activity always have a social and political context; cultural practices are related to power. If the second wave struggled to make the personal political and defined activism in terms of breaking down political, economic, and other institutional barriers to gender equality, then third-wave feminists see the political in an expanded sense. For them, gender and sexual politics are interwoven through-out the cultural practices of everyday life. In other words, culture is always political, and the meanings we make of objects and activities in our everyday lives can be powerful acts of resistance and transformation.

Further Reading: *Bitch* magazine, http://www.bitchmagazine.com; *Bust* magazine, http://www.bust.com; Green, Karen, and Tristan Taormino, eds., *A Girl's Guide to Taking Over the World: Writings from the Girl Zine Revolution*, New York: St. Martin's Press, 1997; Grrrl Zine Network, http://www.grrrlzines.net; Kearney, Mary Celeste, "Producing Girls: Rethinking the Study of Female Youth Culture," in *Delinquents & Debutantes: Twentieth Century American Girls' Cultures*, ed. Sherrie A. Inness, New York: New York University Press, 1998, 285–310; McRobbie, Angela, *Feminism and Youth Culture*, New York: Routledge, 2000; Rosenberg, Jessica, and Gitana Garofalo, "Riot Grrrl: Revolutions from Within," *Signs: Journal of Women in Culture and Society* 23(3) (1998): 809–841.

JESSICA BLAUSTEIN

CYBERFEMINISM. The term "cyberfeminism" emerged in the early 1990s to refer to the potentially powerful exchanges between women in **cyberspace**. It has been associated both with **postfeminism** and third-wave **feminism** as it represents a new "version" of feminism. It can be roughly divided into two strands; one taking inspiration from **Donna Haraway**'s metaphor of the cyborg (1991), and the other taking inspiration from Sadie Plant's argument concerning women, weaving, and the Web. For Haraway, the cyborg is a "myth about transgressed boundaries, potent fusions, and dangerous possibilities"—what women can potentially be in cyberspace—whereas Plant proposed that women should use the new technology for their own revolutionary ends, and she argued in *Zeros + Ones* (1997) that the digital matrix is a new sexual revolution. The term "cyberfeminist" has been used by both theorists and practitioners to refer to feminist activity in cyberspace. It has been claimed, in particular, by artists who use the Web to explore **identity** and what it means to live in a **body** (e.g., Cyberfeminist House and subRosa [http://www.cyberfeminism.net]). Cyberfeminists have been keen to claim the Internet is a means of communication that has more in common with women's exchanges than with men's and that the Internet is a post-gendered space.

Although popular in practice and reflecting a largely youthful group, as the number of "Webgrrrl" and "cybergrrrl" Web sites demonstrates, cyberfeminism has been a contentious field in **feminist theory**. Studies have not supported the argument that the Internet makes gender irrelevant; instead, cyberspace often reproduces traditional aspects of female/male interaction. This is made clear in the fictional representations of cyberspace in cyberpunk novels, which are largely white and masculine worlds (whether techno-utopia or techno-dystopia), as the novels of William Gibson (1984) and Bruce Sterling (1986) illustrate. This raises another problem with cyberfeminism—that of its subject matter. If cyberfeminism is feminism in cyberspace, then it needs to be clear what the latter means. Although cyberfeminism claims to be involved with the Internet, cyberspace includes multiple points of reference in addition to the Internet (e.g., mobile phones, computer games, digital **television**), not all of which fall under the remit of cyberfeminism. Moreover, cyberfeminism has been linked with a vision of cyberspace that claims it is new and represents new possibilities—a view that does not take into account the many ways in which cyberspace is actually quite reactionary.

Cyberfeminism has been questioned for its lack of a political agenda and for the way in which terms such as "post-human" and "post-gender" are used uncritically in cyberfeminist discourses. Indeed, what is clear is that cyberfeminists, like some third-wave feminists, have been eager to proclaim a new space and label without adequately reflecting upon history (feminist or otherwise). With reference to cyberfeminism, lack of historical reflection takes two forms. First, cyberfeminists have been quick to dismiss second-wave feminism as monolithic and anti-technology. Second, cyberfeminists have disregarded the indisputable fact that any new technologies have always consolidated, rather than challenged, traditional female/male relations. There is also the question of access. Who is accessing the Internet and for what purpose? The colonization of cyberspace by pornography (another instance of technology consolidating traditional male/female relations) makes it clear that much of the Internet is not used for revolutionary purposes. Judith Squires argued that the term "cyberfeminism" should be used as a way to investigate the relationship between the body and technology. This is the opposite of what many cyberfeminists claim, which is that the Internet makes the body an irrelevant category. In short, new technologies and feminist politics do not necessarily make a cyberfeminist.

Despite these detractions, there are two areas where cyberfeminism has brought about exciting developments in the field of feminist thought and activism. The first is the development of large, women-centered Web sites, such as www.feminist.com and the **Third Wave Foundation**'s Web site (http://www. thirdwavefoundation.org/). Although these sites may only be accessible to a small proportion of the global population, their presence is testimony to the power of networking and they bode well for the future use of the Internet in feminist activism. The second is the growing strand of female-authored cyberpunk texts and hypertexts, such as those by Pat Cadigan (2002) and Shelley Jackson (2002). And perhaps what is most powerful about cyberfeminism is the image of the cyborg, not necessarily for its transgression but for the rigorous debates that have taken place as a result of Haraway's argument. Tellingly, the cyborg is an image that does not belong solely to cyberfeminism but to larger debates about gender, technology, and the body, as exemplified by Sarah Kember's work (2002). This is an indication of how cyberfeminism will have to engage with the material conditions of women and computers. A feminist in cyberspace is not always a cyberfeminist, and to claim to be a cyberfeminist is not always a political statement. It is these tensions that cyberfeminism might seek to address.

See also Postmodern Theory; *Volume 2, Primary Document 44*

Further Reading: Adam, Alison, and Rachel Lander, eds., *Women in Computing*, Exeter, UK: Intellect Books, 1997; Cadigan, Pat, ed., *The Ultimate Cyberpunk*, New York: ibooks, 2002; Fernandez, Maria, Faith Wilding, and Michelle Wright, eds., *Domain Errors: Cyberfeminist Practices*, New York: Autonomedia, 2002; Flanagan, Mary, and Austin Booth, eds., *Reload: Rethinking Women & Cyberculture*, Cambridge, MA: MIT Press, 2002; Gibson, William, *Neuromancer*, London: Gollancz, 1984; Gillis, Stacy, "Neither Cyborg Nor Goddess: The (Im)Possibilities of Cyberfeminism," in *Third Wave Feminism: A Critical Exploration*, eds. Stacy Gillis, Gillian Howie, and Rebecca Munford, Basingstoke, UK: Palgrave, 2004, 185–196; Haraway, Donna, *Simians, Cyborgs and Women: The Reinvention of Nature*, New York: Routledge, 1991; Jackson, Shelley, *The Melancholy of Anatomy*, New York: Anchor Books, 2002; Kember, Sarah, *Cyberfeminism and Artificial Life*, New York: Routledge, 2002; Plant, Sadie, *Zeros + Ones: Digital Women and the New Technoculture*, London: Fourth Estate, 1997; Squires, Judith, "Fabulous Feminist Futures and the Lure of Cyberculture," in *Fractal Dreams: New Media in Social Context*, ed. John Dovey, London: Lawrence and Wishart, 1996, 194–216; Sterling, Bruce, ed., *Mirrorshades: The Cyberpunk Anthology*, New York: Ace Books, 1986.

STACY GILLIS

CYBERSPACE. Often claimed as a new third-wave feminist space of potential, cyberspace as an idea emerged from cybernetics, the systems of control and communication in animals and machines. Cyberspace is most commonly understood as the exchanges that take place either *with* computer technology or with another individual *through* computer technology, and it is largely concerned with the exchanges of data in information and **communications technology**. But while cyberspace is traditionally referred to as a space accessed via a personal computer, cyberspace is increasingly being understood as also referring to computer games, mobile phones, and digital **television**.

Computing and cybernetics have a long history, with Charles Babbage devising plans in 1833 for an "analytical engine" which, had it been built, would have been able to calculate large equations. Other developments in the nineteenth century for managing large amounts of information included the Hollerith punchcard machine, devised for the U.S. census of 1890. However, it was not until World War II that the first electronic computer was developed. The aptly named Colossus was an extremely large computer programmed via punched paper tape and developed by the British to decode encrypted German messages. Technological developments in the 1950s and 1960s meant that the size of the computers was substantially reduced, although they still were perceived and used, for the most part, as calculating machines for the business and the military. Although Sadie Plant has pointed up a female history of computing in her book *Zeros + Ones* (1997), the use of computers has been deeply gendered and computers were and still are associated with men and masculine modes of behavior. This association is evidenced by the overwhelming numbers of men working in the information technology industry and the myth of the male hacker.

Although computers had become a standard feature in many businesses by the late 1970s, the personal computer was unknown until the computer revolution of the early 1980s. The personal computer was put on the market on August 13, 1981, and within two years it had become *Time* magazine's "Man of the Year." Led by the launch of the IBM Personal Computer in 1981 and the Apple Macintosh in 1984, the computer revolution was a marketing strategy that moved the computer into the home. This step was crucial because it allowed women, many for the first time, to have access to information technologies. The marketing strategies were often, however, reliant upon traditional understandings of gender, with computers marketed as being able to help with women's domestic work through, for example, the organization of recipes and shopping lists. Since the early 1980s, the personal computer has become an indispensable part of many households, although primarily as a leisure activity. However, with less than 20 percent of global households having electricity, let alone Internet access, cyberspace should be understood as a white, Western leisure activity, although it does have the potential to facilitate communication between diverse parts of the world.

The expansion of personal computers in the 1980s and 1990s was matched by an increasing demand for software and by the development of the Internet.

The latter originated in the ARPANET computer network, developed in 1969 at the University of California at Los Angeles to ensure military communication in case of a nuclear attack. In 1983, ARPANET was divided into military and civilian networks, the latter quickly moving beyond the control of any one source and evolving into the Internet of today. A careful distinction should be made between the Internet and the World Wide Web, as they are often wrongly used interchangeably. The Internet is a global communications network connected by fiber-optic cabling. The World Wide Web (or the Web) refers to those small parts of the Internet used most often, consisting of the Internet resources that use Hypertext Transfer Protocol (http) and can be accessed via a Web browser. "Cyberspace" refers to all the electronic geographies of the Internet—not just the Web.

Notions of cyberspace had appeared in various science **fiction** texts over the course of the twentieth century, but those texts that make up the subgenre of cyberpunk are largely regarded as primarily investigating the complexities of human interaction with technology and cyberspace. Indeed, the term "cyberspace" was coined by William Gibson in *Neuromancer* (1984) to designate a "consensual hallucination experienced daily by billions of legitimate operators.... A graphic representation of data abstracted from the banks of every computer in the human system. Unthinkable complexity. Lines of light ranged in the nonspace of the mind, clusters and constellations of data" (51). What is so important about this novel is that, as do later cyberpunk novels, it provides a vocabulary to describe the experiences of the computer revolution. The *Mirrorshades Anthology* (1985), edited by Bruce Sterling, and *The Ultimate Cyberpunk* (2002), edited by Pat Cadigan, serve as good introductions to the range of ideas in cyberpunk. The genre has largely been populated by male authors. The masculine hacker protagonist at the heart of many cyberpunk texts has been critiqued by many, including Pat Cadigan and Kathy Acker in their fusion of cyberpunk and **feminism** and by Neal Stephenson in his reworking of cyberpunk conventions. Concerns about technology and computers have also been addressed in **films**, with Hollywood picking up on the cyberpunk themes of technology and masculinity in such films as *The Matrix* and *Terminator* trilogies.

Cyberspace appears to offer a space in which identities are fluid and can be simulated. Certainly, gender blending and gender crossing (assuming the identity of a different gender) are common elements in many exchanges on the Internet, particularly so in the many chat rooms and MMPORGs (Massively Multiplayer Online Role Playing Games) that populate the Internet. To change one's **identity** in these spaces is only a matter of editing one's description; moreover, one can also have multiple identities at the same time, all displaying various racial, gendered, sexed, etc., characteristics. However, Beth E. Kolko, Lisa Nakamura, and Gilbert B. Rodman's important *Race in Cyberspace* collection (2000) points out the ways in which race is often absent from online identities and cybercultural debates. Similarly, it is not as easy as some have hoped to leave behind the characteristics of the **body** sitting at the computer creating the online identities. The ethics of playing with online identity is also debated regularly; debates that are aggravated by those who use the Internet to groom children for abuse. But while the ethics of identity politics will continue to be debated, what has happened is that rigid notions of what it means to be, for example, male or female are challenged. What these disturbances have done is make problematic the cultural assumptions—which have a long history—that men are more technologically minded, whereas women are not. In short, if one can play with identity online, it raises questions about what identity is and whether it is biological or "natural."

There are two interconnected and commonly used metaphors used to refer to the interaction of humans and technology: the post-human and the cyborg. The term "post-human" is used by critics to refer to the destruction of the rational (male) human individual who has been the subject of critical inquiry for the past 300 years. To be post-human means to be *beyond* the human and all that being human involves: "The human/machine interface becomes a place in which traditional notions of subjectivity and embodiment are potentially abandoned" (Gillis 2002, 209). The cyborg metaphor, which refers to a transgressive mixture of biology and technology, was proposed by **Donna Haraway** and has proven extremely compelling for those who work in cyberspace and **cyberfeminism**. As much time is spent connected to, or working with, machines and technology, the metaphor of the cyborg is extremely pertinent. These two metaphors—the post-human and the cyborg—indicate how the interface between humans and machines is becoming essential to our understanding of ourselves, both in and out of cyberspace.

Katharine N. Hayles (1999) argues that the late twentieth century has seen "a new way of looking at human beings. Henceforth, humans were to be seen primarily as information-processing entities who are *essentially* similar to intelligent machines" (7). An example of this statement is the way in which the language used to describe humans is increasingly technologized, while the language used to describe technology is largely anthropomorphized (i.e., given human characteristics). That is, humans are described as machines and machines are described as human. As more time is spent online—whether for business, educational, or leisure purposes—more critical thinking about what kinds of interactions and communities this new space of cyberspace is creating will emerge.

See also Postmodern Theory

Further Reading: Balsamo, Anne, *Technologies of the Gendered Body: Reading Cyborg Women*, Durham, NC: Duke University Press, 1996; Bell, David, and Barbara Kennedy, eds., *The Cybercultures Reader*, New York: Routledge, 2000; Cadigan, Pat, ed., *The Ultimate Cyberpunk*, New York: ibooks, 2002; Featherstone, Mark, and Roger Burrows, eds., *Cyberspace/Cyberbodies/Cyberpunk*, Thousand Oaks, CA: Sage, 1995; Gibson, William, *Neuromancer*, London: Gollancz, 1984; Gillis, Stacy, "Cybercriticism," in *Introducing Theory at the 21st Century*, ed. Julian Wolfreys, Edinburgh, UK: Edinburgh University Press, 2002, 202–216; Gillis, Stacy, "Cybersex," in *More Dirty Looks: Gender, Pornography* *and Power*, ed. Pamela Church Gibson, London: British Film Institute, 2004, 92–101; Haraway, Donna, *Simians, Cyborgs and Women: The Reinvention of Nature*, New York: Routledge, 1991; Havenden, Fiona, Gill Kirkup, Linda Janes et al., eds., *The Gendered Cyborg: A Reader*, New York: Routledge, 2000; Hayles, Katharine N., *How We Became Posthuman: The Reinvention of Nature*, Chicago: University of Chicago Press, 1999; Kolko, Beth E., Lisa Nakamura, and Gilbert B. Rodman, eds., *Race in Cyberspace*, New York: Routledge, 2000; Plant, Sadie, *Zeros + Ones: Digital Women and the New Technoculture*, London: Fourth Estate, 1997; Sterling, Bruce, ed., *Mirrorshades: The Cyberpunk Anthology*, New York: Ace Books, 1986; Wolmark, Jenny, ed., *Cybersexualities: A Reader in Feminist Theory, Cyborgs and Cyberspace*, Edinburgh, UK: Edinburgh University Press, 1999.

STACY GILLIS

D

DADS AND DAUGHTERS. The third wave of **feminism** has seen major shifts in the role of men in the feminist movement, as many seek to act as allies to feminist advocates in areas such as the struggles to end sexual assault and **domestic violence**. Joe Kelly, with his partner Nancy Gruver, first endeavored to change the face of modern parenthood in 1992, when Nancy and their daughters, Mavis and Nia, began *New Moon: The Magazine for Girls and Their Dreams*, which employed Kelly until 1999. At this point Kelly, Gruver, and Michael Kieschnick cofounded a national nonprofit organization called Dads and Daughters (DADs). DADs' main mission is to encourage fathers to become engaged in their daughters' lives and join other activists in changing American culture's dangerous effects on girls and women.

The organization's extensive Web site uses many common tactics in Internet activism, such as interactive quizzes, weekly e-mail newsletters, and interactive **media** campaigns. Joe Kelly's book, *Dads and Daughters: How to Inspire, Understand and Support Your Daughter* (2002), relies heavily on the idea that American culture is poisonous for girls as it encourages a "gender straitjacket," and it offers strategies to help fathers negotiate such a culture. Critics of the book deplore Kelly's almost total neglect of the particular issues faced by poor and working-class families, families of color, and gay fathers, while supporters applaud the careful attention given to many of the chief concerns of the third wave, including **body** image, **sexuality**, media literacy, **girl power**, and reconstruction of femininity and masculinity.

Further Reading: Kelly, Joe, *Dads and Daughters: How to Inspire, Understand and Support Your Daughter*, New York: Broadway Books, 2002; *New Moon* magazine, http://www. NewMoon.org.

JACKIE REGALES

DECONSTRUCTION. Deconstruction is the name for a philosophy and later a method of literary criticism, but it is also one of the key ideas informing third-wave thinking. Anti-foundationalist in approach, which means that it is a theory that questions the idea of central origins, deconstruction was a part of major writings by the late philosopher Jacques Derrida in the 1960s. His writings began to influence American thinkers in the 1970s and became widespread by the 1980s. Most important to third-wave **feminism** is the way deconstruction shows the way hierarchical, oppositional structures are characteristic of Western thinking. Any idea about what something *is*, Derrida wrote, tends to be defined by its opposite. To name just a few of the most obvious examples, white is defined as the opposite of black, male is the opposite of female, and culture is the opposite of nature. In each of these instances, the characteristics of the first term are seen as the opposite of the characteristics of the second term. Not only are the terms seen as opposites, according to Derrida, but there is a value given to the first term at the expense of the second—the second term is always seen as derivative and less-than. This way of thinking functions on an unconscious level—it is what we assume to be true without thinking about it.

Deconstruction has implications for third-wave feminism because implicitly, then, women are seen not only as the opposite of men but also as having less value than men, just as people of color are seen as both the opposite of whites and as having less value. Derrida questioned this way of assigning meaning to people or anything else. He claimed that because terms like "men" and "women" and the meaning we assign to these terms are essentially a function of language, the meaning is in the language and in the relationships between the words rather than in the men and women themselves. The relationships between these terms and the meanings assigned to them is arbitrary (something that is created by people and therefore subject to change), just as ideas about what "men" and "women" are have significantly shifted over time and related to what culture a man or woman lives in and his or her economic circumstances. Women who do not work are becoming increasingly rare in major-developed countries such as the United States, as well as in the developing world, which has implications for how "women" are understood and what is thought about them. These understandings shift according to any given woman's circumstances, including her race, religion, and economic situation. Derrida argued that these understandings are "always already" shaped by the words we use and the changeable cultural meanings ascribed to them, and that therefore meaning is never stable or fixed definitively. Deconstruction was, for Derrida, the unmasking of the way these words work and revealed the fact that the words do not refer to something beyond themselves that is unchangeable, like some special essence of "woman" or "man." For Derrida and deconstruction there is no fixed essence, only words and the cultural meanings that they carry. Hierarchical meanings that would assign greater value to men than women, then, are social constructions; something people make up, rather than anything fundamental rooted in our bodies or ourselves. Third-wave feminism takes this view as one of its major points of departure, assuming that people can change the way they think about "men" and "women" and that these words and those they refer to can be defined for the better.

See also Binary Oppositions; Essentialism

Further Reading: Jehlen, Myra, "Gender," in *Critical Terms for Literary Study*, eds. Frank Lentricchia and Thomas McLaughlin, Chicago: University of Chicago Press, 1995, 263–273; Johnson, Barbara, "Writing," in *Critical Terms for Literary Study*, eds. Frank Lentricchia and Thomas McLaughlin, Chicago: University of Chicago Press, 1995, 39–49; Smith, Barbara Herrnstein, "Value/Evaluation," in *Critical Terms for Literary Study*, eds. Frank Lentricchia and Thomas McLaughlin, Chicago: University of Chicago Press, 1995, 177–185.

LESLIE HEYWOOD

DEPRESSION. Third-wave feminists came of age in a time when depression was being medically treated by the pharmaceutical industry. In the late 1980s, Prozac, the most widely prescribed antidepressant, was introduced to the U.S. market. Within two years, pharmacies were filling 65,000 prescriptions in the United States alone. Within five years, 4.5 million Americans had taken the supposed "miracle drug." It is not clear whether depression is biological or environmental, but it is certain that women of the third wave are more likely to be medicated than their mothers and grandmothers. This raises the question as to whether millions of young women are being pacified by prescription drugs. In a culture that still offers fewer social and political opportunities for women than for men, female despair may be written off as deficient brain chemistry. The danger is that this diagnosis invalidates the angst of millions of teenage girls and women feeling the pressures of and reacting against the impossibilities and inequalities of cultural standards.

According to the National Institute of Mental Health, 18.8 million Americans per year will experience a depressive disorder. Such disorders can be distinguished by trademark symptoms of persistent sadness, anxiety, emptiness, and lack of interest in former pleasurable activities. The effects of depression can be disabling and in certain cases debilitating; many sufferers experience thoughts of death or suicide.

In 2000, suicide was the third leading cause of death among people fifteen to twenty-four years old—10.4 of every 100,000 persons in this age group—following unintentional injuries and homicide. Suicide was also the third leading cause of death among children ages ten to fourteen, with an average of 1.5 per 100,000 children in this age group. The suicide rate for adolescents ages fifteen to nineteen was 8.2 deaths per 100,000 teenagers, including five times as many males as females. Among people twenty to twenty-four years of age, the suicide rate was 12.8 per 100,000 young adults, with seven times as many deaths among men as among women.

Women experience depression almost twice as much as men. However, men are four times more likely to commit suicide, although women report *attempting* suicide three times more often than men. In many cases, depression is less a problem of brain chemistry than it is a combination of genetic, psychological, and social factors. People born after 1955 are three times more likely to exhibit depression than those born before that time.

Despite the modern popularity of antidepressant medication, depression has always been prevalent in the lives of young women. Hippocrates, esteemed medical writer and physician of ancient Greece, believed that differences in phlegmatic humors determined the temperaments of the sexes. This "disease of young women" he called Melancholia was characterized by "aversion to food, despondency, sleeplessness, irritability, restlessness." A common malady of the nineteenth and early twentieth centuries was hysteria—what is now classified as **eating disorders**, depression, and anxiety. Joseph Breuer and Sigmund Freud's *Psychoanalytic Studies on Hysteria* (1895) focused on this malady in young women, noting that many victims were described as intelligent or even gifted. Those afflicted were perhaps able to perceive more than their peers; as women, they had few outlets for their gifts other than in the domestic realm. According to psychologists Deborah Perlick and Brett Silverstein (1994), incidents of female depression have spiked during periods of changing gender roles, when "large numbers of women aspire to achieve in highly respected areas traditionally reserved for males." But they add that "even during these periods of liberation they realize that being female places them at a disadvantage in these areas, and that the traditional female roles of wife, mother, and homemaker remain relatively undervalued" (90). Such women recognized the limitations of being female and were defeated by a sense of their own powerlessness.

Stories such as Charlotte Perkins Gilman's "The Yellow Wallpaper" (1892) featured women incapacitated by nameless maladies. Overwhelmed between the choice of wifedom, motherhood, and professional success, poet Sylvia Plath wrote in her semi-autobiographical novel *The Bell Jar* (1962), "I felt like a racehorse in a world without racetracks" (62). Though written seventy years apart, both women felt imprisoned by the lesser status of their own bodies.

Today, some girls manifest depression through anorexia or self-mutilation, drug abuse, or alcohol. In any case, it is socially unacceptable for a girl to outwardly express her anguish. Anguish turned inward is what may result in the crisis of **identity** experienced by many girls. Adolescent self-loathing may follow a girl into adulthood and become part of the mature woman's identity. Feelings of worthlessness and emptiness may be latent processing of a consumer culture that values the surface of a product more than its substance. Depression, according to clinical psychologist Mary Pipher, may be a way of grieving for the girl sacrificed at puberty who existed as more than an object. Adolescent girls find themselves susceptible to the targets of **advertising**; the perfect self is always just out of reach, keeping her in a constant state of need. This creates a spiritual hunger that may become temporarily salved by the purchase of material goods. In a world that markets low self-esteem and is indifferent toward female achievement, she learns to see herself in terms of exterior validation. Formerly confident girls find themselves silent both within and outside of the classroom. Girls who feel defeated by the barrage of mixed messages, **double standards**, and unattainable standards of perfection may succumb to depression. Many third-wave feminists would see the high incidence of depression in girls as due to these social problems and argue that social change, as well as medication, are the necessary solutions.

See also Beauty Ideals; Body; Consumerism; Women's Health

Further Reading: Gilbert, Sandra M., and Susan Gubar, "A Feminist Reading of Gilman's 'The Yellow Wallpaper,'" in *The Madwoman in the Attic: The Woman Writer and the Nineteenth-Century Literary Imagination*, New Haven, CT: Yale University Press, 2000; Perlick, Deborah, and Brett Silverstein, "Faces of Female Discontent: Depression, Disordered Eating, and Changing Gender Roles," in *Feminist Perspectives on Eating Disorders*, New York: Guilford Press, 1994; Pipher, Mary, *Reviving Ophelia: Saving the Selves of Adolescent Girls*, New York: Ballantine Books, 1994; Plath, Sylvia, *The Bell Jar*, New York: Bantam Books, 1981; Strock, Margaret, "Plain Talk About Depression," National Institute of Mental Health Web site, http://www.nimh.nih.gov; Wurtzel, Elizabeth, *Prozac Nation*, New York: Riverhead Books, 1994.

LEIGH PHILLIPS

DESIRE, FEMINIST. Third-wave feminists draw on three distinct strands of **feminism** to construct a definition of desire: French feminism, **black feminism**, and materialist feminism. At the intersection of bodily pleasures, socially transformative yearnings, and economic analysis, this generation of feminists makes desire a priority—both as an individualistic commitment to following their bliss and as a resource in stimulating collective action—without ever losing sight of the ways desire can be manufactured, commodified, and used against them.

French feminists have spent a substantial amount of time refuting traditional psychoanalytic theories about "what women want." Freudian notions of "penis envy" and the "Electra complex," along with Lacanian equations of desire with lack, are criticized for being centered on the **male body** and psyche and for defining desire in negative terms. French critic Hélène Cixous redefines desire as *jouissance*, an overflowing of pleasure, figured as an orgasmic delight and flood of bodily fluid. Luce Irigaray similarly inverts negative configurations of the female body in *These Lips Which Are Not One* (1981), asserting that women enjoy a surplus of erotic sensation and a self-sufficient sexual anatomy: the two lips of a woman's vulva are always touching one another, thus the fulfillment of a woman's desire is built into her body, not displaced on to male sex organs or masculine social power.

This reconceptualization of the female body as a site of excess rather than lack provides a foundation for a new feeling of entitlement among young women, well represented by the words of Inga Muscio in *Cunt: A Declaration of Independence* (1998): "Each passing day heralds the emergence of yet another athlete, rock star, activist, artist or politician who reminds women we can do pretty much whatever we want. Signs of the dawning post-patriarchal age are positively rampant" (183). A spectrum of desires—from the self-care of auto-eroticism to the longing for social justice—are presented as integrally connected. Some feminists belittle this connection as masturbatory, yet others see in it the imprint of black feminists such as Audre Lorde, who argues that "[o]ur erotic knowledge empowers us," and **bell hooks** (1990), who asserts, "Surely our desire for radical social change is intimately linked with the desire to experience pleasure, erotic fulfillment and a host of other passions." Desire is a radical energy that women can direct at themselves, each other, and the world.

However, this radical energy has historically been contained by patriarchal institutions. Capitalism, for instance, organizes women's desires around consumer practices, so that joy is translated into dishwashing detergent and the clichéd answer to what women want is too often—with a nod to HBO's series *Sex and the City*—another pair of shoes. Desire is thus paradoxically yoked to a disciplined work ethic in the service of accumulating wealth. Third-wave feminists recognize the dangers of this co-optation and promote politically conscious consumer practices, such as Inga Muscio's concept of "cuntlovin' **consumerism**": supporting women's businesses and art, thereby redirecting women's consumer desire toward feminist goals. **Susan Bordo**, in *Unbearable Weight: Feminism, Western Culture, and the Body* (1993), likewise recognizes women's "desire" to be thin or to have plastic surgery as the product of a patriarchal capitalist consumer culture. Her analyses of anorexia and **advertising** campaigns revolve around the production of gendered desires; women learn to long for precisely those things that mark them as secondary and to perceive these desires inaccurately as individual choices and evidence of their freedom.

This materialist feminist critique is applied with particular force to the institution of **marriage**. The monetary and emotional investment in wedding culture strikes many third-wave feminists as a questionable allocation of resources. Jaclyn Gellar demystifies this social institution in her 2001 book, *Here Comes the Bride: Women, Weddings, and the Marriage Mystique*, by arguing against the tradition of becoming a wife to prove oneself desirable, but her exhaustive inventory of bridal registries, **magazines**, and gown shops demonstrates the force of culture behind this desire: "It is overdetermined by **family** pressure, legal sanction, and the deluge of consumer images linking wedlock to female happiness and self-worth."

The gendering of desire—in which men want, and women want to be wanted—is central to the broader feminist issues of female objectification and the male gaze. Third-wave feminists have experimented with the power dynamics of the gaze, investing the object of the gaze with heretofore unacknowledged power. Their subversive practices range from the quotidian (such as wearing lipstick ironically as a comment on beauty culture and as a parody of vamp iconicity) to the spectacular (such as seeking work in strip clubs and peep shows or performing a concert topless with the word "slut" scrawled on one's belly, as did Kathleen Hanna of the band **Bikini Kill**). Commenting on these "adept manipulations of spectacle," Joanne Gottlieb and Gayle Wald (1994) assert, "Such performance recuperates to-be-looked-at-ness as something that constitutes, rather than erodes or impedes, female subjectivity."

Ani DiFranco, a singer-songwriter-producer of independent **music** and owner of Righteous Babe Records, exuberantly asserts in a song of being motivated by joy, despite a context of patriarchal oppression and sexist bias. This could work as an anthem of third-wave feminist desire. Indeed, the contradictions of desire—wanting to be liberated and wanting to be desired, or wanting to be feminist and wanting to be married—define some of the richest spaces of third-wave feminist analysis.

See also Capitalist Patriarchy; Consumerism; Patriarchy; Sexuality

Further Reading: Bordo, Susan, *Unbearable Weight: Feminism, Western Culture, and the Body*, Berkeley: University of California Press, 1993; Gellar, Jaclyn, *Here Comes the Bride: Women, Weddings, and the Marriage Mystique*, New York: Four Walls Eight Windows, 2001; Gottllieb, Joanne, and Gayle Wald, "Smells Like Teen Spirit: Riot Grrrls, Revolution and Women in Independent Rock," in *Microphone Fiends: Youth Music and Youth Culture*, eds. Andrew Ross and Tricia Rose, New York: Routledge, 1994, 250–274; Hollibaugh, Amber, *My Dangerous Desires: A Queer Girl Dreaming Her Way Home*, Durham, NC: Duke University Press, 2000; hooks, bell, *Yearning: Race, Gender, and Cultural Politics*, Boston: South End, 1990; Johnson, Merri Lisa, ed., *Jane Sexes It Up: True Confessions of Feminist Desire*, New York: Four Walls Eight Windows, 2002; Muscio, Inga, *Cunt: A Declaration of Independence*, Seattle: Seal, 1998.

MERRI LISA JOHNSON

DiFRANCO, ANI. Born in 1970, Ani DiFranco has become a third-wave feminist icon and is admired for her innovative and insightful **music** as well as for her political commitments and dedication to speaking her mind. The self-described "li'l folksinger" began selling tapes out of the trunk of her car. Today she hosts a catalog of more than fifteen albums, all released on her own Righteous Babe Records label. In addition to frequent touring, DiFranco often appears in progressive **magazines** such as *The Nation* and on the independent news show *Democracy Now!* In 2004 she performed at the **March for Women's Lives** in Washington, D.C.

Rock critics describe DiFranco's music as "emotional" and "honest," highlighting the no-bones-about-it approach she takes on issues from gun control to corporate corruption. Journalists also report that DiFranco's use of words like "tampon" and "cunt" often keeps her off the airwaves. Other artists' "bitches and hoes" are not generally a problem for Clear Channel Communications, Inc. (the largest owner of radio stations), but it may be DiFranco's stories of menstrual blood in the corporate boardroom that gets the mainstream **media** jumpy.

In 2001, the *David Letterman Show* refused to let DiFranco perform "Subdivision," a song about modern-day **racism** and segregation, requesting that she play something more "preferable musically." DiFranco declined the invitation and let her fans know about the not-so-subtle act of censorship. This is just one example of what has contributed to her iconic status. Her career highlights third-wavers' insistence that music can be activism and that activists can dance along their way to social justice.

Further Reading: Ani DiFranco's Web site, http://www.righteousbabe.com; Quirino, Raffaele, *Ani DiFranco—Righteous Babe*, Kingston, Ontario: Quarry Press, 2000.

ANNA FEIGENBAUM

DISCRIMINATION AGAINST WOMEN. According to the office of Equal Employment Opportunity, discrimination is defined in civil rights law as unfavorable or unfair treatment of a person or class of persons in comparison to others who are not members of the protected class because of race, sex, color, religion, national origin, age, physical or mental handicap, or sexual orientation. Many would think that by the middle of the first decade in the twenty-first century, the feminist movement—a movement that began in the late 1800s—would have already eliminated discrimination against women. But discrimination against women is as much an issue for third-wave feminists as it has been for feminists in the first and second waves. Although some progress has been made, there is still a strong need for feminist activists of all "waves" to work to combat such discrimination.

Whether latent or overt, discrimination occurs if it includes actions or policies that *result* in discrimination. Women are still denied equal treatment, opportunity, and rights on the basis of sex, as well as on the basis of other identities that women claim, such as race, religion, sexual orientation, and class. Social justice activism is merely one way in which third-wave feminists are collectively trying to fight the pervasive discrimination that still exists.

Legislation is just one example of how today's culture views women and discrimination. The **Equal Rights Amendment (ERA)** was first introduced to congress in 1923 and subsequently introduced and defeated in 1946, 1967, and 1971, and finally defeated in 1982. In 1979, the United Nations General Assembly adopted an international bill of rights for women. The Convention on the Elimination of All Forms of Discrimination against Women **(CEDAW)** promises to give women equal rights in all aspects of their lives, including in the political, health, educational, social, and legal spheres. By accepting CEDAW, states commit themselves to incorporate the principle of equality in their legal system and establish tribunals to ensure the effective protection of women against discrimination. The United States is the only industrialized country that has not signed CEDAW—others not yet signed on include Sudan and Saudi Arabia.

Although some feminists may see such legislation as lip service from the government, it still creates an important mechanism for people and institutions to be held accountable for discriminating actions and policies and has important symbolic value. Third-wave feminists realize that **equal opportunity** often does not mean equal outcome, and they are consequently mobilizing around such vital issues.

However, two major successful legislative provisions prohibiting sex discrimination were Title VII of the 1964 Civil Rights Act, which states that employers cannot discriminate on the basis of sex, race, creed, or national origin, and Title IX of the Education Amendments Act of 1972, which outlawed sex discrimination in educational institutions, including collegiate **sports**. Women and girls have gained the opportunities to pursue an **education** but are still underrepresented in the faculty of colleges and universities. They are less likely to be tenured, are often lower in faculty rank, and earn an average income less than their male colleagues. Vocational education also discriminates against women and girls by steering students onto traditionally male and female career paths; for example, channeling males into plumbing, mechanics, carpentry, and welding, which still yield a higher income than "female" jobs such as childcare, nursing, and cosmetology.

Health policies are another way in which women feel the brunt of discrimination. Insurance companies in the United States cover half of the prescriptions for Viagra but only one-third of the prescriptions for birth-control pills. Health research and treatments also have adverse effects on women. While most fertility research is done on women, it does not account for the 40 percent of infertility that is due to the man. Most fertility treatments and procedures are still actually performed on the woman.

Women's work life is an area that is overwhelmingly laden with discrimination—from pay scale to entry opportunities, as well as promotional capacity. Women currently earn seventy-three cents to the man's dollar. Women are well represented in the overall workforce, but they still make up only 12.5 percent of corporate officers, and the numbers become even more dismal for women of color, as they often run into the "**glass ceiling**"—those barriers many women and people of color experience as they try to reach the upper echelons of corporate America. (The idea is that one can *see* one's way to the top but encounter a "glass ceiling" that prevents one from going any further.) As of 2005, only eight women were CEOs of Fortune 500 companies. Major corporations such as Wal-Mart, Morgan Stanley, and Merrill Lynch have settled multimillion-dollar lawsuits on the basis of sex discrimination. Justice gained through such settlements is certainly a sign of progress, but the work culture itself is still very inhospitable for women to advance their careers. There is often the expectation that employees in promotion-track positions can put in the long work hours necessary to excel. Many women are not able to conform to such expectations because greater household and child-care obligations continue to remain a reality.

More educational and professional opportunities are certainly available to young women today, but these opportunities have also created struggles and conflict. Some will argue that women have to choose between having a **family** or a career; others counter by stating that the "system" or "culture" needs to change instead of women acquiescing to accommodate the current norm. Gendered roles, such as that of caretaker, continue to be a constant source of debate, and current policies such as parental leave are just one indicator of how society views and values these issues. In the United States, only 50 percent of new parents are assured parental leave. Legally they are only granted twelve unpaid weeks, compared with eighteen weeks in Great Britain, ten months in Italy, and almost a full year of paid leave in Norway and Sweden.

In addition to the most tangible forms of sex discrimination, young feminists are acknowledging and theorizing their own internal **racism**, sexism, homophobia, and **heterosexism**. They are raising their own consciousness, becoming aware of other more subtle inequalities, and realizing their own role and establishing steps for change.

See also Wage Gap

Further Reading: Dicker, Rory, and Alison Piepmeier, eds., *Catching a Wave: Reclaiming Feminism for the 21st Century*, Boston: Northeastern University Press, 2003; Heywood, Leslie, and Jennifer Drake, eds., *Third Wave Agenda: Being Feminist, Doing Feminism*, Minneapolis: University of Minnesota Press, 1997; Sparks, E.K., http://www.catalystwomen.org; http://www.niehs.nih.gov/oeeo/disc-def.htm; http://virtual.clemson.edu/groups/womenstudies/ws301/chro3wave.htm; http://www.un.org/womenwatch/daw/cedaw; http://www.yourfuturehealth.com/resources_statistics.htm.

NEL P. SUNG

DIVISION OF LABOR/GENDER ROLES. Division of labor refers to the organization of work into categories determined by sex. Although divisions of labor have changed in Western countries since the early 1980s so that white, middle-, and upper-class women now also often work, a "second shift" mentality still exists where women are expected to work outside the home, raise the children, and do most of the housework. Therefore, division of labor and gender roles are still very much an issue for third-wave **feminism**.

Sociobiologists trace the division of work and gender roles back to prehistory, when men worked as hunters and women labored as gatherers and nurturers. According to such theorists, male dominance emerged as hunting led to warfare and ultimately to the establishment of governments. Although the "man as hunter" hypothesis is influential, it has been criticized, among other reasons, for selecting only evidence that supports its hypothesis, for not addressing the extent of women's roles as gatherers, and for overlooking the fact that both sexes sometimes shared domestic responsibilities.

Feminists tend not to accept that men and women have evolved in ways that would mandate their exclusive labor in separate spheres; however, they are interested in understanding and redressing the inequalities resulting from the division of labor. Marxist feminists locate the rise of inequality in the invention of private property. Once surplus value (extra goods or wealth beyond what is needed to survive each day) had been produced in early societies, men wanted to will their property to their children. According to this view, to ensure that their offspring were their own, men needed to control women's **sexuality** by containing wives in **marriage**. What developed was women's role as unpaid nurturer in the domestic sphere. In Western societies, the Industrial Revolution strengthened this role as men occupied the public sphere of production and women occupied the private sphere of reproduction and consumption of goods—the classic wife and mother role. This division between public and private spheres of labor has structured our understanding of gender roles for at least the last two centuries.

People tend not to see how gender roles—the behaviors, attitudes, and traits associated with males and females—are related to history and culture and that these roles have changed a great deal over time. Instead, they see gender roles as a function of nature or biology. This belief mirrors the common attitude toward gender itself, which is typically conflated with sex. Feminists, however, distinguish between sex and gender: unlike sex, which refers to the biological differences between males and females, gender refers to the social and cultural meanings ascribed to sexual difference. According to Judith Lorber (1994), "Gender is so pervasive that in our society we assume it is bred into our genes. Most people find it hard to believe that gender is constantly created and recreated out of human interaction, out of social life, and is the texture and order of that social life" (14). Because people tend not to think that gender is socially created, they often tend to ignore the ways that they participate in its reproduction.

Yet, gender roles are socially constructed as people develop: people learn to "do gender" based on the expectations of the society in which they live. Virtually as soon as children are born, they are taught the proper behaviors and attitudes associated with masculinity and femininity. Although parents and caregivers may not always impart explicit lessons in gender roles, an understanding of correct gender-role performance influences the ways people treat children of each sex. Socialization comes in many forms: the names children are given, the clothes they wear, the toys they play with, the movies they watch, the games they play—all these things teach children gender roles. Boys are taught to reject femininity and to be "masculine"; that is, active, competitive, aggressive, strong, dominant, and emotionally unexpressive. In contrast, girls learn to be "feminine"; that is, nurturing, cooperative, dependent, sensitive, empathetic, and emotionally communicative.

As children are socialized to perform their gender role appropriately, they internalize rules that limit their behavior. For instance, boys discover that they should not wear dresses, play with dolls, or cry, and girls find out that they should not play football or get into fistfights. Ultimately these rules inhibit the fullest development of a person's humanity; as Gloria Steinem has said, gender is a prison for both men and women. Although Steinem sees the prison of gender as less confining for men—she comments that men's prison is equipped with carpeting as well as someone to bring coffee—there actually seem to be more limitations on the male gender role than on the female one. This is because society ranks the genders: masculinity is valued more highly than femininity. As a result, it is easier—and more strategic—for females to adopt "masculine" behaviors such as independence, competitiveness, and strength, for instance, than it is for males to adopt "feminine" qualities such as nurturance and emotional openness. In fact, displaying such feminine qualities may lead people to make homophobic attacks on a male's "manhood."

Theorists who attribute an epidemic of male violence to masculinity's emphasis on aggressiveness and rejection of emotional expressiveness want to see boys and men freed from the prison of gender roles so that they can embrace traits such as sensitivity, communication, and nurturance. The rethinking of gender roles—and especially of the carefully policed boundaries of masculinity—is a project third-wave feminists have inherited from their second-wave predecessors. While second-wavers used new theories about the social construction of gender to help expand girls' and women's opportunities in **education** and work, the third wave—through new programs in gender studies and men's studies—is adding to these goals in an attempt to reconceptualize masculinity.

Third-wave feminists have grown up in a world where gender roles have expanded for women and the strict sexual division of labor seems like a thing of the past. Having mothers who worked—out of either necessity or **desire** (or both)—taught third-wavers that displaying "masculine" qualities such as assertiveness and competitiveness would serve them well in the public sphere of work. And the fact that most American women work outside the home suggests that women's confinement to the private sphere of nurturance has virtually disappeared. Yet, even as women's labor positions them in the public sphere, sexual divisions remain entrenched: society still tends to see the work of child-rearing as a "feminine" job, one that is undervalued and underpaid (or unpaid). In addition, certain professional sectors, such as law, politics, and business, continue to be structured in ways that reinforce old understandings of the division of labor. Recent debates about the "opt-out revolution"—the choice made by upper-middle-class white women to relinquish professional identities to be full-time mothers—revisit questions about work and **family** initiated by second-wave feminists. However, the conclusions reached by those who are "**opting out**" reinforce the traditional division of labor and diminish feminism's efforts to lobby for new systems that would rethink the division between work and family. Third-wave feminism will need to address the divide between public and private spheres to craft roles, rules, and social policies that make more seamless connections between these realms.

Further Reading: Devor, Holly, *Gender Blending: Confronting the Limits of Duality*, Bloomington, IN: Indiana University Press, 1989; Lorber, Judith, *Paradoxes of Gender*, New Haven, CT: Yale University Press, 1994; West, Candace, and Don Zimmerman, "Doing Gender," *Gender and Society* 1 (1987): 125–151.

RORY DICKER

DIY. DIY stands for "do it yourself" and was one of the early rallying cries of third-wave **feminism**, especially in the Riot Grrrl movement. In general, this slogan invites people to make and do things independently of mainstream consumer culture. The DIY attitude usually reflects at least one of three basic assumptions. The first assumption is that alternative or handmade products are inherently more desirable than mass-produced goods. The second is that paying for mass-produced goods serves the interests of those who already enjoy a disproportionate share of the wealth without benefiting the average consumer in any meaningful way. The third is that reusing existing materials to create something new is more ethical or practical than contributing to the waste that is so prevalent in contemporary U.S. culture. Many people also have explicitly feminist motivations for rejecting commercial goods in favor of alternative products, particularly alternative products that are made by women.

There is a broad range of activities associated with DIY. DIY can refer to something as simple as supporting women's businesses whenever it is possible or practical to do so. It can also refer to much larger projects, such as running an independent bookstore or self-publishing original print material. Many women who embrace the DIY attitude also celebrate traditional women's crafts such as sewing and cooking, and many offer handcrafted clothing, quilts, and baked goods for sale or trade. In addition, many direct their talent and creativity toward products that are of unique interest to girls and women. For example, it is the spirit of feminist DIY that moves some women to make, sell, or purchase handmade, reusable, cloth menstrual pads instead of supporting the manufacturers of more wasteful commercial menstrual products. The spirit of DIY in third-wave feminism today can be seen in many of the women-owned businesses that advertise in third-wave **magazines** such as *Bust* and *Bitch*. *See also* Consumerism; Zines; *Volume 2, Primary Document 13*

Further Reading: Wrekk, Alex, *The Stolen Sharpie Revolution: Zine and DIY Resource Guide*, Portland, OR: Microcosm Publishing, 2002.

MIMI MARINUCCI

DOMESTIC VIOLENCE. Domestic violence was a keystone issue for second-wave feminists, who were very successful in bringing it to national attention and establishing shelters for women in need. But the problem persists today and is very much an issue for third-wave feminists to confront as well.

Domestic violence refers to a range of behaviors, from emotional and sexual abuse, to stalking, to economic coercion, to acts of physical violence. Although the withholding of a paycheck, the killing of a **family** companion animal, and the physical beating of one partner by another may seem to be very different, the common denominator that would make all these acts domestic violence is that they are performed so that one person can achieve and maintain power and control over another person. Women are the vast majority of the victims of domestic violence, and this is one of the most serious human rights violations facing women globally. The United Nations estimates that one in three women in the world will experience sexual or domestic violence in her lifetime, and in the United States as well as globally, a woman is more likely to be injured or killed by a partner or spouse than by anyone else.

Second-wave feminists in the United States and England were the first to recognize violence against women in their homes as a problem and not simply one of the occupational hazards of being a woman. They coined the term "wife battering" to describe what they saw happening to many women, and they opened the first battered women's shelters in the late 1960s so that abused women would have a safe place to go to escape the abuse. They also began broad challenges to the way that the legal and criminal justice systems address violence against women in the home. The term "wife battering" was later replaced with the broader, perhaps more palatable, term, "domestic violence." Feminists have argued that domestic violence is tied to gender roles in society: men in our society are trained to be powerful, assertive, and in control, while women are trained to be passive, submissive, and compliant, and violence against women in the home is one way that these gender roles are maintained. Indeed, for much of human history, women have been considered literally the property of their fathers and then husbands, and domestic violence is simply one way that this ownership is demonstrated. Although current U.S. law does not recognize women as men's property, the cultural manifestations of that property relationship linger. Feminist theorists point to fairy tales as one of many cultural scripts that teach women that their ultimate goal is to be happily married and that they should be willing to sacrifice their own safety to achieve that goal.

The question most commonly asked about victims of domestic violence is, "Why didn't she leave?" Feminist theorists have repeatedly found this question problematic, identifying it as a way of blaming the victim and excusing the perpetrator. This question presumes that a woman who is in a violent relationship will be safer if she exits, when, in fact, a woman is seven times more likely to be killed by her abusive partner while she is leaving or after she has left. In addition, this question places all the responsibility for stopping domestic violence on the victim, when—as feminists have noted—the person doing the abusing is the one whose behavior should change.

Domestic violence has not been a focus of young feminists as much as activism around **rape**; for instance, many universities that now have sexual misconduct policies that respond appropriately to rape (because of young feminist activism) still lack policies that address dating violence and stalking. Perhaps this is because domestic violence is seen as an issue for older women; however, violence in intimate relationships is not a problem exclusive to married couples or to "adults." A growing body of research documents the extent to which coercive behaviors of power and control are enacted within dating relationships. Dating violence and stalking can be particularly acute problems on college campuses, where a victim may live in close proximity to her abuser and have little recourse for escaping him if they attend class together or socialize in similar groups.

There have been a number of significant recent feminist interventions into theories of domestic violence, although these interventions are not necessarily categorized as third wave. Theorists have demanded recognition of how differences in ethnicity, economic circumstance, immigration status, and **sexuality** can affect a woman's experience of domestic violence. For instance, Kimberlé Crenshaw and other feminists of color note that much research and activism on domestic violence assumes a victim who is white, middle class, and a native English speaker. This incorrect assumption harms domestic violence victims who are not only marginalized by gender, but who experience other marginalizing **identity** categories. Their suffering may become invisible, and institutions established to help victims may inadequately respond to their needs or even exacerbate their suffering. Organizations such as the Survivor Project in Portland, Oregon, which addresses violence against **transgender** people, and Incite! Women of Color Against Violence respond to these feminist critiques. In addition, the 2000 reauthorization of the federal Violence Against Women Act provided more explicit provisions for immigrant women, at the instigation of feminist activists and advocates.

Other feminist theorists have addressed the language surrounding domestic violence: writer **bell hooks** uses the term "patriarchal violence," which is broad enough to include violence against children and violence in same-sex relationships, without removing the feminist theoretical understanding of domestic violence as centering on patriarchal power and control. Other scholars suggest "terrorism in the home" or "sexual terrorism" as terms that accurately capture the fear that victims experience and that express the severity of the problem of domestic violence for women globally. Although some scholars have argued that violence against men in heterosexual relationships is as widespread as violence against women, the statistics that support this argument have been widely discredited by social science and criminal justice research.

See also Animal Rights; Marriage; Patriarchy

Further Reading: Crenshaw, Kimberlé Williams, "Mapping the Margins: Intersectionality, Identity Politics, and Violence Against Women of Color," in *The Public Nature of Private Violence: The Discovery of Domestic Abuse*, eds. Martha Albertson Fineman and Roxanne Mykitiuk, New York: Routledge, 1994, 93–118; Ferrato, Donna, *Living with the Enemy*, New York: Aperture, 1991; LaViolette, Alyce, and Ola W. Barnett, *It Could Happen to Anyone: Why Battered Women Stay*, Thousand Oaks, CA: Sage Publications, 2000; Schechter, Susan, *Women and Male Violence: The Visions and Struggles of the Battered Women's Movement*, Boston: South End Press, 1982; National Coalition Against Domestic Violence, http://www.ncadv.org; The Survivor Project, http://www.survivorproject.org.

Alison Piepmeier

DOMESTICITY, CULT OF. The cult of domesticity is something that third-wave **feminism** tends to look at critically and ironically. It is a concept that arose between 1820 and the Civil War, when industrialization created a new middle class. It is a concept that has changed, but one can see many women following it today. The cult of domesticity was included in the concept of "True Womanhood," which itself was based on the following four main principles: piety, purity, submissiveness, and domesticity. These principles defined women's status in society, and maintaining these four values, in this view, equaled happiness and success. The cult of domesticity argued that nurturing work was important to sculpting future generations and therefore encouraged educating women. This concept was in direct opposition to the former idea that women were not competent enough to attend school and be educated. They were, in fact, banned from higher **education** until the late 1800s. The four principles defined the principles and rules women were to follow in maintaining their home while men were out in the workforce. When the shift to industrialization moved work from home to the factories and offices, women were left to maintain the home as a type of sanctuary where the **family** values would be safe, secure, and intact. The world of work was defined as male, and therefore the female world was home. Maintaining a beautiful, ornate home that pleased the wage-earner (the male) was vital. Women maintained a home to which the man could retreat after his hard day's work and be free to express a more human, noncompetitive spirit. Therefore, the family unit (and, therefore, **women's work**) changed from how it contributed to the community to how it maintained and protected its own family values by isolating the family from others. Although women were given an inferior place in society, they were expected to maintain and nurture the "future" of society (their families). This belief encouraged women to be schooled in the domestic or nurturing sciences—teaching, nursing, sewing, cooking, and keeping the accounts for the household. One can see how this directly opposed the understanding that women did not belong in schools with men.

Today, some educated women are "**opting out**"—choosing to stay at home and raise their families rather than join the work force, often after being in the work force (which was a principle that was primary to the first and second waves of feminism). But men should also be able to make this choice. Third-wave feminism is largely critical of anything that claims an essentialist **identity** for women, such as the idea that women are "naturally" more domestic, arguing instead that some men are more domestic than some women, and some women are more domestic than some men, and it should be each individual's choice whether they pursue work outside the home or within the home.
See also Division of Labor/Gender Roles; Education

Further Reading: Friedan, Betty, *The Feminine Mystique*, New York: Norton, 1963; Matthews, Glenna, *"Just a Housewife": The Rise and Fall of Domesticity in America*, New York and London: Oxford University Press, 1989; http://people.uncw.edu/sherrilld/edn200/Schooling_Women.htm; http://www.lbrary.csi.cuny.edu/dept/history/lavender/386/truewoman.html.

KRISTINE SISBARRO

DOUBLE STANDARDS. Although there has been some discussion and change regarding double standards for women and men, especially about questions of **sexuality**, the double standard is alive and well and therefore very much an issue for third-wave feminists. When there is a double standard, there is one set of expectations, rules, or roles for one individual or group and a different, often unequal, set of expectations, rules, or roles applied to another individual or group. Sometimes a double standard is legitimate and necessary. For example, older people typically pay reduced prices for bus, train, or movie tickets because they have no immediate revenue source and live on a fixed income, while other people must pay higher ticket prices. But in the case of women, a double standard usually stems from sexist assumptions about women's inferiority and results in gender inequality. Because of double standards, women are subject to sex-specific pressures and restrictions.

Feminism has always been concerned with double standards and how they result in the subordination of women. First-wave feminist leaders lamented a number of double standards, but they spent most of their energy and resources fighting the double standard in suffrage. In an 1854 address to the New York State Legislature, Elizabeth Cady Stanton (1815–1902) said, "We [women] have every qualification required by the Constitution, necessary to the legal voter, but the one of sex." Activists of feminism's second wave further elaborated, analyzed, and popularized the idea that women are oppressed by sexist double standards. By showing that sexism is a social system reinforced through double standards, second-wave feminists taught women that their individual subordination was not private or personal, but rather part of an enormous social framework with political ramifications (hence the slogan, "the personal is political").

Third-wave feminists have exposed the fact that despite many individual women's gains since the second wave, sexist double standards continue to limit most women, and that double standards against women have become subtler. Thus, despite broad knowledge about feminism in our culture at large, knowledge of the existence of double standards against women remains largely clouded and therefore not acknowledged and rectified.

American women today experience many double standards. In the area of beauty, many people, both women and men alike, believe that being physically attractive is more important for women than for men. In fact, women are commonly judged according to their physical appearance to a degree that men are not. This double standard leads women, far more than men, to spend enormous amounts of money and time trying to alter their appearance to fit a narrow cultural ideal of beauty. The pursuit of this ideal can lead to feelings of low self-worth and a sense of **competition** with other women.

Another double standard for women exists in the area of ambition and success. Boys and men, we are taught, are by nature ambitious, while girls and women inherently lack ambition and the **desire** for public or professional success. However, many girls and women are ambitious and do yearn for public or professional success. To express their ambition yet appear feminine, many girls and women are forced to hide their ambitious impulses, which can lead to destructive feelings of competition and underhanded methods of manipulation to achieve success.

A third double standard exists in the area of parenthood. Mothers, much more than fathers, are held responsible for the caretaking and welfare of their children. Mothers, much more than fathers, are expected to curb or leave their paid work to devote their time to their children. This circumstance results in less income for mothers and fewer opportunities to advance in the workplace or achieve public success—things that fathers are not pressured to relinquish.

The Sexual Double Standard. A fourth double standard, the sexual double standard, is particularly well recognized among feminists. The sexual double standard permits greater sexual freedom for men than for women. It is the idea that males are allowed, even encouraged, to express themselves sexually, while females are supposed to lack sexual desire. According to this logic, there is something fundamentally wrong with females who do have sexual desires and needs. Thus, some girls and women are categorized as "good" (i.e., they lack sexual desire) while others are considered "bad" or "loose" or "slutty" (i.e., they are thought to have and act on their sexual desires).

Our vocabulary reflects the sexual double standard. There are many words and expressions with positive connotations for a sexually active male (e.g., stud, player, stallion, ladies' man, the man, Romeo, Don Juan, Casanova, lover) and very few words or expressions with negative connotations (e.g., womanizer, wolf, "can't keep it in his pants"). Meanwhile, the opposite holds true for females. There are only two positive words to connote a sexually active female (hot or sexy), yet a tremendous number of words and expressions with negative connotations (e.g., slut, whore, ho, tramp, **bitch**, freak, hoochie mama, pig, prostitute, hooker, nympho, harlot, hussy, tart, bimbo, floozy, vixen, minx, loose woman, fallen woman, vamp, wench, slattern, Jezebel, strumpet, skank, sleaze, slag, sexpot).

First-wave leader Victoria Woodhull (1838–1927) shocked Americans with her frank speeches about the need for women to overcome the sexual double standard and take control of their sexuality. Second-wave author Shere Hite (1942–) discussed the sexual double standard in her best-selling book, *The Hite Report: A Nationwide Study of Female Sexuality* (1976), and quoted American women who felt oppressed by the need to act like a "good girl." Third-wave author **Naomi Wolf** (1962–) argued in her memoir, *Promiscuities: The Secret Struggle for Womanhood* (1997), that women must acknowledge their sexual desires and thereby break the connection between being sexual and being "slutty." Leora Tanenbaum (1969–) introduced the term "slut-bashing" to third-wave feminists in her 1999 book *Slut!: Growing Up Female with a Bad Reputation*. Tanenbaum expressed the opinion that "slut-bashing," when teenagers slander and ostracize a girl they believe falls into the "slut" category, is a form of **sexual harassment.**

Although typically only one or two girls are singled out for this kind of harassment at any one time in any particular school, Tanenbaum showed that "slut-bashing" polices all girls' sexuality because it reinforces the sexual double standard. Even if they are not personally singled out for harassment, all girls are made to feel sexually inhibited because they learn the message that sex is bad and wrong. At the same time, however, girls are also made to feel that their sexuality is cheapened: girls labeled "sluts" often are not sexually active in the first place or are no more sexually active than other girls in their peer group. Thus, Tanenbaum argued, "slut-bashing" and the sexual double standard can lead some girls to become more sexually active than they would have been otherwise; these girls believe that it is only a matter of time before they themselves are labeled, so that there is no point in abstaining from sexual activity when they will be punished for their sexuality in any event.

The sexual double standard continues to affect girls as they become adults. It also affects boys and men, who are led to believe that only "good" females deserve to be treated with respect, whereas sexual or "slutty" females are not worthy of respect. As a result of this mindset, some boys and men believe that it is acceptable to coerce a female to have sex if she is considered "slutty" and that she is never entitled to refuse sex.

See also Competition, Women and; Desire, Feminist; Family; *Volume 2, Primary Document 42*

Further Reading: Benedict, Helen, *Virgin or Vamp: How the Press Covers Sex Crimes*, New York: Oxford University Press, 1992; Dobie, Kathy, *The Only Girl in the Car: A Memoir*, New York: Dial, 2003; Hite, Shere, *The Hite Report: A Nationwide Study of Female Sexuality*, New York: Dell, 1976; Stanton, Elizabeth Cady, "Address to the New York State Legislature, 1854," in *Feminism: The Essential Historical Writings*, ed. Miriam Schneir, New York: Vintage, 1972, 110–116; Tanenbaum, Leora, *Slut!: Growing Up Female with a Bad Reputation*, New York: Seven Stories, 1999 (Reprint, New York: HarperPerennial, 2000); Wolf, Naomi, *Promiscuities: The Secret Struggle for Womanhood*, New York: Random House, 1997.

LEORA TANENBAUM

DOWNSIZING. Characteristic of the social, economic, and cultural conditions within which many third-wave feminists grew up, downsizing is a process whereby companies cut costs to ensure the greatest profit. Economic **globalization** has resulted in a steep increase in downsizing. One of the main aspects of globalization is free market capitalism, which involves heavy competition for the lowest price of any of a number of goods. This results in the creation of lower-paying jobs with low benefits (sometimes referred to as "**McJobs**"), the **outsourcing** of jobs, or downsizing by eliminating numerous jobs altogether. Third-wavers, who find themselves confronted with an increasingly competitive job market, are deeply affected by this process.

Downsizing primarily refers to company layoffs in order to cut labor costs, but it has also come to mean the downsizing of workers' benefits as well, which has a similar effect. For example, a company might not hire permanent staff, which would mean a significant benefit package, but will instead have current staff work longer hours and/or hire temporary workers to fill gaps. Temporary work has a direct effect on third-wavers who, faced with bleak choices in the job market, often turn to temp work while looking for a permanent position. Typically, temporary positions are filled through agencies, not the companies themselves, and therefore extensive benefits packages are not an option. **Naomi Klein** has noted the recent rise of temporary work and found that from 1970 to 1998 in the United States, there was a 1,201.5 percent increase in the number of people employed by temp agencies (2002, 265).

Downsizing means an increase in unemployment, and young people's unemployment has also increased. According to the United Nations, although people between the ages of fifteen and twenty-four represent 18 percent of the world's population, they make up 41 percent of the unemployed (2004). The United Nations also found that, in a review of ninety-seven countries, young women made up a higher percentage of the unemployed in two-thirds of those countries. In the United States in 2000, young women ages twenty-five to thirty-four were four times as likely as young men to be looking for work, and young black women in this situation were three times more likely to be living in poverty than their white counterparts (Costello, Wight, and Stone, 2002, 70). Third-wave critics such as Michelle Sidler argue that feminists should use their experience fighting against **patriarchy** to voice their dissent regarding these economic hardships, while recognizing the need to address the interlocking oppressions of the global system, of which patriarchy is only one.

See also Volume 2, Primary Document 32

Further Reading: Costello, Cynthia B., Vanessa R. Wight, and Anne J. Stone, eds., *The American Woman 2003–2004: Daughters of a Revolution—Young Women Today*, Women's Research and Education Institute, New York: Palgrave Macmillan, 2002; Klein, Naomi, *No Logo: No Space No Choice No Jobs*, 2nd ed., New York: Picador, 2002; Sidler, Michelle, "Living in McJobdom: Third Wave Feminism and Class Inequality," in *Third Wave Agenda: Being Feminist, Doing Feminism*, eds. Leslie Heywood and Jennifer Drake, Minneapolis: University of Minnesota Press, 1997, 25–39; "United Nations World Youth Report 2003: The global situation of young people," United Nations Department of Economic and Social Affairs Web site, http://www.un.org/esa/socdev/unyin/wyr/; Women and the Economy, Globalization and Women's Work, UN PAC Web site, 2004, http://www.unpac.ca/g_womenswork.html.

GWENDOLYN BEETHAM

DRAG KINGS. An example of the third-wave sensibility that sees gender as both constructed and constantly shifting, drag kings are female entertainers who don masculine attire and perform as male celebrities or composite characters. Drag kings select celebrities for impersonation for their distinctive style such as Prince, Ricky Martin, Elvis Presley, Michael Jackson, Village People, or N'Sync. Some perform either as males or females. Often kings will create masculine characters for comedy routines. Such performances feature proto-typical characters like lounge lizards, womanizers, cowboys, gangsters/gangstas, and bikers. The characters invented by kings are unambiguously masculine—the types of males who flourish outside middle-class sensibility. Rare are portrayals of clean-cut males, as they lack the qualities most desirable (i.e., visual unique-ness with easily recognizable social affectations). A parody as much as it is a tribute to masculinity, kings exaggerate hypermasculine characteristics and be-haviors such as facial hair and machismo.

Culture and Lifestyle. Most kings identify as **queer** or lesbian. Masculine dress and attitude become part of a king's allure within the queer community. Some kings continue to project their bravado offstage to enjoy masculine priv-ilege. "Boi" culture (lesbians who lead lifestyles resembling those of promiscu-ous gay males) figures prominently in drag king circles. Some kings, while remaining biologically female, live their lives as men.

Drag kings, as they are known today, emerged in San Francisco and London in the 1980s and now exist worldwide. Women throughout history have adopted male dress for reasons other than entertainment, such as military credibility (e.g., Joan of Arc) and freedom of movement (e.g., George Sand). Actresses such as Sarah Bernhardt would play male roles, while others such as Annie Hindle and Gladys Bentley were renowned as male impersonators.

Gender theorist **Judith Butler** characterizes gender as performative and drag as a parody of that performance. In *Gender Trouble*, she writes, "In imitating gender, drag implicitly reveals the imitative structure of gender itself—as well as its contingency" (1999, 175). Drag kings illustrate that gender is a choice for individuals to project according to how they want to be received. Most drag kings compile a colorful biography to complement and rationalize their personas.

Humor and wry observation inform the creation of drag personas. Unlike drag queens, who favor the elegant feminine model, kings gravitate to the thug or outlaw model of masculinity. The Deadbeat Daddies sardonically portray an unflattering masculinity, while TheUnderGrounDKingZ promote a member as an antisocial ex-convict. "Feminem" is one performer's interpretation of Eminem (rapper whose lyrics explore **misogyny** and homophobia). Some feminists believe that these characterizations celebrate the worst in masculinity, but kings revel in the contradiction between their performance and their place in society as women. Pushing boundaries and confronting assumptions about gender while having fun is the drag king agenda.

See also Transgender

Further Reading: Butler, Judith, *Gender Trouble: Feminism and the Subversion of Iden-tity*, 2nd ed., New York: Routledge, 1999; DC Kings Home Page, http://www.dckings.com/; del LaGrace, Volcano, and Judith Halberstam, *The Drag King Book*, London: Serpent's Tail, 1999.

TRACY WALKER

E

EATING DISORDERS. Third-wave activist **Amy Richards** has noted that **body** image "may be the pivotal third wave issue—the common struggle that mobilizes the current feminist generation" (*Adios, Barbie*, 1998, 196). Today's popular culture urges women to be the unattainable size of **fashion** models. Today's woman may find herself empowered in the larger world yet still oppressed by her own self-loathing; a loathing that is produced by messages in the **media** everywhere around her that say she is insufficient as she is and needs to be "fixed" through the consumption of products. The issue is unifying to a great number of women because of its immediacy and the collective hopelessness that they experience. Many turn to **feminism** as an outlet for this frustration. Others may succumb to eating disorders. Feminism allows the woman to gain an **identity** within a community of survivors; to understand that the personal is political and that the body is a stage upon which an ever-changing cultural script acts. Eating disorders mentally and physically diminish a sufferer. Instead of being the public entity that second-wave feminists envisioned, she relinquishes her presence entirely.

Eating disorders are culturally specific, but not exclusively modern, conditions. It is not starvation that is essential to these disorders, but the voluntary act of restricting, increasing, or ejecting food that displays the seriousness of a patient's psychic distress. Primarily a female illness that occurs in adolescence and young adulthood, 8 million women continue to struggle with eating disorders as compared to 1 million males. The term "eating disorder" is usually applied to two conditions: anorexia nervosa and bulimia nervosa. A third type, binge-eating disorder, has been suggested but has yet to be officially approved as a formal psychiatric diagnosis. This disorder affects an estimated 35 percent of males.

An estimated 0.5–3.7 percent of females suffer from anorexia nervosa in their lifetime. Anorexia nervosa literally means "loss of appetite for nervous reasons"; however, it is not so much the loss of appetite as it is the suppression of the urge to eat. Symptoms include compulsive and excessive exercise, avoiding meals, frequent weighing, and fear of fat. Medically, the anoretic is characterized by a slow heart rate, irregular menstrual periods, low blood pressure, reduced body temperature, and a body weight that is 25 percent below normal. The outcome of recovery is not entirely certain; some patients are cured after a single episode, while others spend their lives alternating between relapse and health. The mortality rate among anoretics has been estimated at 0.56 percent per year, or approximately 5.6 percent per decade, which is about twelve times higher than the annual death rate due to all causes of death among females ages fifteen to twenty-four in the general population. The most common causes of death from anorexia are complications of the disorder, such as cardiac arrest or electrolyte imbalance, and suicide. Twenty percent of anoretics will eventually die of starvation or its prolonged side effects.

An estimated 1.1–4.2 percent of females have bulimia nervosa in their lifetime. Bulimia nervosa is an eating and psychiatric compulsive disorder characterized by the consumption of large amounts of food in short periods of time, self-induced vomiting, strict fasting, enemas, vigorous exercise, and abuse of laxatives. This behavior must occur at least twice a week for three months. Bulimia is a disease that is highly addictive and dangerous. While anoretics are grossly underweight, bulimics often maintain a normal weight, and therefore the disease is difficult to detect. Dental problems, chronic heartburn/abdominal pain, and dehydration are common immediate effects. Bulimia can also result in irregular heartbeat, serious medical complications, and death.

The third category falls under "Eating Disorder Not Specified," and it includes persons who regularly binge without engaging in inappropriate compensatory actions and any individual who is recovering from or about to enter one of the "specified" eating disorder categories. Surveys have estimated that between 2 and 5 percent of Americans experience a binge-eating disorder in a six-month period. Symptoms include eating an excessive amount of food within a short period of time (at least two days a week for at least six months). Such individuals do not purge themselves of excessive calories and appear overweight.

Eating disorders often begin by regular dieting and eventually spiral out of control. It is still uncertain why some individuals can diet and maintain healthy eating habits, while others resort to binging, purging, or starvation. Body dysmorphic disorder is an abnormal preoccupation with a perceived defect in one's appearance. Such obsessive insecurity results in disordered eating patterns, the treatment for which usually involves inpatient or outpatient therapy. To contribute to successful recovery, a reasonable body weight must be achieved, along with the treatment of self-esteem/interpersonal problems.

All three categories of eating disorders grant the individual a temporary sense of control, stability, and power because she is able to choose what exits or enters her mouth. Distorted body image, clinical **depression**/psychological disorders, and a history of abuse often accompany disordered eating. One with the illness essentially blames the body for cultural, medical, or familial circumstances beyond the patient's control. The patient relates and reduces all life issues to the body; a body that she struggles to revise into a more controllable form. If the cultural pressure is to conform to an ideal thinness, many women will comply in order to be seen as well behaved and unobtrusive.

The staggering modern emergence of eating disorders provides an excellent example of a **backlash** against feminism and serves as one of the clearest indicators that gender equality has yet to be reached. The United States has the greatest number of "liberated" females but also the greatest number of females with eating disorders. Although women's intellect can be on par with that of men, women's "ideal" body size hovers on emaciation. Author Caroline Knapp writes in *Appetites: Why Women Want* (2003):

> The great anxious focus on the minutiae of appetite—on calories and portion size and what's going into the body versus what's being expended, on shoes and hair and abs of steel—keeps the larger, more fearsome questions of desire blurred and out of focus. American women spend approximately $1 million every hour on cosmetics. This may or may not say something about female vanity, but it certainly says something about female energy, about where it is and is not focused. Easier to worry about the body than the soul, easier to fit the self into the narrow slots of identity our culture offers to women than to create one from scratch, easier to worship at socially sanctioned altars of desire than to construct your own, one that allows for the expression of all passions, the satisfaction of all appetites (52–53).

Backlash is the thrust against the continuing progress of **equal rights**. Though women have joined the workforce and participate in a more accepting climate of gender equality, many are reluctant to call themselves feminists. Post–second-wave culture has suggested that equality has been achieved; therefore, any hindrance to female success must be the fault of the woman. If the culture defines achievement as being a virtually unattainable weight for most women, then competitive women may find themselves struggling to prove their value and competence as an "ideal" career person, parent, and woman. The "ideal" weight as represented by actresses and models represents 5–10 percent of the thinnest American women. Some 90–95 percent of women feel as though they do not measure up. A perfectionist will find every aspect of her professional, personal, and sexual identity always lacking. If she is having difficulty proving her equality in the boardroom while juggling motherhood and maintaining an acceptable figure, she must simply not be "good enough" to handle the responsibilities. To *appear* successful, the career-oriented woman must be thin. It is not thinness, but the implications of thinness created by culture, that suggests a woman's capability for ambition and self-discipline.

Naomi Wolf in *The Beauty Myth* (1992) assures that "a backlash against women's advancement does not originate in a smoke-filled room; it is often unconscious and reflexive, like racism" (3). Incidents of eating disorders have spiked to epic proportions during periods of changing gender roles, according to psychologists Deborah Perlick and Brett Silverstein. Disordered eating increased in the 1920s and often manifests in first-generation female college students. Women are able to perceive the tension between their own achievements and that of the previous generation, as measured by the success of mothers and grandmothers. Considering the implied relations between thinness, success, and female competence, it comes as little surprise that 20 percent of contemporary college women are afflicted with eating disorders.

Since the early 1980s, eating disorders have grown in certain demographics of women because the conditions have been precise for their development. The female anorexia sufferer takes up less room physically to negotiate with the larger place women have composed in the public sphere. Natural curves essential for the function of childbearing become lost, and breast size shrinks. She can no longer menstruate and carry a child to term; her body assumes the form of an adolescent boy's. Second-wave feminism assured that women could be just as good as men. Women found themselves in the boardroom, perhaps unconsciously aspiring to the lean, toned body of a male, a body that said "I am competent." A thin body implies competitiveness and ambition. If one can conquer running on fumes, one can do anything—one is beyond the limitations of the female body. It is culturally assumed that body size relates to eating and fitness habits; therefore, the overweight female might be associated with the quality of slothfulness.

The thin woman is almost perceived as too busy to eat. Her image must be sophisticated and beyond the base, animal desires of hunger and the body it suggests. She is simply acting on a long cultural history of despising and fearing the female appetite. In the Garden of Eden, Eve was seduced by the serpent into eating from the tree of knowledge. This myth is one of the earliest displays connecting hunger and desire with moral weakness. In the contemporary United States, fat implies a sense of weakness. There is a pervading sense that anyone can realize their desires with a little work: if women cannot prove to be as good as men, then it is their own fault. If you are fat, it is your fault. The American Dream is the myth of the self-made man, and now the self-made woman. The woman with an eating disorder has given birth to herself, the product of reinvention in a world of personas.

Eating disorders are initially a private affair and often work as a buffer between the self and the often woman-unfriendly outer world. The complexities of the contemporary woman's struggles to negotiate between herself and the **"glass ceiling,"** herself and men, or herself and **family** become all compiled and reduced into a compact, controllable form. Eating disorders are some of the few avenues of control available to young women, despite "liberation." In fact, many eating disorder sufferers identify as feminists and feel such a sense of desperation that they inscribe it on their bodies. A woman with an eating disorder simultaneously emulates and produces a mockery of cultural standards; instead of achieving anything remotely close to mainstream beauty standards, she announces her body in the form of its absence.

Adolescents are susceptible to the superficial influences of mass media. Popular teen **magazines** have capitalized on the young girl's pursuit of "normal" and the desire of peer approval by featuring ultimately unachievable bodies. Advertisers have marketed the body, often airbrushed to a "perfection" that is unreachable, keeping the girl in a constant condition of need. It is this sense of inadequacy that she may remedy with consumer goods. The message becomes apparent that a girl's or woman's appearance is the sum of her identity.

See also Advertising; Beauty Ideals; Consumerism; Magazines, Women's; Women's Health

Further Reading: Fallon, Patricia A., ed., *Feminist Perspectives on Eating Disorders*, New York: The Guilform Press, 1994; Hesse-Biber, Sharlene, *Am I Thin Enough Yet? The Cult of Thinness and the Commercialization of Identity*, New York: Oxford University Press, 1996; Hornbacher, Marya, *Wasted: A Memoir of Anorexia and Bulimia*, New York: Harper Perennial, 1999; Knapp, Caroline, *Appetites: Why Women Want*, New York: Counterpoint Press, 2003; Richards, Amelia, "Body Image: Third Wave Feminism's Issue?" in *Body Outlaws*, ed. Ophira Edut, Emeryville: Seal Press, 1998; Spearing, Melissa, "Eating Disorder: Facts About Eating Disorders and the Search for Solutions," National Institute of Mental Health Web site, http://www.nimh.nih.gov/publicat/eatingdisorders.cfm; Thompson, Becky, *A Hunger So Wide and So Deep*, Minneapolis: University of Minnesota Press, 1994; Wolf, Naomi, *The Beauty Myth*, New York: Anchor Books, 1992.

LEIGH PHILLIPS

EDUCATION. Education in its most basic form is a process (institutionalized or not) through which knowledge is attained, shared, or constructed. Traditional educational approaches position the teacher as the "knower," the one who transmits information to students who are often expected to be passive recipients. A hierarchy is clear in traditional education, both in structure and in power. The structure of the classroom—the teacher at the head of the class, facing students whose chairs are usually situated in rows—reinforces the notion of education as a hierarchy based on knowledge and power. The teachings of feminist education seek to resist and dismantle systems of power and oppression. Feminist teaching practices challenge traditional methods of student education, and third-wave feminist pedagogy (the art and practice of teaching) involves various approaches, which might include a circular classroom (where students and teacher sit in a circle rather than rows), engagement with the Internet and popular culture, and an explicit connection to communities through activism to put knowledge into practice.

Third-wave feminist pedagogy is student-centered, valuing students as a part of knowledge construction and expression rather than as receptacles for information. The term "engaged pedagogy," adopted by feminist **bell hooks** from philosophical predecessors (including Paulo Freire and Thich Naht Hanh), refers to education as a "holistic process," one that transgresses boundaries that confine students to a rigid, assembly-line approach to learning. Holistic education seeks to treat the whole person, teaching more than facts about particular subjects but connecting learning to the world beyond the classroom through direct engagement with communities, heightened self-awareness and actualization, and practical application(s) of course content. Third-wave feminist educational philosophies are strongly rooted in holistic teaching practices.

Third-wave feminist education encourages not only intellectual development but also personal growth by encouraging student involvement with different communities, activism, and enhanced perspectives of their own world(s). Students are prompted by texts and activities that require them to see through a more critical lens, promoting a "connection between ideas learned in university settings and those learned in life practices," as hooks discusses in *Teaching to Transgress* (1994). Feminist, holistic, third-wave education not only teaches students to be critical thinkers by exposing them to texts and perspectives that challenge them, but it teaches them how to apply knowledge they acquire in practical and meaningful ways.

Third-wave education is pluralistic; that is, different teachers use different strategies. There is also the belief that there is more than one way to construct knowledge, as feminist education values difference, gray areas, and complexity of meaning. Feminist education is an active, evolving process, unbound by traditional methodologies and simultaneously constructing, conveying, and challenging knowledge. Third-wave feminist pedagogical approaches deconstruct and reconstruct the classroom both figuratively and literally, and third-wave pedagogical strategies are clearly modeled after the various theories such feminists use. Challenging traditional methods and purposes of education as well as physical classroom structures (such as the circle format), third-wave feminist education decentralizes authority in ways that reinforce feminist opposition to hierarchies, encourage knowledge transmission through various channels (teacher to student, student to teacher, student to student), and dismantle systems of power that reinforce oppression by establishing authority as necessity. Just as third-wave **feminism** challenges existing political, cultural, and social systems, third-wave pedagogy challenges traditional classroom approaches and settings.

Third-wave educational approaches not only recognize but often connect to students' cultural contexts, encouraging student engagement with cyber and popular culture in a way that asks them to be critical viewers and thinkers about what surrounds them everyday. Some of the more distinct elements of third-wave pedagogy include the indisputable presence of visual culture and **cyberspace** in students' lives and, hence, in teaching strategies, engagement with and responses to popular culture, a heavy emphasis on activism as education, and a focus on global issues.

Service Learning. A significant element of third-wave and much feminist education is a connection to the community as a necessary part of the learning process. Social activism uses tools to enact social change around particular issues, while service learning more explicitly bridges the classroom to the community by using knowledge and skills directly related to the academic objectives of a particular course. Identifying communities in need of service in line with particular course objectives, teachers and students construct assignments to benefit specific communities and meet students' learning needs. Many educational programs formally and institutionally sanction service learning and, in these programs, students earn classroom credit for community work. Not all service learning is feminist, but many feminist classrooms use service learning in varying capacities.

Cyber/Visual/Popular Culture. As cyberculture (along with visual culture) becomes more important in students' lives, education responds to its presence. Harnessing the power, currency, and benefits of cyber-, visual, and popular culture (often one and the same), education can engage students while maintaining rigor and clear objectives, regardless of course content. Because many students in a third-wave context have lived in visual and cyberculture(s) their whole lives, while prior generations lived in primarily print cultures (which transmit meaning through printed texts rather than visual texts), using technology and visuals to construct and transmit meaning can be effective and powerful; such approaches to education are increasingly more common. Approaches might include using Web sites and electronic resources for information and research, creating assignments that ask students to view and challenge representations on the Web and in popular culture, using message boards and online environments for discussion, creating and turning in assignments via the Internet, and assigning students to create Web sites that educate others and reflect their understanding of course material.

Online Education. The development of online education intersects with third-wave feminism both on the timeline and in its connection to cyberculture. Because girls and women have traditionally been geared toward nontechnical fields, online education resists such categorizations by inviting (and in some cases demanding) involvement by both males and females. The currency of online education aligns it more specifically with third-wave feminism; distinguishing it from more general feminist educational practices, as the Internet and third-wave feminism developed and continue to develop simultaneously. A crucial benefit of online education is accessibility. Online classes provide access to education that many students would not have otherwise, such as homebound or nontraditional returning students whose work and life schedules keep them from attending conventional face-to-face classroom settings. Web classes in college are standard, and while some classes might include both Web and face-to-face components, many courses function without students and instructor(s) ever meeting in person. On the other hand, inaccessibility can also be an issue because not everyone has access to the resources that online classes require (such as computers or computer skills), due to financial reasons or otherwise. The use of voice in online classes reinforces feminist constructions of communities because voices online are stripped down to words that resonate without being attached to appearance or other barriers, including student fear of speaking out in large classroom settings. Students who might never speak are encouraged (or required) to use their voice in online classes by responding to texts, materials, and assignments, which is revolutionizing classroom discussion in ways that might never happen in face-to-face settings.

Global Focus. Connecting local communities and concerns to global issues is an important piece of third-wave feminism and third-wave education. Courses dealing with global issues are more common (with or without being third wave or feminist), but connecting to global communities has become an essential part of much third-wave feminist education. Courses on global feminism are most explicit, but other courses linked to global concerns in varying capacities are increasingly common, depending on course content and/or subject matter. Viewing borders as sites of connection rather than sites of distinction transgresses traditional boundaries and teaches individuals to think beyond their own world(s), an important educational component in a world where technology allows for such connection (and also illuminates cultural boundaries, especially for those who do not engage such technology for various reasons, whether economical, developmental, cultural, or otherwise). As industrialized nations move toward **globalization** (the integration and internationalization of world economies), connecting students to other cultures helps them think critically about the implications of globalization and imposing specific cultural standards on others.

See also Communications Technology; Cyberfeminism; Cyberspace; Single-sex Education; *Volume 2, Primary Document 31*

Further Reading: hooks, bell, *Teaching to Transgress*, New York: Routledge, 1994; Maher, Frances A., and Mary Kay Thomson Tetreault, *The Feminist Classroom*, New York: Basic Books, 2001; Mayberry, Maralee, and Ellen Cronan Rose, *Meeting the Challenge: Innovative Feminist Pedagogies in Action*, New York: Routledge, 1999.

LEANDRA PRESTON

EDUT, OPHIRA. Ophira Edut is a publisher, writer, editor, Web developer, and public speaker covering issues such as **body** image, **media**, culture, Jewish issues, and gender. She is one of the founding publishers of *HUES* (Hear Us Emerging Sisters) magazine, a national, multicultural, young women-empowered magazine that was published from 1994 through 1999. Edut started *HUES* magazine as a college project with her twin sister, Tali, and their friend, Dyann Logwood, as a response to the invisibility of women of color, cultures, and body sizes in mainstream **magazines**.

Edut sold *HUES* to New Moon Publishers and became an associate editor for *Ms.* magazine. (*Fierce* magazine took *HUES*' place in 2003, reviving and re-envisioning a young women's magazine to empower women who do not exactly fit the mold of the mainstream media.) Her sister, Tali was already working for *BUILD* magazine, Do Something Foundation's progressive magazine. At the same time, Edut edited *Body Outlaws: Young Women Write about Body Image and Identity* (2000), the first book that explores body image from multicultural young women's perspectives. The 1998 version, *Adios, Barbie: Young Women Write about Body Image and Identity*, was taken off the market after Mattel, the maker of **Barbie**, sued in 1999. Edut is a founding board member of the Independent Press Association and contributing editor for *Ms.* magazine.

See also Magazines, Women's; *Volume 2, Primary Documents 37 and 40*

Further Reading: Edut, Ophira, http://www.ophira.com; *Fierce* magazine, www.fiercemag. com/home.html; Heywood, Leslie, and Jennifer Drake, eds., *Third Wave Agenda: Being Feminist, Doing Feminism*, Minneapolis: University of Minnesota Press, 1997; Ruttenberg, Danya, *Yentl's Revenge: The Next Wave of Jewish Feminism*, Seattle: Seal Press, 2001.

HEATHER CASSELL

ELLIOTT, MISSY. Often thought to be representative of a third-wave sensibility, Missy "Misdemeanor" Elliott (1971–) is a writer, producer, and performer of **hip-hop** and rap **music**. Elliott was born Melissa Elliott in Portsman, Virginia. She was discovered by Devante Swing, of the R&B group Jodeci, while performing with her first group, Sista. Although Sista never successfully recorded, Elliott began making guest appearances with artists like MC Lyte and SWV (Sisters With Voices). With her longtime collaborator Timbaland (Timothy Moseley), Elliott also began writing songs for popular performers including Aaliyah, Ginuwine, Whitney Houston, and Lil' Kim.

In 1997, Elliott released her first solo album, *Supa Dupa Fly*, which topped charts. The music video for the single "The Rain" featured digitally distorted images of Elliott wearing a blown-up garbage bag. Surrealism, humorous videos, and flashy, space-age **fashion** soon became Elliott's trademark.

Hip-hop music is often said to be misogynist, stereotypically referring to black women as "bitches and hos." In this regard, Elliott stands out as a female artist in a field dominated by men. She has used her celebrity status to address many of the negative images popularized in hip-hop music. For example, Elliott frequently speaks out against violence, emphasizing a need for unity and positive self-image. She is open about the domestic abuse she experienced as a child and has made significant donations to anti-violence causes. Unlike many popular female artists, Elliott has not taken on an excessively sexualized persona. Rather, she is portrayed as capable, confident, and strong.

Elliott has been criticized, however, for occasionally reinforcing negative images of black men and women in her songs. Her second album, *Da Real World* (1999), is a good example. In the controversial song "She's a Bitch," Elliott proudly reclaims the term "**bitch**" as positive and powerful. The themes of the song are common to male-produced rap music (such as violence, extreme wealth, power, **sexuality**), but Elliott reverses the traditional gender roles of hip-hop by placing herself as the powerful figure.

Elliott has since become a mainstream celebrity, appearing in **films, television** shows, and commercials. She has released five full-length albums and has collaborated on singles with a wide variety of artists. Elliott frequently experiments with Middle Eastern and Asian styles of music, producing innovatively blended hip-hop. Her use of impromptu nonsense words and playful onomatopoeic sounds give her music a playful, creative sound. Because of her willingness to take risks and experiment with new styles, Elliott is known as one of the most innovative and successful artists today, and she is an inspiration to third-wavers everywhere.

See also Hip-Hop Feminism; Hip-Hop Terms for Women

Further Reading: Missy Elliott Web site, http://www.missy-elliott.com; Morgan, Joan, *When Chickenheads Come Home to Roost: A Hip-Hop Feminist Breaks It Down,* New York: Touchstone, 1999; VIBE/SPIN Ventures LLC, *Hip-Hop Divas,* New York: Three Rivers Press, 2001.

TERESA SIMONE

EMPOWERMENT. Women's empowerment remains a central focus in third-wave **feminism.** The concept of empowerment deals with two elements of cultivating power: internally (as an individual) and collectively. These levels of recognizing, developing, and acting on goals work to advance both personal feelings of esteem and political activism to resist and counteract oppression and injustice in a larger structural sense. The personal and institutional aims of empowerment serve both personal and social goals for change and therefore coincide with the feminist recognition that "the personal is political." A starting point in building an empowered group recognizes that action and inaction alike are politically charged. Like second-wave work, the work of third-wave feminists often emphasizes strategies to build coalitions and community-centered action and research. Liberation from oppressive social systems for individuals and groups are often among the primary goals. The liberationist efforts of third-wave feminists include both analyses of social institutions that reinforce existing systems of dominance and privilege, and practical activism that serves to undermine the power system that maintains inequalities based on factors such as race, gender, class, ability, and sexual orientation.

Efforts to increase empowerment include the exposure of social, political, economic, and cultural influences and aim to cultivate a critical understanding of existing injustices. In fostering a critical understanding of reality (understood as the world, culture, and social systems in it), the ultimate goal of fulfilling human potential is advanced. To develop potential, exposure of inequality and a basic intellectual understanding alone are not the main focus. Instead, empowerment aims to develop self-awareness, self-reflection, and action in response to imposed structures that create powerlessness.

Powerlessness can be understood as a condition of perceived or actual inability and may result from a number of situations. Economic instability, stress, limited access to political power, limited time to develop knowledge of issues or to devote to activist efforts and direct collaboration, limited access to information and resources, and internalized oppression are factors that may contribute to a self-perceived ineffectualness, which may in turn have a negative impact on self-esteem and one's ability to recognize, access, and use available and existing resources.

The dimensions of empowerment respond to and directly counteract powerlessness. Empowerment includes basic personal and social aims, such as enhancing or cultivating an improved sense of self, which may involve developing pride in a particular group **identity** or affiliation (e.g., grouping based on ethnic status, religious membership, or sexual orientation); developing the skills for critical consciousness, which enables an understanding and knowledge of factors that impose powerlessness, so that women can instead contribute to a real sense of internal power or agency (a willful capacity to act); the practical outcomes in developing strategies for action regarding liberation; and the use of existing resources to accomplish social goals.

The goals of empowerment have personal (micro-level) and political or social (macro-level) implications. On the micro-level, empowerment works to transcend the realities and perceptions of a powerless state by dealing directly with the things that interfere with and thereby block an individual's abilities to develop an internal sense of power, and it works to develop clear powers of self-determination and self-actualization (personal autonomy and agency). Subsequent benefits on the personal level can include increased esteem, the recognition and use of assets, community participation, and the achievement of self-established goals.

On the macro or general level, there can be significant social consequences to collective empowerment that results from collaborative work. Groups that pool together individual resources and assets can respond to social problems and issues by intervening on a basic level. Grassroots organizing projects typify the social outcomes possible with collective empowerment strategies.

Several examples of collective empowerment include student groups developed to respond to a campus problem, community boycotts and civic organizations that respond to locally identified problems, cooperative networks of people who form protest groups or organize demonstrations to work on a particular issue or policy, or employee groups that form to respond to workplace issues of fair pay or benefits. Some additional examples of efforts of empowerment include consciousness-raising groups that serve both personal and social goals of empowerment by contributing to individual development and collective strategizing, professional groups that meet to respond to an identified need or problem, or volunteers who develop free tutoring programs or mentor relationships for local children and youth. Consciousness-raising groups serve both personal and social goals of empowerment by contributing to an atmosphere

of action, and such coalition-building efforts facilitate a position of power in spite of the imposed elements of basic social inequality and injustice.
See also Girl Power

Further Reading: Cuomo, Chris J., *Feminism and Ecological Communities*, Routledge: New York, 1998; Freire, Paulo, *Pedagogy of the Oppressed*, New York: Continuum, 2000; hooks, bell, *Teaching to Transgress: Education as the Practice of Freedom*, New York: Routledge, 1994; Third Wave Foundation, www.thirdwavefoundation.org; Turner, Francis J., ed. "The Empowerment Approach to Social Work Practice," in *Social Work Treatment*, New York: Free Press, 1996.

ERIKA FEIGENBAUM

ENVIRONMENTALISM. Many third-wave feminists self-identify as environmentalists, but third-wave environmentalism defies simplistic attempts to classify it into distinct subcategories. It is characterized by respect for the diversity of all life forms, a deep concern about toxic by-products of industrialization and **war**, and skepticism about the fundamental Western socioeconomic value systems and worldviews that condone the rapid spread of materialistic **consumerism** at the expense of earth's biosphere and non-Western cultures. Unlike the predominantly white, middle-class, second-wave feminist movement, third-wave environmentalism's role models are as likely to be from Third World countries or be women of color in the United States. Third-wave ecofeminism draws upon second-wave feminist environmental theory and puts it into action. The grassroots political activism and local environmental clean-up efforts initiated by women and like-minded men of all ages, **education** levels, races, sexual orientations, and socioeconomic classes are manifestations of global third-wave environmentalism.

It is generally agreed that the term "ecofeminism" entered the English language by the late 1970s. There is no agreement, however, as to its actual origin. Some credit the French writer Francoise d'Eaubonne with coining the word in her 1974 essay, "La Feminisme ou la Mort (Feminism or Death)." Ynestra King, an activist and ecofeminist theorist, was among the first Americans to use the term. She taught ecofeminism courses at the Institute for Social Ecology (http://www.social-ecology.org), which was established in 1974. Other second-wave feminists trace the earliest use of ecofeminism to radical feminist theologian Mary Daly. Still others believe that many women around the world "invented" the term on their own throughout the 1970s, an era when networking among feminist scholars and activists had to be conducted without the conveniences of the Internet's e-mail or Web sites. King believes ecofeminism is the third wave of the women's movement.

Regardless of when or where the word originated, the earliest ecofeminists became political activists in response to catastrophic environmental disasters that polluted their towns, killed people outright, and/or resulted in ongoing health problems for the women's families and communities. Multiple miscarriages, serious birth defects, blindness, atypical clusters of cancer, chronic respiratory illnesses, shortened life spans, and uninhabitable land are among the legacies of human-caused ecological disasters, such as the Three Mile Island nuclear plant radiation leak near Middletown, Pennsylvania, on March 28, 1979, and the decades-long quagmire of illnesses and property damage from leakage of industrial and military chemical wastes from Occidental Petroleum Corporation's Love Canal, New York, property. In response to the Three Mile Island leak, King and other women activists organized the Women and Life on Earth: Eco-Feminism in the '80s Conference held at the University of Massachusetts, Amherst, during the Spring Equinox of 1980. Women and Life on Earth, a regional activist network, functioned from 1979 through 1982. In 1999, it was reestablished as an international ecofeminist network via the Internet (http://www.womenandlife.org). Lois Gibbs, a Love Canal housewife-turned-activist, was instrumental in obtaining federal funding for the relocation of her **family** and her neighbors to uncontaminated homes. She cofounded the Center for Health, Environment and Justice (CHEJ) (http://www.chej.org) in 1981 to help people facing other industrial contamination crises learn how to cope with unsympathetic government officials and hostile corporate representatives. CHEJ now sponsors a nationwide initiative—its BE SAFE campaign—to prevent pollution and environmental destruction before it happens.

Second-wave feminists focused on gender when theorizing about the ways dominant patriarchal cultures have oppressed the natural environment. Building onto that foundation, third-wave ecofeminists identify global capitalistic economics as the actual reason for the widespread exploitation and abuse of the environment. When examining who benefits from versus who suffers from the global spread of capitalism, third-wave environmentalists consider the categories of race, sexual orientation, and socioeconomic class, as well as gender. The concept of environmental justice is based on the belief that affluent people of industrialized Western countries, supported by consumption politics, are consuming more than their fair share of the planet's natural resources. A popular bumper sticker captures the mindset of thoughtless consumerism: "The one who dies with the most toys wins." Some people who are satisfied with the economic status quo counter that overpopulation causes poverty and that poor people do not deserve a larger share of the earth's resources for a better quality of life. Nevertheless, U.S. foreign aid packages are often coupled with provisions that bar funding of birth-control resources. Moreover, U.S. foreign aid tends to be available only to countries that have natural resources of interest to multinational corporations or that support a global capitalist economy, regardless of evidence of greater need in countries that do not meet those criteria.

Another popular phrase, "not in my backyard (NIMBY)," summarizes a major controversy in the arena of technological development and environmental protection. Ecofeminist activists learned from Three Mile Island and the Love Canal that economic partnerships between governments and industries result in their placing higher value on corporate profits than on the health of their own employees or the general public. Toxic waste dumps, factories that process dangerous chemicals, and nuclear reactors tend to be placed on less-valued land. Marginalized people, including indigenous populations, the elderly, non-whites, and the poor are most likely to live near industrial waste dumps and unsafe factories. These less-valued groups experience disproportionately higher health risks from technology than do more affluent people. A tragic example of this occurred on December 3, 1984, at the Union Carbide Corporation's pesticide factory in Bhopal, India, which was built in an impoverished residential area. An explosion at the factory released toxic gas that killed more than 3,000 people and injured more than 200,000 others. Native Americans formed the Indigenous Environmental Network (http://www.ienearth.org) in 1990 to combat the long-standing government and industrial practice of turning tribal lands into toxic waste dump sites.

Nonhuman life forms, both plant and animal, are also under constant threat of habitat contamination or destruction and even species extinction from deforestation, over-fishing, war, and other ecologically unsound practices condoned by governments and businesses. In the 1980s, ecologist and winner of the 2004 Nobel Peace Prize Wangari Maathai founded the Green Belt movement in Kenya, a grassroots campaign that eventually grew into more than 6,000 women's groups that planted 20 million trees, replacing the indigenous forest that had been destroyed by clear-cutting. Maathai's leadership restored the ecosystem and improved the quality of life of the rural people who directly depend on natural resources for their survival. The International Society for Ecology and Culture (ISEC) (http://www.isec.org.uk) is a nonprofit organization that promotes decentralized local economies as an alternative to a monopolistic global economy. ISEC's "Ancient Futures Network" seeks to protect both biological and cultural diversity in the industrialized Western and in Third World countries.

Ingrid Newkirk cofounded People for the Ethical Treatment of Animals (PETA) (http://www.peta.org) in 1980. Today, it is the largest **animal rights** organization in the world. In 1982, ecofeminists Marti Kheel and Tina Frisco cofounded Feminists for Animal Rights (FAR) (http://www.farinc.org), a nonprofit national educational organization dedicated to ending all forms of abuse against women, animals, and the earth.

Third-wave ecofeminism also reflects the spiritual elements developed by second-wave theologians. King contends that ecofeminism is the starting point for reconciling humans with the natural environment and enabling people to envision the kind of harmonious, holistic world that ought to exist. Greta Gaard, an ecofeminist activist and theorist, asserts that the same traditional Western patriarchal philosophies that elevated scientific rationalism as a necessary control over the chaotic natural world have been used to justify the devaluation and oppression of women, indigenous colonized peoples, and non-heterosexuals, because their perceived **sexuality** is interpreted to be irrational and evil. Gaard calls for a coalition between heterosexual ecofeminists

and **queer** liberation activists to work together to develop a democratic, ecological social structure that values all people equally and a new Western philosophy that is not threatened by the erotic. Thus, the third-wave ecofeminist movement is subversive. It calls for rethinking the basic relationships between humans and the rest of nature and replacing the scientific paradigm that has dominated Western thought for centuries. Ecofeminists contend that the serious environmental crises around the world are actually battlefields in a global economic war that will determine which people are the most valuable and which people and nonhuman species are valued least by the planet's power-brokers. Ecofeminists oppose socioeconomic value systems that undermine the earth's ability to support life. They believe greed-driven global development is shortsighted and will bankrupt the planet's resources for future generations. Ecofeminists seek the development of alternative, nonexploitative economic and social systems that respect and protect all life forms and their habitats.
See also Capitalist Patriarchy; Consumerism; Globalization

Further Reading: Diamond, Irene, and Gloria Feman Orenstein, eds., *Reweaving the World: The Emergence of Ecofeminism*, San Francisco: Sierra Club Books, 1990; Gaard, Greta, *Ecological Politics: Ecofeminists and the Greens*, Philadelphia: Temple University Press, 1998; Glass, Betty, "Ecofeminism," in *Women's Studies: Core Books*, Association of College and Research Libraries, Women's Studies Section, http://digital.library.wisc.edu/1711.dl/ACRLWSS; Haraway, Donna, *The Haraway Reader*, New York: Routledge, 2004; Mies, Maria, and Vandana Shiva, *Ecofeminism*, London: Zed Books, 1993; Ruether, Rosemary Radford, ed., *Women Healing Earth: Third World Women on Ecology, Feminism, and Religion*, Maryknoll, NY: Orbis Books, 1996; Starhawk, *Webs of Power: Notes from the Global Uprising*, Gabriola Island, BC: New Society Publishers, 2002.

BETTY J. GLASS

ERA/EQUAL RIGHTS/EQUAL OPPORTUNITY. Still an issue of concern to third-wave feminists because the Equal Rights Amendment (ERA) has still not passed, and equal rights and opportunities are still open questions, these three interrelated issues—the ERA/equal rights/equal opportunity—mark an unresolved area of struggle that began at the beginning of the twentieth century. Alice Paul, suffragist and leader of the National Women's Party, penned the ERA in 1921. This was only one year after the passage of the Nineteenth Amendment granting women's suffrage. The ERA stated, "Men and women shall have equal rights throughout the United States and every place subject to its jurisdiction." It called not only for equal rights between men and women but would also give the government the authority to create and interpret legislation to this end. The simply stated amendment was introduced to Congress in 1923. However, many lawmakers and citizens found the ERA extremely controversial because they could not predict precisely what changes that ERA would produce in the social structure of society or familial structures of the home.

The ERA did not pass the House of Representatives in 1923 and it was subsequently reintroduced to Congress every year until 1972. Serious fervor over the ERA was reenergized during the social unrest of the late 1960s and early 1970s. The concept of equality had its roots in the earlier (and still ongoing) movements of abolition, civil rights, and women's rights. Over the course of 100 years, between 1865 and 1965, the passage of key legislation helped create a climate in which the passage of the ERA was possible. The passages of the Thirteenth, Fourteenth, Fifteenth, and Nineteenth Amendments secured emancipation, citizenship for former slaves, black male suffrage, and eventually women's suffrage, respectively, and guaranteed at the very least political rights to previously disenfranchised groups. The Civil Rights Act of 1964 intended to end discrimination based on sex, race, color, religion, or national origin. Title VII, more specifically, prohibited employment discrimination based on the same criteria. Courts have since interpreted Title VII to bar discrimination based on sexual orientation.

The 1960s, the height of the civil rights movement and the Vietnam War, marked a volatile moment in the American consciousness. A reinvigorated women's rights movement and the emergence of strong feminist rhetoric, namely by Betty Friedan (1921–), author of *The Feminist Mystique*, 1963, and Kate Millett (1934–), author of *Sexual Politics*, 1970, also contributed to the formation of a unique political climate that led to the passage of the ERA in 1972. President John F. Kennedy (1917–1963), in an effort to investigate and create equal opportunity, established the Commission on the Status of Women in 1961. Specifically charged with examining **discrimination against women**, the committee recommended and President Kennedy signed into law the Equal Pay Act of 1963. The intention of this act was to eliminate the **wage gap** between men and women in theory, but forty years later it has yet to do so in practice. President Lyndon B. Johnson established affirmative action in 1965. This called for the allocation of jobs and resources to specific groups and mainly affected government and educational institutions, which were required to set up affirmative action programs. Lastly, in 1972, the Equal Opportunities Employment Act established a commission to ensure that the aforementioned legislation was enforced.

The passage of the ERA in 1972 seemed to be at the pinnacle of the women's, feminist, civil rights, and equality movements. The amendment passed the House and then overwhelmingly passed the Senate by a vote of eighty-four to eight on March 22, 1972. Slightly altered from Paul's original text, the 1971 version read, "Equality of rights under the law shall not be denied or abridged by the United States or by any state on account of sex." However, seven years later, as the first ratification deadline approached, supporters managed only to secure thirty of the necessary thirty-eight states for the Amendment's ratification. A large protest in Washington, D.C., successfully pushed through a deadline extension of three years. Supporters of the proposed Twenty-seventh Amendment were unable to rally the necessary number of states needed. At the final ratification deadline, only thirty-five of the necessary thirty-eight states had ratified the amendment. The ERA died in July of 1982.

There has been constant debate by historians and political scientists about why the ERA was not successfully ratified. Both proponents and opponents of the ERA campaigned that its passage would produce substantial changes. The argument was based on the fundamental question: do equal rights mean same rights? Each side critiqued the other for an overexaggeration of the changes the ERA would bring about. Proponents believed that the ERA would create legal equality for women, would allow for women to be drafted and sent to combat in **war** time, would grant full equality with men, would close the wage gap, and would fund medically necessary abortion. The push to pass the ERA was also met with stern opposition.

Backlash against the women's liberation movement, **feminism**, the growth of the political Right, and opposition from conservatives, namely Phyllis Schlafly (1924–), created a powerful countermovement against the ERA. Schlafly, an author and activist, was the leader of both STOP ERA and the Eagle forum. Each was an organization dedicated to the defeat of the ERA based on the belief that it would change **family** structure and put women at risk for military combat. Most importantly, Schlafly campaigned that the passage of the ERA would result in women's loss of family rights in custodial cases or would lessen the sentences for sex crimes against women. In a grassroots effort, she was able to generate enough fear about the possible substantive changes the ERA would make if it were ratified. Schlafly is the most outspoken and well-known opponent of the ERA. She testified in front of thirty state legislatures in opposition to the amendment during the ratification process.

Another factor may have contributed to the ultimate failure of the ERA. There was an enormous amount of controversy regarding the Supreme Court decision of **Roe v. Wade** (1973), which restricted states from denying women access to abortion during their first three months of pregnancy. Decided within a year of the Senate passing the amendment, this decision significantly affected public opinion not just about abortion, but also about women's rights in general. The controversy provided perfect ammunition for opponents of the ERA, who easily equated the passage of the ERA with the sanctioning of abortion. Another theory is that the actual wording of the ERA was broad enough that the enforcement and interpretation of it would have to be outlined by the courts. In other words, it did not precisely spell out what this "new equality" would be.

The fifty-year struggle to pass the ERA and the fact that its ratification was not successful does not mean that equal opportunity was lost or denied. Several states passed legislation similar to that of the ERA. These states included Utah, Virginia, and Illinois (which had not ratified the Constitutional Amendment), and Colorado, Hawaii, New Mexico, Maryland, Massachusetts, Texas, Washington, Pennsylvania, and New Hampshire (which initially ratified the amendment).

In addition, separate legislation has passed and various organizations have formed with the goal of creating equal opportunity. Equal opportunity is not a monolithic concept with a singular meaning. It can mean the absence of discrimination for an individual, governmental, or societal elimination of the possibility of disadvantages, or it can mean that individuals who have or suffer from disadvantages for which they are not responsible are recognized. Equal opportunity is not directly stated as an inalienable right in the Constitution. But some argue that it is inherently implied under the Fourteenth Amendment, which contains the clause of a citizen's right to equal protection under the law.

Further Reading: Halberstam, Malvina, and Elizabeth F. Defeis, *Women's Legal Rights: International Covenants an Alternative to ERA?*, Dobbs Ferry, NY: Transnational Publishers, Inc., 1987; Mansbridge, Jane J., *Why We Lost the ERA*, Chicago: University of Chicago Press, 1986; Pole, J.R., *The Pursuit of Equality in American History*, Revised Edition, Berkeley: University of California Press, 1993; *Roe v. Wade*, 410 U.S. 113 (1973); Steiner, Gilbert Y., *Constitutional Inequality: The Political Fortunes of the Equal Rights Amendment*, Washington, D.C.: The Brookings Institution, 1985; Van Dyke, Vernon, *Equality and Public Policy*, Chicago: Nelson-Hall Publishers, 1990.

JESSICA A. YORK

ESSENTIALISM. A key issue to third-wave feminists, most of whom take an anti-essentialist stance, essentialism remains a point of view to be challenged. In a broad sense, essentialism is the assumption that all members of a particular race, class, gender, or sexual orientation share common characteristics—an assumption that can lead to damaging prejudicial stereotypes of such groups. When applied to gender, essentialism is the belief that because biological differences exist between women and men, women and men are "naturally" different in terms of character and personality as well. Someone who thinks in an essentialist way views men as strong, aggressive, violent, brave, logical, disciplined, lustful, and independent. Women, on the other hand, are seen as weak, passive, gentle, cowardly, emotional, lacking self-control and stamina, lacking in sexual appetites, and highly invested in their relationships with others. Essentialism has a long history in Western culture and philosophy, going at least as far back as ancient Greece (as evidenced by the fact that Aristotle wrote about men being naturally more noble, courageous, and virtuous than women). In the eighteenth century, philosophers such as Immanuel Kant and John Locke argued that the social division of the sexes was justified by the natural differences between male and female bodies. This theory was known as "natural law." Eighteenth-century scientists began studying the **male body** and female **body** and concluded that because males' skulls were larger than females' skulls and females' pelvises were larger than males' pelvises, men were better fit for politics, business, and public life in general, and women, whose smaller skulls presumably indicated lesser intelligence, were best suited to bear children and tend the home.

The implications of an essentialist view of gender are far reaching. Traditional gender roles are, to an extent, based on an underlying **biological determinism**, or the view that "biology is destiny." As a result, women have long had primary responsibility for parenting and housework, and men have been the breadwinners. Even today, men outnumber women in positions of prestige in business and government, and girls and women are not as strongly encouraged to pursue careers in math, science, and technology as boys and men.

Feminists who have wanted to expose and change the social organization of gender have objected to essentialism for its oversimplified and hierarchical definition of what is manly and what is womanly, but feminists have also had to be careful not to fall into the trap of essentializing women as a group themselves. Anyone can see that women do not share a common set of attributes: women (and men) can be aggressive and logical at some times, and passive and emotional at other times. Therefore, feminists have been stuck in a "difference dilemma": politically, feminists need to be able to make claims about women as a group, such as "women must have reproductive freedom" or "science courses need to be redesigned to accommodate women's learning styles." These claims can easily be read as subscribing to essentialist assumptions, but many feminists are willing to take the intellectual risk of essentialism to critique social and economic inequities that cut along gender lines.

See also Division of Labor/Gender Roles; Family; Wage Gap

Further Reading: Guess, Carol, "Deconstructing Me: On Being (Out) in the Academy," in *Third Wave Agenda: Being Feminist, Doing Feminism*, eds. Leslie Heywood and Jennifer Drake, Minneapolis: University of Minnesota Press, 1997; Lay, Mary, "The Computer Culture, Gender, and Nonacademic Writing: An Interdisciplinary Critique," in *Nonacademic Writing: Social Theory and Technology*, eds. Ann Hill Duin and Craig Hansen, Mahwah, NJ: Lawrence Erlbaum Associates, 1996, 57–80; Ritchie, Joy, "Confronting the 'Essential' Problem: Reconnecting Feminist Theory and Pedagogy," in *Feminism and Composition: A Critical Sourcebook*, eds. Gesa E. Kirsch, Faye Spencer Maor, Lance Massey et al., Boston, MA: Bedford/St. Martin's, 2003, 79–102; Schiebinger, Londa, "Introduction," in *Feminism and the Body*, ed. Londa Schiebinger, New York: Oxford University Press, 2000, 1–21; Schiebinger, Londa, "Skeletons in the Closet: The First Illustrations of the Female Skeleton in Eighteenth-Century Anatomy," in *Feminism and the Body*, ed. Londa Schiebinger, New York: Oxford University Press, 2000, 25–57; Snitow, Ann, "A Gender Diary," in *Conflicts in Feminism*, eds. Marianne Hirsch and Evelyn Fox Keller, New York: Routledge, 1990, 9–43; Sorisio, Carolyn, "A Tale of Two Feminisms: Power and Victimization in Contemporary Feminist Debate," in *Third Wave Agenda: Being Feminist, Doing Feminism*, eds. Leslie Heywood and Jennifer Drake, Minneapolis: University of Minnesota Press, 1997.

Clancy Ratliff

EVOLUTIONARY BIOLOGY AND PSYCHOLOGY. Evolutionary biology and psychology have only recently become a major interest to a number of feminists, including those in the third wave. Previously, most feminists criticized evolutionary theory and biology as both a patriarchal and biased discipline that refused to acknowledge its subjective investments in its supposedly "objective" discourse. But more recently, a change in perspective has come about as scientists have discovered links between genetic activity and environmental conditions. In turn, as biologists have come to disprove hypotheses such as **biological determinism**, which they previously upheld, some feminists have decided to enter into the field to scientifically investigate exactly what conditions perpetuate the dominant social order in hopes of learning how to alter the surrounding environment to make certain characteristics, such as dominant versions of masculinity, less evolutionarily fit. This shift has helped to reshape a whole series of questions and open them up to numerous perspectives and possible answers. In this new context of scientific knowledge, third-wave **feminism** is interested in both biology and constructivism.

While both biology and psychology have been used to uphold racist and sexist stereotypes by claiming certain races or genders as innately less intelligent or motivated, they are now being used to investigate the *conditions* that might make it more likely that certain races or genders do not reach the same levels as those with power. Power imbalances are maintained by the unlikelihood of company advancement or less pay for the same work. In such conditions, an evolutionary perspective would uphold that because a **glass ceiling** exists, working hard does not necessarily result in more pay. It does not then make sense for a disempowered individual to work extra hard, because the same results can be obtained without the costs of going the extra mile. If these conditions are altered, the argument goes, then these individuals' behavior would also change, because if the same opportunities were readily and equally available, those individuals who might not be motivated to work hard in an office with a glass ceiling would find themselves working very hard in a world where they could see room for advancement. As a consequence, evolutionary-based disciplines are now being used to dismantle some of the very stereotypes and ideologies they had originally been used to construct. The entering of feminists into evolutionary thought has helped to open up both biological and psychological research to a number of different questions and has allowed space for subjective claims to overcome the previous absolutisms that scientific discourses once took as their purpose to discover in their search for truth.
See also Wage Gap

Further Reading: Brodwin, Paul, "Genetics, Identity, and the Anthropology of Essentialism," *Anthropological Quarterly* 75(2) (2002): 323–330; Penn, Dustin, "The Evolutionary Roots of Our Environmental Problems," *The Quarterly Review of Biology* 78(2) (2003): 275–301; Ridley, Matt, *Nature Via Nurture: Genes, Experience, and What Makes Us Human*, New York: HarperCollins, 2003.

JOSEPH SCHATZ

F

FALUDI, SUSAN. Susan Faludi is a Pulitzer Prize–winning journalist and best-selling feminist author. She was born in New York City on April 18, 1959, to Steven Faludi, a photographer, and Marilyn Lanning Faludi, an editor. Faludi proved to be a capable reporter and social commentator at a young age, reporting on contentious—and often politically charged—issues for both her elementary and high school newspapers. She cultivated her skills as an undergraduate at Harvard University (serving as a writer and then managing editor of the *Harvard Crimson*), often tackling women's issues and later writing one contentious article about sexual harassment on the university's campus. Faludi graduated summa cum laude in 1981 and immediately launched her career in journalism, working for *The New York Times*, *The Miami Herald*, and the *San Jose Mercury News* until she joined *The Wall Street Journal*'s staff in 1990. Just one year later, she was awarded the Pulitzer Prize for explanatory journalism. Her first book, *Backlash: The Undeclared War Against American Women*, was also published in 1991. Inspired by a 1986 *Newsweek* article that labeled **feminism** "the great experiment that failed" and motivated by the prevalence of **media** reports stating that the women's movement's success had left an entire generation of women over the age of thirty manless, lonely, and unhappy, Faludi set out to investigate further. After four years of extensive research, she exposed the myths of women's improved economic and social lives (and the spurious evidence supporting such claims) and concluded that the powerful counter-assaults to women's liberation—the **backlash**—proved only that the feminist struggle was not yet over. The book was a popular success, rapidly climbed to the top of the national bestseller list (and stayed there for nine consecutive months), and it elevated Faludi to the status of cultural icon.

Reviewers praised the book for its timeliness, descriptiveness, and thorough and wide-reaching data, while opponents called it reductive, charging that it was little more than an elaborate conspiracy theory. Despite its critics, *Backlash* won the National Book Critics Circle Award for general nonfiction in 1992. Faludi's second book, *Stiffed: The Betrayal of the American Man*, was published in 1999 and also hit the bestseller lists. Exploring the state of the "modern man" and investigating the collapse of traditional masculinity since World War II, Faludi concluded that men—like women—have been affected by social and cultural forces and have been left feeling powerless. *Stiffed* asserted that men and women must work together, find common cause, and create new paradigms that benefit everyone. Faludi currently lives in California.

Further Reading: Faludi, Susan, *Backlash: The Undeclared War Against American Women*, New York: Crown, 1991; Faludi, Susan, *Stiffed: The Betrayal of the American Man*, New York: William Morrow, 1999.

CANDIS STEENBERGEN

FAMILY. A family is a group of people related through kinship. Various cultures define kinship differently. In the United States, the term "family," or "kin," generally refers to two concepts: extended family and immediate family. For many years, the immediate family referred to a specific family structure known as the nuclear family; however, in the past few decades and along with the rise of third-wave **feminism**, the structure of and ideas about immediate families have changed.

Extended Family. An extended family comprises all the people an individual is related to through a shared genealogy or common ancestry and through **marriage**. People who share a common ancestry are considered blood relatives. The types of familial relationships established by blood include parents, grandparents, children, grandchildren, aunts, uncles, nieces, nephews, and cousins. People related through marriage are considered in-laws, with the exception of the husband-wife relationship.

Nuclear Family. In common use, the word "family" most often brings to mind a person's immediate family. When referred to as a "nuclear family," the immediate family consists of two parents and a child or children sharing a household independent of the parents' families' households. Typically, a nuclear family includes a mother, a father, and their children—the son(s) and daughter(s) who are brother(s) and sister(s) to one another. Once the nuclear family's children reach adulthood, they establish households independent of their parents.

Divisions of Labor in the Nuclear Family. In Western culture, the nuclear family has typically implied a bundle of assumed sex roles, or jobs within the family unit that are divided based on a person's sex. In such a system, the father, as the male, has typically been the breadwinner, and the mother has been a housewife, in charge of the home and the children. Likewise, chores inside the home, such as cleaning and sewing, are assigned to female children, while chores outside the home are assigned to male children.

This sex role system has roots in the colonial era of U.S. history (the 1600s), when families in villages farmed their property, relying on each other for survival. Their divided labor produced all the goods that they needed to live, so every family member had specific responsibilities. However, this system became less prevalent with the rise of capitalism in the 1800s; more people could exchange labor for wages, which they then used to purchase the goods needed to survive. In the early capitalist state, many women worked outside the home until they were married, and men worked outside the home throughout their lifetimes. Because not all of the goods that a family needed to survive had become available for purchase, women still had many important production tasks within the home, such as baking bread and sewing clothing. Over the next two centuries, capitalism became the major model of life, and by the mid-1900s, many families could buy all items they needed with the father's wages. Families no longer needed women to remain at home to produce goods, and they no longer needed to divide tasks between sons and daughters to survive. However, sex role patterns within families continued.

During World War II, most able-bodied American men were sent to **war**. Without enough men to fill all the jobs, millions of single and married women had a chance to work outside their homes. When the men returned from the war, employers and society at large expected women to return to their household roles so that men could have their jobs back. However, polls showed that 80 percent of women wanted to continue working after the war. Some 4 million women were forced to stop working in 1946 when their employers fired them. Later, as women returned to the work force, they faced various forms of discrimination, such as sexual harassment and being fired if pregnant. In the 1960s and 1970s, second-wave feminists struggled to end workplace discrimination. Now, the majority of women in the United States work outside the home, and **discrimination against women** in the workplace has become illegal.

Changes in the Family. Lessening need for divisions of labor within families combined with the widespread availability of employment opportunities for women have dramatically changed the shape of families since the late 1970s. Nuclear families are declining as other types of immediate families are on the rise, and census data show that families have changed more since the late 1970s than they did in the previous fifty years.

Even since the early 1990s, major shifts have occurred. In 1990, nuclear families constituted 39 percent of U.S. households, but by the 2000 census, the percentage of households with nuclear families had dropped to 25 percent. Reasons for this decline include people marrying later than they used to, and more elderly people continuing to live in their own homes as the enormous baby boom generation ages. Furthermore, with a high national divorce rate, many U.S. families have a single parent in the home. The 2000 census showed that single mothers headed 7 percent of all U.S. households, an increase of 25 percent since 1990, and single fathers headed 2 percent of all U.S. households, an increase of 62 percent. The number of households headed by unmarried couples with children also increased sharply. Conservative groups have been concerned about these changes, but efforts to encourage people to live in nuclear families have generally failed.

Although women have increasingly been employed outside the home in the past few decades, a 2002 Census Bureau survey indicated that out of the total number of children under age 15 with two parents at home, 25 percent of them had stay-at-home moms—a slight increase from 1994, when 23 percent had stay-at-home moms. This increase may be partially due to an increase in the Hispanic population, as some Latino cultures more strongly value stay-at-home **mothering**. The 2002 Census Bureau survey indicated that of the 10.6 million children whose mothers decided to stay at home with them rather than seek employment outside the home, approximately 16 percent lived in poverty, as opposed to only 4 percent among children whose mothers worked. The survey also revealed that 189,000 children's fathers were stay-at-home dads, an increase of 18 percent from 1994 to 2002. Parents report that raising children full time is slowly becoming perceived as equivalent to a job; thus, it is logical that staying at home with the children is increasingly acceptable for third-wave fathers.

The feminist movement of the 1960s and 1970s also raised many parents' awareness that the sex roles assumed by them and their children do not occur naturally but by socialization; therefore, many families have made a concerted effort to ensure that all family members participate in a range of household tasks, rather than assigning them based on sex.

Families in the Third Wave. Third-wavers define the word "family" broadly, recognizing many configurations of adults and children as constituting families. Configurations include interracial families; families with unmarried parents who cohabitate; families with two mothers or two fathers, who may or may not have had a **same-sex union** or **same-sex marriage**; families with the woman as the breadwinner and the man as the primary caretaker of the children and household; and families produced by several marriages. In some circles, it might even include polygamous families, in which a man has more than one wife, or polyandrous families, in which a woman has more than one husband. U.S. law permits only monogamous marriages, however, so plural marriages would not have legal recognition.

Another third-wave trend involves young people returning to their parents' homes after childhood instead of or after attempting to start their own households. Members of **Generation X** have been staying in their parents' homes for longer periods of time, often from the time they graduate college into their late twenties. This means that as they are renegotiating their relationships with the families of their childhood, they are forming new types of families in which all of the children may be adults. When some adult children return to their parents' home, they bring a lover, spouse, or close friend with them, thereby also constituting a different type of family. And with the high divorce rate in the United States, many adult children do not return to the parents they grew up with. They may live with only one parent, or with a parent and his or her lover or spouse, who may have other children living in the home.

Family Names. Immediate family members often share the last name, or surname, of the father, making family naming traditions patrilineal. The woman gives up her own family name, or maiden name, upon marrying, and takes her husband's. At birth, their child receives the father's surname, as well, so that all members of the family share the same name. However, reflecting the many new types of immediate families, naming patterns have been changing.

More married women now choose to keep their maiden names. One might keep her maiden name when she marries; take the husband's name and keep her maiden name as a middle name; take her husband's surname as a middle name; or hyphenate the maiden name and the husband's surname.

In such situations, a couple's children may be assigned surnames in numerous ways. All children born to the couple may be given the father's last name, the mother's last name, or some combination (such as a hyphenation) of both names. Alternatively, some children in the same family might be given differing surnames. For example, daughters might be given the mother's surname, while sons are given the father's surname. With all the naming possibilities, every member of an immediate family could have a different last name.

Some couples have opted to change both the husband and wife's surnames upon marrying. They might decide to share the same hyphenated name, or to create a new surname that combines parts of each original name. Others have created new surnames altogether. This can be seen as a postmodern, third-wave response approach to selecting a surname shared by all members of an immediate family.

See also Division of Labor/Gender Roles; Wage Gap

Further Reading: Armas, Genaro C., "Census Shows Rise in Number of Children with Stay-at-Home Mothers," *The Detroit News*, June 17, 2003, http://www.detnews.com/2003/census/0307/09/census-195821.htm; Benfer, Amy, "The Nuclear Family Takes a Hit," *Salon.com*, June 7, 2001, http://dir.salon.com/mwt/feature/2001/06/07/family_values/index.html; Council on Contemporary Families, "America's Changing Families," Council on Contemporary Families Web site, http://www.census.gov/population/www/socdemo/hh-fam/p20-537_00.html; D'Emilio, John, "Capitalism and Gay Identity," in *The Gender/Sexuality Reader: Culture, History, Political Economy*, eds. Roger Lancaster and Micaela di Leonardo, New York: Routledge, 1997, 169–178; Douglass, Susan, *Where the Girls Are: Growing Up Female with the Mass Media*, New York: Times Books, 1994; Parsons, Talcott, "The Kinship System of the Contemporary United States" in *Essays in Sociological Theory*, New York: Free Press, 1954, 189–194, http://www2.pfeiffer.edu/~lridener/courses/PARSONS3.HTML; Ritchie, Karen, "Marketing to Generation X," *American Demographics* 17(4) (1995).

REBECCA C. HAINS

FASHION. The third wave has claimed fashion as an arena for female-centered fun, feminist politics, and individual self-expression. Many third-wave feminists point to their willingness to embrace fashion as a primary example of their difference from second-wave feminists. However, they unite with their second-wave foremothers by resisting any attempt to coerce girls and women to conform to fashions. Furthermore, they are critical of narrow standards of fashion that exclude some women from participating. Fashion can only be liberating and fun if it is optional for everyone.

Third-wave feminists often characterize second-wave **feminism** as a movement that was implicitly "anti-fashion": a label that many second-wave feminists dispute. **Rebecca Walker**'s third-wave anthology, *To Be Real: Telling the Truth and Changing the Face of Feminism* (1995), captures some of this debate. In Walker's anthology, authors Danzy Senna and **bell hooks** (among others) argue that second-wave feminists were participants in a "revolution ... defined by strict dress codes" and were guilty of neglecting aesthetics in their criticisms of materialism and women's objectification. However, Gloria Steinem countered in her foreword, "Feminism has always stood for the right to bare, decorate, cover, enjoy, or do whatever we damn please with our bodies—and to do so in safety" (1995, xvi).

This debate over the second wave's approach to fashion is evidence of the power of feminism's critics. Like third-wave feminists, second-wave feminists struggled to overcome stereotypes that they were ugly, unfashionable, man-hating lesbians. After members of the women's liberation movement tossed bras, curlers, and fashion **magazines** into a "Freedom Trashcan" in 1968 to protest the Miss America Pageant, the hostile press coined the enduring slur "bra burner" to describe feminists. (Ironically, no bras were burned at the protest.) By labeling feminists as bra burners, critics simultaneously discredited their appearance, their **sexuality**, and their politics. The derogatory term "bra burner" takes the focus away from the feminists' message and implies that feminists are merely discontented with their underclothing. Feminists are presumably easily identified—they would be unfashionably dressed, braless women.

In an effort to combat the restrictive and coercive nature of beauty norms in the 1960s and 1970s, some second-wave feminists did indeed express "anti-fashion" politics. Anti-fashion rhetoric offered feminists a means of challenging the legitimacy of their opponents' criticisms. By wearing unfashionable clothing and refusing to conform to the narrow range of **beauty ideals** imposed on their generation, second-wave feminists expanded the range of aesthetic possibilities for women. Furthermore, they expanded the realm of activism to make attire (for instance, going braless or wearing pants) into a political statement. In this way, second-wave feminists followed the lead of black nationalists, who made the slogan "black is beautiful" a political call for recognition of a more diverse aesthetics.

Third-wave feminists have attempted to avoid acquiring the reputation that they are "anti-fashion," although the stereotype continues to plague feminists today. By linking fashion and feminism, third-wave feminists (particularly self-identified "girlie" feminists, such as the writers for the magazine *Bust*) seek to revive interest among young, media-saturated women in a social movement. Many third-wave feminists, such as Marcelle Karp and Debbie Stoller, authors of *The* Bust *Guide to the New Girl Order* (1999), and **Jennifer Baumgardner** and **Amy Richards**, authors of *Manifesta: Young Women, Feminism, and the Future* (2000), have argued that girls and women do not experience fashion as the oppressive institution that their mothers did. Many describe fashion as a means for female bonding and for affirmation of what is a traditionally female pursuit. They also point to the opportunities that fashion provides for self-expression and creativity.

Because of their emphasis on the pleasures of fashion, third-wave feminists have met with a number of criticisms from the public at large and from second-wave feminists in particular. Most notably, they are accused of uncritically accepting **consumerism** and capitalism—two ideologies that many second-wave feminists viewed as tools for the oppression of women. Third-wave feminists also face accusations of choosing an insubstantial and silly style of activism. They defend their stance on fashion by pointing to the dominant roles that popular and consumer cultures play in shaping the politics of the early twenty-first century. Third-wave feminists, such as Leslie Heywood and Jennifer Drake, editors of *Third Wave Agenda: Being Feminist, Doing Feminism* (1997), argue that women are so inundated with **advertising**, fashion magazines, celebrity styles, and commercially produced images of beauty that a focus on fashion cuts straight to the heart of their experience. Rejection of fashion is impossible to some extent because images so pervade everyday lives in **media** culture today. It is conceivable that some women who find pleasure and **empowerment** from participating in the world of fashion are also strong feminists. Furthermore, an all-encompassing dismissal of fashion as something that enslaves women would unrealistically paint women as "victims" of beauty ideals that they often wholeheartedly embrace. Nevertheless, third-wave feminists agree that one agenda of the feminist movement must be to make pursuit of fashion a choice for individual women.

Despite their reputation for a fashion-friendly approach, third-wave feminists have voiced significant criticisms of fashion. They have tackled the fashion industry's profit-driven objectification of women and girls. Third-wave magazines (such as *HUES, Bust,* and *Bitch*), **zines**, and Web sites (such as the San Francisco–based http://www.About-Face.org) protest advertisements that objectify women's bodies. They point to the exclusionary policies of the fashion industry, which designs fashionable clothing solely for slender women and advertises it with mostly young, white women. By limiting the pleasures of fashion to a select group, designers and marketers teach overweight, nonwhite, and older women that they are inherently unfashionable. Third-wave feminists also grapple with the fact that fashion serves as an indicator of class and status. While some young girls enjoy the pleasures of fashion, others find that a smaller or inexpensive wardrobe can be a roadblock to popularity. Shopping for a new outfit can provide some girls with opportunities to bond in a female-dominated culture at the mall; however, many girls find that the price tags are a quick reminder that the pleasures of fashion are not available for everyone. Girls and women who do not acquire and maintain a fashionable appearance find that their personal relationships and even their careers are disadvantaged as a result. These are just some of the limitations to fashion that third-wave feminists critique. *See also* Girl/Girlies; Victim/Power Feminism

Further Reading: Baumgardner, Jennifer, and Amy Richards, *Manifesta: Young Women, Feminism, and the Future*, New York: Farrar, Straus, and Giroux, 2000; Edut, Ophira, *Adios, Barbie: Young Women Write about Body Image and Identity*, Seattle: Seal Press, 1998; Heywood, Leslie, and Jennifer Drake, eds., *Third Wave Agenda: Being Feminist, Doing Feminism*, Minneapolis: University of Minnesota Press, 1997; hooks, bell, "Beauty Laid Bare: Aesthetics in the Ordinary," in *To Be Real: Telling the Truth and Changing the Face of Feminism*, ed. Rebecca Walker, New York: Doubleday, 1995; Karp, Marcelle, and Debbie Stoller, *The Bust Guide to the New Girl Order*, New York: Penguin Books, 1999; Kilbourne, Jean, *Can't Buy My Love: How Advertising Changes the Way We Think and Feel*, New York: Touchstone, 2000; Wolf, Naomi, *The Beauty Myth: How Images of Beauty Are Used against Women*, New York: W. Morrow, 1991.

BETH KREYDATUS

FEMINAZI. A notable barricade to third-wave **feminism** is the association drawn between feminists and the "feminazi" stereotype. Many who believe in the aims of the third wave refuse identification as such, for fear of being considered a "feminazi." The term is associated with shame, fear, and ridicule for certain women, which shuts out many potential feminists who refuse to resign themselves to a label.

Right-wing radio personality Rush Limbaugh coined the term to portray **abortion** rights advocates as militaristic. Limbaugh, notorious for berating Democrats on his daily talk show, asserts that feminism is a threat to moral society and displays extremism. American women have been reassured by pop culture, the **media**, and history books that equality has largely been won. Lest women critique unresolved issues such as equal pay, job opportunities, and basic requirements to succeed in today's workforce, they are left to consider that feminism allows, according to Limbaugh, "unattractive women easier access to the mainstream." The term has become popularly associated with the act of relinquishing femininity.

"Feminazi" was actually informed by Limbaugh's staunch pro-life viewpoint. Limbaugh singled out the National Organization for Women as a group comprised of such members "obsessed" with abortion rights and lesbian rights. He repeatedly has characterized certain feminists as fascists to force the comparison between abortion and the Holocaust.

Further Reading: Faludi, Susan, *The Undeclared War Against American Women*, New York: Anchor Books, 1991; Rush Hudson Limbaugh III, http://en.wikipedia.org/wiki/Rush_Limbaugh.

LEIGH PHILLIPS

FEMININITY/MASCULINITY. Third-wave **feminism** views characteristics like masculinity and femininity on a continuum, so that men are seen as having many feminine characteristics, and women many masculine characteristics, with the proportions varying from person to person rather than being a result of one's **male body** or female **body**. Traditionally, stereotypes often interpreted masculinity and femininity—the gendered identities assigned to men and women—as terms that were the opposite of each other, defining masculinity in largely positive terms in relation to femininity. Masculinity stood for rationality, strength, and activity; femininity stood for emotion, weakness, and passivity. Second-wave feminism challenged these definitions, and during the 1980s and 1990s there was an even greater change in the way feminists defined masculinity and femininity. First, pro-feminist men began to contribute to academic debate with greater vigor. Second, postmodern academic literature aimed to take apart the **gender binary**, which they considered false. Third, masculinity itself, instead of just femininity and women, became a focus for research. The result was that third-wave feminists now view gender as a continuum, with masculinity and femininity merging together and shifting, rather than being defined in stark contrast to each other.

Judith Butler's *Gender Trouble* (1990) radically challenged the notion that gender was a set of opposite categories belonging to male and female bodies. Butler, a postmodernist, argued that masculinity and femininity were artificial characteristics that had to be "performed" by individuals and were unlinked to biological sex. She likened the performance of gender **identity** to the wearing of clothes: we can pick and choose what clothes we wear and it is the same for our gender identity. Men can therefore perform feminine roles and women can be masculine. An example of this would be people who dress in "drag." In Butler's conception, masculinity and femininity are unstable, difficult to define, and forever open to challenge and change.

Masculinity as a category itself became a focus for feminist research instead of a relational category to femininity. R.W. Connell, in his groundbreaking book *Masculinities* (1995), argued that masculinity itself was just as broad, artificial, and changing a category as femininity. Indeed, he established the notion that there were multiple masculinities and that men could also be oppressed by rigid constructs of gender. In any given society, Connell contended, there is a "hegemonic" form of masculinity; a dominant ideal to which all men are encouraged to embody and achieve. However, it would be impossible for all men to achieve this ideal and some, such as gay or black men, may well be excluded from dominant masculinities. Some feminist authors have criticized Connell and other academics in the "New Men's Studies" movement for downplaying the real benefits and power men have over women. However, the recognition that masculinity and femininity are not opposed and that masculinity itself is a valid site of feminist research has been a major development in **feminist theory**, empirical work, and debate since the early 1990s. Third-wave feminists now view masculinity and femininity as a continuum, and an unstable and continually shifting one at that. They have moved beyond conceptualizing gender as a set of opposite characteristics occurring in a particular biological body.

See also Binary Oppositions; Biological Determinism

Further Reading: Butler, Judith, *Gender Trouble: Feminism and the Subversion of Identity*, 2nd ed., New York: Routledge, 1999; Connell, Robert, *Gender*, Cambridge, MA: Polity Press, 2002; Connell, Robert, *Masculinities*, Cambridge, MA: Polity Press, 1995; Heywood, Leslie, and Shari Dworkin, *Built to Win: The Female Athlete as Cultural Icon*, Minneapolis: University of Minnesota Press, 2003; Whitehead, Stephen, *Men and Masculinities: Key Themes and New Directions*, Cambridge, MA: Polity Press, 2002.

DANIEL CONWAY

FEMINISM, FIRST, SECOND, THIRD WAVES. Although its usefulness has lately been questioned, feminist history is often explained through the metaphor of waves. In the oceanography of the U.S. and British women's movements, "first wave" usually refers to the surge of activism that began in the 1830s and culminated with women's suffrage in 1920 in the United States (1928 in the United Kingdom). The "second wave" describes the resurgence of women's organizing beginning in the mid-1960s and, in the United States, ending—or at least suffering major setbacks—with the defeat of the **Equal Rights Amendment (ERA)** and the advent of the Reagan/Bush era. The "third wave," a term enlivened by multiple meanings, often refers to the period beginning with the Clinton/Gore era and continuing today.

Scholars have questioned the usefulness of these distinctions as a way of organizing feminist history. Some argue that by locating the "first wave" in the nineteenth century, women's theorizing and activism in earlier generations are made invisible. Others ask how to measure where one wave ends and another begins. Still others note that the wave metaphor overlooks activity that takes place between waves.

Despite such qualifications, many agree that the wave metaphor can still be a useful way to describe the different time periods of feminist thinking and organizing over time. The "waving" of feminism raises interesting questions about continuity, generation, and change, particularly for "third-wave" feminists, whose theorizing and activism draws from, and takes place alongside, second-wave predecessors. Does the third wave continue or depart from second-wave concerns? Is the distinction one of age, generation, political cohort, style, theory, or practice? Can second-wave feminists "do" third-wave feminism, and vice versa? These are just some of the ongoing quandaries and definitional challenges the wave metaphor presents for feminists today.

First Wave. For most feminists, the first wave began at the 1848 Seneca Falls Women's Rights Convention. There, Elizabeth Cady Stanton, Jane Hunt, Mary Ann McClintock, Lucretia Mott, Martha Wright, and other anti-slavery activists demanded an end to all discrimination based on sex. To launch their movement, "first-wavers" borrowed theories, tactics, and language from the abolitionist debates around them. A century later, young female radicals would use similar appropriations to counter sexism in the civil rights and New Left movements. This pattern has continued, as girls in the early 1990s grew frustrated with their second-class status in sexist punk subculture and left to create girl bands of their own.

At the Seneca Convention, 260 women and forty men wrote and ratified the "Declaration of Sentiments," a Declaration of Independence inclusive of women. They were inspired by Margaret Fuller's *Woman in the Nineteenth Century* (1845), a feminist manifesto that demanded removal of all barriers to women, and Sarah Grimké's *Letters on the Equality of the Sexes and the Condition of Women* (1838), the first women's rights pamphlet in the United States.

Joining forces with former temperance crusader and abolitionist Susan B. Anthony, the Seneca Falls activists demanded full participation in public and civic life for women. They called for higher **education** and professional opportunities for women and the right to divorce, own property, claim inheritance, win custody of children, and vote. In parallel, they worked to enact the Thirteenth Amendment, which abolished slavery in 1865. Sojourner Truth, a former slave, played a critical role in linking these causes by arguing against abolitionists who sought to enfranchise black men while still denying the vote to women of any race.

In 1920, the Nineteenth Amendment granted women the right to vote. While a momentous gain, there were those who thought that suffrage was not enough. Alice Paul, a key advocate for the amendment and founder of the National Women's Party, introduced the Equal Rights Amendment (ERA) in 1923 to promote women's equality in *every* arena of public life. But many working women and labor groups opposed the ERA to safeguard already-existing protective legislation that women enjoyed.

The first wave is widely assumed to have ebbed as a unified movement following suffrage. In the following years, the successful "suffragist" coalition scattered to other social justice and activist causes, including unionization, anti-poverty, and anti-militarist campaigns.

Suffragists' daughters and granddaughters (women who came of age after 1900) turned their back on their foremothers' politics. During the post–World War I prosperity, many girls just wanted to have fun. Embracing newfound autonomy, younger women experimented with expressive **individualism** and sexual freedom. Following some courageous leads—like Emma Goldman's free love advocacy and Margaret Sanger's birth-control movement—young women proclaimed the right to voluntary motherhood without sacrificing their **sexuality**. They were not, however, interested in "feminism" as such. In 1919, female Greenwich Village literary radicals founded a journal dedicated not to "men and women," but to all "people." Interestingly, they called themselves "post feminist."

Second Wave. The "second wave" refers to the resurgence of women's organizing beginning in the mid-1960s and ending with the ERA's defeat and the advent of the Reagan/Bush era in 1980. Historians generally describe this wave as the confluence of at least two major currents: a radical branch, comprised of younger women focused on "women's liberation"; and a more liberal, "women's rights"–oriented branch, powered by a generation significantly older. Together, these currents catalyzed a mass movement that challenged definitions of public and private life and called for full human rights for women. Though sometimes at odds, they made feminism a widespread movement in a remarkably short time.

The "women's liberation" branch emerged from within the 1960s Civil Rights, anti-Vietnam, and student movements as young women began to look to their own oppression within these liberationist networks. After seeing their experiences trivialized by the movements' male leadership, these women declared that oppression of women generally was not a trivial, private matter, but rather a social problem of national significance. Rallying behind slogans such as "the personal is political" and "sisterhood is powerful," radical feminists met in small groups, explored political meanings in their personal experiences, and sought to root out internalized and external sources of patriarchal oppression. Many women's liberationists made the "political" choice to live as lesbians. By describing lesbianism as something other than sexual deviance, they reframed female homosexuality.

Consciousness raising became the women's liberation movement's main organizing tool, rapidly catching on outside of radical circles. Ms. magazine, founded by Gloria Steinem in 1972, popularized many women's liberation concepts. In practice, radical feminism helped spawn the **women's health** movement; battered women's shelters; **rape** crisis centers; the women's art movement; journals and **zines**, including No More Fun and Games (https://www.greenlion.com); and Lilith (http://www.history.unimelb.edu.au/lilith/), and influential books, such as Kate Millet's Sexual Politics (1970), Shulamith Firestone's The Dialectic of Sex (1970), and Robin Morgan's anthology, Sisterhood Is Powerful (1970).

Celestine Ware's Woman Power (1970) first challenged the emerging second wave to address **racism**—including its own. Ware, a member of the Stanton-Anthony Brigade of New York Radical Feminists, was among the few black women active in the predominantly white, middle-class movement. Alienated by sexism in the Black Power movement that followed the civil rights campaigns, many black women formed their own feminist groups. Some, including Fannie Lou Hamer, Florynce Kennedy, Pauli Murray, and Aileen Hernandez, also partnered with or helped found mainstream feminist forums such as the Women's Action Alliance and the National Women's Political Caucus.

While radical feminists sought to root out sources of patriarchal oppression, a "liberal" current fought for women's rights within mainstream politics. In 1963, a Presidential Commission on the Status of Women (chaired by Eleanor Roosevelt) documented discrimination in employment, unequal pay, lack of social services such as childcare, and continuing legal inequality for women. The Commission activated professional women whose concerns about women's status during the 1950s had found no outlet. Also in 1963, writer Betty Friedan published her groundbreaking book *The Feminine Mystique*, which rallied white, middle-class housewives by identifying the internal and external traps of **domesticity** and suggesting that meaningful work outside the home could solve "the problem that has no name."

In 1966, together with leaders of state commissions on women and with labor union women, Friedan founded the National Organization for Women (NOW). NOW was established to pressure governments to take **discrimination against women** seriously. A modernized version of the 1848 Declaration of Sentiments, NOW's mission was "[t]o take action to bring women into full participation in the mainstream of American society now, assuming all the privileges and responsibilities thereof in truly equal partnership with men." NOW's first target was the newly formed Equal Employment Opportunity Commission (EEOC), which, in 1968, finally barred sex-segregated want ads. Early on, NOW also waged a successful campaign against airlines that forced married stewardesses and those older than 32 to resign; pressured federal contractors and subcontractors to ban sex discrimination; and supported southern factory women who sued Colgate-Palmolive and Southern Bell Telephone for denying women jobs.

Internal tensions within both second-wave branches revealed differences among women as substantial as those between women and men. By 1972, a "gay-straight" split fragmented countless women's liberation groups. Many lesbian women eventually left NOW after a battle over lesbian rights. When the 1967 NOW Convention passed an agenda supporting the ERA and advocating repeal of antiabortion statutes, many labor union women resigned. As during the 1920s, labor women saw the ERA as undercutting legislation that protected women workers. Others thought that reproductive freedom was too radical for the American public to accept and resigned as well. Some then founded the Women's Equity Action League (WEAL), described by its founders as a "conservative NOW."

Second-wave feminists won unprecedented gains for women, including legal redress for **domestic violence**, sexual assault, and sexual harassment; the legalization of abortion; and sex-based integration of institutions from governments to bars to Little League. But just as the 1920 suffrage victory marked a turning point for first-wavers, the 1973 legalization of abortion through **Roe v. Wade** signaled the peak of the second wave. In November 1975, several key progressive states defeated the ERA and the **media** began sounding the movement's death knell. Ronald Reagan's election in 1980 quickly threatened the movement's fragile gains. Concurrently, the New Right was gaining strength, claiming the public spotlight, and responding to the politicizing of sexuality—particularly around the issues of abortion and lesbianism—with public actions of their own.

Between the Waves. For many late-1960s and 1970s activists, the 1980s represented a period of integration, solidification, and institution-building. With oppositional forces gaining and the ERA wavering, mainstream politics became increasingly hostile to feminist ideas. As in the 1930s, many prominent feminists dispersed into other social and professional enclaves. The academy became an important site of feminist activity, as **women's studies** became institutionalized.

In spring 1982, a Barnard conference called "Towards a Politics of Sexuality" broadened discussions of sexual politics by confronting conflicting theories within feminist circles regarding women's sexual victimization and female agency. The anti-pornography movement, born in the late 1970s, primarily emphasized women's sexual victimization. Connecting pornography with violence against women, some anti-pornography feminists presumed a fixed sexual economy in which men were always violent and women always vulnerable. Their assumptions catalyzed a countervailing feminist politics that stressed sexual agency, variety, and pleasure. The "sex debates" paved the way for nuanced feminist stances toward pleasure and danger. These debates continue among third-wave feminists.

Also during the 1980s, the feminism of women of color emerged as a substantial force in scholarship. Theorizing from their experience of multiple oppressions, women of color highlighted class- and race-based assumptions underlying second-wave **feminist theory** and practice. They published essays in several influential anthologies, including *This Bridge Called My Back: Writings by Radical Women of Color* (1981), edited by Gloria Anzaldúa and Cherríe Moraga, and *All the Women Are White, All the Blacks Are Men, but Some of Us Are Brave* (1982), edited by Patricia Bell Scott, Gloria Hull, and Barbara Smith. By expanding the experiences and challenging the assumptions of second-wave feminism, women of color and "third world feminists" helped spark what later became known as feminism's "third wave."

Third Wave. The third wave generally refers to the period from the Clinton Presidency (1992) to the present. Key components of third-wave feminism to date include an emphasis on multiculturalism and diversity; an assumption that the category of "woman" is no longer the only **identity** worth examining; an insistence that the **war** for women's social, political, and economic equality is far from over; a playful attitude toward sexuality; a critical engagement with popular culture; and an embrace of contradiction. Often distinguished by rhetorical and theoretical shifts and generational differences in activist style and affiliation, "third wave" is perhaps best described as a mark of chronological affiliation that denotes a set of shared historical circumstances.

Feminist issues returned to national attention in the early 1990s. In 1991, law professor Anita Hill charged Supreme Court nominee Clarence Thomas with sexual harassment, sparking a national debate about sex and power. Many progressive-minded young women (and men), who came of age during the conservative 1980s, were energized by Hill's televised testimony before the Senate Judiciary Committee, President Clinton's election, **Hillary Clinton**'s powerful presence, and the publication of two influential feminist bestsellers, **Susan**

Faludi's *Backlash* (1992) and **Naomi Wolf**'s *The Beauty Myth* (1991). The early 1990s saw membership in existing women's organizations increase nationwide and the formation of new groups such as African American Women in Defense of Ourselves, Third Wave Direct Action Corporation, and the Women's Health Action and Mobilization (WHAM). New **magazines**, journals, and zines by and about young women and their activism also appeared in the early 1990s, including *HUES* (Hear Us Sisters Emerging), a multicultural feminist zine; *GAYA: A Journal By and About Young Women*; and *Riot Grrrl*, an online zine produced by girls in the punk scene who grew fed up with second-class citizenship in sexist punk subculture.

During the early to mid-1990s, both the U.S. and worldwide feminist movements made advances. Nongovernmental organizations expanded exponentially across the world, establishing women's rights as human rights and making their presence known through international conferences that culminated in September 1995 at the **Beijing Fourth World Conference on Women**.

Despite this resurgent activism and other movement activity, America's conservative political climate during the 1980s had taken a toll. In the early 1990s, polls reported that many young American women were reluctant to identify themselves as "feminists," even though they continued to support women's social, political, and economic advancement. Media pundits interpreted the "I'm-not-a-feminist-but" phenomenon as a telltale sign that the women's movement was dead, and they dubbed young women born after the late 1960s the "postfeminist" generation—another echo from first-wave debates.

In 1992, **Rebecca Walker** (writer Alice Walker's daughter) declared in *Ms.* magazine, "I am not a postfeminist feminist. I am the third wave." Rebutting the "**postfeminism**" label, Walker's "third wave" implies continuity with previous feminist waves. Early third-wave writings are anthologized in Barbara Findlen's *Listen Up: Voices of the Next Feminist Generation* (1995) and Rebecca Walker's *To Be Real: Telling the Truth and Changing the Face of Feminism* (1995). These two collections of personal essays, now read in many women's studies courses, have facilitated the consciousness raising of a new generation. Also influential in naming, shaping, and popularizing early third-wave feminism are the anthology *Third Wave Agenda: Doing Feminism, Being Feminist* (1997), edited by Leslie Heywood and Jennifer Drake; and **Jennifer Baumgardner** and **Amy Richards**' *Manifesta: Young Women, Feminism, and the Future* (2000).

Many third-wave feminists—daughters of women's studies—use second-wave theory and strategy even as they critique it, forging amalgams of feminism that speak to and through contemporary times. Some offer updated renditions of sexual politics through anthologies such as *Jane Sexes It Up: True Confessions of Feminist Desire* (2002), edited by Merri Lisa Johnson; through Web sites such as *Sexing the Political: A Journal of Third Wave Feminists on Sexuality* (http://www.sexingthepolitical.com), published by Krista Jacobs; and through **music, film,** and performance. Others build on second-wave critiques by creating their own media to counter representational practices through which mainstream and alternative culture construct femininity and female sexuality. Through zines such as *Bust* (now a magazine with mass circulation) and *Bitch: Feminist Response to Popular Culture*, Grrrl feminists actively monitor popular culture, contest dominant images of women and girls, and celebrate a new girl culture—and a distinctive "grrrl style"—resistant to patriarchal images.

Third-wave feminism has emerged as part culture, part cause. Composed of multiple, simultaneously flowing currents, third-wave feminism has not coalesced into an easily identifiable political movement. Writers Alison Piepmeier and Rory Dicker, in an introduction to their anthology *Catching a Wave: Reclaiming Feminism for the 21st Century* (2003) noted, "[T]hird wave feminism's political activism on behalf of women's rights is shaped by—and responds to—a world of global capitalism and information technology, postmodernism and postcolonialism, and environmental degradation. We no longer live in the world that feminists of the second wave faced. Third wavers, who came of age in the late twentieth century and after, are therefore concerned not simply with 'women's issues' but with a broad range of interlocking topics ... ranging from protests of the World Economic Forum and welfare reform to activism on behalf of independent media outlets" (10). Third-wave feminists continue to explore the "lived messiness" (Heywood and Drake's term) of third-wave feminist theory and practice in anthologies, including most recently, *The Fire This Time: Young Activists and the New Feminism* (2004), edited by Vivien Labaton and Dawn Lundy Martin.

Naming the third wave has played a major role in pushing forward a multiplicity of feminist agendas. But it has also generated tensions among feminists of different generations. Some third-wavers see second-wavers as "pioneers" but not necessarily as active players forging new terrain. Subsequently, many second-wavers fear being shelved as "classics." Although some second-wavers are reluctant to recognize younger women's activism as sufficiently "feminist," third-wavers insist that theirs is a feminism forged in and adapted to a twenty-first century world. In 2005, third-wave feminism is still in the process of unfolding.

See also Black Feminism; *Volume 2, Primary Documents 1, 2, 5, 6, 11, 12, 15–18, 24, 41, and 52*

Further Reading: Anzaldúa, Gloria, and Cherríe Moraga, eds., *This Bridge Called My Back: Writings by Radical Women of Color*, Watertown, MA: Persephone Press, 1981; Baumgardner, Jennifer, and Amy Richards, *Manifesta: Young Women, Feminism, and the Future*, New York: Farrar, Straus and Giroux, 2000; Baxandall, Rosalyn, and Linda Gordon, eds., *Dear Sisters: Dispatches from the Women's Liberation Movement*, New York: Basic Books, 2000; Cott, Nancy, *The Grounding of Modern Feminism*, New Haven, CT: Yale University Press, 1987; Dicker, Rory, and Alison Piepmeier, eds., *Catching a Wave: Reclaiming Feminism for the 21st Century*, Boston: Northeastern University Press, 2003; Documents from the Women's Liberation Movement, Online Archival Collection, Special Collections Library, Duke University, http://scriptorium.lib.duke.edu/wlm/; Echols, Alice, *Daring to Be Bad: Radical Feminism in America 1967–1975*, Minneapolis: University of Minnesota Press, 1989; Evans, Sara M., Born for Liberty: *A History of Women in America*, New York: The Free Press, 1989; Evans, Sara M., *Personal Politics: The Roots of Women's Liberation in the Civil Rights Movement*, New York: Random House,

1980; Faludi, Susan, *Backlash*, New York: Anchor Books, 1992; Findlen, Barbara, ed., *Listen Up: Voices of the Next Feminist Generation*, Seattle: Seal Press, 1995; Friedan, Betty, *The Feminine Mystique*, New York: Bantam, 1983; Heywood, Leslie, and Jennifer Drake, eds., *Third Wave Agenda: Doing Feminism, Being Feminist*, Minneapolis: University of Minnesota Press, 1997; Hull, Gloria T., Patricia Bell Scott, and Barbara Smith, eds., *All the Women Are White, All the Blacks Are Men, but Some of Us Are Brave: Black Women's Studies*, Old Westbury, NY: Feminist Press, 1982; Johnson, Merri Lisa, ed., *Jane Sexes It Up: True Confessions of Feminist Desire*, New York: Four Walls Eight Windows, 2002; Karp, Marcelle, and Debbie Stoller, eds., *The Bust Guide to the New Girl Order*, New York: Penguin Books, 1999; Labaton, Vivien, and Dawn Lundy Martin, eds., *The Fire This Time: Young Activists and the New Feminism*, New York: Anchor Books, 2004; Looser, Devoney, and E. Ann Kaplan, eds., *Generations: Academic Feminists in Dialogue*, Minneapolis: University of Minneapolis Press, 1997; Millet, Kate, *Sexual Politics*, Garden City, NJ: Doubleday, 1970; Morgan, Robin, ed. *Sisterhood Is Powerful*, New York: Random House, 1970; Nicholson, Linda, ed., *The Second Wave: A Reader in Feminist Theory*, New York: Routledge, 1997; Rosen, Ruth, *The World Split Open: How the Modern Women's Movement Changed America*, New York: Viking, 2000; The Scholar & Feminist Online, www.barnard.edu/sfonline; Sexing the Political: A Journal of Third Wave Feminists on Sexuality, www.sexingthepolitical.com; Siegel, Deborah, *Fighting Words: The Forty Year Struggle for the Soul of Feminism* (forthcoming); Snitow, Ann, Christine Stansell, and Sharon Thompson, eds., *Powers of Desire: The Politics of Sexuality*, New York: Monthly Review Press, 1983; Vance, Carol, ed., *Pleasure and Danger: Exploring Female Sexuality*, Boston: Routledge and Kegan Paul, 1984; Walker, Rebecca, ed., *To Be Real: Telling the Truth and Changing the Face of Feminism*, New York: Doubleday, 1995; Wolf, Naomi, *The Beauty Myth: How Images of Beauty Are Used against Women*, New York: W. Morrow, 1991.

DEBORAH SIEGEL

FEMINIST PUBLISHING. Social movements are often defined by the written materials they produce, and the third wave of American **feminism** is no exception. In fact, the movement was initially identified and defined by anthologies published by the popular press in the mid- to late 1990s. These collections primarily contained first-person essays written by young women, a deeply personal style that has come to represent much of the material to come of out the third wave. Because the movement was seen as appealing to young women of all social classes, their writings and expressions diverged from the feminists of the 1970s. As a result, much of the third wave's rhetoric was expressed through the mediums of that generation: the Riot Grrrl culture of zine creation, which developed from dissatisfaction with punk culture, and the burgeoning sphere of **cyberspace**.

The term "third wave" was initially coined in the mid-1980s through a collection of essays entitled *The Third Wave: Feminist Perspectives on Racism*. Culled from a diverse group of activists and academics, the book was never able to find the support of a mainstream publisher, but its title and content were the first step in articulating the contradictions and ambiguities faced by young women raised in a era where "feminism" was a familiar—albeit controversial—part of the cultural lexicon. Not long after, in the early 1990s, two prominent trials brought renewed **media** interest to feminist issues: the Clarence Thomas–Anita Hill sexual harassment hearings and the William Kennedy Smith **rape** trial. These events galvanized feminists of all ages and from all walks of life, resulting in a new language and forum to discuss **patriarchy**. For the first time, the "slackers" of **Generation X** began to organize around the feminist movement. This increasing public interest in third-wave discourse resulted in the production and publication of several more anthologies, the most significant of which are **Rebecca Walker**'s *To Be Real: Telling the Truth and Changing the Face of Feminism* (1995) and Barbara Findlen's *Listen Up: Voices from the Next Feminist Generation* (1995). The fact that these collections were published through the popular (rather than academic) press is significant in that they established the third wave as residing outside the ivory tower as a social movement that is accessible to the mass population. Contributors wrote about what it means to be a woman of color in the United States, how to navigate life as a working mother, and about the challenges of trying to conform to the late twentieth century's ideal of the "super woman." Publishing in the third wave was defined by women sharing their experiences, and the community that was formed through the page helped solidify the young movement.

Still, the fact that these highly personal, introspective essays were processed through publishing houses made many view them as sanitized and reminiscent of the second wave; a movement criticized for the privilege it granted to the interests of middle-class whites. Including the voices of lower-class women and women of color in the popular press anthologies helped to democratize the movement somewhat, but third-wave leaders realized that the message was still inherently exclusive. When working with a mainstream publisher, certain standards of grammar and diction have to be taken into consideration. And distribution is limited to those who have the money to acquire such books, either through purchase or library acquisition. As a result, third-wavers began to look for alternative ways to disseminate their message while creating community and solidarity within the movement.

One such development was the use of **zines**, a community-based form of journalism. Zines are typically created by cutting and pasting material onto a page before photocopying and stapling them together. The medium is frequently adopted by social movements because its **DIY** (do it yourself) accessibility allows virtually anyone to publish anything. Through zines, young feminists from all walks of life could articulate their concerns in whatever medium they were most comfortable with (e.g., **poetry**, prose, or illustration) for very little money.

The close association of zines with the third wave developed from the Riot Grrrl movement of the early 1990s. Unofficially led by Kathleen Hanna, former lead singer of the band **Bikini Kill**, the Riot Grrrl movement encouraged young women to find a space within traditional male spheres where they could express themselves. For third-wave feminists, this philosophy was felt most keenly in the **music** and publishing industries.

Zines are primarily distributed through informal channels of communication; the publications that came out of the third wave were no exception. Young women traded zines with one another and purchased them at independent bookstores and coffeehouses, acts that not only provided them with a sense of community but also established unity against the dominant consumer culture. Hanna cofounded Riot Grrrl Press, a clearinghouse of zines published by women and girls, making it even easier to access these sometimes hard-to-find publications.

The highly personal nature of zines often makes their publication dependent on the time and resources of the creator. Because of this fact, zines often go out of print after a couple of months. However, of the scores of zines created during this era, several have evolved into actual glossy **magazines** that continue to espouse third-wave sentiments. *Bust*, created by Debbie Stoller and Marcelle Karp in 1993, is one example. Lisa Jervis and Andi Zeisler's *Bitch: A Feminist Response to Pop Culture* is another. Both titles originated as low-budget, shoestring publications that were transformed into quarterly magazines with significant readerships. In 1999, Stoller and Karp even published a popular press anthology of their zine's most poignant essays and interviews entitled *The* Bust *Guide to the New Girl Order*.

Despite the fact that their association with mainstream printing companies makes these publications more available to audiences, critics maintain that, by going glossy, *Bust* and *Bitch* have relinquished the ideals of the third wave. Each publication is now dependent on **advertising** dollars and readership to survive. Critics of the move believe that this affiliation with the mainstream signifies the incorporation of the third-wave sensibilities into the dominant culture. Many see this as the first step toward sanitizing the movement and thus nullifying its message of female **empowerment**.

For many, the Internet boom of the mid-1990s provided a means through which third-wave discourse could be disseminated widely without the interference of companies who may not be motivated by feminist interests. Many zines have corresponding Web pages where issues are bought and advertised. Feminist-centered cyber communities provide a space where women can "chat" about issues relevant to their lives and find information relevant to their interests. Like paper zines, self-publishing online is also relatively easy, as long as the producer has access to a computer and the appropriate software.

Technical advances in the early and mid-1990s help democratize the feminist movement in ways unheard of at any other point in history. The proliferation of the zine movement and the popularity and accessibility of the Internet made the gap between producer and consumer smaller than in virtually any other mass medium. These advances in publishing undoubtedly helped spread the messages of the third wave, thereby introducing a new generation to feminism.

See also Cyberspace; *Volume 2, Primary Document 35*

Further Reading: *Bitch* magazine, http://www.bitchmagazine.com, *Bust* magazine, http://www.bust.com; Taormino, Tristan, ed., *Girls Guide to Taking Over the World: Writings from the Girl Zine Revolution*, New York: St. Martin's, 1997; Walker, Rebecca, ed., *To Be Real: Telling the Truth and Changing the Face of Feminism*, New York: Doubleday, 1995.

KRISTEN KIDDER

FEMINIST THEORY. Feminist theory represents a range of scholarship that aims toward a systematic analysis of oppression and focuses on ending oppressions including those based on race, class, gender, sexual orientation, ability, and other social categories. Feminist theory, considered as an umbrella term, encompasses issues and approaches to theoretical and practical problems arising from the systems of oppression as they affect individuals and groups. Third-wave feminists are identified by a timeline of women who came of age primarily in the 1980s and 1990s. Third-wave feminists, informed by second-wave critiques of the feminist movement and its scholarship, have responded with a serious rethinking of fundamental concepts of **feminism**.

Often influenced by the work of women of color, working-class women, and others who fall outside the dominant categories of privilege, third-wave accounts of feminism attempt to resist essentialist notions of "woman" and strive toward complicating, rather than simplifying, reducing, or making universal claims about "all women." Third-wave feminist approaches include close attention to "intersectional" investigations of oppression that rely on careful consideration of positions of privilege and marginalization related to factors other than gender and sex. By beginning with complicated and multifaceted notions of position, much third-wave work also discusses the goals of coalition-building across such differences. Particular attention to the failures of mainstream feminism (historically) to respond to differences between women helps third-wave scholars advance liberatory goals in theory and practice.

Third-wave feminists are popularly divided into respective groups that entail their areas of emphasis. Though the emphases sometimes appear with different labels, an alternative to the complicated "intersectional" approach is also readily identifiable. Several themes emerge from this popularized body of work. Self-described "power feminism" follows a tradition of **individualism** that asserts the success of earlier feminist goals. Primarily, "power feminists" emphasize the entry of some women into competitive workforce markets and their subsequent individual achievements as representing the success of **equal rights** movements. The popular characterization of feminism in a "postfeminist" perspective often neglects attending to the ways in which differences in economic class, race, or other categories of privilege have restricted access and opportunities to all women and may instead focus, as suggested, on individuals and their accomplishments. The alternative to "power feminism" pays attention to systems of power and privilege, rather than emphasizing individuals.

Further Reading: Findlen, Barbara, ed., *Listen Up: Voices from the Next Feminist Generation*, Seattle: Seal Press, 1995; Heywood, Leslie, and Jennifer Drake, eds., *Third Wave Agenda: Being Feminist, Doing Feminism*, Minneapolis: University of Minnesota Press, 1997; Sommers, Christina Hoff, *Who Stole Feminism?: How Women Have Betrayed Women*, New York: Simon and Schuster, 1994; Walker, Rebecca, ed., *To Be Real: Telling the Truth and Changing the Face of Feminism*, New York: Doubleday, 1995; Wing, Adrien Katherine, ed., *Critical Race Feminism*, 2nd ed., New York: New York University Press, 2003.

ERIKA FEIGENBAUM

FICTION, THIRD-WAVE. Third-wave fiction can be defined as writing that possesses or performs a third-wave feminist sensibility in its embrace of **hybridity** and contradiction over purity and either/or modes of thinking. Third-wave fiction is most often produced by emerging **Generation X** or Generation Y writers, but the work of some established writers can be understood as prefiguring or participating in third-wave literary production. Although third-wave fiction takes on many forms and themes, two major trends in third-wave fiction may be delineated: postmodern multicultural literature and punk postmodernism.

Third-Wave Fiction and Postmodern Multicultural Literature. First, a substantial group of writers work in the tradition of postmodern multicultural literature, in which **identity** markers relating to race, class, gender, and nation are disrupted or redefined. Third-wave writers continue the work of established postmodern multicultural writers in their turn to genres such as the historical novel and the coming-of-age narrative, in the use of folklore and the spoken word, in the commitment to representing both violence and beauty, and in the focus on the lives of girls and women. For example, Edwidge Danticat's works of fiction—*Breath, Eyes, Memory* (1994), *Krik? Krak!* (1995), *The Farming of the Bones* (1998), and *Behind the Mountains* (2002)—lyrically explore various aspects of Haitian history and contemporary Haitian life. Lois-Ann Yamanaka uses Hawaiian Creole English and sharp wit to narrate stories about working-class Japanese Americans living in Hawaii, as in *Wild Meat and the Bully Burgers* (1996), *Blu's Hanging* (1997), and *Heads By Harry* (1999). Clearly, these and other third-wave writers like Monica Ali and Jhumpa Lahiri are in dialog with the work of established authors such as Toni Morrison, Bharati Mukherjee, and Leslie Marmon Silko. Perhaps these three writers could be called first sightings of the third wave in their insistence on exploring the sometimes violent messiness of individual, communal, and national identities in the context of **globalization**.

Third-wave writers are also expanding the canon of postmodern multicultural literature in four significant ways. First, third-wave fiction often begins with the assumption that so-called marginal identities are normative or, conversely, that the normative is marginal, as in ZZ Packer's sharply realistic short story collection, *Drinking Coffee Elsewhere* (2003), and Jeffrey Eugenides' Pulitzer

Prize–winning *Middlesex* (2002), which features a hermaphrodite narrator. Second, third-wave fictions often emphasize the humor in cultural hybridity and cross-cultural exchange, as in Zadie Smith's *White Teeth* (2001) and Gish Jen's *Mona in the Promised Land* (1997). Third, characters in third-wave fiction often resist identity categories in favor of embracing the fluidity of identity. Examples include Jen's protagonist, Mona, and Eugenides' protagonist, Cal, as well as Danzy Senna's protagonist Birdie in *Caucasia* (1999). Finally, third-wave fiction writers engage popular culture critically and with pleasure. All of the texts mentioned do this to some extent, but this tendency is particularly evident in David Foster Wallace's work, especially the short story collections *Girl with Curious Hair* (1996) and *Brief Interviews with Hideous Men* (2000). Eugenides and Wallace are included in this discussion of third-wave feminist writing because of their interest in the serious and/or satiric representation of gendered subjectivity.

Third-Wave Fiction and Punk Postmodernism. Another substantial group of third-wave writers can be read as punk postmodernists. Their sometimes autobiographical fictions are set in contemporary urban subcultures (usually lesbian) and variously explore sex, drugs, violence, **music**, low-wage work, gender identity, travel, and friendship. Representative books include Erika Lopez's *Tomato "Mad Dog" Rodriguez* trilogy: *Flaming Iguanas: An Illustrated All-Girl Road Novel Thing* (1998), *They Call Me Mad Dog: A Story for Bitter, Lonely People* (2001), and *Hoochie Mama: The Other White Meat* (2001); **Michelle Tea**'s *The Passionate Mistakes and Intricate Corruption of One Girl In America* (1998) and the Lambda Award–winning *Valencia* (2000); and Tribe 8 singer Lynn Breedlove's *Godspeed* (2003). A magical realist version of punk postmodernism can be found in Francesca Lia Block's five *Weetzie Bat* books, which are aimed at a young adult audience and were published between 1989 and 1995.

Third-wave punk postmodernist fiction begins with Lesbian Avengers cofounder Sarah Schulman's East Village novels of the 1980s and 1990s. Representative titles include *Girls, Visions and Everything* (1986), a girl-centered revision of Beat author Jack Kerouac's sex-spirituality-travel narratives; and *People In Trouble* (1990), which Schulman claims as the stolen pretext for the acclaimed Broadway show *Rent*. Kathy Acker's novels *Blood and Guts in High School* (1984), *Don Quixote* (1986), and *Empire of the Senseless* (1988) are other important pretexts for third-wave punk postmodernist fiction. Critics often note the similarity between Acker's writing and the work of Beat writer William Burroughs, which, together with Schulman's invocation of Kerouac, indicates an interesting link between third-wave punk postmodernist fiction writers and the male Beats. This literary lineage also suggests that Beat poet, memoirist, editor, and activist Diane diPrima is an important and unacknowledged precursor for third-wave literature.

The lush experimental writing of Carole Maso and Jeannette Winterson should also be understood as informing third-wave punk postmodernism, particularly because of their representations of female **desire** and lesbian **sexuality**.

As with Lynn Breedlove, it can be argued that Maso and Winterson *are* third-wave writers in sensibility, although they are generationally second wave.

Other Trends in Third-Wave Fiction. Important third-wave women writers that do not clearly fit either of these trends in third-wave fiction include Nicola Barker, Aimee Bender, and A.L. Kennedy, all of whom share an affinity for creating quirky and difficult characters and exploring the nooks and crannies of contemporary life. Representative works include Barker's *The Three Button Trick* (1999), Bender's *The Girl in the Flammable Skirt* (1999), and Kennedy's *Indelible Acts* (2003), all of which are short story collections.

"Chick lit" is a highly lucrative form of popular fiction aimed at young(ish) women readers. More postfeminist than third wave, chick lit books are sisters to **television** shows such as *Ally McBeal* and *Sex and the City* and feature young urban women dealing both awkwardly and gracefully with their careers, love lives, and consumer choices. The success of Helen Fielding's **Bridget Jones's Diary** (1996) gave birth to the genre. Other early chick lit includes Laura Zigman's *Animal Husbandry* (1998) and Melissa Banks' *The Girls' Guide to Hunting and Fishing* (1999). With the creation of chick lit imprints such as Red Dress Ink and Strapless at major publishing houses, the number of chick lit titles has exploded in the 2000s.

It should be noted that the anthologies *Chick-Lit: Postfeminist Fiction* (1995) and *Chick-Lit 2 (No Chick Vics)* (1996), edited by Cris Mazza and Jeffrey DeShell, predate the popular usage of terms like "chick lit" and "third wave." Mazza and DeShell were prescient in collecting irreverent and experimental work by women writers and in their refusal to include victim and recovery narratives in these collections.

Third-Wave Fiction and Literary Criticism. No critical discussions of third-wave fiction have been published, although there have been some courses and conference papers that consider the topic. There are several possible reasons for this lack of sustained critical attention. First, nonfiction has dominated third-wave literary production, as writers have focused on memoir and essay to do the work of defining third-wave **feminism**. For example, early collections such as *Listen Up* (1995), *To Be Real* (1995), and *Third Wave Agenda* (1997) sought to differentiate third-wave feminism from second-wave feminism in terms of ethos and historical context, while embracing the second-wave feminist view that the personal is political. Second, the emergence of third-wave writing in the 1990s and 2000s has coincided with the dominance of nonfiction in the publishing industry, so that the category "third-wave writing" has come to be defined as nonfiction by publishers and, perhaps, by readers. Note the proliferation and relative success of collections marketed as "third wave" by publishers eager to tap into both textbook and trade book markets: *The* Bust *Guide to the New Girl Order* (1999), *Manifesta* (2000), *Body Outlaws* (2000), *Breeder* (2001), *Young Wives' Tales* (2001), *Listen Up* (2001, 2nd ed.), *Colonize This!* (2002), and *Catching a Wave* (2003). Third, what could be understood as "third-wave feminist fiction" is simply not marketed as such, perhaps because writers and publishers view such a label as a marketing limitation, especially in light of the attention paid to "emerging writers." And fourth, third-wave fiction is usually written by writers still establishing their reputations, and third-wave writing often troubles established ways of approaching feminist and women's literature.

See also Writers, Fantasy/Science Fiction

Further Reading: Acker, Kathy, *Essential Acker: The Selected Writings of Kathy Acker*, New York: Grove Press, 2002; Ali, Monica, *Brick Lane*, New York: Scribner, 2003; Barker, Nicola, *The Three Button Trick*, New York: Ecco, 1999; Bender, Aimee, *Girl in the Flammable Skirt*, New York: Doubleday, 1999; Block, Francesca Lia, *Dangerous Angels: The Weetzie Bat Books*, New York: Harper Trophy, 1998; Breedlove, Lynn, *Godspeed*, New York: St. Martin's Press, 2002; Danticat, Edwidge, *The Farming of Bones*, New York: Penguin, 1999; Eugenides, Jeffrey, *Middlesex*, New York: Picador, 2003; Jen, Gish, *Mona in the Promised Land*, New York: Vintage, 1997; Kennedy, A.L., *Indelible Acts*, New York: Knopf, 2003; Lahiri, Jhumpa, *Interpreter of Maladies*, New York: Houghton Mifflin, 1999; Lopez, Erika, *Flaming Iguanas: An All-Girl Road Novel Thing*, New York: Simon and Schuster, 1998; Maso, Carole, *Defiance*, New York: Plume, 1999; Mazza, Cris, and Jeffrey DeShell, *Chick-Lit 2 (No Chick Vics)*, New York: FC2/Black Ice Books, 1996; Mazza, Cris, *Chick-Lit: Postfeminist Fiction*, Evanston, IL: Northwestern University Press, 1995; Packer, ZZ, *Drinking Coffee Elsewhere*, New York: Riverhead, 2003; Schulman, Sarah, *People in Trouble*, New York: Penguin, 1990; Senna, Danzy, *Caucasia*, New York: Riverhead Books, 1999; Smith, Zadie, *White Teeth*, New York: Vintage, 2001; Tea, Michelle, *Valencia*, Seattle: Seal Press, 2000; Wallace, David Foster, *Brief Interviews with Hideous Men*, New York: Back Bay Books, 2000; Winterson, Jeannette, *Oranges Are Not the Only Fruit*, New York: Grove Press, 1997; Yamanaka, Lois-Ann, *Wild Meat and the Bully Burgers*, New York: Harcourt, 1997.

JENNIFER DRAKE

FILM, THIRD-WAVE. A hallmark of the third wave is that it is engaged in creating popular culture, not just consuming and critiquing it. As Debbie Stoller, the cofounder of *Bust* magazine, put it after moving to New York with a PhD in Psychology of Women from Yale University, "Since my work was about women and **media**, I wanted to make better media for women. I wanted to change the media directly rather than complain to other people about how bad it was" (*Bust* magazine Web site, www.bust.com). In the world of film, this third-wave instinct to create media has meant that women, and feminists in particular, have a greater range of subjects to depict and have roles both behind the scenes and out front in films. They have both pioneered new genres (as seen in **queer** girl love stories such as *The Incredibly True Adventures of Two Girls in Love* [1995]) and proved that the old ones are not just male domains (as in teen sex/romance flicks with male protagonists, such as *Valley Girl* [1983] and *Fast Times at Ridgemont High* [1982]).

The act of having consciously feminist women and women who simply grew up in a feminist culture creating film has resulted in work that explores the boundaries of what is allowed in the mainstream and challenges an earlier (second-wave) definition of what is allowed in **feminism**. To wit, some directors and writers make work under the banner of feminism that a generation ago would be understood simply as misogynistic, such as Mary Harron's controversial film *American Psycho* (2000), based on the book by Bret Easton Ellis, which tells the story of a consumerist serial killer. Harron, who also made the 1996 film *I Shot Andy Warhol*, about unhinged protofeminist and *SCUM Manifesto* (1968) scribe Valerie Solanas, defends her film (and the book) as a "satire" of **consumerism**.

It is perhaps no coincidence that third-wave feminism garnered national attention in 1992, the year after the film *Thelma and Louise* was released. Of course, there were other percolating factors in the culture besides this film. For instance, the loose collection of punk rock feminists known as Riot Grrrl hosted their first conference in July in Washington, D.C.; the student group Students for and Orwellian Society (SOS) organized a successful boycott on college campuses against Domino's Pizza for their support of Operation Rescue, an antiabortion group; and the **Third Wave Foundation** embarked on Freedom Summer '92, a cross-country voter registration drive that brought 20,000 new voters into the election. Meanwhile, young women attended the April 1992 March for Choice on Washington, designed to counter the increasing threat to women's access to abortion. Among others, actress/activist Susan Sarandon, one of the stars of *Thelma and Louise*, took the stage and demanded reproductive freedom for all. The roaring and positive response from the crowd was both an acknowledgment of Sarandon's efforts as a women's rights crusader and of her character in *Thelma and Louise*.

Thelma and Louise, written by Callie Khouri, is the story of an Arkansas waitress and her Hausfrau best friend. They shoot a rapist and take off on the lam in a 1966 T-bird. Between that act and the movie's end, the two escape their familiar, boring, repressed, and abusive lives and embark on an adventure into the unknown as they head to Mexico. Along the way they vanquish sexist cops, best a disgusting, sexually harassing trucker, and ditch both a clueless husband and a too-little/too-late boyfriend. Thelma even has a sexual awakening (finally!) to rival anything Betty Dodson or Nancy Friday might advocate, and with a young, never-so-charming-again, and often shirtless Brad Pitt. (Thelma and Louise are never topless.) The glorious characters of Thelma (Geena Davis) and Louise (Susan Sarandon) and the utter success of the film signified a break with a recent **backlash** era of film. Suddenly, a feminist journey and independent women did not have to be seen as unnatural or as the enemy.

The filmmakers could not have anticipated this, but the film was released after a year of assaults on women's issues. The Senate Judiciary Committee had humiliated Anita Hill during Clarence Thomas' Supreme Court confirmation hearings and William Kennedy Smith had escaped a date **rape** conviction while his accuser was excoriated in the press. On a larger social justice front, an all-white jury found that the Los Angeles Police Department was *not* guilty of mercilessly beating an unarmed motorist named Rodney King, despite a video-tape to the contrary. It also intersected with a growing frustration with Hollywood for the constant perpetuation of the stereotypical female characters who are docile and demure or vixen and vicious, perhaps peaking with Alex Forrest (played by a rail-thin Glenn Close), the scariest single woman ever, who kills her lover's (Michael Douglas) daughter's bunny and nearly his hearth-warming wife (Anne Archer) in the 1987 blockbuster *Fatal Attraction*.

Thelma and Louise became feminism's revenge for these on-and-off screen oppressions. It seemed to provoke a collective up-tick in female **empowerment**, and suddenly every woman had a sassy response to street harassers and sexist remarks alike: "Have you seen *Thelma and Louise?*" The complex mix of defi-ance, vulnerability, and humor captured in the film resonated with younger women in particular, who, not unlike *Thelma and Louise*, were prompted to reject the sexism they were confronting in their own lives and create new books, new films, and a surge of new activist groups, including third-wave groups such as Lesbian Avengers, the Third Wave Foundation, WAC (Women Artists Coalition), and Culture Babes.

Second-wavers had paved a substantial road for younger women in film, most of it dedicated to raising consciousness about the dearth of opportunity for women in film, the limited range of female characters portrayed, and the blithe acceptance of anti-woman violence and **misogyny** in films. Even a confection as delightful as Woody Allen's first comedy, *What's New Pussycat?* (1965), featured countless scenes of men making unwanted advances on women. While third-wavers watched *Grease* (1978) and *ET* (1982), second-wave women fought for women to be represented on the silver screen as more than sex objects and to be behind the scenes as directors and studio executives. Second-wave fem-inists successfully broke down the assumption that women could not be direc-tors or screenwriters and that, given the huge number of female audience members, Hollywood might even benefit from having more women decision-makers.

Just as in other fields that were wholly dominated by men thirty years ago, today women are more integrated into the film industry than ever before. Still, women are far from equal. According to the Celluloid Ceiling Study, "In 2003, women comprised only 17 percent of individuals working in key behind-the-scenes roles on the top 250 domestic grossing films. This is the same percent-age of women who worked on the top films of 1998. Approximately one out of five films released in 2003 employed no women directors, executive producers, producers, writers, cinematographers, or editors." Sherry Lansing has been the head of Paramount Motion Pictures since 1990, but she is the only woman to be president of any major studio. Amy Pascal is a Vice Chairman at Sony Records and is credited with spiking their box office sales. Marlene Gorris became the first woman director *ever* to win an Oscar for a feature film. She won the Academy Award for the best foreign film for the matriarchal movie *Antonia's Line* in 1996. A woman has yet to win the award in the non-foreign film category. Sofia Coppola won best screenplay for her creation *Lost in Translation* (2003), but not best director. It is a sign of progress, however, that Coppola was nominated for best director. Only two other women have ever been nominated: Lina Wertmüller for *Seven Beauties* (1976) and Jane Campion for *The Piano* (1993).

The second-wave success at integrating the film industry had a profound influence on the young women of today, who have never known a time when women could not be the power players and decision makers. Access was not something they perceived as a problem: heightened expectations are a signature feature of third-wave feminism. Third-wave women were raised with feminism in the water, advantages such as Title IX and abortion rights, and the rhetoric that girls were as valuable as boys (*Free to Be You and Me* [1974] was the ethos, if not always the reality, of the era). Third-wavers experienced more freedom from sexism and could imagine more possibilities. This freedom infused the third wave with confidence, something that has been interpreted as both an asset (women "have better 'shit detectors,'" as Gloria Steinem often points out) and as negative (self-esteem without historical or political consciousness often results). Interpretations aside, this unique perspective positioned third-wavers to launch a unique and creative counterattack to the decades-long perpetuation of Hollywood's sexism. Rather than simply complaining and demanding equal numbers, a lovely, diverse dawn of third-wave feminist film was ushered in.

Cinematically, third-wavers were exposed to 1970s feminist film heroines (such as Norma Rae, from *Norma Rae* [1979], and single mom Alice, from *Alice Doesn't Live Here Anymore* [1974]) and to the anti-heroic killers (in Dutch director Marlene Gorris' *A Question of Silence* [1983]). In the early 1980s, as the backlash was picking up steam, Gorris released *A Question of Silence* (1983), her fictional film about the criminal investigation of three women who do not know each other but decide to spontaneously murder a condescending male shopkeeper. The women kill this man, as it becomes clear through the investigation, simply for being a male agent of the **patriarchy**. It was a startling last gasp of the angry wing of the second wave, slicing through the culture (at least for those who viewed art films) like a knife. What made it feminist (besides the filmmaker) was that the women, who killed with impunity, were very sympathetic characters.

The third wave also drew from the tremendously popular John Hughes films of the early 1980s, such as *16 Candles* (1984), *The Breakfast Club* (1985), *Pretty in Pink* (1986), and *Some Kind of Wonderful* (1987). These films had the tried-and-true teen bait of hot stars, girls to admire for their bravado and their wardrobe, and great soundtracks, but they differed in that they depicted heroines who were not the Gidgets and Debbie Reynolds kewpies of their mother's generation of teens. These new teen-flick heroines were outsiders, such as James Dean in *Rebel Without a Cause* (1955). They were also "regular" girls who thought about their clothes and had crushes, or were, as in the case of Mary

Stuart Masterson in *Some Kind of Wonderful* (1987), tomboys who played drums but still got the guy. By the 1980s, girls were suitable subjects for the outsider role, thus giving viewers a greater imagination of what women could be, and more to the point, that they could be outsiders and be rewarded. The barrier to acceptable female behavior was pushed to a new limit.

Third-wave feminist filmmakers, then, responded to both the feminism they grew up with (and this history of feminist film) and the mainstream film culture that they were raised in. *Girlfight* (2000), *Chutney Popcorn* (2000), and *The Incredibly True Adventures of Two Girls in Love* (1995), for instance, do not share much by way of themes or characters, but they are all three clearly third-wave films. In other words, there is no formal definition for determining what makes a film third wave or even what ingredients make it feminist. It is more a feeling evoked in the viewer than concrete evidence; it is more a confidence than a correct answer.

Third-wave films often tackle previously under-the-radar issues such as bisexuality, transgenderism, and female serial killers and often use humor as a way to get at otherwise difficult and challenging subjects, such as surrogate parenting, being called a "slut," or the drive to have **cosmetic surgery**. They capture current dilemmas, not third-wavers' mother's dilemmas (such as in the case of *Mean Girls* (2004), which grew out of Rosalind Wiseman's nonfiction feminist bestseller *Queen Bees and Wannabes* (2002) and posits strategies for understanding girl bullies). *Lovely and Amazing* (2001) presented the myriad of ways that women are dealing with their **body** image. For instance, is it "bad" to be thin, even if one is naturally that way? In what way do thin people affect other people's image of themselves? How does race factor into images of beauty? Are black women exempt from the beauty pressures on white women? If so, how does that point to the ways in which **racism** both relieves women of color from some of the stereotypical female roles and at the same time reinforces their lack of privilege as females?

Meanwhile, men are also a topic of third-wave film, both in the surreal critique of 1980s stock brokers in *American Psycho* (2000) and in the *Fight Club* (1999), with its riff on similar themes of masculinity and capitalism. A more coherent and successful film than *American Psycho*, *Fight Club* can be viewed as the filmic companion to **Susan Faludi**'s 1999 book *Stiffed*. The film raises the questions of how men, especially working-class men, are struggling with their own **identity** crises in a still sexist but feminist-influenced society. How can men escape the pressure to be masculine? On the topic of gender, *The Crying Game* (1992) and, more poetically, *Orlando* (1993) challenge the viewer's assumptions about what makes a real woman or man. *Legally Blonde II* (2003), in the pink and blonde get-up of a very anti-feminist film, asks the question that most feminists should be asking themselves: How can I make a difference? These are cursory interpretations of each of these films, but the point is that if one is an informed viewer, one can bring feminist politics to any film, either to be inspired by it or to challenge its limitations. There will never be complete agreement on what a feminist film is (or even what feminism is, for that matter). In the third-wave view, feminist films are not made just by women.

The most profound advancement for feminists in film is the rise of the independent films, which, even if not mainstream, have certainly created their own significant tributary. In the era of third-wave feminism, independent films challenged the blockbusters for money and popular appeal. In 1997, when Frances McDormand won best actress for her role in *Fargo* (in which she portrays a pregnant, rural sheriff), it signaled that feminism had finally made an impact on Hollywood. In her acceptance speech, McDormand said, "We five women [nominees] were fortunate to have the choice, not just the opportunity, but *choice* to play such rich, complex female characters. And I encourage writers and directors to keep these really interesting female roles coming, and while you're at it you can throw in a few for the men as well" (McDormand, Oscar Acceptance Speech, 1997). Oscars for Marcia Gay Harden, Hilary Swank, Halle Berry, and Charlize Theron followed up McDormand's sense that roles for women were improving by winning best-actress awards for their performances in *Pollock* (2000), *Boys Don't Cry* (1999), *Monster's Ball* (2001), and *Monster* (2004), respectively, epitomizing the fact that the independent film world commanded respect. Each of these actresses was indebted to the woman she portrayed, knowing the difficulties that some women face on a daily basis. These otherwise alternative films are more likely to tackle difficult issues; take a risk by including less glamorous actors; and scrap together a budget to make an important film, even if financial gain is not a likely result. The subject matter is the motivation, not the visual affects. Sundance is now common parlance, like Hollywood, and the Independent Film Channel captures audiences in the same numbers as Cinemax and HBO. As feminism's impact continues to be felt, it is felt in the independent films first.

With all of these accomplishments comes a new challenge: even with women behind the scenes, women are not much better represented. Women's roles are still often limited to wife, mother, sexually promiscuous woman, or dangerously manipulative woman. They are likely to be rescued, depressed, and ditzy. Third-wavers are left to contend with the fact that as much as women can accomplish what men can, women can also be as sexist and self-hating or as silly and frivolous as society presumes they are. Having a female director is not a guarantee that the content will be feminist, and women are just as capable of exploiting characters. And more to the point of the uniqueness of third wave, what one feminist viewer finds offensive and exploitative, another finds humorous or accurate. See Elle Woods, Reese Witherspoon's character in *Legally Blonde I* (2001) and *II* (2003). Some feminists take her manicured old-school femininity to imply that nowadays one has to be perfectly feminine to be a feminist. These feminists believe one must have the expensive clothes, the interest in high heels, the lap dog, the standing hair appointment, and the law degree from Harvard. Others relish the fact that Elle, far from being a perfect embodiment of what a feminist "typically" looks like or values, can buck that pressure and still have a feminist core.

In a way, determining what makes a film feminist cannot be left to anyone but the beholder. Instead of asking others whether a film was feminist, third-wavers are turning that question on themselves. Were the director, producer, and/or writer female? What about the traditionally male jobs of director of photography and boom operator, and the traditionally female jobs of hair and makeup? Did the film use Asian, black, or Hispanic actors, underscoring that the race of the character is rarely relevant to a story unless its plot is about race? Did it represent issues otherwise marginalized by society? Did it use humor to bring in an unexpected audience to the political underpinnings of the film? Were stereotypes challenged? In the era of third-wave feminism, the real film critic is the individual who brings her own ability to read the text of the film. To do so is the privilege and the responsibility of having grown up with feminist resources, critiques of sexism, women behind the scenes, and a growing tradition of feminist film at their disposal (if not always immediately accessible).

Returning to the putative beginnings of a third wave sensibility in film, *Thelma and Louise*, on the surface, had a negative outcome. The two rebels do not ever make it to Mexico to drink "margaritas by the seaside, mamacita," as Louise puts it. Instead, the two are cornered by cops and FBI agents right at the edge of the Grand Canyon, where they are outnumbered and have no chance of escaping prison. Rather than surrender, they "keep going" over the edge. They die, of course, but not within the confines of the movie. The last image is of freedom. Their personal journey is a three-day crash course in second-wave **consciousness raising** and transformation. A feminist question is begged with the film's last image of the two of them in Louise's turquoise T-Bird, suspended (if only for a moment) above a great chasm. They found freedom, but now what? Third-wave feminist filmmakers continue to answer the question begged by a previous generation and portray what it means to be a bit freer.

Further Reading: Inness, Sherri, ed., *Action Chicks: New Images of Tough Women in Popular Culture*, New York: Palgrave, 2004; Lauzen, Martha M., "The Celluloid Ceiling: Behind-the-Scenes and On-Screen Employment of Women in the Top 250 Films of 2003," executive summary, School of Communication, San Diego State University, San Diego, CA, 2003; NYWIFT Web site, http://www.nywift.org; Reel Women, http://www.reelwomen.org/.

JENNIFER BAUMGARDNER
AMY RICHARDS

FILMMAKERS, FEMINIST. A feminist filmmaker claims a feminist **ideology**, vocalizes the role **feminism** plays in filmmaking in challenging codes, modes of production, and distribution, and makes **films** that explore intersectional issues of race, gender, class, age, **sexuality**, sexism, **misogyny**, homophobia, and movements for social change (e.g., women's rights, **domestic violence**). There have been a number of feminist filmmakers in the second wave, and as their gains and successes have opened up possibilities for younger women, third-wave filmmakers are an active part of the cinematic scene.

Third-Wave Feminist Films/Filmmakers. Live Nude Girls Unite (www. livenudegirlsunite.com) is a documentary by Julia Query, a former **women's studies** major and self-proclaimed feminist stripper, and Vicky Funari that directly addresses feminist labor struggles and the sex wars and engages an intersectional analysis in its feminist film praxis.

Aishah Shahidah Simmons' film, *NO! The Documentary* (2000), explores the issues of race, gender, homophobia, **rape**, and misogyny from a black feminist lesbian perspective. Simmons is an independent feminist filmmaker.

Further Reading: Juhasz, Alexandra, *Women of Vision*, Minneapolis: University of Minnesota Press, 2001; Kaplan, E. Ann, *Feminism & Film*, New York: Oxford University Press, 2000; Women in the Director's Chair, http://www.widc.org; Women Make Movies, http://www.wmm.com; http://www.notherapedocumentary.org.

Rachel Raimist

G

GENDER BINARY. "Gender binary" refers to the social organization of two genders: man and woman. Third-wave **feminism** is invested in challenging this way of thinking. Binary logic functions as a system wherein two groups are seen as polar opposites, also known as dichotomies. Such a polarization creates a hierarchy of meaning, whereby one term holds value and its binary opposite does not. Examples include: man/woman, male/female, and masculine/feminine. Traits associated with the first term, "man," "male," and "masculine," include, for instance, "rational," "active," and "strong." The flip side, "woman," "female," and "feminine," is viewed as "irrational," "passive," and "weak." The first term in a binary is usually seen as superior and it depends on the second term for its meaning. The gender binary reinforces a view of gender divided into two clear-cut groups—men and women—and does not account for multiple experiences of gender but rather collapses gender variation into an either/or logic.

In U.S. society, binary gender roles are institutionalized. One is either a boy or a **girl** and this either/or gendering is the first thing decided in a newborn's life. There are severe social and moral penalties for gender nonconformity including ostracism, harassment, and physical violence.

Feminist scholars have been challenging the implications of a binary system for many years and argue for a more complex understanding of gender (and other markers of difference as well, such as race, **sexuality**, and ability). For instance, in her book *Borderlands/La Frontera* (1999), Gloria Anzaldúa describes what it is like to live with racial hybridity (being of mixed race), which she characterizes as living at the "borderlands," neither one place or another. Anzaldua refers to her cultural multiplicity as "mestiza consciousness"; a shifting of **identity** and integrity that cannot be reduced to a polarized existence.

Contemporary work in gender theory counters simplistic binary logic. In her essay in the 2002 book *GenderQueer: Voices from Beyond the Sexual Binary*, Joan Nestle describes a process of coming to a new understanding of gender and takes into account the faultiness of a prescribed gender binary. She states, "[W]hat I have come to understand is that there are pluralistic gender histories, pluralistic challenges to the male/female, woman/man, lesbian, **butch/femme** constructions and identities as I had come to know them" (9). Riki Wilchins, editor of the 2002 collection of essays *GenderQueer*, exemplifies third-wave thinking about the performative nature of gender and states that "for although it looks like something we *are*, gender is always a *doing* rather than a being. In this sense, *all gender is drag*. And as with any drag, there's always the chance that we'll do something wrong, fall off the stage, do something unscripted" (12). He explains that "gender is about the freedom of disengaging from the binary system of gender identity and the need to develop the pride and courage to survive the daily" (16).

A world divided into men and women, where only two genders are possible, is a fixed and rigid world of gender. Third-wave feminists and activists continue to challenge all things binary.

See also Binary Oppositions; Deconstruction; Queer; *Volume 2, Primary Document 57*

Further Reading: Anzaldúa, Gloria, *Borderlands/La Frontera*, 2nd ed., San Francisco: Aunt Lute Books, 1999; Feinberg, Leslie, *Transgender Warriors*, Boston: Beacon Press, 1996; Nestle, Joan, Clare Howell, and Riki Wilchins, *GenderQueer: Voices from Beyond the Sexual Binary*, Los Angeles: Alyson Books, 2002; Pratt, Minnie Bruce, *S/He*, Ithaca, NY: Firebrand Books, 1995.

KRIS GANDARA

GENERATION X. "Generation X" is a term used to describe the age cohort born between 1964 (the end of the Baby Boom generation) and 1981 (the beginning of Generation Y), although those boundaries are debated. This group is considered the foundation of the feminist third wave, but like other generational designations, the term "Generation X" is viewed as an attempt to characterize the approximately 59 million people born during that time period and cannot possibly speak for them all. The name came into vogue in the early 1990s as a way of describing the generation following and set in opposition to the values and **identity** of the post–World War II baby boomers.

The term "Generation X" was originally linked to studies of alternative youth and their subculture, first in the early 1950s as the name of a project by Robert Capa, and then in 1964 as the title of a novel by Charles Hamblett and Jane Deverson. British rocker Billy Idol adopted the name for his 1970s punk rock band, and writer Douglas Coupland later popularized it in his novel *Generation X: Tales for an Accelerated Culture* (1991). It was after the publication of Coupland's book that the **media** appropriated the term, using it to describe a group of alienated, overeducated, underachieving slackers who listened to grunge music, drank mochas, and railed against their **McJobs**. Coupland's characters became a template for the Generation X figure who would appear in subsequent popular **film** and **television**: restless, listless, cynical, info laden, critical of **consumerism** and status seeking, and largely unconcerned with issues of gender.

Coupland's novel gave rise to terms aimed at defining the generation, such as "Boomer Envy"—envy of material wealth and long-range material security accrued by older members of the baby boom generation by virtue of their fortunate births—and "Clique Maintenance"—the need of one generation to see the generation following it as deficient so as to bolster its own collective ego. It is this perceived hostility that caused some Generation X third-wavers to part ways with their second-wave foremothers and what they viewed as the "bra burning," Betty Friedan–inspired activism associated with them such as the push to get women in the workforce. Largely because of the success of the second wave, such issues were perceived by some third-wave feminists as out of touch with third-wave concerns.

The figure of the alienated and apathetic Generation Xer fascinated popular **media**. Newsmagazines like *Time* and *Newsweek* both featured cover stories on the phenomenon, hoping to "pin down" the exact nature of this cohort of twenty-somethings. Those falling under the designation often resisted the term just as strenuously, causing media to label the group "resistant to categorization." The 1994 cover story in *Newsweek* used as its gimmick the demythologization of Generation X, or "The 13th Gen." The myths they named served as a picture of how larger mainstream culture had come to understand this group of twenty-somethings as slackers, damaged children of divorce, homogeneously white, and fascinated by Kurt Cobain, the tragic figure and icon of grunge rock. All of these myths are also rooted in the popular film, television, music, and fictional imagery associated with Generation X. For example, the magazine *Jane* was created by and for Generation X, both of them putting a new voice to the old consumerism. Coupland's term "obscurism," or, "the practice of peppering daily life with obscure references (forgotten films, dead TV stars, unpopular books, defunct countries, etc.) as a subliminal means of showcasing both one's **education** and one's wish to disassociate from the world of mass culture" characterized the generation's alleged disenchantment with and fixation on mainstream culture.

Because Generation X was the first demographic group for whom MTV and television were integral to their childhood memories, it seems fitting that they are often defined by and identified through associations with film, television, and music. Some popular Generation X actors include Janeane Garofolo, Winona Ryder, Ethan Hawke, Ben Stiller, Ben Affleck, Matt Damon, and Molly Ringwald. Notable movies include *Slacker* (1991), *Reality Bites* (1994), and *Chasing Amy* (1997). The television shows of the Generation X childhood include *The Smurfs*, *The Land of the Lost*, *The Bionic Woman*, *Charlie's Angels*, and the *Dukes of Hazard*; in adulthood this generation has been associated with

Beavis and Butthead, *The Simpsons*, *Friends*, and, of course, MTV. Grunge music from Seattle was a defining force for this group in the 1990s, and the prominent bands included Pearl Jam and Nirvana. Generation X authors include Michael Chabon, David Foster Wallace, and Bret Easton Ellis. Many of these cultural icons of Generation X embodied the alleged values of the demographic: nonconformity and disillusionment with the value of rules, resistance and rebellion, mistrust of the baby boomer generation's choices and values, and disaffection.

Although Generation Xers are often portrayed as apathetic, third-wave **feminism** and its focus on the junctures between capitalism, commodification, and sexism emerged from them. Even though some skeptical culture brokers and disenchanted second-wavers claim that feminism had "skipped a generation," feminist commentators such as **Naomi Wolf**, **Jennifer Baumgardner**, **Amy Richards**, and **Rebecca Walker** came of age with Generation X. The Riot Grrrls movement was also born during this time. These writers introduced concepts such as the Third Shift and the Beauty Myth, addressed the **empowerment** of female **sexuality**, and recognized the prevalence of date **rape** and **sexual harassment**. The third wave is also sometimes characterized by strong critical voices who question what they see as an increasingly institutionalized rather than activist feminism. Generation X feminists continue to propel the third wave as they are joined by the Millennials (also known as "Generation Y"). These feminists are picking up the feminist torch, hoping to address issues of concern to young women such as the feminization of poverty, global feminisms, pay equity, gay-lesbian-bisexual-**transgender-queer** issues, and reproductive rights.

Further Reading: Coupland, Douglas, *Generation X: Tales for an Accelerated Culture*, New York: St. Martin's Press, 1991; Giles, Jeff, and Susan Miller, "Generalizations X," *Newsweek*, June 6, 1994: 62–64; Howe, Neil, and William Strauss, *Millennials Rising: The Next Great Generation*, New York: Vintage Books, 2000; Shugart, Helen, "Isn't It Ironic?: The Intersection of Third-Wave Feminism and Generation X," *Woman's Studies in Communication*, 24 (2005): 131–168; http://www.thirdwavefoundation.org/.

HOLLY HASSEL
JESSICA LOUREY

GILLIGAN, CAROL. Generationally second wave but influential on and debated by the third wave, internationally acclaimed psychologist and writer Carol Gilligan (1936–) plays a significant role in the development of research focusing on the moral development of women and adolescent **girls** and the ways that women deal with conflict resolution. She is well known for her claims that women and men have different moral and psychological tendencies: that men think in terms of rules and justice while women are more inclined to think in terms of caring and relationships. Social constructionist feminists (who contend that gender differences are socially constructed rather than physiologically scripted) disagree with Gilligan and distinguish her fundamentals as "difference **feminism**" (which relies on the premise that men and women are inherently different).

In the early 1970s, Gilligan challenged developmental psychologist Lawrence Kohlberg's research on moral development and justice because of its patriarchal perspective and gender-biased methodologies. Her critique and response to Kohlberg's research was published in her most renowned work, *In a Different Voice: Psychological Theory and Women's Development* (1982). She has authored and coauthored numerous books and publications. Her principal publications in addition to *In a Different Voice* are *Women, Girls, and Psychotherapy: Reframing Resistance* (1991), *Meeting at the Crossroads* (1992), *Between Voice and Silence: Women and Girls, Race and Relationship* (1995), and *The Birth of Pleasure* (2002). Gilligan was appointed to Harvard University's first position in gender studies in 1997 and is an interdisciplinary professor at New York University.

Further Reading: Gilligan, Carol, *Between Voice and Silence: Women and Girls: Race and Relationships*, Cambridge, MA: Harvard University Press, 1996; Gilligan, Carol, *In a Different Voice: Psychological Theory and Women's Development*, Cambridge, MA: Harvard University Press, 1982.

LEANDRA PRESTON

GIRL/GIRLIES. The third wave aspires to transform associations with sex stereotypes by reframing these perspectives so that they become empowering. "Girl" traditionally suggested inferiority and weakness. Using "girl" as a term of familiarity fleshes out the stereotype of female simplicity. Third-wave feminists control their own **representation** and declare meaning as something that is not permanently fixed.

The early 1990s Riot Grrrl movement incorporated gender politics into a punk rock, girl-focused subculture. The former notion of "girl" was revised into "grrrl," a growl that disavows powerlessness. Meanwhile, books such as Mary Pipher's *Reviving Ophelia* (1994) celebrated the possibilities of girl culture before the repressive onset of adolescence. This literature inspired musicians like **Bikini Kill**'s Kathleen Hanna to embrace certain symbols associated with girlhood. "Girlies" are those who embrace stereotypical elements of **femininity**. Plastic barrettes, baby-doll dresses, and baby-tees commonly adorned female vocalists and came to be associated with the Riot Grrrl movement. Out of "girlie" culture came *Bust* magazine, an alternative to most **magazines** for young women that enforce conventional passivity. *Bust*, the magazine of the "new girl order," reclaims pin up models and representations of women from the 1950s and infuses these symbols with **identity** politics.

See also Music

Further Reading: Carlip, Hillary, *Girlpower: Young Women Speak Out*, New York: Warner Books, 1995; Gilligan, Carol, *Meeting at the Crossroads: Women's Psychology and Girls' Development*, New York: Ballantine, 1993; Pipher, Mary, *Reviving Ophelia: Saving the Selves of Adolescent Girls*, New York: Ballantine, 1994.

LEIGH PHILLIPS

GIRL POWER. "Girl power," a term first made popular in the mid-1990s by the British pop group The Spice Girls, has been considered a popularized version of third-wave **feminism** and, alternately, the antithesis of feminism. Like third-wave feminism, **girl** power does not believe that one's feminist message must be dressed in unfeminine attire; rather, it celebrates the feminine in women and girls while it promotes their strength. Girl power reclaims the **body** as a site of power through **sports** and physical assertion, celebrates pluralities of female **identity**, values **femininity** and at the same time values female **empowerment** and equality, and refuses to dismiss female **sexuality** as a symbol of weakness or objectification. However, unlike much of the third-wave feminist movement, girl power does not move beyond the notion of girls harnessing their own personal power. Though it talks to girls, implying some coalition amongst its constituents, girl power discourse rarely encourages collective social change. It focuses on individual empowerment rather than group change or collective action. Girl power can be seen in two distinct, yet overlapping, ways: as a watered-down feminist position available as a stylish accessory, and as a popularized yet meaningful and widespread embodiment of some third-wave feminist positions.

In 1996, The Spice Girls, a British pop group consisting of five female performers each representing a different characteristic—Scary Spice, Posh Spice, Baby Spice, Sporty Spice, and Ginger Spice—released their first single, "Wannabe." Decked out in miniskirts, plunging necklines, and go-go boots, and adorned with makeup and girly flourishes, the Spice Girls appeared to be marketing themselves as stereotypical pop stars who were using their sexualized bodies to sell their **music**. At the same time, the rhetoric produced by the Spice Girls took a position closer to third-wave feminist beliefs. Not only did their first single privilege female friendship over romantic relationships (which was a far cry from the girl groups of preceding decades), but the Spice Girls declared their "girl power" and claimed in the liner notes of their first album that girl power was the feminism of the nineties. The Spice Girls promoted a notion of power that was both feminine and feminist; they celebrated the athletic beside the cute, and the spicy rage at being oppressed beside the **desire** to be decorated with the trimmings of femininity.

This user-friendly feminist tag was quickly picked up by popular **media** as the contemporary slogan of girlhood. Just after the release of the Spice Girls single, Donna Shalala, then Secretary of Health and Human Services, launched a mediated "Girl Power" public health campaign designed to empower girls to resist engaging in risky health behaviors. The **Powerpuff Girls**, a cartoon series about three sisters named Bubbles, Buttercup, and Blossom, also epitomized girl power. Not only did these girls wear pastel dresses and have cute names, they also saved their small town from evil.

Girl power has entered the everyday lexicon. Seeing its popularity and accessibility, the entertainment, clothing, toy, cosmetics, and **advertising** agencies

quickly adopted the term, producing **magazines, television** shows, T-shirts, and makeup that marked girls as sexy, sporty, spicy, and sweet.
See also Magazines, Women's

Further Reading: Budgeon, Shelley, "'I'll Tell You What I Really, Really Want': Girl Power and Self-Identity in Britain," in *Millennium Girls: Today's Girls around the World,* ed. Sherrie Inness, Lenham, MD: Rowman & Littlefield, 1998, 115–143; Douglas, Susan, "Girls n' Spice: All Things Nice?" *The Nation,* 265 (1997): 21–24; Riordan, Ellen, "Commodified Agents and Empowered Girls: Consuming and Producing Feminism," *Journal of Communication Inquiry* 25 (2001): 279–297.

EMILIE ZASLOW

GIRLS INCORPORATED. Girls Incorporated (Girls Inc.) is a charitable, non-profit organization with a mission "to inspire all girls to become smart, strong, and bold." Headquartered on New York's Wall Street, it offers programs to **girls** ages six to eighteen at 1,000 sites across the United States and Canada. It also educates and informs the public about girls' strengths and needs and advocates for an equitable society. Founded in 1945 as the Girls Clubs of America and renamed Girls Inc. in 1990, its roots extend to the first Girls Club, which was established in 1864.

Girls Inc. shares many third-wave feminist goals. For example, third-wavers draw attention to the varying needs of girls of differing races and classes. Girls Inc. is attuned to this variance, with most centers located in high-risk, low-income areas. Another similarity is attention to the **media.** Many third-wavers claim that media consumption raised their feminist consciousness and that they enjoyed and criticized it simultaneously. Girls Inc. raises girls' consciousness through its Media Literacy program, which helps girls think critically about media messages and stereotypes.

Other Girls Inc. programs seek to prevent pregnancy; foster girls' interests in mathematics, the sciences, and technology; build resistance against peer pressure; mentor youth leadership projects; and encourage physical fitness. Their widely circulated "Girls' Bill of Rights" is available in eight languages.
See also Advertising

Further Reading: Girls Inc., Information Central Web Site, http://www.girlsinc. org/ic/index.php; *Harris Interactive,* "Girls Hit the Political Scene: Not Only to Be Seen but Heard," http://www.harrisinteractive.com/news/printerfriend/index.asp? NewsID=286.

REBECCA C. HAINS

GLASS CEILING. The glass ceiling is a barrier that prevents qualified people from attaining senior management-level positions within corporations and organizations because of cultural, sexist, racist, classist, homophobic, and transphobic prejudices, attitudes, and practices.

At the beginning of the 1990s, just as **Generation X** women began to enter the workplace, the concept of the "glass ceiling" began to first take hold. In

March 1986, the *Wall Street Journal* published a special report about the workplace called "The Corporate Woman: Room at the Top: U.S. Industry, Despite Some Advances, Remains Mostly Devoid of Women in Senior Posts." It described the obstacles women faced as they worked their way up the "corporate ladder." A year later the Department of Labor published "Workforce 2000," a study about the changes in the workforce, coining and defining the term "glass ceiling." Despite the economic and employment projections at the time, young women rapidly excelled, moving up the management ladder in certain industries dominated by women such as human resources, public relations, and retail. These successes are often cited by managers, politicians, and organizations to show that women have top management positions in corporate America and that the glass ceiling is no longer a factor. However, the reality is that even in industries where women dominate, senior management positions are still held by men and there are many professional fields, such as technology and finance, which remain predominantly a male domain.

What is categorized as women's particular potentialities begins at different stages during their **education** when **girls** are tracked into vocational or college prep fields. These categorizations are largely based on **family** financial support, class, race, and potential for future leadership. Many organizations, such as the National Women's Law Center, studied and reported on the tracking of girls into subjects that are "traditionally female" rather than allowing girls to choose between more advanced technical and vocational courses, which can lead to higher-paying jobs and careers. Tracking girls into "female" vocations and professions continues as they grow into women and enter the workplace. Hampering women's advancement in the workplace are challenges in obtaining a college degree; managers' preconceived ideas about women's career goals; family responsibilities; lack of a strong network, mentors, membership in professional organizations; and other tools that help them gain experience, opportunities, and support.

See also Single-Sex Education; Wage Gap

Further Reading: Costello, Cynthia B., Anne J. Stone, and Vanessa R. Wight, *The American Woman 2003–2004: Daughters of a Revolution—Young Women Today*, New York: Palgrave 2003; Stith, Anthony, *Breaking the Glass Ceiling: Racism and Sexism in Corporate America: The Myths, the Realities and the Solutions*, Orange, NJ: Bryant & Dillon, 1996; Woo, Deborah, *Glass Ceilings and Asian Americans: The New Face of Workplace Barriers*, New York: Alta Mira Press, 2000; http://www.advancingwomen.com/; http://www.catalystwomen.org; http://www.ethnicmajority.com; www.theglassceiling.com/; http://www.womensleadership.com/.

Heather Cassell

GLOBALIZATION. The term "globalization" became popular in the 1990s as a way to describe economic restructuring and the widening of the reach of the global free market economy. Globalization involves large shifts in economic, political, and cultural processes. The global move toward free market capitalism began in the 1970s and, with the advent of modern technology, grew to an even larger scale in the 1980s and 1990s. Third-wave feminists tend to be critical of the gross inequities that have resulted from many economic policies of globalization. Yet, from a third-wave perspective, there are also positive aspects of globalization, such as the growth of technology, which shortens distances and blurs boundaries. Regardless of its positive or negative aspects, globalization has changed the way that third-wavers "do **feminism**," a change actively shaped by the young women and men who came of age in this global era.

There is no one definition of the process of globalization. However, critics generally agree on the basic principles of globalization: the economic structure of globalization promotes free market capitalism by developed countries (the "global north") to countries of the developing world (the "global south"). Institutions such as the International Monetary Fund (IMF), the World Bank, and the World Trade Organization (WTO), and treaties like the North American Free Trade Agreement (NAFTA) are instrumental in promoting global capitalism. The power given to these institutions and to multinational corporations that control large sums of global capital leads to increasing privatization of resources and lessens the power of individual states, resulting in profound political and cultural change. Therefore, globalization can be thought of as several intersecting processes involving not only economic restructuring, but political and cultural shifts as well.

"Economic globalization" describes the process in which countries are encouraged to open their borders to the international capitalist market system. Free trade is also encouraged, which critics argue often results in large power inequities between the richer countries of the global north and poorer countries of the global south. For example, the practice of free market capitalism has led to a new international division of labor, with large companies based in the global north taking advantage of cheaper, less restrictive labor in the global south. This results, critics say, in the exploitation of southern workers. Feminists also critique the gendered nature of this process, because a disproportionate number of those affected by this exploitation are women.

The wide reach of economic globalization, together with another main tenet of globalization, the development of technology, has resulted in the formation of a new global political climate. People around the world have been able to unite in common causes such as social justice, **environmentalism**, and labor rights. The women's movement has benefited from this aspect of globalization, which has made events such as the UN World Conferences on Women (Mexico City, 1975; Nairobi, 1985; Beijing, 1995) possible, and has also resulted in the formation of international conventions on women's rights, such as the Convention on the Elimination of all Forms of **Discrimination** against Women (**CEDAW**). These actions show that the process of globalization challenges deeply entrenched attitudes about gender all over the world. However, even those who have benefited from global political activism argue that the increasing globalization of society results in a type of cultural hegemony, whereby the culture and practices of the global north are exported to the global south.

Third-wave feminism, strongly influenced by these critiques, seeks at its base to recognize the diversity within the feminist movement and thus the various ways (negative *and* positive) globalization affects women and men from different cultures, races, and classes.

Beneficial or Destructive. Some proponents of globalization argue that inequuities resulting from economic restructuring are not as bad as opponents would claim, and that the opening of markets brings growth and benefits to all. Others argue that globalization is flawed in its current state, but that this is due to policies of institutions such as the IMF. Third-wave feminists tend to align more closely with what is commonly referred to as the anti-globalization movement, or the "movement of movements." This perspective arises partly because the third wave's roots are steeped in U.S. women of color and Third World feminists' critiques of the second-wave feminist movement, and partly because their lives are so affected by the globalization process. Nevertheless, this does not mean that young feminists are "anti" globalization in all of its forms. In fact, third-wavers have benefited from globalization in many ways (e.g., by using the Internet as a networking tool to organize with other like-minded young women from Texas to Taiwan). However, third-wave feminists also recognize that women are more likely than men to lack Internet access and/or even the basic literacy skills needed to use computers. As this example illustrates, although increasingly more people are affected by globalization, they are often less able to access the power that globalization can offer. The United Nations reports that the gap between the richest in the world and the poorest is growing: the 200 richest people on earth have assets greater than the combined incomes of more than 2 billion of the poorest, the majority of whom are women. In the United States in particular, the economic restructuring processes of **downsizing** and **outsourcing** have left many young women jobless or with a low-skill, low-benefits **McJob**. In addition, globalization has resulted in the increased privatization of health insurance, **education**, and other resources critical to women (and men), as states are encouraged to spend more on opening their markets and less on social programs. Awareness of these growing inequalities leads many third-wavers to argue that several aspects of globalization result in a power shift that focuses on profit rather than well-being, a process that adversely effects all (and particularly young) women.

Activism. Third-wave feminists are working against globalization's inequities, arguing that "another world is possible." Organizations working for social justice, such as National Women's Alliance and Sister Action for Power, use a global perspective in their work, incorporating third-wave notions of diversity and inclusion. Groups such as the Radical Cheerleaders and the Pink Bloc participate in anti-globalization demonstrations against the movement's symbols of global injustice, the World Bank, the IMF, and the multinationals. Bringing a third-wave perspective to protesting, the Radical Cheerleaders turn a stereotypically **"girly"** sport into a subversive act, while the Pink Bloc uses theatrical tactics. As these examples show, and the women involved in a student-run,

student-led, third-wave conference at Beloit College in Beloit, Wisconsin, in 2004 assert, the influence of globalization means that third-wave feminism "seeks to foster a more inclusive and complicated dialogue than has been imagined possible to this point." Like the anti-globalization movement, third-wavers use varied and alternative sites of resistance to voice their concerns with the complex effects of power shifts stemming from the globalization process. For example, a global factory run by a multinational corporation may bring jobs to a particular area, but if those jobs are targeted at women because they can be paid lower wages, then more jobs may not be a good thing. Both movements' concern with how these shifts affect everyone differently is highlighted by the fact that their work supports a wide range of causes, including environmentalism, "traditional" women's rights, immigration rights, **queer** rights, prison reform, indigenous rights, and anti-**racism**. For third-wavers, like the second-wave women of color before them, whose critiques they have taken up and adapted, "[t]here is no such thing as a single-issue struggle because we do not live single-issue lives" (Audre Lorde, the Audre Lorde Project, 2004).
See also Volume 2, Primary Documents 32 and 33

Further Reading: Association for Women's Rights in Development (AWID), http://www.awid.org; Audre Lorde Project, http://www.alp.org; Beloit College, Third Wave Feminism Conference, April 3–4, 2004, http://www.beloit.edu/~thirdwav/whatis.php; Bhagwati, Jagdish, *In Defense of Globalization*, New York: Oxford University Press, 2004; Blackwell, Maylei, Linda Burnham, and Jung Hee Choi, eds., *Time to Rise: US Women of Color—Issues and Strategies*, Women of Color Resource Center, 2001, http://www.coloredgirls.org/; Dicker, Rory, and Alison Piepmeier, eds., *Catching a Wave: Reclaiming Feminism for the 21st Century*, Boston: Northeastern University Press, 2003; Heywood, Leslie, and Jennifer Drake, eds., *Third Wave Agenda: Being Feminist, Doing Feminism*, Minneapolis: University of Minnesota Press, 1997; Klein, Naomi, *No Logo: No Space No Choice No Jobs*, 2nd ed., New York: Picador, 2002; Labaton, Vivien, and Dawn Lundy Martin, eds., *The Fire This Time: Young Activists and the New Feminism*, New York: Anchor Books, 2004; Mohanty, Chandra Talpade, "'Under Western Eyes' Revisited: Feminist Solidarity through Anticapitalist Struggles," *Signs: Journal of Women in Culture and Society* 28(2) (2002): 499–535; Morgan, Robin, ed., *Sisterhood Is Forever*, New York: Washington Square Press, 2003; Naples, Nancy, and Manisha Desai, eds., *Women's Activism and Globalization: Linking Local Struggles and Transnational Politics*, New York: Routledge, 2002; National Women's Alliance, http://www.nwaforchange.org/; Stiglitz, Joseph, *Globalization and Its Discontents*, London: Penguin, 2002; United Nations, *World Youth Report 2003: The global situation of young people*, http://www.un.org/esa/socdev/unyin/wyr/; United Nations Development Fund for Women (UNIFEM), http://www.unifem.org; Women and The Economy, UN Platform for Action Committee, http://www.unpac.ca/; Women's Environment and Development Organization (WEDO), http://www.wedo.org; World Social Forum, http://www.wsfindia.org/anotherworld.php.

GWENDOLYN BEETHAM

GUERRILLA GIRLS. A powerful example of third-wave feminist performative activism, the Guerrilla Girls are a New York City–based activist group originally created to protest the relative exclusion of women and people of color from the artistic canon. Although they will admit to being artists in their own right, the actual **identity** of the Guerrilla Girls is a closely guarded secret. In interviews, members assume the names of dead females artists, and during public demonstrations the group members conceal their appearance by pairing gorilla masks with sexually provocative clothing. The group encourages participation from the general public by making their materials, which generally contain statistics regarding the racial and gender makeup of prominent American artistic groups, readily available online and in **magazines**. Supporters are then able to copy and distribute in public spaces all over the world, bringing the message of the Guerrilla Girls to an even larger audience. As a result, the group aligns itself not only with the traditionally masculine narrative of the masked avenger—that mysterious hero who performs acts for the public good without receiving credit—but also with the **DIY** (do it yourself) ethos of third-wave **feminism**.

The Guerrilla Girls were originally inspired by a 1985 show at the Museum of Modern Art, entitled *An International Survey of Painting and Sculpture*. Although the curator boasted that the exhibit was a showcase for "significant" contemporary artists, of the 169 people included, only thirteen were women, and people of color were excluded entirely. After some research, the group discovered that this percentage was common and that minority populations had been experiencing a **backlash** in the **art** world since the 1970s. Their mission, then, was clear: to make the public aware of the masculine bias inherent not only in museums and galleries, but in the culture at large. The Guerrilla Girls began picketing in costume in front of local museums and sending press releases to various publications. Their message of protest has taken the form of billboards, bus **advertising**, magazine spreads, and letter-**writing** campaigns. They regularly distribute their newsletter, *Hot Flashes from the Guerrilla Girls*, as a way to monitor **racism** and sexism in the art world.

These less-than-conventional tactics have brought the Guerrilla Girls vast **media** attention, which has translated into credibility and influence with many art critics. However, the group's activism is not solely focused on museums. Since the mid-1990s, the issues taken up by the Guerrilla Girls have expanded to include **war** protests, gay and lesbian equality, and reproductive freedom—virtually any cause on the contemporary feminist agenda. In more recent years, their message has been more personal, as the Girls seek to deconstruct cultural notions of womanhood and "empower women to create their own stereotypes." The primary thread running through their activism is the attempt to make the invisible visible.

See also Empowerment; *Volume 2, Primary Documents 48 and 49*

Further Reading: Guerrilla Girls, *Bitches, Bimbos, and Ballbreakers: The Guerrilla Girls' Illustrated Guide to Female Stereotypes*, New York: Penguin, 2003; Guerrilla Girls, *Confessions of the Guerrilla Girls*, New York: HarperCollins, 1995; Guerrilla Girls, *The Guerrilla Girls, Bedside Companion to the History of Western Art*, New York: Penguin, 1998.

KRISTEN KIDDER

GUINIER, LANI. An icon for many third-wave feminists, Lani Guinier (1950–) is a prominent anti-racist, feminist legal scholar, writer, and activist. A graduate of Radcliffe College and Yale University of Law, Guinier worked for the NAACP Legal Defense Fund during the 1980s and litigated cases dealing with voting rights in the south. In 1988, Guinier accepted a professorship at the University of Pennsylvania, a post she held for a decade. In 1993, she came to public attention when President Bill Clinton nominated her to be the first black woman to head the Civil Rights Division of the Department of Justice. Guinier was an ideal candidate as she had served in the Civil Rights Division during the Carter administration; however, conservatives attacked Guinier's views on democracy and voting, and Clinton withdrew her nomination. She used this experience as a public platform to draw attention to issues of race, gender, and democratic decision-making and has argued for public discussion on these issues. One means of achieving this goal of public discussion was the formation of the Web site *Racetalks* (http://www.racetalks.org), created by Guinier and Susan Sturm to facilitate public discussion about issues pertaining to race and gender equity. In 1998, Guinier joined the Faculty of Law at Harvard University, becoming the first black woman tenured professor in the history of Harvard Law School. Guinier has published many books, including *The Tyranny of the Majority* (1994), *Becoming Gentlemen: Woman, Law Schools and Institutional Change* (1995), and *The Miner's Canary: Rethinking Race and Power* (2002). In 1998, she published her personal and political **memoir**, *Lift Every Voice: Turning a Civil Rights Setback into a New Vision of Social Justice*.

Further Reading: Guinier, Lani, *Lift Every Voice: Turning a Civil Rights Setback into a New Vision of Social Justice*, New York: Simon and Schuster, 1998.

ROBYN S. BOURGEOIS

H

HALBERSTAM, JUDITH. Lesbian gender theorist Judith "Jack" Halberstam (1961–) is the author of the groundbreaking book, *Female Masculinity* (1998). "If what we call 'dominant masculinity' is taken to be a naturalized relation between maleness and power," Halberstam argues, "then it makes little sense to examine men for the contours of that masculinity's social construction" (2). Halberstam's leading premise affirms that masculinity is not reducible to the **male body**. She calls for the consideration of a female-centered masculinity that takes various forms, like those embodiments found in **drag kings**, stone butches, and female-to-male **transgender**isms. Halberstam suggests that in thinking about multiple expressions of gender, a complex history of alternative masculinities and also a greater understanding of the relationships between gender, sex, and **sexuality** are gained.

Halberstam earned a BA from the University of California, Berkeley (1985), and an MA and PhD from the University of Minnesota (1989, 1991). She is associate professor in the Department of Literature at the University of Southern California, where she teaches Critical Theory, **Film** and Popular Culture, Gender Studies, Nineteenth Century Literature, and **Queer** Studies. Halberstam has won awards for her contributions to gender theory including the Compton Noll Award for Best LGBT Essay (2001), Publisher's Triangle Judy Grahn Award for Lesbian Nonfiction for *Female Masculinity* (1999), and two Lambda Book Award nominations for *Female Masculinity* (1999).

Halberstam's work in minority genders and sexualities also includes *The Drag King Book* (1999), *Skin Shows: Gothic Horror and the Technology of Monsters* (1995), *Posthuman Bodies* (1995), and numerous articles in **cultural studies** and feminist theory and queer theory journals. She writes a regular film review column for *Girlfriends* magazine.

Further Reading: Halberstam, Judith, *The Drag King Book*, London: Serpent's Tail, 1999; Halberstam, Judith, *Female Masculinity*, Durham, NC: Duke University Press, 1998; Halberstam, Judith, Web site, http://www.egomego.com/judith/home.htm.

Kris Gandara

HAMM, MIA. Adopted as an icon by many third-wave feminists, two-time Olympic gold medalist (1996, 2004) and Olympic silver medalist (2000), U.S. Soccer's Female Athlete of the Year for three consecutive years (1994–1996) (five times over the course of her career), and the current record holder for goals scored in international **competition**, Mia Hamm (1972–) is synonymous with U.S. women's soccer. Attractive and personable, Hamm achieved iconic status and brought soccer into the mainstream with success in the 1996 Olympics and 1999 Women's World Cup. As a spokesperson for a number of products, Hamm demonstrated the marketability of the strong female athlete. Her **Nike** commercials unabashedly demonstrated strength and success and a series of Gatorade ads paired her with basketball superstar Michael Jordan, in which anything he did, she did better. Despite her success as a spokesperson, however, Hamm earned no more than $2 million annually in her prime—far less than comparable male athletes.

Arguably the best all-around women's soccer player for more than a decade, her charitable work makes her not only a top athlete, but a role model off the field as well. Founded in 1999, The Mia Hamm Foundation is dedicated to raising funds and awareness for bone marrow diseases and the encouragement and **empowerment** of young female athletes.

See also Sports; Women's Professional Sports Organizations

Further Reading: Longman, Jere, *The Girls of Summer: The U.S. Women's Soccer Team and How It Changed the World*, New York: HarperCollins, 2001; The Mia Hamm Foundation Web site, http://www.miafoundation.org.

Faye Linda Wachs

HARAWAY, DONNA. A prominent U.S. feminist scholar and thinker who has been immensely influential for the third wave, Donna Haraway is most famous for her essay "A Cyborg Manifesto: Science, Technology, and Socialist-Feminism in the Late Twentieth Century" (1991), a work that bridges between second- and third-wave **feminism**. Earlier versions were published in 1983 and 1985, and Haraway did a wonderful job of seizing the cyborg from the militaristic imagery of Hollywood **films** and offering it to feminists as a symbol of a globally connected, contemporary version of **identity** that many find inspiring. Her work is controversial and some find it inaccessible. Yet her ironic and experimental style of **writing**—ranging across **fiction**, multiple theories, and popular culture—has been almost as influential in stimulating third-wave feminist thinking as has her content. Haraway's insistence on arguing "for pleasure in the confusion of boundaries and for responsibility in their construction" (151) is a call to action for third-wavers desirous of a serious but playful politics. Another key essay is "Situated Knowledge: The Science Question in Feminism and the Privilege of Partial Perspective" (1991), which deepens third-wave feminist understandings of the links between women's political agency and structural inequalities. Both essays are published in her seminal book, *Simians, Cyborgs and Women* (1991). She is professor at the History of Consciousness Program at University of California, Santa Cruz.

Further Reading: Haraway, Donna, *Simians, Cyborgs and Women: The Reinvention of Nature*, New York: Routledge, 1991.

ANN KALOSKI-NAYLOR

HERNÁNDEZ, DAISY. Daisy Hernández (1975–) is a writer, editor, researcher, and public speaker focusing on **feminism**, women of color, and **queer** issues. Many of her essays and articles have been published in third-wave anthologies, such as *Listen Up: Voices from the Next Feminist Generation* (2001), *Sex and Single Girls: Straight and Queer Women on Sexuality* (2000), and *Without A Net: The Female Experience of Growing Up Working Class* (2003). Hernández coedited *Colonize This!: Young Women of Color on Today's Feminism* (2002) with Bushra Rehman, the first collection in twenty years of essays by women of color about their perspectives on feminism.

Hernández wrote a column for *Ms.* magazine from 2000 through 2001 and assisted Gail Collins with research for her book, *American Women: Four Hundred Years of Dolls, Drudges, Helpmates, and Heroines* (2003). Hernández wrote editorials and reported for the *New York Times* from 2002 to 2003 before becoming an Editing and Writing Fellow at *ColorLines* magazine. In May 2004, she was the keynote speaker at the Visions of Feminism Conference and delivered a speech titled "Board v. Board and Feminism." She is actively involved with Women in Literature and Letters (WILL), a grassroots collective of women of color writers. *See also Volume 2, Primary Documents 9 and 22*

Further Reading: *ColorLines* magazine, http://www.colorlines.com; Moreno, Robyn, and Michelle Herrera Mulligan, eds., *Border-Line Personalities: A New Generation of Latinas Dish on Sex, Sass, and Cultural Shifting*, New York: Rayo 2004.

HEATHER CASSELL

HETEROSEXISM. Heterosexism refers to an attitude that discriminates against non-heterosexuals while presenting heterosexuality as though it were the only "normal," acceptable form of sexual expression. Heterosexism is an attitude that many third-wave feminists are dedicated to challenging. Just as sexism keeps women locked in a subordinate position and **racism** acts to exclude certain races from the dominant culture, heterosexism effectively denies lesbian, gay, bisexual, and **transgender** people the rights and privileges granted to heterosexual individuals and couples. In response, corresponding activist and academic movements, including third-wave **feminism** and **queer theory**, have formed to comprehend, confront, and defeat these prejudices. Examples of heterosexism in action include laws against sodomy, the ban against openly lesbian women and gay men in the **military**, refusal to allow same-sex couples to attend high school dances, and the prohibition on **same-sex unions/gay marriage**. Marriage itself grants innumerable rights unavailable to same-sex couples. Arguably, heterosexist attitudes also foster the fear and hatred responsible for the verbal threats and violent crimes aimed at sexual minorities.

However, heterosexism also works on a subtler but no less insidious level beyond the law. For instance, teachers may ignore verbal taunts and harassment aimed at a gay student, or a supervisor may pass over a gay employee and promote a less qualified, straight worker instead. People who engage in heterosexism are not always aware they are doing so, as this attitude is deeply ingrained into the social fabric, causing people to unconsciously silence and harm sexual minorities. Like homophobia, heterosexism is pervasive in society, operating both overtly and invisibly.

In addition to dealing strictly with **sexuality**, heterosexism also restricts the behaviors, mannerisms, and **identity** options available to women and men. As heterosexism targets "gay acting" individuals such as effeminate men and strong, assertive women, people wishing to escape this **discrimination** and hostility are forced to adopt conventional gender roles (e.g., stoic masculinity or passive **femininity**), which dictate everything from what one wears to how one walks and talks. Such adoptions, in turn, help to solidify stereotypical views of the proper places for women and men, which ultimately perpetuates the unequal balance of power between genders in society. Consequently, heterosexism and sexism work together to maintain the status quo.

Feminists and queer activists work to dismantle the system that propagates sexism and heterosexism. This activism involves demands for civil rights and economic justice, and it raises awareness of how and why these prejudices operate. Working to end heterosexism, then, promises new opportunities for members of the gay, lesbian, bisexual, and transgender community, and it also promotes a new freedom for all women and men looking for ways to live that break with traditional gender roles.

See also Compulsory Heterosexuality

Further Reading: Blumenfeld, Warren J., *Homophobia: How We All Pay the Price*, Boston: Beacon Press, 1992; Human Rights Campaign, http://www.hrc.org.

Sean Murray

HILL, LAURYN. Lauryn Hill (1975–) is a groundbreaking rapper, singer, and songwriter who is a true third-wave icon. With fellow Fugees band members Prakazrel Michel and Wyclef Jean, Hill won two Grammy Awards for *The Score* (1996), and her first solo album, *The Miseducation of Lauryn Hill* (1998), won

a record-breaking five Grammy Awards. Hill conceived of *Miseducation* as a version of historian Carter G. Woodson's *Mis-education of the Negro* (1933), a book about the detrimental impact of schools on African Americans and the need to develop more Afrocentric curricula. Hill's album "schools" listeners and creates a multi-voiced autobiography by combining rap, gospel, reggae, and soul with lyrics that explore male-female relationships, motherhood, corruption, spirituality, and black global cultures. After settling a lawsuit brought against her over *Miseducation* songwriting credits, Hill took a break from public life. She reappeared with *MTV Unplugged No. 2.0* (2002), surprising critics and fans with emotional songs delivered in a folk/rap style over simple guitar accompaniment. While this raw album was viewed by some critics and fans as evidence of a breakdown, from a third-wave perspective Hill's departure from her star persona is not perplexing. It is precisely Hill's ability to explore multiple voices and to craft a raggedly lush wholeness out of complex and contradictory parts that makes her work so exemplary of the third wave.
See also Music

Further Reading: Cleage, Pearl, "Looking for Lauryn," *Essence* 33(3) (2002): 88–94; Dangerfield, Celnisha L., "Lauryn Hill as Lyricist and Womanist," in *Understanding African American Rhetoric: Classical Origins to Contemporary Innovations*, eds. Ronald Jackson II and Elaine Richardson, New York: Routledge, 2003; Touré, "Lady Soul," *Rolling Stone*, February 1999, 46–54; Touré, "The Mystery of Lauryn Hill," *Rolling Stone*, October 2003, 75–79.

JENNIFER DRAKE

HIP-HOP FEMINISM. Hip-hop **feminism** is a growing part of third-wave feminist movements, addressed in recent anthologies including *Catching a Wave* (2003), *Colonize This!* (2002), *Listen Up* (2001), *Third Wave Agenda* (1997), and *To Be Real* (1995). These works bring serious attention to women in hip-hop, critique feminist rap, and begin to bridge spaces between **feminist theory**, **black feminism**, and hip-hop feminism.

Much of the third-wave hip-hop feminist **writing** articulates the need to connect hip-hop practice and feminist beliefs within spaces of contradictions. In "Sexism and the Art of Feminist Hip-Hop Maintenance," from *To Be Real* (1995), Eisa Davis wrote, "Hip-hop gave me a language that made my black womanhood coherent to myself and the world" (127). Understanding that hip-hop's sexism dominates mainstream outlets, she acknowledged her ability to practice feminism within those spaces, stating, "I don't fit into a puritanical, dualistic feminism that recognizes only indignant innocence ... or unenlightened guilt.... I don't have to choose" (127).

In "Can I Get a Witness?" from *Colonize This!* (2002), Shani Jamila, artist, academic, and activist, wrote, "As women of the hip-hop generation we need a feminist consciousness that allows us to examine how **representations** and images can be simultaneously empowering and problematic" and urged that "[t]he most important thing we can do as a generation is to see our new positions as power and weapons to be used strategically in the struggle rather than as spoils of **war**" (392). In *When Chickenheads Come Home to Roost: My Life as a Hip-hop Feminist* (1999) (published later as *A Hip-Hop Feminist Breaks It Down*, 2000), **Joan Morgan** called this generation the "post-Civil Rights, post-feminist, post-soul children of hip-hop" and examined the **misogyny** of rap **music** and stereotyping of black womanhood through her personal narrative. Some criticize the book as limited in focus and style and not scholarly enough; still, Morgan, a widely published writer, has spent much of her career writing women in hip-hop into history, reaching large readerships, and exemplifying hip-hop feminist praxis.

Check It While I Wreck It: Black Womanhood, Hip-Hop Culture, and the Public Sphere (2001) by scholar Gwendolyn Pough and other numerous academic articles offer feminist critiques of hip-hop, specifically rap music such as Queen Latifah's "Ladies First" and her Afrocentric imagery. Some of this work, which has made important theoretical strides, counts expletives and tracks terms that degrade women, and it analyzes mainstream music video imagery and the participation (or lack thereof) of women in rap. Some writers look beyond mainstream outlets (e.g., commercial radio, BET, and MTV) for "underground" "femcees" but still fail to address that there is a lack of artists who claim or self-name as feminist.

Female rapper Mystic is argued to have a feminist consciousness because she articulates a rejection of the reduction of hip-hop women into dichotomous stereotypes. She criticizes the fact that there are usually only two stereotypes, either the gold digger or the straight, politically active woman, and argues that black women are more complicated than this. Many cite her as an example of hip-hop feminist praxis, although she does not wholeheartedly embrace this label. In fact, she asserts, "I'm not like some political poster child or some feminist poster child, I'm just kind of like your regular woman, [your] regular chick." Many who write about women in hip-hop fall into the conundrum of present day "sex war" arguments that stem from second-wave feminisms. For example, a *Washington Post* article written by Kristal Brent Zook," The Mask of Lil' Kim; What Lies Behind the Hip-Hop Artist's Raunchy Image? A Businesswoman, a Feminist ... an Enigma," (September 30, 2000) quoted journalist asha bandele, who argued, "I do not believe that [Lil'] Kim is in control of her image because there's nothing powerful about it.... It's a caricature." Yet in the same article, Lil' Kim claims a feminist title, stating overtly, "I'm a feminist." Less problematic artists such as Mystic, Queen Latifah, and countless others who center their raps on women's experiences do not claim a feminist title.

Further problematic in hip-hop feminist writing is the lack of attention to anything beyond rap music. Complex and contradictory, hip-hop also includes visual **art** (graffiti and murals), auditory and poetic manifestations (dj-ing, music production, and rap), dance forms (b-girling/b-boying), and hip-hop **films** (*Boyz'N the Hood* [1991] and *Nobody Knows My Name* [2001]). Hip-hop's main outlet is no longer solely radio but also the Internet (e.g., *The Wake Up Show*), hip-hop **theater** (e.g., *Hip-hop Theater Festival*), and hip-hop **television** (*Russell Simmons' Def Poetry Jam*). Hip-hop is multi-genre (including but not limited to conscious rap, commercial rap, underground, and spoken word), multigenerational, multiracial, multiethnic, and multicultural. This lack of limitations—in form, space, or participants—is embedded in hip-hop ideologies and cultural practices, which allows them to be accessible and spread. B-girls like Asia One (who has produced the B-boy Summit for over ten years in Los Angeles, CA) mentors young b-girls and battles with them as part of her b-girl collective, No Easy Props. This summit is a community-oriented hip-hop event that presents the history of hip-hop culture along with showcasing the skills of bboying and bgirling—the hip-hop term for breaking and breakdancing. All-female collectives, such as Sisterz of the Underground, mentor elementary students in after-school hip-hop programs. Teachers and activists use hip-hop as a teaching tool in their classrooms. This work can be seen firsthand at El Puente, an alternative high school in Flatbush, Brooklyn, New York, and also through the accomplishments of the organization sistaiisista, "the freedom school for women of color," which offers workshops on self-defense, **women's health**, and so on. Individual activists also make great strides. For example, Sarah Jones, a playwright, poet, and activist, made history by suing the Federal Communications Commission (FCC) for its ban of her celebrated song, "Your Revolution," which cites popular rap lyrics and imagery but also adds a feminist twist, exemplifying social change through hip-hop feminisms.

Feminists and women-centered hip-hop practitioners make **films**, do graffiti, dj, promote, teach, mother, and "live hip-hop," as the popular hip-hop saying goes. Hip-hop feminism is the need for a more encompassing theoretical frame that expands on postmodernism, offering a broadened view of hip-hop beyond rap, and theory. New theories are needed to interrogate power, gender construction, and **performativity**, specifically performances of **femininity** and masculinity. There is still a need for alternative communities engaged in hip-hop feminism.

Further Reading: Forman, Murray, "Movin' Closer to an Independent Funk: Black Feminist Theory, Standpoint, and Women in Rap," *Women's Studies* 23 (1994): 35ff; Hernández, Daisy, and Bushra Rehman, eds., *Colonize This!: Young Women of Color on Today's Feminism*, Seattle: Seal Press, 2002, 392; Keyes, Cheryl L., "'We're More Than a Novelty Boys': Strategies of Female Rappers in the Rap Music Tradition," in *Feminist Messages: A Coding in Women's Folk Culture*, ed. Joan Newton Radner, Urbana: University of Illinois Press, 1993; Morgan, Joan, *When Chickenheads Come Home to Roost: A Hip-Hop Feminist Breaks It Down*, New York: Touchstone, 1999; Pough, Gwendolyn, *Check It While I Wreck It: Black Womanhood, Hip-Hop Culture, and the Public Sphere*, Boston: Northeastern University Press, 2004; Roberts, Robin, "'Ladies First': Queen Latifah's Afrocentric Feminist Music Video," *African American Review* 28 (1994): 245–55; Walker, Rebecca, ed., *To Be Real: Telling the Truth and Changing the Face of Feminism*, New York: Anchor Books, 1995, 127.

RACHEL RAIMIST

HIP-HOP TERMS FOR WOMEN. Rap's discourse, as part of black vernacular, is an expression of signifying in which the orator (rapper) plays with language to critique, unsettle, and reconfigure dominant meanings through (re)signification. This terminology can be confusing because many words have double meanings that depend on context and reception and develop through the constant reinvention of terms. For example, "**bitch**" (also biatch, batch, renc, bizzo, cave bitch, gansta bitch, the baddest bitch, ride or die bitch) is used as both derogatory (as in rapper Compton's Most Wanted's rap "U's a Bitch") and as a self-claimed word for women's **empowerment** (as in rapper Lil' Kim's "Queen Bitch"). Similarly, the word "ho"/"hoe" (also referenced as hoochie, trick, skeezer, skalywag, and groupie) usually means a hooker or a whorish woman but is also used by a master of ceremonies as a call-and-response to simply hype the audience ("everybody say ho" and the audience responds with "ho, ho"). The double meaning has led to confusion among some cultural outsiders.

Some musicians rely on metaphoric bird imagery (e.g., chicken, chickenhead, duck, ghetto bird, pigeon) and refer to women who cluck (talk) a lot and walk around aimlessly (like a chicken with its head cut off). For instance, note rapper Notorious B.I.G.'s verse in Total's "Can't You See": "chickenheads be cluckin," which refers to women who talk too much and cannot keep a secret. He expands this meaning in "Unbelievable" when he says, "Chickenheads be cluckin' in my bathroom, fuckin." Here, he analogizes the back-and-forth motion a woman's head makes during oral sex to the pecking of a chicken. In *When Chickenheads Come Home to Roost: My Life As a Hip-Hop Feminist* (1999), **Joan Morgan** complicates the negative sexual image of a "chickenhead," naming herself as simultaneously "chickenhater" and envious, seeing her "STRONG-BLACKWOMAN" feminist self needing to be more "chicken" to make it in a hip-hop world.

Women are also called "honey"/"honey dip", suggesting a woman's sweetness, and "dime"/"dimepiece," indicating beauty as ranked by a ten, or various ice cream flavors (e.g., Wu-Tang's "Ice Cream"). This implies the different flavors of women—"French vanilla" (white), "caramel" (Asian or other brown-skinned), "butapecan" (Puerto Rican), and "chocolate deluxe" (Black). Other terms reflect the feminine **body** such as "chassie" and "skirt" or define women who connect with men for material gain such as "golddigger." Terms such as "babymama" and "hoodrat," among others, have reached mainstream status and are used in Hollywood **films** and commercial **media**, often perpetuating stereotypes of black womanhood.

Finally, terms of endearment for women including "boo," "shorty," "wiz," and "Earth" from the 5 Percent Nation teachings of mother as "Old Earth," and wife or wifey as Earth (e.g., Method Man and Mary J. Blige's "All I Need"), although seemingly positive significations, reveal a heterosexist framework. Still, many terms signify empowered women who are "down" for hip-hop, such as "queens," "fly-girls," "sistas," "homegirls," and "b-girls" (derived from "break girl"

or "Bronx girl," from the male form "b-boy," to specify a dancer who breaks to breakbeat records, but which has expanded to also include the many women who claim to be hip-hop).
See also Volume 2, Primary Documents 3 and 30

Further Reading: Morgan, Joan, *When Chickenheads Come Home to Roost: My Life as a Hip-Hop Feminist*, New York: Touchstone, 1999; Pough, Gwendolyn D., *Check It While I Wreck It*, Boston: Northeastern University Press, 2004; Vibe/Spin Ventures, LLC, *Hip-hop Divas*, Three Rivers Press, 2001.

RACHEL RAIMIST

HISTORY, POSTMODERN. Feminism's engagement with the discipline of history has been complicated and intellectually significant. Much time has been spent attempting to write women *into* history proper: to tell the stories of women who had been left out completely from traditional history's grand narratives (which were largely the tales of events and the men who were involved). If, as some historians argue, the first wave of feminism (from the Enlightenment era until the middle of the twentieth century) stressed equality, rights, liberation, and emancipation, the concept of women's history itself emerged right alongside. While sexual **identity** was deemed inessential to that history, women as active, autonomous agents certainly were essential, and they became protagonists in novels and political players in their own right. Sexual identity became more significant in the telling of women's pasts with the second wave, whose historians stressed the differences of women—while challenging the hegemony of masculine values in society—by differentiating between sex and gender (sex as the biological component of being, gender as the social and cultural interpretation of it), and by also confronting rigid gender roles assigned to women. Equality, they argued, relied heavily on **binary oppositions**: women being equal to man; feminine the equivalent to masculine. As a result, feminist histories began a more radical transformation and focused more on constructing a history that valued women, their struggles, and their work as significant to the development of society. By undercutting the universality of *history* as exclusionary to half of the population, the discipline of history was dramatically reinvented.

Third-wave feminists have taken that methodology one step further, examining difference not in terms of opposites, but rather as a phenomenon that is constantly constructed, reconstructed, performed, and deconstructed. Building from the work of Jean François Lyotard, Jacques Derrida, and **Judith Butler**, postmodernism significantly altered views on twentieth-century women's history and led to a critical examination of earlier ways of studying and **writing** the past—as well as whose story became part of those histories. That involves a rejection of grand narratives, a dismissal of universal theories, ideas, and stories of the past, and an engagement with more polymorphous and groundless difference. History, like sexual identity, is textual: constantly shifting, continually in production, and always open to question. Feminism is as disparate and multifaceted as the feminists who purport it, and the multiple histories of feminisms

must be written, critiqued, and rewritten as such to effectively disrupt false boundaries and to destabilize traditional, monolithic history to expose diverse and often opposing experiences and positions. Although the third-wave historical project has only just begun, the combination of postmodern strategies for deconstructing history, new and newly found writings by women of color, postcolonial theory, and poststructuralist studies have again altered the way in which feminism is documented and feminist history is read and recorded. In many ways, feminist scholars have been forced to think, read, and write in a unprecedented hypercritical and self-reflexive manner, in a way that undermined much of what feminist historical practice (and the reading of texts that have since become "historical") had come to rely on as "sound" methodology.
See also Deconstruction; Postcolonial Feminism

Further Reading: Jenkins, Keith, ed., *The Postmodern History Reader*, New York: Routledge, 1997; Laslett, Barbara, Ruth-Ellen B. Joeres, Mary Jo Maynes, Evelyn Brooks Higginbotham, and Jeanne Barker-Nunn, eds., *History and Theory: Feminist Research, Debates, Contestations*, Chicago: University of Chicago Press, 1997; Lerner, Gerda, *Why History Matters: Life and Thought*, New York: Oxford University Press, 1997; Scott, Joan Wallach, *Feminism and History*, New York: Oxford University Press, 1996.

CANDIS STEENBERGEN

HOOKS, BELL. One of the third wave's most widely cited influences, bell hooks (1952–) was born Gloria Jean Watkins in Hopkinsville, Kentucky. Hooks' pseudonym honors both her grandmother (whose name she took) and her mother. She received her BA from Stanford University in 1973, her MA in 1976 from the University of Wisconsin, Madison, and her PhD in 1983 from the University of California, Santa Cruz. In 1981 hooks published her first book, *Ain't I A Woman: Black Women and Feminism*, which challenges some of the historical stereotypes about black women. She has since authored, or coauthored, scores of books detailing her theories, research, and commentary as they relate to feminism, class, love, gender and/or race relations, pedagogical theories and practices, black women, and most recently, black men. She has also penned several children's books and **poetry** collections and has taught at some of the nation's most prestigious colleges and universities. A prolific feminist scholar and black intellectual, and a vocal cultural and social critic, it is common to find at least one of her books on the recommended reading lists of most **women's studies** and **cultural studies** syllabi. "Passionate," "freethinking," and "bold" are but a few adjectives to best describe hooks' voluminous legacy to black literary intellectualism. In fact, the *New York Times* described her as "the only woman in recent years who is readily identified as a member of that select group known as 'black public intellectuals.'" She lives in Greenwich Village, New York City.
See also Black Feminism; *Volume 2, Primary Documents 20, 23, and 26*

Further Reading: hooks, bell, *Ain't I a Woman: Black Women and Feminism*, Boston: South End Press, 1981; hooks, bell, *Bone Black: Memories of Girlhood*, New York: Henry

Holt, 1996; hooks, bell, *Killing Rage: Ending Racism*, New York: Henry Holt, 1995; hooks, bell, *Salvation: Black People and Love*, New York: Perennial, 2001; hooks, bell, *Teaching to Transgress: Education as the Practice of Freedom*, New York: Routledge, 1994; hooks, bell, *We Real Cool: Black Men and Masculinity*, New York: Routledge, 2003; *When Angels Speak of Love*, New York: Pocket Books, 2005; hooks, bell, *Wounds of Passion: A Writing Life*, New York: Henry Holt, 1997.

MURIEL L. WHETSTONE-SIMS

HYBRIDITY. The third wave tends to embrace hybridity, or mixture, as a way of conceptualizing experience. Hybridity emphasizes that personal, familial, and national identities are complex and shifting in the context of **globalization**, because globalization creates a world in motion: people leave home seeking economic opportunity; jobs are moved from country to country by corporations seeking profit; information, images, and ideas from various cultures circulate via the Internet, **television**, movies, and **music**; **wars** and other forms of violence cause mass migrations; tourism is a major international industry; and people must operate as different selves in different locations. Hybridity, then, assumes cultural contact, understood both positively and negatively. Sometimes cultural contact happens through exchange and dialog, as when musicians introduce each other to their cultures' ways of playing an instrument or composing a song, or when people from various countries work together on a particular issue, such as how to stop global warming. At other times cultural contact takes violent forms, as in the nineteenth-century slave trade linking Europe, Africa, and the Americas, or in any situation of empire-building or war. Appropriation and exoticization are other forms of cultural contact, as when non-Native Americans purchase and display Native American ritual objects as decorative **art** or when non–African Americans take on elements of hip-hop style. And sometimes multiple kinds of cultural contact are happening at once: exchange *and* appropriation, for example. Whatever forms cultural contact takes, the individuals and cultures involved will be changed, sometimes radically so and sometimes in unequal ways. Third-wave experience has been defined by people and cultures in motion and the multicultural spaces that this creates, and hybridity is a particular way of understanding multiculturalism in terms of global flows and networks rather than through **binary oppositions**, such as West/East, North/South, us/them.

Hybridity operates both as a metaphor for understanding the complexity of contemporary experience *and* as a lived reality. In the sciences, hybridity refers to the genetic mixing of two different species; the *Oxford English Dictionary*, that definitive source for word genealogies, uses the negative terms half-breed, cross-breed, and mongrel to define the hybrid. Many scholars in **art** history, literary and **cultural studies**, and the social sciences have questioned the use of "hybridity" as a way to conceptualize experience by pointing out that the term has a negative connotation concerning race-mixing. Critics of the term are concerned that a simple celebration of hybridity as a metaphor for contemporary experience will trivialize the very real difficulties that have faced mixed-race people, as well as lead to an ignorance of how cultural hybridization can be shaped by power imbalances between cultures. On the other hand, as Professor Steven Yao has pointed out, scientific definitions of hybridity imply that seemingly natural categories can be disrupted, which opens ways to reconsider who and what is "natural" or "normal." The third wave embraces hybridity for this radical potential and with a critical understanding of the contradictions embedded in the concept.

See also Asian American Feminism

Further Reading: Anzaldúa, Gloria, *Borderlands/La Frontera*, 2nd ed., San Francisco: Aunt Lute Books, 1999; Fusco, Coco, *English Is Broken Here: Notes on Cultural Fusion in the Americas*, New York: The New Press, 1995; Gómez-Peña, Guillermo, *Dangerous Border-Crossers: The Artist Talks Back*, New York: Routledge, 2000; Jones, Lisa, *Bulletproof Diva: Tales of Race, Sex and Hair*, New York: Anchor Books, 1995; Lippard, Lucy, *Mixed Blessings: New Art in a Multicultural America*, New York: Pantheon, 1990; Omi, Michael, and Howard Winant, *Racial Formation in the United States: From the 1960s to the 1990s*, 2nd ed., New York: Routledge, 1994; Smith, Zadie, *White Teeth*, New York: Vintage, 2001; Yao, Steven G., "Taxonomizing Hybridity," *Textual Practice* 17(2) (2003): 357–379.

JENNIFER DRAKE

I

IDENTITY. "Identity" in the third-wave feminist sense draws on historical definitions but has its own take as well. Identities are ways in which people come to understand who they are in relationship to others and the social world. An individual's social identity is made up of all one's social statuses (i.e., positions held in society). Social identities can come from the groups a person involuntarily belongs to (i.e., sex, race, ethnicity, disability) or groups that one joins and willingly becomes a member (e.g., athlete, drug user, religious adherent). Social movements, such as a women's movement, also shape an individual's self. Social movement scholars argue that when people come together to enact social change, they also create a unified and oppositional way of seeing the world. Collective identities are more than ideologies (i.e., set of beliefs) and instead emerge out of a shared sense of injustice that also draws life experiences of a group. This identity can alter an activist's conception of self and can politicize everyday life.

"Feminist" is a collective identity, adopted by individuals but created through interaction with a group. Because group interactions and memberships vary, so do the types of feminist identity that are created. In the past, scholars have identified feminist identities by the theoretical frameworks they seemed aligned to, such as radical, liberal, Marxist, socialist, or lesbian **feminism**. However, these theory-based distinctions fail to capture the complexity of feminist identities. Individuals can adopt a variety of beliefs and ideas from different theories and often do not fit any one ideological category. Instead, by focusing on how groups of activists create a shared sense of who they are and how that is different from the dominant society (and other feminist identities), scholars can better capture the complexity of identity construction.

One essential aspect of creating a feminist identity is the construction of boundaries to distinguish members from non-members. By doing so, movement communities develop what is called "an oppositional consciousness," which helps to define their position and issues. Social movement communities cannot construct impenetrable boundaries between themselves and society but must find ways to interact with the groups and institutions they seek to change. This process of negotiation, where practices of everyday life (e.g., wearing a T-shirt with the words "**bitch**" or "cunt") affirm the identities embraced by participants, contributes to the formation of a shared group consciousness. The degree of boundary construction and negotiation is determined by the group's goals, targets, and ideologies. For example, some groups interact freely with the dominant culture (e.g., feminists who lobby politicians for change), whereas other groups may construct strong boundaries between themselves and the rest of society (e.g., feminists who believe in women-only space and events). In sum, collective identities are oppositional in that by adopting the identity of "feminist," an individual is signifying her/his participation in a social change effort and that he/she is different (to a degree determined by the strength of boundaries) from the dominant society.

In groups that draw participants from different classes, races, ethnicities, and sexual orientations, finding shared interests and articulating them is difficult and can exclude marginalized groups. Therefore, creating an identity to increase a group's position can also have the unintended effect of reinforcing the very social categories that create intragroup tensions. For example, in certain strands of both the nineteenth- and twentieth-century American women's movement, the construction of the category *woman* was synonymous with white, heterosexual, married, middle-class women's experiences, ignoring the grievances of other women, particularly women of color, lesbians, and poor women. Therefore, the attempt to create single feminist identity has created (and continues to create) dissension in groups, communities, and the entire U.S. women's movement.

The term "third-wave feminist" is often used to identify young women and men who are involved in feminism in the twenty-first century. The construction of contemporary or third-wave feminist identities is shaped not only by participants but also by the larger social and political culture. The designation of the "third wave" extends from the concept of a "political generation," which is a group of people who have formative experiences at approximately the same point in their lives and develop a common framework for seeing the world. Young women and men in the twenty-first century enter into feminism in a society dramatically shaped by earlier feminists and other forms of activism. Through the efforts of earlier feminists, a variety of cultural events exist, ranging from feminist **theater**, cruises, and **music** and **comedy** festivals to camps, day-care programs, and **women's studies** courses. Young **girls** and boys can read non-gendered children's books, listen to feminist music, and attend summer camps organized around gender equity. In addition, feminism is embedded in the institutions in which third-wave feminists spend their lives, such as their families, schools, and religious/spiritual institutions.

Close examination of third-wave feminism shows that this diffusion of feminist **ideology** into the culture and structure of society, along with the debates and dissentions experienced by earlier feminists results in a multitude of contemporary feminist identities. These identities range from feminists who work for change through existing social structure (e.g., the political and **education** systems), to individuals who reject societal labels and conventions in their everyday life (e.g., **drag kings**, **queer** feminist activists, **wiccans**, pagans, and anti-racist and anti-**globalization** activists).

Further Reading: Melucci, Alberto, *Nomads of the Present: Social Movements and Individual Needs in Contemporary Society*, Philadelphia: Temple University Press, 1989; Reger, Jo, "Organizational Dynamics and the Construction of Multiple Feminist Identities in the National Organization for Women," *Gender & Society*, 5 (2002): 710–727; Taylor, Verta, and Nancy Whittier, "Collective Identity in Social Movement Communities: Lesbian Feminist Mobilization," in *Frontiers in Social Movement Theory*, eds. Aldon Morris and Carol M. Mueller, New Haven: Yale University Press, 1992, 104–129.

JO REGER

IDEOLOGY. An ideology is a set of beliefs, values, and attitudes that explains how people view the world and justify that view. Third-wave **feminism** has no single, unified ideology. Ideologies are ongoing creations, resulting as people interact with the broader society. Members of a social movement adopt similar ideologies that explain their grievances and targets and strategies for change. Contemporary feminist ideologies are rooted in past debates and controversies and are shaped by the political, social, and cultural environments. Contemporary feminists embrace a variety of ideologies. However, ideologies most often characterized as third wave can be grouped into three major themes that connect to and influence each other. These are inclusiveness and diversity, gender as a social constraint, and the individual as a primary site of feminist activism.

The need for an inclusive movement emerged from earlier periods of feminism when issues relevant to groups of nonwhite, non–middle-class women were often ignored in terms of the movements' goals and strategies. Women of color struggled to align themselves with white feminist groups, which articulated "women's" issues only from their own experiences. Lesbians were labeled a "menace" and were purged from groups such as the National Organization for Women. Working-class women often found that their economic issues were not addressed. These exclusionary dynamics led to an articulation for inclusiveness and a call for women to realize that their social positions hinged on more than gender, and that they instead resulted from a matrix of social identities including class, race-ethnicity, religion, and **sexuality**.

The second ideological theme comes from an intertwining of lesbian, bisexual, gay, and **transgender** ideas on the fluidity of sexuality (e.g., **queer**) and the work of feminist theorists, such as **Judith Butler** and Judith Lorber. Butler and Lorber illustrate how gender is a socially constructed performance and not a biological determinant, allowing feminists to challenge gender and sexual dichotomies (i.e., man/women, male/female, heterosexual/homosexual) by adopting more fluid notions of themselves and portraying that through dress, appearance, pronoun usage, and renaming oneself. The social phenomena of **drag king** shows, where biological women perform and "do" masculinity, illustrates this ideological theme.

The idea of challenging gender through everyday actions is an example of the third theme: centering the individual as the primary site of feminist activism. Contemporary feminists are seen as doing an everyday feminism that springs from issues in their own lives, as opposed to having issues articulated by a local or national feminist organization. In this sense, contemporary feminists draw upon the 1960s and 1970s feminist notion that the "personal is political" and are enacting the political in their lives and actions. Focusing on the individual as the site of activism is a change from the strategy of focusing on legal, political, and/or cultural institutions as the source of oppression and the targets of change. Every day, individualized action seeks to change the broader culture, not only the institutions within it.

Further Reading: Butler, Judith, *Gender Trouble: Feminism and the Subversion of Identity*, New York: Routledge, 1990; Collins, Patricia Hill, *Black Feminist Thought: Knowledge, Consciousness, and the Politics of Empowerment*, New York: Routledge, 1990; Lorber, Judith, *Paradoxes of Gender*, New Haven, CT: Yale University Press, 1994; Moraga, Cherríe, and Gloria Anzaldúa, eds., *This Bridge Called My Back: Writings by Radical Women of Color*, Berkeley, CA: Third Woman Press, 2002.

JO REGER

INDIVIDUALISM. Individualism is the assertion that puts the individual or self at the forefront of all things. Third-wave **feminism** differentiates itself from its forerunner, second-wave feminism, by drawing on the multiple identities of the individual, redefining terms, and further exploring the concept of intersectionality—the way different aspects of one's **identity** are related. Young feminists of the third wave celebrate the pluralities of race, color, ethnicity, socioeconomic status and class, sexual orientation, nationality and geography, physical disability, and age to broaden the boundaries of previous feminisms that were often narrow in scope or altogether skipped over such characteristics. While **queer** women and women of color started mobilizing in the 1970s, their voices became most visible at the onset of the third wave. Queer women and women of color are claiming their own identities and demanding that their diverse experiences are recognized and validated.

The irony of the third wave is that the overwhelmingly American "rugged individual" premise, the concept that has brought women together in sisterhood, is also what has created, driven, and perpetuated **competition** and capitalism. However, individualism is still a central energy to a lot of third-wave subscribers, as many were reared in environments that reaped the rewards of foremothers' struggles with class, race, geography, and nationality. Third-wavers have had the luxury of growing up in a world that told them to be strong and self-assured. These messages have also created young women who do not claim to be feminist and do not recognize feminism as something with which they can identify. These are the same women who have been fed the American myth of equal opportunity and assimilation and were told that the women's movement was something of the past. Third-wave feminists are actively trying to dispel this dangerous myth by promoting ideas of inclusion and sisterhood while maintaining their individual multiple identities.

Third-wave **magazines** and online **zines** such as *Bust,* **Bitch,** and *Riot Grrrls* evolved out of the punk rock movement and created a space for young women to abandon traditional ideas of **femininity,** claim their innate individual power, and redefine themselves as they see fit. While Riot Grrrls' refusal to be "nice" is clearly third-wave ingenuity, the individualism within the third wave also embraces those **girlie** feminists who aim to drive out the myths of "**feminazis**" and educate young independent women, especially those known for opening sentences with, "I'm not a feminist, but ..." However, such individualistic ideals have created contention among feminists and cause many to wonder if it is still possible to have a collective feminist movement if feminists are to truly claim their individualism. Regardless, third-wave feminism has created a space where women of diverse backgrounds can discuss such divisive issues and raise their consciousnesses to new terms and conditions to make their individual voices heard.

Further Reading: Dicker, Rory, and Alison Piepmeier, eds., *Catching a Wave: Reclaiming Feminism for the 21st Century,* Boston: Northeastern University Press, 2003; Freedman, Estelle B., *No Turning Back: The History of Feminism and the Future of Women,* New York: Ballantine Books, 2002; Hernández, Daisy, and Bushra Rehman, eds., *Colonize This!: Young Women of Color on Today's Feminism,* New York: Seal Press, 2002; Heywood, Leslie, and Jennifer Drake, eds., *Third Wave Agenda: Being Feminist, Doing Feminism,* Minneapolis: University of Minnesota Press, 1997.

NEL P. SUNG

ISLAMIC FEMINISM. Islamic **feminism** is a general term to describe the work of Muslim women to improve the status of Muslim women globally. It is important to differentiate between Muslim feminists and Islamic feminists. Muslim feminists are women or men, some practicing Muslims and some of Muslim background, who are feminists. Islam may or may not matter to their feminism and may be treated as a potential ally in the fight for women's rights or a patriarchal and anti-feminist force, or as both simultaneously. Islamic feminists, however, are practicing Muslims who use Muslim tradition and belief to empower themselves and other women and as a framework for expanding women's rights. They emphasize the pro-woman history of Islam, including its early prohibitions on female infanticide; the fact that sharia, Islamic law, significantly improved women's rights within the seventh-century Arabian context; and the powerful symbols of early Muslim women. These symbolic women include Khadijah, the first wife of the Prophet Muhammad and first convert to Islam, who was a prominent businesswoman; Aisha, Muhammad's favorite wife, a major religious leader after his death and a political figure in the early Muslim community; and Fatima, the Prophet's daughter and a political actor in the breakup of Islam into Sunni and Shia sects. In contrast to some Western feminisms, and similarly to some **postcolonial feminisms**, most Islamic feminists believe in the importance of recognizing women as parts of cultural, religious, and **family** networks and of improving the status of women within these networks rather than by giving them independence from them. Beyond these starting points, however, Islamic feminists have different ways of using Muslim tradition to empower women. Some emphasize the importance of reinterpreting the Qur'an, the Muslim holy book, in ways that empower women, including by emphasizing the Qur'an rather than the hadith, or traditions and sayings of the Prophet, which are less empowering to women than men. These feminists argue that Islam in general terms proclaimed believing women and men to be equal in all ways in the sight of God; when it gave specific legal provisions, it substantially improved women's status. So, Islamic feminist scholars such as Amina Wadud argue that the Qur'an must be read as a document compelling progress toward human equality and social justice. She uses it to advocate for women's **equal rights** in the family and under the state, and Islamic feminists in Muslim countries argue concretely that this sort of interpretation lends itself toward the banning of practices such as polygamy, which are discouraged and limited, if permitted, in the Qur'an. Islamic feminists who emphasize reinterpretation can often find ways to make common cause with non-Islamic feminists, especially in countries where Islam is a politically powerful tool. For instance, in Egypt, Islamic and non-Islamic feminists joined forces to argue for a revision of **marriage** law that gave women more rights to control the terms of the marriage contract, using arguments based on what women are entitled to receive in the Qur'an and arguments based on women's rights without reference to Islam. However, another group of Islamic feminists argue that Islam provides a complete system for empowering women on their own terms, and that women are equivalent to men as believers but are different in their social position. These Islamic feminists often believe that women have a duty to stay home and care for children, but that this is an exalted position that demands respect from husbands and the state, or that women and men must be strictly separated in social life both so that they maintain sexual propriety and so that men and women treat each other equally. Some of these women may be involved with Islamist movements, commonly called **religious fundamentalisms** or political Islam in the United States, while others may be acting out of pure religious conviction. Many specific women's issues are common to all types of Islamic feminism. Marriage law is a very important issue; Islamic feminists argue against polygamy and in favor of women being given more control over the conditions of the marriage contract and the terms of divorce, including the right of a woman to maintain custody of her children, her ability to seek a divorce, and limits on her husband's ability to divorce her. Another major point is inheritance law; sharia gives women a smaller portion of inheritance than men, but in many Muslim countries women do not receive even that amount, so some Islamic feminists argue for a more equitable inheritance law while others argue for a different enforcement of the sharia-based law. Islamic feminists have worked to end female genital mutilation, a pre-Islamic practice in parts of Africa, by arguing that it is anti-Islamic. Outside of legal reform, Islamic feminists put a great emphasis on women's **empowerment**, including providing social services, literacy classes, and work skills training for women, and they also offer classes and study sessions to teach women about Islam and about the ways they can use Islam to empower themselves. An issue much on the minds of Western feminists is the wearing of various types of veils that cover women's hair or faces, and dress that conceals the **body**. Many Islamic feminists wear various sorts of veils, or *hijab*, while others do not. However, Islamic feminists insist that the veil is a symbol of personal devotion and propriety, and they do not believe that women should be compelled to wear a veil unless they choose to do so. But, Islamic feminists argue that women who choose to wear veils should not be deprived of the ability to enter public life, and they oppose the policies of countries such as Turkey, where veiled women may not be sworn in as members of parliament, or France, where young women are not allowed to veil in school.

See also Religion and Spirituality

Further Reading: Ahmed, Leila, *Women and Gender in Islam: Historical Roots of a Modern Debate*, New Haven, CT: Yale University Press, 1992; Fernea, Elizabeth Warnock, *In Search of Islamic Feminism: One Woman's Global Journey*, New York: Doubleday, 1998; Mernissi, Fatima, *The Veil and the Male Elite: A Feminist Interpretation of Women's Rights in Islam*, trans. Mary Jo Lakeland, Reading, MA: Addison-Wesley, 1991; Wadud, Amia, *Qur'an and Woman: Rereading the Sacred Text from a Woman's Perspective*, 2nd ed., New York: Oxford University Press, 1999.

EMILY REGAN WILLS

K

KLEIN, NAOMI. Naomi Klein (1970–) is a Canadian activist and journalist whose work criticizes the trends of **consumerism** and the monolithic influence of conglomerate corporations. Klein's involvement in organizing the 1999 **Seattle protests** and her 2000 book, *No Logo*, represent the third-wave feminist commitment to ending oppressions on many levels. Klein's work deals with the effects of the increasingly globalized economy, largely dominated by North American corporations, and its impact on people and the environment worldwide. Klein's work reflects a characteristically broad scope that connects individual choices and issues to global matters of exploitation. Typical of **cultural activism**, her critique contributes to a growing dissatisfaction among the third-wave generation feminists who are aware of the culpable role that consumer habits in North America play in the exploitive labor conditions that result from companies going overseas to maximize profits.

Klein's critiques of the brand-name mindset identifies that the onslaught of advertisements contribute to individual concerns over authenticity and beliefs about personal success. On the social level, her work identifies the wider-scale dangers posed by consumerism. Product manufacturing, often occurring in nations with unregulated labor, involves the exploitation of labor and frequently the environment. By connecting the dots between so-called "First-World" consumption and Third-World manufacturing, Klein calls in to question the culture of "marketplace values."

See also Globalization

Further Reading: Klein, Naomi, *No Logo*, New York: Picador USA, 2000; Viner, Katherine, "Hand-To-Brand Combat: A Profile of Naomi Klein," Common Dreams News Center Web Site, http://www.commondreams.org/cgi?file=/views/092300-103.htm.

ERIKA FEIGENBAUM

L

LATINA FEMINISM. A distinct part of the third wave, Latina **feminism** is a general term to describe the movement and worldview of feminists who identify as Latinas. Latina and Latino are gendered nouns that refer to individuals who are from a Latin American country or are of Latin American descent and reside in the United States. Hispanic is another term often used to describe people of Latin American descent. The term Hispanic has been criticized, however, because it overemphasizes the Spanish European ancestry of Latin Americans. Many Latin Americans have Spanish ancestry as well as indigenous and/or African ancestry.

At 13 percent of the population, Latinos currently are the largest minority group in the United States. Latinos have immigrated to the United States from a number of Latin American countries. Latin America includes Mexico, parts of the Caribbean, and all of Central and South America. Some Mexican Americans have ancestors who lived in the Southwest before the United States conquered the land from Mexico in the 1800s. Most Latinas living in the United States are of Mexican, Puerto Rican, Central American, or Cuban heritage or nationality. Mexicans represent the largest nationality among Latinos in the United States; approximately 58 percent of the Latino population is Mexican.

Latinas are a diverse group because they represent many nationalities, ethnicities, and cultures. How strongly a Latina identifies with her Latin American heritage may depend in part on whether she is a native to the United States or an immigrant. More than 60 percent of Latinas residing in the United States were born there, while approximately 40 percent of Latinas are immigrants. Latina immigrants are likely to speak Spanish, whereas Latinas who were born in the United States are likely to speak English. Many Latinas, especially second-generation immigrants, are bilingual.

Latinas have a long history of involvement in the struggle for equality and justice. Latinas' involvement in the fight for equality has extended beyond the traditional areas of women's rights to include advocacy on behalf of workers and other disadvantaged groups. For example, Dolores Huerta, a pioneer Latina feminist and leader of the United Farm Workers Union, played an important role in organizing farm workers in their fight against exploitative working conditions. Latina feminists have also fought alongside revolutionaries in Mexico, Cuba, and Central America. Today, many Latina feminists are involved in the human rights movement at the domestic and international levels.

Latinas have also participated in the mainstream women's rights movement. During the second wave of feminism, Latina feminists fought for women's equality and reproductive rights. One of the most celebrated Latina reproductive rights activists was Helen Rodriguez-Trias, a Puerto Rican physician who helped expand access to **abortion** and reduce forced sterilization of Latinas in the 1970s. Despite their involvement, Latinas, along with other women of color who identify as feminists, have criticized the predominately white mainstream women's movement for failing to adequately represent and advocate on behalf of Latinas. Specifically, Latina feminists have argued that the mainstream movement has not fully addressed the intersecting forms of oppression and injustice that affect women who are racial/ethnic minorities.

To address the specific needs and challenges facing Latinas, Latina feminists developed a Latina feminism movement, which reflects the diversity of the Latina population. As a result, there is no single definition of Latina feminism; Latina feminism means different things to different Latinas. Although Latina feminism has many forms, most Latina feminists share the common goal of eliminating the intersecting forms of oppression that Latinas experience because of their unique identities. Latinas face inequalities and **discrimination** as a result of their gender, race, ethnicity, and immigration status. Many Latinas, especially those who are immigrants, also face cultural and linguistic barriers. Lesbian Latinas often experience homophobia and **heterosexism**. Certain cultural practices, such as *machismo* and *marianismo*, and religious beliefs can also contribute to the subordination of Latinas. Recognizing that Latinas are subject to sexism, classism, **racism**, heterosexism, and xenophobia and that they experience these forms of prejudice in the general society and the Latino community, Latina feminists aim to challenge all social systems and structures that perpetuate inequalities and advocate for social justice for all Latinas. Their agenda includes eliminating racial, gender, and socioeconomic inequalities, as well as politically empowering Latinas and their communities.

Latina feminism is also influenced by a **desire** to improve Latinas' quality of life. Latinas disproportionately suffer from high rates of school drop-out, unemployment, poverty, and teen pregnancy. Latina feminists, aware of the problems many Latinas face, focus on issues that relate to the economic and spiritual well-being of Latinas and their families. Through scholarship, public **education**, and political advocacy, Latina feminists advocate for Latinas in the areas of employment, poverty, education, health, childcare, and reproductive rights.

Although these are the overarching goals of Latina feminists, the movement itself takes many forms. For example, Chicana feminism is a Latina feminist movement that focuses on how inequalities in the areas of race, class, gender, and **sexuality** affect Chicanas—women or **girls** of Mexican descent who were born or raised in the United States. People began to use the term Chicana/o to describe themselves during the Chicano movement of the1960s and 1970s. In this movement, Mexican Americans advocated for civil, political, and socioeconomic rights for their community. They also fought against the pervasive racial inequality that existed at the time. The Chicana feminist movement emerged from this **identity**-affirming Mexican American movement as well as the mainstream feminist movement. Chicanas are credited with **writing** many of the pioneering works of the Latina feminist movement.

Mujerista is another Latina feminist movement. A Mujerista is a Latina who is fighting against gender and race/ethnicity–based oppression in Latino communities and in society at large. The Latina feminists who created the term "Mujerista" were responding to concerns that the word feminist has negative connotations among Latinas, especially those who consider themselves religious. They also believed that the feminist movement did not account for the racial/ethnic inequalities that Latinas face in the United States and that the feminist movement had not taken the Latina perspective seriously.
See also Volume 2, Primary Documents 9, 22, 28, and 61

Further Reading: Anzaldúa, Gloria, *Borderlands/La Frontera: The New Mestiza*, San Francisco: Aunt Lute Press, 1987; Ikas, Karin Rosa, *Chicana Ways: Conversations with Ten Chicana Writers*, Reno: University of Nevada Press, 2002; Latina Feminist Group, *Telling to Live: Latina Feminist Testimonios*, Durham, NC: Duke University Press, 2001.

ANGELA HOOTON

LEWINSKY, MONICA. Former White House intern Monica Lewinsky came to the public's attention in the mid-1990s after she was subpoenaed by lawyers in the Paula Jones **sexual harassment** lawsuit against Bill Clinton, when he was governor of Arkansas. At the time Lewinsky denied any sexual relationship with President Clinton, but it was later uncovered in secretly recorded conversations with her confidante, Linda Tripp, who worked at the Pentagon, that she indeed did have a sexual relationship with the president.

Like many women of her generation who grew up exposed to second-wave **feminism**, Lewinsky evokes the contradictions inherent in many young women's sexual and professional lives, as she uses discourses associated with "power feminism" and "**victim feminism**." In many ways she symbolizes the problems women of the third-wave face: while benefiting from many second-wave efforts, there are still barriers and contradictions to deal with, such as negotiating a sexual and professional **identity**. Lewinsky has been characterized as a victim, a tramp, and even an opportunist by critics, and indeed, it seems from all accounts fairly difficult to put any one label on her actions. The daughter of wealthy Beverly Hills, California, parents, Lewinsky came to the White House in 1995 as a twenty-one-year-old intern, where she first met Clinton. They began an on-again, off-again relationship in November, which Clinton finally ended one year later.

Lewinsky's cultural celebrity resulted in an appearance on *20/20* with Barbara Walters in March 1999 to promote her book *Monica's Story*. She was also featured in a diet plan ad campaign, before venturing into business with her own line of women's handbags. Lewinsky was also the host of a short-lived reality **television** series called *Mr. Personality*.

Further Reading: Liebovich, Louis, *The Press and Modern Presidency: Myths and Mindsets from Kennedy to Election 2000*, Westport, CT: Praeger, 2001; Monica Lewinsky Web site: http://www.therealmonica.com.

Natasha Patterson

LIL' KIM. A good example of third-wave feminist contradiction, Lil' Kim (1975–), born Kimberly Jones, is the stage name of the hip-hop artist and celebrity also known as "Queen Bee." Jones became known through her association with Notorious B.I.G., the legendary hip-hop artist also known as Biggie Smalls. Biggie helped launch Jones' career as the only female performer in Junior M.A.F.I.A.'s 1995 debut album. A year later, Jones released her debut solo LP, *Hard Core*, which immediately became a hit. In 1997, Biggie was murdered by gunshot in Los Angeles (only weeks before his second album, *Life After Death*, was released). The death of her mentor affected Jones, and her recording career briefly slowed. However, in 2000, Jones released her second album, *Notorious K.I.M.*, on the record label she founded, Queen Bee Records. The album, an obvious tribute to Biggie, was immediately successful, solidifying her career as a solo artist. Jones has consistently expanded her career, acting in **films** and making countless guest appearances with other hip-hop artists.

While her **music** is very popular, Jones remains a controversial public figure. She is often critiqued as reinforcing stereotypical and negative **media** images of black women. However, others applaud Jones as a powerful and intelligent marketer, able to capitalize on popular ideals and sell herself as a celebrity. Jones' lyrics and persona are explicitly sexual, and she is frequently portrayed as a gold-digger, or a woman who uses her lovers to become wealthier. Alternately, Jones portrays herself as rich, powerful, and independent. Her songs frequently imply sexual dominance, such as when she orders men to perform oral sex.

Although she gets her nickname from her short stature, Jones' more obvious trademark is her hair, a constantly shifting assortment of multicolored wigs. Because she sometimes wears long blonde wigs and colored contact lenses, Jones has been accused of catering to racist standards of beauty. Others contend that Jones' over-the-top image is ironic, highlighting the fact that such ideals are constructed and may be obtained with sufficient money. Notably, however, Jones does not only portray white-centered standards of beauty but has used wigs and costuming to suggest a variety of ethnic stereotypes (e.g., harem **girl**, Cleopatra, geisha, mafia gangster).

Jones' manipulations of her **body** (her significant weight loss after her first album, and her breast implants and nose job) have been highly publicized. Jones has defended herself, arguing that such modifications enhance her image as a celebrity. Her video "How Many Licks" exploits this issue, portraying Lil' Kim as an edible candy doll available in three fantasy styles. The video, which shows Jones as she is molded on a factory production line, is a playful acknowledgment that Lil' Kim, the celebrity, is a marketed ideal. Despite her critics, Jones' appeal to popular fantasy, her tough, sexy attitude, and her talent continue to make her an immensely popular artist.

See also Hip-Hop Feminism; Music

Further Reading: Lil' Kim Official Web site, http://www.lilkim.com; Pough, Gwendolyn, *Check It While I Wreck It: Black Womanhood, Hip-hop Culture, and the Public Sphere*, Boston: Northeastern University Press, 2004; VIBE/SPIN Ventures LLC, *Hip-Hop Divas*, New York: Three Rivers Press, 2001.

TERESA SIMONE

LIPSTICK LESBIAN. The term "lipstick lesbian" originated in the early 1990s and has several associated definitions. The most common is a "lesbian who is beautiful, stylish, or markedly feminine"; that is, a lesbian who has all the conventional feminine signs such as long hair, makeup, or high heels. Some use lipstick lesbian synonymously with "femme lesbian," but this is not always the case because others believe there is a difference between the two. Disputably, the difference is that a "lipstick lesbian" is more defined by outward appearances and a femme lesbian is defined more by a deep **identity** rather than an outward appearance. It is also suggested that they differ in that lipstick lesbians only want to date other feminine lesbians, whereas femme lesbians want to date more masculine lesbians, but this difference is disputed because it inaccurately generalizes across personalities and preferences. Some lesbians are offended by the term "lipstick lesbian" because it is often used to describe other lesbians in a derogatory way. Some lesbians think that it minimizes them because it may have to do with the assumption that wearing makeup/looking pretty can only be to attract men (and therefore any lesbian wearing it is still trying to appeal to men in some way). Third-wave feminists do not see feminine signifiers as negative and see affirmative possibilities for identity through their use.

See also Butch/Femme

Further Reading: Cogan, Jeanine, and Joanie M. Erickson, *Lesbians, Levis and Lipstick: The Meaning of Beauty in Our Lives*, Haworth Gay and Lesbian Studies, http://www.wordspy.com/words/lipsticklesbian.asp; http://www.belladonna.org/lipglossary.html.

KRISTINE SISBARRO

LOVE, COURTNEY. An icon to many third-wave feminists and self-proclaimed feminist, grunge singer/songwriter Courtney Love (1964–) was born Love Michelle Harrison and later renamed Courtney Michelle Harrison by her mother. Known for both her wild behavior and her **music**, Love has been called everything from the "queen of grunge" to a "rock 'n roll diva." In 1989, Love formed Hole, a band that released three full-length albums that discussed the difficulties of womanhood, from prostitution to fame, on a backdrop of distorted guitars and Love's screaming vocals. In 1992, she married grunge band Nirvana front man Kurt Cobain, who later committed suicide. Characteristic of the patriarchal culture she criticizes, Love's style and music were overshadowed by the **media**'s depictions of her court dates and tabloid escapades relating to drug charges and child custody. Although her music, especially 1994's "Doll Parts," attacked stereotypes of beauty and **femininity** and challenged ideas of female autonomy and was a major feminist intervention, her outspoken criticisms were often used to dismiss her. Her early image, dubbed "kinderwhore" for her short baby-doll dresses, bleached blonde hair, and smeared lipstick, provoked the media to call her the icon for the new wave of feminist rockers. Despite granting her "icon" status, however, the media always represented Love according to the very sexist stereotypes she was trying to question—as a sexualized object. Outside criticism of her personal life and views has been a major part of Love's career, from those who claim she profited from both Cobain's life and suicide to *Vanity Fair*'s article claiming that Love used heroin while she was pregnant with her daughter, Frances Bean, to her image change in later years to a slick, surgically enhanced star. Love is a controversial symbol of many of the contradictions inherent in third-wave **feminism**.
See also Music

Further Reading: Brite, Poppy Z., *Courtney Love: The Real Story*, New York: Simon and Schuster, 1997; Courtney Love Internet Movie Database, http://www.imdb.com/name/nm0001482/; O'Dair, Barbara, ed., *Trouble Girls: The Rolling Stone Book of Women in Rock*, New York: Random House, 1997; Raphael, Amy, *Grrrls: Viva Rock Divas*, New York: St. Martin's Griffin, 1996.

BREA GRANT

M

MAGAZINES, MEN'S. General-interest magazines were the first kind to appear in the United States, becoming popular in the last two decades of the nineteenth century. Magazines geared specifically toward women, such as the *Ladies' Home Journal*, preceded those geared toward men. *Esquire*, a general-interest men's magazine still in existence today, was founded in 1933, the worst year of the Depression, by William Randolph Hearst. One of its trademarks was the inclusion of **writings** by top literary men of the day, including F. Scott Fitzgerald and Ernest Hemingway. *GQ* is a peer of *Esquire*. Appearing in 1931 as *Apparel Arts*, then known as *Esquire's Apparel Arts*, and later changing its name to *Gentleman's Quarterly* before settling on its current incarnation in 1983, it is published in different international versions today and is devoted to high-class living, from haute couture to the latest **sports** cars.

Appreciation (some might call it objectification) of beautiful women has always been a major facet of men's magazines. This was especially true in the 1960s, when *Esquire's* popularity increased because of the "Vargas Girls," women featured in each issue in titillating paintings by Alberto Vargas. Vargas had been marketing such work since 1919. Pictures of women became a more important part of men's magazine content in the latter half of the twentieth century, probably due in large part to the emergence of *Playboy* magazine.

Playboy, founded in 1953 by Hugh Hefner, was similar to *Esquire*, although it is known today as a much racier magazine. The combination of thought-provoking stories and journalism with pinup **girls** was designed to appeal to a wide range of men, and the images were coy in a way that made them more appropriate than pornographic literature distributed in a more clandestine **fashion**. *Playboy*, whose first centerfold was Marilyn Monroe, also counted many of the day's top male scribes among its contributors—Norman Mailer, Joseph Heller, and John Updike are just a few. Interviews with presidents and other figures important to global politics, such as Fidel Castro, added to the magazine's acceptability. Still popular today, including many versions published internationally, *Playboy* has always aimed to speak to a male sensibility that is cosmopolitan, debonair, and heterosexual.

In the final decade of the twentieth century, a new breed of men's magazines appeared. Including examples such as *Maxim*, *FHM* (*For Him Magazine*), and *Stuff*, these magazines do not aim to be cerebral. Including crass jokes, a high graphics-to-text ratio, and scantily clad (though not nude) girls aplenty, this proliferation reflects, perhaps, a **desire** of the modern man to have a brief escape from reality and the high-stress lifestyle of the modern age. It may also be a response to the number of women rapidly rising to positions in business and politics equal to those that have been considered men-only for many years: an affirmation that women are best seen and not heard and are safest when objectified. A survey of articles appearing recently in *Maxim* includes the following: "Sex Express: How to Spot the Girl with a Condom in Her Purse" (June 2002), "'Dost Thou Cometh Here Often?' *Maxim*'s Unbelievable History of Sex" (February 2001), and "Tonight's the Night! 40 Totally Unfair Pick-Up Tricks" (May 2004).

For young men, as well as women, magazines have long been one of the tools through which they form ideas about what society expects of them. In both the articles and the advertisements, there are silent instructions about the "appropriate" way for men to act in all aspects of their lives, from career to leisure time to romantic relationships. However, most contemporary American mass-**media** publications still fail to accurately portray the diversity of the country itself or the numerous possibilities open to either gender today.

See also Pornography, Feminism and

Further Reading: Gauntlett, David, *Media, Gender and Identity: An Introduction*, New York: Routledge, 2002; GQ magazine, http://www.GQ.com; http://www.fhm-magazin.de; http://www.maximonline.de; Werkmeister, Meike, "Men's Magazines in Germany," http://theoryhead.com/gender/germany.htm.

JESSICA MANACK

MAGAZINES, WOMEN'S. Women's magazines have been identified as both friend and foe to third-wave feminists. On one hand, numerous feminists have criticized women's magazines for presenting and perpetuating unrealistic ideals for women such as "super mom/woman" ideals. Others critique the magazines for failing to show more than one **beauty ideal**: young, white, and thin, which often results in women feeling inadequate. On the other hand, feminists have learned that the magazine format is a powerful form and in numerous ways have co-opted the magazine format to create feminist space.

History. The first mass circulation magazine for women published in the United States began in 1792. Before the Civil War, women's magazines in this country were aimed toward the elite. After the Civil War, however, technological advances, in conjunction with the Postal Act of 1879, made the cost affordable to middle-class (the vast majority of whom were white) women, exponentially expanding the magazine's target audience. To be sure, consider that in 1865 there were 700 women's magazines, but just two decades later in 1865 there were 4,400 women's periodicals. The leaders of the pack, known as the "Big Six," emerged during this time, and half of them are still in publication today. These are *McCall's, Ladies Home Journal,* and *Good Housekeeping.* From the outset, **advertising** has played a fundamental role in the development and content of women's magazines. Indeed some journals, such as *McCall's,* were started with the explicit aim of product promotion.

Historically, women's magazines have been commercial, with profits motivating their production, but a handful of early publications served as a voice for the feminist community. For example, Elizabeth Cady Stanton and Susan B. Anthony published a weekly entitled *The Revolution* in 1868. Furthermore, a limited number of journals were specifically aimed toward racial and ethnic minorities, including *The Women's Era* (1894–1903), which targeted African American women, and *American Jewess* (1895–1899).

The modern era of women's magazines began after World War II, when **television** became a serious challenge to magazine consumption. Indeed, readers turned to magazines less and less for relaxation and entertainment and more for informational purposes. By the 1960s, a mixed group of carryovers from the Big Six and newcomer magazines had established themselves as leaders of the women's magazine industry, and they were dubbed the "Seven Sisters." They were *Ladies Home Journal, McCall's, Good Housekeeping, Family Circle, Women's Day, Redbook,* and *Better Homes and Gardens.*

The beginning of the 1970s began a vast wave of niche magazines, such as *Essence,* that targeted the African American women's audience; *Teen, YM, Seventeen,* which catered especially to teens and young women; and **fashion** magazines *Elle* and *Mirabella.* Although these magazines failed to reach the masses in the way that the Seven Sisters did, they are highly popular with advertisers because they allow for more targeted advertising.

During the explosion of women's niche magazines, feminist magazines have emerged as well. *Ms.* was established in the early 1970s after it was tested with a 300,000-circulation trial run. Remarkably, all 300,000 copies were sold out in eight days. This trial yielded some 26,000 subscriptions and more than 20,000 letters from readers. *Ms.* has had financial difficulty over the years, in large part because of its commitment to keep out advertising that poses a conflict of interest with its text, yet it is still in print, more than three decades after it began. *Ms.* was certainly the most celebrated magazine to come out of the second wave, but it was not alone. For example, *Off Our Backs,* which describes itself as a news journal, began publication in 1970, making it the nation's oldest feminist magazine that is still in publication. *Lilith,* which caters to Jewish women, began publication in 1976 and also remains in print today.

The emergence of third-wave **feminism** has brought a new crop of feminist magazines. *Bust: Voice of the New Girl Order* and **Bitch**: *A Feminist Response to Pop Culture* are among the most popular. Furthermore, there is an expanding variety of niche magazines within the subset of feminist magazines, such as feminist **music** magazines like *Venus* and *Rock Grrl*.

In addition to what is available at the local newsstand, numerous third-wave feminists, not satisfied with the content of mass publication magazines, have taken matters into their own hands and written, published, and distributed their own **zines**. These homemade, small-circulation publications discuss the entire spectrum of issues facing young feminists today and range from sex workers rights, to being a feminist teenage mom, and everything in between. Zines are widely celebrated among many young feminists because they allow for an open dialog about real issues faced by women that are not discussed by mainstream society. In addition, not only do they allow for the disenfranchised to have a voice, they also allow for women who do not share the experiences of the zine writers to have an inside look into topics they may otherwise never be exposed to.

Critique of Mainstream Women's Magazines. Despite the ever-increasing number of feminist magazines and zines, they are very much niche magazines and do not have the mass circulation that the Seven Sisters have.

Many feminists claim that mainstream women's magazines are in the business of selling fantasies so their readers will in turn buy products. Common to these magazines are portrayals of women in "super mom" roles who effortlessly balance their family and work lives and have plenty of time left over for self-beautification, or the idea that all women should be waif thin. Indeed, some feminists will suggest that portraying unrealistic ideals of women as normal entices women to buy a product. Consider, for example, today's culture's obsession with thinness. The last few decades have seen the "ideal" woman size shrink as the profit margins of the diet industry have dramatically increased. Consider in 1991 the diet industry was estimated to be worth $33 billion a year annually, whereas in 2004 the industry is estimated to be worth $50 billion a year.

See also Volume 2, Primary Document 35

Further Reading: Grrrl Zine Network Web site, http://www.grrrlzines.net/; Wolf, Naomi, *The Beauty Myth*, New York: Anchor Books, 1991; Zuckerman, Mary Ellen, *A History of Popular Women's Magazines in the United States, 1792–1995*, Westport, CT: Greenwood Press, 1998.

Laura Gladney-Lemon

MALE BODY. Feminist theorists have always been concerned with the **body** and its impact on meanings of gender and **sexuality**. Second-wave feminists concentrated mainly on female bodies. Germaine Greer, in the book *The Female Eunuch* (1970), traced how the female body had been defined by Western society. Greer pointed out that a woman's gender and sexual **identity** were tied to her biological sex, and drawing on the **writings** of psychologist Sigmund

Freud, her body was defined as lacking a penis. Thus, a woman's body was defined as being less than a man's. The result of this conclusion was that women were viewed as less capable than men and their physical differences, such as being able to have children and being generally physically weaker than men, created oppressive and restrictive ideologies of **femininity** and the roles women were expected to play in society. Second-wave feminist academics, therefore, sought to reclaim and celebrate the female body and consequently liberate women from the oppressive gender ideologies; the male body was only in focus insofar as it was seen as being defined by culture as superior.

In the late 1970s and early 1980s, the French philosopher Michel Foucault widened and intensified the focus on the body. Foucault believed that power in society operated on an individual level and that it was more worthwhile to study power at this level, than, for example, to focus attention on the state. In *Discipline and Punish* (1979) and *The History of Sexuality* (1978), Foucault traced how understandings of the body had changed throughout history so that society could be controlled and regulated. Ideas of appropriate sexual identity had been worked into meanings of the body in the late nineteenth century, and gay men and lesbian women had become stigmatized as a result. The body in contemporary culture, according to Foucault, was a site of power struggle, with gays and some women resisting what society had deemed "natural" practices for their bodies.

Third-wave feminists investigate the male body in its own right and seek to further destabilize the assumed links between the body, gender, and sexuality. **Judith Butler**, in *Gender Trouble* (1999) and *Bodies That Matter* (1993), built on Foucault's theories and challenged the notion that gender identity and sexuality are tied to the body (even though society assumes that they are). Butler accepted that assumptions are made about how a man or woman's body should be and what is therefore appropriate sexual behavior. However, she believes that sexuality, gender, and **desire** are fluid and artificial and untied to anyone's body: masculinity can be embodied by a woman's body as easily as femininity can be embodied by a man's. A gay man's desires are practically no different from a heterosexual man's desires; both bodily desires are equally as constructed and changeable. The male body, in this conception, performs its gender identity like wearing clothes. Butler believes that men who dress in drag perform a feminine gender identity and reveal how false mainstream society's understandings of the body, gender, and sexuality really are.

There are other ways in which the male body is investigated by third-wave feminists. It has long been noted that the imagery of the male body in society has been a powerful means for political, economic, and social leaders to create the society they desire. One example of this power can be seen in the effects of militarization on society and the male body. The British government in the Victorian era was shocked and concerned when a large proportion of the men who volunteered to fight in the Boer War were physically unfit for service. As a result, the government encouraged the Boy Scout movement and team **sports** to be played in school; they created hegemonic ideals in society where boys were encouraged to be physically fit, competitive, and tough. Boys who were fit and sporty would make good soldiers and protect Britain's empire and power. This example makes Foucault's point that the male body is a political tool upon which power concerns are at the center. Although this is a historical example, any nation that has an army and conducts **war** will need to encourage men to mold their bodies and conduct themselves in a way that suits the government's needs, and contemporary Western society is just as, if not more, militarized than Victorian Britain.

Cultural Studies academics base their research on the understanding that culture has political consequences, and they look at how culture affects the way men view and use their bodies and the related impact this has on identity. In the 1980s, the culture of Western societies began to dramatically change as free market and pro-capitalist governments encouraged consumer spending and a love of material possessions and advancement. Advertisements, movies, and men's spending habits and lifestyles began to change, creating new understandings of the male body. Second-wave feminists realized advertisements presented women as objects to be owned, desired, and gazed upon by men and that women as a group were viewed as consumers and spenders whereas men worked and earned the money. In the 1980s and 1990s, however, men became major material consumers. Consumer goods such as aftershave, clothes, and hair-care and facial products have become as much a part of achieving the perfect male body as they have always been a part of women's lifestyles. It had been commonplace for women to be erotically placed and scantily dressed in **advertising** images; images of men came to be presented in the same way. Third-wave feminists have wondered whether advertisements aimed at men, presenting male models in provocative and even homoerotic poses, have led to men becoming as much objects of desire as women once were. The 1990s Calvin Klein aftershave CKOne and its accompanying advertising campaign has been viewed as an example of the changing understandings of the male body in society. In the advertisements were male and female models whose bodies appeared to be very similar, and whose sexuality could be interpreted as straight or gay. It seemed as if Butler's point about the body, gender, and sexuality had been incorporated into Klein's appeal to his consumers. Gone are the days when the female body was petite and "feminine" and men muscular, tough, macho, "masculine," and heterosexual. The images associated with the male body will continue to change and adapt, and the way men view themselves and their role in society will always be a target of feminist research.

See also Consumerism; Magazines, Men's

Further Reading: Butler, Judith, *Bodies That Matter: On the Discursive Limits of Sex*, New York: Routledge, 1993; Butler, Judith, *Gender Trouble: Feminism and the Subversion of Identity*, 2nd ed., New York: Routledge, 1999; Chapman, Rowena, and Jonathan Rutherford, eds., *Male Order: Unwrapping Masculinity*, London: Lawrence and Wishart, 1988; Edwards, Tim, *Men in the Mirror: Men's Fashion, Masculinity and Consumer*

Society, New York: Continuum, 1997; Foucault, Michel, *Discipline and Punish: The Birth of the Prison*, Harmondsworth: Penguin, 1979; Foucault, Michel, *The History of Sexuality*, New York: Pantheon, 1978; Greer, Germaine, *The Female Eunuch*, New York: Penguin, 1971; Watson, Jonathan, *Male Bodies: Health, Culture and Identity*, Philadelphia: Open University Press, 2000.

DANIEL CONWAY

MANJI, IRSHAD. Irshad Manji (1968–) is a Canadian Muslim lesbian and feminist, **television** host and producer, and writer. First known for her work with the Canadian television program *Queer Television*, her major work to date is the controversial and best-selling book *The Trouble with Islam: A Muslim's Call for Reform in Her Faith* (2004). In the book, Manji describes her problems with modern Islam, especially its poor treatment of women and intolerance for other religions, which she blames on an overly literal interpretation of the Qur'an, an absence of critical thinking, and tribal notions of Muslim community. She argues that Western Muslims and non-Muslim allies should engage in a reformation through *ijtihad* (critical thinking and reevaluation of ideas). She emphasizes the need to empower Muslim women, specifically through the creation of microcredit programs, which are small-lending development programs that give women the ability to start their own businesses and establish financial lives apart from **family** members. Throughout her book, Manji connects her gender consciousness to her problem with Islam, discussing her father's abuse of her mother, the gender segregation and **discrimination** in the *madrassa* (Islamic school) she attended in her youth, and Muslim homophobia. Her book sparked intense reactions, positive and negative, from Muslims and non-Muslims. Many applaud her for breaking through silences in Muslim communities about problems; others are disturbed by her quickness to vilify Islam as a system and her lack of historical perspective. Some consider her brash and outspoken manner refreshing; others find it adolescent and alienating. Manji has received death threats for her outspokenness and her **sexuality**. Besides *The Trouble with Islam*, Manji is the author of *Risking Utopia* (1997). She lives in Toronto with her partner.
See also Islamic Feminism

Further Reading: Manji, Irshad, *The Trouble with Islam: A Muslim's Call for Reform in Her Faith*, New York: St. Martin's Press, 2004; Muslim Refusenik: The Official Website of Irshad Manji, author of *The Trouble with Islam*, http://www.muslimrefusenik.com/.

EMILY REGAN WILLS

MARCH FOR WOMEN'S LIVES. After a culmination of a week of events, 1,150,000 people, many of them third-wave feminists, marched on the National Mall in Washington, D.C., on April 25, 2004, to voice opposition to the government attacks on women's reproductive rights and health. The march was to uphold choice, justice, access, health care, **abortion**, and global and **family** planning and was a collaborative effort among seven organizing groups and other cosponsors including the American Civil Liberties Union, Black Women's Health Imperative, Feminist Majority, NARAL Pro-Choice America, National Latina Institute for Reproductive Health, National Organization for Women, and Planned Parenthood Federation of America. Marchers also included more than a hundred actors and artists, and many participants carried signs and shouted assertions such as Our Bodies Our Lives; Don't Mess with Texas Women; Liberty is Freedom of Choice; Vote As If Your Life Depends on It; It's Her Choice, Y'all; I Love Michigan Vaginas; Against Abortion? Have a Vasectomy; Pro-faith Pro-family Pro-choice; sex-ed = safe sex; Physicians for Reproductive Choice and Health; Grandma Marched, Mom Marched, Now I March; We Demand Emergency Contraception Over the Counter; No Mandatory Pregnancy; and Keep Abortion Legal.

Over the past several years, many of women's reproductive rights and health options have been challenged by lawmakers. The "Global Gag Rule," which prevents access to reproductive information internationally, was reintroduced. The current Supreme Court, with many justices close to retirement, hangs on a one-vote favor of women's reproductive rights and health. The Partial-Birth Abortion Ban, created in 2003, is one of several strategies to eventually destroy the reproductive rights that **Roe v. Wade** granted in 1973. Current officials for the Department of Health and Human Services deny government assistance to single mothers and cohabitating couples and promote **marriage** to women needing that assistance. Additionally, federal funding cannot currently be used for abortion. Most counties in the United States lack abortion providers. Forty-four million Americans do not have health insurance, the preponderance of who are women and children.

Because of these attacks on women's reproductive rights and health, the March for Women's Lives chose to focus on choice, justice, access, health care, abortion, and global and family planning. The goal was to increase access to safe and affordable family planning and reproductive services to women, regardless of location or income, while also ensuring that women have the right of choice to have children or not and thus have control over their own bodies. The march also addressed global and domestic polices that affect **women's health** and reproductive rights while also looking at how women are treated by medical institutions based on age, race, and income.

Further Reading: March for Women's Lives Web site, http://www.marchforwomen. org/; Sanger, Alexander, *Beyond Choice: Reproductive Freedom in the 21st Century*, New York: Public Affairs, 2004; Solinger, Rickie, *Beggars and Choosers: How the Politics of Choice Shapes Adoption, Abortion, and Welfare in the United States*, New York: Hill and Wang, 2001.

LAURA MADELINE WISEMAN

MARRIAGE. In the United States today, "marriage" usually denotes a state-and/or church-sanctioned monogamous union between two consenting, unrelated, heterosexual adults, which grants them certain rights and obligations.

Couples can be married in a civil ceremony by an official representing the state or in a religious ceremony by a church official. In some states, couples living together for an extended period of time are married by "common law," without a civic or religious ceremony.

Marriage in the Third Wave. The shape of marriage has changed with the rise of third-wave **feminism**. In 1970, the average age at marriage was 20.8 years for women and 23.2 years for men. However, as of 1997, the average age at marriage had risen to 25 years for women and 26.8 years for men. There are many reasons for this change. For example, being a single woman does not have the stigma that it once did, and third-wavers are disinclined to rush into a marriage. Many young adults want to earn a degree, establish a career, and be financially stable before marrying. They also want to avoid the high rate of divorce that plagued their parents' generation in the 1980s.

Third-wave couples are open to a variety of arrangements within a marriage. The post–World War II suburban ideal was the husband as breadwinner and the wife as homemaker. Today, many wives work outside the home, and the third-wave ideal is for the wife and husband to share the housework and finances as equal partners. Many married couples plan to remain childless and other couples are waiting longer to have children. Some women choose to stay home once their children are born, but there is an increasing acceptance of stay-at-home dads, too.

In another major cultural shift, same-sex couples and their supporters are advocating for legalization of **same-sex unions/gay marriage**. Vermont legalized same-sex unions in 2000 and Massachusetts legalized same-sex marriages in 2004, though this has since been repealed. Conservative groups oppose same-sex marriage, arguing that only heterosexual marriage is natural. Third-wave feminists might argue that marriage is not "natural," but rather an institution that was created and defined by people. Its definitions and requirements have shifted across time and space.

Shifting Definitions and Requirements. A church or state authority's approval has not always been a prerequisite of marriage. In the medieval world, couples who had intercourse and/or who cohabited were assumed to be married. Gradually, the Catholic Church restricted the definition of marriage, finally making marriage a sacrament that a priest must administer.

Another variable is monogamy versus polygamy. In the non-Western world, polygamy has long been normal: in the pre-Islamic Arab world, a man could marry as many women as he wished, but the Qur'an restricts Islamic men to four wives at most, each of whom he must treat equally. Polygamy was also practiced in U.S. territories in the 1800s with the approval of the Church of Jesus Christ of Latter-day Saints (the Mormon Church), but the Church had banned it by 1890 in response to the U.S. government's outlawing of polygamy in 1882.

The degree of relatedness acceptable in a couple seeking to marry has also changed. For example, in early France, one could not marry someone descended from great-great-great-great-great grandparents. Then, in the year 1215, this restriction was reduced, so that only the descendents of one's great-great grand-parents were off limits. What constitutes kinship has been redefined according to the needs and social mores of the time.

Finally, there were once numerous state bans on interracial marriage, but the U.S. Supreme Court ruled them unenforceable in 1967. Although there are still areas where interracial marriage is stigmatized, every state whose constitution prohibited interracial marriage has repealed that ban; South Carolina and Alabama were the last to officially do so, in 1998 and 2000, respectively.

Rites and Obligations of Marriage in the United States. Marriage grants a couple various rights and obligations. On a social level, marriage permits a couple to engage in sexual intercourse and to have children with society's approval. It also grants social acceptance and understanding of the intense emotional bonds between couples. On a legal level, marrying generally confers upon a couple and their children certain economic benefits such as tax breaks, health insurance benefits for an employed person's spouse and children, property rights, and inheritance. Rights vary from state to state.

Marriage also implicitly obliges the couple to remain sexually and emotionally faithful to one another. Extramarital affairs are usually grounds for divorce; a legal dissolution of a marriage. Marriages can also end through annulment, which declares a marriage was not valid from its beginning. Ending a marriage dissolves the rights that had been conferred upon the couple. Any property they shared is split between them, but if the partners had unequal stakes in the marriage, a court may order alimony and/or child support payments from one party to the other.

See also Volume 2, Primary Document 53

Further Reading: Davis, Natalie Zemon, "Ghosts, Kin, and Progeny: Some Features of Family Life in Early Modern France," *Daedalus* 106(2) (1977): 87–114; Martin, Laura, Ame Theriault, and Sarah Yost, "Introduction to Islam and Women in Islamic Cultures," *Women, the Visual Arts, and Islam,* http://www.skidmore.edu/academics/arthistory/ah369/intro.html; Phillips, Lisa E., "Love, American Style," *American Demographics* 21(2) (1999): 56–57; Ross, Ellen, and Rayna Rapp, "Sex and Society: A Research Note from Social History and Anthropology," in *The Gender/Sexuality Reader: Culture, History, Political Economy,* eds. Roger Lancaster and Micaela di Leonardo, New York: Routledge, 1997, 153–168; "150 Years of Church History," *Tambuli,* April 17, 1980, http://library.lds.org/nxt/gateway.dll/Magazines/Liahona/1980.htm/tambuli%20april%201980%20.htm/150%20years%20of%20church%20history.htm; Wood, Owen, "In Depth: Same Sex Rights," *CBC News Online,* http://www.cbc.ca/news/background/samesexrights/timeline_world.html.

REBECCA C. HAINS

McJOB. The term "McJob" was coined in 1991 by author Douglas Coupland to describe a "low-pay, low-prestige, low-dignity, low-benefit, no-future job in the service sector." The increase of McJobs is an outcome of the process of **globalization.** One of the main aspects of globalization is global, free-market capitalism. Accordingly, McJobs result from the efforts of corporations (and increasingly the public sector in the form of privatization of services) to make a larger profit. Companies are often downsized, which involves cutting costs to ensure the greatest profit. One result is the creation of lower-paying jobs with few benefits. On the other hand, another major aspect of globalization is the advance and export of technology, which has led to an increasingly polarized work environment and an increasing gap between the rich and poor. To avoid being stuck in a McJob in today's workforce, **education** and training in highly skilled fields are required, rather than merely desirable. This development leads to increasingly competitive job market for young people with varying levels of educational background, but those without the means to achieve a higher education are particularly affected. Women disproportionately lose out: in 2000, women high school graduates earned around 75 percent as much as their male counterparts, which is about the same as males without a high school degree.

The fact that "McJobdom" affects both men and women means not only that third-wavers must realize that men are losing out as well but also that "gender equality in the workforce does not automatically bring economic progress." However, McJobdom does affect young women disproportionately. Young women are faced not only with under- and unemployment but also with the reality that women are paid less than men in nearly every sector. In 2000, women ages twenty-four to thirty-five made only 60 percent of the income of their male peers (Costello, Wight, and Stone, 2002). **Patriarchy** also has a color: young black and Latina women tend to be more heavily concentrated in lower-paying jobs with higher unemployment rates. All women are concentrated in "feminized" sectors, which tend to be lower-paid and have less benefits than sectors dominated by men. In 2003, according to the Department of Labor, women were 93.6 percent of secretaries, 93.2 percent of receptionists, and 84.6 percent of housekeepers.

See also Downsizing; Outsourcing

Further Reading: Costello, Cynthia B., Vanessa R. Wight, and Anne J. Stone, eds., *The American Woman 2003–2004: Daughters of a Revolution—Young Women Today*, Women's Research and Education Institute, New York: Palgrave Macmillan, 2002; Coupland, Douglas, *Generation X: Tales for an Accelerated Culture*, New York: St. Martin's Press, 1991; Klein, Naomi, *No Logo: No Space No Choice No Jobs*, 2nd ed., New York: Picador, 2002; Sidler, Michelle, "Living in McJobdom: Third Wave Feminism and Class Inequality," in *Third Wave Agenda: Being Feminist, Doing Feminism*, eds. Leslie Heywood and Jennifer Drake, Minneapolis: University of Minnesota Press, 1997, 25–39; United Nations, *World Youth Report 2003: The Global Situation of Young People*, http://www.un.org/esa/socdev/unyin/wyr/; Women's Bureau, Department of Labor, http://dol.gov/wb; Women and the Economy, UNPAC, http://www.unpac.ca/.

GWENDOLYN BEETHAM

McLACHLAN, SARAH. Sarah McLachlan (1968–) is a Canadian singer/songwriter and activist known for her atmospheric folk-pop sound and emotional ballads. Her **music** is very different from the angry punk of Riot Grrrl that was defining third-wave feminist music in the early 1990s, so she is not necessarily considered a third-wave icon. However, in 1994, McLachlan asked singer Paula Cole to open for her on her upcoming tour, a decision that prompted one concert promoter to ask, "Are you sure you want to put two women on the same bill?" The statement stuck with McLachlan and three years later she launched Lilith Fair, an all-women touring music festival, as a response to the male-dominated music industry and festivals such as Lollapalooza. In doing so, McLachlan created one of the most public and extensive feminist festivals to come out of the third wave. "This was meant to make a needed point to the industry—to show that this could be done and that there is such a wealth of talented women making music out there," McLachlan explained (as cited on her Web site below). The festival was met with much criticism from those opposed to its all-women structure, as well as from those who thought it was not feminist enough. Despite the criticisms, Lilith Fair was the top-grossing festival tour of 1997. Over the three years the festival played, it featured more than 100 female musicians and raised more than $7 million for a variety of charities. In 1998, McLachlan was awarded the Elizabeth Cady Stanton Visionary Award for advancing the careers of women in music.

Further Reading: Childerhose, Buffy, *From Lilith to Lilith Fair: The Authorized Story*, New York: St. Martin's Press, 1998; Prasad, Anil, "A Fair of the Heart," http://www.innerviews.org/inner/mclachlan.html; Sarah McLachlan's Web site, http://sarahmclachlan.com.

HELENA KVARNSTROM

McROBBIE, ANGELA. Angela McRobbie (1954–) is a feminist scholar and cultural critic. Although not self-identified as a "third-wave feminist," McRobbie's groundbreaking research on the "lived lives" of young women and **girls**, most notably working-class girls, has provided third-wave scholars with invaluable insight into how popular culture relates to both young women specifically and gender more generally.

In particular, McRobbie draws on earlier sociological **writings** and research on subcultures, which have tended to focus primarily on the cultural and social experiences of young men (i.e., mods) to provide a counter-picture of working-class girls' lives, especially as it relates to popular culture, such as young women's **magazines**, club cultures/**music**, and **fashion**. As McRobbie commented, "What I wanted to get was a picture of the way the young women saw themselves as women. Consequently I was interested in their views on **education**, on work and employment, on **family** life, **domesticity** and inevitably on **sexuality**." McRobbie's work has been a major stepping stone for contemporary work on young women and popular culture, as well as **feminism** and culture, providing critical insights into how many major **cultural studies** concepts (i.e., **ideology**, subculture, etc.) relate to women and gender.

McRobbie is a prolific writer and the author of numerous articles and books including *In the Culture Society: Art, Fashion, Popular Music* (1999); *Feminism and Youth Culture: From Jackie to Just Seventeen* (1991); and *Feminism for Girls: An Adventure Story* (1981).

See also Magazines, Women's

Further Reading: Hollows, Joanne, *Feminism, Femininity and Popular Culture*, Manchester: Manchester University Press, 2000; Walters, Suzanna Danuta, *Material Girls: Making Sense of Feminist Cultural Theory*, Berkeley: University of California Press, 1995.

NATASHA PATTERSON

MEDIA. Third-wave **feminism** began emerging as a distinct entity in the early 1990s, just as the media was going through a rapid transformation into the digital era. Previous generations had the nightly news, the daily paper delivered to the front door, and **magazines**, but there was a limited amount of media through which to sift. These sources were trusted and respected; news was not to be criticized or sneezed at. Suddenly in 1993, the World Wide Web became accessible to more than government officials and computer geeks. Once just listservs and e-mail, the Internet quickly spawned Web sites (accompanied by a necessity for every traditional institution or venue to have one), streaming video, chat rooms, blogs, and **zines**. The Internet revolution brought enhanced accessibility, but with that it brought new problems. Personal opinions in lieu of reporting, lazily fact-checked articles, and unsubstantiated rants looked, at first glance, just like those old trustworthy primary sources. With twenty-four-hour-news cycles, the omnipresent Internet, and advertisements and political appeals infiltrating **television** sitcoms and movies, the media is an increasingly indistinct entity. It is everywhere and it seems to be everything—a comment some make about third-wave feminism itself.

History. For the feminist movement of the sixties and early-seventies—referred to here as the second wave but by most women as the Women's Liberation Movement (WLM)—the media was one of their main targets in their quest to demand equality and dismantle the **patriarchy**. Second-wave feminists had two very specific complaints: women were excluded from creating the media, and women were represented in essentially two limited roles (sex pot and hausfrau). Women were not producers of the nightly news or the "most trusted voice in America," and they were not even in charge of the major women's magazines; instead, men presided over the **marriage** articles and chicken recipes at *Ladies Home Journal* and *Good Housekeeping*. Women were "**girl** re-porters," assigned to cover the bake-offs or innovative hair treatments, or they were *de facto* editors but had those responsibilities publicly minimized with job titles such as secretaries or fact checkers.

Media women responded to this oppressed status by both infiltrating the mainstream media and creating a vibrant alternative free from the conventional standards of "acceptable" media. To infiltrate, they employed legal and activist tactics. For instance, Susan Brownmiller and other pioneers of the WLM organized protests and other actions, most famously the *Ladies Home Journal* sit-in, in which 100 feminists occupied editor John Mack Carter's offices for eleven hours until he negotiated with them to produce a one-time feminist supplement for which he paid them $10,000. The women used the money to establish the first Women's Center in New York. On the legal front, some women in the media sued their employers for sex **discrimination**, as happened successfully at *Newsweek* in 1970 and the *New York Times* in 1974. Meanwhile, the mere existence of a feminist movement—and debates about sexism and women's rights in the culture—emboldened average women working at major media venues to refuse to tolerate a climate that reduced or delegitimized their contribution to the media. Women themselves were gaining enough confidence and power to influence what writers were commissioned and what stories were prioritized. In fact, the WLM often insisted that only women cover their **abortion** speak-out and their Miss America Pageant protests. Finally, the movement created feminist alternative media in the form of journals or publications (that resembled the zines of today) such as *No More Fun and Games*, independent magazines such as Boston's *Sojourner* and D.C.'s *Off Our Backs*, and a mainstream news magazine called *Ms.* More than any other one entity, *Ms.* came to represent wide-reaching feminist media, just as the National Organization for Women (NOW) represented feminist organizing in shorthand more than any of the other hundreds (perhaps thousands) of feminist groups.

The second wave took on the media as one of its many battles, winning victories that helped to create the media space that third-wave feminists grew up with and now often work in and most definitely consume. Second-wavers altered the landscape in many ways but left third-wavers with a new and distinct challenge: they were no longer reacting just to mainstream "sexist" media (which had, of course, become much more inclusive due to feminist agitating), but to *feminist* media that did not entirely address their priorities and sensibilities. Describing patriarchy, demanding **abortion** rights, and detailing satanic ritual abuse were not topics that many younger women gravitated toward—especially having been raised with the ideals (if not always the reality) of *Free to Be . . . You and Me* (1974) and legalized abortion.

During the eighties and early nineties, a shift began to occur. First, there was a period of feminist critique from within. The richest time for that was probably the 1980s, when feminists of color, lesbians, and feminists with disabilities created theories, journals, and books that would become dominant texts—books such as the anthology *This Bridge Called My Back* (1981), **bell hooks'** *Ain't I a Woman* (1981), Sarah Lucia Hoagland's *Lesbian Ethics* (1989), and the magazine *Disability Rag* (now online as the *Ragged Edge*), to name just a few. After that, third-wave feminists began creating their own media that drew from early WLM feminism and the intrafeminist critiques. In the same way that second-wavers initially pounded on the door to be let in to mainstream (male-run) media before creating their own, younger feminists stopped asking second-wave magazines to invite them in and forged a media for themselves. The feminist media world began expanding again to meet the needs of a new generation. Oftentimes the feminist associations were clear, as is the case with **Bitch**, the subtitle of which is *Feminist Response to Pop Culture*. Other times it was more subtle (and perhaps subversive), such as the many prominent third-wave feminist writers working at mainstream women's magazines. Noted younger feminist writers such as Noelle Howey, who is an editor at *Glamour*; Barbara Findlen, editor of *Listen Up* (1995), once the executive editor at *Ms.* magazine and who now works at the Disney-owned *Family Fun*; and **Tara Roberts**, who worked for years at *Essence* before leaving to create independent feminist magazine *Fierce*, have all argued that any contribution they made to influence these population publications with their feminist values was as profound as their contribution from the feminist margins.

Other self-described third-wavers directed their feminist energies toward creating or working for publications that were not explicitly feminist, but rather progressive or alternative, such as *ColorLines* and *Clamor*. Instead of supporting a media that was distinctly feminist, third-wavers located and prioritized feminism from within a radical movement or mainstream publications, thereby making those spaces more prone to a feminist agenda that did not overlook women.

A New Sensibility. In addition to replicating or riffing on second-wave feminist strategies—infiltrating/integrating the media and creating alternatives—third-wavers began asserting a change in sensibility from their foremothers. Younger consumers of the feminist media were grappling with the fact that they found *Ms.* to be boring and outdated and they actually enjoyed reading *Glamour*, *Essence*, and *Elle*. Their "Better Butt Now" articles or the magazines' celebrity worship did not categorically offend them. In fact, some women found these magazines to be a reflection of their own personal dramas and conflicts—or at least a fairly harmless diversion. In contrast to the second wave, third-wavers did not always feel reduced to sex object or girlfriend by these magazines—they knew that the messages might be simplistic but that their own lives were much, much more complex. They did not go to *Glamour*—or any magazine—for an accurate reflection of a woman, and women were better represented generally out there in the culture because there simply were more women in public life.

Moreover, the magazines were now created by female—often feminist—editors and designers. Third-wave feminists could enjoy the ads for low-rider jeans and the article on the best bikini wax, precisely because they were also reared with a feminist critique of these images and associations. They did not want to or have to repudiate these magazines; they could enjoy them and at the same time acknowledge the limitations of the women's magazine form. Countless women are still offended by the advertisements that sell women's bodies along with products, however. Women of all ages continue to critique this public display of sexism but have begun to challenge their own behavior as much as they attack the perpetuation of this limited and stereotypical image.

Third-wavers' increased ability to negotiate the mainstream has courted some condemnation as feminism "lite" or is said to be a product of patriarchal brainwashing. *Bitch* and *Bust*, two wonderful third-wave feminist magazines, are examples of the "mainstream underground," rather than the "underground underground," tiers that point to the media's ineluctable link with capitalism—never a site of righteous feminism. The most famous article asserting this "young feminists are stupid" line was the 1998 *Time* magazine cover story, "Is Feminism Dead?" which featured photos of Susan B. Anthony, Betty Friedan, Gloria Steinem, and Ally McBeal to make the point that women who loved both equality and shoes were hopelessly retrograde. The third-wave's complex embrace of both feminism and the entities that feminists once thought they could only critique signals progress, though, more than backsliding or fear of feminism. Younger women and men grew up noting that feminists' disavowal of women's magazines, **fashion**, and **advertising** did not make them go away. Moreover, third-wavers are not part of a pop culture generation so much out of choice—they simply grew up in a more media-saturated time (and younger feminists did not create MTV, they just grew up with it). Instead of spending time debating the merits of **girlie** magazines or the pervasiveness of selling sex and the perfect **body**, many believe feminists should prioritize discerning how to read and interpret the media. It is time to retire the feminist binary of good and bad media, where good = independent, but struggling and bad = commercially viable and mainstream. Because feminists are a hodgepodge—diverse in identities and interests—feminist media should reflect that.

The best way to assess third-wave's contribution to media is to look at the publications created by this generation of feminists: *Bitch, Bust, Rockrgrl, HUES*, and more recently, *Fierce*; and countless zines, including *Riot Grrrl, Bamboo Girl*, and *I'm So Fucking Beautiful*, among them. Other publications such as *Venus, Teen Voices*, and *On Our Backs* were created by third-wavers but not necessarily marketed to a distinctly third-wave audience. By making their own media, younger women sidestepped a full-on rejection of their feminist predecessors (needing *Ms.* to speak for them or cover their work, for instance). Within the pages of these magazines, third-wavers began speaking for themselves and they named their own heroines—Nomy Lamm, **Rebecca Walker**, Sarah Jones—as well as prioritized their own distinct issues—*what if I want to be housewife?* and *why does everyone I know have an* **eating disorder**? Artists such as **Ani DiFranco**, Kara Walker, Alix Olson, and Jill Scott, who were creating and influencing culture, were profiled in these media. The politics of the generation—**globalization**, sweatshop labor, and **transgenderism**—were investigated and debated.

The creators also got to make up their own business rules. At *Bitch*, for instance, everyone is paid the same, and at *Bust*, they do not find underwear ads offensive, so they use them to generate revenue. The creators of these magazines might not be rich or have mainstream success, but they have launched their own careers on their own terms. Carla DeSantis of *Rockrgrl* and Tara Roberts of *Fierce* are publishers. Meanwhile, this third-wave media provides opportunities for young writers—many got their start as writers by being published in *Girlfriends* and *Bust*. Even those with some mainstream success used these publications to write the stories they really wanted to write. Perhaps because the editors themselves have received countless rejection letters, they are more willing to take a chance on a stranger and even a strange idea. They do not always agree entirely with everything they print, but they agree that the writer or reporter was onto something—and in that way they promote a very basic journalistic approach and print the news.

Sassy Says: Girl Is Good. In creating "a media of their own," younger women took a page not from *Ms.*, but from *Sassy*, a feminist-y and very cool teen magazine. What *Ms.* did for the second wave of feminism, *Sassy* did for this generation of feminists. In the same way that third-wavers' mothers remember buying the first issue of *Ms.* or the magazine's coining of the term "battered women" in an early cover story, the creators of *Bust* and *Bitch* make an explicit connection between their work and *Sassy*'s. The creation of this magazine symbolizes the birth of third-wave media, and a good majority of third-wave print media has a direct correlation to this one-time successful magazine. Sisters **Ophira Edut** and Tali Edut, creators (with Dyann Logwood) of the now defunct *HUES* magazine interned at *Sassy* one summer and modeled their multicultural feminist magazine after it. When then-Nickelodeon employees Marcelle Karp and Debbie Stoller wanted to create a magazine that spoke to their sensibilities of young women, they envisioned it as "*Sassy* for grown-ups." Many prominent third-wave writers (Diane Paylor and Majorie Ingall, to name two) and mainstream editors such as Christina Kelly (of *Jane* and *YM*) and Kim France (of *New York* magazine and *Lucky*) started their careers at *Sassy*.

Bust's cofounder and editor Debbie Stoller sums up *Sassy*'s appeal:

> I was so into *Sassy*, riot grrrl was starting to pick up steam, there was this Dutch magazine called *Obzay* that I used to read that was great, and I was frustrated that *Ms.* was so dumb. I felt disconnected to everything feminist and the only thing to latch onto that really made sense was *Sassy*. All of my girlfriends read it. I was responding to the pleasure principle of *Sassy*. The way that they spoke to girls—and it seemed to me to be girls of all ages—was respectful, but had a sense of fun and pleasure where as all of the other magazines were like "don't do this and don't do that, being a woman is so hard and sucky." *Sassy* used language girls of all ages used, made the right cultural references, it made me laugh and it made me feel good about being a girl. I thought *Sassy* caught on to what was so important about empowering people. It wasn't just about giving them a good role model—it was not just about the negative things that need to be changed about being female in this society. You had to embrace the positive stuff and that would go along way toward empowering people" (*Bust Guide to the New Girl Order*, 1999, p. 36).

Beyond the influences listed, *Sassy* helped to marshal the growing trend of zines, which were actively promoted through Christina Kelly's "Zine of the Month" feature, giving visibility and a way to connect to countless **DIY** (do it yourself) media makers. Zines themselves are perhaps third-wavers' biggest and most unique contribution to the media and, being under the radar, are the least "tainted by **capitalism** and the vagaries of turning a profit." Some were meant to be distributed only among friends; some were published diaries. Others were encompassing and appealing enough to the mainstream to grow into full-fledged magazines with glossy pages and paid contributors, such as *Bitch* and *Bust*. Jennifer Bleyer characterizes the boom-time for zines in "Cut-and-Paste Revolution: Notes from the Girl Zine Explosion," her essay in the anthology *The Fire This Time* (2004):

> From the late-eighties to the mid-nineties, thousands of zines sprouted up like resilient weeds inside the cracks of the mainstream media's concrete.... After Xerox machines became widely accessible and before the explosion of the Internet, there was a brief moment during which people realized that they could make their own rudimentary publications on copy paper, fasten them with staples, and send them out along the zine distribution thoroughfares that coursed across the country, without any permission or guidance whatsoever (52).

Zines were demoted as the popularization of the Internet made media more accessible to more people than ever. Early sites such as www.feminist.com, Disgruntled Housewife, hip-mama, and Cybergrrl (the first three are still thriving) brought girlie feminist concerns and organizing to the Web; today blogs and ezines are catapulting a new independent female voice into publishing. Now more than ever, anyone can be a writer and everyone can be expert. Although this is great for ensuring that multiple voices are heard and for reflecting the diversity of feminism, there is a drawback in the "infinite potential" of the Internet. Every time someone has a conflict or an issue, they can simply splinter off and create their own media. This **individualism** is often secondary to community and compromise within feminism. When it comes to creating a responsible and accurate media, third wave's prioritizing of the free-for-all market has to be balanced with the danger of being limitless and unbound by any shared vision or goal. In other words, having a bullhorn of our own does not relieve third-wavers of the responsibility to effectively build a movement.

The Future. Third-wave feminists support a plethora of options and do not believe in any one feminist line, but they also strategize and imagine ways to bring these disparate voices together under the banner of third-wave feminism. Third-wave feminists see that it is important to use their consumer power and their behavior as a barometer of what they truly value, rather than what they would like to project as their values. If they think what *Bitch* has to say is as important and credible (or more) than the *New York Times*, then they should be happy that the March for Women's Lives was covered in *Bitch* and not focus on the fact that the *Times* ignored it. Actively giving value to third-wave and independent media will do more to change that unequal landscape than constantly blaming the mainstream for not being inclusive enough.

At least a dozen years into its own **identity**, the third wave is infiltrating the media on many fronts—both mainstream and independent. Collectively, the margins third-wavers create could be stronger than the center, but only, of course, if third-wavers stop buying their own bad press.

See also Cyberspace; Magazines, Men's; Magazines, Women's; *Volume 2, Primary Document 35*

AMY RICHARDS
JENNIFER BAUMGARDNER

MEMOIR. Memoir has been an important venue for third-wave **feminism**. Many prominent third-wave feminists have written a memoir, broadly defined, and this has been one major way third-wave feminists have publicized their ideas. Memoir as a literary form is distinct from the plural *memoirs*, which is largely what was written before 1990. Memoirs are similar to autobiography; books typically written by notable people telling the stories of their lives. Although books in the older tradition are still written, such as President Bill Clinton's blockbuster memoir *My Life*, the newer form of literary memoir has become as popular, or more popular, than **fiction**. Literary memoir, as distinct from *memoirs*, is written by ordinary people and, rather than covering a whole life, is focused on only one short period in someone's life or on one particular incident or theme. Greater attention is given to the **writing** itself—it is more than a recitation of life events. This kind of memoir started to be popular in the early 1990s, with books such as Elizabeth Wurtzel's *Prozac Nation* (1994) and Frank McCourt's *Angela's Ashes* (1996). The two forms have often been confused, but memoir rather than *memoirs* has been the most important form for third-wave feminists.

The rise of memoir as a popular form gave a venue to third-wave feminists for whom telling aspects of their life stories was one of the most effective ways of conveying their political message. Important third-wave feminist books like **Joan Morgan**'s *When the Chickenheads Come Home to Roost* (1999) and Inga Muscio's *Cunt* (2002) feature a first-person narrator telling the stories from her own life that demonstrate a particular political point, thus combining personal narrative and critical social analysis and literally putting the second-wave feminist slogan "the personal is political" into powerful use. Morgan's book showed some of the differences between second- and third-wave feminism through her stories of how circumstances have changed, making feminism something different for her generation. Muscio covers topics from birth control to **rape** to popular culture, all in a first-person voice that weaves in her own experiences. **Rebecca Walker**'s *Black, White, and Jewish* (2002) is focused on one of the third wave's most powerful themes: the experiences of biracial **girls** and women in an American culture that is increasingly bi and/or multiracial and still obsessed with racial distinctions. Walker's powerful story of her life gives voice to these themes, showing how difficult it still is to be biracial in a culture that can only see divisions, while at the same time conveying the sense that her experience is increasingly the normal experience of American life because so many people are now biracial or multiracial. Ariel Gore's *Atlas of the Human Heart* (2003) uses her experiences of travel and self-discovery to reflect on third-wave feminist concerns intimately related to women's experiences, including single motherhood. Leslie Heywood's *Pretty Good for a Girl* (2000) chronicles the experiences of a female athlete who competes in the generation post Title IX. (This civil rights legislation of 1972 mandated that women's **sports** be funded equally to men's.) Each text focuses on a different formative aspect of third-wave experience that distinguishes third-wave feminist views.

Some of the most important third-wave feminist writings have taken the form of short memoir, pieces that are collected with other similar writings focused around a particular theme. Although these do not technically fall under the definition of literary memoir, these short pieces nonetheless use each writer's experience to make a larger point about that experience and show just how much social ideas about race, class, and gender affect individual lives and in turn how these individuals then organize to affect the larger culture. Rebecca Walker's *To Be Real* (1995) and Barbara Findlen's *Listen Up* (1995) include diverse voices of woman who use their lives to reflect on their feminism. Ariel Gore's collection *Breeder* (2001) gives voice to the subject of motherhood. **Tara Roberts'** collection *Am I the Last Virgin?* (1997) gives voice to the sexual challenges young African American women face, and discusses the choice to remain a virgin until marriage. For all these writers, the complications of their own lives function as a resource to draw on when trying to formulate and think through their feminism. Their feminism is their lives.

See also Writing, Third-Wave Feminist; *Volume 2, Primary Documents 2, 3, and 5*

Further Reading: Gore, Ariel, *Atlas of the Human Heart*, Seattle: Seal, 2003; Heywood, Leslie, *Pretty Good for a Girl*, Minneapolis: University of Minnesota, 2000; Hornbacher, Marya, *Wasted*, New York: Harper Perennial, 1999; Morgan, Joan, *When Chickenheads Come Home to Roost*, New York: Simon & Schuster, 1999; Roberts, Tara, ed., *Am I the Last Virgin?* New York: Simon Pulse, 1997; Walker, Rebecca, *Black, White, and Jewish*, New York: Riverhead, 2002; Wurtzel, Elizabeth, *Prozac Nation*, New York: Riverhead, 1997.

LESLIE HEYWOOD

MEN'S MOVEMENT. Like the women's movement, the men's movement is composed of several different groups, organizations, and individuals, all with different ideals of what men's issues are, and therefore how the men's movement should be defined. There are several aspects of the men's movement, ranging from the pro-feminist, anti-sexist movement to the right wing's anti-feminist, reactionary movement. Men's involvement in the third-wave feminist movement falls toward the former, seeking, like third-wavers in general, to be more inclusive and critiquing the roots of *all* inequity, whether patriarchal, racist, or classist.

History. The challenge to traditional gender roles (what feminist theorist Gayle Rubin in 1975 named the "sex/gender" system) that began in the 1960s and 1970s resulted not only in the "second wave" of **feminism**, but also in several manifestations of the men's movement. As gender roles began to change significantly, it was inevitable that men would respond. This response, however, has been extremely varied.

The "men's rights" movement, which began in the 1970s as a direct result of the women's rights movement, countered many of the tenets of feminism and often did not recognize that the power structure that oppressed women also oppressed men. Instead, the mostly white, middle-class men of the "men's rights" movement were "anti-feminist" in the sense that many did not question the power structures of **patriarchy**, **racism**, and classism that prevented equality, but argued that they were not benefiting from the movement to end women's oppression. Truly, much of second-wave feminism itself did not focus on the oppression of men, nor did it take into account racial and class differences among women. Critiques by women of color, such as the women of the Combahee River Collective, brought these issues to the forefront. Women of color such as **bell hooks** also began to address the ways in which masculinity, like its counterpart **femininity**, was also constructed and that both had variations based on race, class, and social status. Men of color also responded to the **racism** inherent in the men's movement with books like *Muy Macho: Latino Men Confront Their Manhood* (1996) and *Black Men on Race, Gender, and Sexuality* (1999).

In the mid-1990s, the mythopoetic men's movement marked a further move away from a pro-feminist stance, as men sought to find the mythical roots of masculinity. Fed by popular books such as Robert Bly's *Iron John* (1990), these (mostly white, middle-class, heterosexual) men embarked on weekend trips that were supposed to result in the attainment of "lost" manhood. Around the same time, however, gender theorists both inside and outside of academia began to envision a more progressive, less divisive "men's movement" in the form of masculinities studies. Authors such as Robert Connell and Michael Kimmel examined masculinities in all of their nuances, arguing for a perspective of masculinities and a men's movement that was relational to, and would not isolate itself from, the women's movement and **women's studies**. Like feminist studies and practice, masculinities studies attempts to examine power structures, articulating ways in which power can be more equitably distributed, to the benefit of *all* people.

Feminist Response. Feminists reacted to all of these movements with both hope and skepticism, as explored in *Women Respond to Men's Movement* (1992) and *Stiffed: The Betrayal of Modern Man* (1999). However, as bell hooks and other feminists importantly note, women should play a role in ending men's investment in the patriarchal power structure and vice versa. Hooks suggests that one of the ways women can help men in this endeavor is to reject "traditional" hypermasculinity and be "seduced by violence no more" (1994).

Contemporary feminists are influenced by both the critiques of feminists of color and critiques of earlier manifestations of the men's movement. Therefore, third-wavers seek at their base to be all encompassing and include men's voices in many of their books and organizations. *The Fire This Time* (2004), for example, features male coauthors in two pieces: one on the feminist roots of the independent **media** center (Indymedia), and one on organizing domestic workers. In 2004, third-wave feminist **Rebecca Walker** edited a collection of both men and women's **writings** on contemporary masculinity. In addition, the profeminist National Organization of Men Against Sexism (NOMAS), with roots dating back to the late 1970s, has members of all genders who seek to fight against racism, classism, *and* sexism. However, as the third-wave "movement" itself is not easily categorized, neither is men's involvement. Indeed, in the tradition of the third wave, myriads of men's perspectives and concerns are acknowledged.

Further Reading: Brod, Harry, and Michael Kaufman, eds., *Theorizing Masculinity*, Thousand Oaks, CA: Sage, 1994; Carbado, Devon W., ed., *Black Men on Race, Gender and Sexuality: A Critical Reader*, New York: New York University Press, 1999; Connell, Robert W., *Masculinities*, Cambridge: Polity, 1995; Connell, Robert W., *The Men and the Boys*, Cambridge: Polity, 2000; Eng, David, *Racial Castration: Managing Masculinity in Asian America*, Durham, NC: Duke University Press, 2001; Faludi, Susan, *Stiffed: The Betrayal of Modern Man*, London: Chatton and Windus, 1999; Gonzalez, Ray, ed., *Muy Macho: Latino Men Confront Their Manhood*, New York: Anchor Books, 1996; Hagan, Kay Leigh, ed., *Women Respond to the Men's Movement*, San Francisco: Pandora, 1992; hooks, bell, *Outlaw Culture: Resisting Representations*, New York: Routledge, 1994; hooks, bell, *The Will to Change: Men, Masculinity, and Love*, New York: Atria, 2004; Kimmel, Michael, ed., *The Politics of Manhood: Profeminist Men Respond to the Mythopoetic Men's Movement*, Philadelphia: Temple University Press, 1995; Labaton, Vivien, and Dawn Lundy Martin, eds., *The Fire This Time: Young Activists and the New Feminism*, New York: Anchor Books, 2004; Men Can Stop Rape, www.mencanstoprape.org; Men Stopping Violence, www.menstoppingviolence.org; National Organization for Men Against Sexism, www.nomas.org; Walker, Rebecca, ed., *To Be Real: Telling the Truth and Changing the Face of Feminism*, New York: Anchor Books, 1995; Walker, Rebecca, ed., *What Makes a Man: 22 Writers Imagine the Future*, New York: Riverhead, 2004.

GWENDOLYN BEETHAM

MILITARY, WOMEN IN THE. During the women's suffrage movement, most women and men were against women joining the military. In Western society, **war** has been gender specific. Young boys and men were conditioned to believe that aggression was associated with masculinity whereas young **girls** and women were conditioned to believe that peace was associated with **femininity**. The argument was that women were inherently nurturing. Most third-wave feminists reject this argument.

Women in developing countries such as Mexico, Guatemala, and El Salvador and many African countries have been involved in battle for years. Up to this day, women are not assigned ground combat roles in the U.S. military. The military women with the highest rank are in the airforce and the navy. The navy created the organization WAVES (Women Accepted for Volunteer Emergency Service) in July 1942. Most WAVES were assigned to administrative roles. WAVES did not accept African American women during World War II.

During the third wave of **feminism**, many young women are being encouraged and recruited to join the military, whereas during the women's suffrage movement and the second wave of feminism women were encouraged to be homemakers, vouch for peace, and subsequently apply to college or go to work. Third-wavers would suggest that it is a woman's right to engage in combat in a war. Feminists today dispute the notion that women are naturally inclined to be peaceful.

Most women who benefited from World Wars I and II were white. Although they did not actually fight in these wars, they played integral roles behind the scenes. These women worked in medical, administrative, and communication fields and supported war.

Bell hooks, lecturer, feminist author, and professor of English at City University of New York, writes in *Feminist Theory*, "An example of the distorted perception of women's reality that is being described by some activists who discuss women and militarism is the popular assumption that 'women are natural enemies of war.' Many anti-war activists suggest that women as bearers of children, or the potential bearers of children, are necessarily more concerned about ending war than men—the implication being that women are life affirming. We who are concerned about feminism and militarism must insist that women (even those who are bearers of children) are not inherently non-violent or life affirming" (54).

Although women have been trained for combat in the U.S. military, they have not actually engaged in battle on ground. Shoshana Johnson, the first African American POW (prisoner of war) in the war on Iraq, became a celebrated military woman in 2003. The objective of feminists of the third wave is to encompass stories and issues of women of all backgrounds, race, and classes. Jessica Lynch, who along with Johnson also belonged to the 507th Maintenance Company from Fort Bliss, is another female soldier who made the headlines. Lynch's story of capture and survival was turned into a movie and a book. There were many objections to the amount of publicity and retirement benefits Lynch received, as Lynch was white and "All American." It was believed that some of her story was fabricated by outside sources to make it more sensational. The fact that Johnson and Lynch were celebrated opened discussion all over the country regarding women in the military. Was this national attention given to them because they were female POWs or U.S. soldiers? Some critics claimed that the national and almost sympathetic nature of the **media** attention was one indication that America was still not comfortable with the notion of women in the military. For most third-wave feminists, who do not believe in inherent differences between men and women, both women and men should be able to serve or not serve as their values and conscience dictate.

Further Reading: Burrelli, David F., "Women in the Armed Forces," www.fas.org; Davis, Angela, *Women, Culture and Politics*, New York: Random House, 1989; Elshtan, Bethke Jean, *Women and War*, New York: Basic Book, 1987; hooks, bell, *Feminist Theory: From Margin to Center*, 2nd ed., Cambridge, MA: South End Press, 2000; Swerdlow, Amy, *Women Strike for Peace: Traditional Motherhood and Radical Politics in the 1960's*, Chicago: University of Chicago Press, 1993.

JACKIE JOICE

MISOGYNY. Misogyny, which derives from the Greek roots "misein" (to hate) and "gyne" (woman) is the term for all forms of hatred of women, although in today's world, it is generally taken to mean a society-wide belief system of hierarchy by gender. Some theories about the sources of misogyny include psychoanalytic suggestions that men are jealous of women's ability to reproduce and nurture life and to provide sexual pleasure, or that there is a deep-rooted resentment in men that their mothers "abandon" them in the inevitable separation that eventually occurs between infant and mother. What is certain is that it has existed, to varying degrees, in most major male-dominated societies as far back as documentation reaches.

Modern manifestations of misogyny take many forms, from **sexual harassment, rape,** and other forms of assault against women, to the use of derogatory names for women and for female genitalia. Female genital mutilation is an example of a misogynist tradition that has endured for centuries and is still taking place in several countries. The Chinese practice of foot binding is another example of a society's imposition on women. Some would say that current Western practices of beauty modification such as plastic surgery and the use of botox are related to misogyny. These practices may be seen as manifestations of hatred of women. Also, in many cultures, for many years into the modern age, women were seen as the property of their husbands.

Authors who have written specifically about misogyny include **bell hooks.** Her essay "Sexism and Misogyny: Who Takes the Rap? Misogyny, Gangsta Rap, and The Piano" (2000) deals with the topic, referencing a genre of **music** that typically refers to women in derogatory terms. Andrea Dworkin is another prominent author whose work often deals with sexual violence against women, based in part on her own experiences.

Interestingly, some men have begun publicizing the term "misandry," which also has its roots in Greek, only with the root "andr" for "man." Discussion of this phenomenon, however, is not as common as that of misogyny.
See also Hip-Hop Terms for Women

Further Reading: Dworkin, Andrea, *Woman Hating*, New York: Dutton, 1974; hooks, bell, *Feminist Theory: From Margin To Center*, 2nd ed., Cambridge, MA: South End Press, 2000; Millett, Kate, *Sexual Politics*, New York: Avon, 1971.

JESSICA MANACK

MORGAN, JOAN. Joan Morgan (1968–) is a distinguished hip-hop journalist and feminist cultural critic. She began her journalism career freelancing for the *Village Voice* and other national **magazines** before joining *Essence* magazine first as an editor-at-large, and later as executive editor, responsible for the day-to-day managerial responsibilities of the editorial team. Morgan is best known in feminist circles, however, as the author of *When Chickenheads Come Home to Roost: My Life as a Hip-Hop Feminist* (1999), nine original, personal essays that are brutally honest and honestly critical. Morgan defines chickenheads as women who use sex to gain protection, wealth, or power. Her book is an exploration of the modern black woman's life, the complexity of choices faced by black women who consider themselves feminists, and a world where "truth is no longer black and white but subtle, intriguing shades of gray" (62).

When Chickenheads Come Home to Roost is Morgan's "search for an up-to-date, functional **feminism**," according to one critic, "one that claims 'the powerful richness and delicious complexities inherent in being black **girls** now.'" Reviews of her book described her as fresh, witty, and irreverent, noting that she is one of most original, perceptive, and engaging young social commentators in America today. *When Chickenheads Come Home to Roost* is required reading in many feminist classrooms interested in dissecting and discussing the relevance of feminism and the contemporary black woman. Morgan was born in Jamaica, raised in the South Bronx, graduated from Wesleyan University, and currently lives in Brooklyn where she is raising her son.

See also Black Feminism; *Volume 2, Primary Document 3*

Further Reading: Morgan, Joan, *When Chickenheads Come Home to Roost: My Life as a Hip-Hop Feminist*, New York: Touchstone, 1999.

MURIEL L. WHETSTONE-SIMS

MOSS, KATE. Supermodel Kate Moss (1974–) who was born in England, began modeling at the age of fourteen after catching the eye of a modeling scout in the JFK airport in New York. Known for her thin figure and youthful look, Moss has appeared in **film, music** videos, and on **television.** She has been featured in **magazines** such as *Allure*, *Harper's Bazaar*, and *Vogue* and has modeled for designers such as Versace, Chanel, and Dolce & Gabbana. Throughout the 1990s Moss was one of the most recognizable and highest-paid supermodels, earning approximately $10,000 a day and representing the zeitgeist of this **fashion** era. At the age of eighteen, Moss became the face of Calvin Klein, posing barely dressed for his underwear ads and nude for Obsession perfume. Because of Moss' childlike appearance, these ads invoked charges that Calvin Klein's fashion campaign was child **pornography.** Feminists continue to be concerned that **media** images of young, thin models such as Moss are related to problems young women face with anorexia and other **eating disorders.** For some third-wave feminists, however, the fact that Moss has "imperfect" freckles and is a bit shorter than average runway models points to expanding ideas of beauty in the world of high fashion, pop culture, and for everyday women and **girls**. The emergence of Moss' well-known waif look in the early 1990s coincided with the baby-doll-dresses-and-combat-boots look that many Riot Grrrls (Babes in Toyland, Hole) wore during the same era. These young women reappropriated pop culture symbols of **femininity** and, through the use of fashion, refused to have their standards of politics or gender defined by anyone but themselves.

See also Beauty Ideals

Further Reading: Moss, Kate, *Kate: The Kate Moss Book*, New York: Rizzoli, 1997.

SHIRA TARRANT

MOTHERING. In many ways, the questions facing the third wave concerning motherhood resemble those faced by the second wave. How can work and motherhood be balanced? What would equal parenting look like, and how can it be achieved? Can motherhood be feminist, and if so, how? Third-wavers find themselves struggling to formulate answers, taking into consideration very different ideas about parenting, **feminism**, and relationships.

Current dialog about motherhood is influenced by many factors, such as the third-wave attempt to reclaim and reconfigure many traditions and institutions that were rejected or found wanting by second-wave feminism. Third-wave feminists have reclaimed and interrogated artifacts and rituals of the more traditional ideas of **femininity** including **Barbie**, the color pink, makeup, housework, and crafts. For mothers, the idea of staying home to raise children and choosing not to work full-time for pay, is perceived by some to be regressing to the days of *The Feminine Mystique*, whereas others see it as the most feminist way possible to raise their children.

Many third-wave mothers are heavily influenced by the ideas of William Sears, who terms his philosophy "attachment parenting." Attachment parenting (AP) relies on the theory that the most important and precious bond in a child's life is with the mother, and that the optimal way to develop such a bond is to keep the child as physically close as possible at all times. This theory results in such practices as extended breastfeeding, "baby-wearing," and the **family** bed. Many women find this school of thought to be inspiring and groundbreaking—a way to develop a close, solid bond with their children and to model for them the ideas of empathy, tenderness, respect, and consideration. Also, they believe that AP ideas support raising children in an anti-consumerist model, because many AP mothers do not believe in strollers, cribs, or much of the traditional equipment for raising children. However, AP philosophies are often misused to enhance **competition** between mothers as they attempt to be more AP than each other, resulting in bitterness, resentment, and feelings of inferiority. Others argue that the AP movement implicitly values stay-at-home mothers over working mothers without taking into account individual choices and needs.

The division between working and stay-at-home mothers dates from the Industrial Revolution, which sent many poor mothers into factories and emphasized at the same time the importance of having upper-class women be the "Angel in the House." Now, at the turn of the twentieth-first century, the debate has been recast as a debate over the nature of work, as many women argue that they are doing the most important work in the world by raising children, and others argue that they cannot possibly stay home and should not be made to feel guilty as a result. This debate is influenced by the third-wave philosophy that feminism should make it possible for all women to design and achieve their own choices, according to their own version of feminism. Other feminists argue that in reality, the "mommy wars" are greatly exaggerated by the mainstream **media** in an attempt to divide women and prevent them from feeling solidarity as mothers who are still oppressed in many ways by American culture and institutions. Some groups are redefining work and career, such as Mothers and More, who believe that most women can and should spend their careers "sequencing" in and out of paid work.

Motherhood is still one of the most radicalizing experiences that many women encounter, and that truth is reflected for the third wave in the explosion of **media** for mothers, relying heavily on personal experiences of isolation, joy, and confusion. The third wave's characteristic concerns with media and media literacy have resulted in publications for every type of parent (pagan, **queer**, of color) alongside mainstream novels exploring the lives of working mothers and stay-at-home mothers alike. *Hip Mama*, a **zine** begun by Ariel Gore in the early 1990s, is for many the ultimate handbook for the third-wave school of parenting. Gore, a single mother formerly on welfare, became the spokeswoman for modern mothers, even debating former Speaker of the House and outspoken conservative Newt Gingrich on MTV about the welfare-to-work programs so prevalent in the 1990s. Her books, Web sites, and magazine explore and redefine ideas about motherhood, focusing on supporting mothers who may feel marginalized because of their race, class, age, **sexuality**, or countercultural or feminist beliefs. **Magazines** such as *Mothering* focus more on issues such as breastfeeding, vaccinations, and organic foods that are relevant to AP and other mothers who practice "natural" parenting.

While in many areas, third-wave women are at the forefront of changing ideas about parenting and motherhood, other third-wavers are **opting out** of motherhood altogether. Many do not believe in monogamy, others still think that choosing to "breed" is a nonfeminist choice, and still others believe that it would be impossible to reconcile their lives of activism with parenting. The pages of **Bitch** magazine saw a typical debate when some women resented those who "make the choice to have a kid and then expect organizations and feminism to accommodate them," and mothers argued that parenthood changed their entire notions of what is revolutionary and activist and deepened their commitment to social change. Many third-wave women simply do not think that dialog about motherhood has a place in their lives as feminists and activists.

Books such as *Manifesta* (2000) and *Cunt* (2002) were criticized for exclusively examining the mother-child relationship from the viewpoint of the daughter, while motherhood is frequently omitted or neglected in third-wave documents and discussions.

The members of the third wave of feminism are remaking motherhood in accordance with their own theories and views on society, as have generations of feminists before them. However, as a generation, the third wave still has much work to do in the project of integrating feminist practices into the institution and practice of motherhood.

See also Division of Labor/Gender Roles; Magazines, Women's; *Volume 2, Primary Document 54*

Further Reading: Crittenden, Ann, *The Price of Motherhood: Why the Most Important Job in the World Is Still the Least Valued,* 2nd ed., New York: Owl Books 2002; Douglas, Susan, and Meredith Michaels, *The Mommy Myth: The Idealization of Motherhood and How It Has Undermined Women,* New York: Free Press, 2004; Friedan, Betty, *The Feminine Mystique,* New York: W.W. Norton, 2001; Gore, Ariel, and Bee Lavender, eds., *Breeder: Real-Life Stories from the New Generation of Mothers,* Seattle: Seal Press, 2001; O'Mara, Peggy, *Natural Family Living: The Mothering Magazine Guide to Parenting,* New York: Atria, 2000; Rich, Adrienne, *Of Woman Born: Motherhood As Experience and Institution,* New York: W.W. Norton, 1995; Sears, Martha, and William Sears, *The Attachment Parenting Book: A Commonsense Guide to Understanding and Nurturing Your Baby,* Boston: Little, Brown, 2001; http://www.mothersandmore.org/; http://www.hipmama. com; http://www.mothering.com; http://www.mothersoughttohaveequalrights.org.

JACKIE REGALES

MULTIRACIALISM. As a demographic category, "multiracialism" refers to individuals who have ancestors of several or various races. Some multiracial individuals have terms to describe their racial background: *métis* (First Nations and French Canadian); *mestiza/mestizo* (individuals with a white/Native American or white/Hispanic racial background, and mixed-raced Philipino Americans); and *mulatto/mulatta* (Latin American and white or black). Multiracial individuals are also referred to by such derogatory terms as *half-breed* or *half-caste.* Multiracialism also refers to anything made up of, involving, or acting on behalf of various races. This includes the recognition of living in a society made up of a variety of racial groups. Finally, multiracialism can refer to equality of political **representation** and social acceptance in a society made up of various races.

Multiracialism in all of these forms has been extremely important to third-wave **feminism**. One of the major critiques made against both first- and second-wave feminism was their neglect of race issues. Some feminists argued that these previous waves focused primarily on white, middle-class women and ignored women of color. Feminists such as **bell hooks**, Patricia Hills Collins, and Gloria Anzaldua drew attention to this neglect of race in first- and second-wave feminism and called for a more inclusive multiracial feminism. These feminists argued for a feminism that fully incorporated women of color, saw political and social equality between feminists of various races, and included race as an issue for feminists to address in their critiques of patriarchal society. Indeed, third-wave feminism has been committed to an inclusive movement that takes into consideration issues of race. Not only has such feminist work focused on issues of race in patriarchal society, but it has also critically examined the privileging of white feminists over feminists of color.

Multiracialism as a demographic category has also played an important role in third-wave feminism. The work of Gloria Anzaldúa drew attention to the status of mixed-race women in patriarchal society. Not fitting into the tidy racial categories created by society to legitimate white racial dominance, mixed-race individuals offer an important challenge to hierarchies of race. Indeed, many feminists view multiracialism as an important site for critical interrogations of racist society. In conjunction with the work of feminists of color, multiracial feminists have added yet another dimension to third-wave feminism's analyses of racial issues.

Further Reading: Anzaldúa, Gloria, *Boderlands/La Frontera—The New Mestiza*, San Francisco: Aunt Lute Books, 1999; hooks, bell, *Feminist Theory—From Margin to Centre*, Cambridge, MA: South End Press Classics, 2000; Mixed-race Online Encyclopedia Listing, http://encyclopedia.thefreedictionary.com/Mixed-race.

ROBYN S. BOURGEOIS

MULTISEXUALITY. Multisexuality is a term with multiple meanings. Multi-sexual can be used as a demographic category to describe an individual who has intimate relations with both people of the same sex and the opposite sex. In this sense, multisexual carries the same meaning as the term "bisexual." Multisexuality has also been used as a synonym for *polygamy*, referring to sexual relations with more than one individual or sexual relations outside of a committed relationship with the consent of both parties involved in the relationship. Multisexuality can also be used to describe a society or group that is made up of a variety of individuals with different sexual identities. In fact, multisexuality is the recognition of the variety of sexual relations practiced by members of a society. This variety of sexualities may include heterosexuality (intimate relations with the opposite sex), homosexuality (intimate relations with the same sex), and bisexuality (intimate relations with both the same and opposite sex). In recent years, a new "sexual" **identity** has emerged: the *metrosexual*. Coined in 1994 by Mark Simpson, popular usage defines the metrosexual as a narcissistic urban male who spends a great deal of time and money on his appearance and lifestyle. Some define the metrosexual as a man who seems stereotypically gay except that his sexual orientation is heterosexual. Some examples of metrosexual males include British soccer star David Beckham and American actors Brad Pitt and George Clooney. The identification of the metrosexual has been important, as the recognition of a heterosexual male partaking in and enjoying stereotypically female and male homosexual activities (such as grooming and shopping) challenges both gender and sexual stereotypes.

Indeed, the reference to *multisexuality*, and the multiple sexual identities in society, has challenged the commonly perceived notion of sexuality being composed of only two sexualities: heterosexuality and homosexuality.

Multisexuality has played an important role in third-wave **feminism**. Like women of color, lesbian and bisexual feminists argued that both first- and second-wave feminism focused on white, middle-class heterosexual women and neglected the experiences of **queer** women. Feminists such as Joan Nestle, Audre Lorde, and Gloria Anzaldúa argued for a more inclusive feminism that included recognition of the sexual differences. Third-wave feminism has actively moved toward a feminism that includes issues of sexuality. This research not only explores sexuality within patriarchal society, but it also examines the privilege of white heterosexual feminists in relation to their lesbian and bisexual counterparts. Furthermore, third-wave feminism has moved beyond a recognition of multisexuality's focus on sexual relations and has expanded to include examination of the multiple sex/gender identities in society, such as **butch** (a masculine lesbian), femme (feminine lesbian), and the **transgender** (individuals who were born as male but have transformed themselves into female and vice versa). In this sense, third-wave feminism recognizes the true diversity and multiplicity of sexual identities in society and is building a feminism that takes these identities into consideration in their analyses of patriarchal society.
See also Volume 2, Primary Document 57

Further Reading: Howell, Clare, and Riki Wilchins, *GenderQueer: Voices from Beyond the Sexual Binary*, Los Angeles: Alyson Publications, 2002; Katz, Jonathon Ned, *The Invention of Heterosexuality*, New York: Plume Books, 1995; Lorde, Audre, "Scratching the Surface: Some Notes on Barriers to Women and Loving," in *Sister Outsider—Essays and Speeches by Audre Lorde*, Freedom, CA: The Crossing Press, 1984, 45–52.

ROBYN S. BOURGEOIS

MUSIC. Third-wave music has played a central role in the production and dissemination of third-wave **feminism**. There are several reasons for this. First, music is a particularly powerful **art** form; it helps people to forge community, to assert individuality, to achieve public voice, to seek transcendence of material circumstances, and to imagine alternative ways and new worlds. The **media**-savvy and pop culture–loving third wave grew up with music's help and has consistently tapped music's power.

Second, in the context of **globalization** and mass media, music has the potential to be an important **education**al and informational tool. Third-wave punk and hip-hop subcultures have made particular use of music as an alternative media outlet, but even mass-marketed music can tell stories and express points of view that do not tend to be heard in other mainstream media outlets. This was particularly apparent while listening to the lyrics and delivery of women's popular music of the 1990s.

Third, musical forms are rooted in particular cultures even as they are shaped by cross-cultural contact, whether that contact takes the form of collaboration or appropriation or both. The third wave thrives within the complexity of musical genealogies because these complexities seem to "keep it real," reflecting the contradictoriness of personal and national histories. The practice of sampling across the musical spectrum enacts this complexity.

Fourth, music is an art that depends upon voice and **body**, and it draws on verbal and visual forms of **representation**. As such, it has been a particularly fruitful site for explorations of key third-wave feminist concepts such as the problems and pleasures of female embodiment; the complexity of a politics of voice (whisper, yell, conversation, ventriloquism, strategic silence); the critique and celebration of girliness and beauty culture; and the performance of gender.

It is not just coincidence that women in music attained major visibility in the 1990s at the same time that third-wave feminism began to be named and claimed. Whether or not the musicians—or their fans, for that matter—used the "f-word" to claim feminism as theirs, women's music in the 1990s gave the third wave a very public presence.

The 1990s: Riot Grrrl. Riot Grrrl emerged in the punk music scene in Olympia, Washington, in 1991, following in the footsteps of 1970s and 1980s women punk revolutionaries such as Patti Smith, Deborah Harry of Blondie, Poly Styrene of X-Ray Spex, Kim Gordon of Sonic Youth, Kim Deal of the Pixies, and Exene Cervenka of X. Intent on claiming punk as an empowering social space, committed to the punk values of telling harsh truths and **DIY** (do it yourself) creativity, and given permission to pick up guitars and mics by the punk embrace of three-chord amateurism, Riot Grrrls got loud together and proclaimed **girl** love. Groups such as **Bikini Kill** set up female-only areas in the mosh pit and passed out pamphlets calling for revolution girl style. Musicians such as Bikini Kill's Kathleen Hanna sometimes performed with words like SLUT scrawled across their bodies; the intention was to show through performance that such words are used against girls to mark or brand them, and to harness the power of these words through aggressive appropriation and parody. Girls wrote songs about female sexual **desire**, the sexual victimization of girls, the "rules" of **femininity**, and female friendship and also began self-publishing and distributing **zines** of their art and **writing**. Riot Grrrl music and zines began to spread through concerts, the Internet, and word of mouth, and girls around the country began to affiliate with Riot Grrrl and create their own local actions.

Riot Grrrl cultural work both extends and departs from the cultural work of the second-wave feminist movement. The in-your-face performance of social scripts for female embodiment can be seen as a third-wave contribution to feminist activism, a contribution that owes more to the work of performance artists such as Carolee Schneeman and Adrian Piper than to women's movement art, most famously represented by Judy Chicago's *Dinner Party*. On the other hand, Riot Grrrl zine making can be understood as a print form of **consciousness raising**, descending from second-wave face-to-face consciousness-raising groups, manifesto writing, and the radical **feminist publishing** movement.

And Riot Grrrl music addresses many of the issues addressed by second-wave "womyn's music," albeit in a much more sonically aggressive **fashion**. In fact, Bikini Kill's drummer Tobi Vail coined the third-wave term "grrrl" as a seriously humorous revision of the second-wave term "womyn."

The first overview of Riot Grrrl appeared in the national press with the publication of Emily White's "Revolution Girl Style Now" in the July 10–16, 1992, edition of *L.A. Weekly*. White's article presented a thoughtful discussion of Riot Grrrl in the context of contemporary **youth culture** and feminism, but the media coverage of Riot Grrrl that followed sent the Grrrls, who were believers in controlling the dissemination of one's own image and words, running for cover. This spate of mainstream interest in Grrrl culture (and, as the Grrrls feared, the misrepresentation of it as "just" girl culture), effectively predicted the emergence a few years later of girl culture as a mass-market phenomenon.

The Riot Grrrl refusal to use popular culture as a tool to share their ideas beyond the confines of the punk scene—or, viewed another way, their desire to create their own institutions and their refusal to sell out—exists in interesting counterpoint to grunge queen **Courtney Love**'s decision to seek the power that comes with national exposure—or, viewed another way, to succumb to the myth of star power. As Emily White observes in the 1997 piece "The Great Indie Debate," "As Love slagged the riot grrrls in public, and the riot grrrls slagged Love, sometimes it seemed as if the **wars** these female bands were waging were petty, small-town affairs. But they also reflected feminist issues that had had long lives: Do you separate from the sexist world or try to engage it?"

The 1990s: Pop Music's "Angry Women." In the 1990s, a number of women chose to engage the sexist world or to perform as if sexism did not exist. Building on the noise made by all-female and mixed-gender bands fronted by women in the late 1980s and early 1990s (the Pixies, the Breeders, the Throwing Muses, Babes in Toyland, Salt-n-Pepa, Lunachicks, L7, Team Dresch, Tribe 8, Queen Latifah, and Hole among them), a wide variety of women performers hit the pop rock scene in the mid 1990s. Here is a representative list of album releases by year. In 1993: Belly (Tanya Donnelly), *Star*; Bikini Kill, *Pussy Whipped*; Melissa Etheridge, *Yes I Am*; P.J. Harvey, *Rid of Me*; Queen Latifah, *Black Reign*; **Liz Phair**, *Exile in Guyville*. In 1994: Tori Amos, *Under the Pink*; **Ani DiFranco**, *Out of Range*; Hole, *Live Through This*; Madonna, *Bedtime Stories*; **Sarah McLachlan**, *Fumbling Toward Ecstasy*; Me'Shell Ndegéocello, *Plantation Lullabies*. In 1995: Bjork, *Post*; Ani DiFranco, *Not A Pretty Girl*; Jewel, *Pieces of You*; Natalie Merchant, *Tiger Lily*; Alanis Morrisette, *Jagged Little Pill*; No Doubt (Gwen Stefani), *Tragic Kingdom*; Joan Osborne, *Relish*. And in 1996: Cibo Matto, *Viva! La Woman*; Ani DiFranco, *Dilate*; the Fugees (**Lauryn Hill**), *The Score*; Sleater Kinney, *Call the Doctor*. In 1996, Morrisette swept the Grammys, and singles by Morrisette, Etheridge, Jewel, Merchant, and Osborne hit the Top 40 charts, leading the music industry to name it the year of the woman in rock. Women musicians and fans greeted this news with mixed emotions. The popularity of women in rock showed that "chicks rock," but it also threatened women musicians with overexposure, trivialization through market categorization as "*women's* rock," and the erasure of the differences between them. The positive fan reception and mixed media coverage of the Lilith Fair, a summer festival that featured all women musicians and toured nationally from 1997–1999, demonstrated the pros and cons of the "women in rock" label.

Like Janis Joplin, Joan Armatrading, Chrissie Hynde, Joni Mitchell, Joan Jett, and Ma Rainey before them, women in the 1990s appropriated rock's rebel yells, travel narratives, love songs, and sexual bravado in a variety of ways, with a shared commitment to the lyric and sonic expression of women's stories and points of view. In their book *The Sex Revolts: Gender, Rebellion, and Rock and Roll* (1999), Simon Reynolds and Joy Press delineate four strategies that mark what they call "the scattered history of female rock rebellion." Although such categories can be limiting and most musicians mix them up in practice, they are useful starting points for understanding the ways in which women in the 1990s engaged rock's male-centered rebel traditions.

First, some women musicians appropriate the position of male rebel so as to play (with/as) boys. For example, P.J. Harvey sings loud and raucous rock, taking on male and female subject positions in her lyrics but always singing from the perspective of the person in power. In contrast, Liz Phair's *Exile in Guyville*, written as a response to the Rolling Stones' *Exile on Main Street* (1972), presents roughly voiced lyrics that tell stories from the perspective of the dominator, the victim, and the confused. Both versions of gender-bending resonated with male and female alternative rock fans, perhaps an indication of the ways that women and men are identifying themselves through mixing masculine and feminine social scripts.

Second, some women musicians create "feminine" rock so as to revise and claim rock's primal power. For example, Courtney Love certainly appropriates the position of male rebel in her sonic delivery and punk rock lifestyle, but her poignantly pissed-off lyrics and 1990s Kinder-whore look simultaneously perform and disintegrate "the feminine." Alternatively, as Reynolds and Press argue, Tori Amos' beautifully voiced sexual and religious confessions, accompanied by her lush piano playing, act to feminize the role of rock rebel as she "rewrit[es] the classic dynamic of breaking loose from **domesticity** and sexual repression as the story of the Prodigal Daughter." And folk-oriented musicians Natalie Merchant and Jewel lay claim to the singer-songwriter tradition in rock, the "feminine" side of rock that has historically been most hospitable to women.

Third, some women musicians take on a variety of personas so as to play with and against the social construction of femininity. Madonna is the most obvious example of this strategy; performing as boy toy, material girl, Marilyn Monroe, dominatrix, spiritual seeker, mother, and many more, she mines female archetypes and stereotypes to find the next self to perform. Cultural critic Gayle

Wald identifies another way that 1990s women in rock don various female personas in an essay about how Gwen Stefani of No Doubt performs versions of "girlhood" and "girliness." Wald also notes an interesting link between Madonna's appropriation of black, gay drag performance and Stefani's appropriation of Jamaican ska performance enroute to the creation of "rebellious" rocker femininities. On the one hand, cultural mixing is a central feature of third-wave art and experience. On the other hand, these kinds of appropriations open up critical questions about the differences between cultural exchange and cultural appropriation.

Fourth, some women musicians rebel against **identity** itself, choosing contradiction and flux over self-definition, or claiming mixture and multiplicity as modes of self-definition. Although most of the musicians mentioned can be understood as favoring these strategies to various degrees, as do many women and men who identify as third wave, Me'shell Ndegéocello and Ani DiFranco best embody these strategies in their music and in their self-representations. Ndegéocello remixes R&B, soul, funk, jazz, and rap, earning comparisons with Curtis Mayfield and Al Green. She also calls herself the female Bruce Springsteen and hit the charts in 1994 with "Wild Night," a duet with Heartland rocker John Mellencamp. DiFranco calls herself a folk punk rocker. She reforms those genres by linking them, and she has stretched them further at various times to include a horn section, the Buffalo Symphony Orchestra, spoken-word **poetry**, jazz, and electronica. Both women are openly bisexual and playfully mix boyishness and girlishness in their appearance, and their lyrics favor mixture as well; their songs are by turns (or all at once) intimate confessionals, neighborhood stories, sexy grooves, and political manifestoes.

Whatever their strategies, pleasures, or politics, women musicians of the 1990s invigorated pop rock when it seemed to be floundering, and they performed (for) the third wave in its joyful and angry and contradictory variety. In contrast, the pop music scene in the early twenty-first century seems to privilege the teen divas' mass-produced vocal stylings, and although interesting exceptions hit the charts—Macy Grey comes to mind—the music that *sounds* like the third wave is back to being independent, even if it is major label.

Twenty-first Century Trends. Third-wave women in rock are alive and well. In recent releases, Kathleen Hanna's new band Le Tigre throws a feminist dance party on *Feminist Sweepstakes* (2001); Me'shell Ndegéocello raps and sings across contemporary blacknesses on *Cookie: The Anthropological Mixtape* (2002); Tori Amos seeks America on the post–9/11 road album *Scarlet's Walk* (2002); Ani DiFranco sinews her way through pro-environment and anticorporate rhymes on *Evolve* (2003); and Sleater Kinney and P.J. Harvey keep howling on *One Beat* (2002) and *Uh Huh Her* (2004), respectively.

As the century turned, the third wave also went looking for different sounds, and musicians turned to old-school music for inspiration while continuing to make it new. There are several possible reasons for this interest in sounds of the past. First, third-wave musicians and fans are getting tired of particular ways of voicing power and anger, particularly after seeing "girl culture" and "angry women" co-opted and remade (again) as stereotype. Second, the third wave is seeking alternatives to the money-hungry moves of corporate **globalization**, as well as new knowledge to keep growing. And third, they are just doing that third-wave thing: messing around, seeking surprise connections between differences, and reconfiguring genealogies.

The music of hip-hop feminists such as Jill Scott, Angie Stone, and Erykah Badu takes up where the Native Tongues movement of the late 1980s left off in its search for smart and positive lyrics matched to music that moves. This music has been dubbed neo-soul for its smoky 1970s a.m. radio feel, its grown-up appeal in contrast to pop R&B's focus on the teen market, and its emphasis on vocal phrasing rather than overpowered delivery. Writing songs that narrate what hip-hop scholar Michael Anthony Neal calls "sista-girl" stories, these singers find critical accompaniment in **Joan Morgan**'s 1999 book *When Chickenheads Come Home to Roost: My Life as a Hip-Hop Feminist*, a key text for black, third-wave feminism.

Rockers such as Tanya Donnelly and Kristen Hersch have turned to making non-mainstream country music in recent albums, joining alternative country singers like the Be Good Tanyas, Neko Case, Iris DeMent, Gillian Welch, and Lucinda Williams. These musicians all explore what legendary music critic Greil Marcus dubbed "the old, weird America"; an America comprised of whiskey and mayhem, illicit love and murder; an America populated by visionaries and hard workers traveling back roads, haunted by poverty and God and Satan and their own deeds; an America where "race records" and "hillbilly records" were sold in separate stores but addressed many of the same themes; an America that can look a lot like our own. Third-wave, alt-country, and neo-soul women are recuperating the cultural histories of working-class and poor people, especially women. They also bring earlier women musicians with them to the feminist table: Ma Rainey, Billie Holiday, Mahalia Jackson, Nina Simone, Maybelle Carter, Loretta Lynn, Wanda Jackson, Hazel Dickens, and Dolly Parton among them.

Women of all ages converged to attend the 29th Michigan Womyn's Music Festival in August 2004, and second- and third-wave musicians shared the womyn's music stage. The 2004 festival lineup featured newcomers such as Magdalen Hsu-Li, Laura Love, and spoken word artist Alix Olson alongside long-standing members of the womyn's music community like Tret Fure and Lucie Blue Tremblay and comedian Kate Clinton. The event of the weekend was the staging of the Hothead Paisan rock opera, based on Diane DiMassa's "homicidal lesbian terrorist" comic book superhero of the 1990s. The cast represented an eclectic feminist genealogy and included folk punk rocker and Righteous Babe Records founder Ani DiFranco; Animal Prufrock, creator of the opera and formerly of the Righteous Babe group Bitch and Animal; Lynne Breedlove, Tribe 8 singer, punk feminist novelist, and the first woman to bring a mosh pit and mock castration to the Michigan Womyn's Music Festival in

1994; gritty-sweet singer-songwriter Ferron, who emerged onto the womyn's music scene in the late 1980s; the buzz-cut fitness guru Susan Powter, whose rallying cry is "Stop the Insanity!"; percussionist and drum teacher Ubaka Hill, a regular participant in the womyn's music scene; Alyson Palmer of the funk rock performance art group Betty; and Toshi Reagon, genre-bending singer-songwriter and daughter of Bernice Johnson Reagon, founder of the well-known African American a capella group Sweet Honey in the Rock.

See also Girl/Girlies; Hip-Hop Feminism; *Volume 2, Primary Documents 3, 30, 34, and 41*

Further Reading: Davis, Angela, *Blues Legacies and Black Feminism*, New York: Random House, 1998; Dawidoff, Nicholas, *In the Country of Country: A Journey to the Roots of American Music*, New York: Vintage, 1997; Gaar, Gillian, *She's a Rebel: The History of Women in Rock and Roll*, 2nd ed., Seattle: Seal Press, 2002; Garrison, Ednie, "U.S. Feminism Grrrl Style! Youth (Sub)Cultures and the Technologics of the Third Wave," *Feminist Studies* 26 (2000): 141–171; Guralnick, Peter, *Sweet Soul Music: Rhythm and Blues and the Southern Dream of Freedom*, Boston: Back Bay, 1999; Juno, Andrea, *Angry Women in Rock: Volume One*, San Francisco: Juno Books, 1996; McDonnell, Evelyn, and Ann Powers, eds., *Rock She Wrote: Women Write About Rock, Pop, and Rap*, New York: Dell, 1995; Michigan Womyn's Music Festival Web site, www.michfest.com; Morgan, Joan, *When Chickenheads Come Home to Roost: A Hip-Hop Feminist Breaks It Down*, 2nd edition, New York: Simon and Schuster, 2000; Neal, Mark Anthony, *Soul Babies: Black Popular Culture and the Post-Soul Aesthetic*, New York: Routledge, 2002; O'Brien, Lucy, *She Bop 2: The Definitive History of Women in Rock, Pop and Soul*, New York: Continuum, 2002; O'Dair, Barbara, ed., *Trouble Girls: The Rolling Stone Book of Women in Rock*, New York: Rolling Stone Press, 1997; *Pop Matters: The Magazine of Global Culture*, http://www.popmatters.com; Reynolds, Simon, and Joy Press, *The Sex Revolts: Gender, Rebellion and Rock 'n' Roll*, Cambridge, MA: Harvard University Press, 1999; *Rockrgrl* magazine, http://www.rockrgrl.com; Savage, Ann, *They're Playing Our Songs: Women Talk About Feminist Rock Music*, Westport, CT: Praeger, 2003; Wald, Gayle, "Just a Girl? Rock Music, Feminism, and the Cultural Construction of Female Youth," *Signs* 23(3) (1998): 585–610; Whiteley, Sheila, *Women and Popular Music: Sexuality, Identity and Subjectivity*, New York: Routledge, 2000.

JENNIFER DRAKE

N

NATIONAL GIRLS AND WOMEN IN SPORTS DAY. Engaged with a third-wave feminist sensibility that is highly supportive of women and **girls in sports,** National Girls and Women in Sports Day (NGWSD) was chartered by Congress in 1986. National Girls and Women in Sports Day represents a growing recognition of the importance of sport and fitness participation for girls and women and validates female athletic achievement. The first NGWSD, held in 1987, served as a memorial for Olympic volleyball standout and advocate for equal opportunities for girls and women in sports, Flo Hyman. National Girls and Women in Sports Day is supported by the National Girls and Women in Sport Coalition, which is made up of Girls Scouts of the USA, **Girls Incorporated,** National Association for Girls and Women in Sport, the Women's Sports Foundation, and the YWCA of the USA. National Girls and Women in Sports Day plays a key role in continuing to raise public awareness about the importance of participation in a range of sports and fitness activities for girls and women. Since its inception, the climate for girls and women in sports has improved considerably, and the participation rates of women and girls have not only increased, but the range of sports in which women regularly participate has expanded. When chartered, the number of boys participating in high school sports outnumbered girls by a ratio of seventeen to one, whereas today the disparity is less than three to two. Events such as NGWSD have played an important role in validating and creating these opportunities. Held annually in February, NGWSD continues to raise awareness and expand vital opportunities for girls and women around the country.

Further Reading: Macy, Sue, and Jane Gottsman, *Play Like a Girl: A Celebration of Women in Sports*, New York: Henry Holt, 1999; Women's Sports Foundation Web site, http://www.womenssportsfoundation.org www.aahperd.org/ngwsdcentral.

FAYE LINDA WACHS

NIKE. The athletic wear company Nike, which was founded in the mid-1960s by Phil Knight and Bill Bowerman, revolutionized the athletic shoe market. However, by the mid-1980s Nike sales were stagnating and it appeared the sneaker **wars** would be lost to competitors such as Reebok that had recognized the importance of the female market. With women now buying as many athletic shoes as men, Nike quickly shifted from a broad-based appeal to focused marketing that targeted athletic female consumers as well. The ensuing **advertising** campaigns became emblematic of the shifting cultural iconography of the female athlete. It was not simply that ads presented strong female athletes in **sports** apparel but that Nike's advertising campaigns featured female athletes and slogans that deliberately marketed feminist sensibilities. For example, the 1996 campaign featured the positives of sport for women articulated with the "If you let me play" campaign. Subsequent campaigns used humor and irony to critique ideologies that had limited women's participation in athletics. The subject of much controversy, "Nike **feminism**" is critiqued for marketing **empowerment** through the consumption of products made by exploiting women in developing countries. Critics contend that rather than being a harbinger of change, the Nike advertisements simply reflect the increased purchasing power of some women (those reflected in their advertisements). Regardless, Nike's presentation of strong, empowered women combined with a discourse of women's entitlement to sport marks an important shift in cultural iconography surrounding the female form, especially the fit female form, and visually represents third-wave ideals that would combine codes of masculinity and **femininity**.

Further Reading: Cole, C.L., and A. Hribar, "Celebrity Feminism: Nike Style Post Fordism, Transcendence, Consumer Power," *Sociology of Sport Journal* 12(4) (1995): 347–369; Dworkin, S.L., and M. Messner, "Just Do What?: Sport, Bodies and Gender," in *Revisioning Gender*, eds. Judith Lorber, Beth Hess, and Myra Max Ferree, Thousand Oaks, CA: Sage Publications, 1999, 341–64; Heywood, Leslie, and Shari L. Dworkin, *Built to Win: The Female Athlete as Cultural Icon*, Minneapolis: University of Minnesota Press, 2003; Lafrance, Melissa R., "Colonizing the Feminine: Nike's Intersections of PostFeminism and Hyperconsumption," in *Sport and Postmodern Times*, ed. Genevieve Rail, Albany, NY: SUNY Press, 1998.

FAYE LINDA WACHS

O

OPRAH. Oprah Winfrey (1954–) is a talk show host, producer/creator, actress, educator, and philanthropist. In the late 1980s, Oprah transformed the talk show format with her award-winning **television** program, *The Oprah Winfrey Show*, and in the process became an international icon. While Oprah's relationship to third-wave **feminism** is not at once obvious or clear, she does acknowledge and pay tribute to the influential women who came before her even as she recognizes the problems that women still face today. Indeed, Oprah's talk show often speaks to tensions between **"victim/power feminism,"** and in many ways Oprah's own life speaks to the contradictions and complications that many young women in the dominant culture face today.

Moreover, Oprah's talk show does aspire to some notion of feminism or, at the very least, a female-centered standpoint, as her show addresses and attempts to deal with many facets of women's lives, from economic issues to personal relationships. Indeed, it has been noted that Oprah is "better able to recognize the shifting and intersecting agendas of class, gender and 'race' than much **feminist theory**" (Squire, as quoted in Hollows, 2000, 107).

Oprah grew up in Mississippi and has been working in the television industry since the age of nineteen. She is also the creator of *O, The Oprah Magazine*; *Oprah's Book Club*; and *Oprah's Angel Network*; as well as having acted in a number of **films**, most notably *The Color Purple* (1985), which earned her an Academy Award nomination. Oprah, one of the most powerful women in the entertainment industry, is a major cultural force.

Further Reading: Decker, Jeffrey Louis, *Made in America: Self-Styled Success from Horatio Alger to Oprah Winfrey*, Minnesota: University of Minnesota Press, 1997; Heywood, Leslie, and Jennifer Drake, eds., *Third Wave Agenda: Being Feminist, Doing Feminism*,

Minnesota: University of Minnesota Press, 1997; Hollows, Joanne, *Feminism, Femininity and Popular Culture*, Manchester: Manchester University Press, 2000; Oprah Winfrey Web site, http://www.oprah.com.

Natasha Patterson

OPTING OUT. On the surface, opting out, the "choice" for young women (and some young men) to leave the workplace for an unspecified number of years or to reduce their employment from full-time to part-time schedules to raise children or focus on other **family** needs during their career, is perceived to be "traditional" and returning to socially accepted "gender roles." Opting out is not usually perceived as a way to continue to break down the barriers in the workplace. Yet young parents who can afford to opt out are creating new paths for balancing the multiple responsibilities in their lives during crucial years where they are building their careers and raising children, especially if one takes into consideration the fact that men as well as women are "opting out." Third-wave **feminism** encourages a look at both sides of "opting out": the men and the women who choose this path.

A range of factors contribute to decisions to "opt out." Women continue to experience sexism. They experience wage **discrimination**, with the exception of a few industries. They experience exhaustion from the second shift; the combination of full-time work and family responsibilities. They experience the fear that if they work long hours, they are not good mothers. Conflicts in this issue range from finding good childcare to society's acceptance of women who stay exclusively at home. Since raising children and caring for family needs still tends to be seen as **women's work**, women in some cases are less stigmatized than men for doing this. Women responding to the combination of these factors are making up what the **media** has labeled as the "Opt-Out Revolution."

However, the **media** has ignored the sizable population of men who have decided to "opt out" and serve as the full-time caretaker for their children while their partner works outside the home. The fact that the **Generation X** demographic women, who statistically have higher levels of **education** than men, and, responding to second-wave feminism and the ambition it enabled in women, sometimes also are more achievement-oriented and have higher-paying jobs with better benefits than men, means that there is a phenomenon of gender reversal that is working out well for many families. In an era of **downsizing** and part-time work where many younger people's identities do not center around jobs, many men do not conflate as much of their **identity** with their work life. Furthermore, many men do not have the kind of career achievement orientation that many feminist women do and much prefer the work of raising children and choose to be the partner who is the primary caretaker.

The **media** attention, however, has mostly focused only on the women who have made this choice, and they have furthermore focused on a small population of well-educated white women exiting highly demanding professions such as law, medicine, or business, and who are also married or in partnered relationships with high-earning professionals. These women, who choose to opt out as a way to balance their career and family obligations, benefit from having the best of both worlds. For many American women and men, however, this "choice" does not exist because many work in part-time "**McJobs**" with few benefits, which is a reality that the media has chosen to ignore.

See also Mothering; Outsourcing; Wage Gap

Further Reading: Crittenden, Ann, *The Price of Motherhood: Why the Most Important Job in the World Is Still the Least Valued*, New York: Metropolitan Books, 2001; Eddie, David, *Housebroken: Confessions of a Stay-at-Home Dad*, New York: Riverhead Books, 2003; http://www.fatherville.com/stay-at-home-fathers.shtml; http://feministmothersathome.com/; http://www.generationmom.com/; http://www.mochamoms.org/; http://20ishparents.com/; McKenna, Elizabeth Perle, *When Work Doesn't Work Anymore: Women, Work, and Identity*, New York: Delta 1998; Orenstein, Peggy, *Flux: Women on Sex, Work, Love, Kids, and Life in a Half-Changed World*, New York: Anchor Books, 2000; Williams, Joan, *Unbending Gender: Why Family and Work Conflict and What to Do About It*, New York: Oxford University Press, 1999.

HEATHER CASSELL

ORLAN. Recognizably "third wave" in her willingness to call attention to the ambivalent pain, power, and pleasure associated with Western **beauty ideals** and the pressures on women to meet them, Orlan is a French transdisciplinary performance artist. Very little detail is known about Orlan's history (or her real name) other than she is the first artist to use her **body**, plastic surgery, and the **media** as her medium. She was born on May 30, 1947, in Saint-Etienne, France. Her interest in performance **art** dealing with the female body—particularly how it has been treated in the history of **art**—emerged publicly for the first time at the age of seventeen in her hometown. In 1977, her performance piece "Le Baiser de l'Artiste" ("the artist's kiss" but could also be slang for "the **rape** of the artist"), performed just outside the French art fair at the Grand Palais, featured a life-size replica of Orlan's torso-turned slot machine (which rewarded users, for five francs, a real kiss from the artist herself). It sparked scandal from onlookers and the artistic community alike and solidified her reputation as a provocative and controversial performance artist. In 1982 (before the development of the Internet), Orlan founded the first electronic art magazine, *Art-Accèss Review*, on the Minitel, and she moved to Paris the following year and became a lecturer in fine art at L'École Nationale des Beaux-Arts in Dijon. While 1978 marked her first surgical performance, it was not until 1990 that her work—self-described as "Carnal Art"—launched her into the international spotlight. That year witnessed a marked shift in Orlan's focus (and an increase in controversy): the operating room became her studio as she launched a series of surgical procedures/performances that interrogated the social pressures weighted on the female body for beauty's sake, using her own body—her face in particular—as her canvas. Building on a decade's worth of work on **identity, feminist theory**, psychoanalytic theory, Christian iconography, and the baroque, "The Reincarnation of Sainte Orlan" (also referred to as "Image—New Images") involves a complete "rebirth" of the artist: a complete physical reconstruction shaped through a series of highly publicized plastic surgeries. Her goal is to refigure different sections of her face to match (albeit in a more exaggerated manner) the facial structures of icons of "feminine beauty," including the forehead of Leonardo da Vinci's Mona Lisa, the chin of Botticelli's Venus, the mouth of François Boucher's Europa, and so on. Orlan creates a living composite of impossibility that simultaneously illustrates both the unattainable aim of ideal feminine beauty and the horrifying process of attempting it. Each performance is meticulously crafted: costumes have been **fashion**ed by famous designers, remnants (photos and **film** footage) are sold to fund the expensive undertakings, and Orlan insists on being conscious to maintain complete control over the production's choreography. Her website, launched in 2000, is the official home/database for her "oeuvre."

Further Reading: Best, Victoria, *Powerful Bodies: Performance in French*, New York: Peter Lang, 1999; Brand, Peg Zeglin, *Beauty Matters*, Bloomington: Indiana University Press, 2000; Jones, Amelia, *Body Art: Performing the Subject*, Minneapolis: University of Minnesota Press, 1996; Kauffman, Linda S., *Bad Girls and Sick Boys: Fantasies in Contemporary Art and Culture*, Berkeley: University of California Press, 1998; Orlan's Official Web site: http://www.orlan.net; Phelan, Peggy, and Helena Reckitt, *Art and Feminism*, Boston: Phaidon Press, 2001.

Candis Steenbergen

OUTSOURCING. In today's global economy, companies often outsource, or subcontract, either part or all of their production. Companies are also **downsizing**, and low-benefit, low-paying **"McJobs"** are created. All of these processes involve cutting costs (i.e., employees and/or benefits) to increase overall profit. According to **globalization's** structure of free market capitalism, the more that can be made for less, the better. Outsourcing effects not only third-wave women inside the United States who are jobless or faced with low-paying jobs as a result, but women around the world, many of whom work for pennies a day in global factories created to increase profits.

Outsourcing is similar to "off-shoring," which involves moving factories to locations outside of a particular country (often the United States) to gain access to workers who will accept lower wages and/or benefits. Outsourcing involves contracting out any part of a corporation's production to manufactures to increase profits, *in-* or *outside* of a particular corporation's home country. However, the "off-shoring" of outsourcing is common, especially to export processing zones (EPZs), many of which were created under trade treaties, such as the North Atlantic Free Trade Agreement (NAFTA). Factories in EPZs, and maquiladoras (factories along the Mexican/U.S. border), offer tariff-free or duty-free export, resulting in more profit. However, this profit does not reach the worker. Because many global factories are also outside of international labor regulations, working conditions are poor, and pay and benefits are low. Sweatshops (factories with extremely poor working conditions) exist inside the United States as well, making up an estimated 50 percent of garment factories. Garment manufacturing is a main outsourcing industry, but outsourced production includes everything from electronics to plastics to auto parts.

Girls and women, particularly ages fifteen to twenty-two, are the overwhelming majority (90 percent) of sweatshop workers. In the United States, many of these workers are recent immigrants and/or women of color. Manufacturers see women as ideal for these jobs because of their "nimble fingers," which are needed for intricate work. Many feminists, however, argue that women are ideal for these jobs because companies are able to pay them less according to the sexual **division of labor**, where **women's work** is not considered "inside" the typical means of production. Many third-wave feminists, particularly women of color and immigrant women, have organized against the exploitation of these workers.

See also Capitalist Patriarchy

Further Reading: Blackwell, Maylei, Linda Burnham, and Jung Hee Choi, eds., *Time to Rise: US Women of Color—Issues and Strategies*, Oakland, CA: Women of Color Resource Center Publications, 2001; Elson, Diane, and Ruth Pearson, "Nimble Fingers Make Cheap Workers," *Feminist Review* 7 (1981): 87–107; Feminist Majority, Feminists Against Sweatshops, http://www.feminist.org/other/sweatshops/; Fuentes, Annette, and Barbara Ehrenreich, *Women and The Global Factory*, New York: Institute for Communications, 1982; Kamel, Rachael, and Anya Hoffman, eds., *The Maquiladora Reader: Cross-Border Organizing Since NAFTA*, American Friends Service Committee, 1999; Labaton, Vivien, and Dawn Lundy Martin, eds., *The Fire This Time: Young Activists and the New Feminism*, New York: Anchor Books, 2004; Louie, Miriam Ching Yoon, *Sweatshop Warriors: Immigrant Women Workers Take on the Global Factory*, Cambridge, MA: South End Press, 2001; National Mobilization Against Sweatshops, http://www.nmass.org/nmass/index.html; Sweatshop Watch, http://www.sweatshopwatch.org; Women and The Economy, UNPAC, http://www.unpac.ca/.

GWENDOLYN BEETHAM

P

PATRIARCHY. Patriarchy (from the Greek roots "patria," which means "**family**"; and "archy," which means "rule") initially applied to a male head of family exerting autocratic rule, then by extension it applied to government ruled by senior men. Second-wave feminists believed liberals failed to challenge the fundamentally biased distribution of power, authority, and access to primary resources. The concept "patriarchy" denotes this general system, where social practices, institutions (church, family, state), and cultural images organize the power that men exert over women.

Prefiguring third-wave interest in the **body** and **queer theory**, second-wave feminists distinguished between sex, gender, and sexual orientation. The woman's body, according to poet Adrienne Rich, is the terrain on which patriarchy is erected; power is exerted through the use and control of women's bodies and **sexuality**. Legal scholar Catharine MacKinnon drew attention to the fact that patriarchy attempts to control reproduction and construct women's sexuality, so women become objects for men. A woman's sexuality always embodies power, a **compulsory heterosexuality**, where "feminine" is defined in terms of, and subservient to, "masculine." Radical feminist Andrea Dworkin echoed this analysis of sex and sexuality in her work on **pornography** and intercourse. Dale Spender showed how language internalizes these "patriarchal imperatives," Kate Millett analyzed forms of **representation** in literature, and Laura Mulvey used psychoanalysis to analyze how the feminine is portrayed in **film**.

Third-wave cultural theory has its roots in works such as those cited above.

Radical feminists, such as Millett, considered patriarchy a universally exploitative system, so pervasive it appears natural, and analytically distinct from economic forms of production and exploitation. For Shulamith Firestone, the "biological" family, with its division of reproductive labor, is at the root of a sex-based class system. Marilyn French argued that patriarchy is the paradigmatic mode of oppression: sex-based domination leads necessarily to other forms of hierarchy. Second-wave socialist and Marxist feminists presented alternatives to this one model of oppression, finding intersections between ethnic, gender, and class exploitation under an even more total system "**capitalist patriarchy**."

Third-wave feminists consider these accounts problematic. First, the essentialist tendency to universalize throughout history and cultures implies that that all women, regardless of ethnicity or class, have common experiences of oppression. Middle-class white women were seen to be generalizing from their own standpoint and failing to recognize the fact that some women are much more "oppressed" than others. Second, when speculating on the origins of patriarchy, second-wave feminists were prone to base their arguments on biology, psychology, or "natural dispositions": naturalism. Third, the attempt to unite theories of patriarchy and capitalism floundered as Marxism itself struggled to retain academic plausibility. However, some, for example Alison Jaggar, argued that patriarchy does not assume a universal form, and most others would agree with MacKinnon that what it means to be a man or woman is a social process and open to change.

The concept of patriarchy is pivotal to **feminist theory**. By rejecting the universalizing nature of the concept "woman" and the idea of universal, systematic oppression that ignores differences in economic and social status between women, the task facing third-wave **feminism** is to rethink ideas of power in a way that can ground political action.

See also Essentialism

Further Reading: Bryson, Valerie, *Feminist Political Theory: An Introduction*, Basingstoke: Macmillan, 1992; Tong, Rosemary, *Feminist Thought: A Comprehensive Introduction*, London: Unwin Hyman, 1989.

GILLIAN HOWIE

PERFORMATIVITY. Performativity is the concept that gender is a daily, habitual, learned act based on cultural norms of **femininity** and masculinity. Third-wave **feminism** is based on this idea. The concept was popularized by the work of **Judith Butler**, who was influenced by theorists who studied "speech acts," or the power of authoritative words to both say and do at the same time. One example is, "I now pronounce you man and wife." According to Butler, gender works in much the same way. Growing up, many **girls** learn countless subtle ways to groom and arrange their bodies to be feminine and attain approval as "normal" in a culture that puts people into one of two categories: man or woman. For example, girls internalize stereotypically feminine acts such as wearing dresses and makeup, shaving underarms and legs, sitting with legs crossed, and playing with dolls (which, it could be argued depending on the kind of play, is a preparation for the adult woman's traditional gender role of raising children). Women and men continually "cite" these gender norms in their day-to-day behavior, usually without realizing it. Even the simple act of filling out a form and circling the "Mr." prefix is a performance of gender. Most often, gender is among the first things one notices about another person, and that is not so much a result of biological differences as it is a result of these stylizations of the **body** and habits of mind supplied by cultural norms. Such norms are oppressive because a person's social legitimacy and normalcy depends on conforming to one of the two genders.

Since the 1970s, feminists have insisted upon the difference between sex and gender. In 1975, Gayle Rubin argued that a predominately heterosexual society that institutionalizes **sexuality** in **marriage** and the **family** unit needs two—and only two—genders, and a causal relationship does not exist between sex and gender; in other words, one's sex does not determine one's gender. Butler extends the sex/gender distinction by saying that neither gender *nor sex* is natural; they are only naturalized through repetition and people's belief in the correct performance of their designated sex and gender; their designated term in the man/woman binary. Butler claims that there is no authentic, innate man or woman behind or before the entry into culture, society, and language.

Some theorists have critiqued performativity as a concept that can be misinterpreted as a simple putting on or taking off of genders: today I'll perform as a man, tomorrow as a woman. That performativity is based on cultural norms, however, makes it much more complex; consider, for example, the act of cross-dressing. If a teenager goes to school in drag, he or she will likely get beaten, harassed, or at least laughed at. Others have argued that performativity reduces the importance of the physical body. However, we can only know the body through language and culture, and that what we interpret as sex is an effect of the discourse surrounding *gender*. Most people assume that although a person can claim to be a man or a woman, the person's sex is a fixed, objective reality, but in the case of an infant with ambiguous genitalia, we see how powerfully gender norms act on the body. Sometimes, it is hard to discern whether an infant has a large clitoris or a small penis. To protect the child from ridicule, doctors and parents will often opt to surgically alter the genitals into a more feminine shape.

Butler points out that there are several ways to expose and undermine gender norms, including creating many new genders, making fun of gender through parody, and rejecting being categorized as either "man" or "woman." We can see many genders in **transgender** and gender**queer** discourse, including the use of terms such as stone butches, baby butches, daddies, cowboys, masters, Boy Scouts, dandies, princes, knights, and tranny bois. Genderqueers, drag queens, and **drag kings** also play with gender by embodying caricatures of extreme masculinity or femininity. The androgynous 1980s character "Pat" from *Saturday Night Live* is an example of what Butler calls resisting "cultural intelligibility." In the **comedy** sketches, other characters ask Pat questions, trying to tease out which of the two genders Pat is. All the questions are parodies of gender stereotypes. For example, they ask Pat whether he or she wants a drink: "Would you like a beer or a cosmopolitan?" Pat always resists interpretation, saying something like, "Oh, I shouldn't. I just took an antihistamine." Although many feminist theorists, including transgender theorists and activists, see parody, the rejection of gender categories, and the proliferation of genders as potent political strategies, other theorists critique this kind of strategy, arguing instead that performative political strategies such as those just mentioned aestheticize "gender expression" at the expense of correcting social inequities that harm women.

See also Biological Determinism; Feminist Theory

Further Reading: Butler, Judith, *Bodies That Matter: On the Discursive Limits of "Sex,"* New York: Routledge, 1993; Butler, Judith, *Excitable Speech: A Politics of the Performative,* New York: Routledge, 1997; Butler, Judith, *Gender Trouble,* New York: Routledge, 1999; Butler, Judith, "Imitation and Gender Insubordination," in *Literary Theory: An Anthology,* eds. Julie Rivkin and Michael Ryan, Malden, MA: Blackwell, 1998, 722–730; Campbell, Karlyn Kohrs, "The Discursive Performance of Femininity: Hating Hillary," *Rhetoric and Public Affairs* 1(1) (1998): 1–19; Rubin, Gayle, "The Traffic in Women," in *Literary Theory: An Anthology,* eds. Julie Rivkin and Michael Ryan, Malden, MA: Blackwell, 1998, 533–560; Snitow, Ann, "A Gender Diary," in *Conflicts in Feminism,* eds. Marianne Hirsch and Evelyn Fox Keller, New York: Routledge, 1990, 9–43.

CLANCY RATLIFF

PHAIR, LIZ. A singer/songwriter many take to be an example of a third-wave feminist, Liz Phair (1967–) was born Elizabeth Clark Phair. Her debut album, *Exile in Guyville* (1993), released on Matador Records, brought her to the forefront of women in rock. Through the use of acoustic and electric guitars and her playful vocals, Phair confronted gender stereotypes with explicit lyrics and sexual subversion. While *Exile in Guyville* sold more than half a million albums, most of the press focused on her dirty, dissatisfied lyrics, such as her calling herself a "blow-job queen." Critics saw her as a rich **girl** getting attention for misbehaving while fans believed she was the feminist role model for **Generation X**. *Rolling Stone* named her Best New Female Artist. In 1994, she released her second album, *Whip-Smart,* which was more personal and less sexual and brought her attention from major **media** outlets. In 2003 she released a slick self-titled album on Capitol Records. Indie rock fans criticized her for cleaning up her style for a radio audience and for working with the mainstream recording team, The Matrix, who are responsible for pop stars like Britney Spears, while others congratulated Phair on the album's new, mature sound.

See also Music

Further Reading: Liz Phair Web site, http://www.lizphair.com; O'Dair, Barbara, ed., *Trouble Girls: The Rolling Stone Book of Women in Rock,* New York: Random House, 1997.

BREA GRANT

POETRY. Feminist poetry in the late twentieth century shaped possibilities for the third-wave feminist poets of the early twenty-first century. Poets such as Adrienne Rich, Sapphire, Lucille Clifton, and Gloria Anzaldúa, whose work appeared between 1951 and 1996, demonstrated the power of poetry as a **consciousness-raising art**. These poems told stories that had never been told, shared visions of revolution, and demonstrated that a written text can empower women to join a movement. Feminist poets continue to empower their readers by making a connection between the personal and the political.

This is the basis for the poetry written by third-wave feminists, which includes the work of Elizabeth Alexander, Honor Moore, and many others. The freedom contemporary poets have to write about (and publish) their personal struggles and observations is due in great part to the feminist poets of the 1950s and 1960s who made **writing** a healing and "revolutionary" act.

Two popular forms of poetic feminist expression have emerged. The first can be classified as "written word" and can manifest as traditional poetry. The second form of expression, which has grown immensely in recent years, stems from "oral tradition" and takes the form of "spoken word," or live poetry. The poet recites her work either from memory or creates work spontaneously in front of the audience. This kind of presentation has created works that "break down" the elite division between readers and nonreaders by making poetry more accessible to those who do not have the resources to obtain books. It has become the preferred form of art for many young poets. Spoken word bends the rules of traditional poetry. A blend of poetry and performance monologue, spoken word is a poetic expression that continues the trend of consciousness-raising writing established by earlier feminist writers.

A theme found in both forms of expression is the act of reclaiming what has previously been denied or unrecognized. Instead of creating poetry concerned with portraying a homogenous front—the point of view of the primarily white, middle, and upper classes—poets create a unique space on the page where the culture and language are specific to a particular group of people and express their particular views. When they participate in the "telling the untold" school of poetry, third-wave poets tackle sexism, **racism**, homophobia, and poverty and express the realities of their particular locations—geographic, socioeconomic, and/or gender based. In doing so, these poets demonstrate a multitude of unique visions and the diversity that exists in poetry today.

See also Tea, Michelle

Further Reading: Academy of American Poets, http://www.poets.org; Anzaldúa, Gloria, *Making Face, Making Soul/Haciendo Caras: Creative and Critical Perspectives by Feminists of Color*, San Francisco: Aunt Lute Book, 1990; Florence, Howe, *No More Masks!: An Anthology of Twentieth-Century American Women Poets*, New York: Harper-Perennial, 1993; Gillan, Maria Mazziotti, and Jennifer Gillan, eds., *Unsettling America*, New York: Penguin, 1993; Various, *My Words Consume Me: An Anthology of Youth Speaks Poets*, San Francisco: McSweeny's, 2000.

GRISELDA SUAREZ

POLITICAL PARTICIPATION. Political participation can be defined in many ways. In the traditional sense of the term, political participation means just that: involvement in the political arena. However, **feminism** has a long history of subverting what it means to be involved in politics and challenging the meaning of the "political." "The personal is political" has been one of feminism's slogans since the early 1970s. This phrase signifies that women's issues, such as reproductive rights, which were traditionally considered to be in the realm of the personal, are also political. Third-wave feminists have both adopted this phrase and adapted it to apply to a wide range of causes, from **queer** rights to anti-**globalization**. Despite the fact that young women are often critiqued for not being political enough, there is strong evidence of both traditional and activist political involvement, although perhaps not in their foremothers' "traditional feminist" manner.

Feminist Political Tradition. During the "first wave" of the feminist movement (the period in the late nineteenth and early twentieth centuries), traditional political participation was the main goal: women were organizing for the right to vote. Women in the "second wave" of the feminist movement organized both in and outside of "traditional" political venues, holding "**consciousness-raising**" meetings to identify "personal" issues that were considered "political" under "the personal is political" slogan. There were debates within the feminist movement as to whether change on these issues could come from outside the political realm, or whether more women should participate inside traditional political channels such as the Senate, House of Representatives, and local elected positions. During this period, women of color also critiqued the movement's way of addressing the "political," arguing that women of color's experiences were often absent. While agreeing that the political system needed to change to recognize the needs of all women, the question became: Change for whom and for what?

In politics, the first and second waves of feminism produced many successes. Women now have the right to divorce, the right to **abortion**, and the right to own property. Many third-wavers cannot imagine a time when this was not so. However, as with other areas where sexual **discrimination** persists (such as the **wage gap** between women and men), there is still a long way to go for women in the political realm. Women are still severely underrepresented as elected officials. In fact, the United States ranks fifty-second in the world in the percentage of women holding elected office. A woman has yet to be elected as president or vice president, although they have run for these offices. Several organizations seek to involve young women in politics in this traditional sense, such as The White House Project's *Vote, Run, Lead Initiative.* However, building on the second wave's tradition of activism "outside" and the critiques of women of color, third-wavers seek not only to become politically involved but also to transform the way women do politics.

New Grrrl Politics. Because of their nontraditional ways of practicing feminist politics, third-wavers are often assumed to be politically apathetic. For example, third-wavers often use popular culture as a means to politicize the personal in the form of "zines," or, like the Riot Grrrls, through popular **music**. Many third-wave **writings**, such as those anthologized in *To Be Real* (1995) and *Colonize This!* (2002), are personalized explorations of what it means to be a young (feminist, person of color, bisexual, or all of the above) woman, rather than declarations of third-wave political theory. However, these writings also echo the "second wave" consciousness-raising meetings and therefore can be read as the third wave's version of "the personal is political." Other writings (along with many young women's organizations), such as *Manifesta* (2000) and *The Fire This Time* (2004), tackle the political in a more direct way, offering experience, **DIY** (do it yourself) advice and, in the case of *Manifesta*, a "thirteen-point agenda."

The nontraditional nature of third-wave political participation makes coalition building essential and new forms of technology, such as the Internet, have made building coalitions easier. However, the way(s) in which young feminists are "doing politics" in the era of globalization has been the cause for critique by some second-wavers and the **media**, who charge that this type of participation has not led to one cohesive young feminist "movement." Because young women and men are not united under one "label," these critics suggest that young people are politically uninvolved. Upon closer inspection, it is evident that third-wavers *are* involved, and that their causes are many. In addition to get-out-the-vote projects, third-wavers also organize across class, race, gender, and **sexuality** on issues that vary from economic justice to environmental **racism**. Moreover, this type of organization "allow[s] more young women and men to claim feminism as a framework not just for activism but for living. What some may see as a detrimental fragmentation within the feminist movement, [third wavers] understand to be a place of power."

See also Environmentalism; Seattle Protests; Third Wave Foundation; *Volume 2, Primary Document 46*

Further Reading: Baumgardner, Jennifer, and Amy Richards, *Manifesta: Young Women, Feminism, and the Future*, New York: Farrar, Straus and Giroux, 2000; Dicker, Rory, and Alison Piepmeier, eds., *Catching a Wave: Reclaiming Feminism for the 21st Century*, Boston: Northeastern University Press, 2003; Hernández, Daisy, and Bushra Rehman, eds., *Colonize This!: Young Women of Color on Today's Feminism*, Seattle: Seal Press, 2002; Heywood, Leslie, and Jennifer Drake, eds., *Third Wave Agenda: Being Feminist, Doing Feminism*, Minneapolis: University of Minnesota Press, 1997; hooks, bell, *Feminist Theory: From Margins to Center*, Boston: South End Press, 1984; Labaton, Vivien, and Dawn Lundy Martin, eds., *The Fire This Time: Young Activists and the New Feminism*, New York: Anchor Books, 2004; Moraga, Cherríe L., and Gloria E. Anzaldúa, eds., *This Bridge Called My Back: Writings by Radical Women of Color*, 3rd ed., Berkeley, CA: Third Woman Press, 2002; Naples, Nancy, and Manisha Desai, eds., *Women's Activism and Globalization: Linking Local Struggles and Transnational Politics*, New York: Routledge, 2002; Phillips, Anne, ed., *Feminism and Politics*, New York: Oxford University Press, 1998; Rock the Vote, http://www.rockthevote.org; Siegel, Deborah, *Fighting Words: The 40-Year Struggle for the Soul of Feminism*, forthcoming; Third Wave Foundation, www.thirdwavefoundation.org; Walker, Rebecca, ed., *To Be Real: Telling the Truth and*

Changing the Face of Feminism, New York: Anchor Books, 1995; The White House Project, http://www.thewhitehouseproject.org; Women of Color Resource Center, http://www.coloredgirls.org; Young Women's Task Force, National Council of Women's Organizations, http://www.womensorganizations.org.

GWENDOLYN BEETHAM

PORNOGRAPHY, FEMINISM AND. Pornography has become a litmus test for feminists, a measure of one's commitment to the cause of overthrowing the **patriarchy** or of one's pleasure in chic transgression against establishment **feminism**. It is such a loaded topic that many women avoid discussing it at all, perceiving it as a trap or an empty intellectual exercise. For this reason, Lynn Chancer's balanced discussion of pornography in **feminist theory**, *Reconcilable Differences: Confronting Beauty, Pornography, and the Future of Feminism* (1998), may be the most important text on the subject for the contemporary women's movement. She begins by replacing the simplistic misnomers of anti-porn and anti-censorship feminists with a framework of "relative emphases," acknowledging that both sides of the debate are interested in liberating female **sexuality** as well as critiquing the sexism of traditional pornography, but noting that they diverge on the matter of which goal to prioritize.

Chancer's preference for the anti-censorship side leads her to outline first the strengths of Nadine Strossen's arguments in defense of pornography. The key elements include the preservation of civil liberties on the basis of the First Amendment, a resistance to sexual repression, and a critique of any single-issue feminist agenda. The First Amendment protects free speech, and it has been invoked in many legal cases regarding pornography, a defense made famous by the Larry Flynt trial. Mainstream pornography such as *Hustler* magazine has, however, not been the main target of obscenity cases against pornography. Whereas ordinances against obscenity are often presented in the guise of **family** values—protecting women, children, and an ethical way of life—they have in reality been used consistently to restrict women's reproductive and sexual freedom, to obstruct **sex education** for women and children, and to target the publications of gay, lesbian, and minority artists. Chancer emphasizes the absurdity of this turn of events. Feminist-authored ordinances against pornography have been co-opted by moral conservatives to censor erotic lesbian publications in Canada, for instance, instead of the violent heterosexual porn the authors had in mind.

Further, in a culture that often demonizes sexuality, pornography appeals to some women because it is a genre that speaks freely about sex, indulges shamelessly in sexual pleasure, and allows the viewer to look at sex with a "frank stare," in writer and sex activist Carol Queen's words. The feminist rhetoric of disgust with porn may, as Professor and author Laura Kipnis argues, stem from class bias; she interprets the genre as a carnivalesque display of the improper or socially seditious **body**. Chancer asserts, "Even if one grants that pornography frequently contains conventionally sexist images" (67), its effects are not limited to sexism, "[f]or it also contains imagery arguably freeing in effects, especially since it is generally socially taboo to express and acknowledge sexual feelings" (71). Finally, the problem of a single-issue agenda appears in a number of feminists' **writings** against the anti-porn position. Chancer asks the rhetorical question, "Why would regulating pornography necessarily contribute to weakening a still male-dominated society, rather than strengthening the hand of a state that feminists cannot control?" Gayle Rubin made the same point many years earlier: "Anti-porn propaganda often implies that sexism originates within the commercial sex industry and subsequently infects the rest of society," but the sex industry merely "reflects the sexism that exists in the society as a whole" (301–2). Rubin rejects antiporn rhetoric because it "criticizes non-routine acts of love rather than routine acts of oppression, exploitation, or violence." Chancer points to Strossen's explanation of the single-issue agenda appeals to some feminists: "pornography is an easy target, an easy answer." In other words, it makes sexism feel more manageable.

Chancer turns from Strossen to Catharine MacKinnon and Andrea Dworkin, the leaders of the antipornography movement and authors of the first city ordinance against pornography, after which other ordinances have been modeled. In a section devoted to the resonances of the MacKinnon/Dworkin position, Chancer provides an overview of the concept in **cultural studies** of "hegemony": the unconscious level on which individuals internalize social systems of inequality and come to see their place in them as natural and right. It is on this level that pornography can be seen as destructive, as it provides a set of sexual images that consistently eroticize female subordination, male domination, and ethnic stereotypes. As a limited set of male-centered fantasies, hegemonic pornography positions women as the material through which men pursue pleasure. Female **desire** is represented only as the desire to service male bodies. Because men overwhelmingly own the pornography industry, the feeling of alienation many women experience when viewing porn may arise from the fact that "pornography, like patriarchy itself, indeed is not *fully* in their/our/ women's interests." Nevertheless, most contemporary feminist writers on this subject lean toward a more complex analysis than the antiporn angle provides, and Chancer demonstrates this sophistication in attending to the very real concerns raised by antiporn feminists while arguing that one can *both* advocate against censorship *and* formulate serious challenges, critiques, and protests of the objectionable and discriminatory content of pornography. In tune with trends in feminist cultural studies that acknowledge active audiences' responses to pop cultural texts, including pornography, Chancer concludes by reminding readers that despite the sexism and other limitations of this genre, "many can still find pleasures in niches, in cracks, through reimaginations." Indeed, women who work in the porn industry or actively consume its products will play an important role in shaping the feminist discussions of pornography to come.
See also Pornography, Feminist; Pro-Sex Feminism

Further Reading: Chancer, Lynn, *Reconcilable Differences: Confronting Beauty, Pornography, and the Future of Feminism*, Berkeley: University of California Press, 1998; Cornell, Drucilla, ed., *Feminism and Pornography*, New York: Oxford University Press, 2000; Doyle, Kegan, and Dany Lacombe, "Porn Power: Sex, Violence, and the Meaning of Images in 1980s Feminism," in *"Bad Girls"/"Good Girls": Women, Sex, and Power in the Nineties*, eds. Nan Bauer Maglin and Donna Perry, New Brunswick, NJ: Rutgers, 1996, 188–204; Hooijer, Katinka, "Vulvodynia: On the Medicinal Purposes of Porn," in *Jane Sexes It Up: True Confessions of Feminist Desire*, ed. Merri Lisa Johnson, New York: Four Walls Eight Windows, 2002; Kipnis, Laura, *Bound and Gagged: Pornography and the Politics of Fantasy in America*, New York: Grove, 1996; McElroy, Wendy, *XXX: A Woman's Right to Pornography*, New York: St. Martin's Press, 1995; Strossen, Nadine, *Defending Pornography: Free Speech, Sex, and the Fight for Women's Rights*, New York: New York University Press, 1995; Williams, Linda, *Hard Core: Power, Pleasure, and the "Frenzy of the Visible,"* Berkeley: University of California Press, 1989.

Merri Lisa Johnson

PORNOGRAPHY, FEMINIST. Third-wave feminists are largely uninterested in the distinction between **pornography** and eroticism that prompted so much debate among second-wave feminists. In place of this debate over "good" and "bad" images, third-wave feminists reject the constraints of political correctness on **representations** of **desire** (dubbed "sexual correctness" by some scholars). Feminist pornography for this generation is heavily influenced by marginalized or nonnormative sexualities—including gay and lesbian, **transgender**, **butch/ femme**, and sex-worker activists—and is devoted to reducing the stigma surrounding sexual pleasure in **feminism** and U.S. culture. As sex educator and feminist pornographer Carol Queen asserts, "Until we honor the full spectrum of consensual erotic desire, none of us will be truly free to pursue our own." In this sense, the emerging third-wave position on feminist pornography builds on the sex-positive feminism of the 1980s.

By Lesbians, for Lesbians. Since the mid-1980s, the lesbian feminist pornographic magazine *On Our Backs* has explored the diversity of lesbian **sexuality**, playfully resisting the seriousness of feminist **writing** in the news journal, *Off Our Backs*, while expanding the range of **body** types represented in mainstream pornography by featuring women with short hair, piercings, tattoos, nonsurgically enhanced breasts, and a range of ethnicities. In a similar vein, the Canadian lesbian feminist performance **art** collective, Kiss and Tell, produced *Her Tongue on My Theory* (1994), an art book that depicts its members in bondage scenes. Asserting that images made in a context of pleasure and mutual respect are not the same as images made in a context of oppression or coercion—even if the images themselves look very similar—the members of Kiss and Tell refuse to be "good" feminists or "good" lesbians.

This sense of irreverence infuses the work of Shar Rednour and Jackie Strano, co-owners of S.I.R. Video (an acronym for Sex, Indulgence, and Rock and Roll) and producers of the lesbian pornographic double feature **film**, *Hard Love* and *How to Fuck in High Heels* (2000). This **Generation X** filmmaking team endorses butch/femme gender play, complete with strap-on dildo. Rednour is part of the movement within lesbian feminist pornography to present femme sexuality as powerful, replacing the traditionally passive **femininity** of mainstream porn (she is often the one wielding the dildo). Their newest film, *Sugar High Glitter City* (2001), borrows a parodic aesthetic of excess from contemporary **girlie** culture to create a new tongue-in-cheek genre of adult film: "dykesploitation." Independent lesbian porn thus takes back the "male" gaze, turning objectification into the stuff of satire.

Straight but Not Narrow. Among heterosexual feminist pornographers, there is a similar desire to break free of traditional sexual imagery that fetishizes male ejaculation and puts women in the subordinated role. Participants often engage in gender role reversals, experimenting with the fluidity of power in sexual intercourse. Two popular videos on male anal eroticism—*Bend Over Boyfriend* 1 (1998) and 2 (1999)—combine porn with **sex education** in a mission to promote more give-and-take in heterosexual eroticism (directed by Rednour and Strano, and featuring Carol Queen and her partner Robert Morgan). In some ways, the distinction between lesbian and heterosexual feminist pornography is a false one—as some work in both genres and have worked together at Good Vibrations and Fatale Video—because feminist pornography as a whole is interested in dismantling clear boundaries between different kinds of sex to avoid hierarchies of privilege and rigid **identity** categories. Queen coined the term "pomosexual" (a combination of postmodern and homosexual) to designate this priority of calling categories into question. **Susie Bright** (former columnist for *Playboy* and feminist sex educator) joins Queen in drawing attention to the straight closet in which many heterosexuals find themselves repressing alternative desires.

Lisa Palac comes out of the closet as a "girl pornographer" in *The Edge of the Bed: How Dirty Pictures Changed My Life* (1998), a **memoir** of her transition from feminist-induced frigidity toward porn to the delight of producing her own erotic texts. As a writer for *On Our Backs* and later in an experimental 2-CD project of aural pornography with husband Ron Gompertz—*Cyborgasm* 1 and 2—Palac has spearheaded explorations of cybersex, affirming the value of masturbation as an end in itself and as a satisfying form of "safer sex."

The Internet has been instrumental in making feminist pornography more widely available. In 1998, Heather Corinna founded *Scarlet Letters: A Journal of Femmerotica*, a Web site devoted to sex-positive feminist erotic writing. Together with coeditor Hanne Blank, well known for her contributions to the subgenres of fat-positive and **transgender** erotica, Corinna adds to the element of "genderfuck" in feminist porn with her own term, "genrefuck," for art that denies the separation of erotic from non-erotic as artificial and indicative of a sex-negative society. Although feminist pornography is a small field, limited by financial constraints and marketplace demands, those in the business believe it is poised to expand.

See also Pornography, Feminism and; Pro-Sex Feminism

Further Reading: Bright, Susie, *Full Exposure: Opening Up to Your Sexual Creativity*, San Francisco: HarperCollins, 1999; *Kiss and Tell, Her Tongue on My Theory*, Vancouver: Press Gang, 1994; Palac, Lisa, *The Edge of the Bed: How Dirty Pictures Changed My Life*, Boston: Little, Brown, 1998; Queen, Carol, ed., *Pomosexuals: Challenging Assumptions about Gender and Sexuality*, San Francisco: Cleis, 1997; Queen, Carol, *Real Live Nude Girl: Chronicles of a Sex-Positive Culture*, San Francisco: Cleis, 1997; *Scarlet Letters: A Journal of Femmerotica*, http://www.scarletletters.com; Stan, Adele, ed., *Debating Sexual Correctness: Pornography, Sexual Harassment, Date Rape, and the Politics of Sexual Equality*, New York: Dell, 1995.

MERRI LISA JOHNSON

POSTCOLONIAL FEMINISM. Postcolonial **feminism** is an example of non–age-related third-wave feminism. Like third wave generally, it works to develop its explanations from women themselves while breaking down binary notions of either/or by, among other things, recognizing the differences among women. In the United States, the increasing interest in postcolonial feminism can be seen in the publication of several special issues of leading feminist journals featuring postcolonial feminism.

The roots of this feminism extend back into second-wave feminism. Gloria Anzaldúa, **bell hooks**, and Chandra Talpade Mohanty are examples of women who have called for the recognition of the differing meanings for feminisms in non-Western cultures. Postcolonial feminism today, however, also operates more extensively across geographical and intellectual borders. Intellectually, it criticizes the Western scientific paradigm for its assertions of universality, arguing that its knowledge claims are simply knowledges that have been developed by one group of people at one historical time and place. Theoretically, postcolonial feminism works to extend the analysis of the intersection of sexism with ethnicity, class, and **heterosexism**, to include the still existing negative effects of Western colonialism. More recent phenomena, the capitalist global economy, development projects in the southern hemisphere, and events such as environmental **racism** in the United States are viewed in postcolonialism as neocolonial and a continuation of the European expansion begun in 1492.

The capitalist global economy and its impacts are of crucial importance to postcolonial feminists. This feminism is linking local and global concerns important to women's lives. Women are especially affected by development projects, both by the destruction of resources on which they depend and by the dislocation of immigration. Postcolonial feminists alert their audience to the fact that in the so-called developing world, women and their children, in particular, are severely affected by insufficient food, the increasing cost of living, declining services, and eroding economic and environmental conditions.

These adverse neocolonial impacts often spawn resistance by Third World women, who from the vantage point of their particular locations understand the costs of development and how these costs are occurring. They are most often the ones in the forefront of actions to stop this damage. Some of their more familiar protest examples are in environmental and ecological movements. The Chipko Movement, as described by internationally known ecofeminist and leader in the anti-**globalization** movement, Vandana Shiva of India, is an example. It began when village women of Himalayan India organized to protect their forests from contractors' axes. In the United States, in the environmental justice movement, a movement responding to the disproportionate location of environmentally polluting projects near where people of color and/or poor live, most activists are women. Perhaps more importantly, Third World women have numerous ongoing sites of resistance, which include "self-help" movements for housing or infrastructure, soup kitchens, "mothers' movements" for human rights, movements against fundamentalism and communal violence, International Monetary Fund protests, and so on. Globalization has been accompanied by a tremendous growth in activism to increase women's participation in development activities in the "South"—the word used most frequently in globalization discourse to refer to the developing world.

Third World economic development, which often impairs women's ability to provide basic needs for their children and themselves, raises important questions about how Western First World feminists should understand and engage with these continuing effects of colonial history. In their attempt to understand the situation of many Third World women, First World postcolonial feminists make use of differing analyses. Some enlarge on a Marxist-feminist analysis by demonstrating the relationship between the process of capital accumulation and the sexual division of labor, arguing that the economic and social **empowerment** of women is necessary for "real" economic development to take place in the Third World. Correspondingly, there has been a sizeable growth in research on women's exclusion from development programs. Another related **body** of literature, often ecofeminist, demonstrates the relationship between women and sustainable development, especially the effectiveness of women's centuries-old farming practices. This literature deconstructs the notion that development means progress and criticizes the accompanying belief that industrial capitalism is a natural process in which environmental destruction is often a necessary spillover effect. Postcolonial feminism benefits from analysis that begins from the perspectives of those involved—communities of poor women of all colors in both affluent and neocolonial nations. Mohanty advises that beginning with affected women's voices provides the most inclusive way of thinking about a more concrete and expansive vision of social justice.

A promising aspect for women who must still deal with the negative race and class effects of an earlier colonial diaspora can be seen in the struggles of some of these women to empower themselves by redefining and valorizing their identities. Chicana/Mexican feminist Gloria Anzaldúa worked to create new ways of seeing from the location/dislocation of border-crossing women. From her experience, Anzaldúa imaged an emerging Chicana/Mexican woman, the new mestiza, who not only crosses geopolitical borders but also cultural and ethnic borders, and as a result is able to develop the advantage of multifocal vision. The new mestiza is politically cognizant of what goes on in these different "worlds" and therefore is capable of seeing matters from many different angles. The new mestiza can link Western women's often unicultural perceptions to other worldviews. The new mestiza's multifocal vision provides a way to think about aligning U.S. movements for social justice with worldwide movements of decolonization.

Postcolonial feminism acknowledges the differences among the world's women and understands the importance of theorizing from their situated and embodied viewpoints. It is an especially relevant strain of feminist thought, particularly in this time of rapidly globalizing economies.

See also Environmentalism; Latina Feminism

Further Reading: Basu, Amrita, Inderpal Grewal, Caren Kaplan, and Liisa Malkki, eds., "Globalization and Gender," *Signs* (special issue) 26(4) (2001); Narayan, Uma, and Sandra Harding, eds., "Border Crossing: Multicultural and Postcolonial Feminist Challenges to Philosophy," *Hypatia* (special issue) 13(2/3) (1998); Vavrus, Frances, and Lisa Ann Richey, eds., "Women and Development: /Rethinking Policy and Reconceptualizing Practice," *Women's Studies Quarterly* (special issue) 29 (3/4) (2003).

COLLEEN MACK-CANTY

POSTFEMINISM. Postfeminism invokes different meanings in different contexts. This complexity makes the term difficult to define and is central to the tension sometimes noted between third-wave and postfeminism. There are two primary uses of the term postfeminism. In the United States, especially in the popular press, postfeminism is a catchphrase used to (1) categorize those who recognize past feminist gains but deny the label "feminist" (including those who claim "I'm not a feminist, but ...") and (2) to explain a **backlash** against **feminism** (almost a return to a pre-feminist state) or attacks on current feminism from individuals who claim a feminist **identity**. Postfeminism is also used in Europe and by many U.S. academics to describe a theoretical position that grapples with changing definitions of individuals and identities.

The presence of postfeminism is evidence of the ambiguity surrounding contemporary feminism. Although third-wave feminism incorporates a changing landscape of definition without rejecting the past, some postfeminists praise the golden era of feminism while lambasting those engaged in what they see as the promotion of women's victim status. Other postfeminists seem to suffer from a lack of information or access to stronger examples. An article in *Time* magazine, for example, juxtaposed second-wave examples of activism and leadership with mass **media representations** of women (such as the **television** character Ally McBeal) who are far from feminist role models. It failed to acknowledge the vibrant examples of feminist activism and leadership that are present in a range of arenas. Such examples make it clear that feminism is alive and well—a notion more compatible with third-wave feminism.

Popular Postfeminism. In the United States, popular culture and **media** usages of postfeminism originated in the 1980s and generally refer to rejections or critiques of feminism from the "daughters" of the second-wave feminists. Postfeminists tend to critique representations of women as victims, which they see in campaigns against date **rape, sexual harassment,** and **pornography.** Postfeminists often acknowledge being *products* of feminism while rejecting *affiliation* with feminism. This can be seen especially in the case of writers such as Katie Roiphe, the daughter of a second-wave feminist, who rejects many aspects of contemporary feminism. Popular postfeminism is seen in books and newspaper articles proclaiming the death of feminism, suggesting that all that is left of feminism is Ally McBeal or Helen Fielding's famous fictional character **Bridget Jones,** or implying that feminism is now irrelevant. In the United States, the media's declarations of postfeminism were one key to the crystallization of third-wave feminism. Writer **Rebecca Walker,** for example, distinguished her identity from this sense of postfeminist apathy: "I am not a postfeminism feminist," she wrote in *Ms.* in 1992. "I am the Third Wave."

Third wave sees popular postfeminism as problematic in overlooking the many remaining feminist struggles, as well as in turning a blind eye to those currently engaged in feminist activism, who see this work as far from over. Postfeminism can be seen as a **backlash**—a reactionary position set in opposition to perceptions of second-wave feminism. Many postfeminists posit a division between so-called **victim feminism** (which they generally identify with feminism's second wave) and power feminism or equality feminism (which they often advocate as the solution to the problem of victim feminism). This animosity toward second-wave feminism suggests a dissatisfaction with the struggle for equality, even as it claims affiliation with liberation and achievement.

Some postfeminists depoliticize feminist issues, seeing their own struggles with **domestic violence** or equal employment opportunities as individual experiences rather than in the context of a feminist struggle or as symptoms of sexism. Many of the women interviewed for books and articles expressing women's dis-identification with feminism have engaged in this depoliticization. Several women cited in Rene Denfeld's 1995 book, *The New Victorians: A Young Woman's Challenge to the Old Feminist Order,* express the separation between their own experiences and the more generalized "woman's experience" that has benefited from the feminist movement. Some active feminists, including many in the third wave, see this disavowal of feminism as demonstrating ignorance of the multifaceted nature of feminism. This dissatisfaction can be seen in bumper stickers (sold by the National Organization for Women [NOW] and other organizations) proclaiming, "I'll be post-feminist in the post-**patriarchy.**"

Postfeminism in the Media. The mainstream media are in part to blame for the perceived growth of popular postfeminism. *Time* magazine and others published feature stories examining the so-called death of feminism. However, activists and authors such as **Jennifer Baumgardner and Amy Richards** (*Manifesta,* 2000) argue that while the look of feminism may be changing or diversifying, it is far from over. What some see as evidence of *post*feminism—a change in patterns of activism, different organizations, a lack of celebrity leaders—others see as evidence of an *evolution* of feminism.

Susan Bolotin's 1982 *New York Times Magazine* article assessed the current state of feminism and found that many young women were supportive of women's rights but did not self-identify as "feminist." Bolotin argued that since the definition of feminism was unclear and fraught with stereotypes, many women believed in **equal rights** (her definition of feminism) without labeling themselves feminists—a situation she labeled "post-feminism."

The *New York Times* followed this with a 1986 editorial by Geneva Overholser that explained "What 'Post-Feminism' Really Means." Overholser suggested that "post-feminism" was commonly used to describe women's dissatisfaction with the balance of home and career within the guise of liberation. Her examples included women who took the opportunity to pursue careers outside the home and found either that they **desire**d more focus on home and **family** or that being in the workforce was not as satisfying as they had hoped. Overholser argued that the solutions to these problems generally entailed women's shift back to the home— a change she suggests is more *pre*-feminist than postfeminist.

Time magazine is another source of these varying presentations of feminism. A December 1989 cover story asked, "Is there a future for feminism?" and determined that "feminism is not dead." Three years later, following the publication of **Susan Faludi**'s *Backlash*, the cover story examined "the **war** against feminism." The article highlighted Faludi's argument that feminism is blamed for women's disappointment with the balance between work and home and classified the two possible roles that existed for women in the 1980s: men-hating career woman or blissfully postfeminist mothers.

In 1998, *Time* contributed another story on feminism with a cover that asked, "Is Feminism Dead?" and featured a photo of the character Ally McBeal as the face of current feminism. The article's author, Ginia Bellafante, contrasted examples of the potent 1970s feminism of protests and liberation with 1990s examples of triviality and ineffectual activism she characterized as "stylish fluff." Bellafante's article was met with a flood of responses and critiques from novelist Erica Jong, *The Nation* columnist Katha Pollitt, and NOW.

Postfeminist Authors. In addition to the mainstream media's analyses regarding the state of feminism, the media latches onto authors who grapple with these issues. Authors most often associated with postfeminism include Katie Roiphe, Rene Denfeld, and, in some cases, **Naomi Wolf**. Because of their age and a surface identification with some aspects of feminism, they are frequently classified as third-wave feminists, although many feminists categorize their work as postfeminist in spirit. These authors often receive generous media attention and are heralded as spokespeople for their generation.

These postfeminists often claim a feminist identity while critiquing what they perceive to be the wayward feminist mainstream position. Roiphe, for example, identifies herself as a feminist but argues that mainstream/liberal feminism has shifted into a pattern of "victim feminism" or prudishness. Roiphe and Denfeld suggest that many young women do not consider themselves feminist because the movement is ill-defined or preoccupied with an anti-male, anti-sex agenda ("victim feminism" or the oddly named "gender feminism").

Naomi Wolf's 1991 book, *The Beauty Myth*, built on the notion of the backlash to explain how notions of women's beauty are used to constrain women's employment growth and stifle their self-esteem. Wolf looked to a "peer-driven feminist third wave" as a source of activism and change and as a way to counter "the fib called postfeminism."

Wolf's 1993 book, *Fire with Fire*, took a different angle. The book aimed to explain what Wolf perceived as an estrangement between feminism and women's identification with the women's movement. Wolf made a similar argument to that of Roiphe and Denfeld: feminism had been sidetracked and had become a movement of "victim feminism" in which women are seen as pure beings in need of protection. Roiphe simply presents her dissatisfaction with the current state of feminism as she sees it, but Denfeld and Wolf offer similar plans for the future of feminism. Denfeld identifies as an "equality feminist" who suggests that feminism focus solely on ensuring equality of rights and opportunities. Wolf's contribution, which she calls "power feminism," focuses on a similar claim to women's equality. Although in some ways a manifesto for a new feminism, Wolf's book is often read as yet another critique of feminism based on a stereotype.

Theoretical Postfeminism. There is another distinct use of the term postfeminism more prevalent in academic discourse and outside the United States. This alternative use suggests the intersection between feminism and other theories and debates, including postmodernism, post-structuralism, psychoanalytic theory, and postcolonialism. Building on the work of theorists such as **Judith Butler** and Teresa de Lauretis, academic postfeminism critiques the very notions of identity and equality that are central to some feminist **writings**. It further acknowledges and incorporates questions of difference, multiplicity, and ambiguity. Theoretical postfeminism suggests, following postmodernism, that categories such as "man" and "woman" are no longer capable of explaining gender experience; thus, questions of identity, and feminist identity, must be reexamined.

This usage of academic postfeminism is aligned with, rather than opposed to, third-wave theories. Theoretical postfeminism can be understood as the shift from a feminism based on struggles for equality to one that acknowledges debates around difference. In fact, scholar Amanda Lotz argues that this category of postfeminism can be understood as a type of third-wave feminism, rather than its antithesis. Instead of positioning itself in opposition to second-wave thinking, or offering critiques of "victim feminism," this postfeminism builds on many of the fundamental issues suggested by second-wave feminism.

Many academics use postfeminist theory to engage in cultural critiques of social institutions that position women and men as polar opposites. This both encourages a move toward parity and critiques institutions claiming some stability of the categories "woman" or "man." As such, this theoretical position is in step with a third-wave push for awareness of the intersectionality of identities (gender, **sexuality**, race, class, etc.). However, unlike a popular postfeminist position, this theoretical stance does not simply argue for "equality" with no move to change the underlying systems that perpetuate gross inequalities. Instead, theoretical postfeminism grapples with questions of power and structure that fortify gender distinctions and social institutions.

See also Binary Oppositions; Postmodern Theory; *Volume 2 Primary Documents 1, 4, 11, 14, 16, and 41*

Further Reading: Brooks, Ann, *Postfeminisms: Feminism, Cultural Theory and Cultural Forms*, New York: Routledge, 1997; Denfeld, Rene, *The New Victorians: A Young Woman's Challenge to the Old Feminist Order*, New York: Warner Books, 1995; Lotz, Amanda, "Communicating Third-Wave Feminism and New Social Movements: Challenges for the Next Century of Feminist Endeavor," *Women and Language* 26(1) (2003): 2; Modleski, Tania, *Feminism Without Women: Culture and Criticism in a "Postfeminist" Age*, New York: Routledge, 1991; Phoca, Sophia, and Rebecca Wright, *Introducing Postfeminism*, New York: Totem Books, 1999; Roiphe, Katie, *The Morning After: Sex, Fear, and Feminism*, Boston: Little, Brown, 1994; Whelehan, Imelda, *Modern Feminist Thought: From the Second Wave to "Post-Feminism,"* New York: New York University Press, 1995; Wolf, Naomi, *Fire with Fire: The New Female Power and How It Will Change the 21st Century*, New York: Random House, 1993.

JONAROSE JAFFE FEINBERG

POSTMODERN THEORY. Although the term "postmodern" emerged from and has had an impact on a range of cultural forms and disciplines including architecture, literature, human sciences, philosophy, the **visual arts**, and **feminism**, it resists any simple definition. Like **feminist theory**, postmodern theory encompasses various meanings and positions and, in turn, has produced a range of (often opposing) readings and understandings. Since the 1980s there has been a proliferation of debates concerning postmodernism, questioning both what it is and how valuable it is as an intellectual and social position.

The term "postmodern" inevitably implies an engagement with the modern. On one hand, the "postmodern" is understood as a periodizing concept insofar as it challenges the emphasis on reason, rationality, progress, and science associated with modernity. "Modernity" is another nebulous and contested term, though it is generally considered to denote a way of life informed by the changes brought about by industrialization, urbanization, and the rise of capitalism in Western society since the eighteenth century. For literary critic Frederic Jameson, postmodernism is the "cultural logic of late capitalism," a period characterized by new modes of consumption and production, technological developments, the role of the mass **media**, and so on. On the other hand, it is understood as a set of aesthetic styles and practices identified with playfulness, self-consciousness, and fragmentation, as well as a breaking down of the boundary between "serious" and "popular" (or "high" and "low") cultural forms. Thus, although postmodernism shares some of the aesthetic practices of modernism, its attitude toward them is different: while modernism is characterized by a nostalgia and mourning for lost unity, postmodernism celebrates fragmentation and discontinuity. One of the most influential theories of the postmodern is offered by the French philosopher Jean-François Lyotard in *The Postmodern Condition: A Report on Knowledge* (1984). Here, Lyotard discusses how developing technology transforms systems of knowledge, bringing about a crisis of faith concerning the possibilities of producing an objective explanation of reality. Importantly, Lyotard sees the postmodern condition as characterized by the collapse of "grand narratives" (e.g., Marxism, Modernity) that seek to legitimize systems of knowledge in an attempt to stabilize and order society, and the emergence of smaller, local, multiple, and competing narratives.

Suspicious of the ideas about truth, objectivity, and absolute knowledge that shape Western culture, postmodern theory offers a view of the world that is uncertain, contingent, and fragmented. It challenges the humanist conceptualization of a coherent and unified self and instead emphasizes subjectivity as fluid and shifting. Insofar as postmodern theory both destabilizes traditional definitions of gender and offers a space for marginalized and minority voices, it shares some common ground with feminist thought. Nevertheless, the various and often conflicting meanings and understandings shaping postmodern theory are mirrored by the vicissitudes characterizing its crossroads with feminism. In particular, some feminists have expressed a concern that postmodern theory's emphasis on the fragmentation, even dissolution, of **identity** poses a threat to the politics of a feminism founded on a conception of women as social subjects. For example, philosopher and feminist theorist Linda Alcoff asks how we can "ground a feminist politics that deconstructs the female subject?" In their exploration of the uneasy relationship between postmodernism and feminism, feminist theorists Nancy Fraser and Linda Nicholson highlight a tension between a line of philosophical enquiry that posits a distrust of grand narratives and an interest in politically grounded social criticism and action. They argue, however, that the intersection of postmodern theory and feminist criticism could be mutually advantageous: while feminism sheds light on the male-centered perspectives of postmodern theory (its marginalization of an analysis of gender), postmodern theorizing redresses a universalizing and essentializing tendency in feminist thought (which, by positing gender as the most important category of social difference, privileges heterosexist and ethnocentric claims about female identity).

In its emphasis on destabilizing fixed definitions of gender and rejection of unitary notions of "woman" and "feminism," third-wave feminism is clearly informed and shaped by postmodern theory, as well as other anti-foundationalist discourse such as **postcolonialism** and poststructuralism. Emerging in a period of late capitalism, third-wave feminism is "as much a product of 'postmodern cultural conditions' as it is a product of the First and Second Waves, or **women's studies**, or the media **backlash**, or violence" (Garrison, 148). Third-wave feminist ideas about **identity** embrace notions of contradiction, multiplicity, and ambiguity, building on postmodern theory's critique of ideas about the unified self and engaging with the fluid nature of gender and sexual identity. Third-wave feminist writer and Professor Ednie Kaeh Garrison argues that the postmodern nature of third-wave feminism is demonstrated in a number of ways: for example, its problematization of the categories of "woman" and "feminism," its emphasis on networking, and its deployment of democratized technologies. Performers such as Madonna and **Courtney Love** have been described as "postmodern feminists" because of their playful experimentation with and subversion of gender codes and roles. However, they have also been criticized for representing a tendency to privilege individual style over collective politics—a criticism that has also been made of third-wave feminism.

See also Cyberfeminism; Cyberspace; Postfeminism

Further Reading: Alcoff, Linda, "Cultural Feminism Versus Post-Structuralism: The Identity Crisis in Feminist Theory," in *Feminism and Philosophy: Essential Readings in Theory, Reinterpretation, and Application,* eds. Nancy Tuana and Rosemarie Tong, Boulder: Westview, 1995, 434–456; Fraser, Nancy, and Linda Nicholson, "Social Criticism without Philosophy: An Encounter Between Feminism and Postmodernism," *Theory, Culture and Society* 5(2/3) (1988): 373–394; Garrison, Ednie Kaeh, "U.S. Feminism—Grrrl Style! Youth (Sub)Cultures and the Technologics of the Third Wave," *Feminist Studies* 26(1) (2000): 141–170; Heywood, Leslie, and Jennifer Drake, "Introduction," *Third Wave Agenda,* Minneapolis: University of Minnesota Press, 1997; Hutcheon, Linda, *The Poetics of Postmodernism: History, Theory, Fiction,* New York: Routledge, 1988; Jameson, Frederic, "Postmodernism, or the Cultural Logic of Late Capitalism," *New Left Review* 146 (1984): 53–92; Lyotard, Jean-François, *The Postmodern Condition: A Report on Knowledge,* Manchester: Manchester University Press, 1984; Nicholson, Linda J., ed., *Feminism/Postmodernism,* New York: Routledge, 1990; Soper, Kate, *Troubled Pleasures: Writings on Politics, Gender and Hedonism,* London: Verso, 1990; Walker, Rebecca, "Being Real: An Introduction," in *To Be Real: Telling the Truth and Changing the Face of Feminism,* ed. Rebecca Walker, New York: Anchor, 1995, xxix–xl.

REBECCA MUNFORD

POWERPUFF GIRLS. Definitely an expression of "**girl power**" and sometimes seen as an example of third-wave **feminism**, *The Powerpuff Girls* is an Emmy award–winning cartoon about three sisters, superhero kindergarteners Blossom, Bubbles, and Buttercup, who fight crime for the City of Townsville. Their father, Professor Utonium, produced them in an experiment intended to create the perfect little **girl**. He combined sugar, spice, and everything nice, but a drop of "Chemical X" accidentally fell in, creating an explosion from which the Powerpuff Girls were born.

Each sister has a unique personality reflecting sugar, spice, or everything nice. Bubbles, the blonde, is very sweet, speaks every language, loves coloring, and can talk to animals. Buttercup, the brunette, is the toughest fighter, and she would rather play rough than study. Blossom, the redhead, is the nice, smart, and articulate leader, who often tries reasoning with foes. The girls' superpowers include super strength, the ability to fly, and laser eye-beams.

They are not just strong—they are also cute, with big eyes, little dresses, and Mary Jane shoes. Thus, they are icons of third-wave girl power, whose combination of strength and **femininity** defies the stereotype that girls are weak and passive and that only men can be powerful. For example, the episode "Members Only" depicts supermen who assume the girls are inconsequential but whom the girls easily defeat—and later rescue. This philosophy is commodified in Powerpuff merchandise featuring phrases such as "Girls rule, boys drool." Overall, the girls' embodiment of "power" and "puff" constitutes a powerful third-wave feminist statement.

The cartoon also contains elements of power feminism, a problematic form of feminism that some consider part of the third wave; it argues against the idea that women are victims of an oppressive **patriarchy**. The episode "Equal Fights" pits the girls against a villain whose unfair caricature of second-wave, victim-oriented, radical feminist rhetoric persuades them that men oppress the females of Townsville.

Their foes, mostly males, include their arch-nemesis, the monkey Mojo Jojo; the cross-dressing devil figure, Him; the unicellular, wannabe bad guys, the Amoeba Boys; the green-skinned mutant teen ruffians, the Gangrene Gang; and the brutish hillbilly, Fuzzy Lumpkins. The girls respond to crises reported by the Mayor of Townsville and his extremely intelligent yet shapely assistant, Ms. Bellum, but as empowered third-wave girls, they plan and execute their missions independently.

Craig McCracken created the show in 1992, when he was a twenty-year-old sophomore studying character animation at the California Institute for the Arts. It debuted as "Whoopass Girl Stew" at Spike and Mike's Twisted Festival of Animation, premiering as a series in its current form on Cartoon Network in 1998. A full-length feature **film** appeared in **theaters** in 2002.

See also Empowerment; Girl/Girlies

Further Reading: Hains, Rebecca, "Power(puff) Feminism: *The Powerpuff Girls* as a Site of Strength and Collective Action in the Third Wave," in *Mediated Women: Representations of Popular Culture*, 2nd ed., Marian Meyers, Cresskill, NJ: Hampton Press, forthcoming; Hains, Rebecca, "The Problematics of Reclaiming the Girlish: The Powerpuff Girls and Girl Power," *Femspec* 5(2), 2005; Havrilesky, Heather, "Powerpuff Girls Meet World," *Salon*, July 2, 2002, http://archive.salon.com/mwt/feature/2002/07/02/powerpuff/; Lloyd, Robert, "Beyond Good and Evil: To the Utterly Adorable Ass-Kicking Superheroics of the Powerpuff Girls!" *LAWeekly*, November 24–30, 2000, http://www.laweekly.com/ink/01/01/features-lloyd.php.

REBECCA C. HAINS

PRO-SEX FEMINISM. In 1982, the Scholar and Feminist IX Conference at Barnard College, "Towards a Politics of **Sexuality**," gave rise to a split between factions of feminists, variously dubbed pro-sex vs. anti-sex or anti-censorship vs. anti-**pornography** feminists. The terms "pro-sex **feminism**" and "anti-sex feminism" have been problematized as simplistic and divisive. Andrea Dworkin, frequently invoked as icon and spokesperson for the anti-sex side, once wryly suggested that "sex-negative" is the term used to dismiss or discredit ideas, particularly political critiques, that might lead to the deflation of men's sexual privilege. Likewise, in a collection of essays from the infamous conference, Carole Vance argues that "pro-sex" misleadingly suggests a narrow opposition to anti-sex or anti-porn feminism and connotes a mindless embrace of sex. She offers the term "feminist sex radical" as a more accurate label. Pro-sex or sex-positive feminists balance attention to "pleasure and danger" as they seek to make more things possible and permissible for women to say, do, think, or fantasize about. Despite the limitations of terminology, the values espoused by pro-sex feminists—an expansion of sexual freedom despite a context of patriarchal oppression and a commitment to telling the truth about our most complex **desires**—continue to be important to many third-wave feminists.

Pro-sex feminism usually refers to a segment of the women's movement that defends pornography, sex work, sadomasochism, and **butch/femme** roles, but it also recuperates heterosexuality, intercourse, **marriage**, and sex toys from separatist feminist dismissals. Although the label came into **fashion** in the 1980s, this position within feminism has a longer history, reaching back to the Free Love feminists of the nineteenth century who advocated sex outside of marriage and educated women about birth control. Indeed, the link between sexual freedom and **sex education** remains salient today; many pro-sex feminists (Annie Sprinkle, Carol Queen, Candida Royalle) are also sex educators. A thread of utopianism runs through this feminist history, including the belief that sexual pleasure is a useful force in countering oppressive social forces, from capitalism to imperialism to Puritanism to sexism itself.

This approach to sex has been caricatured as "orgasm politics" or "do-me feminism," but such critics miss the genuinely hopeful and utterly serious motivations behind pro-sex feminism. Because women have historically been socialized to repress their sexual desires (e.g., nice **girls** wait until marriage) and have consistently been misled about their sexual anatomies (think of Freud on the clitoral orgasm as a sign of immaturity), and because young women in the current moment are still taught to take responsibility for aggressive or violent male desire, but are not taught how to say "yes" or "no" unequivocally in a sexually critical moment, the commitment of pro-sex feminists to developing what sex activist Lynn Phillips calls "a discourse of female pleasure without penalties" is truly urgent.

Pro-sex feminism often grows out of the need to rectify exclusions by other feminists, intervening in charges against the lavender menace (lesbians), the leather menace (sadomasochists), and heterosexual collaborators (straight women). Because third-wave feminism also positions itself as more inclusive than the second wave, it shares a natural affinity with pro-sex feminism, preferring unresolved tensions between politics and practices in place of judgmental prescriptivism. The sexual libertarianism of pro-sex feminism appeals to a generation born after the sexual revolution and socialized during the highly individualist period of the 1980s. Sex activist Lynn Chancer further explains this preference as analogous to the mind/**body** problem in philosophy: discussions of sexism "tend toward the disembodied and conceptually abstract," whereas pro-sex feminism errs on the side of embodiment, sometimes leaving larger "political economies of **patriarchy**" incompletely disassembled. There is a longing among young women for **feminist theory** that addresses how to live in *this* world in *these* bodies; how to engage sexually within the current social organization. For this reason, pro-sex feminists are sometimes criticized for being assimilationist. Chancer counters this charge, arguing that it is absurd to condemn individual practices for making the best of the available options. Third-wave feminists may recognize their own troubling experiences in the work of anti-sex feminists, including Andrea Dworkin's analysis of penetration as an expression of ownership for men and a trade for emotional intimacy for women, but they do not know how to take them home—into relationships, into bedrooms, into conversations with male romantic partners. Pro-sex feminism offers a more nuanced analysis of sex, power, and fantasy and is consistently more interested in discussing sex *as it is*, rather than as it should be.

Sex-worker activists constitute a major subset of pro-sex feminism. In addition to exposing heterosexuality as an economic system, sex-worker feminism works to reverse the whore stigma (by which sex workers are marginalized and "good" women are disciplined). In *Whores and Other Feminists* (1997), Jill Nagle returns to the problem of exclusion in feminism: "Whores … are the dykes of the nineties, the lavender menace whom it's still considered okay to ostracize." Given the flow of sex workers into academic feminism and vice versa since the mid-1990s, it is perhaps not surprising to see this tension begin to subside, as author Wendy Chapkis suggests it has: "The slut, the dyke, and the whore are thus embraced by Sex Radicals as a potent symbolic challenge to confining notions of proper womanhood and conventional sexuality." **Queer** theorists have also played an important role in shaping pro-sex feminism, adding force to philosophies of pleasure as a legitimate end in itself, separating intercourse from reproduction or emotional intimacy, and de-centering penetration in favor of oral sex and full-body eroticism.

See also Desire, Feminist; Queer Theory; Sex Shops, Feminist; *Volume 2, Primary Document 52*

Further Reading: Chapkis, Wendy, *Live Sex Acts: Women Performing Erotic Labor*, New York: Routledge, 1997; Johnson, Merri Lisa, ed., *Jane Sexes It Up: True Confessions of Feminist Desire*, New York: Four Walls Eight Windows, 2002; Nagle, Jill, ed., *Whores and Other Feminists*, New York: Routledge, 1997; Vance, Carole S., ed., *Pleasure and Danger: Exploring Female Sexuality*, London: Pandora, 1989; Warner, Michael, *The Trouble with Normal: Sex, Politics, and the Ethics of Queer Life*, New York: Free Press, 1999.

MERRI LISA JOHNSON

Q

QUEER. Shedding its link to a homophobic past, the term "queer" now celebrates the unity and diversity of the progressive gay movement of the present and is consequently connected to third-wave **feminism**'s critique of social attitudes and policies that oppress minorities. Over the years, "queer" has held multiple meanings, demonstrating a range of different, often-contradictory connotations depending on who is using the word and to whom it is applied. Although "queer" itself simply describes someone or something that departs from what is considered "normal" or expected, it developed into a slur for homosexuals that could be used as a noun, as in, "Is she a queer?" or an adjective, as in, "He is so queer." In this context, the term reinforces notions of heterosexuality as normal, natural, and desirable, at the expense of same-sex attraction, which is cast as abnormal, unnatural, and perverse. Difference, seen in this light, is inherently negative, whereas conformity is valued. Such usage also reaffirms the concept of **sexuality** as consisting of exact opposites (e.g., straight/queer) rather than a fluid spectrum of attraction and **desire** that a person may experience over a lifetime or on a regular basis. A popular school-yard game, "Smear the Queer," often played by boys, exemplifies how the word queer is used to signify both scorn and separateness, as the object is to designate one player as different from the rest of the group and then proceed to chase, swarm, and pummel him to the ground.

In recent years, "queer" has been wrested from the exclusive control of homophobic individuals and groups and is instead used by sexual minorities as a term denoting pride in being different from the constructed norm. Similar to the way in which individuals of African descent may use the word "nigger" to refer to each other, lesbians, gays, bisexual, and transgendered people use "queer" as a term of solidarity that embraces their outsider sexual status. This shift is also evident in popular culture, as **television** shows and other **media** sources that celebrate sexual difference employ queer in their titles and content.

However, the new life of queer is not simply a response to those who would use it to disparage sexual minorities and reaffirm heterosexuality as the norm. Somewhat ironically, queer also signifies a reaction to what is perceived as the shortcomings of earlier gay and lesbian liberation movements. According to this critique, labels such as "gay" often represented the agenda of upper-class white men who wished to affirm their similarities with mainstream culture. Consequently, gay tended to operate in an exclusionary way, serving the aims of some, while ignoring the demands of sexual minorities who were also people of color and/or lower class. Queer, then, is an attempt to recognize the unity required to establish political clout, while acknowledging the diversity of views and needs among the people who wield the label.

In fact, queer has developed into such a broad umbrella category that even people who do not identify themselves as experiencing or acting on same-sex attraction have begun to use the term to refer to themselves or their sexual practices. "Straights" identifying themselves as queer often do so to signify their desire to push beyond the sexual boundaries established by conservative culture and may engage in activities such as gender role reversal and sado-masochistic play.

Within the academic world, queer is frequently used as a verb to describe a way of approaching a subject so that the voices and identities of sexual minorities are reclaimed from a heterosexual context that strives to submerge and silence them. For example, a literary scholar may queer a novel by exploring how subtle references to a character's behavior and relationships point to sexual desires that depart from the established norm.

See also Heterosexism; Queer Theory

Further Reading: Jagose, Annamarie, *Queer Theory: An Introduction*, New York: New York University Press, 1997; Sullivan, Nikki, *A Critical Introduction to Queer Theory*, New York: New York University Press, 2003.

SEAN MURRAY

QUEER THEORY. Queer theory, like third-wave feminism, is both a critique of the dominant culture and a response to earlier liberation movements; in this case, the gay and lesbian liberation movement. In terms of its critique of the dominant culture, queer theory proposes that the very structures that gird our society are opposed to sexual diversity and are therefore the proper targets of activism aimed at bringing an end to homophobia, **heterosexism**, and rigid gender roles. For example, capitalism, with its unique ability for swallowing everything in its path and churning it back out ready for safe consumption by the masses, is perceived as threatening because of its potential to take the queer out of queer, thereby transforming divergent **sexuality** into identities and expressions more palpable for mainstream tastes. This process can be witnessed in the growing number of **television** programs that depict gays and lesbians as just like everyone else, individuals happy to be part of consumer culture and content to accept the status quo. Queer theory, then, urges us to reexamine elements of our society that are automatically viewed as harmless, beneficial, eternal, or universal. In fact, queer theory shares with feminism the goal of exposing how social dynamics such as male power and heterosexual privilege are not permanent, sweeping truths but are based upon specific cultural and historical factors. Concerning political action, queer theory holds that sexual minorities, because of their status as outsiders, have the capacity for objectively analyzing, challenging, and changing oppressive social structures. Choosing to act otherwise is to cooperate with the system that encourages prejudice against people who do not fit within the established norm.

Queer theory attempts to take a more complex approach than the strategies advocated by, say, the lesbian and gay activists of the 1970s. Whereas earlier generations of sexual minorities attempted to pave inroads to better access the economic privileges and civil rights of the mainstream, activists guided by queer theory are cautious about adopting tactics that could lead to their absorption into the dominant culture for the reasons listed. The debate over legalizing **same-sex unions/gay marriage** illustrates the basic division between these two schools of thought. Proponents of gay **marriage** argue that the issue is worth fighting for because of the countless civil rights and economic benefits, in addition to the appearance of legitimacy, that marriage provides couples with. However, many in the queer community oppose wasting valuable time, energy, and resources on securing the right to legally wed, reasoning that the institution of marriage, by imposing an uneven balance of power and demanding the unrealistic vow of monogamy, is itself irreparably flawed.

In addition to developing a more radical critique of mainstream culture, queer theory is sensitive to the ways in which earlier liberation movements assumed a universal set of interests and agendas that was quite often more connected to white, financially well-off men. So, for instance, a strategy aimed at removing barriers to sexual minorities may assist Caucasian males while inadvertently failing to achieve justice for women and/or people of color. Queer theory also recognizes that sexual orientation may or may not be the most important aspect of a person's **identity**. For one person, the act of coming out and claiming a queer identity may be the defining characteristic of her identity; for another, gender and/or racial identity and all of their implications may take priority over queerness. In essence, queer theory strives to address the complex realities of those claiming queer identities, rather than assuming a universal collection of political aims.

Despite its objective of creating a united coalition that also recognizes difference among the queer community, queer theory's use of the term "queer" is not embraced by all. To many, that label can never lose the offensive and violent overtones created by anti-gay individuals desiring to alienate and ridicule those with sexual **desires** that depart from what is considered normal. As noted, some reject the notion that an umbrella term such as "queer" can accurately describe such a diverse community.

In terms of its academic roots, queer theory owes much to theorists such as Michel Foucault and Eve Kosofsky Sedgwick. Foucault, a gay man, attempted to refute the notion of the "repressive hypothesis" in his influential work, *The History of Sexuality: An Introduction, Volume 1* (1978). According to the repressive hypothesis, diverse forms of sexual expression have long been stifled in the West due to a socioeconomic system that emphasizes the reproductive potential of relationships. Therefore, the heterosexual married couple is the necessary unit for producing the next generation of laborers, whereas homosexuality is shunned because it fails to generate offspring. Foucault, on the other hand, argued a very different, almost opposite case. He theorized that although various forms of sexual expression apart from heterosexuality have indeed existed throughout history, the nineteenth century's medicalization of same-sex attraction gave homosexuality its name. This naming and documentation enabled homosexuality to develop into an identity, rather than simply a behavior that anyone could engage in. Although this classifying and describing of homosexuality in medical and psychological professions routinely labeled it a disorder to be cured, it also created the channels through which the homosexual could emerge as a person with a voice. Ironically, then, the last century has witnessed an explosion of sexual identities and possibilities due to forces that initially aimed to contain and eliminate them. Concerning his direct impact on queer theory and activism, Foucault's great contribution is the optimistic insight that with every label and prohibition established by the dominant culture comes yet another available channel for the oppressed to make themselves heard.

Sedgwick's *Epistemology of the Closet* (1990) is another landmark book in the development of queer theory. Using the literature of famous authors such as Herman Melville and Oscar Wilde, she explores how the emerging importance of the categories of homosexual and heterosexual often lies buried within the text. Her work ultimately helped open the door for establishing courses and departments that focused on gay and lesbian issues at many colleges and universities. However, many queer scholars are also sensitive to the ways in which establishing queer theory as a formal course of study might have a normalizing effect on a movement aiming to critique the forces of normalization.
See also Consumerism; *Volume 2, Primary Document 57*

Further Reading: Foucault, Michel, *The History of Sexuality: An Introduction, Volume 1*, New York: Vintage Books, 1978; Sedgwick, Eve Kosofsky, *Epistemology of the Closet*, Berkeley: University of California Press, 1990; Sullivan, Nikki, *A Critical Introduction to Queer Theory*, New York: New York University Press, 2003; Toibin, Colm, *Love in a Dark Time*, New York: Scribner's, 2002.

SEAN MURRAY

R

RACISM. In U.S. culture, racism occurs when groups of people are discriminated against because of their real or perceived membership in a racial group. Race in itself is a concept discussed, debated, and redefined by feminists. Third-wave feminists understand race as physical attributes—such as skin color, eye color, or facial structure—that occupy different social and political positions in different cultures. The notion of "race" has been defined different ways during different moments in history. For example, some thinkers, such as Charles Darwin, defined race as a solely biological characteristic. Many contemporary feminist thinkers, however, also acknowledge that biological characteristics, such as skin color, play an important role in defining race. In addition, they claim that different cultures have different systems and hierarchies of "race." Therefore, because race does not constitute a concrete category across cultures and historical moments, the concept of "race" is specific to both history and location.

The mutability of racial categories does not mean, however, that all "races" receive the same access to social, political, and economic resources. In many cultures, racial minorities are subjected to prejudice and **discrimination**. Racism can be overt, covert, and even unintentional. Many white feminists have participated in racist projects and have since been critiqued by women of color. Women of color, who identified as "U.S. Third World feminists," initiated this critique, which began in the late 1970s and continued into the 1980s and 1990s. Most importantly, these critiques are what many younger feminists name as the point of departure for third-wave **feminism**.

(White) Womanhood and the First Wave. Understanding the role of racism in the history of feminism is important for third-wavers because its historical legacy in the United States has greatly influenced "third-wave agendas," and

many third-wave feminists (of all racial backgrounds) espouse anti-racist theories and practices. As early as the mid-nineteenth century, women of color spoke out about the differences between their experiences and the experiences of white women. In a speech made in Akron, Ohio, in 1851, a freed slave, Sojourner Truth (originally named Isabella Baumfree) asked, "Ain't I a Woman?" In this speech, Truth responds to dominant beliefs about womanhood in the nineteenth century and points to the narrowness of these beliefs. Later coined "The Cult of True Womanhood," nineteenth-century ideas about womanhood recognized women for their purity, piety, submissiveness, and **domesticity**. Realistically, very few women were able to uphold these ideals, and many contemporary feminist theorists recognize that only middle-class white women were able to conform to these standards. Several first-wave feminists took issue with "The Cult of True Womanhood." Feminists such as Elizabeth Cady Stanton and Sarah Grimké challenged these beliefs about women in their writings. Nonetheless, race remained invisible in their texts. The exclusion of women of color and issues of race from the first and second waves of feminism serves as another important rallying point for the third wave. It is the recognition of race's erasure from previous feminist movements that marks the third wave as a distinct wave of feminism. Critiques of feminism by women of color were important catalysts for the third wave of feminism. Sojourner Truth's remarks set the stage for critiques of (white) feminism that came about during the second wave.

In her speech, "Ain't I a Woman?," Sojourner Truth declared "[t]hat man over there says that women need to be helped into carriages, and lifted over ditches, and to have the best place everywhere. Nobody ever helps me into carriages, or over mud-puddles, or give me any best place! And ain't I a woman?" (http://www.fordham.edu/halsall/mod/sojtruth-woman.html). To put Truth's statement in its historical context, most black women in the early- to mid-nineteenth century were slaves. Truth was a free woman when she gave this speech, but she was nonetheless born into slavery and became free in 1827.

This "idea" of woman was only available to those who had the economic means to subsist in a single-wage household. Furthermore, only non-slave women had the option of keeping their **family** together (and even then they were vulnerable) without interference from slave owners. Essentially, only free middle- and upper-class white women could fulfill this lauded idea of womanhood. Feminist scholar Hazel Carby has aptly named this historical trope "The Cult of True Womanhood." Some theorists also label this set of "womanly" characteristics as "The Cult of Domesticity." Sojourner Truth could not adhere to the Cult of True Womanhood because of her position as a former slave. In her speech, she asks, "Ain't I a woman?" to question dominant ways of thinking about womanhood. Importantly, these "ideas" about womanhood not only existed in the minds of individuals; many feminists claim that these "ideas" oftentimes affected the material conditions of women's lives.

The Simultaneity of Oppressions in the Second Wave. The second wave of feminism has been labeled as a "white women's movement." This is because many writings that are characterized as "second wave" focus mainly on the experiences of white, middle-class women. Women of color, who identified as U.S. Third World feminists or womanists, critiqued the second wave of feminism for ignoring the ways in which different women have different experiences. In 1977, the Combahee River Collective, a group of black feminists, published "A Black Feminist Statement." In this document, they explore the history of Black women's activism and point to the ways in which different identities such as race, class, and gender intersect. In other words, they argue that women have different experiences because women occupy different positions in society and that not all of these positions are equal. A woman can be white, lower class, and heterosexual, or black, middle class, and lesbian. Women are Latina, Asian American, and biracial; lower class, middle class, and upper class in different periods in their lives; and heterosexual, lesbian, bisexual, or transgendered. The Combahee River Collective claims that one's different social positions inform one's **identity** simultaneously. The simultaneity of oppressions in race, sex, and class has been of utmost importance to third-wave feminism.

In the early 1980s, many women of color continued to critique the second wave. Chicana feminists Gloria Anzaldúa and Cherríe Moraga published *This Bridge Called My Back: Writings by Radical Women of Color* in 1981. A collection of **poetry**, political writings, **consciousness-raising** essays, and visual **art** that examine the intersections oppressions, *This Bridge Called My Back* continues to be an important text for third-wave feminists. It not only widened the terms of feminism to include women of color and Third World women, it also presented a challenge to the traditional ways of perceiving knowledge production (i.e., knowledge is produced only by intellectuals who write in highly sophisticated language) by showing that analytical thinking about gender can take place through multiple artistic, as well as literary, mediums (e.g., literary texts, poems, and **visual art**). This expansion of analytical tools is also a key component of third-wave feminism.

Writer Alice Walker has also addressed the race problem in feminism, and her essay "Womanist" defines several characteristics of black feminists and feminists of color. Walker was writing at the same time as Anzaldúa and Moraga, and like *This Bridge Called My Back* (1981), "Womanist" (and the book in which it appears, *In Search of Our Mothers' Gardens*) points to the ways that women of color negotiate their multiple identities. Walker's essay is more of a celebration of feminists of color, and less of a critique of white feminism. However, Walker's essay "Womanist" ends with the well-known statement: "Womanist is to feminist as purple is to lavender." This not only implies that "feminist" is a "lighter" term than "womanist," it also creates a space for feminist-minded women of color to identify without taking on a presumably "white" feminist **identity**.

Acknowledging Privilege, Acknowledging Whiteness. The critiques of the second wave by women of color resulted in a reexamination of **feminist theory** and practice. Women of color carved out their own spaces in academic and activist communities while continuing to work across racial groups with white women and other women of color. Many white feminists responded to these criticisms and sought to make their work and activism more inclusive of different racial identities. The process was often difficult. There is still much work to be done before third-wave feminism can be truly all-inclusive.

Critiques by women of color led many white women to examine their "whiteness" as a racial category. In her essay "White Privilege: Unpacking the Invisible Knapsack" (1989), Peggy McIntosh wrote about the various social and cultural privileges associated with white identities. Many white, third-wave feminists recognize the social implications of their whiteness and explore the ways in which their racial identity is implicated in the oppression of people of color. This critique does not mean that *all* white, third-wave feminists are involved in these critiques, and some third-wavers have been criticized for their treatment of race despite their good intentions. For example, it has been argued that Eve Ensler's **The Vagina Monologues** portrays the experiences of women of color in the United States and in the Third World (as well as **queer** women) without taking into account the complexities of their lives.

Colonize This!: Young Women of Color on Today's Feminism (2002) is a third-wave anthology that addresses race and racism in contemporary feminism. Despite the claim of racial inclusiveness in the third wave, many of the writers write of the marginalization of race in contemporary feminist movements. For example, in the essay "Heartbroken: Women of Color Feminism and the Third Wave," Rebecca Hurdis discusses the difficulties for contemporary feminists of color and points out that some third-wavers continue to render race invisible. Hurdis writes that *Manifesta: Young Women, Feminism, and the Future* (2000) authors **Jennifer Baumgardner and Amy Richards** market their book as *the* definitive text for the third wave. Hurdis disagrees and claims that *Manifesta* "is a great book for the college white woman who has recently been inspired by feminism" and that it is "astounding" that *Manifesta* includes "no extensive discussion of women of color feminism." Hurdis remains optimistic, nonetheless, and claims that *Manifesta*'s erasure of race "raised a need for creating a lineage" for feminists of color, and she goes on to discuss the ways in which women of color are actively working to create a "third space" that is inclusive of their multiple identities.

See also Black Feminism; Latina Feminism; Representation, Third-Wave Use of; *Volume 2, Primary Documents 9 and 29*

Further Reading: Anzaldúa, Gloria, and Cherríe Moraga, eds., *This Bridge Called My Back: Writings By Radical Women of Color*, 3rd ed., Berkeley: Third Woman Press, 2002; Esquibel, Catrióna Rueda, 1997–2003, *Queer Chicana Fictions*, http://www.chicana-lesbians.com; http://womens-studies.ohio-state.edu/jotas; Frankenberg, Ruth, *White Women, Race Matters: The Social Construction of Whiteness*, Minneapolis: University of Minnesota Press, 1993; Hernández, Daisy, and Bushra Rehman, eds.,

Colonize This!: Young Women of Color on Today's Feminism, New York: Seal Press, 2002; hooks, bell, *Feminist Theory: From Margin to Center*, 2nd ed., Cambridge, MA: South End Press, 2002; Lorde, Audre, *Sister Outsider: Essays and Speeches*, Berkeley: Crossing Press, 1984; Nam, Vickie, *YELL-Oh Girls!: Emerging Voices Explore Culture, Identity and Growing Up Asian American*, New York: HarperCollins, 2001; Smith, Barbara, ed., *Homegirls: A Black Feminist Anthology*, New York: Kitchen Table-Women of Color Press, 1983. Walker, Alice, *In Search of Our Mother's Gardens: Womanist Prose*, New York: Harcourt, Brace, Jovanovich, 1983.

MARY SITZENSTATTER

RAPE. Rape is as much an issue for third-wave **feminism** as it was for the second wave. Rape is a sexual act performed against the victim's will; it is a particularly intimate violation of a victim's **body** and autonomy. Current legal definitions (which vary from state to state) identify rape as unlawful sexual penetration of the vagina, anus, or mouth. This includes penetration from foreign objects such as a bottle, and it includes male and female victims and heterosexual and homosexual rape. What makes the sexual penetration unlawful is that it is accomplished without the consent of the victim, and the perpetrator knows—or has reason to know—that the victim does not consent. In other words, even if victims do not scream, fight, or cry, if they do not consent or are not able to consent then any sexual penetration that occurs is rape. Rape is a crime of epidemic proportions: approximately 600,000 women are raped in the United States every year, and one in five women in the world will experience an attempted or completed rape in her lifetime. Perhaps more disturbingly, in anonymous surveys of male college students in the United States and England, one-third admitted that they would rape a woman if they knew that they would not be caught (Rape, Abuse, and Incest National Network, www.rainn.org).

Second-wave feminists are responsible for current legal and social definitions of rape: beginning in the late 1960s, they argued for legal reforms that made rape a prosecutable crime, and they created rape crisis centers and appropriate medical responses to rape. Through social science research as well as through **consciousness-raising** groups and speak-outs, they named the problem of rape and determined that it is part of the patriarchal functioning of our society. Feminist scholars Susan Brownmiller, Diana Russell, and Susan Griffin argued that rape is an act that perpetuates the **patriarchy** by keeping women fearful and keeping men in charge. They suggested that rape is tied to gender roles in society: men in our society are trained to be powerful, assertive, and in control, while women are trained to be passive, submissive, and compliant. Rape is one way that these gender roles are manifested and maintained.

Third-wave feminists have benefited from the groundbreaking work of second-wave theorists, and they have continued activism and theory surrounding violence against women. Many young feminists in the early 1990s were radicalized by the prominent rape trials of men such as boxer Mike Tyson and

William Kennedy Smith. Anti-rape activism is an area in which second- and third-wave feminists often work together without the generational conflicts that may characterize other areas of activism and scholarship. For instance, many communities hold speak-outs and Take Back the Night marches against rape—these are forms of activism developed in the second wave that now involve multiple feminist generations. Feminists of all generations continue to dispute rape myths, such as the myth that rape is a crime committed by black men against white women (the vast majority of rapes are within the same ethnic or racial group) or that rapists are deranged psychopaths (most rapists are everyday men who believe that they are entitled to sex).

One focal point for third-wave activism around sexual violence is acquaintance rape. Nearly 70 percent of rapes are committed by someone the victim knows, despite the common rape myth that rapists are strangers (advice for women to look under their cars in parking lots, for instance, presumes an attacker who is a stranger). Third-wave feminists have been instrumental in publicizing and raising awareness about this fact. Rape in general is the least reported and the least prosecuted crime, and acquaintance rape is even more difficult to prosecute; indeed, many people believe that if a woman is raped by someone she knows, she must have wanted it. This rape myth blames the victim, and third-wave feminists have been outspoken in their opposition to victim blaming and in their demand that acquaintance rape be recognized as a crime. This demand often takes the form of activism. For instance, students at Brown University in the early 1990s, appalled at the number of acquaintance rapes that the administration was ignoring, undertook a kind of vigilante justice, listing in a women's bathroom the names of men who were rapists.

Anti-rape activism has emerged in other ways in university communities. Students at Antioch College, Columbia University, and Georgetown University succeeded in implementing stronger sexual misconduct policies on campus, and some of this activism has become national through student groups such as SAFER and SpeakOut. Most third-wave anthologies include essays that address violence against women. Third-wave activists have promoted women's self-defense; this has taken the form of **zines** such as *Free to Fight! The Self-Defense Project*, cheers such as "Shoot the Rapist" by Radical Cheerleading squads, and scholarly explorations. The third wave has also pushed for a broader understanding of how rape affects women of different ethnicities, economic backgrounds, and sexualities. For instance, the Survivor Project in Portland, Oregon, addresses violence against **transgendered** people.

Men became involved in anti-rape work in the 1980s and 1990s. Although this work is not easily categorized as either second or third wave, men's involvement in feminism is embraced by many third-wavers. Male activists have noted that men are also victims of rape—in 2002, one in every eight rape victims was male—but that even in cases of male rape, men are the vast majority of the perpetrators. Although most men are not rapists, most rapists are men. Men's feminist work on rape by such activists as Jonathan Stoltenberg,

Jackson Katz, and Michael Kimmel has tended to emphasize the social construction of masculinity as crucial to the understanding of violence against women.

Postfeminist discussion around rape has been controversial. Critics such as Katie Roiphe and Camille Paglia critiqued feminist anti-rape activists for emphasizing women's victimization, and they suggested that the rape crisis identified in feminist writings was a creation of feminist hysteria rather than an accurate reflection of gender relations.

See also Victim/Power Feminism

Further Reading: Brownmiller, Susan, *Against Our Will: Men, Women and Rape*, New York: Simon and Schuster, 1975; Buchwald, Emilie, Pamela R. Fletcher, and Martha Roth, eds., *Transforming a Rape Culture*, Minneapolis: Milweed Editions, 1993; Gold, Jodi, and Susan Villari, eds., *Just Sex: Students Rewrite the Rules on Sex, Violence, Activism, and Equality*, Lanham, MD: Rowman and Littlefield, 2000; McCaughey, Martha, *Real Knockouts: The Physical Feminism of Women's Self-Defense*, New York: New York University Press, 1997; Rape, Abuse, and Incest National Network, http://www.rainn. org; Schulhofer, Stephen, *Unwanted Sex: The Culture of Intimidation and the Failure of Law*, Cambridge, MA: Harvard University Press, 1998; Smith, Merril D., ed., *Encyclopedia of Rape*, Westport, CT: Greenwood Press, 2004.

ALISON PIEPMEIER

RELIGION AND SPIRITUALITY. In June of 2003, the Young Women and Leadership program of the Association for Women's Rights in Development held a discussion with thirty-five young women from the African continent in Capetown, South Africa, to determine what they thought about contemporary religious debates and the compatibility of formal religion and **feminism**. The moderators found that although religion is often relegated to the fringes of women's lives and treated as antithetical to feminist principles, many feminists do not think religion is inherently oppressive to women. In reality, religion and spirituality play an important role in many young feminists' lives. Young women throughout the world embrace their religious and spiritual beliefs and are in favor of finding ways to combine their religious and feminist values into a coherent belief system.

Third-wave feminists have worked both within and outside of traditional religious channels in pursuit of their spiritual, personal, and political goals. Since the 1980s, women from a number of different faiths have challenged the notion that there is no place for women in organized religion. Rather than abandon their faith, many religious women have labored to open up and transform the institutions from which they have been excluded or marginalized. Alternatively, women have also sought spiritual growth in less organized religious practices, ranging from solitary spiritual journeys rooted in traditions from many different faiths to goddess religion tied specifically to women's concerns and feminist practice. Regardless of the spiritual path they choose, it has become clear to many third-wave feminists that one should not and does not have to choose between feminism and spiritual or religious growth. Additionally, older women's religious organizations are reorganizing and adapting to the rise of third-wave feminism, and more young women are getting involved in women's religious organizations and creating their own organizations, **zines**, and Web sites to reflect their worldview and religious/spiritual outlook.

Christian Feminism. Christian Feminism is a broad term used to describe an informal movement for women's equality rooted in the Christian faith. It is an interfaith and intergenerational movement that welcomes women and men interested in using Christian teachings as a basis for supporting women's **empowerment** and equality between the sexes.

Although there are many independent groups committed to the Christian feminist vision throughout the world, the Christians for Biblical Equality is perhaps the most well known. Christians for Biblical Equality is a nonprofit organization made up of both individuals and churches from more than eighty denominations who believe that the Bible should be interpreted holistically and thematically to highlight the idea of the fundamental equality of men and women of all racial and ethnic groups. They see the continual reexamination and reinterpretation of the Bible as central to Christian faith and practice. They believe that women's talents should be recognized and used at all levels of teaching, preaching, and worship as small group leaders, counselors, facilitators, administrators, ushers, communion servers, board members, and pastors. According to Christians for Biblical Equality, women should be given the full benefit of their spiritual equality with men in both their personal and professional relationships.

Catholic Feminism. Although the Catholic Church is among one of the most criticized religious traditions in terms of its treatment and attitudes toward women, Catholic women have been laboring for decades to promote the equality of the sexes within the church. The Women's Ordination Conference was founded in 1975 and incorporated and opened its first office in Washington, D.C., in 1977. Since then, the group has developed a set of five principles that has guided their work. These include reclaiming the church's early tradition of equality among disciples, recognition for the variety of ministries in the Roman Catholic Church, promotion of inclusive spiritualities that are both liberating and feminist in orientation, and supporting ministries that meet the spiritual needs of the people of God while celebrating the diversity of gender, race, ethnicity, **sexuality**, language, and symbol.

As the Women's Ordination Conference has developed, its purpose remains strong while adapting to the changing world and the position of women within it. In 1995 the Women's Ordination Conference created the Young Feminist Network to address the spiritual and religious needs of young feminist women and men. The Young Feminist Network bills itself as a "community of Catholic feminists committed to transforming themselves, the church, and the world through grace, prayer and activism." As part of this mission, Young Feminist Network has committed itself to supporting young adults who want to integrate their faith and feminism, challenging gender **discrimination** within the church and society at large. They are working toward a transformation of the structures of the Catholic church so that these structures become fully inclusive of women, affirming, and participatory, encouraging young women and men to participate in parishes or small faith-based groups, and providing visible leadership opportunities for young Catholic feminists. Young Feminist Network also tries to educate young feminists about their faith through the distribution of pamphlets, articles, and reading lists and through educational programs such as summer retreats, leadership training workshops, and mentoring programs.

Jewish Feminism. Young Jewish feminists are also attempting to merge their spiritual and feminist principles. Although Jewish feminism is not a new phenomenon, the tone and character of Jewish feminist organizations have changed since the 1980s. The concerns and focus of the women, who established and have been publishing the Jewish feminist magazine *Lilith* since 1977, do not speak entirely to the new generation of Jewish feminists. Third-wave Jewish feminists are a heterogenous group. They differ widely with regard to the nature and practice of their faith and their feminism offering diverse interpretation of both aspects of their **identity**. On their paths to establishing a "Jewishly informed feminism" that suits their modern lives, the younger generation has successfully used the Internet and zines as forums for exploring the intersection between their religious, spiritual, and feminist concerns. Charlotte Hongiman-Smith's successful zine, *Maydeleh: a zine for nice Jewish grrrls*, is a primary example of the type of work coming from the younger generation. The purpose of *Maydeleh* and zines/Web sites of its ilk is to provide a forum for young activist Jewish women to discuss matters of faith, religious practice, culture, and community. It is also intended to be a corrective to the lack of attention to Jewish matters in mainstream **media** and the lack of attention to women in mainstream Jewish **magazines**.

Buddhist Feminism. There are many forms of Buddhism (e.g., Chinese, Korean, Japanese, Tibetan, Zen). Many American Buddhists have been critical of the elements of Buddhism that they feel to be oppressive and stifling for women. In recent years this has resulted in the increased participation of women in Buddhism. In contrast, women in Asia generally have a much less prominent role in Buddhism. Since at least the 1990s, the legitimacy of ordaining women as nuns has become a major topic of discussion within the Buddhist community. In 1998, three women in southeast Asia were ordained as Buddhist nuns, and many feminists believe that this act would and has brought about a significant advancement for women's rights in that region. This act also speaks to one of the central tenants of Buddhist teaching that all beings, regardless of gender, are inherently equal and interdependent. Thus, through cultivating compassion, equanimity, humility, and wisdom, both men and women can achieve enlightenment. These goals, although lofty, have also served as the guiding principle behind much third-wave feminist thought.

Islamic/Muslim Feminism. Although it is common to assume that Islam and feminism are incompatible, the notion that one can be both a Muslim and feminist is not that alien to many women within the faith. In fact, a significant portion of Muslim women, especially in the United States, identify both as Muslims and feminists. They believe that although the cultural practices surrounding Islamic religious belief may be patriarchal and oppressive, the faith itself is not. Although the road has not been easy, Muslim feminists in the United States have worked hard since the 1990s to promote the more egalitarian aspects of their religion by promoting women's equality within a spiritual context. Like their Christian and Jewish counterparts, Muslim feminists reject the notion that feminist goals cannot be gained within a religious context. Rather, they call for a reinterpretation and reevaluation of Islam through non-patriarchal perspectives, which take into account both history and spiritual teachings. To accomplish these goals, Muslim feminists first have to convince both the men and women of the Muslim community that women have a God-given right and duty to access and interpret Islamic texts and cultural religious practices.

Earth-Based Feminism. A variety of earth-based religions serve as inspiration for contemporary Goddess spirituality, including Native American spiritism, European nature religions (especially witchcraft), westernized Hinduism, Chinese Taoism, Japanese Shintoism, and Buddhism. One of the most self-consciously feminist spiritual paths taken by third-wavers has been Dianic Wicca. Established in 1971 by second-wave feminists, the Dianic tradition is a goddess- and woman-centered, earth-based, and self-consciously feminist denomination of **Wicca**. Interestingly, Dianic Wicca has managed to maintain its relevance for its founding generation of feminists while serving as a powerful and popular religious and spiritual option for many third-wavers. Although there is no official governing religious body, the Los Angeles–based Temple of Diana serves as a national organization of Dianic tradition and is recognized as such by most followers. Dianic Wiccans honor and celebrate the physical and emotional qualities that women share as a result of their common biology and life cycle. Although many of the important figures within Dianic circles are well-known second-wave feminists including Zsuzsanna Budapest, Mary Daly, Starhawk, Ruth Barrett, Doreen Valiente, and Diane Stein, there is a considerable following from young women as well. Dianic Wicca appeals to feminists for several reasons. Unlike traditional Wicca, Dianic Wiccans only worship the Goddess, reasoning that she is the source of all living things and contains all within her (both the female and male principles). Although an overwhelming majority of Dianics worship in female-only circles, there are some mixed-gender Dianic traditions. In addition to spiritual growth and worship, political action is also central to Dianic Wiccans, making them yet another group of feminists who do not adhere to the notion that religion and politics are separate spheres of interest.

Feminism without Religion. Although women from a number of different faiths have made a considerable effort to promote and incorporate feminist principles into their religious beliefs and traditions, there are still a number of women who believe that religion is one of the primary stumbling blocks to achieving women's rights. In particular, The Freedom from Religion Foundation has committed itself to working for the separation of state and church through educational programs and legal actions for a number of violations of the separation of state and church including: prayers in public schools, payment of public funds for religious purposes, government funding of sectarian institutions, and the ongoing church-led campaigns against civil rights for women, gays, and lesbians. The Freedom from Religion Foundation maintains that the most organized and persistent opponent of women's social, economic, and sexual rights has and is organized religion. They also maintain that the Bible is filled with stories of contempt for women's bodies and serves as one of the primary tools aiding Protestant and Catholic coalitions against women's advancement. Unlike Protestant and Catholic women's right's activists, feminists of this persuasion are not interested in reinterpreting the Bible, because they see it as fundamentally flawed.

The Future. Given the diversity of opinions within the feminist community regarding the possibilities for forging a religious worldview and practice that incorporates feminist thought into existing religious and spiritual belief structures, it is clear that there are many issues yet to be decided. Third-wave feminists have benefited from the work second-wave feminists have done within established religious institutions. Their voices are being heard and they may, in the near future, help to realize the goals set forth by their second-wave predecessors while simultaneously setting goals for themselves and future generations of feminist religious and spiritual believers and activists.

See also Islamic Feminism; Religious Fundamentalism; *Volume 2, Primary Document 63*

Further Reading: Adler, Rachel, "Feminist Judaism: Past and Future," *Cross Currents,* 2004, http://www.crosscurrents.org/Adlerwinter2002.htm; Association for Women's Rights in Development, "How are young women thinking and discussing the relationship between formal religion and feminism?" http://www.awid.org/go.php?stid=844; Beliefnet, "Feminist Generation Gap Emerges at Re-Imagining Conference," http://www.beliefnet.com/story/51/story_5117_1.html; Buddhahnet, Women in Buddhism, http://www.buddhanet.net/mag_nuns.htm; Christians for Biblical Equality, http://www.cbeinternational.org/new/about/about_cbe.shtml; Freedom from Religion Foundation, http://ffrf.org/index.php; Honigman-Smith, Charlotte, "Jewish Feminism's Third Wave" *Tikkun,* March/April 2002, http://www.tikkun.org/magazine/index.cfm/action/tikkun/issue/tik0203/article/020351.html; Jewish Orthodox Feminist Alliance, http://www.jofa.org/about.php?T1=highlights; *Lilith: The Independent Jewish Women's Magazine,* http://www.lilithmag.com; *MAYDELEH: a zine for nice Jewish grrls,* http://www.geocities.com/maydeleh/; Muslim Women's League, http://www.mwlusa.org/; New Religious Movements, "Wicca," http://religiousmovements.lib.virginia.edu/nrms/wicca.html; Temple of Diana: A National Organization of Dianic Wicca, http://www.templeofdiana.org/; Women's Ordination Conference, http://www.womensordination.org/pages/projects_femnet.html.

JAIME MCLEAN

RELIGIOUS FUNDAMENTALISM. Religious fundamentalism is a particular type of religious activism and practice that has gained political prominence in much of the world. The term "fundamentalism" was first used in the 1910s and 1920s to describe one of many competing trends of American Protestantism; however, the term came into wide use again in the 1970s to describe first Christian right-wing movements and then movements from many religions. Most scholars agree that fundamentalism is defined by an opposition to the supposed chaos and social disorder promoted by modernity, an emphasis on the perfection and completeness of religious texts, an orientation toward temporal political action and militancy, a deep sense of persecution and **discrimination**, and a socially (and, in the West, financially) conservative worldview. However, there is strong disagreement over whether the term "fundamentalism" is appropriate for describing these movements. Many believe that the term is a misappropriation, linking together widely disparate movements and ignoring the individual circumstances of each one; they see the term "fundamentalism" as a way of eliminating differences between religions and movements and as an easily, and politically facile, way of dismissing challenges to the social order. Other scholars recognize these problems but believe that there are enough connections among different right-wing, anti-modernist religious movements, and that these movements are different enough from other movements, to allow comparative study. Still others believe that, although the term "fundamentalist" may carry insufficient weight intellectually, its use in public discourse makes it a necessary term for intellectual engagement.

Movements called "fundamentalist" have arisen all over the world in many different contexts. In the United States, Christian fundamentalism, both Protestant and Catholic, is a politically powerful force within the Republican Party and advocates against legal **abortion**, the rights of LesbianGayBisexualTransgender people (LGBT), and stronger government action to ensure women's equality. In much of the Muslim world, Islamic fundamentalists encourage the implementation of the *shari'a* (religious law) adherence to a particular construction of Islamic morality, and, in some cases, the violent overthrow of secular states. In Israel, Jewish fundamentalists, who often are part of the Parliamentary majority, advocate for more restrictive definitions of Jewishness, state enforcement of Jewish dietary laws, the Sabbath, and gender segregation. In India, Hindu fundamentalists, whose political party (the Bharatiya Janata Party) was the lead party in the legislature for several years, organized violent attacks on Muslim minorities, urged the creation of a Hindu (as opposed to a secular state), and have been active in resurrecting the religious practice of sati, the burning of widows on their husband's funeral pyres. Other fundamentalisms (Sikhism in India, Buddhism in Sri Lanka, the New Religions in Japan, and others) have also arisen in the past few decades.

While acknowledging the specificity of any given fundamentalism, it is still clear, in looking from case to case, that gender is at the core of many of these fundamentalist systems of thought. There are several ways in which gender is central to fundamentalism's actions. First, a particular construction of the **family**, and of women's essential and natural place within the family and within **marriage**, is a key part of fundamentalism's ideal community. Men and women are considered to have different roles in life. The man's role is to interact with the outside world as breadwinner and leader, and the woman's role is to focus on her home, her husband, and her children. Within Christian fundamentalism, the nuclear family—itself a product of modernity—is considered the proper structure for the Christian family. Hindu fundamentalism encourages women's submission to an extended family. The key to a woman's special, and legitimately respected, position is in her ability to give birth and her supposed special prowess as mother, caregiver, and homemaker. Her reproductive capacity creates her social purpose, which directly contributes to the involvement of fundamentalist women (and men) in campaigns against birth control and abortion. This first point is related to a second: the fundamentalist belief that changes in women's social position are a key part of the social chaos brought by modernity. The increase in women working outside the home, the expansion of political rights to women, and the principles advocated by **feminism** and women's liberation movements are all seen as part of the current catastrophe in social functioning and are fiercely opposed by fundamentalists. Islamic fundamentalists point to advances in women's rights as coming from the West and of being alien to Islam, which gives women all of their proper rights. They brand all feminists and advocates for women's rights as Westernized, a label that can be poisonous in politics in the developing world. Christian fundamentalists in the West put their political muscle behind opposition to abortion, the Equal Rights Amendment (**ERA**), **same-sex unions/gay marriage**, and most other feminist policy changes. Many fundamentalists are focused on ensuring sex-specific proper dress and behavior, especially for women. While many Jewish and Muslim non-fundamentalist women cover their hair (with wigs, hats, or veils) and bodies (with long dresses, stockings, and robes), Jewish and Islamic fundamentalism put special emphasis on the appropriate form of this covering, in some cases to the point of physical attacks on "inappropriately" dressed women and to national legislation on a female dress code.

Although fundamentalisms are avowedly antifeminist, these movements recognize the weight that is given to calls for women's liberation. Most fundamentalists argue that it is modern, secular Western society that degrades women, and that fundamentalism liberates them from that oppressive society and raises them up to new levels of respect. As well, many women actively and voluntarily join and lead even the most rabidly anti-woman fundamentalist movements. For many of these women, belonging to fundamentalist movements gives them an ability to participate in public life. Conservative family members might disapprove of their being involved in political organizing, but women who are involved in fundamentalist organizing often receive approval from family members. Being a religiously proper woman allows women to bargain with patriarchal forces in their lives to achieve status within the household and freedom of movement outside it. So, while fundamentalist movements directly oppose the changes in women's status encouraged by feminism, they can sometimes serve as means for individual women to bargain to improve their own status. *See also* Islamic Feminism; Patriarchy; Religion and Spirituality

Further Reading: Ammerman, Nancy Tatom, *Bible Believers: Fundamentalists in the Modern World.* New Brunswick, NJ: Rutgers University Press, 1987; Berktay, Fatmagül, "The Position and Control of Woman: Central Concern of Fundamentalism Today" and "Fundamentalism in Iran: Challenge to Modernity," in *Women and Religion*, trans. Belma Ötu-Baskett, Montreal: Black Rose, 1998, 147–182; Hawley, John Stratton, ed., *Fundamentalism and Gender*, New York: Oxford University Press, 1994; Sahgal, Gita, and Nira Yuval-Davis, eds., *Refusing Holy Orders: Women and Fundamentalism in Britain*, London: Virago Press, 1992.

EMILY REGAN WILLS

REPRESENTATION, THIRD-WAVE USE OF. Representation quite literally means re-presentation. Representations are the re-presentation of the objects and ideas in the everyday world, such as images, words, and Web sites. Representations are also everywhere—on billboard **advertising, television**, or the sides of buses. Representations allow members of a certain society to "make sense" of the world around them and serve as a way of classifying and characterizing differences. For example, the television show *Buffy the Vampire Slayer* is not a lived experience; instead, it *represents* a lived experience and shows the viewer very specific ways of thinking about gender, race, class, and **sexuality**. This does not, however, mean that representations always reflect cultural "truths." Many third-wave feminists recognize that representations are active agents in gender socialization and create ways of thinking about race, class, gender, and sexuality.

Third-wave feminists define representations as cultural objects that help create meanings about gender within society. Some of these include toys, computer games, television shows, novels, photographs, advertisements, and **magazines**. Representation is very important to the third wave of **feminism**, and many members of the movement use representations to spread their ideas about feminism. Many third-wave feminists critique mainstream representations of gender through their photographs, **fiction, art, poetry**, and **music** (among other formats), and much third-wave activism centers around art and music communities. Third-wave feminists fund and create their feminist art festivals, such as Ladyfest, and from hip galleries to seedy punk bars, third-wave feminists are redefining the ways in which representations create knowledge about women's lives in the past and the present.

Race and Representation. Third-wave uses of representation are greatly influenced by the U.S. Third World feminists. In the 1970s and 1980s, many women of color critiqued the second-wave feminism for failing to account for the experiences of women of color. Chicana feminists Gloria Anzaldúa and Cherríe Moraga published *This Bridge Called My Back: Writings by Radical Women* *of Color* in 1981. This anthology contains autobiographical narratives, political writings, poems, letters, stories, and **visual art**. The composition of the text is important, for not only are the writers addressing their experiences with race and **racism** on a material level, they are also exploring the ways in which race and racism inform the creation of culture. One of the text's major critiques is of the ways in which **feminist theory** is written. Furthermore, the editors and contributors recognize that knowledge production is valuable not only within the "academy," but also outside of the "ivory tower."

Audre Lorde, a well-known black feminist theorist, also comments on the creation of feminist knowledge in her essay "Poetry Is Not a Luxury" (1984). Here, she discusses the importance of recognizing the political power of **poetry**. Lorde, like many other U.S. Third World feminists, stresses the importance of using one's "own" language to comprehend the ways in which one views the world. She explains that critically assessing the "traditional" (i.e., white, Western, and male) ways of producing knowledge results in a "new language" that arises from women's "place of power within." According to Lorde, this new language is poetry, and this poetry should be used for intellectual, as well as political, revolution. Lorde's words are important to third-wave feminists, and many third-wavers seek to incorporate a "new language" into their representations. Furthermore, many third-wavers are also concerned with the women's representations throughout history and the ways in which these representations create meaning about the intersections of gender, race, class, sexuality, and ethnicity.

Feminism Takes on Art History. In the 1970s, second-wave feminists such as Judy Chicago and Linda Nochlin criticized the ways in which women have been represented in art history. They claimed that in the past, women were excluded from the art world, and, indeed, an examination of women's history reveals that women were rarely, if ever, given the chance to explore their artistic talents. (First-wave British feminist Virginia Woolf also explored women's exclusion from artistic and literary circles in "The Story of Shakespeare's Sister" in *A Room of One's Own*.) Furthermore, the intersection of gender with race, class status, and ethnic background also blocked many women from receiving any kind of **education**, let alone one centered in the arts. These various historical realities answer Linda Nochlin's intriguing question: "Why have there been no Great Women artists?"

In *Ways of Seeing* (1972), John Berger claimed that in the history of Western art, "men act and women appear." This concept is of utmost importance for contemporary feminist critics and many claim that in art history, men are subjects and women are objects. In other words, men are active—they are the painters, the generals, the leaders—while women are there simply to be looked at. Feminist **film** theorist Laura Mulvey examines women's "to-be-looked-at-ness" in popular film. Well versed in psychoanalysis, Mulvey writes that in many films (particularly those of Alfred Hitchcock), women are objects of the "male gaze." Although Mulvey's theory has been critiqued and expanded on by other critics, "The Male Gaze," originally published in 1975, is still an important document/concept for third-wavers studying representation.

Third-wave feminists take critics such as Chicago, Nochlin, Mulvey, and Berger seriously and continue to critique mainstream representations of women in the art world. The third-wave feminist art activists the **Guerrilla Girls** use clever tactics and colorful texts in their critiques of the art world. For example, they use such broad mediums as billboards, postcards, political demonstrations, the Internet, and visits to college campuses to educate the masses. Interestingly, a major part of their activist agenda is the sporting of gorilla masks and, quite literally, the Guerrilla Girls hide their faces as they fight (in the trenches) for women's ownership of their representations.

Third-wave feminists also encourage the reclaiming of women's artistic spaces. In the past, domestic arts, such as quilt making, decorating, knitting, and sewing, were viewed simply as women's leisure activities. These creations were not considered works of "great" art. However, many contemporary feminists claim that these items for the home deserve as much recognition as traditional art forms, such as painting and sculpture. Asserting that women were not given the opportunities or means to attend prestigious art schools or to learn the traditionally male-dominated ways of creating art, third-wave feminists contend that women's creations in the past, present, and future must be viewed through the lens of women's omission from the "traditional" world of art.

Representations and Resistance. Third-wave feminists believe that representations are powerful tools in Western cultures. Therefore, they also claim that representations can be used strategically to combat dominant stereotypes about gender. This oppositional use of representation is called resistance. Many representations of women in popular culture position women primarily as objects, but third-wave feminists argue that some representations show strong, independent, feminist-minded women. This, however, does not mean that *all* representations of women are positive, and many third-wavers continue to combat—and critique—oppressive representations of women. Lastly, Angela Y. Davis explains in *Blues Legacies and Black Feminism* (1998) that women blues singers resisted dominant troupes of **femininity** with their music and performances. Women of color have continually used representations as modes of resistance to both racism and sexism. As the U.S. Third World feminists influenced the shift to the third wave, the contributions of women of color to third-wave uses of Representation also helped shape a distinctly third-wave feminist movement.

From Audre Lorde to the Guerrilla Girls, second- and third-wave feminists stress the importance of representation and its significant role in the creation of ideas about gender. Television characters such as Buffy (the Vampire Slayer), Xena (Warrior Princess), and Roseanne have been claimed by third-wave feminists as strong, independent women who represent positive role models for third-wavers. Comic Margaret Cho and bands such as Le Tigre, Sleater-Kinney, and Sweet Honey in the Rock are representative of feminist performers. And finally, Selena, Dar Williams, **Ani DiFranco, Liz Phair, Courtney Love, Missy Elliott**, and Me'shell Ndegéocello are important for third-wavers who seek feminist voices in popular **music** and culture.

See also Volume 2, Primary Documents 48 and 49

Further Reading: Chicago, Judy, *Women and Art: Contested Territory*, New York: Watson-Guptill, 1999; Davis, Angela Y., *Blues Legacies and Black Feminism*, New York: Vintage, 1998; Douglas, Susan, *Where the Girls Are: Growing Up Female with the Mass Media*, New York: Random House, 1994; Guerrilla Girls, *Bitches, Bimbos and Ballbreakers: The Guerrilla Girls' Illustrated Guide to Female Stereotypes*, New York: Penguin, 2003; Guerrilla Girls, *The Guerrilla Girls' Bedside Companion to the History of Western Art*, New York: Penguin, 1998; Heywood, Leslie, and Jennifer Drake, *Third Wave Agenda: Being Feminist, Doing Feminism*, Minneapolis: University of Minnesota Press, 1997; hooks, bell, *Black Looks: Race and Representation*, Boston: South End Press, 1992; Morrison, Toni, *Playing in the Dark: Whiteness and the Literary Imagination*, New York: Vintage, 1993; Walker, Alice, *In Search of Our Mothers' Gardens: Womanist Prose*, San Diego: Harcourt Brace Jovanovich, 1983.

MARY SITZENSTATTER

REPRODUCTIVE TECHNOLOGIES. New reproductive technologies, or NRTs, are medical interventions in the processes of reproduction. Reproductive technologies allow more women and families to have or not have children and thus are of concern to third-wave **feminism**.

The categories of reproductive technologies include the prevention of fertility through birth control, and additionally, emergency contraception; the fostering of fertility through sperm donation, by which a woman is impregnated with sperm from someone other than her partner; egg donation, by which a woman conceives with an egg donated by another; sperm and egg freezing; in vitro fertilization (IVF), in which a woman's eggs are fertilized by sperm outside her **body** and the fertilized embryo is then implanted in her uterus; alternative fertility or **family** formation including embryo adoption, in which a donated egg and sperm IVF takes place; embryo freezing; surrogate mothers, which is bearing a child under contract; embryo and fetal screening, including amniocentesis; genetic screening and ultrasound; and delivery room procedures including fetal monitors, caesarian sections, planned deliveries, and drugs used during delivery.

Access to birth-control technologies has widened, although most recently it has been under attack by fundamentalists on the religious right, with pharmacists refusing to fill prescriptions because of their "faith." Birth-control methods are safe and highly effective. The accessibility and safety of birth control vary by method. Prevention of the transmission of sperm to the egg can be accomplished through female and male condoms, spermicides, intrauterine devices (IUDs), oral contraceptives (birth-control pill), RU-486, diaphragm or cervical cap, the birth-control patch, injections, hormonal vaginal contraceptive rings, tubal ligation, vasectomy, and implants (which have been taken off the market). Norplant, which involved capsules inserted into a woman's arm that emitted hormones over a prolonged period, was an example of a birth control known to be marketed or enforced on low-income women and women of color. Many women were left with the implant in their arms and had difficulty finding health care professionals to remove them. The birth-control pill has widespread use and success and is becoming increasingly accessible and affordable. There are even new birth-control pills, such as Seasonale, which defer the menstrual period to only four times per year, which may give women additional control over their body.

Emergency contraception consists of hormonal pills taken after having unprotected sex or having the copper T IUD put into the uterus within seven days of unprotected sex. Feminists continue fighting for emergency contraception without a prescription.

Assistive technologies such as fertility treatments, IVF, and egg, sperm, and embryo donation allow single women, infertile women and couples, disabled women and couples, postmenopausal women, and lesbian/gay couples to have children, but they remain extremely expensive and have a low success rate. Fertility treatments, IVF, and egg donation are known to be physically demanding processes so the lack of success is particularly difficult. Fertility clinics need egg donors and typically seek donors who are young and college-educated from specific racial or ethnic groups. These donors receive financial compensation for increasing their hormone levels to allow the eggs to increase in size for easier extraction via a surgical procedure. This allows women to help other women and allows families to be created that otherwise could not be, but the process is expensive, like many NRTs, and inaccessible to most.

Embryo freezing allows for postponed childbearing, which increases women's control over reproduction while preserving the state of the fertilized egg. Embryo freezing may also allow women being treated for a disease to have the embryo implanted after completing treatment. Embryo donation may result from embryonic cryogenics, allowing a woman or couple to provide the potential for reproduction to another person or couple.

Surrogate mothers refer to women who bear a child under contract. This may or may not involve sperm or egg donation from those in contract with the mother and allows families seeking children greater opportunity and financial compensation to the surrogate mother.

Screenings such as amniocentesis, ultrasound, and genetic screening increases women's knowledge about their fetus and can contribute to the birth of healthy children. Simultaneously, some feminists caution full-scale approval because there can be race-, sex-, or disease-based genetic selection with risk of the eugenic weeding out of certain peoples. While increased knowledge and control in the reproductive process remains key for women, asking questions about the ethics behind the procedures is critical.

Delivery room procedures including fetal monitors, caesarian sections, delivery techniques, and the use of drugs may allow women a more comfortable and safe delivery in certain situations. The increased technology attempts to ensure the baby's health in addition to the mother's. Increasing rates of cesarean sections and planned deliveries have some feminists concerned about who exactly is in control of the birth process.

NRTs are designed to widen choices but remain restricted to those who can afford them. Health insurance rarely covers assistive reproduction techniques. So if NRTs are liberating for women, they must be liberating for all women, in the control of all women, and available to all women.

Class and race **discrimination**, historically, have played into reproductive technologies. Poverty, limited life choices, and the capitalist marketplace itself can shape the availability, purchase, sale, and use of NRTs. Increased access and scrutiny are goals to ensure the right of every woman to decide what medical procedures she wishes done on or to her body.

Reproductive technologies are chances to ameliorate involuntary childlessness and involuntary childbearing while allowing increased choice and control. Increased access to reproductive choices for women is important, but third-wave feminists can simultaneously critique the system to ensure or monitor that these technologies are not used against women as a form of eugenics and that women freely choose them. If NRTs violate a woman's right and access to choice, the encouraging of the compulsory bearing of children by women or questions of financially profiting from NRTs will be probed. Increased medicalization of reproduction may mean the ability for families to form or not form, or women to conceive who once could not, but many believe this should not mean increased control over women's bodies by the medical establishment. Lastly, for women with diseases and disorders that impede reproduction, a third-wave sensibility demands that the underlying problems of pollution, toxicity, and untreated diseases that affect women and men that necessitated the NRTs be addressed as well.

Further Reading: Becker, Gay, *The Elusive Embryo: How Women and Men Approach New Reproductive Technologies*, Berkley: University of California Press, 2000; Hartouni, Valerie, *Cultural Conceptions: On Reproductive Technologies and the Remaking of Life*, Minneapolis: University of Minnesota Press, 1997; Lublin, Nancy, *Pandora's Box: Feminism Confronts Reproductive Technology*, Lanham, MD: Rowman & Littlefield, 1998; Van Der Ploeg, Irma, *Prosthetic Bodies: The Construction of the Fetus and the Couple as Patients in Reproductive Technologies*, New York: Springer, 2001.

AMI LYNCH

RICHARDS, AMY. *See* Baumgardner, Jennifer, and Richards, Amy; *Volume 2, Primary Document 41*

RIOT GRRRLS. *See* Alt Culture; Bikini Kill; Music; Third-Wave Catch Phrases.

ROBERTS, TARA. Tara Roberts (1970–) is the founder and publisher of *Fierce* magazine, an online and print magazine designed for women who want to "live juicy, wild, uncompromising, untamed, unapologetic lives." For women of color in particular, Roberts is a visionary on a mission to give voice to women regularly ignored by most mainstream "women's" **magazines**. "*Fierce* is for all of us," writes Roberts in her publisher's letter. "*Fierce* is feminist, it's womanist, and it's beyond these words. *Fierce* stands for all women everywhere defining themselves, coming up with new language that moves beyond politics, beyond color, beyond class." Inspired by a dream and birthed with a whole lot of enthusiasm and bodaciousness, Atlanta-based *Fierce* magazine debuted in May 2003 to rave reviews and public acclaim.

Roberts graduated cum laude in 1991 from Mount Holyoke College in South Hadley, Massachusetts, and from New York University, where she earned an MS in publishing. She began her career at *Essence* magazine in 1993 as an editorial assistant in the Arts and Entertainment Department and was eventually promoted to the position of editorial director of *Essence Online*, before moving to *Heart & Soul* magazine as its lifestyle editor. Roberts' book, *Am I the Last Virgin?: Ten African American Reflections on Sex and Love* (1997) is a collection of first-person essays by young black women exploring their own sexual coming-of-age experiences. Before leaving New York for Atlanta, Roberts also taught journalism at Syracuse University.

See also Black Feminism; Magazines, Women's; Womanism/Womanist

Further Reading: *Fierce* magazine, http://www.Fiercemag.com; Roberts, Tara, ed., *Am I the Last Virgin?: Ten African American Reflections on Sex and Love*, New York: Simon Pulse, 1997.

MURIEL L. WHETSTONE-SIMS

***ROE v. WADE* AND RECENT CHALLENGES.** Of crucial importance to third-wave **feminism**, *Roe v. Wade* is the U.S. Supreme Court case, decided in 1973, that guaranteed a constitutional right to an **abortion** during the first six months of pregnancy. Before the Court's ruling, most states prohibited abortion, although most allowed an exception when pregnancy threatened the woman's life. The Court overturned these state prohibitions in *Roe v. Wade*. The Court ruled that states could restrict abortions only during the final three months of pregnancy. Along with *Doe v. Bolton*, a case where a poor, married mother of three from Georgia wanted an abortion but state law required permission from a panel of doctors and hospital officials, the *Roe* decision legalized abortion.

The Case. Until the second half of the nineteenth century, most states chose not to restrict abortion, but by the end of the nineteenth century, most states had adopted statutes that made it a crime to either perform or obtain an abortion except to save the life of a pregnant woman.

The restrictive measures in the United States began in an effort to increase the population and to increase medical control over women's bodies. Most of these nineteenth-century statutes were still in effect in 1970, when Norma McCorvey, a pregnant woman from Dallas, challenged a Texas abortion law. Using the pseudonym "Jane Roe," McCorvey sued Henry Wade, the Dallas County district attorney, to allow her to have an abortion. The Texas law banned abortions in that state, except when the pregnancy physically threatened the life of the pregnant woman, which was not applicable to Roe, but as a poor, single woman she did not want to bear a child she could not afford to raise. Financial burdens and two other children prevented her from traveling to a state where abortions were legal.

Roe and her attorneys asked the federal district court to declare that the Texas abortion statute violated her right to privacy under the Constitution and that no one else should be prosecuted. Sarah Weddington argued for the prosecution that a woman's right to make childbearing decisions free of governmental compulsion was fundamental to her right to control her own life.

A three-judge panel in Texas ruled in favor of Roe that the Texas abortion laws violated the Ninth and Fourteenth Amendments, which guarantee privacy rights and should protect a woman's choice to have an abortion. Roe and Wade both appealed to the U.S. Supreme Court when the district attorney refused to forbid future abortion prosecutions.

The Supreme Court heard arguments for *Roe v. Wade* in December 1971. Finally, in January 1973, the Court decided seven to two in favor of Roe.

Right to Privacy. Based on the right of privacy, the Court struck down many state anti-abortion statutes. Justice Harry Blackmun argued that the state's right to protect the fetus increased as a pregnancy advanced. This decision established the right to an abortion and also gave states the right to intervene in the second and third trimesters of pregnancy to protect the woman from abortion procedures deemed dangerous while protecting the "potential" life of the fetus. Blackmun noted the constitutional protections guaranteeing that the government will not intrude into its citizens' privacy without a legal cause but that privacy is not absolute, leading Blackmun to develop compromise guidelines during the later stages of pregnancy.

Medical Considerations. Blackmun pointed out that initially abortion statutes were partly designed to protect the life of a pregnant woman from abortion procedures previously considered dangerous. As of 1973, Blackmun noted that abortion posed less of a danger than pregnancy and childbirth. So Blackmun concluded that the state should have a responsibility to ensure that abortions be performed safely, but now that abortion was safe in the first and second trimesters it should be legal.

The Court argued that during the second trimester an abortion posed a greater threat to a woman's health, so the state could regulate abortion only to protect the health of a pregnant woman. Blackmun stated that in the third trimester, the fetus may be considered capable of living with medical intervention outside the uterus, so that at the third trimester of pregnancy, the state has a responsibility to protect the life of the fetus, supplanting the privacy concerns of the woman unless the pregnancy threatens her life. The Court rejected the Texas law's idea that a fetus had "person" protection under the Fourteenth Amendment.

Challenges to Roe. Repeated challenges, since 1973, have narrowed *Roe's* scope but have not overturned it. The Court has allowed some states to impose restrictions that make an abortion difficult to obtain, particularly for low-income women and teenagers. The 1977 Hyde Amendment withdrew state funding for abortion for poor women. The Court has also upheld state laws requiring that pregnant girls younger than the age of eighteen must notify at least one parent before obtaining an abortion.

In a 1989 case, *Webster v. Reproductive Health Services*, the Court limited *Roe*'s scope but upheld Missouri's ban on the use of public facilities, employees, or funds for any abortion-related purpose and increased states' leeway in regulating abortion. Then in 1992, in *Planned Parenthood v. Casey*, the Court reaffirmed the abortion rights granted in *Roe v. Wade*, while permitting further restrictions, and declared Pennsylvania's Abortion Control Act constitutional in part but struck down husband notification. In 1994, *Madsen v. Women's Heath Center* put clinics that provide pregnancy and abortion counseling on the same statute as hospitals that are protected from service disruptions. The Child Custody Protection Act criminalizes an adult accompanying a minor to get an abortion across state lines if the home state's laws were violated. In 2001, the Unborn Victims of Violence Act gave states the right to see the fetus as having legal status if hurt or killed when a federal crime is committed. Women's rights advocates are concerned about the implications for reproductive rights. From 1995 to 2000 Congress passed, but President Bill Clinton vetoed, a bill that would ban rare, late-term abortion, called "partial-birth abortion" by its critics. Subsequent attempts by many states to ban this method were contested in the courts, and in 2000 the Supreme Court voided laws that do not include an exception when the woman's health is endangered. A federal bill banning the procedure was passed in 2003 and signed into law but was quickly challenged in the courts. The core components of the *Roe v. Wade* decision remain intact.

Opponents of abortion have used more militant tactics in recent years in attempts to disrupt the operations of facilities that perform abortions, and some extremists have resorted to bombings and assassination. Reproductive rights proponents continue their struggle to protect the rights guaranteed by *Roe v. Wade*.

Further Reading: Faux, Marian, *Roe v. Wade*, New York: Cooper Square Publishers, 2000; National Abortion Rights Action League, Pro-Choice America, NARAL Web site, http://www.naral.org; Planned Parenthood Federation of America Web site, http://www.plannedparenthood.org.

AMI LYNCH

ROSE, TRICIA. Tricia Rose (1963–), a feminist scholar and cultural critic, is committed to pursuing projects that break new ground. Her book, *Black Noise: Rap Music and Black Culture in Contemporary America* (1994), was the first substantial study of rap **music** and hip-hop culture. Perhaps because Rose came of age in New York as rap music and hip-hop culture were emerging there,

the book presents a particularly nuanced discussion of rap music, including its relationship to New York's 1970s urban development policies, its innovative uses of technology, its aesthetic strategies, and its complex racial and sexual politics. *Black Noise* has become a canonical text in **cultural studies**, and its attentiveness to exploring and contextualizing rap's contradictions serves as a model of third-wave feminist approaches to scholarship. Another project, entitled *Longing to Tell: Black Women's Stories of Sexuality and Intimacy* (2003), was the first oral history about black women's **sexuality**. Working against centuries of stereotypes about black women's sexuality, the book presents the stories of twenty women in their own words. These twenty were culled from hundreds of interviews Rose conducted with women across the United States. *Longing to Tell* is an important addition to the group of third-wave **consciousness-raising** texts that includes Barbara Findlen's *Listen Up* (1995) and Rebecca Walker's *To Be Real* (1995), particularly because it bridges the second and third waves in its attention to the experiences of black women from different generations and backgrounds.
See also Black Feminism; Hip-Hop Feminism

Further Reading: Inoue, Todd, "Get Real," http://www.metroactive.com/papers/metro/07.10.03/rose-0328.html; Rose, Tricia, *Black Noise: Rap and Black Culture in Contemporary America*, Hanover, NH: Wesleyan University Press, 1994; Rose, Tricia, *Longing to Tell: Black Women's Stories of Sexuality and Intimacy*, New York: Farrar, Straus and Giroux, 2003; Ross, Andrew, and Tricia Rose, *Microphone Fiends: Youth Music and Youth Culture*, New York: Routledge, 1994; Tricia Rose Web site, http://www.triciarose.com.

JENNIFER DRAKE

RuPAUL. Often seen as an example of the kind of gender fluidity the third wave most values, flamboyant performer (Andre Charles) RuPaul (1960–) was born in San Diego, California, in 1960. His interest in **fashion** dates back to his earliest years. His artistic output dates back to the early 1980s, when he began creating **music** (as part of RuPaul and the U-Hauls), **television** programs, **film**, and books in Atlanta, Georgia. When he moved to New York later in the decade, he rose to prominence in the club scene, where his trademark became bright, exaggerated, and flamboyant drag outfits. Approaching seven feet of height in heels, RuPaul's enormous bouffant coifs also helped to define his so-called Glamazon style. After becoming 1990s "Queen of Manhattan," he focused on developing his singing career, having signed a contract with Tommy Boy Records in 1991. He remains best known for the song "Supermodel (You Better Work)." An ode to the well-known models of the moment, it gave popular culture the catch phrase "sashay, chantay." The 1990s also saw his major motion-picture debut in Spike Lee's *Crooklyn* (1994). RuPaul also appeared in roles in *The Brady Bunch Movie* (1995), *To Wong Foo, Thanks for Everything! From Julie Newmar* (1995), and *But I'm a Cheerleader* (1999). RuPaul was one of the first people to bring drag to the American masses, even having his own talk show and variety program, *The RuPaul Show*, which enjoyed a 100-episode run. Demonstrating his **desire** to use his fame in positive ways, he became the first face of M.A.C. CosmeticsVivaGlam campaign. All the proceeds from sales of their VivaGlam lipstick are donated to assist men, women, and children living with **AIDS**.

Further Reading: RuPaul, *Lettin It All Hang Out: An Autobiography*, New York: Hyperion Books, 1995; RuPaul, Red Hot, http://www.rupaul.com.

JESSICA MANACK

S

SAME-SEX UNIONS/GAY MARRIAGE. Gay **marriage** (or same-sex marriage) is the union of two individuals of the same sex. Like heterosexual marriage, same-sex marriage may be a religious or civil ceremony. A highly controversial topic, gay marriage has been portrayed as both the pioneer civil rights issue of the new millennium and a symptom of societal and moral decline. For third-wave feminists, who tend to identify across **identity** categories such as gay/straight, the conflict or controversy seems unwarranted.

Conflict surrounding gay marriage centers on whether couples in homosexual relationships should be allowed the same rights and privileges offered to heterosexual couples. The topic may be oversimplified as a debate over the morality of homosexuality. However, many heterosexual couples support same-sex marriage. Contrarily, many homosexuals do not support same-sex marriage, arguing that marriage reproduces structures of inequality.

Opponents tend to argue that marriage, by definition, is a union between a man and a woman. This definition of marriage is often, but not always, framed within a Judeo-Christian religious belief system, arguing that God disallows homosexuality. Opponents contend that same-sex marriages threaten nuclear **family** structures, creating the conditions in which socially unacceptable family structures (polygamy, bigamy, incest, bestiality) could also become legal. Opponents also argue that allowing same-sex marriages could harm children's development or encourage homosexuality.

Supporters of same-sex marriage tend to argue that gay marriage is an issue of civil rights and equality under the law: for homosexuals to have full and equal citizenship, they must be afforded the same status as heterosexuals. Marriage, supporters argue, is a status granted by state governments rather than religious authorities. Regarding the decline of nuclear family structures, supporters' arguments split. Some supporters contend that nontraditional families have dramatically increased during the last half-century. Legalized same-sex marriage, they argue, will not create nontraditional families but, rather, will offer protection to already-common types of families.

Opponents claim that legally allowing same-sex couples to marry would create an increased financial burden on government. Supporters, however, argue that all citizens are taxpayers and thus equally deserving of rights and protections. Opponents object to framing gay marriage as an issue of civil rights. Some argue, for example, that the black civil rights movement addressed true incidences of **discrimination** against black citizens, but the gay marriage movement seeks special rights for a small minority.

Supporters point out that same-sex marriage allows not only privileged tax status as a couple, but hundreds of other benefits including access to health insurance and pension plans, the right to hospital visitations, and authority over emergency medical decisions. These benefits, supporters argue, are also routinely denied to unmarried heterosexual couples. Legalized same-sex marriage, they argue, is not an issue of special interest to homosexuals but to any couple not offered the same rights as married heterosexuals.

Opponents of same-sex marriage frequently cite the decline of the traditional nuclear family. However, social anthropologists argue that the nuclear family is a relatively recent kinship structure, linked to industrial and post-industrial economic and labor conditions. In human history, families have been arranged in countless configurations.

Historically, in many cultures, gay marriage has been tolerated and even embraced. For example, ancient Greek, Roman, Chinese, and Japanese cultures all had instances of same-sex unions. Most recorded same-sex marriage practices in history have been between men. Although lesbian relationships have existed historically, lesbians may not have married because of their lesser social and economic status as women. Frequently, marriages were between an adult man and a younger boy, a practice known as pederasty. Although this marriage practice has not formally existed for thousands of years, opponents of gay marriage often use this historical fact to argue that allowing gay marriage encourages pedophilia.

Currently, same-sex marriages are legal only in the Netherlands, Belgium, and Canada. However, Denmark, Finland, France, Germany, Greenland, Iceland, Norway, Portugal, and Sweden allow civil unions. Civil unions, available to unmarried heterosexual couples as well as homosexual couples, offer official status to eligible domestic partners. Civil unions typically offer most of the rights and protections of marriage but are not equal to legal marriage. Other countries, such as Spain and Cambodia, have indicated that they will legalize same-sex unions in the near future.

In the United States, a small number of cities, counties, and states have attempted to challenge federal legislation by allowing same-sex marriages or civil unions. The U.S. movement to legalize same-sex marriage can be traced back to the 1971, when two gay men filed a claim to marry on the basis that there was no specific prohibition against gay marriage. The Minnesota Supreme Court ruled against them. In the following years, similar attempts to legally marry were occasionally successful. However, many states began drafting legislation explicitly barring homosexual couples from marrying. For example, same-sex marriages were legalized in Hawaii in 1993, after the State Supreme Court ruled that prohibitions against gay marriage violated laws against sex discrimination. By 1998, the Hawaii Constitution was amended to restrict marriage to heterosexual couples.

Partially in reaction to developments in Hawaii, in 1996 President Bill Clinton signed the Defense of Marriage Act (DOMA). This federal law limits the definition of marriage to a union of one man and one woman. The law also provides that each state may determine whether to recognize same-sex unions. As a result, thirty-eight states have drafted laws prohibiting the recognition of same-sex unions. More recently, the Bush Administration proposed the Federal Marriage Amendment, which not only defines marriage as a union of one man and one woman but also prohibits states from recognizing same-sex unions.

Currently, both Massachusetts and Vermont have legalized same-sex unions. Some areas of California and Oregon briefly offered same-sex unions; however, both were issued court orders to stop. Although same-sex marriages have been legalized in some areas, these marriages are not recognized by the federal government or by most states. Therefore, fighting for gay rights and gay marriage tends to be an issue of activism for third-wave feminists.
See also Heterosexism; Religion and Spirituality

Further Reading: Baird, Robert, and Stuart Rosenbaum, *Same-Sex Marriage: The Moral and Legal Debate*, New York: Prometheus Books, 1997; Ontario Consultants on Religious Tolerance, "Same-Sex Marriages and Civil Unions", Religious Tolerance Web site, http://www.religioustolerance.org/hom_marr.htm; Wardle, Lynn, ed., *Marriage and Same-Sex Unions: A Debate*. Westport, CT: Praeger Publishers, 2003.

TERESA SIMONE

SEATTLE PROTESTS. At the end of November and the beginning December 1999, an estimated 50,000–100,000 protesters, many of them third-wave feminists, gathered in the streets of Seattle to protest the ministerial meeting of the World Trade Organization (WTO).

The Seattle protests were especially unique because they attracted numerous organizations that put aside their political differences to protest a common enemy: the WTO. Labor and environmentalists joined with many other diverse individuals and groups ranging from church fellowships, to anarchists, to nonviolent direction action activists. Even members of the ultra conservative reform party and as well as libertarians came out to oppose international trade. Third-wave feminists' involvement in this broadly coalitional movement serves as an example of what sociologist Anita Harris calls characteristic of the movement: it is not always visible *as* **feminism** because the fights take on gender issues among a number of other, interrelated problems.

Impressively (in terms of demonstrating a new form of activism), this protest spread beyond the streets of Seattle. In addition to those protesting in Seattle, on November 30 there were solidarity protests around the United States in Atlanta, Amherst, Austin, Baltimore, Louisville, Montpelier, Morgantown, Nashville, Philadelphia, Santa Cruz, and Washington, D.C. Around the world, protest locations included Canada, Iceland, England, Ireland, Wales, Portugal, France, Switzerland, the Netherlands, Germany, Italy, Greece, the Czech Republic, Turkey, Israel, Pakistan, India, South Korea, the Philippines, and Australia.

The protests in Seattle were effective insofar as they caused the WTO meetings to be disrupted: the official opening ceremony was delayed and subsequently canceled. Furthermore, the meetings ended without any agreements being made. This was accomplished in part by surrounding the WTO meeting sites with a human blockade, which prevented delegates from attending the meetings.

The protesters faced serious adversity. Not only was it cold and rainy but the protesters were also met with strong police resistance, especially after a small number of protesters caused property damage by breaking windows and overturning garbage containers and newspaper boxes. According to most accounts, the police used rubber bullets and pepper spray and went so far as to arrest not only the few causing property damage but countless peaceful protesters as well. At the end of the week, there were close to 600 protest-related arrests.

As often happens today in other contexts, where the **media** expects feminists to focus only on gender, it was noted by many in attendance that there was a lack of a strong feminist presence. Just as third-wave feminism is often accused of "not really being feminism" because it is focused on other issues in addition to gender, these claims could be countered by saying that feminists are not simply feminists—they are also members of labor, environmental groups, churches, etc. Thus, feminists were there as factions of other organizations, and feminisms are an important component of each of these political and social entities. Given that most workers in the developing world are girls and women, WTO policies certainly are of interest to women and feminists. Third-wavers see that the public needs to get used to the idea that feminism is now in dialog with a number of other issues such as race, **globalization**, and national identities and can no longer be seen as a movement that is only focused on one kind of women in one location.

See also Environmentalism

Further Reading: Harris, Anita, *Future Girl*, New York: Routledge, 2004; University of Washington WTO Seattle Collection, http://content.lib.washington.edu/WTOweb/; Yuen, Eddie, George Katsiaficas, and Daniel Burton Rose, *The Battle of Seattle: The New Challenge to Capitalist Globalization*, New York: Soft Skull Press, 2001.

Laura Gladney-Lemon

SEX EDUCATION. From books, community networks, and workshops, to foundations and self-published and distributed **zines**, sex **education** and sexual health have been defining issues for third-wave **feminism**. Today most Americans agree that some kind of sex education should be taught in schools, but debates abound over *what* kind is the right kind. There is no doubt that the third wave has a stake in such debates.

Generally speaking, there are three approaches to sex education in schools. The abstinence-plus approach (also commonly referred to as the comprehensive approach) teaches abstinence from sexual intercourse before **marriage** as the preferred method of birth control, but it provides detailed information about all other methods of birth control as well as information about **abortion**. Abstinence-plus sex education communicates a full understanding of the risks of sexually transmitted diseases (STDs) and often includes topics such as **sexual harassment**, **rape**, and sexual abuse. Beyond the facts, this approach also encompasses young people's psychological and emotional preparedness about sex, pressures to have sex, and communication skills. There is another comprehensive sex-education curriculum that does not stress abstinence as the preferred choice, but teaches kids how to make responsible decisions about sex. Such an approach will include abstinence as one choice among many, and it will cover all of the rest of the topics as listed.

Since at least the early 1990s, the third approach, abstinence-only sex education, has been strongly supported by social conservatives in the United States and received substantial federal funding from Congress in 1996 as part of its welfare reform package. Abstinence-only sex education teaches that abstinence from sexual intercourse (and some say any kind of sexual activity; the definition of abstinence varies) is the only way to prevent STDs and pregnancy outside of marriage. This approach also teaches that a monogamous, married, heterosexual relationship is the only standard for sexual activity. Most proponents of abstinence-only sex education assume that any education about contraception might encourage sexual activity. When birth control is mentioned at all, it is usually talked about in terms of its failures. Abortion is not discussed, and adoption is promoted for pregnant teens. The curriculum often warns of the dangers of alcohol and drug abuse, and it teaches teens how to reject sexual advances. Abstinence-only educators will use scare tactics such as tragic stories about unwanted pregnancies, faulty birth control, and STDs to strike fear into teenagers. More recently, oral sex has been added to many abstinence-only curricula, so that kids will realize that it, too, carries great risks. As of 2004, about one-third of public secondary schools teach abstinence-only sex education. The privileging of abstinence-only sex education over the last several years, and perhaps even more prominently in the current presidential administration, has led to heated debates about sex, gender, the **body**, **religion**, **media**, and education in contemporary American culture.

Third-wave feminists unanimously agree with many others, including the Office of the Surgeon General and the Centers for Disease Control, that the abstinence-only curriculum may be both ineffective and unrealistic in its approach to sex education. They strongly disagree that more knowledge about birth control will lead to increased sexual activity, and they believe that abstinence-only methods mislead kids into believing that birth control is completely ineffective in the prevention of STDs and teen pregnancy, thereby equipping teens with nothing in the face of sexual activity. Other than abstinence, controversial topics within sex education include access to contraception without parental knowledge or consent, oral sex, and homosexuality (many Americans who believe it is okay to teach kids about homosexuality, for example, only believe that kids should be informed in a "neutral" way, without being told whether it is acceptable or not).

There are several defining characteristics and guiding principles of third-wave feminism that would factor into any third-wave approach to sex education:

1. Committed to *choice* in the deepest way, the third wave is open to various genders, sexualities, and sexual practices, and third-wave feminists communicate to young women and girls that it is cool to be anything— abstinent or sexually active, bisexual, gay, or straight.

2. The third wave also thinks the only way to be cool about sex is to be smart about sex. Younger generations of feminists believe that the only effective approach to educating girls and young women about safe sex is not to shield them from all the facts, but to provide them with as much *information* as possible about the very real risks involved with being sexually active; about the pressures associated with sex; about STDs and unplanned pregnancy; and about sexual harassment, sexual abuse, and rape. For the third wave, knowledge is power, so access to information about sex—in schools and elsewhere—is vital for young women, especially in a society that packages and sells sex all around them. They believe in talking about sex in everyday language and in the frankest, "realest" way possible. Young women, especially, need a sex education that is based on their everyday lives, that sidesteps lofty ideals and weighty moral platforms, and that gives them a space to work through the confusing and mixed messages about **sexuality** that confront them daily from pop culture, **family**, and sexual partners. Third-wave feminists also believe in linking personal sex education and sexual health—the kind that kids get in schools and the tips that so many young women read in **magazines**—to politics. For example, sex education needs to acknowledge the link between the increase in STDs among young women and the fact that men are not regularly screened for STDs as women are. Young people need to be informed about the politics of gender and health care that do not reimburse ob-gyn services as much as they reimburse health care for men.

3. Beyond information, third-wave feminism stresses the importance of *communication* to safe, smart sex and sexual health. A truly comprehensive sex education encompasses far more than just the facts to include

communication skills so that kids are able to talk openly and freely with friends, family, and, most importantly, sexual partners. One of the major goals of the third wave is to break long-held patterns and codes of silence and shame that have circulated around sex, birth control, STDs, pregnancy, and sexual orientation, so that girls and women realize they are not alone. With books, conventions, workshops, and Internet sites, younger generations of feminists have helped young women voice their questions and concerns about sex within supportive and open-minded communities.

4. If new generations of feminists have provided places for girls and women to voice their concerns about sex, they have also shaped spaces in which young women can voice their curiosities and **desires**. Third-wave feminists passionately believe in sexual freedom as strongly as they believe in reproductive freedom. They also think that acknowledging the pleasures of sex should be part of a comprehensive sex education—alongside the risks and complications that sexual activity entails. Just as they have a fundamental right to know and control their own bodies (second-wave feminists did a great job of making women's own bodies less mysterious to themselves with the publication of the Boston Women's Collective's *Our Bodies, Ourselves* in 1973; the 8th edition of *Our Bodies, Ourselves* was published in 2005), girls and women also have a right to *desire* as active agents in the world, not vulnerable creatures who need to be protected from others' sexual desires. Perhaps one of the biggest problems with abstinence-only sex education approaches, and even with many current comprehensive models of sex education, is that they always assume girls to be in the position of having to resist their partners' sexual advances. Such approaches teach girls how to say no and when it is okay to say yes, but they do not acknowledge that girls, too, can actively desire and enjoy sexual activity. New generations of feminists believe that girls need an alternative and safe space to explore their own bodies and acknowledge their own pleasures. They believe that sexual expression and pleasure need to be liberated not only from the language of fear and violence but also from ideals of marriage and procreation. While they deeply respect girls' and women's choice to be abstinent and include that choice as part of a comprehensive curriculum, they embrace sex as something positive and pleasurable for those who are ready to take that important step, and many critique the concept of "losing of virginity" because it implies something negative.

5. For the third wave, the overall sexual health of girls and young women is so important that one might imagine sex education to be one crucial component of an overall sexual health curriculum. For younger feminists, to be sexually healthy is to be free to make one's own choices, to be fully equipped with all kinds of knowledge, to be part of a strong and supportive community of friends and mentors, and to be able to express one's feelings and desires about even the most sensitive sex-related issues. Sex

education for sexual health extends beyond the classroom to other spheres of young women's everyday lives: to the Internet, which has served as an important resource for information and a basis for community; to books, zines, and magazines; to **music**; and to workshops, clubs, and organizations. Furthermore, sex education for sexual health does not discuss sex and sexuality in a vacuum. The most effective books and Web sites connect sex education in very concrete ways to other things such as overall health, **sports, art**, music, school, family life, and popular culture.

6. Third-wave feminists see boys and men as part of the fight and part of the solution. When it comes to sex education, they also think that information and communication are absolutely essential for boys. Moreover, they believe that dominant norms of masculinity prevent boys from gaining the full knowledge they need and communicating about sex in healthy ways. Younger feminists demand *gender equity* in heterosexual relationships; they assume that men should always take an active role in thinking about birth control and general sexual health. Basically, they think it is essential that men take as much responsibility as women in such relationships and that they are held accountable for taking the necessary steps for safe sex, from birth control to sexual health. Third-wave feminists do not believe that women should have to do all of this important work in an equal relationship. Furthermore, gender equity applies not just in sexual relationships, but in *all* relationships in the social world. A comprehensive sex education, therefore, requires feminist education for both sexes that extends beyond the bedroom, so to speak, to all spheres of social life.

See also Reproductive Technologies; Virginity Movement

Further Reading: Baumgardner, Jennifer, and Amy Richards, *Manifesta: Young Women, Feminism, and the Future*, New York: Farrar, Straus and Giroux, 2000; The Boston Women's Health Book Collective, *Our Bodies, Ourselves for the New Century: A Book by and for Women*, 8th ed., New York: Touchstone, 2005, http://www.feminist.com/resources/ourbodies/index.html; Columbia University's Health Education Program, *The "Go Ask Alice" Book of Answers: A Guide to Good Physical, Sexual and Emotional Health*, New York: Henry Holt, 1998, http://www.goaskalice.columbia.edu; Drill, Esther, Heather McDonald, and Rebecca Odes, *Deal With It: A Whole New Approach to Your Body, Brain and Life as a Gurl*, New York: Pocket Books, 1999, http://www.gurl.com; Fine, Michelle, "Sexuality, Schooling and Adolescent Females: The Missing Discourse of Desire," *Harvard Educational Review* 58(1) (1988): 29–53; Gray, Heather M., and Samantha Phillips, *Real Girl Real World: Tools for Finding Your True Self*, Seattle, WA: Seal Press, 1998; National Public Radio, the Kaiser Family Foundation, and Harvard University's Kennedy School Poll: Sex Education in America, http://www.kff.org/kaiserpolls/pomr012904oth.cfm; Planned Parenthood's Web site for teenagers: http://www.teenwire.com; Scarleteen: Sex Education for the Real World, http://www.scarleteen.com; Walker, Rebecca, "Lusting for Freedom," in *Listen Up: Voices from the Next Feminist Generation*, ed. Barbara Findlen, Seattle, WA: Seal Press, 1995, 95–101.

JESSICA BLAUSTEIN

SEX SHOPS, FEMINIST. Inspired by second-wave **consciousness-raising** groups, woman-owned sex shops have come to embody the sex-positive attitudes and politicized consumptive practices prevalent in third-wave **feminism**.

In 1974, Dell Williams opened the first mail-order catalog and store offering sex toys and **sex education** products specifically for women. The store, located in New York City, was called Eve's Garden and was inspired by Betty Dodson, who had recently self-published *Liberating Masturbation* and was holding masturbation workshops. In 1977, Joani Blanks, a sex therapist, educator, and founder of Down There Press, opened Good Vibrations in San Francisco. Since that time, the number of woman-owned sex shops has grown and now includes Toys in Babeland, A Woman's Touch, and Come As You Are. The advent of the Internet further expanded the market and proved an ideal way for many people to access sex shops from the privacy of their own homes. Most of the shops now have online ordering and several stores have opened that operate solely through the Internet, including Libida and Extra Curious.

These stores strive to create clean, safe, and sex-positive environments in which women can feel comfortable and even empowered in their shopping experience. The products are displayed openly and the customers are able to ask questions about the merchandise. The new group of consumers created by woman-owned sex shops and the sex-positive ideals of the third wave has also spurred a demand for better and more diverse toys. New, innovative specialty products, such as Vixen dildos and harnesses, have been developed and greatly expanded the variety of sex aides now available for women and their partners.

The mission of most woman-owned sex shops is not only to sell products but also to provide sex education and a sex-positive culture for their customers. Staff are trained to be sex educators who can give customers informed, accurate information. Good Vibrations even has a staff sexologist, Carol Queen. Some stores hold seminars and presentations, organize outreach programs for schools and other organizations, and a number of shops offer extensive education and information through their Web sites. For example, Toys in Babeland's site includes an advice column, how-to's, sex tips, a glossary, and an advocacy section called Sex Act that alerts readers to pertinent political issues. Libida includes an advice column that was at one time written by sex-positive activist **Susie Bright**. Making purchases from these stores is considered by many third-wave feminists to be a way of investing in the feminist community, politicizing the act of consumption itself. In return the shops are thought to sell both empowering products and philosophies.

Some critique these shops for promoting sexual **empowerment** through **consumerism**. Although many do see woman-owned sex shops as spaces of liberation and sites of feminist activism, some question whether sexual liberation can be bought and what the political implications are of Western women empowering themselves through products made by underpaid workers in Third World countries. The consumer **empowerment** issues raised by woman-owned sex shops are central to third-wave feminism itself.

See also Pro-Sex Feminism

Further Reading: Eve's Garden Web site, http://www.evesgarden.com; Good Vibrations Web site, http://www.goodvibes.com; Jackson, Karen, "Grandma's Secret: The History of the Vibrator," Sex For Women Web site, http://www.sexforwomen.net/vibrators.htm; Semans, Anne, and Cathy Winks, *The Good Vibrations Guide to Sex: The Most Complete Sex Manual Ever Written*, San Francisco: Cleis Press, 2002; Toys in Babeland Web site, http://www.babeland.com.

HELENA KVARNSTROM

SEX TOURISM/SEX WORK. Sex tourism is the practice in which tourists are encouraged to engage in sexual relations with people of the destination country or region. This is promoted by developing and expanding already existing sex work industries originally intended for local residents. Third-wave **feminism** recognizes that legal statutes as well as strict migration laws are keeping many of the workers in a state of dependence, yet to participate in sex tourism/sex work is a choice with many complexities, requiring respect for all the workers. Not restricted to any country or city, though it may be more visible or prevalent in some regions where it has been constructed to be so, sex tourism accounts for a large portion of all tourism.

The type of clientele changes from different destinations. **Queer**-positive sex tourism has begun to grow in certain areas. Pedophile clients, with the use of the Internet, continue to grow in numbers. Female sex tourists are reputed to frequent certain Caribbean Islands more often than any other group, whereas the stereotype of the Western and Japanese man being the main client of the southeast Asian sex industries is somewhat false given that the bulk of clients are men from nearby countries. **AIDS** has not diminished the sex tourism industry; however, many studies reveal that clients are increasingly demanding younger workers as a precautionary measure.

The prevalent image of the middle-aged white man having sex with Third World or "foreign" sex workers has lead to fierce critiques of colonialism, cultural imperialism, and the commodification of **sexuality** by feminists worldwide. To develop an analysis of sex tourism, one must examine the structural inequalities of the economic phenomenon of "**globalization**." Global capitalism has prompted the considerable development of sex industries that specifically cater to certain groups, most often Western men. Some critics argue that sex tourism is a product of foreign-dominated economies relying on tourist currencies to repay debts to the International Monetary Fund and the World Bank. It is the popular **representation**s such as the Eastern European hairdresser/prostitute or the Asian masseuse/prostitute that sustain political mobilization against sex tourism internationally, but this mobilization is weighed down with second-wave advocacy language in that the **identity** of the sex worker is often seen as fixed: the dichotomy of rich Western male/poor Third World female, reinforcing the idea of a "powerful subject/disempowered Other."

Although it is important to recognize economic, political, and social bases of inequalities for sex workers, some of the critiques by Western feminists continue to convey the hegemonically constructed identities of "oppressor" and "victim" by presenting them as fixed identities and subject positions. Often they argue that the sex workers of certain ethnicities have been "eroticized" and forced to project submissiveness and sexual desirability for their clients. These critiques offer little room for the workers themselves to shape and negotiate **identity**. This tendency to view these sex workers primarily as victims needing guidance and help, while hypercritically often taking the stance that Western sex workers can and are able to choose sex work as their profession, is a continuation of colonialism and **racism**.

As a result, Western feminist activists who campaign against sex tourism sometimes align themselves against the actual workers. For example, in the 1980s a major campaign against the U.S. **military** "comfort women" in the Philippines was not supported by women in the sex industry, because the arguments of colonial domination did not resemble the specific ways these relations between the U.S. men and the sex-working women played out in daily life. The closure of the base in Olongapo City, Olongapo, resulted in the women being forced to return to rural areas and work lower-paying, more strenuous jobs.

When sex workers themselves discuss the subject, many view the situation as being a negotiated tension between their free will to enter prostitution and the constraints that make the sex industry an opportunity for them. Many see sex work as an alternative to lower-paying service and industry jobs. But for some of the workers, the negotiations are more confining, or nonexistent. With sex tourism it is often not only the clients who travel, but it is the workers themselves who travel for the job. Many are illegal immigrants with the threat of deportation, which often keeps them in oppressed relationships with traffickers and pimps. There is evidence that many young women are sold, often into debt bondage (where they must work off the debt incurred from travel and prices demanded by the traffickers, etc.) in exchange for money for their families. The list of people who profit from the sex industry (traffickers, recruiters, etc.) is long, whereas the sex workers must struggle against direct disadvantages undermining their ability to have control and continuing relationships of dependence. Clients are rarely stigmatized or prosecuted by society or the law, whereas the sex workers must deal with society's morality and social and legal pressures. The legal statutes dictating the sex industry, combined with strict migration laws, allow it to continue to grow underground and keep many of the workers in a state of dependence. And yet, one will often hear the argument that the supply of workers creates the demand, and not the other way around. When considering the issue of sex tourism, third-wave feminism is sensitive to and cognizant of both power imbalances and sex-worker agency.

Further Reading: Bauer, Thomas, and Bob McKercher, eds., *Sex and Tourism: Journeys of Romance, Love and Lust*, New York: Haworth Hospitality Press, 2003; Ehrenreich, Barbara, and Arlie Russell Hochschild, eds., *Global Woman: Nannies, Maids, and Sex*

Workers in the New Economy, New York: Metropolitan Books, 2003; Kempadoo, Kamala, and Jo Doezema, eds., *Global Sex Workers: Rights, Resistance and Redefinition*, New York: Routledge, 1998.

AMY MILLER

SEXUAL HARASSMENT. Sexual harassment is a legal term that encompasses all unwanted verbal and/or physical behavior of a sexual nature. Sexual harassment includes undesired physical contact, sexually explicit remarks, and other behaviors that contribute to an inappropriate workplace climate. Such remarks may range in scope from solicitations for sexual favors, comments that draw attention to someone's **body** or attire, to creating an inhospitable work environment by posting lewd or explicit photos in public spaces. Sexual harassment is officially defined by the Equal Employment Opportunity Commission (EEOC) and is described as a form of sex **discrimination** that violates Title VII of the 1964 Civil Rights Act. Under this act, unwelcome sexual advances in workplace and educational settings that hinder an individual's ability to fulfill his or her duties or that contribute to an intimidating, offensive, or hostile environment are identified by the law as illegal.

As is characteristic of third-wave feminist work, recent attention to sexual harassment critically and carefully attends to the ways in which social categories such as race, class, ability, and sexual orientation interplay with gender in sexual harassment cases. For instance, current scholarship is aware and attentive to the ways in which **racism** and classism infuse sexual harassment cases. The "believability" of a sexual harassment victim is seldom a matter of gender alone, and the victim's economic status, ethnic or "racial" identity, and **sexuality** will often play into the analysis and **media** exposure granted to the case, as will similar categories of the perpetrator's identity. Bringing to the forefront of sexual harassment discussions an examination of persistent racist, classist, and other stereotypes about promiscuity enable a more complicated reading of the issues involved in sexual harassment. Such readings employ an "intersectional" approach. Additionally, the link between culturally feminized jobs, such as in-home child care and domestic work, and the economic devaluation of such jobs, raise significant moral and policy-level concerns regarding the enforcement of sexual harassment laws in households.

There are five basic dimensions encompassed by sexual harassment laws, and the legal perimeters established by sexual harassment laws are significant in the securing of women's rights and the advancement of feminist aims because they identify a policy-level commitment to certain minimal standards of conduct in employment, educational, and professional settings. First, the law recognizes that sexual harassment is not limited by the gender of the victim, who may be male or female. Second, the harasser need not be in a position of direct or indirect power over the victim. For example, the harasser could be (but need not necessarily be) the victim's supervisor, colleague, client, or non-employee in the workplace (such as a contract worker). Third, it follows that as the harasser is not necessarily the victim's supervisor; the victim's economic well-being or employment status need not be in jeopardy because of the sexual harassment. Fourth, anyone affected by the inhospitable environment created by the harassment may make a claim against the conduct. Even if someone is not the direct "victim" of the harassment, but s/he is witness to it or is otherwise affected by the climate of harassment, s/he is entitled to pursue a lawsuit. Fifth, those subjected to any unwelcome sexual attention or advances, and all the employees exposed to the environment created by the unwanted attention, are entitled to protection under the law. Although the five overarching protections are included in federal sexual harassment law, each state may have slightly different features of protection.

To elaborate, additionally two specific levels of sexual harassment are legally recognized. These more or less break down to include both the victim and the indirectly affected employees. Quid pro quo and hostile environment sexual harassment are the two types. Quid pro quo sexual harassment involves an economic threat; "hostile environment" conditions do not.

In a quid pro quo case, one may be promoted, demoted, or fired as a result of responses to sexual advances or remarks, and this type of sexual harassment may represent a single event or an ongoing situation. Courts have consistently held employers strictly liable for quid pro quo sexual harassment, upholding victims' rights even in cases where s/he originally consented and then changed his/her mind about the sexual conduct.

Hostile environment sexual harassment includes a range of other legal requirements regarding the nature of a professional setting, and a person's employment or economic status need not be in danger in these cases. Primarily, a hostile environment includes conduct that contributes to an inappropriately sexualized atmosphere: the display of sexually explicit photos or calendars, the exchange of sexually explicit "jokes," comments, or invasive, personal questions are examples of behaviors that contribute to an inhospitable, intimidating, or substantially uncomfortable atmosphere. In a general social climate that tolerates the extensive sexualization and degradation of women (or men) outside of the workplace, hostile environment sexual harassment raises interesting questions regarding harassment that occurs in public (rather than private, employment-related) situations.

Three international associations have addressed sexual harassment: the United Nations, the European Communities, and the International Labor Organization. The actions taken by these groups include research and reports on sexual harassment, the issuance of gender-equality mandates, and adoption of resolutions against sexual harassment. The impact of feminized poverty and the exploitation of "Third World" labor by "First World" consumption raises serious and numerous problems requiring improved labor standards that protect workers' rights and access to protection from sexual harassment. Strategies to engender a more organized labor force, internationally, would involve a substantial overhaul of existing employment practices. Third-wave **feminism**'s contribution to work on the issue has largely been in terms of its attention to factors in addition to gender (such as race, positionality, and class) that inform and complicate the problem.

See also Rape

Further Reading: Dell, Heather S., "Making 'Racialized Misogyny' Visible: Internalizing Women and Violence," in *Encompassing Gender: Integrating International Studies and Women's Studies*, eds. Mary M. Lay, et al., New York: Feminist Press, 2002, 272–286; Ehrenreich, Barbara, and Arlie Russell Hochschild, eds., *Global Woman: Nannies, Maids, and Sex Workers in the New Economy*, New York: Henry Holt, 2002; http://www.de.psu.edu/harassment; http://www.eeoc.gov/facts/fs-sex.html; http://www.feminist.org/911/harass.html; Morrison, Toni, ed., *Race-ing Justice, Engendering Power: Essays on Anita Hill, Clarence Thomas, and the Construction of Social Reality*, New York: Pantheon, 1992; Razack, Sherene H., *Looking White People in the Eye: Gender, Race, and Culture in Courtrooms and Classrooms*, Toronto: University of Toronto Press, 1998, 56–87 and 130–156; Webb, Susan, *Shockwaves: The Global Impact of Sexual Harassment*, New York: Master Media, 1994.

Erika Feigenbaum

SEXUALITY. Sexuality has been a centerpiece in all three major "waves" of feminist history, from the fight for birth control in the 1920s, to the fight for **abortion** rights and **rape** laws in the 1970s, to current debates over **sex education**, date rape, and the politics of the baby tee. Feminist authors Nan Bauer Maglin and Donna Perry identify sexuality as the "lightning rod for this generation's hopes and discontents (and democratic visions) in the same way that civil rights and Vietnam galvanized [their] generation in the 1960s." Indeed, third-wave feminists have seized upon the legacies of Kate Millet's "sexual politics," Erica Jong's "zipless fuck," and Adrienne Rich's "**compulsory heterosexuality**," pushing for an adequate theory of sexuality that takes into account second-wave feminist critiques of intimacy and institutionalized sexuality while simultaneously forging an individualist **feminism** that embraces disruptive sexualities and advocates an entitlement to pleasure and erotic knowledge.

The term "sexuality" is sometimes used as shorthand for sexual orientation—homosexual, heterosexual, bisexual, or transsexual—constituting an axis of **identity** comparable to race, gender, and social class that positions the individual in a web of social relations and power differentials. Despite the potential usefulness of acknowledging sexual orientation as a site of self-naming, group allegiance, and **discrimination** or privilege, it is fairly common to encounter resistance to these categories, especially among third-wave feminists. In an era shaped by pop singer Madonna's postmodern sexual posturing, actress Anne Heche and the phenomenon of the "hasbien" (a woman who experiments with lesbianism and returns to heterosexuality), and the widespread trend of bisexual chic, boundary-crossing is more norm than exception. Actress Sandra Bernhardt's appearance on the sitcom *Roseanne* might serve as a touchstone for this turn away from rigid sexualities: as a married woman who leaves her husband to date a woman, and then breaks up with the woman to date her former husband, she is asked pointblank by Roseanne to identify herself as straight, gay, or bisexual. Her response—"Don't box me in!"—is a rallying cry that resonates in a culture that has accommodated theories of gender as **performativity** (something one does, not something one is). Gay historian Jonathan Katz has demonstrated that sexual behavior only came to signify sexual identity less than a hundred years ago. Recent years have seen a return to pre-modern discourses of sexuality, separating sex acts from stable identity categories and making coalition possible between straight and gay interests under the elastic label of "**queer**."

Straight with a Twist. In addition to fluid boundaries between sexual orientations, **feminist theory** has moved in the direction of examining fluid boundaries *within* sexual orientations, exploring the possibility of "many heterosexualities" or "alternative heterosexualities," for instance. Heterosexuality, commonly depicted in feminist writing as compulsory and conflated with sexism and **heterosexism**, is being split into less monolithic categories: hegemonic heterosexuality versus feminist heterosexuality (Carol Smart), queer heterosexuality (Lynne Segal, Calvin Thomas), or noncomplicitous heterosexuality (Carol Siegel). Within an alternative heterosexuality, male and female partners forge roles for themselves apart from gender traditional gender roles and power imbalances. Beyond simple inversions—stay-at-home dads and working mothers—one finds rich reworkings of gender difference outside frameworks of polar opposition. As straight couples take their cue from gay culture, sexuality is separated from the reproductive imperative and from state-sanctioned forms of heterosexuality (**marriage**, monogamy, and the nuclear **family**). Whereas certain (anti-sex or separatist) feminists accuse women who choose to be in heterosexual relationships and claim to enjoy heterosexual intercourse of having a "male-identified" sexuality, others assert women's right to indulge in sexual freedoms and pleasures historically accorded only to men. The prefix "hetero" thus comes to stand for differences within and between gender roles, not the eroticization of power struggles or patriarchal hierarchy.

"Slut" Bashing. The virgin/whore dichotomy continues to organize female sexuality, and not just in locker rooms. Sexuality is often the grounds on which separatist feminists condemn third-wave feminists. Just as Madonna's **music** videos prompted political debate in the 1980s, grunge rocker **Courtney Love**'s hypersexuality is derided as "ostentatious sluttishness" by Germaine Greer, a second-wave feminist who groups Riot Grrrls and the Spice Girls together under the appellation of "bimbo feminism" and dismisses interpretations that applaud Love's persona as a cutting parody of patriarchal sexuality. As today's young women style themselves after Britney Spears (with bare midriffs and navel piercings), some feminists wonder whether the women's movement has failed entirely, but the line between liberated and oppressive sexuality remains unclear. The most astute feminist work on sexuality, therefore,

acknowledges the force of **patriarchy**'s discourses on women's bodies as well as the agency and creative resistance with which women, including teenagers, respond. Leora Tanenbaum achieves this balance in *Slut!: Growing Up Female with a Bad Reputation* (1999), an ethnography of female outsiders in high school. Through a combination of interview transcripts and analysis, Tanenbaum creates a portrait of young women being policed by the slut stigma: "Because 'good' girls can become 'bad' girls in an instant, slut-bashing controls all girls." Yet those who endure this label sometimes find themselves freed of its conformist pressures, able to see through the mechanism as injustice or farce.

Lynn Phillips provides an equally illuminating study of college-age women in *Flirting with Danger: Young Women's Reflections on Sexuality and Domination* (2000). Exploring "what is *not so clear* in women's experiences of their relationships and sexualities" (x), Phillips outlines a series of conflicting cultural discourses that young women use to explain complex heterosexual encounters. For example, the discourse of good womanhood splits into two types: the "pleasing woman" and the "together woman." The "pleasing woman" discourse "stresses morality, sexual 'purity,' and service to men and children" (39). In contrast, the "together woman" discourse promotes a "free, sexually sophisticated" woman who feels entitled to "full equality and satisfaction in her sexual encounters and romantic relationships" (47). Ironically, the qualities of the together woman are often presented in women's **magazines** "as an effective new way of *attracting men*," undermining its actual potential as a liberating discourse and making it a close cousin to the pleasing woman. Neither path permits autonomous sexuality (much less lesbian sexuality).

Another example of these contradictory discourses arises from the question of what constitutes "normal" male heterosexuality. The "normal/danger dichotomy" discourse tells women that "healthy and abusive relationships are mutually exclusive" (52), or, in other words, that "there are 'good guys' and 'bad guys'" and perceptive women ought to be able to tell the difference. This discourse elides the pervasive facts of **domestic violence** and date rape, in which the good guy (father, boyfriend) can turn into the bad guy (abuser, rapist) within the course of a single evening. Alongside these false categories sits the "male sexual drive" discourse, an idea of male heterosexuality as naturally aggressive and hard to control: "By warning young women, 'Don't start what you're not willing to finish,' the male sexual drive discourse serves to remind them of their vulnerability and subordinate status relative to men" (58). Within this landscape of contradictory discourses, young women cobble together explanations of their experiences that consistently excuse individual men and patriarchal culture while taking responsibility on themselves "when things go badly."

Despite this bleak picture of pressure and ambivalence, many problems of sexuality are inflated. Girls are not for the most part giving blowjobs in the back of the school bus; children are not having intercourse in middle school in epidemic numbers. The narrative of moral decline more often serves conservative ends (abstinence-only education, chastity pledges) than the feminist goals of sexual and economic autonomy. The use of sexuality to control or condemn young women—whether by the patriarchy or by feminists—counts as slut-bashing, a form of violence against which the authors of *Manifesta: Young Women, Feminism, and the Future* (2000) urge third-wave feminists to protest.

Outercourse. Sexuality has historically been harnessed in the United States to capitalist consumer culture: Americans sublimate erotic energy into hard work and hedonistic consumption. An economy of scarcity in which women's resources of chastity and pleasure must be rationed out, and in which the idiom of respectability invests this scarcity with a social class dimension and moral component, drives mainstream discussions of sexuality. It is something women must "save" for their husbands. In place of this anxiety-producing business model of sexuality, queer theorists and artists advocate an economy of plenty, or of excess. There is more than enough sexual energy to go around, without holding back or directing one's eroticism into "productive" fields such as work, marriage, or reproduction. The *un*domestication of **desire** leads to a freer exchange of erotic energy, both in culture, as positive feelings and enjoyment are directed at each other and the world around us rather than the abstract accumulation of wealth, and in personal practices, as couples explore the overflowing pleasures of outercourse (nonpenetrative sex) and women seek out "the clitoral truth" with a burgeoning arsenal of pocket rockets and anatomical knowledge.

Alternative visions of sexuality are not highly visible in the current moment, but they are available if one knows where to look. Greenery Press in San Francisco is devoted to expanding the range of available sexualities. *The Ethical Slut: A Guide to Infinite Sexual Possibilities* (1997), known in certain circles as the bible of polyamory, redefines slut as a positive term denoting openmindedness and courage rather than stigma. After offering a reexamination of sexual ethics from a perspective of nonpossessiveness, nonjealousy, and mutual respect that applies equally well to monogamous relationships as to nonmonogamy, authors Dossie Easton and Catherine Liszt imagine a "slut utopia" premised on pluralism, the belief that "there can be as many ways to be sexual as there are to be human, and all of them valid." Rather than being (merely) about hedonistic abandon or having sex with anything that moves, as bisexual and polyamorous people are often cast, ethical sluthood is a challenge to "get bigger than our programmed judgments."

For young women, the Internet is an incomparable resource on sexuality and an important site through which to access wider visions of erotic bodies, identities, and behaviors. For this reason, Judith Levine has protested the filtering of the Internet in *Harmful to Minors: The Perils of Protecting Minors from Sex* (2002), arguing that such censorship does not protect women and children; it helps keep them ignorant. Levine lists several Web sites of interest to girls seeking information about sexuality, including Go Ask Alice! (http://www.

goaskalice.columbia.edu) and http://www.gURL.com. For the twenty-something and thirty-something generation, Krista Jacobs produces the Web journal, *Sexing the Political,* where third-wave feminists are publishing the sexual polemics of a new academic generation.

See also Desire, Feminist; *Volume 2, Primary Documents 42 and 52*

Further Reading: Chalker, Rebecca, *The Clitoral Truth: The Secret World at Your Fingertips,* New York: Seven Stories, 2000; Damsky, Lee, ed., *Sex and Single Girls: Straight and Queer Women on Sexuality,* Seattle: Seal Press, 2000; Easton, Dossie, and Catherine Liszt, *The Ethical Slut: A Guide to Infinite Sexual Possibilities,* San Francisco: Greenery, 1997; *Go Ask Alice!* Columbia University's Health Q&A Services, http://www.goaskalice. columbia.edu/; Jacobs, Krista, ed., *Sexing the Political: A Journal of Third Wave Feminists on Sexuality,* http://www.sexingthepolitical.com/; Kamen, Paula, *Her Way: Young Women Remake the Sexual Revolution,* New York: Broadway Books, 2002; Maglin, Nan Bauer, and Donna Perry, eds., *"Bad Girls"/"Good Girls": Women, Sex, and Power in the Nineties,* New Brunswick, NJ: Rutgers University Press, 1996; Phillips, Lynn M., *Flirting with Danger: Young Women's Reflections on Sexuality and Domination,* New York: New York University Press, 2000; Scarlet Teen: Sex Education for the Real World, http://www. scarletletters.com/; Segal, Lynne, *Straight Sex: Rethinking the Politics of Pleasure,* Berkeley: University of California Press, 1994; Sex, etc.: A Web site by Teens for Teens, http:// www.sxetc.org/; Siegel, Carol, *New Millennial Sexstyles,* Bloomington: Indiana University Press, 2000; Tanenbaum, Leora, *Slut!: Growing Up Female with a Bad Reputation,* New York: Seven Stories, 1999.

MERRI LISA JOHNSON

SINGLE-SEX EDUCATION. Single-sex **education** seeks to foster learning by teaching individuals in same-sex environments rather than standard coeducational settings. Single-sex education is particularly crucial for women, as many argue the positive educational benefits of such classrooms are essential in a patriarchal society, claiming that coeducational environments are often biased, and single-sex education attempts to balance such inequities. Single-sex educational programs act as vehicles to enhance academic achievement among girls and attempt to provide more empowering and effective settings than co-educational classrooms by providing equitable education. The third wave is often ambivalent about this latest move, which can be seen as fostering assumptions of essential differences between genders, which the third wave does not believe. However, single-sex education may be seen as a form of strategic **essentialism**, an endorsement of gender difference for a larger purpose (i.e., the educational success of women and girls), and viewed in this way, third-wave **feminism** would be more supportive.

The bases for single-sex classes vary, but advocates of single-sex education believe that single-sex settings improve girls' academic performance and attitude toward multiple subjects, encourage girls to pursue jobs in male-dominated fields, promote autonomy, and minimize gender bias cultivated in coeducational settings. Advocates of single-sex education argue that girls thrive when educated apart from boys, claiming that girls in coeducational classrooms are called on less frequently and receive significantly less teacher attention than boys. Advocates also argue that despite the progress of feminism, women and girls are still relegated to their gendered roles in coeducational settings, asserting that students demonstrate a stronger commitment to academics when removed from the biases inherent to mixed-sex environments.

Many feminists—including much of the third wave—oppose single-sex education, resistant to claims that boys and girls are innately or essentially different. Opponents of single-sex education argue that coeducational settings better prepare girls and boys to function in a coeducational world, and that isolating them from one another stunts their ability to form and maintain mixed-sex relationships. Other arguments against coeducation include a rejection of claims that boys and girls have inherently different learning styles and interests, challenging studies that seek to prove that single-sex settings improve academic performance and claims that mixed-sex schools perform just as well as single-sex schools when given the same advantages (smaller class sizes, larger budgets, and motivated, high-performing students with involved parents). Since its passage in 1972, opponents claim that single-sex education is a violation of Title IX of the Educational Amendments, which states that "No person in the United States shall, on the basis of sex, be excluded from participation in, be denied the benefits of, or be subject to **discrimination** under any educational programs or activity receiving federal financial assistance," and aims to prevent sex discrimination in education, complicating single-sex programs when admission criteria challenges equal access. Though Title IX does not specifically disallow single-sex schools, it does require that districts provide comparable facilities, courses, and services to boys and girls, preventing public programs directed toward women and girls only. For this reason, most single-sex programs are private and do not receive federal funding. With the passage of the No Child Left Behind Act in 2002, however, Congress defined single-sex schools as acceptable "innovative educational programs" that were permitted to use public funds, reviving single-sex education, particularly in public institutions.

Many feminists, including those in the third wave, view the No Child Left Behind provision as a step backward for women and girls, as it does not require that educational institutions receiving public funding provide equal resources and opportunities for girls and protect against sexual discrimination. As legislation changes, so does the status of single-sex education; however, despite legislation, feminists attempt to balance inequities in all educational programs. *See also* Women's Colleges

Further Reading: National Organization for Single-Sex Public Education, http://www. singlesexschools.org/evidence.html; Salomone, Rosemary, *Same, Different, Equal: Rethinking Single-Sex Schooling*, New Haven, CT: Yale University Press, 2003; Streitmatter, Janice L., *For Girls Only: Making a Case for Single-Sex Schooling*, New York: SUNY Press, 1999.

LEANDRA PRESTON

SOAPBOX, INC. A progressive third-wave feminist speaker's bureau promoting cultural and political experts, Soapbox, Inc. is the brainchild of **Jennifer Baumgardner and Amy Richards**. They decided, after their book tour for *Manifesta: Young Women, Feminism, and the Future* (2000), which they cowrote, and listening to the many women and men at colleges and universities, organizations, bookstores, and other speaking venues around the United States, that there was a need for a speaker's bureau for a new generation of activists.

Baumgardner and Richards brought all of their resources together and opened their doors for business in 2002. Soapbox, Inc., under Baumgardner and Richard's direction, not only represents a new generation of cultural and political experts, but is an example of the diversity and complexity of third-wave leadership. Soapbox, Inc. is more than an agency that represents this generation's "it" leaders; it offers tools to assist with fundraising for and planning events, as well as promoting unknown authors and requesting reasonable speaker fees. Soapbox, Inc. is an example of third-wave **feminism** combining do-it-yourself (**DIY**) networking and collaboration (inherited from the second-wave movement) with **media** savvy and broadening the definition of feminism beyond a movement just for women, to a "few good men" as well. Currently, Soapbox, Inc. represents forty-two speakers.

Soon after Soapbox, Inc. started, Baumgardner and Richards were representing third-wave feminist leaders, such as **Ophira Edut**, **Rebecca Walker**, Paula Kamen, Debbie Stoller, Farai Chideya, **Irshad Manji**, Hanna Blank, Lisa Tiger, Lisa Jervis, Leora Tanenbaum, Inga Muscio, Daniel Sinker, and many other third-wave activists, writers, artists, and business leaders. Soapbox, Inc.'s speakers cover topics such as "Radical Domesticity: Why Martha Stewart Is Not the Anti-Christ," "Women Are as Good as Men and Women Are as Bad as Men: Morality and Accountability," "What a Feminist Looks Like: The True Diversity of Feminism," "Can Men Be Feminists?," "Why Are Feminists the Only Ones Who Aren't Allowed to Shop? How to Be a Feminist in a Capitalist Culture," "CR for the 21st Century: Pedicures, Book Clubs, Listservs, and Other Spaces Where Women Raise Consciousness," "Is the Women's Movement Racist?" "Who's the Next Gloria? Feminist Leadership Today," and "Practical Solutions to Probable Questions: Or How to Get a Job, Use Your Degree, Start a Foundation, and More." Other topics range from sexual orientation, transgender/transsexual issues, **sexuality**, relationships, **racism**, being biracial, money, **religion**, to **media**, and more.

Baumgardner and Richards integrated their intergenerational work, discussions and events with second- and third-wave feminists addressing current events. Richards and Baumgardner started organizing intergenerational events while Richards was Gloria Steinem's personal assistant and cofounded and organized events for the **Third Wave Foundation** and Baumgardner worked for Ms. magazine. Richards and Baumgardner added Gloria Steinem, Andrea Dworkin, Marcia Gillespie, and other well-known second-wave feminists to their roster of speakers.

See also Cultural Activism; *Volume 2, Primary Document 41*

Further Reading: Baumgardner, Jennifer, and Amy Richards, *Manifesta: Young Women, Feminism, and the Future*, New York: Farrar, Straus and Giroux, 2000; http://www.manifesta.com; http://www.ophira.com; http://www.rebeccawalker.com; http://www.soapboxinc.com.

HEATHER CASSELL

SPORTS. Of great interest to third-wave feminists as an activist strategy or site of engagement, modern sports emerged in the mid-1800s with the advent of industrialization. As work and **family** life transitioned to adapt to the changes wrought by industrialization, gender roles entered a state of flux. Sports became an arena in which the meanings of gender and gender **identity** could be publicly debated. In the early days of modern sports, women's bodies were viewed as fragile, delicate, and unsuitable for a host of endeavors. Ironically, though working-class women and women of color often participated in grueling physical labor, idealized women's bodies were viewed as unsuitable for any type of physical exertion. Such ideologies were used to limit women's participation in public life and de-feminize "othered" women (i.e., women who were not white, straight, and middle or upper class). Sports became an arena in which such ideologies could be reinforced but also challenged. The differences in sporting experiences for women from a range of class backgrounds, racial identities, and/or sexual orientations reflected struggles, conflicts, and contradictions in the culture at large. In the post–World War I era, middle- and upper-class women saw an expansion of amateur opportunities and a shift in iconography to the "athletic girl." Sports also provided working class women and women of color opportunities for social mobility and a means to challenge raced and classed ideologies of **femininity**. At the same time, middle-class women found strenuous **competition** discouraged, and working class and women of color found sexual exploitation and the stigma of mannishness foisted on athletes problematic. These trends continued through the 1970s. With the advent of the women's movement, creating opportunities for women in all facets of public life, including sports, became an important goal. Since then, opportunities for women have expanded significantly in terms of both opportunities and the range of organized sports to which women have access. Moreover, women athletes saw an increase in **media** attention, sponsorship dollars, and institutional opportunities. The marketing of current athletic icons reveals the complex interplay of the simultaneous reification of and challenge to traditional ideologies, economic forces, and a changing cultural climate.

Since the inception of modern sport, two key issues have been central to feminist debates: access to opportunities and the nature of women's sports. In the first case, creating opportunities for girls and women has been and remains essential. The tremendous success since the early 1980s in expanding opportunities for women is evident in the closing of the gap in the proportions of boys and girls playing high school sports, Title IX, and the expansion of women's amateur and professional opportunities. Debates, however, center on what these opportunities should look like. Some laud the expansion of women's sports institutions that are the corollaries of their male counter parts, but others lament that the worst of men's sports is infiltrating women's sports. Proponents of this view contend that women-centered sports should have a markedly different ethos from men's, avoiding the detrimental effects of professional competition, such as performance-enhancing substances, injury, and unethical business practices. A key area of contention is the marketing of female icons as sex symbols. Some laud the display of sexy athletes, arguing new images dispel historical conflations of athletic and male, remove the stigma of "manishness" and/or lesbianism, draw more spectators to women's sports, and allow female athletes a measure of financial success. Others contend that the sexual objectification of female athletes reinvigorates ideologies that are detrimental to women. Third-wave theorizing allows one to understand these issues as interrelated and not mutually exclusive positions.

Third-wave feminists build upon the success of the second wave's struggles for access, acceptance, and support. But with this access has come a more complicated set of issues and problems that have engendered a host of new theoretical insights, debates, and issues. Key to current third-wave theorizing in sports is understanding the complexity of social location/experience and contradictions engendered. In the first case, sport continues to provide an arena in which ideologies about raced, gendered, classed, and sexualized bodies are simultaneously problematized. Recognizing the vast array of experiences, **desires**, and interpretations of practices across groups reveals identity as a complex matrix. Moreover, as access increased, sports became a forum in which women with a range of issues related to sport and/or gender could meet, form coalitions, and gain a broader perspective on social issues. In the second case, third-wave sport theorizing acknowledges the complex and often contradictory array of social forces at work. A key example is the complicated relationship between women's sports and **sexuality**. Because sports were viewed initially as male appropriate, female athletes faced the stigma of "mannishness" and eventually lesbianism. Because women's sports carried this stigma, in many cases women's sports become a haven for "othered women," some of whom were/are gay/lesbian/bisexual/transsexual. While women's sports struggle to dispel the "myth" that there are lesbians in sports, it also has become a place in which women have been able to publically acknowledge non-heterosexual status. Professional and amateur sports often select "heterosexy" athletes for promotion, and endorsement dollars tend to follow the most conventionally attractive, but not necessarily most skilled, female athletes. For example, tennis player Ana Kournikova earned more than most of her rivals with her lucrative endorsement contracts, despite having never won a major tournament. Yet, there is increasing acceptance of lesbian athletes, and it is no longer impossible to obtain sponsorships once "out."

Finally, third-wave perspectives require a critical interrogation of assumptions about sport, athletes, and gender simultaneously. This critique, however, must extend to the blanket assumptions made by feminist sports scholars in the past, such as the condemnation of competition and professionalism. From a third-wave perspective, current struggles in sport must acknowledge the wide range of ways to participate in sports, from highly competitive to recreational forums.

See also Body; Hamm, Mia; National Girls and Women in Sports Day; Nike; Williams, Venus, and Williams, Serena; Women's Professional Sports Organizations; *Volume 2, Primary Documents 2 and 5*

Further Reading: Cahn, Susan, *Coming on Strong: Gender and Sexuality in Twentieth Century Women's Sports*, New York: The Free Press, 1994; Hall, M. Ann, *Feminism and Sporting Bodies*, Champaign, IL: Human Kinetics, 1996; Hargreaves, Jennifer, *Sporting Females: Critical Issues in the History and Sociology of Women's Sports*, New York: Routledge, 1994; Heywood, Leslie, and Shari L. Dworkin, *Built to Win: The Female Athlete as Cultural Icon*, Minneapolis: University of Minnesota Press, 2003; Sandoz, Joli, and Joby Winans, eds., *Whatever It Takes: Women on Women in Sports*, New York: Farrar, Straus and Giroux, 1999.

FAYE LINDA WACHS

T

TAKE YOUR DAUGHTER TO WORK DAY. Take Your Daughter to Work Day, created by the Ms. Foundation, took place on the fourth Thursday in April and ran for ten years, from 1993 to 2002. This event was geared to allow mothers and fathers to bring their daughters to work to create opportunities for girls to envision their future employment in all types of fields, besides those that were gender-specific. It hoped to provide attention to adolescent girls, nurture girls' leadership and **education**, increase self-esteem, and provide one-on-one time with their parent. It can be seen as one of the activist strategies that bridges second- and third-wave **feminism** and that opened intergenerational dialog.

In 2003, Take Your Daughter to Work Day was replaced by Take Our Daughters and Sons to Work Day by the Ms. Foundation to further evolve its original program and change its initial focus. This shows a particularly third-wave orientation, as third wave has argued from the beginning that men and boys need to be part of any activist or policy position regarding gender. The new program hopes to make work environments **family**-friendly and provides children, ages eight to twelve, with an opportunity to explore jobs for their future, teach them about the realities of the work world, and show them the daily lives of adults in that world. Its goal is to encourage daughters and sons to explore connections between education and their future workplace while also considering the difficulties and challenges that adults face when balancing family and work lives.

Further Reading: Ms. Foundation for Women: Changing the Way the World Works, http://www.ms.foundation.org; Take Our Daughters and Sons to Work: A New Generation at Work, http://www.daughtersandsonstowork.org.

LAURA MADELINE WISEMAN

TEA, MICHELLE. An award-winning third-wave lesbian feminist writer, poet, public speaker, and spoken word performance artist, Michelle Tea (1971–) is a cofounder of Sister Spit, the all-girl open mic **poetry** group that started in San Francisco and zigzagged across the United States as the Rambling Road Show between 1994 until 1997, when the group disbanded. Tea's works include a collection of **poetry**, *The Beautiful: Collected Poems* (2003); the highly acclaimed *Valencia* (2000), which explored the tumultuous and torrid love affairs of a San Francisco dyke; and *Chelsea Whistle* (2002), a semi-autobiographical novel about her childhood. Tea has also edited numerous anthologies, such as *Without a Net: Anthology of Writing by Working-Class Women* (2004), exploring the life histories of young women who are working class. Other anthologies Tea edited tackle subjects such as sex and punk rock. Tea writes for the *San Francisco Bay Guardian*, Nerve.com, *Girlfriends Magazine*, and other publications. Tea travels the nation on the Sex Workers Art Show Tour and organizes the RADAR Reading series at the San Francisco Public Library.
See also Volume 2, Primary Document 21

Further Reading: http://www.purpleglitter.com/michelle_tea/; http://www.sisterspit.com/spitindex.html; http://www.sfbg.com/38/40/x_psychic_dream.html; Tea, Michelle, *The Passionate Mistakes and Intricate Corruption of One Girl in America*, San Francisco: Semiotext(e), 1998; Tea, Michelle, *Pills, Thrills, Chills, and Heartache: Adventures in the First Person*, Los Angeles: Alyson Publications, 2004; Tea, Michelle, *Rent Girl*, San Francisco: Last Gasp, 2004; Tea, Michelle, ed., *Beyond Definition: New Writing from Lesbian and Gay San Francisco*, San Francisco: Manic D Press, 1994; Tristan Taormino, ed., *Best Lesbian Erotica 2004*, San Francisco: Cleis Press, 2003.

HEATHER CASSELL

TELEVISION. Feminist ideas have been presented, represented, and misrepresented in television since the emergence of second-wave **feminism** in the late 1960s. Shows in the 1970s, 1980s, and 1990s—such as *The Mary Tyler Moore Show* (1970–1977), *Wonder Woman* (1976–1979), *Murphy Brown* (1988–1998), and *Roseanne* (1988–1997)—offer examples of U.S. television's portrayal of and engagement with second-wave feminism and the women's movement. Series in the mid-1990s and early 2000s, such as *Buffy the Vampire Slayer* (1997–2003), *Xena: Warrior Princess* (1995–2001), *Sex and the City* (1998–2003), and *Alias* (2001–), are informed by and address third-wave feminist themes and concerns. However, the relationship between feminism and popular culture is complex, and television has been a crucial site for the **representation** and negotiation of feminist *and* anti-feminist ideas. While series such as *The Mary Tyler Moore Show* presented images of independent, "liberated" women, most representations of popular versions of feminism since the 1970s have focused on specific characters and stereotypes as I will detail next.

One of the dominant caricatures of the 1980s and early 1990s was that of the shoulder-padded, power-driven career woman. While this figure became a commonplace in **films** such as *Working Girl* (1988) and *Disclosure* (1994), she has a television precedent in the figure of Alexis in the incredibly popular prime-time soap opera *Dynasty* (1981–1989). In *Backlash: The Undeclared War Against Women* (1992), **Susan Faludi** argued that the 1980s (the "**backlash decade**") saw the marginalization of women in U.S. prime-time television. This was a time when single women (especially independent and ambitious ones) almost disappeared from the small screen, as both sitcoms and films focused on fathers. Moreover, Faludi identified a wave of films and television programs in the late 1980s that represented the sexually and professionally independent woman as either a pathological monster or a neurotic spinster (as seen in *Fatal Attraction* [1987] and *Thirtysomething* [1987–1991]). The proliferation of representations of empowered young women on television since the mid-1990s has been positioned as a response to both the gains and limitations of second-wave feminism, as well as to the anti-feminist representations of independent women associated with the backlash of the 1980s.

Feminist Television Criticism and the Soap Opera. In *Screen Tastes: Soap Opera to Satellite Dishes* (1997), the feminist critic Charlotte Brunsdon identifies four main categories of scholarship within the field of feminist television criticism: (1) investigations of the situation of women working within the television industry; (2) considerations of the presence of women on the television screen; (3) detailed analyses of television programs as "texts"; and (4) audience studies. Early feminist approaches to television, and the media more generally, tended to use a realist paradigm and to focus on questions about "images of women." Such approaches were concerned with comparing **representations** of **femininity** with the reality of women's lives, and challenging stereotypical (and often demeaning) images of women, which, it was argued, functioned to normalize and perpetuate traditional sex roles. Therefore, feminist critiques of popular modes of femininity were central to an understanding of women's oppression and how girls and young women were socialized into "feminine" behaviors and mores.

One of the most important areas for feminist television criticism was the soap opera. The soap opera has traditionally been situated as a "trashy" cultural form—not least because of its categorization as a "women's genre" (the term soap opera comes from U.S. radio serials in the 1930s that were sponsored by soap powder manufacturers and so directly aimed at female audiences). In the 1970s, feminist critics focused on how daytime television programs presented unrealistic and stereotypical images of women; in other words, how these programs offered a limited view of women's roles, which were most frequently located within familial and domestic contexts. One of the difficulties with this kind of analysis is that it presupposes an idea about a certain version of "reality" and the "realities" of women's experiences.

In the late 1970s, theorists started to consider how genres like the soap opera traditionally identified with and consumed by women articulated aspects of women's experience. This formed part of a broader movement in **cultural studies** and literary studies to both reevaluate and recuperate "women's genres" (e.g., the romance). Within the context of television studies, critical attention shifted to how women viewers were actively involved in constructing meaning from these televisual texts, rather than simply being passive consumers of traditional images of femininity. In her influential study *Loving with a Vengeance: Mass-Produced Fantasies for Women* (1984), which offered a feminist analysis of popular cultural forms from Harlequin novels to U.S. daytime soap operas, Tania Modleski explored the pleasure of the soap opera in relation to women's position within the domestic sphere. Rather than seeing the soap opera as "feminine" in a negative way, she repositioned it as a positive expression that plays with dominant narrative forms. Through a discussion of its formal features, Modleski argued that the soap opera emphasizes interruption, repetition, and distraction, all of which are also characteristic of domestic labor. On one hand, then, the soap opera confirms and reaffirms traditional female roles; on the other hand, however, it can be understood as offering a radical aesthetic that disrupts and even subverts the ostensible order of the realist text. In *Watching Dallas: Soap Opera and the Melodramatic Imagination* (1985), the feminist critic Ien Ang theorized the pleasures of watching soap operas and explored how audiences actively construct meaning. Ang argued that a soap opera such as *Dallas* offers its viewers pleasure by enabling "melodramatic" identifications. Although the soap opera world is clearly fictional, it nonetheless offers a kind of emotional or psychological reality: its exaggerated crises and storylines function metaphorically. In highlighting questions of class, ethnicity, and nationality, such studies examining the international reception of soap operas, in particular *Dallas*, forced a reevaluation of what constituted the otherwise homogenous and universalizing category of the "female audience."

Third-Wave Feminism and Television. From Buffy and Xena, to Ally McBeal and Carrie Bradshaw, to Lisa Simpson and *Farscape's* (1999–) Aeryn Sun, there has been a proliferation of empowered young women on television since the mid-1990s. These characters, and their respective series, can be seen to address a number of the concerns and themes of third-wave feminist writing, and their ascendance on the small screen has been linked to third-wave feminism's active role in popular culture. One of the dominant and most contentious features of these series is that they often celebrate both the gains of second-wave feminism and the paraphernalia (or "trappings") of traditional femininity (which were perceived by many second-wave feminists as central to women's oppression). In this respect, these television series speak to and of third-wave feminism's reconsideration of the relationship between feminism and popular culture and, especially, its reassessment (and celebration) of popular modes of femininity. For example, many of these series exhibit an emphasis on—and a even fascination with—the pleasures derived from **fashion**. Carrie Bradshaw in *Sex and the City* takes a conspicuous pleasure in fashion, as she playfully mixes Manolo Blahnik shoes with vintage items. The impeccably made-up Buffy Summers in *Buffy the Vampire Slayer* undertakes complex martial arts moves in stylish clothes and designer footwear. Strong and independent, yet embracing their "femininity," the female characters in these shows are aligned with a form of "**Girlie**" feminism (often identified with third-wave feminism), which does not posit traditional femininity (makeup, fashion, high heels, etc.) at odds with female **empowerment**, but rather central to it.

A discussion of the extent to which these series both address and articulate third-wave feminist concerns and themes was initially eclipsed by their positioning as manifestations of "postfeminist" ideas. Of particular interest is the treatment of *Ally McBeal* (1997–2002). In June 1998, *Time* magazine ran a cover story asking "Is Feminism Dead?" Its cover mapped the progression of the feminist movement through pictures of four women: Susan B. Anthony, Betty Friedan, Gloria Steinem, and Calista Flockhart (the actress who played Ally McBeal). The television character Ally McBeal thus came to represent a generation of self-involved and individualistic young women who were no longer politically engaged but preoccupied with sex, relationships, and fashion. Nevertheless, more recently feminist critics have highlighted the ways in which *Ally McBeal* plays with some of the conflicting inheritances of feminism, in particular the tension between enjoying the benefits of second-wave feminism's political agendas, while claiming the right to choose individual definitions of feminism. In their depiction of female sexual confidence and pleasure, and critique of **marriage** and **family** life, such series also offer a response to the anti-feminist messages of the 1980s and early 1990s. *Sex and the City* is particularly progressive in its frank and open discussion of female **sexuality**, giving air time to previously taboo subjects such as masturbation, orgasms, and **abortion**, and validating the choices of young women for whom marriage and family life is not necessarily a primary goal. Moreover, the series is notable for the prominence it gives to the bonds of female friendship, providing a positive model of female solidarity and companionship previously marginalized on prime-time television.

Some of the most compelling and subversive female characters to appear on the small screen since the mid-1990s have emerged from contemporary action television. There has been an eruption of television series offering representations of smart, savvy, independent, physically powerful, and even overtly sexy female action heroes: for example, *Buffy the Vampire Slayer*, *Xena: Warrior Princess*, *Dark Angel* (2000–2002), *Alias*, and *La Femme Nikita* (1997–2001). The ass-kicking heroes of these television series not only fight back against their oppressors and aggressors but also against images of women as passive victims. In doing so, they draw on and develop the role of the female action hero in shows of the 1960s and 1970s (e.g., *Wonder Woman*, *Charlie's Angels* [1976–1981], and *The Avengers* [1961–1969]). However, tough and independent, but also attractive and traditionally "feminine," the new female action hero is clearly defined as a girl hero. She is physically powerful and agile but often incredibly glamorous as well. As in *Sex and the City* and *Ally McBeal*, fashion is a dominant theme: Sydney Bristow in *Alias* relies on numerous costume changes to negotiate her dual identity as graduate student and CIA double agent, and

Nikita in *La Femme Nikita* often appears in a range of designer evening wear. Critics such as Charlene Tung have noted how, at the same time as embracing the traditional signs of femininity, these new female action heroes use their bodies as weapons: they possess "killer bodies" in both senses of the term.

The new generation of female action heroes occupying the television landscape challenge and subvert conventional gender roles and expectations. According to author Elyce Rae Helford, the "female action-adventure hero is composed equally of herstory, affirmative action, equal opportunity, and repudiation of gender **essentialism** and traditional feminine roles" (2000, 293). A product of feminist consciousness and the gains of the women's movement, these action heroes dramatize many of the conflicts central to third-wave feminist theorizing: their battles are fought against both traditional patriarchal frameworks and inherited feminist models. *Buffy the Vampire Slayer* in particular has attracted a substantial amount of critical debate concerning its feminist credentials within the context of third-wave feminism. Perhaps more so than her ass-kicking contemporaries, Buffy can be seen to embody a number of third-wave feminist themes and concerns insofar as she exemplifies the contradictions and paradoxes shaping young women's dual negotiation of the spectres of feminist *and* patriarchal discourses (e.g., the tension between individual and collective empowerment, generational conflict, and a renegotiation of the relationship between feminism and popular modes of femininity). One of the main criticisms made against *Buffy the Vampire Slayer* is that it promotes a version of Girlie feminism that is individualistic and without a political agenda. This is a charge that has also been made against other contemporary female action heroes, such as Xena, who have been positioned as "part of the myth of the American Dream, of transcendence, of individual greatness done for the good of others ... female heroes function well within the individualist discourse of **postfeminism**" (Helford, 294).

Certainly, the ascendance of the ass-kicking super girl on the small screen has not been unreservedly embraced. First, at the same time as these popular prime-time series portray empowered and independent young women, there is a concern that they represent the co-option, commercialization, and, consequently, de-radicalization of feminist ideas and politics through their embracing of the "**girl power**" slogan. Nevertheless, as with the career girl, female friendship and solidarity are important themes in many of these series. Although in *Alias* Sydney Bristow's female relationships are mostly antagonistic, both *Buffy the Vampire Slayer* and *Xena: Warrior Princess* offer positive and powerful representations of female friendship and (in the final series of *Buffy*, in particular) female community and collective action. Female bonds are also central to the underlying dynamic of the series *Charmed* (1998–), in which female power is strengthened by the "power of three," as in three sisters. Indeed, although she has not yet received the same amount of critical attention, the girl witch merits attention as another figure embodying some of the themes and concerns of third-wave feminism. Willow in *Buffy the Vampire Slayer*, Sabrina in *Sabrina the*

Teenage Witch (1996–2003), and the Halliwell sisters in *Charmed* offer alternative versions of the female action hero, as well as the more overtly domesticated witches of earlier sitcoms, such as *Bewitched* (1964–1972) and *I Dream of Jeannie* (1965–1970). More than her ass-kicking counterpart, the shape-shifting witch points up the possibility of alternative identities and **desires** within the contemporary television landscape. For example, in *Buffy the Vampire Slayer*, Willow's witchcraft metaphorically dramatizes her awakening lesbian sexuality.

One of the most pertinent criticisms made of contemporary television's depiction of feminism is that it both participates in and perpetuates constructions of white womanhood. In her influential study *Prime-Time Feminism: Television, Media Culture, and the Women's Movement since 1970*, the feminist critic Bonnie Dow highlights how "television's representations of feminism are almost exclusively filtered through white, middle-class, heterosexual, female characters" (xxiii). Further, at the same time as these television programs make readily available images of empowered and independent women, these images are often contained and diluted through the **media**-friendly discourse of girl power.

See also Volume 2, Primary Document 51

Further Reading: Ang, Ien, *Watching Dallas: Soap Opera and the Melodramatic Imagination*, London: Methuen, 1985; Brunsdon, Charlotte, *Screen Tastes: Soap Opera to Satellite Dishes*, New York: Routledge, 1997; Brunsdon, Charlotte, Julie D'Acci, and Lynn Spigel, eds., *Feminist Television Criticism: A Reader*, New York: Oxford University Press, 1997; Dow, Bonnie, *Prime-Time Feminism: Television, Media Culture, and the Women's Movement since 1970*, Philadelphia: University of Pennsylvania Press, 1996; Early, Frances, and Kathleen Kennedy, eds., *Athena's Daughters: Television's New Women Warriors*, Syracuse, NY: Syracuse University Press, 2003; Geraghty, Christine, *Women and Soap Opera: A Study of Prime Time Soap Operas*, Cambridge: Polity, 1991; Gorton, Kristyn, "(Un)fashionable Feminists: The Media and *Ally McBeal*," in *Third Wave Feminism: A Critical Exploration*, eds. Stacy Gillis, Gillian Howie, and Rebecca Munford, London: Palgrave Macmillan, 2004, 154–163; Greven, David, "Throwing Down the Gauntlet: Defiant Women, Decadent Men, Objects of Power, and *Witchblade*," in *Action Chicks: New Images of Tough Women in Popular Culture*, ed. Sherrie A. Inness, New York: Palgrave Macmillan, 2004, 123–152; Helford, Elyce Rae, "Postfeminism and the Female Action-Adventure Hero: Positioning *Tank Girl*," in *Future Females, The Next Generation: New Voices and Velocities in Feminist Science Fiction Criticism*, ed. Marleen S. Barr, Lanham, MD: Rowman and Littlefield, 2000, 291–308; Henry, Astrid, "Orgasms and Empowerment: *Sex and the City* and the Third Wave Feminism," in *Reading* Sex and the City, eds. Kim Akass and Janet McCabe, London: I.B. Tauris, 2004, 65–82; Karras, Irene, "The Third Wave's Final Girl: *Buffy the Vampire Slayer*," *Thirdspace* 1(2) (2002), http://www.thirdspace.ca/articles/karras.htm; Liebes, Tamar, and Elihu Katz, *The Export of Meaning: Dallas*, New York: Oxford University Press, 1990; Modleski, Tania, *Loving with a Vengeance: Mass-Produced Fantasies for Women*, New York: Routledge, 1982; Pender, Patricia, "'Kicking Ass Is Comfort Food': Buffy as Third Wave Feminist Icon," in *Third Wave Feminism: A Critical Exploration*, eds. Stacy Gillis, Gillian Howie, and Rebecca Munford, London: Palgrave Macmillan, 2004, 164–174; Tung, Charlene, "Embodying an Image: Gender, Race, and Sexuality," in *Action Chicks: New Images of*

Tough Women in Popular Culture, ed. Sherrie A. Inness, New York: Palgrave Macmillan, 2004, 95–122.

REBECCA MUNFORD

THEATER. Most scholars trace the origins of theater as a political practice back to Greece's City Dionysia (fifth-century BC), an Athenian festival that included live performance in its celebration of religious and civic pride. Although the plays of that time have since been interpreted by feminist scholars as misogynistic, and the festival itself explicitly excluded women and slaves from participation, its purpose, structure, and impact were deeply tied to emerging notions of democratic participation. In contemporary culture as well, theater and performance continue to be defined by their relationship to democracy, public culture, and cultural politics. Although there has yet to be a theater production explicitly defined as third-wave feminist, the gender, racial, sexual, and economic politics in contemporary theater reflect third-wave concerns.

Feminist theater is one such area in which the relationship between **art** and politics is apparent and can be interpreted. Feminist theater practices mirror the waves of the feminist movement, with the third wave of feminist theater beginning, roughly, in the 1990s and continuing to the present. Following directly on the heels of second-wave feminist theater, the structures, form, and content of third-wave feminist theater is what distinguishes it from its predecessor. For example, second-wave feminist theater practice was largely the product and project of the proliferation of feminist theater collectives that came into existence in the 1970s and 1980s throughout the United States and specifically in New York City. Generally, these organizations were cooperatively run on a volunteer basis with limited budgets and large amounts of collective action. Women's One World Café of New York (WOW Café) is one such example of a collective dedicated to promoting and presenting work by women, about women, and for women-identified audiences. WOW is exceptional, though, in its longevity: of the approximately 160 feminist theaters in existence by the end of the 1980s, very few remain. Also still active is Spiderwoman Theater (in New York). Comprised of Lisa Mayo and her sisters, Muriel and Gloria Miguel, Spiderwoman is the oldest continually performing women's theater company in North America and focuses on issues related to Native American identity and oppression. The second oldest company, Horizons: Theater from a Woman's Perspective (in Washington, D.C.), also continues to produce new work. Although these companies are the exceptions and most collectives from the second wave have since folded, feminist theater practice has not declined; on the contrary, the work and accomplishments of theater practitioners in the 1970s and 1980s expanded and were expanded by the discourse of **feminism** and, in turn, affected the ways in which feminists can and do make theater.

Playwright and performer Peggy Shaw, for example, cofounder of the Split Britches Ensemble (comprised of Shaw, Lois Weaver, and Deb Margolin), got her start with Weaver and Margolin at WOW Café and continues to make feminist theater today, though the definition of what exactly constitutes feminist theater has changed with the times. Her most recent play, *To My Chagrin*, premiered at Jump-Start Performance Company, a community-based theater is San Antonio, Texas. A solo performance, *To My Chagrin* explores Shaw's relationship as a white, butch lesbian with her biracial grandson and the shared masculinity between them. Although the form (autobiographical solo performance), the venue (community-based performance company in Texas), and the content (explorations of race, class, gender **identity**, and **sexuality**) are in some ways different from her earlier pieces with the Split Britches Ensemble, Shaw's work, like that of many contemporary theater practitioners who began in the 1980s, continues to resist male hegemony. Additionally, it addresses sexism's relationship to **racism**, homophobia, and gender-based **discrimination**, and the ways in which all function together to oppress women.

Other mid-career theater practitioners who continue to work in feminism's third wave include playwright Maria Irene Fornes, director Laurie Carlos, and performance artists Holly Hughes, Carmelita Tropicana (Alisa Troyano), Marga Gomez, Deb Margolin, Lois Weaver, and Robbie McCauley.

Since the early 1990s, new artists have emerged whose work addresses issues relevant to contemporary notions of feminism. Like artists who began working more than a decade earlier, the work of these women of the third wave also focuses on multiple and interlocking social issues while situating women's voices and experiences as central and the resistance to women's oppression as critical. Playwright and performer Sarah Jones (*Surface Transit, Women Can't Wait, Waking the American Dream, Bridge and Tunnel*), playwrights Kia Corthron (*Seeking the Genesis; Breath, Boom; Come Down Burning; Cage Rhythm*), Rebecca Gilman (*Spinning into Butter, Boy Gets Girl*), Diana Son (*Stop Kiss*), Naomi Wallace (*The Trestle at Pope Lick Creek, One Flea Spare, Slaughter City, In the Heart of America*), Suzan-Lori Parks (*Imperceptible Mutabilities in the Third Kingdom, Death of the Last Black Man in the Whole Entire Universe, Topdog/Underdog, The America Play, Fucking A*), and Paula Vogel (*Baltimore Waltz, How I Learned to Drive*), to name some, all received notoriety in the 1990s on, although some began their careers earlier. Vogel, for example, was born in 1951 and began writing in college, but her work was frequently rejected. It was not until 1992 that her fantastical play about a brother and sister in search of a cure for A.T.D. (Acquired Toilet Disease), *The Baltimore Waltz*, opened in New York to great success and subsequently won the Obie Award (award for best off-Broadway play). Since then, her work has been produced at theaters such as Circle Repertory (New York), The Goodman Theatre (Chicago), The Magic Theater (San Francisco), Center Stage (Washington, D.C.), and the Alley Theatre (Houston), as well as in Canada, England, Brazil, and Chile. Although Vogel's work tackles issues larger than feminism and her plays are presented in regional venues that have a more expansive mission, Vogel's popularity indicates, among other things, how the ways in which feminism is enacted, and the sites at which feminist theater reaches its public, have changed, and, in some cases, been incorporated into more mainstream politics and culture.

Suzan-Lori Parks is another example of a playwright who emerged in feminism's third wave. In 1989, Parks was named by the *New York Times* as the "year's most promising playwright" and, just one year later, won an Obie for her full-length play, *Imperceptible Mutabilities in the Third Kingdom* (directed by her long-time collaborator, Liz Diamond). In addition to an Obie, she has received a Pulitzer Prize for Drama (*Topdog/Underdog*) and is the 2001 recipient of the MacArthur Foundation "Genius" Award. Her most recent play, *Fucking A* (2003) (directed by Michael Grief at the Public Theater in New York), is a riff on Nathaniel Hawthorne's *The Scarlet Letter* (1850) and more significantly the histories of sexism and racism in America. *Fucking A* is the story of Hester (played by S. Epatha Merkerson), a black woman in a fictitious city, who works as an abortionist to earn money to "buy" her son, Monster (played by Mos Def), out of prison. Centering her narrative on the experience of a woman of color, Parks is able to interrogate the histories of sexism, racism, and economic oppression and encourage her audiences to see the world in which they live and, possibly, re-imagine it.

In 1996, the yet unknown Eve Ensler premiered her play, **The Vagina Monologues**. Ensler interviewed more than 200 women, ranging in age from six to seventy-five, about their vaginas; the result was a series of monologues of women talking openly about their vaginas. It began as a solo performance (featuring Ensler), but it quickly became a three-woman show in constant repertory, often starring well-known actresses (including Susan Sarandon, Winona Ryder, Glenn Close, and Whoopi Goldberg) and serving as a fundraising event for feminist causes. To date, it has been performed in twenty countries and translated into twenty languages, including many productions on college campuses where it reaches young feminists and pre-feminists. In 1998, Ensler launched the V-Day Foundation, a global movement to end violence against women.

When, in 2001, the United States invaded Afghanistan and, later, Iraq, Kathryn Blume, a New York–based actress, founded the Lysistrata Project. More than a thousand theater companies from around the world, including many ad hoc collectives formed for the purposes of the event, organized to stage Aristophanes' ancient Greek **comedy**, *Lysistrata*, on the same day. In the play, the women of Athens, led by Lysistrata, refuse sex with their husbands until they agree to end their **war** with Sparta. This modern interpretation of the classic text enacted a global protest against war and violence. This project connected the political potency of theater to its ancient roots and established its potential for feminist activism. Theater continues to be a valuable activist forum for third-wave feminists.

Further Reading: Canning, Charlotte, *Feminist Theatres in the U.S.A.: Staging Women's Experiences*, New York: Routledge, 1996; Case, Sue-Ellen, ed., *Performing Feminisms: Feminist Critical Theory and Theatre*, Baltimore: Johns Hopkins University Press, 1990; Diamond, Elin, *Unmaking Mimesis: Essays on Feminism and Theater*, New York: Routledge,

1997; Dolan, Jill, *The Feminist Spectator as Critic*, Ann Arbor: University of Michigan Press, 1988; Phelan, Peggy, *Unmarked: The Politics of Performance*, New York: Routledge, 1993; Schneider, Rebecca, *The Explicit Body in Performance*, New York: Routledge, 1997.

JACLYN IRIS PRYOR

THIRD-WAVE CATCH PHRASES. Third-wave **feminism**, like other identifiable movements, has a particular vocabulary associated with it and the activism of particular groups. One of most obvious is "**Girl Power**," but one of the characteristics of this phrase is that many try to claim it. Although its source is nebulous, one line of speculation about the origin is that it arose, as did much third-wave lingo, out of the Riot Grrrl movement. Hillary Carlip, inspired in part by the movement, began putting together a book called *Girl Power* in 1993, which featured fresh, unapologetic, unedited writing by girls from all demographic groups. Riot Grrrls, eager to portray girls as powerful beings and as forces to be reckoned with, also frequently used the phrase "Revolution Girl Style Now!" as a mantra. The Riot Grrrl movement, very dependent on the written word, was spread by fanzines created and distributed across the country. Interestingly, one aspect of the Riot Grrrl movement included a reclaiming of negative language in an attempt to confront the users of such derogations; Kathleen Hanna of the band **Bikini Kill** would often write in marker words such as "slut" on her exposed stomach. This kind of ironic reappropriation of terms previously used to devalue girls is characteristic of some of the most identifiable phrases associated with the third wave.

The confrontational stance of the Riot Grrrls, coupled with scholarship in the 1980s and 1990s that included close scrutiny of girls' self-esteem (or lack thereof) such as **Naomi Wolf**'s book *The Beauty Myth* (1991) and Mary Pipher's *Reviving Ophelia: Saving the Selves of Adolescent Girls* (1994), led to a change in the way girls were written about and discussed. Once the problem of girls' lack of confidence was identified and addressed, moves were made—in girls' magazine articles and other media outlets—to portray girls as smart, strong, powerful people and as capable as boys in all arenas.

In recent years, the phrase "Girl Power" has been plastered on products as wide-ranging as notebooks, jewelry, and clothing; many groups have co-opted the phrase. The Spice Girls, a British pop **music** group, made it their *modus operandi*, although cynicism exists as to their motive. The Spice Girls were able to make quite a bit of money from marketing this slogan and concept in a positive, anger-free way. By the late 1990s, merchandising of this type was widespread, including such sophomoric efforts as products bearing the slogan "Girls Rule, Boys Drool." The original politicizing force had been drained from the language.

Another characteristically third-wave phrase comes from the group **Girls Incorporated** (Girls Inc.). Girls Inc. is an organization devoted to empowering girls and young women. It claims roots that date back 140 years to the Industrial

Revolution, when girls and young women found themselves in new roles as laborers. With the slogan, "Inspiring all girls to be smart, strong, and bold," they aim to educate girls on topics including math, science, health, and **media** literacy. Some of the forms their outreach takes include workshops for girls and **television** commercials. Girls Inc. is an example of intergenerational dialog between the second and third waves and with younger women.

Another recent phenomenon that makes use of what might be termed third-wave catch phrases is the Radical Cheerleaders movement. This is an informal organization of young women around the United States who trade female-friendly chants and rhymes. Women are encouraged to perform these cheers in groups in public. Some of the cheers are housed and circulated on the Internet, while others travel through word of mouth. Topics addressed by Radical Cheerleaders include dieting and **body** image, politics, and **sexual harassment**. These women use the confrontation and energy that typified the Riot Grrrl movement and take their messages straight to the public.

Plenty of men are concerned with sending positive messages to young girls, too. An organization called **Dads and Daughters** holds as their mission statement, "DADs inspires fathers to actively and deeply engage in the lives of their daughters and galvanizes fathers and others to transform the pervasive cultural messages that devalue girls and women." Dads and Daughters is organized by Joe Kelly, whose wife started the young feminist women's magazine *New Moon*. Cross-gender activism is one of the characteristics of third-wave feminism, and Dads and Daughters is a prominent example.

Now, it is common to see words like "smart," "strong," and "bold" used to describe all sorts of initiatives, from government-led body-image **education** programs to, again, merchandise designed to appeal to young girls. Although these catch phrases are most often used in marketing, it is probable that their usage will increase and appear more widely used for other purposes as well.

See also Magazines, Women's

Further Reading: Carlip, Hillary, *Girl Power*, New York: Warner Books, 1995; Girls Inc., http://www.girlsinc.org; Dads and Daughters, http://www.dadsanddaughters.org; Fine, Carla, *Strong, Smart and Bold: Empowering Girls for Life*, New York: HarperResource, 2001.

JESSICA MANACK

THIRD WAVE FOUNDATION. The Third Wave Foundation is the first and only national membership-driven foundation and direct action organization for young women between the ages of fifteen and thirty. The Foundation supports leadership training, **education**, and networking between young feminists and organizations by providing funding, resources, and educational programs.

The Third Wave Foundation was founded as the Third Wave Direct Action Corps by **Rebecca Walker** and Shannon Liss during the summer of 1992 as a direct response to the Clarence Thomas/Anita Hill sexual harassment hearings and the Rodney King verdict and Los Angeles riots. Walker and Liss quickly organized the first Freedom Summer Ride, a cross-country voter registration bus trip—modeled after the 1960s Freedom Rides—with 120 young women and men who registered 20,000-plus voters in twenty-three underserved communities. This direct action inspired young women and men around the nation to join the Third Wave Direct Action Corps and began a network of young feminist activists. Due to the enormous response, the Corps opened its national office in New York City in 1993 and developed the presence of a new generation of feminist activists. In 1995 Walker joined forces with **Amy Richards**, Catherine Gund, and Dawn Lundy Martin and founded the Third Wave Fund to provide financial support for young women's activism, education, small business enterprises, and access to **abortion** services. The Fund operated in conjunction with the Corps until 1997, when the interlinked organizations were combined into the Third Wave Foundation, and Vivien Labaton was named director. By the end of 1995, chapters were established in San Francisco; Madison, Wisconsin; and on college campuses throughout the United States.

The Foundation began to vocalize its mission in 1994 with their newsletter, *See It. Tell It. Change It!* and operated online with ThirdWaveOnline. The Foundation established its presence by producing large public events around New York City, such as Info-Parties, the Young Women's Film Festival in collaboration with New York University, and hosted fundraiser dinners and speaking events in New York, San Francisco, and Los Angeles. The Foundation also produced educational workshops, such as the Why Vote? workshop series, to educate young women about the importance of voting and **political participation**; the Young Donor Conference and the Why Give? campaign, to educate young wealthy people about philanthropy; the I Spy Sexism campaign, to take action against organizations, businesses, and people practicing **discrimination** based on gender, race, or sexual orientation; and an intergenerational lecture series with well-known second-wave leaders, such as Gloria Steinem and Alice Walker, and third-wave feminists to bridge the generation gap. In 2000 the Foundation established its annual summer road trip ROAMS (Reaching Out Across MovementS), a networking tour bringing young women activists together with social justice organizations in underserved communities.

Further Reading: Baumgardner, Jennifer, and Amy Richards, *Manifesta: Young Women, Feminism, and the Future*, New York: Farrar, Straus and Giroux, 2000; The Third Wave Foundation, *See It. Tell It. Change It! Newsletter*, New York: Third Wave Foundation, http://www.thirdwavefoundation.org; Walker, Alice, *To Be Real: Telling the Truth and Changing the Face of Feminism*, New York: Anchor Books/Doubleday, 1995.

HEATHER CASSELL

TRANSGENDER. Transgender is a term that applies to a broad range of individuals and is used positively in the third wave. It includes people who are intersex (born with both male and female genitalia), people who are transsexual (in the process or who have completed surgically changing their sex from male to female [MTF] or female to male [FTM]); and people who are genderqueer and/or tranies (people who are transgender but choose not to go through the medical and surgical process to change their bodies to the male or female sex, and people who are straight, but identify themselves with a different gender than their physical **body** would dictate).

Being accepted into the third-wave feminist movement as a transgender/transsexual person can sometimes be seen as parallel to lesbians being accepted into the feminist movement during the 1970s and 1980s, when the National Organization for Women (NOW), led by Betty Friedan, termed lesbians the "lavender menace" and actively worked to exclude them from NOW. Transgender/transsexual people experienced similar difficulties being accepted into women's communities and women-only spaces during the 1990s, as MTFs were perceived either as not being "real women" or FTMs as traitors for transitioning into men, therefore acquiring and embracing the privileges of being male. However, because third-wave feminist thinking explicitly questions the **gender binary** male/female and generally has a non-essentialist approach to thinking about gender, transgender fits much more fully into third-wave understandings of gender and **sexuality** than did second-wave thinking, which especially in its cultural feminist incarnation tended to cling to essentialist definitions of gender (women as "naturally" more peaceful, moral, nurturing, etc.).

The transgender movement began to pick up its pace during the late 1980s and throughout the 1990s with new medical technologies that made gender transformation more possible. The psychological diagnosis of Gender Identity Disorder (the persistent belief that an individual is the opposite sex of what they appear to be physically, i.e., a girl stating she is a boy or a boy stating that he is a girl), which was originally defined in 1980 by the American Psychological Association in the *Diagnostic and Statistical Manual of Mental Disorders*, was redefined in 1987 and again in 1994 to distinguish between girls who identified as tomboys and girls who *truly* identified as being boys (by stating that they wanted a penis or insisting on only wearing boys clothes), and boys who had an intense **desire** and identification with girls and wanted to be girls. The clarification of the definition of Gender Identity Disorder allowed transgender/transsexual people to request medical treatments such as hormone therapy and actual sex reassignment surgery to alter their physical sex to match their gender, while it simultaneously allowed for the option of remaining in the body they were born with and existing as intersex or genderqueer.

The process to reassign sex takes a long time. First, transgender/transsexual people need to undergo psychological and medical examination to determine whether they qualify for sex reassignment surgery. Second, transgender/transsexual people need to dress and live their lives as the opposite sex for a minimum of one year before receiving professional recommendation to proceed with surgical and medical treatments to transition into the sex they identify as. Once this part of the process is completed, transgender/transsexual people need to get the money to pay for their surgery and hormone treatments, which are very expensive. The physical and psychological transition from one sex to the other is only the beginning of the challenges transgender/transsexual individuals face. During and after surgery, many health complications can occur including heart problems, problems with their reproductive organs leading to cancer, and other life-threatening medical conditions.

The increasing number of people opting to change their sex to match their gender causes a great deal of debate within the feminist, gay, lesbian, and bisexual movement, and society at large. There is a lot of confusion about and hostility toward transgender/transsexual individuals because they are viewed as being "different" and as not fitting into a clear definition of male or female. Contributing to hostile feelings toward transgender/transsexual people is the difficulty with identifying their sexual orientation and the way they necessarily add another subgroup to the gay, lesbian, and bisexual community. For example, a straight man who was once married and had a **family** who then transitions into a lesbian woman is much easier for many to understand than a lesbian who transitions into a man and becomes a gay man. To complicate matters further, many transgender/transsexual people who identify as heterosexual do not want to be connected with the gay, lesbian, and bisexual community because they do not identify as being gay, lesbian, or bisexual or the social and political issues related with that community. They simply want to lead "normal" lives and be happy.

Leading a normal life after changing genders and sex is a challenge. Often legal issues concerning employment, family (such as child custody), and safety and **discrimination** cause more complications because the legal system and society are not equipped with words or language to define and articulate rights for transgender/transsexual people. There are many misconceptions and myths about transgender/transsexual people, such as the perception within the heterosexual community that transgender/transsexual people are deviant and the perception within the gay, lesbian, and bisexual community that transgender/transsexual people do not have political goals and are even homophobic.

Beyond binding legal issues, MTFs and FTMs have a difficult time finding a community where they feel they can be themselves and live freely. For example, in the early 1990s when MTFs wanted access to feminist organizations and women-only spaces before their complete transition and after their surgery, a great deal of debate was generated about what a "real woman" actually is and MTFs were and continue to be viewed suspiciously by women. MTFs who identify their sexual orientation as lesbian were met with even more hostility within the lesbian community. Some lesbians perceive MTFs as not being "true lesbians" because they were once men, and lesbians do not want MTF lesbians to have leadership roles in their organizations because, from this point of view, the MTFs display "male" leadership qualities, which alienate many lesbians. On the other side, FTMs are considered by some feminists and lesbians to be traitors because they choose to change their sex from female to male and receive the benefits of being male in society. The exclusion and prejudice of FTMs and MTFs in women's spaces and activism has led to transfeminism. All of these problems are related to essentialist definitions of "male" and "female," "men" and "women," none of which the third wave would subscribe to.

Transfeminism. Transfeminism is conceptually very third wave and is a movement of FTMs, MTFs, intersex, and genderqueer and trannies to identify, define, and link similar issues of oppression between the transgender and feminist movements. These issues include health and reproductive rights, sexuality, violence against women, body image, employment, family rights, and others. Through examining intersex, transgender, transsexual, and genderqueer experiences, transfeminists have identified a number of related areas between the transgender and feminist movements. First, transgender activists and transfeminists define the mutilation of intersex children by doctors and families to assign a gender and surgically "correct" the child's genitalia to match the assigned gender as abuse. Denying intersex, transgender, transsexual, and genderqueer individuals the basic right to decide to proceed with surgical and medical (taking hormones) altercations to their physical body is perceived to be directly related to women's rights to proper health care, reproductive rights, and the right to make their own medical decisions. Second, transfeminists link issues of violence as a shared problem that both transgender people and women face. Since the release of *Boys Don't Cry,* a 1999 **film** based on the true story of Brandon Teena and his violent death in 1992 for being transgender, reports of violence against and deaths resulting in violence because of an individual's transgender status are in the news and are entering the public's consciousness. Third, transfeminists connect issues of body image—altering their bodies to fit into societal standards to identify as a boy or a girl—to the right to embrace the body they feel most comfortable in. It is the transfeminist and transgender perspective that is much more identifiably "third wave" with its insistence on gender as a malleable cultural construction and the lack of essentialist qualities belonging to bodies of either assigned biological gender.

See also Essentialism; *Volume 2, Primary Documents 57 and 62*

Further Reading: Bornstein, Kate, *Gender Outlaw: On Men, Women and the Rest of Us,* New York: Routledge, 1995; Burke, Phyllis, *Gender Shock: Exploding the Myths of Male & Female,* New York: Anchor Books, 1996; Courvant, Diana, "Strip!" in *Adios, Barbie: Young Women Write About Body Image and Identity,* ed. Edut, Ophira, Seattle: Seal Press, 1998, 104–113; Currah, Paisley, and Shannon Minter, *Transgender Equality: A Handbook for Activists and Policymakers,* San Francisco: National Center for Lesbian Rights and Policy Institute of the National Gay and Lesbian Task Force, 2000; Devor, Holly, *FTM: Female to Male Transexuals in Society,* Bloomington: Indiana University Press, 1999; Fausto-Sterling, Anne, *Sexing the Body: Gender Politics and the Construction of Sexuality,* New York: Basic Books, 2000; Feinberg, Leslie, *Transgender Warriors: Making History from Joan of Arc to Dennis Rodman,* Boston: Beacon Press, 1997; Howell,

Clare, Joan Nestle, and Riki Wilchins, *Genderqueer: Voices from Beyond the Sexual Binary*, Los Angeles: Alyson Publications, 2002; http://www.colage.org/kids/kids_w_trnsgndr_prnts.html; http://www.gendertalk.com/; http://www.gpac.org/; http://www.nclrights.org/projects/transgenderproject.htm; http://www.ntac.org/; http://www.planetout.com/; http://www.tgguide.com/; http://www.transgendercare.com/default.asp; http://www.transgenderlaw.org/; Kirkland, Anna, "When Transgender People Sue and Win: Feminist Reflections on Strategy, Activism, and the Legal Process," in *The Fire This Time: Young Activists and the New Feminism*, eds. Vivien Labaton and Dawn Lundy Martin, New York: Anchor Books, 2004, 181–219; Koyama, Emi, "The Transfeminist Manifesto," in *Catching a Wave: Reclaiming Feminism for the 21st Century*, eds. Rory Dicker and Alison Piepmeier, Boston: Northeastern University Press, 2003, 244–259; O'Keefe, Tracie, *Finding the Real Me: True Tales of Sex and Gender Diversity*, San Francisco: John Wiley and Sons, 2003; Wheeler, Anne, *Better Than Chocolate*, British Columbia: Vidmark/Trimark, 2002; Whittle, Stephen, *The Transgender Debate*, Reading, UK: Garnet, 2001.

HEATHER CASSELL

TRANSNATIONAL FEMINISM. Transnational **feminism** refers to the ways in which women's movements around the globe are interconnected in both their theories and practices. Not usually identified with third-wave feminism in the media (which is often mistakenly associated with **postfeminism**, or derogatorily and reductively associated with middle-class white girls who like lipstick), transnational feminism is actually a powerful example of ideas central to third-wave feminism. Transnational feminisms recognize that women face many similar situations in relation to **patriarchy** around the globe. Nonetheless, the transnational third wave avoids making broad generalizations about women's experiences and instead calls for theories and practices that recognize the differences between cultures and also addresses the ways in which cultures are connected through such vehicles as the global economic system and mass global communication. With the rise of **globalization**, as well as communication mediums such as the Internet, many feminists contend that distances between people, at least on a metaphorical level, are lessening. This means that people around the globe are increasingly connected. However, all connections are not equal, and often Western women are unintentionally implicated in non-Western women's oppression.

Transnational feminism requires analytical skills and knowledge of feminist history, because third-wavers have new frameworks for conceptualizing women's experiences in different parts of the world. Many contemporary feminists are highly critical of Western first- and second-wave feminisms' treatment—in both theory and practice—of non-Western women. Much recent scholarship examines the ways in which past "global sisterhoods" are embedded with unequal power relations, which stem from privileging Western beliefs about non-Western people. Many contemporary feminists critique feminisms of the past for failing to recognize the culturally specific gender relations in non-Western nations and states. They point to the ways in which patriarchal belief systems and politics manifest differently in different cultures. This does not, however, mean that third-wave feminists conceptualize *all* women as facing the *same* patriarchy. Quite the contrary, as transnational feminist frameworks consider women's oppression, in both the past and present, as culturally and historically specific. Nor do third-wave transnational feminists simply argue that Western belief systems (such as liberalism or capitalism or Christianity) are inherently *better* than non-Western belief systems. Instead, transnational feminism reconceptualizes the past to better understand the social, political, economic, and cultural complexities of the present.

Defining Transnational. Contemporary feminist terminology has moved away from the term "international" and instead uses the term "transnational." It is important to distinguish between these two terms, because their meanings have different implications. "International" quite literally signifies "between nations" and suggests that nations are separate entities. Some feminist thinkers continue to use "international" as their preferred term for discussing global relations. However, beginning in the early 1990s, many feminists, including those in the third wave, replaced the term "international" with "transnational." Stressing the complex relationships between nations, transnational points to the ways that "other" nations exist not only outside of a nation but also *within* a nation. The term also refers to the ways in which the rise of global capital in both historical and contemporary societies link nations through the global economic system. During the process of colonization, as well as globalization, many nations relied on products and workers from other nations. The results of this are not only economic, but cultural and social links among many nations were also forged. Therefore, the term "transnational" refers to the ways in which nations are not separate entities, but instead are constantly engaged in economic and cultural exchanges.

The term "transnational feminism" refers to ways in which women's movements around the globe negotiate their activism and ideas with each other. The use of transnational implies that these women's groups recognize the ways in which patriarchy works on both local and global levels. It also suggests that feminist groups (especially Western feminists) recognize that patriarchy is not a phenomenon only in "underdeveloped nations"; instead, transnational feminism implies that women's groups explore the linkages between local and global patriarchal practices. Feminist scholars such as Inderpal Grewal and Caren Kaplan contend that transnational feminist theories and practices stress the free flow of information and capital across borders and examine their effects on women's lives.

First World, Third World, and the Transnational Power of Naming. Contemporary feminist critics claim that the term "Third World" should be used with caution. These critics contend that members of the Third World did not choose this name—it was placed on them by members of the First World. Some feminists' claim that the use of "First," "Second," and "Third" world result in a hierarchy—and the privileging of First World cultures and societies.

Therefore, when third-wavers use the term "Third World," they do so with care and recognize that this term does not adequately represent the experiences and ideas of those women living in the so-called Third World. Furthermore, many contemporary feminist critics also view the use of "underdeveloped" in descriptions of Third World countries as problematic and contend that "development" does not necessarily mean "better."

Third-wave feminism recognizes that women have different experiences and actively make room for the women's diversity in their theories and practices. As feminisms of the past were critiqued by women of color in the United States, new ways of thinking about identity emerged and helped shape the third wave. It is important to recognize that not only women of color who were born in the United States were involved in these critiques. In fact, many Third World women criticized white feminists for failing to account for the complexities of Third World women's experiences. These critiques took place mainly in the academy, and many feminist academics, such as Chandra Mohanty and Gayatri Spivak, claimed that many Western feminists approached Third World women in a way that demeaned them and failed to take into account differential power relationships between women. Mohanty, Spivak, and other writers criticized some Western academics for failing to account for the ways in which Third World women face very different experiences in different parts of the world.

Feminist Movements and Global Sisterhood. There are many problems with conceptualizing different transnational feminisms as inextricably linked. The power relations between nations can sometimes negate the possibility of a "global sisterhood." In other words, women from Western countries sometimes fail to recognize these power relationships and the ways in which the history of feminism intersects with colonial and postcolonial histories. Like the problematic relations between women of color and white women in so-called First World nations, international feminist relations have also been wrought with misperceptions and inequalities. For example, during the first wave of feminism, many white, Western women participated in imperialist projects. Embarking on the project of "civilizing the natives," these women—some in the name of feminism—sought to better the social, political, and cultural situations of non-Western women. Despite these good intentions, some Western women missionaries and imperialists viewed non-Western people as "uncivilized barbarians," whose women were especially oppressed. Because many non-Western women were colonized in the age of imperialism and colonialism, contemporary feminist thinkers oftentimes discuss the ways in which **representations** of non-Western peoples are still viewed through the eyes of colonialism. This means that Western people continue to conceptualize non-Western people as barbaric and uncivilized. Non-Western women are oftentimes conceptualized as lacking any personal agency and being a helpless victim to a brutal patriarchy that Western women have since transcended. However, not all first- and second-wave feminists intentionally or unintentionally sought to colonize non-Western women. Individuals negotiate dominant belief systems and there are always examples of personal transgressions. Yet there are many examples of white women's role in imperial and missionary conquests, and it is seen to be imperative that third-wavers understand this complex feminist history in order to build stronger transnational alliances.

Transnational Frameworks and Third-Wave Feminism. Thinking cross-culturally without privileging one's own culture is difficult. Having a framework with which to analyze such topics as sati, female genital cutting (FGC), the veil, or personal autonomy in non-Western contexts allows some third-wave feminists to "make sense" of cross-cultural phenomena, without simply viewing it through a Western lens. For example, in discussions about FGC, some third-wave feminists depict those women who undergo this practice as victimized and oppressed. However, other third-wave feminists recognize that it is important to understand the context in which this culturally specific practice takes place before making any broad claims about women's status. As well, although sisterhood and solidarity are necessary tools in feminist movements, there is also a time for separatism. It is this blending of solidarity and separatism, past and present, difference and commonality, and local and global that marks transnational third-wave feminism.

In "Arrogant Perception, World Traveling and Multicultural Feminism: The Case of Female Genital Surgeries" (1997), Isabelle R. Gunning suggests a three-part method for thinking critically about cultures other than one's own. Gunning's first suggestion is to see oneself in one's historical context. Therein, if contemplating FGC in non-Western countries, one would first pay attention to the ways in which women's genitals have been treated in Western contexts and would examine the historical circumstances under which these practices took place. Many intersexed persons—those born with genitalia that conforms to neither male nor female—have had involuntary surgeries on their genitals in Western culture. Second, Gunning advices seeing oneself as the "'other' sees you." Therefore, she suggests exploring the ways in which one's own cultural practices could be viewed as "barbaric" or "uncivilized" by non-Western peoples. Last, Gunning advises that we see the "other" in the other's context. This means that one must first understand the complex historical, social, economic, political, and cultural implications of FGC before attempting to analyze the situation or making broad claims about FGC. This kind of historical and cross-cultural awareness is a mandatory part of transnational feminism, and third-wave feminists make this part of their feminist praxis.

See also Racism; Volume 2, Primary Documents 9, 33, and 45

Further Reading: Anzaldúa, Gloria, *Borderlands/La Frontera: The New Metiza*, San Francisco: Aunt Lute Books, 1987; Enloe, Cynthia, *Bananas, Beaches and Bases: Making Feminist Sense of International Politics*, London: Pandora Press, 1989; Gunning, Isabelle, "Arrogant Perception, World Traveling and Multicultural Feminism: The Case of Female Genital Surgeries," in *Critical Race Feminism: A Reader*, ed. Adriene Katherine Wing, New York: New York University Press, 1997; Hernández, Daisy, and Bushra

Rehman, eds., *Colonize This!: Young Women of Color on Today's Feminism*, New York: Seal Press, 2002; James, Stanlie, and Claire Robertson, *Genital Cutting and Transnational Sisterhood: Disputing U.S. Polemics*, Chicago: University of Illinois Press, 2002; Jayawardena, Kumari, *The White Woman's Other Burden: Western Women and South Asia during British Colonial Rule*, New York: Routledge, 1995; Kincaid, Jamaica, *A Small Place*, New York: Farrar, Straus and Giroux, 1988; Naples, Nancy, and Manisha Desai, eds., *Women's Activism and Globalization: Linking Local Struggles and Transnational Politics*, New York: Routledge, 2002.

MARY SITZENSTATTER

V

THE VAGINA MONOLOGUES. A series of monologues based on interviews with more than 200 women, *The Vagina Monologues* have grown from a one-actress production by the author, Eve Ensler, to star-studded assemblies performed across the United States. In the monologues, the female voice is used to explore issues related to the female **body** and **sexuality** and addresses how these are normally considered taboo. Using humor, anger, and pain, the monologues deal with a variety of issues pertaining to women's oppression and addresses issues such as **rape** as a war crime, women's sexual lives, and the female anatomy.

Overwhelmed with audience members' personal "vagina" stories, Ensler, with the help of activists from Feminist.com, created the V-Day organization in 1997. The mission of V-Day is to end violence against women by increasing awareness and raising funds to support organizations working to ensure women's safety. The funds that are collected through ticket sales, donations, **advertising**, and merchandise are distributed to grassroots and field organizations. In 1999, the V-Day organization established the college initiative, which gave universities and colleges permission to perform the production and use the proceeds in their communities as long as they followed organizational guidelines. Within five years, *The Vagina Monologues* went from being performed at sixty-five colleges and universities to 602, and it has raised more than $14 million worldwide.

The Vagina Monologues has spread on university campuses at a time when there is ambiguity over the state of contemporary **feminism**. Although Ensler does not consider the monologues feminist, they have mobilized feminists on college campuses by helping establish communities in which young feminists can bond and share experiences. *The Vagina Monologues* has become an empowering experience and a vehicle for activism in environments that are often hostile to feminism.

See also Theater

Further Reading: Ensler, Eve, *The Vagina Monologues*, New York: Villard, 2001; Reger, Jo, and Lacey Story, "Talking about My Vagina: Two College Campuses and the Influence of the Vagina Monologues," in *Different Wavelengths: Studies of Contemporary Feminism*, ed. Jo Reger, New York: Routledge, 2005.

LACEY STORY

VICTIM/POWER FEMINISM. In the early 1990s, authors such as Katie Roiphe (*The Morning After: Rape, Fear, and Feminism on Campus*, 1993) and **Naomi Wolf** (*Fire with Fire: The New Female Power and How It Will Change the Twenty-First Century*, 1993), who the media sometimes considers third-wave feminists, along with anti-feminist authors such as Camille Paglia (*Sex, Art, and American Culture: Essays*, 1992), suggested that mainstream **academic feminism** was ideologically misguided, as well as alienating to young women, because of its emphasis on women as sexual and economic victims of men and patriarchal culture. Wolf coined the term "victim feminism" to refer to this style of feminism and offered an alternative, "power feminism," that would emphasize women's strengths and abilities. According to these authors, victim feminism emphasizes the ways in which women are victimized—physically, economically, and politically—by the **patriarchy**. These authors suggest that feminism overstresses women's victimization because this ensures the continued need for feminism, and they argue that this approach infantilizes women. Power feminism, on the other hand, is an **ideology** that suggests that women can achieve as much as men and argues that feminism should emphasize and capitalize on individual women's abilities to achieve within the current social structure. Wolf's articulation of power feminism asks women "to fantasize political retribution for an insult to sex, to claim and use money, and to imagine and enjoy winning."

These concepts have been controversial within feminist communities. Roiphe, Wolf, and Paglia have been criticized for presenting an incomplete or distorted picture of feminism; in addition, power feminism was criticized because its emphasis on women's individual achievements will tend to benefit those women who are already privileged—white, middle- and upper-class straight women—and do little to change the status of women who are structurally more disadvantaged, such as women of color and poor women. Feminists who study violence against women have taken issue with the label "victim feminism," arguing that articulating the extent to which women are victimized—through **rape** and **domestic violence**, for instance—is not the same thing as making women into victims. A different sort of critique came from feminists of color such as **bell hooks**. Hooks agrees with the frustration with academic feminism that has led to the label "victim feminism." She suggests that the argument that women are universally victims inappropriately glosses over the differences among women. However, hooks notes that the spokeswomen for power feminism, all of whom are white, seem to ignore not only the issue of race but also the work of feminists of color. Although victim feminism and power feminism received a great deal of mainstream **media** attention in the early and mid-1990s, by the turn of the twenty-first century the terms had become less common.

Further Reading: hooks, bell, *Outlaw Culture: Resisting Representations*, New York: Routledge, 1994; Maglin, Nan Bauer, and Donna Perry, eds., *"Bad Girls"/"Good Girls": Women, Sex, and Power in the Nineties*, New Brunswick, NJ: Rutgers University Press, 1996; Sorisio, Carolyn, "A Tale of Two Feminisms: Power and Victimization in Contemporary Feminist Debate," in *Third Wave Agenda: Being Feminist, Doing Feminism*, eds. Leslie Heywood and Jennifer Drake, Minneapolis: University of Minnesota Press, 1997, 134–149; Wolf, Naomi, *Fire with Fire: The New Female Power and How It Will Change the Twenty-First Century*, New York: Random House, 1993.

ALISON PIEPMEIER

VIRGINITY MOVEMENT. Whether or not teens are having sex has been the preoccupation of parents throughout many generations, but one that has been given more attention in the 2000–2008 Bush administration with its exclusive funding for abstinence-only **sex education**. The virginity movement can be seen as both politically driven and as a response to the ever-increasing, commodity-based **sexuality** of American consumer culture. Since the mid-1990s, the virginity movement has taken shape in two forms: abstinence-based education and virginity pledges. Not only has the number of abstinence-based sexual education programs increased, but millions of teenagers have also "pledged" to abstain from sexual intercourse until **marriage**. There are a variety of reasons for the sustained popularity of these movements. The first is fear. The fears of the consequences of sexual intercourse include unwanted pregnancy, sexually transmitted diseases, and the risk HIV/**AIDS**. For other individuals it is spiritual commitment based on religious vows or an emotional demonstration of personal control.

The pledge movement began in 1993. It was initiated by members of the Southern Baptist Church. Since the early 1990s, this group and others like it have acquired more than 2.5 million signatures of adolescents willing to pledge to stay virgins until **marriage**. These abstinence commitments, as they are sometimes called, are usually solicited from teens in a public setting such as at school or church. Debate ensues over the use of the dynamic of peer pressure to get teens to sign. Studies have shown that teens feel more comfortable making a commitment in solidarity or as a group. The pledge movement is the focus of researchers and the federal government who question the efficacy of it in delaying sexual intercourse among teens.

In July 2000, Columbia University researchers Peter S. Bearman and Hannah Brückner conducted a study entitled, "Promising the Future: Virginity Pledges as They Affect Transition to First Intercourse." This was a longitudinal study of more than 90,000 teens across the country in grades 7–12. The study concluded that the efficacy of the pledge depended on two variables: the age of the teen pledging and the social environment of the pledger or student. For teens older than eighteen, the pledge did not delay sexual intercourse. For sixteen and seventeen year olds, the pledge resulted in the delay of sexual intercourse by eighteen months compared with non-pledgers. The social environment of the student, meaning whether or not the teen was in a relationship with someone from the same school or outside, changed the results of the study. However, the study did not examine the possible increase of other forms of sexual activity—oral or anal sex—which could still expose them to sexually transmitted diseases, among adolescents who did not break the pledge.

Support for the virginity movement is not wholly tied to religious organizations. Although loosely organized, there are approximately eighty separate programs and organizations involved in the virginity pledge movements. There are also more than 700 abstinence-based sexual education programs, many of which receive federal funding. The most prominent of such organizations is True Love Waits, led by Paul Turner and Jimmy Hester. Opposition to the virginity movement is primarily focused on the issue of whether or not to provide federal funding for programs that promote abstinence-only–based education. Opponents fear that this form of education will result in students not being properly taught about the use of contraception and the prevention of sexually transmitted diseases. Therefore, teens are left lacking the appropriate knowledge to deal with sex and its possible consequences when they finally decide to have it.
See also Religion and Spirituality

Further Reading: Bearman, Peter, and Hannah Bruckner, "Promising the Future: Virginity Pledges and First Intercourse," *American Journal of Sociology* 106(4) (2001); Benards, Neal, *Teenage Sexuality: Opposing Viewpoints*, St. Paul, MN: Greenhaven Press, 1988; Sommers, Michael, and Annie Sommers, *Everything You Need to Know About Virginity*, New York: Rosen Publishing Group, 2001.

JESSICA A. YORK

VISUAL ART. Third-wave visual **art** combines the social and political agendas of feminist art with specific third-wave concerns and typically uses new visual media for its expression. Issues that are of concern to third-wave feminists are the major focus of third-wave visual art, such as race and multiculturalism, **sexuality**, pop culture and its impact on perceptions of gender **identity**, the role of new information and **communication technologies**, and how to respect diversity in feminist thought and practices.

Visual art can best be described as creative expression and artistic output that uses one, or a combination, of the visual media. Visual art is open and broad, as it can be any form of art that the audience is able to see. The media available for artistic expression have changed over time as new media sources became available, so visual art itself has changed over time as well. Early cave paintings are visual art, as are drawings, printmaking, sculpture, photography, fiber arts, filmmaking, and other methods and media of expression. Contemporary visual art includes digital and electronic art, e-mail art, ASCII character art, Internet art, Web art, video art, found art, graffiti, comic books, interactive installations, and many others. Visual art may make use of one medium for expression or make use of several media simultaneously. Visual art may be expressed in two dimensions, such as drawing or photographs, or in three dimensions, such as sculptures or woven tapestries.

Feminist visual art is about creatively and authentically expressing the social world from a distinctly female perspective. The feminist art movement has a political component, in that it typically asks the audience to reflect on women's roles and identities in society as negatively expressed through **patriarchy**. It is also critical of the dominant patriarchal structures that benefit male artists and their artistic works and devalue the output of female artists. Female artists have fought to participate in cultural production and to be accepted as legitimate artists in their own right.

Third-wave visual art is part of the larger feminist art movement. Third-wave visual art often draws on and uses traditional notions of **femininity**. Some of the artists are doing so deliberately to subversively challenge social norms of gender roles and appropriate sexual behaviors for women. Third-wave **feminism** reclaims the right for women to express their identities in a multitude of ways, including "**girlie**" activities such as playing with cosmetics, dressing up, and shopping, and this is reflected in third-wave visual art. Sylvie Fleury uses high-class boutique shopping bags, **fashion** magazine covers, trendy designer shoe boxes, and even shattered Chanel makeup compacts to create her visual art installations. Fleury's work explores the connections and intersections between women, their roles as consumers, and their roles as objectified commodities used to sell products. However, some third-wave feminist artists have been criticized for using these damaging stereotypes without question or criticism or political motivation. By reclaiming feminine attributes in their work, these artists are arguably reinforcing demeaning traits allocated to women. Third-wave visual art is often ambiguous, complex, full of contradictions, and open to a variety of interpretations by the audience.

One dominant theme in third-wave visual art is the expression of women's **sexuality**. Women in mainstream **media** and art are typically sexually objectified—reduced to **body** parts available for male consumption. Their sexuality is constructed as being heterosexual and for male pleasure. Third-wave visual art challenges the objectification of women's bodies and their sexuality, often in playful and creative ways. For example, the Boxing Katrina series by the artist Katrina is a collection of life cast sculptures of the artist's vulva and genitalia. Her work is in reaction to the negative social attitudes about women's vaginas that make women uncomfortable with their own bodies and female sexuality.

Many third-wave visual artists take on pop culture's role in creating and maintaining dominant gender stereotypes as a social issue requiring critical analysis. **Advertising** and **fashion** are two main venues of pop culture that third-wave visual artists have challenged. The **Guerrilla Girls**, a New York–based collective of women artists founded in 1985, have modified major highway and city billboards to call attention to how advertising commodifies and objectifies women and to address current social issues. In 2003 they modified a Trent L'Ottscar billboard to comment upon the lack of female **representation** in politics and in Hollywood. Their activist art is designed to subvert dominant culture by using humorous images and statements to challenge their audiences. Their book on masculinist traditions in art history, *The Guerrilla Girls' Bedside Companion to the History of Western Art* (1998), playfully explores the real world of women artists historically and their fight for recognition.

Growing up with computer and electronic technologies already deeply embedded within the contemporary social landscape, many third-wave visual artists are using the Internet and computers as their forums for feminist artistic expression. The VNS Matrix, a collective of three Australian female artists, use the Internet and other electronic-based media to challenge the cultural perception that technology is male domain. Their 1994 installation, *All New Gen*, merges a computer game with video screens playing Quicktime videos, textual commentary, and photographs. The audience participates as a team of female heroes who join *All New Gen* out to take down Big Daddy Mainframe.

Third-wave visual art brings together the larger political concerns of the women's movement, the challenges experienced by the feminist art movement, and the contemporary social issues confronting third-wave feminists. Visual art is a creative forum by which third-wave women can challenge, subvert, and critique contemporary culture in ways that are authentic to their own lives and experiences.

See also Girl/Girlies; *Volume 2, Primary Documents 48–50*

Further Reading: Bloom, Lisa, ed., *With Other Eyes: Looking at Race & Gender in Visual Culture*, Minneapolis: University of Minnesota Press, 1999; *Genders* Online Journal, http://www.genders.org/index.html; Guerrilla Girls, The, *The Guerrilla Girls' Bedside Companion to the History of Western Art*, New York: Penguin Books, 1998; Jones, Amelia, ed., *The Feminism and Visual Culture Reader*, New York: Routledge, 2002; Robertson, George, Melinda Mash, and Lisa Ticknew, eds., *The Block Reader in Visual Culture*, New York: Routledge, 1996.

JENNIFER BRAYTON

W

WAGE GAP. The wage gap is the disparity between women's and men's wages (taking into account racial backgrounds) when they have the same qualifications and level of work experience. Young women today, depending on the industries they work in, experience a greater earning power, but on average continue to experience a large percentage of difference in their wages compared with those of white men with the same education levels and qualifications working in the same positions. The wage gap has equalized in the eighteen to twenty-four demographic in entry level positions but increases the further one goes up the economic ladder.

In 1963 the Equal Pay Act made it illegal for employers to pay different wages to men and women who are in the same positions and do the same work. Despite the new law, the wage gap persists even with additional legislation, such as the Fair Pay Act and the Paycheck Fairness Act, because of a number of reasons: race, age, level of **education**, chosen profession, and regional differences. Compounding the issues are myths, such as the idea that men are the providers for their **family**; wage secrecy, forbidding employees to discuss and compare their wages; and problems with enforcing the laws. Taking these factors into account when calculating and assessing the wage gap between men and women, a 2003 report by the U.S. General Office of Accounting states that women on average currently earn $.80 to every $1.00 a white man earns and the wage gap widens more for African American women who earn $.66 and Latinas who earn $.54 per every $1.00 a white man earns.

Many men are aware of the wage gap. According to a study done by the *Washington Post*, the Henry J. Kaiser Family Foundation, and Harvard University in 1998, 43 percent of men believe that men in general do not want women to advance in the workplace and therefore make it difficult for women to get promotions. Impacting women's progress in the workplace and wages are the facts that men gain a 2 percent increase in their wages if they have children and women with children lose an estimated 2.5 percent in their earnings. The significance of the 20 percent wage gap means that women continue to economically benefit through **marriage**. If women did earn equal pay on par with white men, according to the Bureau of Labor Statistics, their income would raise by $4,000, taking half of the population of women and their families out of poverty. According to a study by the AFL-CIO in 1999, closing the wage gap will raise women's wages by 13 percent and men's wages by 1 percent. Overall, closing the wage gap benefits both men and women, raising the standard of living for their families, and some men are starting to understand the necessity and benefits.

See also Discrimination against Women; Glass Ceiling

Further Reading: Costello, Cynthia B., Anne J. Stone, and Vanessa R. Wight, *The American Woman 2003–2004: Daughters of a Revolution—Young Women Today*, New York: Palgrave, 2003; http://www.aflcio.org/issuespolitics/women/equalpay/CaseForEqualPay.cfm; http://www.aflcio.org/issuespolitics/women/equalpay/FactSheetHowEqualPayHelpsMen. cfm; http://www.catalystwomen.org; http://www.dol.gov/wb/; http://www.house.gov/ maloney/press/108th/20031120NewGlassCeiling.html; http://www.iwpr.org/pdf/C355.pdf; http://www.pay-equity.org/; http://www.nwlc.org/details.cfm?id=1437&section=newsroom; http://www.washingtonpost.com/wp-srv/national/longterm/gender/gender22a.htm; http:// www.washingtonpost.com/wp-srv/politics/polls/vault/stories/98gender_data_a.htm; Orenstein, Peggy, *Flux: Women on Sex, Work, Love, Kids, & Life in a Half-Changed World*, New York: Anchor Books, 2000.

HEATHER CASSELL

WALKER, REBECCA. One of the founders of third-wave **feminism** and the coiner of the term "third wave," activist, author, mother, and daughter of African American author Alice Walker and Jewish attorney Mel Leventhal, Rebecca Walker (1969–) was born in Jackson, Mississippi, where her parents were active participants in the Civil Rights Movement. Their divorce when she was eight years old forced Walker to split her time and her young life between two very different worlds: her mother's, where she was often considered too white; and her father's, where she was thought to be too black. As a result, Walker grew up with loneliness and confusion to keep her company, depended on a tough crowd, promiscuous sex, and drugs for comfort, and at the age of fourteen she faced an unplanned pregnancy and had an **abortion**. By the time she changed her last name to Walker, she was a stronger individual preparing herself for Yale University, where she graduated cum laude in 1992.

Walker, named by *Time* magazine as one of fifty influential American leaders under forty, is now a prominent feminist activist, author, and public speaker in her own right. Her books include an edited collection of essays, *To Be Real: Telling the Truth and Changing the Face of Feminism* (1995), which explores young women's struggles to reclaim and redefine feminism, and *Black, White, and Jewish: Autobiography of a Shifting Self* (2000), a moving account of self-discovery and self-acceptance. Her most recent work includes the anthology *What Makes a Man: 22 Writers Imagine the Future* (2004), a collection of essays that ponder the question of contemporary masculinity, and which looks at how feminism has helped to shape the other gender. She has written for many national publications and her work is widely anthologized. She is also a co-founder of the only national, activist, philanthropic organization serving women ages fifteen to thirty—the **Third Wave Foundation**—and has won numerous awards for her activist work. She divides her time between New York City and Northern California where she raises her **family**.

See also Volume 2, Primary Documents 1, 5, 64, and 65

Further Reading: Rebecca Walker's Web site, http://www.rebeccawalker.com.

MURIEL L. WHETSTONE-SIMS

WALLACE, MICHELE. Feminist scholar and cultural commentator, Michele Wallace (1953–) is most well known as the author of the seminal book *Black Macho and the Myth of the Superwoman* (1978), which set off a firestorm of fierce debate and intense dialog—within and beyond the black community—about the consequences of black sexual politics defined as adverse to black women. Upon the release of the book in the late 1970s, *Ms.* magazine featured Wallace on its cover and, at that time, she became an overnight celebrity in activist circles whose work was both vilified and glorified.

Wallace earned her BA in English at the City College of New York in 1974, and in 1999 she completed a PhD in Cinema Studies at New York University. While pursuing her undergraduate degree, Wallace cofounded Women Students and Artists for Black Art Liberation (WSABAL), "an activist and polemical unit to advocate the kinds of positions in the **art** world which are now identified with the **Guerrilla Girls**." She is a professor of English at the City College of New York and the CUNY Graduate Center and the author of a number of books, among them *Black Popular Culture*, and *Invisibility Blues: From Pop to Theory* (1990).

See also Black Feminism

Further Reading: DuPlessis, Rachel Blau, and Ann Snitow, eds., *To Hell and Back: On the Road with Black Feminism in the 1960s and 1970s: The Feminist Memoir Project—Voices from Women's Liberation*, New York: Random House, 1998.

MURIEL L. WHETSTONE-SIMS

WAR. War is an armed conflict between two or more nations or groups. Ordinarily wars were between groups of men fighting over land, resources, and for or against dominion. War is an issue for **feminism** because women have traditionally been excluded from the **military** except in service or support roles, and this exclusion reinforced traditional gender role stereotypes. Feminism has been divided on women in the military. Many women supported World Wars I and II and Vietnam. Many women from the suffrage movement and the second wave of feminism supported men going to war and women tending to the homefront. Many women took over the jobs of servicemen while they were defending the United States. Many women also wanted to join the armed forces. Third-wave feminists tend to take an anti-essentialist position toward war, which is that if women want to fight in the military, that is their choice, and they are not limited by old stereotypes that say they are weaker or naturally more peaceful than men.

The actual definition and concept of war has shifted since around the mid-1980s. The definition of war for many third-wavers goes beyond that of military conflict. Today many young feminists are concerned with the acts of aggression and violence perpetrated by corporations and the effect this has on humanity. This constant aggression—in the name of "economic progress"—is waged upon Third World countries in which ultimately women and children suffer the most. During the act of war women are raped and tortured, and children are left orphaned and starving. Similar situations occur when a country's economic status is weakened by World Bank interventions rather than helped by them.

The slogan "war against drugs" was coined during the Reagan administration. At that time in many of the United States' urban and suburban areas, there was an influx of drug use, drug trafficking, and violence. This "war against drugs" crossed international borderlines with the Iran/Contra crisis and the invasion of Panama by the U.S. military. Wars can be waged upon ideas, theories, and inanimate objects. The first war that occurred during third-wave feminism's time was the Gulf War, waged by former President George H. W. Bush. Most influential have been the post–9/11 war on the Taliban (a group of young male Muslim extremists that operated in Afghanistan and suppressed Afghanistan's citizens, especially women) and Muslim extremist and al Qaeda leader Osama bin Laden, and the U.S. attack on Iraq. The slogan "war on terrorism" became part of American popular culture and engendered ample debate. Many politicians and U.S. government officials and officials abroad, as well as many third-wave feminists, questioned the declaration of war on a noun or **ideology**. Although third-wave feminism supports the idea of women in the military if they freely choose (and are not forced to by economic considerations) to participate, and does not see women as inherently more peaceful, most feminists in the third wave have challenged this latest manifestation of war. *See also* Essentialism

Further Reading: Alonzo, Hyman Harriet, *The Women's Peace Union and the Outlawry of War 1921–1942*, Knoxville: University of Tennessee Press, 1989; Costello, B. Cynthia, Shari Miles, Anne J. Stone, eds., *American Woman: 1999–2000: A Century of Change—What's Next?* New York: W.W. Norton, 1998; hooks, bell, *Feminist Theory: From Margin to Center*, 2nd ed., Cambridge, MA: South End Press, 2000; Labaton, Vivien, and Dawn Lundy Martin, eds., *The Fire This Time: Young Activists and the New Feminism*, New York: Anchor Books, 2004; Woodward, Bob, *Plan of Attack*, New York: Simon and

Schuster, 2004; Ziegler, Susan, "Find A Cure for War: Women's Politics and the Peace Movement in the 1920's," *Journal of Social History* 24 (1990): 69–86.

JACKIE JOICE

WHEDON, JOSS. Joss Whedon (1964–) is best known as the creator of the hit **television** series *Buffy the Vampire Slayer* (1997–2003), which followed the life of Buffy Summers, a teenage girl who is "chosen" to fight vampires and other demons as part of an ancient line of other female vampire slayers. Always working metaphorically to comment on young people's lives, the show begins with Buffy's entrance into Sunnydale High School, a school metaphorically and literally placed over a hell mouth. The show follows Buffy and her compatriots through college.

Whedon was a women's studies major at Smith College in Northampton, Massachusetts. In several interviews he has said that he was trying to create an alternative feminist role model in the character of Buffy. He was critically reclaiming the ubiquitous blonde girl victim of the horror movies—the character who, ostensibly because of her **femininity** and weakness, always dies in that genre. *Buffy the Vampire Slayer* is an ironic reworking of that stereotype, featuring a blonde girl who is stronger than any demon, not to mention any guy, and whose responsibility it is to save the world again and again. In addition to *Buffy*, Whedon is the writer and creator of the series *Firefly* (2002), co-creator of the BTVS spin-off *Angel* (1999–2004), cowriter of Disney's *Toy Story* (1995), and writer of the *Alien: Resurrection* (1997). He also wrote several issues in a series called *The Astonishing X-Men* (2004, 2005) for Marvel Comics. In his ironic dismantling of the traditional stereotypes of femininity, Whedon is an outspoken proponent and quintessential example of the cultural practices of third-wave **feminism**.
See also Volume 2, Primary Document 51

Further Reading: IGN Entertainment Inc., "An Interview with Joss Whedon," Film-Force, http://filmforce.ign.com/articles/425/425492p1.html; In Joss We Trust, MSN Entertainment, News, http://www.entertainment.msn.com/news/article.aspx?news=122421; Joss Whedon dot Net, http://www.josswhedon.net; Joss Whedon, Internet Movie Database, http://www.imdb.com/name/nm0923736/; Whedonesque: Joss Whedon Web log, http://whedonesque.com.

BREA GRANT

WICCA. Wicca, sometimes called Wicce, The Craft, or The Old Religion by its practitioners, is a neo-pagan earth-centered **religion** founded in England by Gerald Gardner in the mid-twentieth century. Although some Wiccans are feminists, Wicca itself is not rooted in feminist belief or practice. Feminists are attracted to Wicca because it emphasizes balance and equality between the genders. Although no particular religious practice is related to third-wave **feminism**, Wicca's emphasis on equality makes it, like Unitarianism, appealing to many feminists.

There is no central authority or doctrine in Wicca. Many traditions fall under the general classification of Wicca. The most well-recognized traditions include Gardnerian, Alexandrian, Welsh Traditional, Dianic, Faery, and Seax-Wica. "Eclectic" Wiccans borrow from a number of traditions and favor a more spontaneous style of worship.

Although most Wiccans are solitary practitioners, many still choose to meet in small autonomous groups known as "covens." Ranging in size from three to thirteen people, covens can be of mixed gender, or all female or male. The groups are often headed by a High Priestess, priest, or both, but each member is considered to be a priestess or priest in her/his own right. These groups differ in structure, organization, practice, and focus but all adhere to the same general code of ethics.

Wiccans follow a core ethical statement called the Wiccan Rede, which states "an ye harm none, do what ye will." This means that as long as one's actions do not harm others or oneself, one is free to do as one wants. This is especially important where the use of magic is concerned, because the Law of Return states that an individual's actions, both good and bad, return to her/him three times over.

Wiccans believe in balanced polarities (including the feminine and masculine). These aspects are embodied in two deities known as the Goddess and God. The Goddess has three faces corresponding to various cycles in nature: the Maiden, the Mother, and the Crone. The Horned God, also known as the Hunter, is worshiped as the masculine side of nature. He represents fertility and is considered the controller of life and death.

In addition to the Goddess and the God, some Wiccans recognize a number of deities and through the use of magic attempt to channel the energy contained in nature to get closer to these gods. Although *practicing* magic is not required, a belief in magic is central to Wicca. In lieu of a permanent house of worship in which to practice magic, Wiccans create a sacred space by "casting a circle" using elements representing air, earth, water, and fire.

Most Wiccans, regardless of tradition, hold religious celebrations on Esbats, or nights of the full moon, and on Sabbats, the cycle of eight seasonal days of celebration throughout the year known as the Wheel of the Year. The exact dates of the Sabbats vary from year to year but generally fall within a two-day period. There are four minor and four major Sabbats. The minor Sabbats include: Yule (The Winter's Solstice), Ostara (Spring Equinox), Litha (Summer's Solstice), and Mabon (Autumnal Equinox). The major Sabbats are Imbolc (Candlemas), Beltane (Fertility celebration), Lammas (Celebration of Lugh/First Harvest), and Samhain (Year's End/Year's Beginning).

Further Reading: Adler, Margot, *Drawing Down the Moon: Witches, Druids, Goddess-Worshippers, and Other Pagans in America Today*, New York: Penguin, 1997; The Church and School of Wicca, http://wicca.org/; Covenant of the Goddess, http://www.cog.org/; Farrar, Janet, and Stewart Farrar, *A Witches' Bible: The Complete Witches' Handbook*, Seattle, WA: Phoenix Publishing, 1996; Gardner, Gerald B., *Witchcraft Today*, New York: Citadel Press, 2004; Hutton, Ronald, *Triumph of the Moon: A History of Modern Pagan Witchcraft*, New York: Oxford University Press, 2001; McLelland, Lilith, *Out of* *the Shadows: Myths and Truths of Modern Wicca*, New York: Citadel Press, 2002; Wicca for the Rest of Us, http://wicca.timerift.net/index.html; "Wicca": The Religious Movement's Homepage Project, http://religiousmovements.lib.virginia.edu/nrms/wicca.html; "Wicca" Religious Tolerance, http://www.religioustolerance.org/witchcra.htm; The Witches League for Public Awareness, http://www.celticcrow.com/; The Witch's Voice, http://www.witchvox.com/.

Jaime McLean

WILLIAMS, VENUS, AND WILLIAMS, SERENA. Tennis star Venus Starr Williams was born June 17, 1980, in Lynwood, California, and her younger sister Serena Williams, also a tennis star, followed on September 26, 1981. The sisters took the tennis world by storm, heralding a new era for women's tennis. In September 1999, seventeen-year-old Serena won the U.S. Open and became the first African American woman to win a Grand Slam Singles title since Althea Gibson won five in the 1950s. Venus emulated her younger sister's success with victories in two Grand Slam events—Wimbledon and the U.S. Open—in 2000. Venus then went on to capture the gold medal in singles in the Sydney Olympics and, partnered with Serena, also won gold in the doubles events. Venus successfully defended her Wimbledon title in 2001. Both sisters continue to compete in and win Grand Slam singles and doubles events. Breaking down both race and class barriers, the Williams sisters demonstrated that two African American women who do not hail from an upper-class background could dominate in a sport often thought of as a "country club" game.

The Williams sisters have embraced their iconic status and work hard to be positive role models for girls and women in **sports**. The Williams sisters' savvy use of **media** allowed them to bring urban African American cultural styles to the foreground. Not only tennis players, but **fashion** designers who trained at the Art Institute of Florida, Venus and Serena are also known for bringing more modern urban sensibilities to tennis fashion. Demonstrating that strength and style are not mutually exclusive, the Williams sisters unabashedly celebrated physical strength combined with a host of signifiers of **femininity**, something indicative of third-wave sensibilities. Everything the Williams sisters have done in their career—from challenging gender, race, and class stereotypes to combining elements of the traditionally masculine and traditionally feminine—is indicative of a third-wave feminist sensibility and approach.

Further Reading: Rineberg, Dave, *Venus & Serena*, Hollywood, FL: Frederick Fell Publishers, 2002; Venus and Serena's Official Web site, http://www.venusandserenawilliams.com.

Faye Linda Wachs

WOLF, NAOMI. Naomi Wolf (1962–), author and social critic, was born in California and later studied at Yale University and as a Rhodes Scholar at Oxford University. Widely and frequently published today in major periodicals and newspapers, with most of her books still in print, she made her mark with *The Beauty Myth: How Images of Beauty Are Used Against Women* (1991). This international bestseller attacked modern **media** and **advertising**, targeting their unrealistic standards of beauty as the source of much of modern female insecurity and lack of confidence, as well as the perpetuation of the beauty and diet industries. Wolf's writings have made her one of the most prominent third-wave thinkers. Her other books, written in response to inequality and **misogyny**, include *Fire with Fire: The New Female Power and How It Will Change the 21st Century* (1993), which encourages women to embrace their power, veering away from an approach in which women are the "victims" of **patriarchy**; *Promiscuities: The Secret Struggle for Womanhood* (1997), which deals with the virgin/whore roles that seem like the only options for girls; *Misconceptions: Truth, Lies and the Unexpected on the Journey to Motherhood* (2001), which discusses the difficulties of childbirth; and *The Treehouse: Eccentric Wisdom from My Father on How to Live, Love and See* (2005). Wolf is a popular speaker on feminist issues and is one of the cofounders of the Upstate New York–based Woodhull Institute for Ethical Leadership, which aims to create new feminist leaders. The Institute is named after Victoria Woodhull, who, in 1872, was the first female to run for the office of President of the United States.

See also Beauty Ideals; Postfeminism; Victim/Power Feminism; *Volume 2, Primary Documents 4 and 13*

Further Reading: Royce Carlton Incorporated, http://www.roycecarlton.com/speakers/wolf_information_kit.html; Wolf, Naomi, *The Beauty Myth: How Images of Beauty Are Used Against Women*, New York: Perennial, 1991; Wolf, Naomi, *Fire with Fire: The New Female Power and How It Will Change the 21st Century*, New York: Random House, 1993; Wolf, Naomi, *Misconceptions: Truth, Lies and the Unexpected on the Journey to Motherhood*, New York: Anchor, 2003; Wolf, Naomi, *Promiscuities: The Secret Struggle for Womanhood*, New York: Ballantine, 1998; Woodhull Institute for Ethical Leadership, http://www.woodhull.org.

JESSICA MANACK

WOMANISM/WOMANIST. A key development in second-wave **feminism** that influenced third-wave feminism and its attention to differences between women, the term "womanist" was originally coined by black feminist author Alice Walker, who introduced the expression in her 1983 volume of essays, entitled *In Search of Our Mothers' Gardens: Womanist Prose*. According to Walker in the opening pages of this book, the term "womanist" has four basic meanings. First, a womanist is "a black feminist or feminist of color," the opposite of "girlish, frivolous, irresponsible, not serious." Womanist is derived "from the black folk expression of mothers to female children, 'You acting womanish' (i.e., like a woman)" and usually referred "to outrageous, audacious, courageous, or *willful* behavior. Wanting to know more and in greater depth than is considered 'good' for one. Interested in grown-up doings. Acting grown up. Being grown up. Interchangeable with another black folk expression: 'You trying to be grown.' Responsible. In charge. *Serious*."

Second, a womanist was also, according to Walker, "a woman who loves other women, sexually and/or nonsexually. Appreciates and prefers women's culture, women's emotional flexibility ... and women's strength. Sometimes loves individual men, sexually and/or nonsexually. Committed to survival and wholeness of entire people, male and female. Not a separatist, except periodically, for health. Traditionally universalist ... Traditionally capable" (xi).

Third, a womanist "loves **music**. Loves dance. Loves the moon. *Loves* the Spirit. Loves love and food and roundness. Loves struggle. *Loves* the Folk. Loves herself. *Regardless*" (xii).

And the fourth, and perhaps most often quoted definition, "womanist is to feminist as purple is to lavender" (xii). Walker explained in a 1984 *New York Times Magazine* interview that "I don't choose womanism because it is 'better' than feminism.... Since womanism means black feminism, this would be a nonsensical distinction. I choose it because I prefer the sound, the feel, the fit of it, because I cherish the spirit of the women (like Sojourner [Truth]) the word calls to mind, and because I share the old ethnic-American habit of offering society a new word when the old word it is using fails to describe behavior and change that only a new word can help it more fully see" (*New York Times Magazine*, January 8, 1984, p. 27). With their introduction, "womanist" and "womanism" became known as racially defined terms in that they became specific definitions for black feminists and other feminists of color; terms intended to define African American women apart from the white feminists dominating mainstream feminist movements. By making reference to the black folk expression, "You acting womanish," Walker centralizes black women's historic, yet marginalized, roles within those feminist movements. Third-wave feminism sees itself as informed by this kind of awareness of differences between women.

See also Black Feminism

Further Reading: Collins, Patricia Hill, "What's in a Name? Womanism, Black Feminism, and Beyond," *The Black Scholar* 26 (Winter/Spring) (1996); Walker, Alice, *In Search of Our Mother's Gardens: Womanist Prose*, New York: Harcourt Brace Jovanovich, 1983.

MURIEL L. WHETSTONE-SIMS

WOMEN'S COLLEGES. Women's colleges are dedicated to promoting and expanding educational opportunities for women. Founded during the mid- to late nineteenth century, when advanced **education** was largely inaccessible to women, women's colleges provide learning experiences for women that might never be available in coeducational settings. Women's colleges began training women in many of the traditionally male disciplines and were the only institutions where women could study science, mathematics, law, and philosophy. By providing equitable educational settings for women, women's colleges meet challenges that women in coeducational settings face, such as discrimination within the classroom, discouragement from pursuing traditionally male-dominated fields, and social pressures that steer women away from academics. Providing women with practical job training in addition to intellectual development, most women's colleges ensure that women have access to quality higher education.

The history of women's colleges is strongly linked to women's suffrage and current women's movements in the United States. The development of seminaries (private secondary schools for young women) during the early 1800s was the beginning of expanded higher educational opportunities for women. Most seminaries initially trained women in traditionally feminine trades such as teaching, while reinforcing gender roles by preparing women to be wives or nuns; however, seminaries were a foundation for women's colleges and strengthened women's college programs that transgressed such gendered boundaries. As women's colleges developed, so did curriculums and goals, encouraging women to pursue nontraditional careers and opportunities, and they expanded opportunities for women significantly. When women finally obtained the right to vote in 1920, they could work toward other forms of liberation, such as a right to education.

During World War II, when so many men were drafted, women found increased opportunities within higher education. Just as women were recruited into traditionally male-dominated areas of the work force during World War II, they were recruited into traditionally male spheres within education, as students and teachers in both coeducational institutions and women's colleges. As women's roles in American society changed, women pursued different educational and career opportunities to fulfill those roles. As a result of such changes, women's colleges expanded their programs, and when the **war** ended, women's colleges remained a more viable option for women.

During the sixties and seventies, legislative changes prohibited single-sex public institutions, threatening existing women's educational programs. Many women's colleges became coeducational, merged with all-male educational institutions, or closed down altogether, and several all-male higher educational institutions were forced to admit women. Some women's colleges survived on generous endowments from private individuals or reconfigured their programs to meet necessary criteria to remain open as public universities (such as admitting men, while still remaining predominantly female), but in general, women's educational programs struggled to survive under such legislation.

Women's colleges in the United States today are part of a broader range of higher education opportunities available to women. Different types of women's colleges include independent private colleges, religiously affiliated private colleges, and public four-year universities. Most women's colleges are private; only three public women's colleges currently exist in the United States (Mississippi State University for Women, Douglass College of Rutgers University, and Texas Woman's University). Legislation on **single-sex education**, such as Title IX (which prohibits gender discrimination in publicly funded educational institutions), forbids public colleges from prohibiting males and is largely responsible for fluctuations in the visibility and proliferation of women's colleges. Private women's colleges thrive as **feminism** provides more options for women, including choices between coeducation and women's colleges, both public and private, providing positive models and futures for women, and challenging and transgressing limitations of coeducational programs. Third-wave feminism has an ambivalent stance toward women's colleges because of the way they seem to uphold essentialist definitions of gender.

See also Essentialism

Further Reading: DeBare, Ilana, *Where Girls Come First: The Rise, Fall, and Surprising Revival of Girls' Schools*, Women's College Coalition, http://www.womenscolleges.org.

LEANDRA PRESTON

WOMEN'S HEALTH. Women's health covers a broad range of issues: reproductive rights (e.g., access to contraception, **abortion**, prenatal care), preventative care for diseases (both physical and mental), research and testing for new drugs with women's particular physiology in mind, private and public insurance coverage for women, and public and private health advocacy organizations that effect the health and well-being of women. Young women today have more access and knowledge about their own health care and well-being because of access to health care and **education**, but women's health issues continue to be underrepresented in the **media**, and women continue to be misdiagnosed and mistreated in medical facilities and underinsured. Although historically a product of second-wave **feminism**, a focus on women's health remains a concern in the third wave.

One of the largest influences on women's health was the women's health movement, which began during the early twentieth century with Margaret Sanger, the founder of Planned Parenthood and the birth-control pill. The movement exploded during the 1970s with new policies directed at serving women's health, especially that of low-income women and children, and with the publication of pamphlets and books, community meetings, and **consciousness-raising** circles that grew and expanded into formal organizations throughout the 1980s and 1990s. The women's health movement brought specific health issues, such as breast cancer, the effects of smoking, and many other health care issues that affect women into focus, forcing researchers, government health institutes, medical professionals, and insurance providers to acknowledge and actively improve the quality and care of women's health and well-being.

One of the first policies focused on women's health was Title X of the Public Health Service Act, the first federal program to provide **family** planning services to poor women. Family planning was a major focus for the women's health movement, and efforts resulted in the relaxation of laws prohibiting distribution of contraceptives to single people (1972) as well as the Supreme Court's ruling in 1973 on **Roe v. Wade,** which decriminalized and legalized a women's right to choose **abortion** as a private medical decision. However, three years later, the Hyde Amendment eliminated federal funding for abortion services with a few exceptions. In 1978 The Pregnancy Discrimination Act was enacted and amended to the Civil Rights Act of 1964 to ban **discrimination** against pregnant women in the workplace. As the women's health movement grew into the 1980s and 1990s, more policies protecting women's health, organizations and research institutions researching issues specifically related to women's health, and media attention on women's health issues began to reach public consciousness.

The women's health movement also taught women how to take control of their own health and well-being by providing education through pamphlets and workshops and with the publication in 1970 of the Boston Women's Health Book Collective's *Women and Their Bodies*, which later became *Our Bodies, Ourselves*, a comprehensive women's health reference guide for women and girls at every stage of their lives. (The most recent edition of *Our Bodies, Ourselves* was published in 2005.) The Boston Women's Health Book Collective believed in providing accurate expert advice and information about women's health issues in an accessible way, so that women could create social change in the health care system, especially as women make up a majority of the health care industry as employees, consumers, and health decision makers for their families. Yet women were underrepresented when decisions about their health were made in the doctors' office, according to governmental policies based on medical research that had been done on men. The Boston Women's Health Book Collective expanded from the kitchen table and library meetings to the Women's Health Information Center in 1980, and the collective was influential in the founding of the National Women's Health Network, the first health advocacy membership organization.

The women's health movement made significant progress with raising awareness about women's health issues, creating access to health care and informing an entire generation of young women and men who are conscious of women's health issues and who are actively engaged in their buying decisions in relation to their health. Still, women's health care issues, such as insurance coverage for contraceptives and proper diagnosis for physical and mental health conditions, remain underrepresented.

Health Insurance. Young women mostly have access to health care coverage through their employer or through Medicaid or Medicare, yet women who work part-time, are in low-paying jobs, or who are self-employed either pay more for their health coverage or are less likely to be covered. According to employment and insurance statistics for women between the ages of twenty-five and thirty-four, white women are most likely to have employer-sponsored health care coverage, followed closely by black and Hispanic women. White and black women have similar rates of employer-sponsored coverage in their own names, but as employer-sponsored family coverage decreases due to high costs for health care coverage, the rate of coverage for black women becomes fewer than one in ten. Latinas in the same age group have the lowest rates of employer-sponsored health insurance coverage overall, most likely because a large proportion of Latinas are employed in low-paying, non-unionized, and/or part-time jobs that do not offer health benefits. Out of low-income women in the twenty-five to thirty-four age group, only 16 percent with incomes below the federal poverty level have employer-sponsored insurance, compared with

89 percent of women who earn incomes that are three times above the poverty level or higher. This increases their health risks, because most poor women cannot afford to pay for their own insurance coverage and additional health care costs.

For many poor women, Medicaid is their best option for health care coverage. Medicaid offers health care coverage with very little out-of-pocket costs. Studies and reports show that poor women covered by Medicaid go to the doctor's more often for regular check ups and have developed relationships with doctors and medical staff, which positively affect their health and well-being. The positive effects of Medicaid coverage for poor women dropped dramatically after the passage of welfare reform—specifically the Personal Responsibility and Work Opportunity Reconciliation Act in 1996—due to new regulations and young, low-income women's misunderstandings about their qualifications for enrollment after cash benefits were eliminated.

Young women who do not receive health benefits through their employers, Medicaid, or Medicare have the lowest rates of health care access, do not go to the doctors on a regular basis, and are unsatisfied with their medical care when they do see a physician. Forty-three percent of poor women between the ages of twenty-five and thirty-four are uninsured: nearly one in five young women do not have health insurance. The ethnic breakdown of uninsured young women is as follows: 35 percent are Latinas, 22 percent are black, and 14 percent are white women. Health information about young Asian/Pacific Islander and Native American women as well as transgender women is virtually non existent.

The leading health risks for young women besides accidents (sudden accidents, assault, and suicide), which are the leading cause of death for women between twenty-five and thirty-four years of age, are heart disease, cancer, mental illnesses such as **depression**, which can lead to suicide and reproductive health factors, and **AIDS**. Two of the best ways young women can prevent heart, cardiovascular, and even mental problems are by eating properly and getting enough exercise. Other major health risks that are preventable but have serious effects on women's health are smoking and alcohol. Health-related problems with smoking that directly affect women include infertility, problems with the menstrual cycle, heart disease, cancer, and emphysema. According to the Substance Abuse and Mental Health Services Administration and National Institute on Drug Abuse studies, white women tend to smoke more than Black and Latina women, despite growing up with public health warning announcements. White women also have higher rates of drinking alcohol than do Black and Latina women.

Heart and cardiovascular disease and cancer rank in the top five illnesses that cause death for women between the ages of twenty-five and thirty-four, according to both the National Center for Health Statistics (2001) and the National Health and Nutrition Examination Survey (2002). These health issues are linked to high cholesterol, diabetes, hypertension (when blood pressure remains high for long periods of time causing stress on the heart, blood vessels, and other organs), obesity, drinking (alcohol), and smoking. Recent studies show that hypertension and cholesterol among young women are decreasing, but rates of obesity continue to increase.

Obesity has been linked with increased risks for heart disease, cardiovascular disease, diabetes, osteoarthritis (most common form of arthritis, caused by the loss of cartilage in the joints, which leads to loss of movement), as well as some varieties of cancer, such as breast (after menopause), endometrium (extra blood causing blood clots in the uterus and in other parts of women's bodies), colon (the intestine that removes food waste from the **body**), kidney (removes liquid waste from the body, stimulates red blood cells, and helps control blood pressure), and esophagus (the tube food follows from the throat to the stomach). Black women experience higher rates of obesity than do white or Hispanic women. Medical and nutrition experts stress the benefits of exercise and eating properly to manage weight as well as other positive effects, yet according to the U.S. Health and Human Services Surgeon General Report (1999), more than 60 percent of women do not meet recommendations for physical activity, and decreases in physical activity are more common among women than men as well as among people who have a lower income and level of education.

There are many healthy ways to manage weight, yet women make up 90 percent of people struggling with **eating disorders**, which include anorexia (starving and rapid weight loss), bulimia (forced vomiting after eating—particularly binge eating), and binge eating (eating huge amounts of food and then controlling weight gain by vomiting leading to bulimia), according to the National Eating Disorders Association. Eating disorders on the surface are related to body image and food but often are the result of much deeper emotional and psychological issues.

Women are more affected by mental health issues than men are. According to the CDC's Vital and Health Statistics Survey in 2003, 14 percent of women feel sad or hopeless all of, most of, or some of the time, and 18 percent of women feel nervous most of the time. Men only felt this way 8 percent and 13 percent of the time, respectively. On top of feeling sad all, most, or some of the time, women were more likely than men to have feelings of everything being an effort, worthlessness, or hopelessness. Families that were poor felt this way twice as much as families that were doing financially well. Black and Hispanic adults (gender and percentages were not specified) felt nervous and anxious as well as hopeless, worthless, and sad all or most of the time. Studying and evaluating mental and anxiety disorders among women is new to physicians and psychologists, so there is little information available to understand mental disorders, especially for young women, despite statistics sited by the American Psychiatric Association that the first sign or experience of depression is experienced during the mid-twenties (this statistic is not gender-specific).

Reproductive health remains to be one of the most pressing issues for young women, especially because young women are becoming sexually active at younger ages (median age is seventeen years old) and marrying at later ages (median age is 25.1 years). Access to and use of proper reproductive health care including regular Pap check-ups, educational materials about sexually transmitted infections and diseases and HIV/AIDS, effective contraceptives, **abortion**, fertility treatments, pregnancy and child birth, and post-pregnancy and infant health needs are vital to the well-being of young women and their families.

Further Reading: Boston Women's Health Collective, *Our Bodies, Ourselves*, New York: Touchstone, 1998; Costello, Cynthia B., Anne J. Stone, and Vanessa R. Wight, *The American Woman 2003–2004: Daughters of a Revolution—Young Women Today*, New York: Palgrave 2003, 93–126; Hornbacher, Marya, *Wasted: A Memoir of Anorexia and Bulimia*, New York: HarperCollins, 1998; http://cis.nci.nih.gov/fact/3_70.htm; http://www.carilion.com/yw/index.html; http://www.cdc.gov/cancer/npcr/uscs/index.htm; http://www.cdc.gov/nccdphp/sgr/ataglan.htm; http://www.cdc.gov/nccdphp/sgr/women.htm; http://www.cdc.gov/nchs/fastats/women.htm; http://www.cdc.gov/ncidod/omwh/; http://www.4woman.gov/YWHS/2002/; http://www.healthywomen.org/; http://www.nationaleatingdisorders.org/p.asp?WebPage_ID=337; http://www.ourbodiesourselves.org/; http://www.womens-health.org/; http://www.youngwomenshealth.org/; http://www2.camh.net/education/public_forums/thereishelp_campaign.html; http://www.4woman.gov/owh/.

HEATHER CASSELL

WOMEN'S HISTORY MONTH. Women's History Month became official in 1987 and celebrates the accomplishments of women throughout history every year in March. Schools, religious organizations, and communities celebrate during the month with presentations, performances, essay and poster contests, parades, discussions, and debates on famous historical women such as Anne Hutchinson, Harriet Tubman, and Rachel Carson. Before the 1970s, little was known about women's lives throughout history. In California in 1978, the Education Task force of the Sonoma County Commission on the Status of Women instigated a Women's History Week to support and expand International Women's Day, March 8. Women's History Week met with great public support and continued to grow and develop in that community. In 1979, a conference was held to further promote Women's History Week in communities across the United States, while also making moves to gain a Congressional Resolution for this celebration. By March of 1980, President Jimmy Carter gave a Presidential Message to encourage the celebration of Women's History Week. That same year, the National Women's History Project (NWHP) was founded to create a clearinghouse of information on women's history and the celebration of Women's History Week. By 1987, a Women's History Month Resolution was approved by Congress with strong bipartisan support in both the House and the Senate. Since 1992, a Presidential Proclamation continues to endorse this international event.

Further Reading: MacGregor, Molly Murphy, *National Women's History Project*, National Women's History Project Web site, http://www.nwhp.org.

LAURA MADELINE WISEMAN

WOMEN'S PROFESSIONAL SPORTS ORGANIZATIONS. Since the mid-1980s, there has been considerable growth in professional opportunities for female athletes. However, the recent failures of high-profile professional soccer and softball leagues demonstrate the difficulties faced by supporters and athletes. Women's professional **sports** organizations exist at a number of levels. Some feature salaried athletes and boast lucrative **media** contracts, but others are professional in name only. Probably the highest-profile league is the Women's National Basketball Association (WNBA). Founded in 1997, it quickly supplanted its **competition** the American Basketball League (ABL), founded in 1996 (eight months before the founding of the WNBA). The ABL folded in 1998, unable to compete with the WNBA, whose relationship with the NBA facilitated access to media contracts and coverage. Women's professional soccer saw the founding of the Women's United Soccer Association (WUSA) in 2001, but because of the same lack of media sponsorship that plagued the ABL, it continues to struggle and its future remains unclear. Reduced to a traveling team in 2004, funding is being sought to allow WUSA to survive. However, the Women's League (W-USL), which had served as a minor league to the WUSA, continues to offer opportunities. A similar fate befell the Women's Professional Softball League. In 1975, a women's professional softball league was inaugurated, but the league folded in 1979. More recently, the Women's Professional Fastpitch Softball League was founded in 1996 and was soon after renamed the Women's Professional Softball League (WPSL). Despite boasting the top softball players in the world, the league struggled and subsequently folded in 2001. Several women's professional football leagues have emerged since the late 1990s, including the National Women's Football Association (NWFA), founded in 2000; the Women's Professional Football League (WPFL), founded in 1999; and the Independent Women's Football League (IWFL), founded in 2003, although founding dates are difficult to pin down as some teams have switched leagues, and some leagues have merged, separated, and evolved. Leagues play American tackle football, a sport that few women have had an opportunity to participate in. Numerous baseball leagues have existed in the past and currently exist, but many are player supported, rather than professional. The All American Girls Professional Baseball League (1943–1954) was started to fill the void left when minor leagues closed down during World War II and represents one of the better known women's opportunities. Unable to sustain attendance in the advent of the television age, the league succumbed to poor attendance and financial losses. The Colorado Silver Bullets offer a single team opportunity for women to play baseball against men's teams. The Silver Bullets played their inaugural game on Mother's Day in 1994, and the team continues to compete today.

Current leagues hope to avoid the pitfalls of the past, high travel costs, poor attendance, and scant media attention. As demonstrated by the WNBA's success, the bulk of profits and operating costs are earned through media contracts, so the pursuit of these seems necessary to success. Historically, women's sports leagues have lacked the media support, sponsorship, and audience building activity necessary to maintain a professional sports league. The increase in media outlets, such as the expansion of cable networks and Web-based media, may facilitate change along these lines.

In addition, numerous regional leagues, including, but not limited to football, baseball, rugby, and softball, exist across the United States. In smaller leagues, players are often unpaid and may pay their own travel expenses. These leagues are significant because they offer women the opportunity to gain experience in and demonstrate women's proficiency at sports—often sports traditionally deemed inappropriate for women. Women's participation in sports that have traditionally been defined as "male" and in women's professional sport leagues is a major concern for third-wave **feminism** because ideas about athleticism and the **body** are one of the last holdouts for assumptions about gender **essentialism**.

See also Hamm, Mia; Nike

Further Reading: Smith, Lisa, ed., *Nike Is a Goddess: The History of Women in Sports*, New York: Atlantic Monthly Press, 1998; http://www.coloradosilverbullets.org/; http://members.aol.com/booinla/; http://www.soccernova.com/working/women/leagues.htm; http://www.womensfootballassociation.com; http://www.wnba.com/.

FAYE LINDA WACHS

WOMEN'S STUDIES VERSUS GENDER STUDIES. Women's studies programs developed in the late 1960s and early 1970s as an aspect and a manifestation of the second wave of **feminism**. Second-wave feminists were informed and shaped, in part, by the Civil Rights movement, and by the New Left, both of which advocated for changes in political institutions. As a part of the Civil Rights movement, black studies programs (and later, ethnic studies programs) had already been established to challenge traditional curriculum, and women's studies programs used them as models for building a program and challenging the institution and the canonical **body** of academic knowledge. Women's studies programs were initiated, in part, as a place to theorize, enact, and initiate feminist activist ideals, in particular within the field of education. In this sense, they were seen as the academic branch of feminism.

Colleges and universities have long been bastions of male power and influence. The numbers of females as faculty and as students were historically limited, and the curriculum taught was traditionally male-centered and biased. In 1960, only 19 percent of all faculty in U.S. colleges and universities were female. By 1995, that number had stabilized at 35 percent. In 1972, females received 44 percent of all Bachelor's degrees, though that number rose to 56 percent by 1997. However, in 1972, females received only 16 percent of PhDs awarded, and by 1997 that number had risen to 39 percent.

In addition to demographics, traditional curriculum was perceived as male-centered, focusing on men, men's history, men's literature, and men's issues. Consequently, the explicit goals of women's studies programs were to include women and women's issues in the curriculum and to alter the fundamental structure of the institution of education. Further, because the institution is individualistic and hierarchical, women's studies faculty introduced communal and collective teaching, scholarship, and learning as part of a feminist ideal. Because feminist **ideology** recognizes the interconnectivity of all knowledge, women's studies programs are fundamentally interdisciplinary, a notion that already challenges the traditional institutional structure. Women's studies professors were often dedicated to a new, radical pedagogy, which was consciously aware of the ways in which traditional modes of teaching perpetuated inequalities. They introduced nonhierarchical and collaborative teaching methods and included students in discussions instead of lecturing. These teaching techniques are now common within other disciplines in higher education.

The first women's studies programs were established in 1969 at San Diego State University and Cornell University. By 1976, the number of universities or colleges offering courses in women's studies had increased to more than 250. In 1978 the number was more than 300; in 1989 it was more than 500, and in 2000 it had reached 600.

However, it is now being debated whether women's studies is the best name for what takes place within these programs, and some programs are changing their names to replace "women" with "gender." This shift is, in part, the consequence of the shift from second-wave feminism to third-wave feminism and attempts to address the universalization of the category of "woman." According to the women's studies Web site at the University of Maryland, as of July 2004 there were 399 programs, departments, majors, or minors offered in women's studies. In addition, there are fifty-two that offer a degree in women's and gender studies, thirty-two in gender studies, four in feminist and gender studies, and three in feminist studies. In addition, there is one program in Jewish women's studies; one in Africana women's studies; one in ethnic and women's studies; three in women's, gender, and **sexuality** studies; two in multicultural and gender studies; one in ethnic and gender; one in gender and sexuality; one in feminist, gender, and sexuality; one in religion, gender, and sexuality; one in sex, gender, and reproduction; one in feminist psychology and women's sexuality; one in feminist, gender, and sexuality; one in women, science, and technology; and one in masculine and feminine studies.

Those who advocate for the shift to gender studies suggest that the name is more inclusive; that it engages men in the conversation as well as women, and that the idea of gender necessarily includes men, because everyone has a gender. They also argue that the change would help programs that are now beginning to suffer a drop in enrollment and a lack of institutional support. In addition, they suggest that gender is a relational system, and therefore "women" cannot be examined without also examining "men." Ideologically, third-wave feminists have argued that the category "women" does not exist as a universal and that the shift to gender studies would eliminate the reduction of all women to a white, middle-class, heterosexual standard. Finally, they argue that the name women's studies perpetuates the universality of men as the norm. In this sense, women are defined as whatever men are not.

Those who contend that the original name should be kept argue that it shifts the focus away from the original intent of women's studies. Although the numbers of women within the academy have improved, and the content of the curriculum across all disciplines reflects, to some degree, the influence of a female-centered object of inquiry, the institution remains fundamentally male-centered. They argue that women's studies continues to empower women who were formerly disempowered within the education system. In addition, they argue that it would shift away from the sexual inequality that still exists in society. Furthermore, they argue that the term "gender studies" is too limiting. Women's studies examines all aspects of women's lives, but gender studies concentrates only on the question of gender. Finally, they contend that the name shift accommodates men. Although women's studies has always included and been open to men, most men have felt uncomfortable within a field of study called women's studies. As women have historically been marginalized within the curriculum, many see the shift to gender studies as step backward, making room for men in a space that had been carved out for women.

Nevertheless, as more programs attempt to be more inclusive, to expand the definition of woman, to incorporate the plurality of sexualities, to recognize the interrelation of gender, ethnicity, sexuality, and class, to represent the changes in society at large, and to represent the incorporation of women's studies ideologies and practices into the academy, the names of these programs will reflect these shifts in priorities. Given the third wave's emphasis on these ideas, many in the third wave would align themselves with gender studies.
See also Feminism, First, Second, Third Waves

Further Reading: Aaron, Jane, and Sylvia Walby, eds., *Out of the Margins: Women's Studies in the Nineties*, London: Falmer Press, 1991; Butler, Johnella E., and John C. Walter, eds., *Transforming the Curriculum: Ethnic Studies and Women's Studies*, Albany, NY: SUNY Press, 1991; Cranny-Francis, Anne, Wendy Waring, Pam Stavropolous, and Joan Kirby, eds., *Gender Studies: Terms and Debates*, London: Palgrave Macmillan, 2003; Howe, Florence, ed., *The Politics of Women's Studies: Testimony from Thirty Founding Mothers*, New York: The Feminist Press, 2000; Howe, Florence, and Paul Lauter, *The Impact of Women's Studies on the Campus and the Disciplines*, Washington, D.C.: The National Institute of Education, 1980; Hull, Gloria T., Patricia Bell Scott, and Barbara Smith, eds., *All the Women Are White, All the Blacks Are Men, but Some of Us Are Brave: Black Women's Studies*, Old Westbury, NY: The Feminist Press, 1982; Moraga, Cherríe, and Gloria Anzaldúa, eds., *This Bridge Called My Back: Writings by Radical Women of Color*, Watertown, MA: Persephone Press, 1981; O'Barr, Jean Fox, *Feminism in Action*, Chapel Hill: The University of North Carolina Press, 1994; O'Connor, Blumhagen, Kathleen Johnson, and Walter D. Johnson, eds., *Women's Studies: Contributions in Women's Studies, Number 2*, Westport, CT: Greenwood Press, 1978; Polity Press, *The Polity Reader in Gender Studies*, Cambridge, MA: Polity Press, 1994; Queen, Carol, and Lawrence Schimel, *Pomosexuals: Challenging Assumptions about Gender and Sexuality*, San Francisco: Cleis Press, 1997; Scott, Joan Wallach, ed., *Women's Studies* on the Edge, Bloomington: Indiana University Press, 1999; Stimpson, Catherine, and Nina Kressner Cobb, *Women's Studies in the United States*, New York: Ford Foundation, 1986.

RITCH CALVIN

WOMEN'S WORK. Women's work is any labor, either paid or unpaid, that women are traditionally expected to do. Women's work is a third-wave feminist issue because in the twenty-first century women expect to work, either in a job that supports their livelihood or in a chosen profession, no matter their class and financial status. According to the Federal **Glass Ceiling** Commission, women and minorities make up 57 percent of the workforce in the United States, and the number continues to increase. According to Catalyst, a research, networking, and advocacy organization for professional and business women, women in the workforce will increase by 10 million by 2010. In addition to the increased number of women working, in another study, *Women and Men in U.S. Corporate Leadership: Same Workplace, Different Realities* (2004), Catalyst established that nearly as many women as men have set goals to make it into the executive office. Contrary to **media** stories about women who have "opted out"—that is, jumped off the career track to have children—Catalyst found that women are satisfied with their careers and the choices they made to get to where they are.

Historically, women's work has been housework and raising children, but taking a position as a housekeeper or a governess qualified as valid employment opportunities for many single women. It was not until the nineteenth and twentieth centuries that women's work expanded into nursing, social work, and **education**. By the end of the twentieth century, women began to and continue to enter many professions such as law, medicine, politics, finance, and other professional fields that were once dominated by men. Although women continue to enter the workplace in record numbers, barriers to advancing, such as the **wage gap**, sexism, **sexual harassment**, and other issues in every industry, continue to limit women's contributions and advancement. Women face challenges that range from their exclusion from the informal social networks that lead to career advancement, to being interrupted by coworkers and **family** during projects, to their work and contributions being undervalued and not recognized, to sexist and racist behavior in the workplace.

Housework and raising children remains to be women's responsibility, as very few daily tasks and very little accountability is assigned to men. According to the United Nations Development Programme's Human Development Report, in 1995 women's unpaid and underpaid labor was estimated to be worth $1.4 trillion in the United States and up to $11 trillion globally. The International Wages for Housework Campaign, an organization devoted to getting women's unpaid work to be recognized and measured by governments as labor that should be included in national and global calculations for production, has been successful in their lobbying endeavors through their International Women Count

Network (IWCN). As of 2002, legislation for counting women's unpaid labor in two nations, Trinidad/Tobago and Spain, has passed, and many other nations, such as Canada, Japan, and Australia, are working on surveys to determine the time spent on unpaid housework. The importance of including women's unpaid work in production calculations is that this will provide a more accurate measure of all of the following: what it really takes for a society to actually function; how much inequality remains to be eliminated; the myths about men as the "breadwinners"; and women's contributions to society, therefore establishing entitlement to legal, economic, civil, and other rights to better their lives. An assessment of the value of women's unpaid work will raise the value of all labor in general.

Women's work in general is undervalued, and industries where women dominate from general labor up to management positions continue to be underpaid, as in professional fields such as nursing, social work, and education. Increasingly, women are taking more leadership roles in nonprofit organizations, labor unions, and government in both local and national positions, but there continues to be a gender imbalance in leadership roles and wages. According to a report about executive positions in nonprofit organizations compiled by the Department of Economics and Institute of Labor and Industrial Relations in 2000, nearly 19 percent of all nonprofit organizations are run by women. Since union organizing began in the nineteenth century, women have participated in strengthening union organizing through their leadership and support, but women remain underrepresented in leadership roles and executive and board positions in unions. Currently, there is only one woman, Wendy Thompson, president of UAW Local 235 in Detroit, who holds a national executive union position out of the 111 national unions. However, this is changing as women's membership increases while men's participation in unions continue to decline, and as the larger society devalues unions and union organizing. Women's increased membership in unions is shifting the focus of their policies and goals to consider and actively mobilize around sexism, children, medical, and other issues that affect women and their families as a whole.

Women are rapidly advancing in government positions. As of 1997, women made up 33.4 percent of official and administrator positions in local and state government. This was a 2.1 percent increase since 1990. Women also make up 42.8 percent of Federal workers, according to the U.S. Office of Personnel Management, yet women continue to be assigned to administrative support positions rather than leadership roles. While women make up the support team in many federal, state, and civil service jobs, women have gained important elective and appointed offices. At the beginning of the twenty-first century, women hold 13.6 percent of the seats in Congress, 14 percent of the seats in the Senate, and 13.6 percent of the seats in the House of Representatives, and three women serve as delegates to Guam, the Virgin Islands, and Washington, D.C. Across the nation, women hold seventy-nine state-elected executive seats. Women's leadership in government agencies and elected offices has proven to improve women's and girls' lives, as well as better family well-being through creating public policies and passing legislation that takes multiple issues into account, such as the Family Medical Leave Act of 1996, that affect men, women, girls, and families.

Women are making their way into positions of power and influence not only in the government and public sector but also in corporate America. Here their progress has been slower. According to the U.S. Bureau of Labor Statistics and Catalyst, as of 2005 only eight women have been promoted to Chief Executive Officer (CEO) positions in Fortune 500 companies in the United States. According to a Catalyst study in 2001, women make up 12.4 percent of Fortune 500 and 10.9 percent in Fortune 1000 companies board of directors. Most women remain trapped in mid-management and in "pink collar" administrative and clerical support jobs, positions that do not lead to advancement and are low paying. According to the U.S. Department of Labor statistics in 2002, 1.5 million jobs were administrative support and office management in a number of industries. The industries where women have been successful rising to the top are often retail, public relations, human resources, and publishing. However, where women dominate the upper levels of the workforce, their salaries are lower than in male-dominated industries such as securities (trading stocks), technology, or science. Women's best bets for success in corporate America are to seek out industries that are in transition, such as those going through deregulation or restructuring or that are fast growing. Yet women continue to strive for management and executive level positions in more traditional professions until they are faced with the realities of being passed up for promotions, being left out of the unofficial social networking, struggling to find mentors, and other factors that keep them from reaching the top.

In the face of these challenges, many women choose to take positions in smaller companies where they have more control of their professional and personal lives or strike out onto their own by opening their own businesses. According to data collected by the Center for Women's Business Research, an organization for women business owners, in 2002 nearly half of all privately owned businesses in the United States were either co-owned or owned by women and employed 18.1 million people. Women's businesses in 2002 generated $2.3 trillion. Women have been business owners in the United States since colonial times to the present, and the number of women going into their own businesses continues to grow. Owning a business provides women with the control and flexibility to manage their professional and personal lives, resulting in greater satisfaction.

See also Opting Out

Further Reading: Center for Women in Government, "The Changing Government Workforce in States and Localities 1990–1997," New York State Library, Albany, New York: 2000, http://www.nysl.nysed.gov/scandoclinks/ocm50554870.htm; Costello, Cynthia B., Anne J. Stone, and Vanessa R. Wight, eds., *The American Woman 2003–2004: Daughters of a Revolution—Young Women Today*, New York: Palgrave, 2003; Hallock,

Kevin F., *The Gender Pay and Employment Gaps for Top Managers in U.S. Nonprofits*, Urbana-Champaign: University of Illinois Press, 2002; http://college.hmco.com/history/readerscomp/women/html/wh_039900_womensbureau.htm; http://college.hmco.com/history/readerscomp/women/html/wh_019600_laborunions.htm; http://seattlepi.nwsource.com/brothers/156308_joyce28.html; http://womenshistory.about.com/library/prm/blwomeninlaborunions1.htm; http://www.bls.gov/oco/print/ocos127.htm; http://www.business.uiuc.edu/hallock/Papers/gender01122002.pdf; http://www.catalystwomen.org/bookstore/files/tid/tidbits04.pdf; http://www.catalystwomen.org/press_room/factsheets/COTE%20Factsheet%202002.pdf; http://www.census.gov/Press-Release/www/2000/cb00-47.html; http://www.ceogo.com/OTHER/WOMENCEOS/; http://www.cluw.org/; http://www.cwig.albany.edu/2000BookPDFBuild.pdf; http://www.enterprisingwomenexhibit.org/; http://www.equalrights.org; http://hdr.undp.org/reports/global/1995/en/pdf/hdr_1995_overview.pdf; http://www.inmotionagazine.com/glass.html; http://www.labornotes.org/archives/2002/10/i.html; http://www.9to5.org; http://www.opm.gov/employ/women/intro.htm; http://www.womenlegislators.org/facts/; Tannen, Deborah, *Talking from 9–5: Women and Men at Work*, New York: Quill, 2001; U.S. Office of Personnel Management, "Introduction," *Guide to Recruiting and Retaining Women in the Federal Government*, Washington, D.C.: June 1998, 1–2.

HEATHER CASSELL

WRITERS, FANTASY/SCIENCE FICTION. Science **fiction** and fantasy, once derided genres, are experiencing increased popularity within millennial popular culture and have always been a resource for third-wave **feminism**. Within science fiction history and criticism, Mary Shelley (1797–1851) is considered to be the "mother" of science fiction. She gave birth to the genre with the publication of her novel, *Frankenstein, or, the Modern Prometheus* (1818). In her novel, she warns of the dangers of scientific experimentation for the wrong reasons and argues for scientific responsibility. After Shelley, science fiction became identified with male writers such as Jules Verne (1828–1905) and H. G. Wells (1866–1946), and during the late-nineteenth and early-twentieth centuries, science fiction was driven primarily by the rapid scientific and technological changes in society and was often a glorification of scientific achievement.

Defining science fiction has always been both difficult and contentious. However, science fiction critic and scholar Darko Suvin provides a model and methodology for defining science fiction, distinguishing it from mainstream fiction and differentiating between science fiction and fantasy. According to Suvin, science fiction is defined by the "new element" (*novum*) that is introduced into the fictional world. This new element can be introduced into the Actants (characters, aliens), the Social Order (society, social structure, government), the Topography (landscape, machinery), or the Natural Laws. The first three produce a sense of estrangement or newness that distinguishes science fiction from mainstream fiction, but introducing a *novum* into the Natural Laws differentiates science fiction from fantasy. These new elements give rise to questions such as what it means to be human, and how our society should be organized. Raising these kinds of questions makes it possible to explore questions of gender, race, **sexuality**, and **patriarchy**. However, these questions were not explored much until the 1960s.

In the 1960s, a major shift took place within the field of science fiction. The New Wave was heralded in with the publication of two influential anthologies: *Dangerous Visions* (1967), edited by Harlan Ellison, and *England Swings* (1968), edited by Judith Merril. While nineteenth-century and early-twentieth century science fiction was characterized by hard science, plot-driven stories, and very little literary value, New Wave science fiction of the 1960s was characterized by a turn away from hard science toward the "soft sciences"—psychology, sociology—and toward a more literary aesthetic. As a consequence, more women began writing and reading science fiction.

Because of the ways in which it analyzes and questions human beings and their relationship to one another and to society, science fiction became the primary medium for second-wave feminists' expression of a **desire** for social change. These feminist science fiction writers tended to adopt traditional genre forms (space opera, alien contact) and adapt them by adding strong female characters or by feminizing the narrative. However, they were particularly adept at using the form of the utopian or dystopian novel. Examples include Monique Wittig's *Les Guérillères* (1969), Suzy McKee Charnas's *Walk to the End of the World* (1974), Naomi Mitchison's *Solution Three* (1975), Joanna Russ' *The Female Man* (1975), Marge Piercy's *Woman on the Edge of Time* (1976), Sally Miller Gearheart's *The Wanderground* (1978), Pamela Sargent's *The Shore of Women* (1986), Margaret Atwood's *The Handmaid's Tale* (1986), and Sherry S. Tepper's *Gate to Women's Country* (1988). These novels tended to examine patriarchal social structures and the effects on women, but they also tended to represent women as a homogeneous whole, rather than represent the individuality and difference of women. Consequently, the utopian novel begins to disappear as the third wave began to focus more on difference and individuality.

One of the writers who best exemplifies the desire to represent women in their diversity and individuality is Octavia Butler. One of the two most prominent African American science fiction writers, Butler has written the five-volume *Patternist* series (*Patternmaster*, 1976; *Mind of My Mind*, 1977; *Survivor*, 1978; *Wild Seed*, 1980; and *Clay's Ark* 1984), the three-volume *Xenogenesis* series (*Dawn*, 1987; *Adulthood Rites*, 1988; *Imago*, 1989), and the *Parable* series (*Parable of the Sower*, 1993; *Parable of the Talents*, 1998). In these novels, Butler introduces racial and ethnic diversity into her narratives, and she examines the question of otherness through alien contact. Butler was once the only female woman of color writer in the field, but writers such as Jewelle Gomez (*The Gilda Stories*, 1991), Tananarive Due (*The Between*, 1995), and Nalo Hopkinson (*Brown Girl in the Ring*, 1998) have recently joined her.

Another important development within the field of science fiction was the emergence of cyberpunk in the mid-1990s. Although the generic characteristics are complex, two significant elements are the emotionless characters and the incorporation of technology into people's lives and bodies. Whereas the second-wave feminist science fiction writers often shunned technology as a masculine mode of oppression and exploitation and tried to revalue emotion as a positive characteristic, writers such as Pat Cadigan (*Synners*, 1991), Laura J. Mixon (*Glass Houses*, 1992), Amy Thomson (*Virtual Girl*, 1993), and Wilhelmina Baird (*Crashcourse*, 1993) create strong female characters who are hard, cold, and emotionless and who have embraced technology fully.

The area where third-wave science fiction is most apparent is in **film** and **television**. The films *Alien* (1979), *Aliens* (1986), *Alien 3* (1992), and *Alien Resurrection* (1997) introduce Ellen Ripley, a strong, intelligent female protagonist who displays a balance between masculine and feminine characteristics. She guns down aliens with one hand while holding onto Newt, the young orphaned girl she rescues, with the other. The films *The Terminator* (1984) and *Terminator 2: Judgment Day* (1991) introduce Sarah Connor, who similarly battles the robots that threaten her son, John. Neither of these women advocates a utopian space, but rather they fight their own battles for personal survival.

Late-1990s and early-2000 television series such as *The X-Files* (1993–2002), *Xena, Warrior Princess* (1995–2001), *Buffy the Vampire Slayer* (1997–2003), *Dark Angel* (2000–2001), *Alias* (2001–) all feature young women who are technologically savvy, skilled in physical combat, culturally or media-connected, and, sometimes, comfortable with their sexuality. While Xena, Max from *Dark Angel*, and Sydney from *Alias* exploit their sexuality to further their fight, Scully from *The X-Files* and Buffy are much more cautious about embracing their sexuality. Regardless of these differences, science fiction in its written and visual modalities has become a major resource for and expression of third-wave feminist thinking.

Further Reading: Barr, Marleen S., *Future Females: A Critical Anthology*, Bowling Green, OH: Bowling Green State University Popular Press, 1981; Barr, Marleen S., *Future Females, the Next Generation: New Voices and Velocities in Feminist Science Fiction Criticism*, Lanham, MD: Rowman & Littlefield, 2000; Barr, Marleen S., *Lost in Space: Probing Feminist Science Fiction and Beyond*, Chapel Hill: University of North Carolina Press, 1993; Flanagan, Mary, and Wayne Booth, *Reload: Rethinking Women and Cyberculture*, Cambridge, MA: MIT Press, 2002; Helford, Elyce Rae, *Fantasy Girls: Gender in the New Universe of Science Fiction and Fantasy Television*, Lanham, MD: Rowman & Littlefield, 2000; Kuhn, Annette, *Alien Zone: Cultural Theory and Contemporary Science Fiction Cinema*, New York: Verso Press, 1990; Larbalestier, Justine, *The Battle of the Sexes in Science Fiction*, Middletown, CT: Wesleyan University Press, 2002; Lefanu, Sarah, *Feminism and Science Fiction*, Bloomington, IN: Indiana University Press, 1988; Penley, Constance, *Close Encounters: Film, Feminism, and Science Fiction*, Minneapolis: University of Minnesota Press, 1991; Roberts, Robin, *A New Species: Gender and Science in Science Fiction*, Urbana, IL: University of Illinois Press, 1993; Russ, Joanna, *To Write Like a Woman: Essays in Feminism and Science Fiction*, Bloomington, IN: Indiana University Press, 1995; Wolmark, Jenny, *Aliens and Others: Science Fiction, Feminism, and Postmodernism*, Iowa City: University of Iowa Press, 1994.

RITCH CALVIN

WRITING, THIRD-WAVE FEMINIST. Reflecting the increasingly wide usage of the term "third wave" in contemporary vocabulary, third-wave writing constitutes a steadily expanding list of publications. By definition, writers that can be defined as adding to a **body** of third-wave analysis represent those women who have grown up in a world already shaped by feminist activism, with the result that they take the freedoms for which their foremothers had to fight for granted. However, although an intrinsic element in third-wave thought is a rejection of the idea that one can only call oneself a "feminist" if one signs up to a set list of objectives and beliefs, all third-wave writers are in agreement that women are still unfairly treated in a society which remains biased in favor of men, and that further activism is necessary if the female gender is to achieve real equality. Broadly speaking, therefore, their writings seek to alert women to remaining areas of discrimination and propose various strategies to resist them. What this entry will do is look at the role played by such books in defining what "third-wave **feminism**" actually means, what cultural issues it particularly focuses on, and topics that have emerged as areas of disagreement amongst third-wave writers themselves.

A good example of an early publication that outlines an area of concern that has become central to third-wave feminism is Naomi Wolf's first book, *The Beauty Myth* (1991). Wolf specifically addresses middle-class women in affluent Western societies who have benefited the most from the social and political changes brought about by second-wave feminism, arguing that although women in such societies are freer than they have ever been, they are still being oppressed by what she calls "the beauty myth": the feeling that they still have to conform to certain stereotypes of feminine appearance. However economically or social powerful a woman might be, she can still be psychologically oppressed by the feeling that she is a failure if she is not thin enough, stylish enough, and young enough. Moreover, hugely profitable industries have arisen to help women keep looking thin, stylish, and young. Women have been persuaded that to work on their appearance is an investment that will help them advance socially and professionally, and they are therefore prepared to spend a large amount of time and money on their faces and bodies. But, Wolf asserts, this can lead to psychological and physical damage. Self-loathing for not being "beautiful" can manifest itself in ever more extreme behavior, such as risky cosmetic surgical procedures, bulimia, and anorexia.

In her conclusion, Wolf speculates on ways in which the beauty myth can be counteracted and argues that that it can only be done through the development of a feminist third wave that would uncover and analyze the propaganda that force women into an unhealthy relationship with their own bodies. Women cannot beat the beauty myth alone—indeed, it thrives by forcing women into critical and competitive relationships with each other—and they must therefore work together to develop a more diverse, pleasurable, and self-fulfilling concept of female beauty.

Naomi Wolf has come to occupy a slightly awkward position within third-wave feminism, because she is seen by some to represent a conservative, even backward-looking, point of view. However, the last chapter of *The Beauty Myth* reveals it to be a typically third-wave text in several ways, and not just because of its deliberate use of the term itself. First, it asserts that although the "beauty myth" is wrong, this does not mean that women should necessarily deny the pleasures and satisfaction to be gained by the manipulation of body image. Second, it upholds a concept of diversity in its rejection of any one standard by which "beauty" might be measured. Third, it refutes a simplistic definition of oppression. For Wolf, men are not necessarily the enemy: instead, the beauty myth is the result of cultural forces that are primarily played out within and between women themselves.

Such an approach—a concern with the pleasures and dangers of self-fashioning, an embracing of diversity and difference, and a more sophisticated understanding of oppression which does not place the blame any one gender, class or cultural group—have all become important areas of analysis within third-wave feminist writing. The examination of such concepts leads to a renegotiation with the term "feminist" itself, since a question that is frequently raised in third-wave writing is the extent to which young women who have grown up in a world shaped by a previous generation of feminist activists perceive "feminism" as a label they can attach to themselves.

A form of publication that appears particularly suited to the kind of third-wave approach outlined above is the anthology, because its format allows many different views to be expressed without having to iron out the differences between them. The last ten years or so have seen the appearance of a number of influential essay collections, including *Feminist Fatale: Voices from the "Twentysomething" Generation Explore the Future of the Women's Movement* (1991), edited by Paula Kamen; Barbara Findlen's *Listen Up: Voices from the Next Feminist Generation* (1995); *To Be Real: Telling the Truth and Changing the Face of Feminism*, edited by Rebecca Walker (1995); Leslie Heywood and Jennifer Drake's *Third Wave Agenda: Being Feminist, Doing Feminism*; and **Ophira Edut**'s *Adios, Barbie* (1998). What all these books have in common is a **desire** to articulate a sense of the third wave as a movement that can encompass different points of view and a whole range of different lifestyles and preoccupations.

Acting on this belief, many of the essays included in such collections take the form of first-person, autobiographical narratives that testify to the multiplicity of female experience. In *To Be Real* (1995), for example, Naomi Wolf's critique of the **marriage** industry sits alongside Jason Schultz's argument that men should develop a feminist sexual sensitivity. **Bell hooks** writes on the need to include an aesthetic dimension to the black liberation movement, and Donna Minkowitz confesses to finding **rape** fantasies erotic. None of these accounts can be assimilated into some kind of homogenous party line, as they focus on a variety of topics and are narrated from a wide range of subject positions—Korean American attorney, white lesbian feminist, black sex worker, blue-collar Chicana, white heterosexual male feminist, black homosexual journalist—none of which is privileged over another. *Listen Up*, which was also published in 1995, is very similar, as it includes the voices of black, white, Jewish, Christian, atheist, Chicana, heterosexual, lesbian, bisexual, middle-class and working-class women united in a medley of accents, angles, and preoccupations. What all the writers have in common is their commitment to feminism; but race, gender, sexual orientation, class, and occupation inescapably influence even that. The message that is central to all these collections of essays, therefore, is that there is no one way to be a feminist. Modern feminism emerges in these publications as inclusive and flexible, not as a set of conditions with which everyone that wishes to call themselves "feminists" must agree.

However, on occasion third-wave writing tends to emphasize this belief by suggesting that their ideas constitute a point of departure from the more inflexible **ideology** of the second wave, which is intolerant of young women's attempts to transform the movement. The contributors to *To Be Real* and *Listen Up*, for example, seem anxious to distance themselves from the cultural stereotype of the second-wave "women's-libber"—humorless, intolerant, bra-burning, and unkempt. Indeed, older feminists' attempts to comment on or participate in third-wave debates have sometimes been regarded rather warily. Gloria Steinem, a prominent activist in the second-wave feminist movement—who not only wrote a foreword to *To Be Real* but also has continued to publish her own feminist manifestos, such as *Revolution from Within* (1992) and *Moving Beyond Words* (1994)—was labeled a "dinosaur" in some quarters of the third-wave movement. And in 1998, when Phylis Chesler published a direct address to her feminist successors, *Letter to a Young Feminist*, it received only luke-warm reviews from its intended audience.

Furthermore, third-wave writing's use of the anecdotal and the autobiographical can raise problems. On the one hand, the use of personal testimonies constitutes a powerful way of alerting readers to the many facets of female experience in contemporary culture. But on the other, these stories may not appear to be situated within a framework that would look for the common links between them in order to construct a wider, more analytical examination of the social roles allocated to women within society.

This is one of the points made in Leslie Heywood and Jennifer Drake's introduction to *Third Wave Agenda: Being Feminist, Doing Feminism* (1997). While they acknowledge the value of the personal story in third-wave writing, the editors also stress that the essays contained in their collection constitute an attempt to combine the personal with a more incisive analysis grounded in cultural theory. In addition, they express a concern that some of the contributors to earlier publications are in danger of appearing to belittle the achievements of the second wave. Contradicting the notion that the second wave solidified into an inflexible system that either actively excluded or deliberately ignored many facets of female experience, Heywood and Drake assert that the embracing of contradiction is in fact a view that second and third waves have in common. Instead, one of *Third Wave Agenda*'s primary concerns is to separate "third wave" from another term with which it is often assumed to be analogous: "**postfeminism**." Heywood and Drake characterize postfeminism as an inherently conservative movement; a vantage point from which its white, middle-class spokeswomen can mount attacks on the feminist politics of the second wave. The third wave, on the other hand, should be regarded as the natural successor to the second-wave struggle, not its antagonist. The third wave's belief in the assimilation, but not the elimination, of difference, is therefore presented in this book as the next phase of feminism, which is evolving to reflect the increasingly multifaceted, divergent nature of modern women's lives, seeking out connections without denying the existence of irreconcilable differences.

In fact, conflict and difference emerges as a central topic in several third-wave analyses. In *Bitch: In Praise of Difficult Women* (1999) and *Catfight: Rivalries Among Women—From Diets to Dating, from the Boardroom to the Delivery Room* (2002), Elizabeth Wurtzel and Leora Tanenbaum reject idealistic notions of "sisterhood." Wurtzel's first book, the autobiographical *Prozac Nation* (1997), won her public notoriety as a controversial and outspoken cultural commentator, a reputation she sought to further in her study of women who are socially disruptive. Wurtzel interweaves cultural analysis with the personal and confessional: her epilogue, for instance, explores how she feels about still being single and childless at the point of turning thirty. Each chapter of *Bitch* examines a different "bitchy" persona: the femme fatale, the sexually obsessive teenager, the madwoman, the wife, the woman who remains faithful to a violent man. What all these figures have in common is their enormous capacity to damage themselves, those around them, or both. Although potent cultural icons—a point Wurtzel makes through reference to a range of examples drawn from literature, **film**, and the media—none of them are sympathetic figures for feminism. Wurtzel, however, tries to rehabilitate, or at least rationalize, the disruptive patterns of behavior these women exemplify, arguing that any female who transgresses social norms runs the risk of being labeled a **bitch**, when in fact she may just be trying to achieve some kind of autonomy out of limited range of options. Wurtzel does not discount the seductiveness of the bitch persona, which is associated with exhibitionism and unrestrained behavior, but she also seeks to uncover the damage and desperation that lurks beneath the glamorous façade.

Leora Tanenbaum's *Catfight* similarly rejects the idealistic notion that feminism has led to increased cooperation between women. The target of her analysis, though, is not just the mad, bad, and dangerous but also all women everywhere. Echoing Naomi Wolf's argument regarding the persistence of the beauty myth published twelve years earlier, Tanenbaum claims that feminism's success has not eliminated competitive female relationships; on the contrary, it has deepened them. Thanks to feminism, women have far easier access to roles outside the home, yet they are still constrained by traditional models of **femininity** that pressures them to marry, have children, and maintain a high standard of attractiveness. Tanenbaum maintains that the adoption of such feminine roles automatically entails entering into a competitive relationship with other women. And, as Wolf has said of the beauty myth, Tanenbaum observes that the consequence of all this rivalry is isolation and self-hatred, since the cycle of conflict is never-ending. There is always another battle to be fought, which is a tragic misdirection of energy that would be better used in continuing the fight for **equal rights**. Consequently, Tanenbaum argues that women should accept themselves and their many and various lifestyles and ambitions, in the understanding that in order to effectively work to change the world around them, they must band together personally, professionally, and politically.

However, although Tanenbaum includes in her conclusion a list of suggestions as to how individual women can begin to establish supportive relationships between themselves—complimenting others on their appearance, mentoring junior colleagues in the workplace, helping a new mother with childcare, and so on—the issue of how women might begin to effect change within the wider political arena is not dealt with quite so explicitly. A criticism frequently leveled at third-wave feminism is that it is purely concerned with frivolous images of personal **empowerment** (e.g., the right to wear lipstick and short skirts and still be a feminist), but that it has not evolved a political agenda that would make it an effective successor to the second wave.

Such a critique is the starting point for the monumental *Manifesta: Young Women, Feminism, and the Future* by **Jennifer Baumgardner and Amy Richards**, published in 2000. Its ambitious project is to define the modern feminist movement, its relationship with its precursors, what its objectives should be, and how such objectives could be achieved. Like many commentators within the third wave, Baumgardner and Richards are particularly preoccupied with tracing the links between past and present manifestations of feminism and to issue a new call to activism. Although they acknowledge that there are many young women who hesitate to call themselves feminists, Baumgardner and Richards argue that they have nevertheless inherited a legacy which is, whether acknowledged or not, inescapably feminist. They describe how a crusading third-wave feminism has become an integral part of American culture, manifesting itself in such bodies as Third Wave Direct Action and **Third Wave Foundation**, the Riot Grrrl movement of the early nineties, and the "**Girlie**" ideology promoted in **magazines** such as *Bust* and *Bitch*. In typical third-wave fashion, though, Baumgardner and Richards do not seek to eliminate the differences between these various movements but argue that, taken together, they indicate a rising tide of feminist activism within American society that is, slowly but surely, making gains for women at every level. Toward the end of the book, the authors issue their thirteen-point "third-wave manifesta." This takes the form of a series of objectives toward which the new feminist movement should work, such as encouraging young women to identify themselves as feminists, encourage men to take more responsibility for sexual health and **family** plan-ning, to increase the public visibility of lesbian and bisexual women, and to make the workplace more responsive to women's needs.

Manifesta is not the last word on third-wave feminism—it was, after all, published nearly five years ago—but it does self-consciously position itself as a pivotal text within the movement. The tenor of Baumgardner and Richards' argument is that the third wave has reached the point where it must take itself seriously as a mature and effective force for change. Young feminists should negotiate with their older predecessors in order to impress upon them that they have reached maturity and no longer need to be "mothered," however benignly. The various manifestations of the third wave should agree to work towards the general directives contained within the book's "manifesta." Fur-thermore, each individual who identifies herself (or himself) as a feminist should be aware of their individual power to act as an effective activist who contrib-utes towards the success of the larger movement.

In conclusion, it can be said that third-wave writing constitutes a vibrant addition to the feminist canon. Like second-wave theory before it, it represents the diversity of the movement, combining personal testimony with sophisticated cultural and political analysis, and it does so often in the same volume. Some of the main issues it deals with are the attempt to renegotiate the relationship between young and old feminists; the examination of the significance of beauty and body image within a feminist context; and the redefinition of the relation-ships between women and men, and between women themselves. Finally, much third-wave writing acts as a call to action for young women who are seeking for a form of feminism which is uniquely their own. It is time for the next generation to redefine the feminist movement in accordance with their own immediate and pressing concerns.

See also Beauty Ideals; Competition, Women and; Feminism, First, Second, Third Waves; Postfeminism; Victim/Power Feminism; Wolf, Naomi

Further Reading: Baumgardner, Jennifer, and Amy Richards, eds., *Manifesta*, New York: Farrar, Straus and Giroux, 2000; Edut, Ophira, ed., *Body Outlaws*, rev. ed., Emeryville, CA: Seal Press, 2003; Findlen, Barbara, ed., *Listen Up* (expanded edition), Emeryville, CA: Seal Press, 2001; Freedman, Estelle, *No Turning Back*, New York: Ballantine Books, 2003; Heywood, Leslie, and Jennifer Drake, eds., *Third Wave Agenda*, Minneapolis: University of Minnesota Press, 1997; Kamen, Paula, ed., *Feminist Fatale*, New York: Plume Books, 1991; Tanenbaum, Leora, *Catfight*, New York: Seven Stories Press, 2002; Walker, Rebecca, ed., *To Be Real*, New York: Anchor Books, 1995; Wolf, Naomi, *The Beauty Myth*, New York: W. Morrow, 1991; Wurtzel, Elizabeth, *Bitch*, New York: Doubleday, 1998.

Sarah Gamble

Y

YOUTH CULTURES, FEMINIST. Today a group of young people, whose age range moves downward to include girls as young as thirteen, are partaking in feminist youth cultures. In keeping with third-wave **feminism** generally, their judgments are based on the lived experiences of girls themselves and not just on external and/or abstract ideas. In further keeping with third wave, these girls break down binary notions of either/or dualistic thinking by recognizing the differences among girls and girlhood. Youth cultures are an attempt to move beyond the traditional notion of female adolescence as the experience of "becoming women" (who marry men) and toward an understanding of girlhood as a distinct period in a female's life cycle. Youth cultures make space available for conversation that is determined by youth. In them, girls express themselves and recognize the importance of their lived experiences. They relate their own ideas and receive those of other young women through such instruments as zines, videos, and **music**. In these ways, youth cultures help girls foster their own **empowerment**.

Youth cultures reclaim the label "Girl" from its usual association with immaturity. Girlhood itself is seen as socially constructed and therefore differing over time and geography. Instead of romanticizing girlhood, it is accepted that, in a patriarchal and often misogynist society, many female adolescents face oppressions as their bodies transform from symbols of childhood and innocence to mature **sexuality**. It is recognized that even today in the United States where female youth is allegedly liberated, girls now are encumbered by a "double future." They must prepare to become both homemaker and paid laborer.

While there are many versions of these cultures, at their core they are seen by feminist youth cultures scholars like Kum-Kum Bhavani, Kathryn R. Kent, and Frances Winndance Twine as a place for youth to exercise agency. This ability, however, is usually constrained, within the intersections of age, gender, sexuality race/ethnicity, religion, nationality, and class oppressions. While girls are conscious actors, they are also ones who negotiate their identities within their class, cultural, and racial/ethnic contexts. Examples of girls' constrained agency can be seen in contemporary U.S. literary works such as *The House on Mango Street* (1991) by Sandra Cisneros and *Beloved* (1987) by Toni Morrison.

Feminist youth today do, nonetheless, have a variety of ways to express resistance. Among these are the above mentioned zines, videos, music, comics, and other such forms of expression. Additional examples include sex radicalism, public policy work, environmental activism, and socialist youth activity. These examples illustrate that while the spheres of the larger dominant culture and of commodity capitalism are sites of domination, they also contain sites where resistance can occur.

Youth cultures are important to Western feminism today. They emphasize areas that have not received adequate attention in the past. Recently published university press books reveal an increasing number of ethnographies, historical studies, music studies, and sociological analyses of girls. While these works tend to remain Euro-American and predominantly heterosexual in focus, related activities in the larger popular culture often do not. The experimental works of white lesbian U.S. video artist Sadie Benning and Chicana author Catriona Rueda Esquibel are illustrative. Bhavnani, Kent, and Twine, the feminist youth culture scholars noted, state that Benning's videos of herself in her bedroom are individual privatized acts of cultural production that can be seen as forms of activism that have potentially wide-ranging political and community-building effects. In "Memories of Girlhood: Chicana Lesbian Fiction," Esquibel specifically describes the formation of girls' sexual identity in Chicana communities. She also notes the presence of these girls in popular culture areas: visual, musical, technological, and print. Numerous other productions of videos ethnographies, zines, Internet groups, and music by youth exist today.

Riot Grrrl is seen by many scholars who study girls' youth cultures in the United States (such as Ednie Kaeh Garrison) as illustrative of the young feminist movement. Riot Grrrl was a group of young, independent female rock groups that began playing in the early 1990s. Networks of Riot Grrrls have been created from the fans of this movement, with chapters across the United States. Riot Grrrls encourage other girls to stand up for themselves. The most common means of communication for the Riot Grrrl community, the zine, can work as a method of empowerment. Zine activity is self-motivated, political activism that a girl can do entirely independently. The Internet provides a space where many girls can comfortably challenge something they do not believe in. When girls feel isolated because they disagree with the dominant culture, they have a network of people (albeit in **cyberspace**) they can turn to and rely on. The feminism of Riot Grrrl is self-determined and grassroots. It gives girls room to decide for themselves who they are, while providing a viable alternative to the popular media-created ideals. For these "punk rock girls" and for other girls and women who produce zines and music that are not necessarily punk, the production of a new movement space is politically powerful.

Feminist youth culture is an important aspect of **feminist theory** and activism in the United States today. In youth cultures like Riot Grrrl, where girls are able to theorize from their own experiences, many girls are empowered to defy patriarchal attempts to define their personhood and sexualize them. The Riot Grrrl example of youth cultures supplies a forum through which girls can both express themselves and support one another. It provides a model of (very) young women empowering themselves to resist patriarchal identity formation. They do so at a time in their lives when the patriarchal culture generally exerts a particularly heavy hand in silencing them, while demanding highly sexualized gender conformity of them. The importance of resistance to both patriarchal and capitalist commodity culture on the part of pubescent girls probably cannot be stressed enough.

See also Communications Technology; McRobbie, Angela; Music, Zines

Further Reading: Bhavnani, Kum-Kum, Kathryn R. Kent, and Frances Winddance Twine, eds., "Feminism and Youth Cultures," *Signs* (special issue) 23(3) (1998); Garrison, Ednie, "U.S. Feminism—Grrrl Style Youth (Sub)Cultures and the Technologics of the Third Wave," *Feminist Studies* 26(1) (2000): 141–169.

COLLEEN MACK-CANTY

Z

ZINES. A crucial third-wave feminist tool for activism and expression, although "zine" is short for "magazine," the term does not refer to all **magazines**. It is usually reserved for underground pamphlets that are assembled and distributed independently of mainstream commercial publishing companies. The zine is seen as one of the most important third-wave feminist outlets and forms of expression. As alternative publications, zines are not restricted by established conventions regarding style and content. This freedom is a primary motivation among zine publishers, and the resulting zines are as different as the writers and artists who create them. Some zines are professionally typeset and printed in batches as small as 1,000 copies, but most are assembled by hand in even smaller batches of a few copies to a few hundred copies. Some are photocopied collections that combine cut-and-paste collage with handwritten, typed, or drawn elements, while others use more sophisticated desktop publishing and graphics software. Indeed, the increased availability of photocopiers and personal computers has enabled many otherwise ordinary people to publish their own zines. The construction of a zine can range from several stapled sheets of office paper to an intricately sewn booklet of handmade paper. Some zines are released in scheduled installments, and some are released sporadically. Some contain artwork, **poetry**, or **fiction**, and some contain personal narratives or social and political commentary. These amateur publications are reminiscent, on the one hand, of the political pamphlets circulated in the pre-Revolutionary, eighteenth-century United States and U.K. and, on the other hand, of high school newspapers and church newsletters. In recent years, many zines have begun to offer online content to reiterate or reinforce their print content. Some even exist exclusively online, though these are more accurately referred to as electronic zines, or e-zines.

Zines are often linked to a specific activity, lifestyle, or subculture. There are zines associated with vegetarian cooking, punk rock, and science fiction, to name just a few examples. Other examples include zines published by feminists, often with an explicitly feminist focus. Many feminists, particularly those identified as the third wave, embrace the **DIY** (do it yourself) attitude that is characteristic of zine publishers, and many participate in well-defined subcultures that serve as informal networks for the circulation of their zines. As already noted, there is a great deal of variety among zines, and feminist zines are no exception. In fact, their stylistic and thematic variations mirror the variations within third-wave **feminism**. In many ways, third-wave feminism has emerged as a reaction by many younger feminists against the perceived rigidity and exclusivity of earlier forms of feminism. As such, it does not consist of a unified set of attitudes or beliefs. Thus, feminist zines, like the people who create them, are as likely to celebrate the experiences of sex workers as they are to condemn the sex industry as a matter of principle; they are as likely to promote political activism as they are to denounce politics altogether; and they are as likely to feature sewing patterns, recipes, and **fashion** advice as they are to denigrate traditional feminine roles.

A significant insight of third-wave feminism is that experience is inherently subjective, and this subjectivity is often conveyed through the use of personal narratives that make no attempt at objectivity. Many zines employ personal narrative, including some zines that read more like private diaries than magazines in any conventional sense. Even zines that lack such narrative structure, however, including those that consist entirely of material assembled from other sources, also offer insight into the subjectivity of those who control their content. By far the most common are those zines that combine different literary and artistic styles, and these styles may or may not include the personal narrative. In such cases, the subjectivity that is presented to the audience appears in a nonlinear or disjointed form, rather than as an uninterrupted sequence of thoughts or ideas. In this sense, zines are effective, both individually and collectively, at conveying confused, conflicting, or even contradictory responses to the gendered experiences of many girls and women. Third-wave feminism is as interested in exploring the subjectivity of gendered experience as second-wave feminism was in prescribing straightforward strategies for fighting sexism. While this does not mean that activism has no place within third-wave feminism, it does mean that third-wave activism often looks quite different from the activism of second-wave feminists. In many cases, the third-wave struggle against sexism takes place internally, as girls and women work to define or redefine their identities and their feminism. Zines give public expression to this private process.

The subject matter of feminist zines is as varied as the literary and artistic forms through which it is conveyed. For instance, there are zines dedicated to promoting women artists and musicians, as well as zines that highlight local political events; there are zines that employ creative writing to convey visions of a better world, as well as zines that reveal the excruciating details of such painful experiences as **rape** and **abortion**; there are zines that critique the mainstream media, as well as zines that celebrate popular culture; there are zines that address lesbian, bisexual, and transgender identities, as well as zines that explore experiences of heterosexuality and motherhood. It is important to recognize that virtually anyone can publish a zine, and there is no mechanism in place to control content or credentials. Zine publishing requires very little equipment or expertise, and the production costs are often defrayed by charging minimal fees, requesting donations, or arranging trades with other zine publishers. The informality and inclusiveness of zine culture lends itself to the expression of the diverse perspectives and interests within third-wave feminism.

See also DIY; *Volume 2, Primary Documents 50 and 54*

Further Reading: Duncombe, Stephen, *Notes from Underground: Zines and the Politics of Alternative Culture*, New York: Verso, 1997; Green, Karen, and Tristan Taormino, eds., *A Girl's Guide to Taking Over the World: Writings from the Girl Zine Revolution*, New York: St. Martin's Griffin, 1997; Rowe, Chip, *The Book of Zines: Readings from the Fringe*, New York: Owl Books, 1997; Vale, V., *Zines! Volume One*, San Francisco: Re/Search Publications, 1996; Vale, V., *Zines! Volume Two*, San Francisco: Re/Search Publications, 1996.

MIMI MARINUCCI

Selected Bibliography

Acker, Kathy. *Essential Acker: The Selected Writings of Kathy Acker*. New York: Grove Press, 2002.

Adams, Carol. *The Sexual Politics of Meat: A Feminist-Vegetarian Critical Theory*. New York: Continuum, 1990.

Adler, Margot. *Drawing Down the Moon: Witches, Druids, Goddess-Worshippers, and Other Pagans in America Today*. New York: Penguin, 1997.

Ahmed, Leila. *Women and Gender in Islam: Historical Roots of a Modern Debate*. New Haven, CT: Yale University Press, 1993.

Anzaldúa, Gloria. *Borderlands/La Frontera: The New Mestiza*. San Francisco: Aunt Lute Books, 1987.

———. *Making Face, Making Soul/Haciendo Caras: Creative and Critical Perspectives by Feminists of Color*. San Francisco: Aunt Lute Books, 1990.

Auth, Janice. *To Beijing and Beyond: Pittsburgh and the United Nations Fourth World Conference on Women*. Pittsburgh: University of Pittsburgh Press, 1998.

Balsamo, Anne. *Technologies of the Gendered Body: Reading Cyborg Women*. Durham, NC: Duke University Press, 1996.

Barr, Marleen S. *Future Females, the Next Generation: New Voices and Velocities in Feminist Science Fiction Criticism*. Lanham, MD: Rowman & Littlefield, 2000.

——— *Lost in Space: Probing Feminist Science Fiction and Beyond*. Chapel Hill, NC: University of North Carolina Press, 1993.

Bauer, Thomas, and Bob McKercher, eds. *Sex and Tourism: Journeys of Romance, Love and Lust*. New York: Haworth Hospitality Press, 2003.

Baumgardner, Jennifer, and Amy Richards. *Manifesta: Young Women, Feminism and the Future*. New York: Farrar, Straus and Giroux, 2000.

———. *Grassroots: A Field Guide to Feminist Activism*. New York: Farrar, Straus and Giroux, 2005.

Baxandall, Rosalyn, and Linda Gordon, eds. *Dear Sisters: Dispatches from the Women's Liberation Movement*. New York: Basic Books, 2000.

Becker, Gay. *The Elusive Embryo: How Women and Men Approach New Reproductive Technologies*. Berkeley: University of California Press, 2000.

Blackwell, Maylei, Linda Burnham, and Jung Hee Choi, eds. *Time to Rise: US Women of Color—Issues and Strategies*. Oakland, CA: Women of Color Resource Center, 2001.

Blea, Irene I. *U.S. Chicanas and Latinas within a Global Context: Women of Color at the Fourth World Women's Conference*. Westport, CT: Praeger, 1997.

Bloom, Lisa, ed. *With Other Eyes: Looking at Race & Gender in Visual Culture*. Minneapolis: University of Minnesota Press, 1999.

Bordo, Susan. *Unbearable Weight: Feminism, Western Culture, and the Body*. Berkeley: University of California Press, 1993.

Bornstein, Kate. *Gender Outlaw: On Men, Women and the Rest of Us*. New York: Routledge, 1995.

Boston Women's Health Collective. *Our Bodies, Ourselves*. New York: Touchstone, 1998.

Brand, Peg Zeglin. *Beauty Matters*. Bloomington: Indiana University Press, 2000.

Bright, Susie. *Full Exposure: Opening Up to Your Sexual Creativity*. San Francisco: HarperCollins, 1999.

———. *The Sexual State of the Union*. New York: Simon & Schuster, 1997.

Brunsdon, Charlotte, Julie D'Acci, and Lynn Spigel, eds. *Feminist Television Criticism: A Reader*. New York: Oxford University Press, 1997.

Buchwald, Emilie, Pamela R. Fletcher, and Martha Roth, eds. *Transforming a Rape Culture*. Minneapolis: Milkweed Editions, 1993.

Burke, Phyllis. *Gender Shock: Exploding the Myths of Male & Female*. New York: Anchor Books, 1996.

Butler, Johnella E., and John C. Walter, eds. *Transforming the Curriculum: Ethnic Studies and Women's Studies*. Albany, NY: State University of New York Press, 1991.

Butler, Judith. *Bodies That Matter: On the Discursive Limits of Sex*. New York: Routledge, 1993.

———. *Excitable Speech: A Politics of the Performative*. New York: Routledge, 1997.

———. *Gender Trouble: Feminism and the Subversion of Identity*. 2nd ed. New York: Routledge, 1999.

Canning, Charlotte. *Feminist Theatres in the U.S.A.: Staging Women's Experiences*. New York: Routledge, 1996.

Carlip, Hillary. *Girl Power: Young Women Speak Out*. New York: Warner Books, 1995.

Case, Sue-Ellen, ed. *Performing Feminisms: Feminist Critical Theory and Theatre*. Baltimore: Johns Hopkins University Press, 1990.

Chancer, Lynn. *Reconcilable Differences: Confronting Beauty, Pornography, and the Future of Feminism*. Berkeley: University of California Press, 1998.

Chapkis, Wendy. *Live Sex Acts: Women Performing Erotic Labor*. New York: Routledge, 1997.

Cherney, Lynn, and Elizabeth Reba Wise. *Wired Women: Gender and New Realities in Cyberspace*. Seattle, WA: Seal Press, 1996.

Chesler, Phyllis. *Woman's Inhumanity to Woman*. New York: Thunder's Mouth/Nation Books, 2002.

Chicago, Judy. *Women and Art: Contested Territory*. New York: Watson-Guptill, 1999.

Cogan, Jeanine, and Joanie M. Erickson. *Lesbians, Levis and Lipstick: The Meaning of Beauty in Our Lives*. San Francisco: Harrington Park Press, 1999.

Collins, Patricia Hill. *Black Feminist Thought: Knowledge, Consciousness, and the Politics of Empowerment*. New York: Routledge, 1990.

Connell, Robert. *Gender*. Cambridge: Polity Press, 2002.

Cornell, Drucilla, ed. *Feminism and Pornography*. New York: Oxford University Press, 2000.

Costello, Cynthia B., Anne J. Stone, and Vanessa R. Wight. *The American Woman 2003–2004: Daughters of a Revolution—Young Women Today*. New York: Palgrave, 2003.

Costello, Cynthia B., Shari Miles, Anne J. Stone, eds. *American Woman: 1999–2000: A Century Of Change—What's Next?* New York: W.W. Norton, 1998.

Coupland, Douglas. *Generation X: Tales for an Accelerated Culture*. New York: St. Martin's Press, 1991.

Cranny-Francis, Anne, Wendy Waring, Pam Stavropolous, and Joan Kirby, eds. *Gender Studies: Terms and Debates*. London: Palgrave Macmillan, 2003.

Crow, Barbara A., ed. *Radical Feminism: A Documentary Reader*. New York: New York University Press, 2000.

Cuomo, Chris J. *Feminism and Ecological Communities*. Routledge: New York, 1998.

Currah, Paisley, and Shannon Minter. *Transgender Equality: A Handbook for Activists and Policymakers*. San Francisco: National Center for Lesbian Rights and Policy Institute of the National Gay and Lesbian Task Force, 2000.

Davis, Angela Y. *Blues Legacies and Black Feminism*. New York: Vintage, 1998.

———. *Women Culture & Politics*. New York: Random House, 1989.

Davis, Kathy. *Reshaping the Female Body: The Dilemma of Cosmetic Surgery*. New York: Routledge, 1995.

DeBare, Ilana. *Where Girls Come First: The Rise, Fall, and Surprising Revival of Girls' Schools*. New York: Jeremy P. Tarcher/Penguin, 2004.

DeBord, Guy. *Society of the Spectacle*. New York: Zone Books, 1995.

Denfeld, Rene. *The New Victorians*. New York: Warner Books, 1996.

Devor, Holly. *FTM: Female to Male Transexuals in Society*. Bloomington: Indiana University Press 1999.

Diamond, Elin. *Unmaking Mimesis: Essays on Feminism and Theater*. New York: Routledge, 1997.

Diamond, Irene, and Gloria Feman Orenstein, eds. *Reweaving the World: The Emergence of Ecofeminism*. San Francisco: Sierra Club Books, 1990.

Dicker, Rory, and Alison Piepmeier, eds. *Catching a Wave: Reclaiming Feminism for the 21st Century*. Boston: Northeastern University Press, 2003.

Douglas, Susan. *Where the Girls Are: Growing Up Female with the Mass Media*. New York: Random House, 1994.

Douglas, Susan, and Meredith Michaels. *The Mommy Myth: The Idealization of Motherhood and How It Has Undermined Women*. New York: Free Press, 2004.

Dow, Bonnie. *Prime-Time Feminism: Television, Media Culture, and the Women's Movement since 1970*. Philadelphia: University of Pennsylvania Press, 1996.

Drill, Esther, Heather McDonald, and Rebecca Odes. *Deal With It: A Whole New Approach to Your Body, Brain and Life as a Gurl*. New York: Pocket Books, 1999.

Duncombe, Stephen. *Notes from Underground: Zines and the Politics of Alternative Culture*. New York: Verso, 1997.

Early, Frances, and Kathleen Kennedy, eds. *Athena's Daughters: Television's New Women Warriors*. Syracuse, NY: Syracuse University Press, 2003.

Edut, Ophira, ed. *Adios, Barbie: Young Women Write about Body Image and Identity*. Seattle: Seal Press, 1998.

———. *Body Outlaws*. rev. ed. Emeryville, CA: Seal Press, 2003.

Edwards, Tim. *Men in the Mirror: Men's Fashion, Masculinity and Consumer Society*. London: Continuum, 1997.

Ehrenreich, Barbara, and Arlie Russell Hochschild, eds. *Global Woman: Nannies, Maids, and Sex Workers in the New Economy*. New York: Henry Holt, 2002.

Elshtan, Bethke Jean. *Women and War*. New York: Basic Books, 1987.

Ensler, Eve. *The Vagina Monologues*. New York: Villard, 2001.

Fallon, Patricia, Melanie A. Katzman, and Susan C. Wooley, eds. *Feminist Perspectives on Eating Disorders*. New York: Guilford Press, 1994.

Faludi, Susan. *Backlash: The Undeclared War against American Women*. New York: Anchor Books, 1991.

———. *Stiffed: The Betrayal of Modern Man*. New York: 2000.

Fausto-Sterling, Anne. *Sexing the Body: Gender Politics and the Construction of Sexuality*. New York: Basic Books, 2000.

Faux, Marian. *Roe v. Wade*. New York: Cooper Square Publishers, 2000.

Feinberg, Leslie. *Transgender Warriors: Making History from Joan of Arc to Dennis Rodman*. Boston: Beacon Press, 1996.

Feldt, Gloria. *The War on Choice: The Right-Wing Attack on Women's Rights and How to Fight Back*. New York: Bantam Books, 2004.

Fernandez, Maria, Faith Wilding, and Michelle Wright, eds. *Domain Errors: Cyberfeminist Practices*. New York: Autonomedia, 2002.

Fernea, Elizabeth Warnock. *In Search of Islamic Feminism: One Woman's Global Journey*. New York: Doubleday, 1998.

Findlen, Barbara, ed. *Listen Up: Voices from the Next Feminist Generation*. Seattle, WA: Seal Press, 1995.

Fine, Carla. *Strong, Smart and Bold: Empowering Girls for Life*. New York: Harper Resource, 2001.

Fineman, Martha Albertson, and Roxanne Mykitiuk, eds. *The Public Nature of Private Violence: The Discovery of Domestic Abuse*. New York: Routledge, 1994.

Flanagan, Mary, and Wayne Booth. *Reload: Rethinking Women and Cyberculture*. Cambridge, MA: MIT Press, 2002.

Flanders, Laura, ed. *The W Effect: Bush's War on Women*. New York: The Feminist Press, 2004.

Frankenberg, Ruth. *White Women, Race Matters: The Social Construction of Whiteness*. Minneapolis: University of Minnesota Press, 1993.

Freedman, Estelle. *No Turning Back*. New York: Ballantine Books, 2003.

Gaard, Greta. *Ecological Politics: Ecofeminists and the Greens*. Philadelphia: Temple University Press, 1998.

Gellar, Jaclyn. *Here Comes the Bride: Women, Weddings, and the Marriage Mystique*. New York: Four Walls Eight Windows, 2001.

Gillan, Maria Mazziotti, and Jennifer Gillan, eds. *Unsettling America*. New York: Penguin, 1993.

Gilligan, Carol. *Between Voice and Silence: Women and Girls: Race and Relationships*. Cambridge, MA: Harvard University Press, 1996.

Gillis, Stacy, Gillian Howie, and Rebecca Munford, eds. *Third Wave Feminism: A Critical Exploration*. London: Palgrave Macmillan, 2004.

Gold, Jodi, and Susan Villari, eds. *Just Sex: Students Rewrite the Rules on Sex, Violence, Activism, and Equality*. Lanham, MD: Rowman and Littlefield, 2000.

Gore, Ariel. *Atlas of the Human Heart*. Seattle: Seal, 2003.

Gore, Ariel, and Bee Lavender, eds. *Breeder: Real-Life Stories from the New Generation of Mothers*. Seattle: Seal Press, 2001.

Gray, Heather M., and Samantha Phillips. *Real Girl Real World: Tools for Finding Your True Self*. Seattle, WA: Seal Press, 1998.

Green, Karen, and Tristan Taormino, eds. *Girl's Guide to Taking Over the World: Writings from the Girl Zine Revolution*. New York: St. Martin's Griffin, 1997.

Guerrilla Girls, The. *Bitches, Bimbos and Ballbreakers: The Guerrilla Girls' Illustrated Guide to Female Stereotypes*. New York: Penguin, 2003.

———. *The Guerrilla Girls' Bedside Companion to the History of Western Art*. New York: Penguin, 1998.

Hagan, Kay Leigh, ed. *Women Respond to the Men's Movement*. San Francisco: Pandora, 1992.

Halberstam, Judith. *The Drag King Book*. London: Serpent's Tail, 1999.

———. *Female Masculinity*. Durham, NC: Duke University Press, 1998.

Hall, M. Ann. *Feminism and Sporting Bodies*. Champaign, IL: Human Kinetics, 1996.

Haraway, Donna. *The Haraway Reader*. New York: Routledge, 2004.

———. *Simians, Cyborgs and Women: The Reinvention of Nature*. New York: Routledge, 1991.

Havenden, Fiona, Gill Kirkup, Linda Janes, and Kathryn Woodward, eds. *The Gendered Cyborg: A Reader*. New York: Routledge, 2000.

Hawley, John Stratton, ed. *Fundamentalism and Gender*. New York: Oxford University Press, 1994.

Hawthorne, Susan, and Renate Klein, eds. *Cyberfeminism: Connectivity, Critique and Creativity*. North Melbourne, Vic: Spinifex Press, 1999.

Helford, Elyce Rae. *Fantasy Girls: Gender in the New Universe of Science Fiction and Fantasy Television*. Lanham, MD: Rowman & Littlefield, 2000.

Henry, Astrid. *Not My Mother's Sister: Generational Conflict and Third Wave Feminism*. Bloomington: University of Indiana Press, 2004.

Hernández, Daisy, and Bushra Rehman, eds. *Colonize This! Young Women of Color on Today's Feminism*. Seattle: Seal Press, 2002.

Hesse-Biber, Sharlene. *Am I Thin Enough Yet?: The Cult of Thinness and the Commercialization of Identity*. New York: Oxford University Press, 1996.

Heywood, Leslie. *Pretty Good for a Girl*. Minneapolis: University of Minnesota Press, 2000.

Heywood, Leslie, and Jennifer Drake, eds. *Third Wave Agenda: Being Feminist, Doing Feminism*. Minneapolis: University of Minnesota Press, 1997.

Heywood, Leslie, and Shari L. Dworkin. *Built to Win: The Female Athlete as Cultural Icon.* Minneapolis: University of Minnesota Press. 2003.

Hirsch, Marianne, and Evelyn Fox Keller, eds. *Conflicts in Feminism.* New York: Routledge, 1990.

Hogeland, Lisa Maria. *Feminism and Its Fictions: The Consciousness-Raising Novel and the Women's Liberation Movement.* Philadelphia: University of Pennsylvania Press, 1998.

Hollows, Joanne. *Feminism, femininity and popular culture.* Manchester, UK: Manchester University Press, 2000.

hooks, bell. *Black Looks: Race and Representation.* Cambridge, MA: South End Press, 1992.

———. *Feminist Theory: From Margin To Center.* 2nd ed. Cambridge, MA: South End Press, 2000.

———. *Outlaw Culture: Resisting Representations.* New York: Routledge, 1994.

Hornbacher, Marya. *Wasted.* New York: Harper Perennial, 1999.

Howe, Florence, and Paul Lauter. *The Impact of Women's Studies on the Campus and the Disciplines.* Washington, D.C.: The National Institute of Education, 1980.

Inness, Sherrie A., ed. *Action Chicks: New Images of Tough Women in Popular Culture.* New York: Palgrave Macmillan, 2004.

———, ed. *Delinquents & Debutantes: Twentieth Century American Girls' Cultures.* New York: New York University Press, 1998.

———, ed. *Millennium Girls: Today's Girls around the World.* Lanham, MD: Rowman & Littlefield, 1998.

Jagose, Annamarie. *Queer Theory: An Introduction.* New York: New York University Press, 1997.

James, Stanlie, and Claire Robertson. *Genital Cutting and Transnational Sisterhood: Disputing U.S. Polemics.* Urbana: University of Illinois Press, 2002.

Jenkins, Keith, ed. *The Postmodern History Reader.* New York: Routledge, 1997.

Johnson, Merri Lisa, ed. *Jane Sexes It Up: True Confessions of Feminist Desire.* New York: Four Walls Eight Windows, 2002.

Jones, Amelia, ed. *The Feminism and Visual Culture Reader.* New York: Routledge, 2002.

Jones, Lisa. *Bulletproof Diva: Tales of Race, Sex and Hair.* New York: Anchor Books, 1995.

Juhasz, Alexandra. *Women of Vision.* Minneapolis: University of Minnesota Press, 2001.

Juno, Andrea. *Angry Women in Rock: Volume One.* San Francisco: Juno Books, 1996.

Kamen, Paula. *Her Way: Young Women Remake the Sexual Revolution.* New York: Broadway, 2002.

Kaplan, E. Ann. *Feminism and Film.* New York: Oxford University Press, 2000.

Karaian, Lara, ed. *Turbo Chicks: Talking Young Feminisms.* Toronto: Sumarch Press, 2001.

Karp, Marcelle, and Debbie Stoller, eds. *The Bust Guide to the New Girl Order.* New York: Penguin Books, 1999.

Kelly, Joe. *Dads and Daughters: How to Inspire, Understand, and Support Your Daughter.* New York: Broadway Books, 2003.

Kember, Sarah. *Cyberfeminism and Artificial Life.* New York: Routledge, 2002.

Kempadoo, Kamala, and Jo Doezema, eds. *Global Sex Workers: Rights, Resistance and Redefinition*. New York: Routledge, 1998.

Kilbourne, Jean. *Can't Buy My Love: How Advertising Changes the Way We Think and Feel*. New York: Touchstone, 2000.

Kim, Elaine H., ed. *Making More Waves: New Writings by Asian American Women*. Boston: Beacon Press, 1997.

Kimmel, Michael, ed. *The Politics of Manhood: Profeminist Men Respond to the Mythopoetic Men's Movement*. Philadelphia: Temple University Press, 1995.

Kiss and Tell. *Her Tongue on My Theory: Images, Essays and Theories*. Vancouver: Press Gang, 1994.

Klein, Naomi. *No Logo: No Space No Choice No Jobs*. 2nd ed. New York: Picador, 2002.

Knapp, Caroline. *Appetites: Why Women Want*. New York: Counterpoint Press, 2003.

Labaton, Vivien, and Dawn Lundy Martin, eds. *The Fire This Time: Young Activists and the New Feminism*. New York: Anchor Books, 2004.

Larbalestier, Justine. *The Battle of the Sexes in Science Fiction*. Middletown, CT: Wesleyan University Press, 2002.

Lay, Mary M., Janice J. Monk, and Deborah S. Rosenfelt, eds. *Encompassing Gender: Integrating International Studies and Women's Studies*. New York: Feminist Press, 2002.

Lefanu, Sarah. *Feminism and Science Fiction*. Bloomington: Indiana University Press, 1988.

Looser, Devoney, and E. Ann Kaplan, eds. *Generations: Academic Feminists in Dialogue*. Minneapolis: University of Minneapolis Press, 1997.

Lorber, Judith. *Paradoxes of Gender*. New Haven, CT: Yale University Press, 1994.

Lord, M.G. *Forever Barbie: The Unauthorized Biography of a Real Doll*. New York: William Morrow, 1994.

Lorde, Audre. *Sister Outsider—Essays and Speeches by Audre Lorde*. Freedom, CA: The Crossing Press, 1984.

Louie, Miriam Ching Yoon. *Sweatshop Warriors: Immigrant Women Workers Take on the Global Factory*. Cambridge, MA: South End Press, 2001.

Lublin, Nancy. *Pandora's Box: Feminism Confronts Reproductive Technology*. Lanham, MD: Rowman and Littlefield, 1998.

Macy, Sue, and Jane Gottsman. *Play Like a Girl: A Celebration of Women in Sports*. New York: Henry Holt, 1999.

Maglin, Nan Bauer, and Donna Perry, eds. *"Bad Girls"/"Good Girls": Women, Sex, and Power in the Nineties*. New Brunswick, NJ: Rutgers University Press, 1996.

Maher, Frances A., and Mary Kay Thomson Tetreault. *The Feminist Classroom*. New York: Basic Books, 2001.

Manji, Irshad. *The Trouble with Islam: A Muslim's Call for Reform in Her Faith*. New York: St. Martin's Press, 2004.

Mazza, Chris, and Jeffrey DeShell. *Chick-Lit: Postfeminist Fiction*. Evanston, IL: Northwestern University Press, 1995.

Mazza, Chris, Jeffrey DeShell, and Elisabeth Sheffell, eds. *Chick-Lit 2 (No Chick Vics)*. Tallahasse, FL: FC2/Black Ice Books, 1996.

McDonnell, Evelyn, and Ann Powers, eds. *Rock She Wrote: Women Write About Rock, Pop, and Rap*. New York: Dell, 1995.

McElroy, Wendy. *XXX: A Woman's Right to Pornography*. New York: St. Martin's Press, 1995.

McRobbie, Angela. *Feminism and Youth Culture*. New York: Routledge, 2000.

Mernissi, Fatima. *The Veil and the Male Elite: A Feminist Interpretation of Women's Rights in Islam*. Translated by Mary Jo Lakeland. Reading, MA: Addison-Wesley, 1991.

Meyers, Marian, ed. *Mediated Women: Representations of Popular Culture*. Cresskill, NJ: Hampton Press, 1999.

Mies, Maria, and Vandana Shiva. *Ecofeminism*. London: Zed Books, 1993.

Modleski, Tania. *Feminism Without Women: Culture and Criticism in a "Postfeminist" Age*. New York: Routledge, 1991.

Moraga, Cherrie L., and Gloria Anzaldua, eds. *This Bridge Called My Back: Writings by Radical Women of Color*. 3rd ed. Berkeley: Third Woman Press, 2002.

Moreno, Robyn, and Michelle Herrera Mulligan, eds. *Border-Line Personalities: A New Generation of Latinas Dish on Sex, Sass, and Cultural Shifting*. New York: Rayo 2004.

Morgan, Joan. *When Chickenheads Come Home to Roost: A Hip-Hop Feminist Breaks It Down*. New York: Simon and Schuster, 2000.

Morgan, Robin, ed. *Sisterhood Is Forever*. New York: Washington Square Press, 2003.

Muscio, Inga. *Cunt: A Declaration of Independence*. Seattle: Seal Press, 1998.

Nagle, Jill, ed. *Whores and Other Feminists*. New York: Routledge, 1997.

Nam, Vickie. *YELL-Oh Girls!: Emerging Voices Explore Culture, Identity and Growing Up Asian American*. New York: HarperCollins, 2001.

Naples, Nancy, and Manisha Desai, eds. *Women's Activism and Globalization: Linking Local Struggles and Transnational Politics*. New York: Routledge, 2002.

Nestle, Joan, Riki Wilchins, and Clare Howell. *GenderQueer: Voices from Beyond the Sexual Binary*. Los Angeles: Alyson Publications, 2002.

Nicholson, Linda J., ed. *Feminism/Postmodernism*. New York: Routledge, 1990.

O'Barr, Jean Fox. *Feminism in Action*. Chapel Hill: University of North Carolina Press, 1994.

O'Dair, Barbara, ed. *Trouble Girls: The Rolling Stone Book of Women in Rock*. New York: Random House, 1997.

O'Keefe, Tracie. *Finding the Real Me: True Tales of Sex and Gender Diversity*. San Francisco: John Wiley & Sons 2003.

Orenstein, Peggy. *Flux: Women on Sex, Work, Love, Kids, & Life in a Half-Changed World*. New York: Anchor Books, 2000.

————. *Schoolgirls: Young Women, Self-Esteem, and the Confidence Gap*. New York: Random House, 1999.

Penley, Constance. *Close Encounters: Film, Feminism, and Science Fiction*. Minneapolis: University of Minnesota Press, 1991.

Phelan, Peggy. *Unmarked: The Politics of Performance*. New York: Routledge, 1993.

Phelan, Peggy, and Helena Reckitt. *Art and Feminism*. Boston: Phaidon Press, 2001.

Phillips, Anne, ed. *Feminism and Politics*. New York: Oxford University Press, 1998.

Phillips, Lynn M. *Flirting with Danger: Young Women's Reflections on Sexuality and Domination*. New York: New York University Press, 2000.

Phoca, Sophia, and Rebecca Wright. *Introducing Postfeminism*. New York: Totem Books, 1999.

Pipher, Mary. *Reviving Ophelia: Saving the Selves of Adolescent Girls*. New York: Ballantine Books, 1994.

Plant, Sadie. *Zeros + Ones: Digital Women and the New Technoculture*. London: Fourth Estate, 1997.

Pough, Gwendolyn. *Check It While I Wreck It: Black Womanhood, Hip Hop Culture, and the Public Sphere*. Boston: Northeastern University Press, 2004.

Pratt, Minnie Bruce. *S/He*. Ithaca, NY: Firebrand Books, 1995.

Queen, Carol. *Real Live Nude Girl: Chronicles of a Sex-Positive Culture*. San Francisco: Cleis, 1997.

Queen, Carol, and Lawrence Schimel. *Pomosexuals: Challenging Assumptions about Gender and Sexuality*. San Francisco: Cleis Press, 1997.

Rail, Genevieve, ed. *Sport and Postmodern Times*. Albany: SUNY Press, 1998.

Raphael, Amy. *Grrrls: Viva Rock Divas*. New York: St. Martin's Griffin, 1996.

Reger, Jo, ed. *Different Wavelengths: Studies of Contemporary Feminism*. New York: Routledge, 2005.

Reynolds, Simon, and Joy Press. *The Sex Revolts: Gender, Rebellion and Rock 'n' Roll*. Cambridge, MA: Harvard University Press, 1999.

Robbins, Trina. *From Girls to Grrrl: A History of Women's Comics from Teens to Zines*. San Francisco: Chronicle Books, 1999.

Roberts, Robin. *A New Species: Gender and Science in Science Fiction*. Urbana: University of Illinois Press, 1993.

Roiphe, Katie. *The Morning After: Sex, Fear, and Feminism*. Boston: Little, Brown, 1994.

Rose, Tricia. *Black Noise: Rap Music and Black Culture in Contemporary America*. Hanover, NH: Wesleyan University Press, 1994.

———. *Longing to Tell: Black Women's Stories of Sexuality and Intimacy*. New York: Farrar, Straus and Giroux, 2003.

Rosenberg, Jessica, and Gitana Garofalo. "Riot Grrrl: Revolutions from Within." *Signs: Journal of Women in Culture and Society* 23(3) (1998): 809–841.

Ross, Andrew, and Tricia Rose. *Microphone Fiends: Youth Music and Youth Culture*. New York: Routledge, 1994.

Rowe, Chip. *The Book of Zines: Readings from the Fringe*. New York: Owl Books, 1997.

Ruether, Rosemary Radford, ed. *Women Healing Earth: Third World Women on Ecology, Feminism, and Religion*. Maryknoll, NY: Orbis Books, 1996.

Russ, Joanna. *To Write Like a Woman: Essays in Feminism and Science Fiction*. Bloomington: Indiana University Press, 1995.

Ruttenberg, Danya, ed. *Yentl's Revenge: The Next Wave of Jewish Feminism*. Seattle: Seal Press, 2001.

Salomone, Rosemary. *Same, Different, Equal: Rethinking Single-Sex Schooling*. New Haven, CT: Yale University Press, 2003.

Sandoz, Joli, and Joby Winans, eds. *Whatever It Takes: Women on Women in Sports*. New York: Farrar, Straus and Giroux, 1999.

Sanger, Alexander. *Beyond Choice: Reproductive Freedom in the 21st Century*. New York: Public Affairs, 2004.

Savage, Ann. *They're Playing Our Songs: Women Talk About Feminist Rock Music*. Westport, CT: Praeger, 2003.

Schneider, Rebecca. *The Explicit Body in Performance*. New York: Routledge, 1997.

Scott, Joan Wallach. *Feminism and History*. New York: Oxford University Press, 1996.

———, ed. *Women's Studies on the Edge*. Bloomington: Indiana University Press, 1999.

Sedgwick, Eve Kosofsky. *Epistemology of the Closet*. Berkeley: University of California Press, 1990.

Segal, Lynne. *Straight Sex: Rethinking the Politics of Pleasure*. Berkeley: University of California Press, 1994.

Siegel, Carol. *New Millennial Sexstyles*. Bloomington: Indiana UP, 2000.

Siegel, Deborah. *Fighting Words: The 40-Year Struggle for the Soul of Feminism*, forthcoming.

Simmons, Rachel. *Odd Girl Out: The Hidden Culture of Aggression in Girls*. New York: Harcourt, 2002.

Singer, Peter. *Animal Liberation*. New York: Avon Books, 1990.

Smith, Lisa, ed. *Nike is a Goddess: The History of Women in Sports*. New York: Atlantic Monthly Press, 1998.

Snitow, Ann, Christine Stansell, and Sharon Thompson, eds. *Powers of Desire: The Politics of Sexuality*. New York: Monthly Review Press, 1983.

Solinger, Rickie. *Beggars and Choosers: How the Politics of Choice Shapes Adoption, Abortion, and Welfare in the United States*. New York: Hill and Wang, 2001.

Sommers, Christina Hoff. *Who Stole Feminism?: How Women Have Betrayed Women*. New York: Simon and Schuster, 1994.

Spiegel, Marjorie. *The Dreaded Comparison: Human and Animal Slavery*. New York: Mirror Books, 1996.

Stan, Adele, ed. *Debating Sexual Correctness: Pornography, Sexual Harassment, Date Rape, and the Politics of Sexual Equality*. New York: Dell, 1995.

Stith, Anthony. *Breaking the Glass Ceiling: Racism & Sexism in Corporate America: The Myths, the Realities & the Solutions*. Orange, NJ: Bryant & Dillon Publishers, 1996.

Streitmatter, Janice L. *For Girls Only: Making a Case for Single-Sex Schooling*. Albany: SUNY Press, 1999.

Strossen, Nadine. *Defending Pornography: Free Speech, Sex, and the Fight for Women's Rights*. New York: New York University Press, 1995.

Sullivan, Nikki. *A Critical Introduction to Queer Theory*. New York: New York University Press, 2003.

Tanenbaum, Leora. *Catfight: Rivalries Among Women—From Diets to Dating, from the Boardroom to the Delivery Room*. New York: Harper Perennial, 2003.

———. *Slut!: Growing Up Female with a Bad Reputation*. New York: Seven Stories, 1999.

Tannen, Deborah. *Talking from 9–5: Women and Men at Work*. New York: Quill, 2001.

Tuana, Nancy, and Rosemarie Tong, eds. *Feminism and Philosophy: Essential Readings in Theory, Reinterpretation, and Application*. Boulder, CO: Westview, 1995.

Usef, Malike, ed. *Am I the Last Virgin?* New York: Simon Pulse, 1997.

VIBE/SPIN Ventures LLC. *Hip-Hop Divas*. New York: Three Rivers Press, 2001.

Wadud, Amia. *Qur'an and Woman: Rereading the Sacred Text from a Woman's Perspective*, 2nd ed. New York: Oxford University Press, 1999.

Wajcman, Judy. *TechnoFeminism*. Williston, VT: Blackwell Publishing, 2004.

Walker, Rebecca. *Black, White, and Jewish*. New York: Riverhead, 2002.

———, ed. *To Be Real: Telling the Truth and Changing the Face of Feminism*. New York: Anchor Books, 1995.

———, ed. *What Makes a Man: 22 Writers Imagine the Future*. New York: Riverhead, 2004.

Walters, Suzanna Danuta. *Material Girls: Making Sense of Feminist Cultural Theory*. Berkeley: University of California Press, 1995.

Webb, Susan. *Shockwaves: The Global Impact of Sexual Harassment*. Master Media, 1994.

Whelehan, Imelda. *Modern Feminist Thought: From the Second Wave to "Post-Feminism."* New York: New York University Press, 1995.

Whiteley, Sheila. *Women and Popular Music: Sexuality, Identity and Subjectivity*. New York: Routledge, 2000.

Whittle, Stephen. *The Transgender Debate*. Reading, UK: Garnet, 2001.

Wing, Adriene Katherine, ed. *Critical Race Feminism: A Reader*. New York: New York University Press, 1997.

Wiseman, Rosalind. *Queen Bees and Wannabes: Helping Your Daughter Survive Cliques, Gossip, Boyfriends, and Other Realities of Adolescence*. New York: Crown, 2002.

Wolf, Naomi. *The Beauty Myth: How Images of Beauty Are Used Against Women*. New York: W. Morrow, 1991.

———. *Fire with Fire: The New Female Power and How It Will Change the 21st Century*. New York: Random House, 1993.

———. *Promiscuities: The Secret Struggle for Womanhood*. New York: Random House, 1997.

Wolmark, Jenny. *Aliens and Others: Science Fiction, Feminism, and Postmodernism*. Iowa City: University of Iowa Press, 1994.

———, ed. *Cybersexualities: A Reader in Feminist Theory, Cyborgs and Cyberspace*. Edinburgh: Edinburgh University Press, 1999.

Woo, Deborah. *Glass Ceilings and Asian Americans: The New Face of Workplace Barriers*. Lanham, MD: Alta Mira Press, 2000.

Woodward, Kathleen. *Figuring Age: Women, Bodies, Generations*. Bloomington: Indiana University Press, 1999.

Wurtzel, Elizabeth. *Bitch: In Praise of Difficult Women*. New York: Doubleday, 1998.

———. *Prozac Nation*. New York: Riverhead, 1997.

Yuen, Eddie, George Katsiaficas, and Daniel Burton Rose. *The Battle of Seattle: The New Challenge to Capitalist Globalization*. New York: Soft Skull Press, 2001.

Zuckerman, Mary Ellen. *A History of Popular Women's Magazines in the United States, 1792–1995*. Westport, CT: Greenwood Press, 1998.

WEB SITES

Ani DiFranco's Web Site. http://www.righteousbabe.com

Association for Women's Rights in Development (AWID). http://www.awid.org

Audre Lorde Project. http://www.alp.org

Bitch Magazine: Feminist Response to Pop Culture. http://www.bitchmagazine.com

Buddhahnet, Women in Buddhism. http://www.buddhanet.net/mag_nuns.htm

BUST magazine. http://www.bust.com

CEDAW: Treaty for the Rights of Women. http://www.womenstreaty.org

CODEPINK. http://www.codepink.org

DC Kings Home Page. http://www.dckings.com

Documents from the Women's Liberation Movement—An On-line Archival Collection. Special Collections Library, Duke University, http://scriptorium.lib.duke.edu/wlm

Esquibel, Catrióna Rueda. 1997–2003. Queer Chicana Fictions. http://www.chicana-lesbians.com

Eve's Garden Web Site. http://www.evesgarden.com

Feminist Majority, Feminists Against Sweatshops. http://www.feminist.org/other/sweatshops

Fierce magazine. http://www.fiercemag.com

Gay, Lesbian, Bisexual, Transgender, and Queer Encyclopedia Web Site. http://www.glbtq.com

Genders Online Journal. http://www.genders.org/index.html

Girls Inc. http://www.girlsinc.org/ic/index.php

Girl Zine Network. www.girlzinenetwork.com

Go Ask Alice! Columbia University's Health Q&A Services. http://www.goaskalice.columbia.edu

Good Vibrations Web Site. http://www.goodvibes.com

Grrrl Zine Network. http://www.grrrlzines.net

gURL.com. http://www.gurl.com

http://www.theglassceiling.com

http://www.ladyfest.org

http://www.lasculturas.com/lib/libfeminism.htm

http://www.manifesta.com

http://www.ophira.com

http://www.ourbodiesourselves.org

http://www.templeofdiana.org

http://www.womens-health.org

http://www.womensleadership.com

http://www.womensorganizations.org

Jewish Orthodox Feminist Alliance. http://www.jofa.org/about.php?T1=highlights

Lilith: the Independent Jewish Women's Magazine. http://www.lilithmag.com

MAYDELEH: a zine for nice Jewish grrrls. http://www.geocities.com/maydeleh/

Michigan Womyn's Music Festival Web Site. http://www.michfest.com

Muslim Refusenik: The Official Web Site of Irshad Manji, author of *The Trouble with Islam*. http://www.muslimrefusenik.com

Muslim Women's League. http://www.mwlusa.org

National Abortion Rights Action League, Pro-Choice America. NARAL Web Site. http://www.naral.org

National Coalition Against Domestic Violence. http://www.ncadv.org

National Institute of Mental Health Web Site. Spearing, Melissa. "Eating Disorder: Facts about Eating Disorders and the Search for Solutions." http://www.nimh.nih.gov/publicat/eatingdisorders.cfm

National Organization for Single-Sex Public Education. http://www.singlesexschools.org/evidence.html

National Women's Alliance. http://www.nwaforchange.org

National Women's History Project Web Site. http://www.nwhp.org

Planned Parenthood's Web site for teenagers. http://www.teenwire.com

Pop Matters: The Magazine of Global Culture. http://www.popmatters.com

Rebecca Walker's Web Site. http://www.rebeccawalker.com

Reel Women, non-profit organization in Austin, Texas that provides a local support system for women at all levels of experience in the film and video industries. http://www.reelwomen.org

Rockrgrl magazine. http://www.rockrgrl.com

The Scholar & Feminist Online. http://www.barnard.edu/sfonline

Sexing the Political: A Journal of Third-Wave Feminists on Sexuality. http://www.sexingthepolitical.com

Soapbox, Inc. http://www.soapboxinc.com

Society for Women in Philosophy Web Site. http://www.uh.edu/~cfreelan/SWIP/bodyimage.html

Susie Bright's Web Site. http://www.susiebright.com

Third Wave Foundation. http://www.thirdwavefoundation.org

Tricia Rose Web Site. http://www.triciarose.com

United Nations Division for the Advancement of Women (DAW). The United Nations Forth World Conference on Women. The United Nations Web Site. http://www.un.org/womenwatch/daw/beijing/index.html

United Nations Development Fund for Women (UNIFEM). http://www.unifem.org

Women and The Economy, UN Platform for Action Committee. http://www.unpac.ca

Women in the Director's Chair. http://www.widc.org

Women Make Movies. http://www.wmm.com

Women of Color Resource Center. http://www.coloredgirls.org

Women's Bureau, Department of Labor. http://dol.gov/wb

Women's College Coalition. http://www.womenscolleges.org

Women's Environment and Development Organization (WEDO). http://www.wedo.org

Women's Sports Foundation. http://www.womenssportsfoundation.org

Young Women's Task Force, National Council of Women's Organizations. http://www.youngwomenshealth.org

Worse than Queer Web Site. http://www.worsethanqueer.com/slander/pp40.html

FILMS

16 Candles
Bend It Like Beckham
Boys Don't Cry
Chasing Amy
Chutney Popcorn
Fast Times at Ridgemont High
Fight Club
Girls Town
Go Fish

The Incredibly True Adventures of Two Girls in Love
Legally Blonde I and II
The Legend of Billie Jean
Lost in Translation
Lovely and Amazing
Mean Girls
Orlando
Pretty in Pink
Thelma and Louise
Valley Girl
Watermelon Woman

Index

Note: Volume numbers are in **bold** type. Page numbers for main entries or primary documents are in *italic* type.

About the Editor and Contributors

Jennifer Baumgardner is the coauthor, along with Amy Richards, of *Grassroots: A Field Guide to Feminist Activism* (2005) and *Manifesta: Young Women, Feminism and the Future* (2000). She and Richards also own and operate Soapbox, Inc., a lecture agency representing progressive speakers.

Gwendolyn Beetham works for the National Council for Research on Women, New York.

Jessica Blaustein is an independent scholar and seamstress in New York City, where she writes and sews about gender and sexuality, visual culture, architecture, and urban studies. She also works for arts and architecture nonprofit organizations.

Robyn S. Bourgeois is a PhD student in the Department of Sociology and Equity Studies in Education at the Ontario Institute for Studies in Education of the University of Toronto.

Jennifer Brayton is Assistant Professor in the Department of Sociology at Ryerson University in Toronto.

Wendy A. Burns-Ardolino is an Instructor/Reference Librarian at the University of South Carolina-Beaufort.

Ritch Calvin is a Lecturer in Women's Studies at SUNY Stony Brook.

Heather Cassell is an administrative assistant for the Jewish Community Endowment Fund and was founder and co-organizer of the West Coast/San Francisco office of the Third Wave Foundation.

Daniel Conway is a PhD candidate researching masculinities, citizenship, and political objection to military service in the South African Defence Force at Rhodes University in South Africa.

Rory Dicker is a Senior Lecturer in English and Women's Studies at Vanderbilt University.

Jennifer Drake is Associate Professor of English at the University of Indianapolis.

Anna Feigenbaum is a doctoral student in Communication Studies and co-coordinator of the Graduate Group for Feminist Scholarship at McGill University, Montreal.

Erika Feigenbaum teaches philosophy and women's studies at Cleveland State University in Ohio.

JonaRose Jaffe Feinberg is a doctoral student in the Department of Communication at the University of California, San Diego.

Sarah Gamble is a Senior Lecturer in English and Gender at the University of Wales, Swansea.

Kris Gandara is a PhD student in English at the University of Nebraska-Lincoln.

Stacy Gillis is a Lecturer in English at the University of Newcastle, UK.

Laura Gladney-Lemon is a graduate student in the Women's and Gender Studies Department at the University of Texas. She specializes in issues of fat hate and size discrimination.

Betty J. Glass is Associate Professor and Women's Studies Subject Specialist for the University of Nevada, Reno Libraries.

Brea Grant is an American Studies graduate student at the University of Texas.

Rebecca C. Hains is a PhD candidate in Mass Media and Communication at Temple University in Philadelphia, where she is also pursuing a graduate certificate in Women's Studies.

Holly Hassel is an Assistant Professor of English and Women's Studies at the University of Wisconsin–Marathon County.

Leslie L. Heywood is Professor of English and Creative Writing at the State University of New York, Binghamton and the co-editor (with Jennifer Drake) of *Third Wave Agenda: Being Feminist, Doing Feminism* (1997) and the author of *Pretty Good for a Girl: A Memoir* (1998), among other works.

Angela Hooton is a Legislative Staff Attorney for the Mexican American Legal Defense and Educational Fund.

Gillian Howie is a Senior Lecturer in Philosophy at the University of Liverpool, UK.

Rebecca Hurdis is a doctoral candidate in the Ethnic Studies Department at the University of California, Berkeley.

Lisa Miya-Jervis is a writer and activist and the publisher of *Bitch* magazine.

Merri Lisa Johnson is an Assistant Professor of English and Women's Studies at Coastal Carolina University.

Jackie Joice is a writer who lives in Long Beach, California.

Ann Kaloski-Naylor is a Lecturer at the Centre for Women's Studies, University of York, England.

Kristen Kidder is a writer, activist, and long-term contributor to *Bitch* magazine.

Beth Kreydatus is a graduate student at the College of William and Mary, Williamsburg, Virginia.

Helena Kvarnstrom has an MA in Cultural Studies from the University of East London. Her research interests are primarily in sex radicalism, Riot Grrrl, and visual culture.

Jessica Lourey teaches English and Sociology at Alexandria Technical College in Alexandria, Minnesota.

Ami Lynch is a faculty member in Sociology and Women's Studies, George Washington University.

Colleen Mack-Canty is an Assistant Professor of Political Science, The University of Idaho, Moscow.

Jessica Manack is an artist and activist located in Pittsburgh.

Mimi Marinucci is an Assistant Professor at Eastern Washington University with a joint appointment in philosophy and women's studies.

Jaime McLean is a PhD student in History at Michigan State University.

Amy Miller is a community organizer based in Montreal.

Rebecca Munford is a Lecturer in Literature, Culture and Theory at the University of Manchester, UK.

Sean Murray in a PhD student in the English Department at Binghamton University, specializing in gender studies.

Jeff Niesel is the music and arts editor at the *Cleveland Free Times*.

Catherine M. Orr is Associate Professor of Women's and Gender Studies at Beloit College, Wisconsin.

Natasha Patterson is a PhD candidate in the Department of Women's Studies, Simon Fraser University, British Columbia, Canada.

Leigh Phillips is a poet and a PhD student in creative writing at Binghamton University.

Alison Piepmeier is the Associate Director of the Women's Studies Program and a Senior Lecturer in Women's Studies at Vanderbilt University.

Leandra Preston is an Instructor and Program Coordinator of the Women's Studies Program at the University of Central Florida in Orlando.

Jaclyn Iris Pryor is in the Performance as Public Practice Program, Department of Theatre and Dance, University of Texas.

Rachel Raimist is a mother, filmmaker, writer, photographer, and hip-hop feminist. She is pursuing a PhD in Feminist Studies at the University of Minnesota.

Clancy Ratliff is a PhD candidate in Rhetoric at the University of Minnesota.

Jackie Regales is an Instructor in Humanities and American Studies at Anne Arundel Community College, Arnold, Maryland.

Jo Reger is an Assistant Professor of Sociology at Oakland University in Rochester, Michigan.

Amy Richards is the coauthor, along with Jennifer Baumgardner of *Grassroots: A Field Guide to Feminist Activism* (2005) and *Manifesta: Young Women, Feminism and the Future* (2000). She and Baumgardner also own and operate Soapbox, Inc., a lecture agency representing progressive speakers.

Stefanie Samuels is Adjunct Faculty, Women's Studies, York University.

Joseph Schatz is Director of Debate and an Instructor of English and Feminist Evolutionary Theory at Binghamton University.

Deborah Siegel is Director of Special Projects at the National Council for Research on Women and a freelance writer.

Teresa Simone has an MA in Women's Studies from the University of Arizona and participates in feminist hip-hop, Riot Grrrl, and other forms of third-wave activism.

Kristine Sisbarro holds an MA in Women's Studies from Southern Connecticut State University. She works as a Program Officer for a progressive foundation in Connecticut.

Mary Sitzenstatter received her master's degree in Women's Studies from The Ohio State University in 2005.

Candis Steenbergen is a doctoral candidate in Interdisciplinary Studies in Society and Culture at Concordia University in Montreal, Quebec.

Lacey Story is a graduate of Oakland University with dual degrees in Women's Studies and Sociology.

Griselda Suarez is a poet and activist living in Long Beach, California.

Nel P. Sung serves on the Board of the New York City Chapter of the National Asian Pacific American Women's Forum and is currently a Master of Philosophy candidate in Ethnic and Racial Studies at Trinity College Dublin in Ireland.

Leora Tanenbaum is the author of *Slut! Growing Up Female with a Bad Reputation* (2000) and *Catfight: Rivalries Among Women—From Diets to Dating, From the Boardroom to the Delivery Room* (2003).

Emilie Tarrant attends high school in Maryland and is studying art history at Goucher College in Baltimore.

Shira Tarrant is an Assistant Professor of Women's Studies at Goucher College in Baltimore, Maryland.

Samantha C. Thrift is a PhD Candidate in the Department of Art History and Communication Studies at McGill University, Montreal, Quebec, Canada.

Faye Linda Wachs is an Assistant Professor of Sociology in the Department of Psychology and Sociology at California Poly Pomona.

Tracy Walker is a MA candidate in Sociology and Equity Studies at the Ontario Institute for Studies in Education at the University of Toronto.

Muriel L. Whetstone-Sims is a graduate student in Women's Studies at Texas Woman's University in Denton and a professional writer.

Emily Regan Wills is a research assistant in the Political Science Department at Yale University.

Laura Madeline Wiseman is a teacher in the Southwest with interests in women's studies and creative writing. She is a columnist for the magazines *F-WORD* and *Empowerment4women* and an editor for *Inthefray*.

Jessica A. York is a PhD candidate in History and an Adjunct Professor of Women's Studies at Stony Brook University, New York.

Emilie Zaslow is a PhD student in the Department of Culture and Communication at New York University.